RECONCILING EFFICIENCY AND EQU_

Due to the growing influence of economics and economists in competition law and policy discourse and the internationalization of antitrust, the equity–efficiency trade-off debate has played a defining role in the transformation of the dominant paradigm governing competition law enforcement since at least the 1970s. The debate remains crucial today as issues of economic inequality and its interaction with efficiency become of central concern to policymakers and decision-makers in competition law, as well as in other spheres of public policy. Despite their central role in the grammar of competition law on the global plane, the intellectual underpinnings of the interactions between equity and efficiency in the context of competition enforcement have never been examined in-depth. This book aims precisely to fill this gap by discussing novel approaches in understanding the role of efficiency and equity concerns in competition law.

Damien Gerard serves as an official in the Directorate General for Competition of the European Commission and is an academic affiliated with the University of Louvain and the College of Europe, where he also heads the Global Competition Law Center.

Ioannis Lianos holds the Chair of Global Competition Law and Policy at UCL Laws and is Director of the Centre for Law, Economics and Society at UCL Laws. He is also the chief researcher of the HSE Skolkovo Institute for Law and Development.

GLOBAL COMPETITION LAW AND ECONOMICS POLICY

This series publishes monographs highlighting the interdisciplinary and multijurisdictional nature of competition law, economics, and policy. Global in coverage, the series should appeal to competition and antitrust specialists working as scholars, practitioners, and judges.

General Editors: Ioannis Lianos, University College London; Thomas Cheng, University of Hong Kong; Simon Roberts, University of Johannesburg; Maarten Pieter Schinkel, University of Amsterdam; Maurice Stucke, University of Tennessee

Reconciling Efficiency and Equity

A GLOBAL CHALLENGE FOR COMPETITION POLICY

Edited by

DAMIEN GERARD

College of Europe and University of Louvain

IOANNIS LIANOS

University College London

CAMBRIDGE
UNIVERSITY PRESS

CAMBRIDGE
UNIVERSITY PRESS

University Printing House, Cambridge CB2 8BS, United Kingdom

One Liberty Plaza, 20th Floor, New York, NY 10006, USA

477 Williamstown Road, Port Melbourne, VIC 3207, Australia

314-321, 3rd Floor, Plot 3, Splendor Forum, Jasola District Centre, New Delhi - 110025, India

103 Penang Road, #05-06/07, Visioncrest Commercial, Singapore 238467

Cambridge University Press is part of the University of Cambridge.

It furthers the University's mission by disseminating knowledge in the pursuit of education, learning and research at the highest international levels of excellence.

www.cambridge.org
Information on this title: www.cambridge.org/9781108702881
DOI: 10.1017/9781108628105

First published 2019
First paperback edition 2022

A catalogue record for this publication is available from the British Library

Library of Congress Cataloging in Publication data
NAMES: Gerard, Damien, editor. | Lianos, Ioannis, editor. | Fox, Eleanor M.
TITLE: Reconciling efficiency and equity : a global challenge for competition law? / edited by Damien Gerard, College of Europe, University of Louvain; Ioannis Lianos, University College London.
DESCRIPTION: Cambridge, United Kingdom ; New York, NY, USA : Cambridge University Press, 2019.| Series: Global competition law and economics policy
IDENTIFIERS: LCCN 2018038013 | ISBN 9781108498081 (hardback)
SUBJECTS: LCSH: Antitrust law – Social aspects. | BISAC: LAW / Antitrust.
CLASSIFICATION: LCC K3850 .R444 2019 | DDC 343.07/21–dc23
LC record available at https://lccn.loc.gov/2018038013

ISBN 978-1-108-49808-1 Hardback
ISBN 978-1-108-70288-1 Paperback

Contents

Contributors

Mor Bakhoum: Senior Research Fellow, Max Planck Institute for Innovation and Competition

Daniel A. Crane: Associate Dean for Faculty and Research and Frederick Paul Furth, Sr., Professor of Law at the University of Michigan

Dennis M. Davis: Professor of Commercial Law at the University of Cape Town and President of the Competition Appeal Court, South Africa

Josef Drexl: Director at the Max Planck Institute for Innovation and Competition and Honorary Professor at the University of Munich

Ariel Ezrachi: Slaughter and May Professor of Competition Law, University of Oxford; Director, Oxford University Centre for Competition Law and Policy

Alan Fels: Professor at the Melbourne Law School, University of Melbourne

Albert A. Foer: Founder and former President of the American Antitrust Institute

Sir Ian Forrester: Judge of the General Court of the European Union

Eleanor M. Fox: Walter J. Derenberg Professor of Trade Regulation, New York University School of Law

Michal S. Gal: Professor and Director of the Forum for Law and Markets, University of Haifa Faculty of Law

Damien Gerard: Director, Global Competition Law Centre, College of Europe; Visiting Lecturer, University of Louvain

Edward M. Iacobucci: Dean and James M. Tory Professor of Law, University of Toronto, Faculty of Law

William E. Kovacic: Global Competition Professor of Law and Policy, George Washington University Law School; Visiting Professor, King's College London; Non-Executive Director, United Kingdom Competition and Markets Authority

David Lewis: Executive Director, Corruption Watch

Ioannis Lianos: Professor of Global Competition Law and Public Policy and Director, Centre for Law, Economics and Society, UCL Faculty of Laws, UCL; chief researcher, Skolkovo-HSE Institute for Law and Development

Philip Marsden: Inquiry Chair, Competition & Markets Authority, UK; Professor of Competition Law and Economics, College of Europe

Abel M. Mateus: Director at the European Bank for Reconstruction and Development; Senior Research Fellow, Centre for Law, Economics and Society, UCL Faculty of Laws

Petros C. Mavroidis: Professor at Columbia Law School and University of Neuchâtel

Pradeep S. Mehta: Secretary General, CUTS International

Giorgio Monti: Professor of Competition Law, LAW/RSCAS Joint Chair, European University Institute

Damien J. Neven: Professor at the Graduate Institute of International and Development Studies

Simon Roberts: Professor at the University of Johannesburg; Director, Centre for Competition, Regulation and Economic Development

Daniel L. Rubinfeld: Professor of Law at NYU School of Law and Robert L. Bridges Professor of Law Emeritus and Professor of Economics Emeritus at the University of California, Berkeley

D. Daniel Sokol: UF Foundation Professor of Law, University of Florida

Maurice E. Stucke: Professor, University of Tennessee College of Law; counsel at the Konkurrenz Group

Michael J. Trebilcock: Professor of Law, University Professor, University of Toronto, Faculty of Law

Spencer Weber Waller: Interim Associate Dean for Academic Affairs, Director, Institute for Consumer Antitrust Studies, and Professor, Loyola University Chicago School of Law

Diane P. Wood: Chief Judge, US Court of Appeals for the Seventh Circuit; Senior Lecturer in Law, University of Chicago Law School

Preface

Competition Policy at the Intersection of Equity and Efficiency

A Tribute to Eleanor Fox

Ian S. Forrester

It is much more fun to get an advance copy of one's obituary than to have to wait for the day when it is needed. This volume honours someone who stands in no need of an obituary, no need of respectful deference, and no need to cluck about the very remote good old days. Moreover, someone who thankfully shows no prospect of early retirement. Someone who is of today, now, actively engaged in the analysis and shaping of the law. Eleanor Fox.

I should put Eleanor Fox's modernity in context. We have known each other over two centuries, at least. Our recollections jointly and severally are so antique that we cannot forget events which lie at the outer edge of antitrust recollection. It is perfectly natural for sweet young things to regard me, a veteran of the *Magill* case (T-69/89 and C-241 and 242/91), as if I were a survivor of the Battle of Trafalgar. We have both seen great battles, and Eleanor has documented them like a good war correspondent, clearly but not dispassionately.

The law has developed greatly since we were beginners: another way of saying that the law has changed in its theories, processes, prime targets and enforcers. Goals, penalties, civil damages, discounts, licensing, market integration, cartels, leniency and cooperation between agencies – all of these in Europe have seen immense evolution. US law has changed greatly, sometimes in parallel to European, sometimes not.

Eleanor Fox's writings have dealt with antitrust law from many points of view. The aspect which I most appreciate is her coverage of the history. Clearly presenting the choices and recognising the alternative points of view make the history far more compelling than showing it as a triumph of right over wrong. Those who neglect the underlying factual controversy and start with the findings are missing half the fun and most of the understanding of what the case means.

Speaking as an advocate who was on the losing side of many cases, I feel sensitive and negative to case histories which present the losing side as obviously hopeless, doomed; and the winning side as evidently destined for success. Parties go to court because they believe they can win. There are always attractive arguments on both sides. Litigation is driven by antitrust lawyers' market forces: logic, a modest literacy in economics, precedent, factual fairness and advocacy of simplicity with an edge of passion which together can convince courts. Seeing this in historical context is a great merit and Eleanor Fox's writings help us understand that context.

Eleanor Fox's contribution has been immense in another hugely important respect: in the development of competition cultures in Africa, Latin America and Asia. I have seen first-hand how competition disciplines, with a bit of creativity and lots of local knowledge, can transform a developing country and emerging economies.

The Gambia, Swaziland, Cambodia and Bhutan are just a few of the small countries touched by the liberating effect of novel competition law thinking. So far as I know, Eleanor Fox has not yet been canonised by a competition agency in one of these countries, but recognition cannot be far away. She has been for emerging nations, uniquely, a voice for the underdog.

Many competition lawyers say I would love to do pro bono work but opportunities don't come up in my practice. I respectfully disagree. Practising lawyers are endowed with great privileges. Working for no fee is a practitioner's duty, a moral tax upon success and eminence. It is one which Eleanor Fox undertakes routinely and cheerfully.

And then of course there is the teaching and the cluster of excellent pupils who have grown in insight and been launched on their careers through academic exposure to Eleanor Fox. I haven't yet met one who had a bad thing to say about their great mentor.

The participation of so many admirers of Eleanor's contribution to our legal discipline in this volume confirms her unique status.

Introduction

Damien Gerard and Ioannis Lianos

Harnessing the tension between 'equity' and 'efficiency' and achieving the optimal equilibrium between these policy objectives has long been one of the major questions bedevilling economics and, more generally, political philosophy in liberal democracies but also beyond. The opposition between the demands of equity and those of efficiency may seem elusive at first. Yet, the equity-versus-efficiency trade-off debate has played a defining role in the transformation of the dominant paradigm governing competition law enforcement at least since the late 1970s,[1] due to the growing influence of economics and economists in competition law and policy discourse[2] and the internationalization of antitrust. Since then, competition law has mainly focused on economic efficiency and on a narrow view of 'consumer welfare', not only in the competition law systems of developed countries but also in the new systems of competition law adopted by emergent and developing countries in the great leap forward of the 1990s and 2000s, a period during which more than one hundred jurisdictions around the world adopted competition law regimes. Although issues of equity and distributive justice are particularly important in emergent and developing jurisdictions, at least at a symbolic level, in practice there has been an attempt to find ways to integrate these concerns in the mainstream competition law framework, rather than to develop an alternative register of understanding. The narrative of the need for greater global convergence in competition law and the associated technocratic vision of the area could not accommodate fairness or equity concerns, due to the alleged risk of introducing some degree of unacceptable local divergence. Hence, competition law was portrayed as a 'neutral' economic policy tool, devoid of any consideration for social policy concerns.

However, this has not always been the case. At the time of the 1929 Wall Street crash, nation states' economies were relatively open following a wave of globalization spanning the second half of the nineteenth and the beginning of the twentieth

---

[1] A. M. Okun, *Equality and Efficiency – The Big Tradeoff* (Brookings Institution, 1975, republished 2015).

[2] I. Lianos, *La Transformation du droit de la concurrence par le recours à l'analyse économique* (Bruylant/Sakkoulas, 2007); R. T. Atkinson and D. B. Audretch, Economic Doctrines and Approaches to Antitrust (ITIF, January 2011).

centuries. Yet the vast unemployment and economic inequality witnessed during the Great Depression led to a surge of protectionist regulation, as the rudimentary national welfare systems of the time were not able to cope with the extent of the problem.[3] Keynesians understood that the resulting political tensions could render particularly difficult the maintenance of the liberal order and argued for 'embedded liberalism'.[4] For them, public policy including antitrust law in the US (as there was no equivalent tool in Europe at the time, at least not so effective) had to deal with the social question by guaranteeing that competition would be fair, that small and medium undertakings would be protected. Fairness-driven competition law statutes, such as the Robinson Patman Act,[5] were adopted. At the same time, once the temptation of corporatism was abandoned,[6] antitrust was enforced vigorously to protect market access and the process of competition.[7] Hence, at least until the early 1970s, antitrust was conceived of as a form of social regulation aimed at ensuring that small and medium-sized undertakings have access to the market without being smashed by the corporate behemoths, while workers could be protected from 'exploitation' through the institution of countervailing powers, such as the unions.[8] Market access and the protection of the competitive process were essential in order to ensure that markets could be considered as fair and providing equal opportunities to all. The need to ensure systemic resilience in the face of the revisionist forces of fascism and communism constituted the political backbone of the expansion of antitrust law during this period.

---

[3] Note that protectionism was primarily seen as a means to protect domestic industry and jobs. In the US, the Smoot–Hawley Tariff Act (1930), which instigated this round of protectionism, pre-dates the establishment of the US federal welfare system by five years (Social Security Act 1935).

[4] See J. G. Ruggie, 'International Regimes, Transactions, and Change: Embedded Liberalism in the Postwar Economic Order' (1982) 36(2) *International Organization* 379, 393–8 (coining the expression 'embedded liberalism' to describe the emergence of a post-Second World War consensus on the combination of 'internal social policy' with the 'external' trade and financial liberalisation as conditions for domestic stability); S. Pitruzzelo, 'Trade Liberalization, Economic Performance, and Social Protection: Nineteenth Century British Laissez-Faire and Post-World-War II US – Embedded Liberalism', in J. Ruggie (ed.), *Embedding Global Markets – An Enduring Challenge* (Ashgate, 2008), 73, at 76–7 (describing the Keynesian criticisms to the belief that competitive and self-regulating markets will 'endogenously converge' towards optimal economic and welfare equilibria without state intervention, which formed the intellectual foundation of the post-Second World War consensus).

[5] 15 USC § 13.

[6] See e.g. the National Industrial Recovery Act, which created the National Recovery Administration, allowing industries to create a set of industrial 'codes of fair competition' setting industries' prices and wages, establishing production quotas, and imposing restrictions on entry.

[7] It was not until 1937, during the second Roosevelt administration, that the country saw a revival of antitrust enforcement (C. Varney, Assistant Attorney General, Antitrust Division, US Department of Justice, 'Vigorous Antitrust Enforcement in this Challenging Era', remarks prepared for the Center for American Progress, 11 May 2009, available at www.justice.gov/atr/speech/vigorous-antitrust-enforcement-challenging-era).

[8] Which benefited from a regime of antitrust exemption, established by s. 6 of the Clayton Act in 1914, and developed further with the Norris–LaGuardia Act (1932).

In Europe, the purpose of enacting EC, and later EU, competition law in the 1950s was different, precisely because of the absence of a community of solidarity among the peoples of the Member States: its aim was to assist the formation of a common or single internal market.[9] As a corollary, any social policy dimension was left to the policy discretion of Member States,[10] and while some of them made the choice of developing their domestic model of competition law focusing on some form of social regulation of their specific brand of capitalism,[11] others relied for a significant period of time on price regulation and regulation through public ownership of significant parts of their economy.[12] Hence, in contrast to the US model, the EU model of competition was initially conceived as a tool of economic rather than social policy.[13]

At that time, economic integration was to be achieved by means of the gradual erosion of barriers to trade and the expansion of foreign direct investments, although this crucially did not include the free movement of private capital. The aim was to open markets for international trade, while clearly separating the economic field subject to global or regional economic integration rules, and the social field, which was perceived as belonging to the remit of the domestic politics of redistribution. Indeed, neither the text of the GATT, nor that of the European Coal and Steel Community or the EEC treaties included any social dimension, as each of them pursued the sole aim of reversing the 'disintegration' of the world economy that spawned from the national protectionist legislation of the previous two decades.[14]

---

[9] For a recent restatement, see e.g. E. M. Fox and D. Gerard, EU Competition Law – Cases, Texts and Context (Elgar, 2017), pp. xii–xiii and 1–32.

[10] This may be explained by the strategy of neo-functionalism followed by the EC (EU), as the Member States ascribed authority to supranational institutions for activities based in areas of agreement between them, every function left to generate others gradually. This did not initially cover social regulation.

[11] On the development and the influence of German ordoliberalism, a specific form of neoliberalism, on German competition law, see H. Rieter and M. Schmolz, 'The Ideas of German Ordoliberalism 1938–1945: Pointing the Way to a New Economic Order' (1993) 1(1) *European Journal of the History of Economic Thought* 87; D. Gerber, 'Constitutionalizing the Economy: German Neo-Liberalism, Competition Law, and the "New" Europe' (1994) 42(1) *American Journal of Comparative Law* 25; A. Nicholls, *Freedom with Responsibility: The Social Market Economy in Germany 1918–1963* (Clarendon Press, 1994). Although some groups in ordoliberal thought were quite close to neoclassical economics, other groups were inspired by the principle of 'social market economy' (V. Vanberg, 'The Freiburg School: Walter Eucken and Ordoliberalism' (Freiburg Discussion Papers on Constitutional Economics 04/11, 2004), available at www.econstor.eu/handle/10419/4343)).

[12] This would be the example of all other Member States founding the EU. The relatively little role of competition law as a tool of social regulation may also be explained by the European social model which relies on the constitution of a powerful social welfare state.

[13] This may also explain why the EU model of competition law did not initially include merger control, as economic concentration was not considered a problem, to the extent that it could lead to economies of scale and the emergence of European industrial champions, this being added at a later stage, and was certainly not conceived of at the time of the adoption of the EUMR as a social policy tool.

[14] Starting with the Smoot–Hawley Tariff Act 1930, 19 USC, ch. 4, in the US.

Competition (or antitrust) law, in the early post-Second World War period, were therefore thought of as being animated by different principles to trade law. In the US, 'populist' antitrust was, to a certain extent, a tool of social regulation designed to ensure that smaller firms had a fair chance of participating in the economic expansion generated by trade liberalization in spite of the rise of economic concentration with the development of multinationals. In contrast, as the EU was not endowed with any redistributive purpose or mechanisms, at least during the first decades of its existence, competition law was perceived as a tool to promote the competitive process, not only for microeconomic efficiency reasons but also for broader macroeconomic aims: the constitution of a European single market.

The Chicago cultural revolution of the 1970s and 1980s changed beyond recognition the US model of antitrust by transforming it from a tool of social regulation, dealing with the social question, to an instrument aiming to promote economic efficiency, making heavy use of the toolkit of neoclassical economics in interpreting the law.[15] The current neoliberal model of competition law that emerged from this 'economics-based model' of competition law focuses on consumer welfare/surplus, that is, the ability of consumers to benefit from lower prices and higher output. The issue of the allocation of that surplus between different groups of consumers, for instance the most vulnerable ones, or more generally defining a standard for a fair allocation of this surplus, is in principle ignored because it raises complex questions of distributive justice, which neoclassical economics assumes away.

Focusing on the allocation of the surplus would have transformed competition law (antitrust) to a form of social policy, something to which the adepts of the Chicago revolution were categorically opposed. Social policy concerns about redistribution and inequality are thought of in the discipline of neoclassical economics to be normative questions involving difficult value judgements that each nation state and their elected officials have to decide. It was also thought that social policy (compensating the losers) would be better achieved by tools other than competition law, such as taxation or the welfare state. The distinction between positive and normative was nevertheless

---

[15] See e.g. Y. Brozen, 'Competition, Efficiency and Antitrust' (1969) 3 J. *World Trade L.* 65; R. H. Bork, *The Antitrust Paradox: A Policy at War with Itself* (Basic Books, 1978); R. A. Posner, 'The Chicago School of Antitrust Analysis' (1979) 127 *University of Pennsylvania Law Review* 924. On the Chicago antitrust 'revolution', see among the many publications, H. Hovenkamp, 'Antitrust Policy after Chicago' (1985) 84(2) *Michigan Law Review* 213. According to this paradigm, antitrust law presumably animated by various concerns, such as justice and social stability, had to be interpreted with only economic efficiency as being the only value of interest: W. Davies, 'Economics and the "nonsense" of law: the case of the Chicago antitrust revolution' (2010) 39(1) *Economy and Society* 64. There are various ideological factors that may explain the Chicago revolution, but, in our opinion, a significant one was the prevalent view among political personnel at the time in the US, in particular after the 1973 oil crisis, that the US economy was in decline, in comparison to the more economically efficient Japanese and German economies. Promoting economic equality and social cohesion and stability therefore lost ground in favour of economic efficiency as the primary goal of competition (antitrust) law, the Chicago antitrust revisionists relying on the consensus among economists at the time that there was a trade-off between inequality and growth.

conveniently forgotten by the practical emphasis of Chicago economists on the sole aim of economic efficiency in all areas of social policy, including taxation. There was also no mechanism, at the international level, to deal with the social consequences of the global expansion of markets and economic concentration. Each state was left on its own to deal with the social dimension of the global economic concentration.

The idea that antitrust was moving towards a 'new equilibrium' became an important feature of the global competition law discussion throughout the 1980s,[16] 1990s and early 2000s, as competition law also was also expanding geographically. Although not as influential as in the US, this model has also gained acceptance in Europe, where the case law of the EU courts and the decisional practice of the European Commission have been moving steadily towards a 'more economic approach'.[17]

This consensus was occasionally broken by disagreements between the US and the EU over a 'wide' or a 'narrow' approach in defining economic efficiency, consumer welfare and the protection of the competitive process,[18] as well as discussions over the need to provide developing countries with the necessary policy space for choosing a different model to the competition law mainstream allowing them in particular to focus on poverty alleviation and more generally to reflect local conditions of imperfect markets and imperfect institutions.[19]

In recent years, the consensus seems to have shifted again as economic inequality is now thought to be related to the rise of economic concentration and market power.[20] Various 'official' voices, even in the developed world, are now arguing in favour of reconsidering fairness and equality concerns as part of the core underpinnings of competition law and policy.[21] Moreover, beyond the realm of antitrust,

---

[16] E. M. Fox, 'Modernization of Antitrust: A New Equilibrium' (1981) 66 *Cornell L. Rev.* 1140.

[17] See e.g. J. Bourgeois and D. Waelbroeck, *Ten Years of Effects-based Approach in EU Competition Law: State of Play and Perspectives* (GCLC Annual Conference Series) (Bruylant, 2013), 302.

[18] E. M. Fox, 'We Protect Competition, You Protect Competitors' (2003) 26(2) *World Competition* 149.

[19] E. M. Fox, 'Antitrust, Economic Development and Poverty: The Other Path' (2007) 13 *Southwestern Journal of Law and Trade in the Americas* 211.

[20] See, J. Stiglitz, 'America Has a Monopoly Problem – and It's Huge', *The Nation* (23 October 2017); D. Wessel, 'Is Lack of Competition Strangling the U.S. Economy?', *Harvard Business Review* (March–April 2018). Other authors have also assessed the negative effects of the reduction of competition and the higher levels of concentration on the reduction of business dynamism, the decline of both the capital and labour shares, the high profitability for some firms only, this leading to interfirm inequality, the deterioration of the job ladder and of the labour market situation overall (S. Barkai, Declining Labor and Capital Shares (London Business School, 2017), available at www.london.edu/faculty-and-research/academic-research/d/declining-labor-and-capital-shares#.WrTDAkxFz4g); R. Decker, J. Haltiwanger, R. S. Jarmin, J. Miranda, 'Where Has All the Skewness Gone? The Decline in High-Growth (Young) Firms in the U.S. (NBER Working Paper series, Working Paper 21776, December 2015); J. Furman and P. Orszag, 'A Firm-Level Perspective on the Role of Rents in the Rise in Inequality' (Washington, DC: Council of Economic Advisers, 2015, noting that due to market concentration, firms are earning outsized profits, particularly in health care and finance).

[21] M. Vestager, EU Competition Commissioner, Competition for a Fairer Society (speech at 2016 Global Antitrust Enforcement Symposium, Georgetown, 20 September 2016, https://ec.europa.eu/commission/commissioners/2014-2019/vestager/announcements/competition-fairer-society_en); R. Hesse, US Acting Assistant Attorney General, 'And Never the Twain Shall Meet? Connecting Popular and Professional

issues of inequality and its interaction with efficiency have become of central concern to policy and decision-makers across various public policy spheres. Yet, despite their central role in the grammar of competition law on the global plane, few scholars have explored the intellectual foundations of the interactions between 'equity' and 'efficiency' in the context of competition/antitrust law. There seems indeed to be significant resistance towards integrating equity and fairness concerns in competition law and conceptualizing this area of law from a social contract perspective.

This book aims precisely to fill this gap. It builds on a symposium co-organized by the Global Competition Law Centre at the College of Europe and the Centre for Law, Economics and Society at University College London, which took place in Brussels in June 2016 with a view to acknowledging and engaging with Professor Eleanor Fox's contribution to the field of competition policy. During her already long and illustrious academic career, Eleanor Fox has authored a body of work directly engaging with the conceptualization of the relationship between 'efficiency' and 'equity', drawing lessons for US antitrust law, EU competition law and the competition law systems of emergent and developing countries. Furthermore, Fox has written on and influenced various transformations in competition policy since the 1980s, in the US and worldwide. Her scholarship is characterized by a willingness to uncover the diversity of approaches underlying antitrust enforcement, to deny the superiority of any single paradigm and to bridge differences in order to foster understanding. In a world where antitrust enforcement has become truly global, antitrust standards have turned into a prevalent form of business regulation and antitrust enforcement has to cope with fast-paced innovation, Professor Fox's scholarship appears distinctively compelling indeed. This said, the present volume is not conceived as a *Festschrift* but as a standalone contribution to one of the most important challenges of modern competition law: the intersection of efficiency and equity. In effect, this book aims to provide critical insights into one of the most difficult and important questions of modern competition law by means of a compilation of original articles drafted by some of today's leading global competition law experts engaging with the psyche of competition law and the balance, or Faustian pact,[22] achieved between 'efficiency' and 'equity'.

The book is structured in three parts. Part I, entitled 'Framing the Tension between Equity and Efficiency as a Global Challenge for Competition Policy: the Vision of a Pioneer', introduces the work of Professor Eleanor Fox insofar as it has

---

Visions for Antitrust Enforcement' (speech at 2016 Global Antitrust Enforcement Symposium, Georgetown, 20 September 2016, www.justice.gov/opa/speech/acting-assistant-attorney-general-renata-hesse-antitrust-division-delivers-opening). For discussion, see D. Gerard, 'Fairness in EU Competition Policy: Significance and Implications' (2018) 9 *J. Eur. Comp. Law & Practice* 211.

22 F. M. Rowe, 'The Decline of Antitrust and the Delusions of Models: The Faustian Pact of Law and Economics' (1983–4) 72 *Geo. L. J.* 1511.

inspired the development of a body of literature on the interaction between competition law and equity concerns. Judge Diane Wood focuses on Eleanor Fox's role as a pioneering woman, 'known not just for her contributions to competition law but also for her role as mentor and role-model to generations of women who followed her' and on Professor Fox's 'relentlessly individual and clear vision of antitrust', which as she notes is 'a vision sharpened by the fact that she saw through assumptions others were making'. Philip Marsden and Spencer Weber Waller then focus on Professor Fox's work on the emergence of international competition law, to which her contribution has been remarkable, and the 'cosmopolitan' perspective she has instilled in this new field.

Part II, 'Reconciling Equity and Efficiency: the Challenge of Making Markets Work for People', presents inequality, poverty, discrimination and development as alternative (or complementary) narratives for competition law. This part engages with three important challenges to which modern competition law is confronted.

The first challenge, which forms the first section of Part II, is the need to develop solid theoretical foundations ensuring that competition law is anchored in the social contract that cements societies together, in other words, to ensure that competition law and markets work for people.

Ioannis Lianos's chapter examines the difficulties of the mainstream paradigm of competition law in integrating equality concerns, and sketches a theoretical framework for a more synergetic relation between efficiency and equity, without however giving in to the sirens of populism. Lianos claims that if one is to take equality concerns seriously, it becomes essential to provide a solid theoretical framework that would engage with the arguments put forward by those defending the status quo. Taking a social contract perspective, and noting the hybrid nature of competition law, which is a tool of economic order, but also a form of social regulation, Lianos explores how the mainstream paradigm of competition law focusing on consumer welfare addresses distributive justice issues only in an indirect and incidental way. He then turns to the institutional argument often opposed by the proponents of the status quo, that other institutions, such as taxation, may be more effective than competition law at dealing with inequalities, finding that this argument does not stand up to serious scrutiny. Lianos also critically engages with the argument that there is a trade-off between equality and efficiency. The final section of his chapter revisits the thorny question of what is to be equalized. Drawing on the idea of 'complex equality', he presents the contours of a fairness-driven competition law, solidly anchored to the social contract.

Michal Gal's contribution further explores the social contract perspective in competition law. Gal argues that competition law constitutes an important part of the social contract standing at the core of market economies, which conceptualizes the relationship between the state and its citizens, as well as among citizens, and legitimizes state action. Her chapter seeks to unveil the assumptions underlying the role of competition laws as part of that social contract. She then explores whether

these assumptions further the goals of the social contract, namely total and individual welfare. In light of recent challenges to the welfare effects of market economies,
Gal seeks specifically to determine whether equality and inclusive growth objectives
should play a more pronounced role in the competition laws of developed jurisdictions, and if so, by what means.

The discussion then moves to focus on emergent and developing economies,
which have for a long time struggled with the integration of equity concerns in their
competition laws, and which have a wealth of experience on the specific adjustments to be made so as to make the competition law tool equity compatible.

Abel Mateus's chapter explores the impact of oligarchies on competition and
development, by studying the contrasting cases of Egypt and Turkey. Efficient and
competitive markets are crucial for the process of investment and technological
upgrading that is the backbone of development. This process is short-circuited in
developing countries because exploitative institutions and norms reserve non-
tradables to public enterprises or politically connected firms, closing entry, and/or
protect sectors of tradables by non-tariff barriers and other exclusionary practices.
The consequence is that most of the population is squeezed to the informal sector
and bound to struggle side by side with those firms. These themes are central to the
events in Arab countries that shook the world and triggered ongoing armed conflicts.
From there, Mateus's chapter discusses the factors that led to crony capitalism and
pathways for gradual reform.

The following chapter by Pradeep Mehta develops further the argument that
competition reforms are for the benefit of ordinary people. Various barriers –
economic, political and social – which have blocked access to resources and
opportunities for a huge portion of the population have been major contributors
to continuing global poverty. Removing those barriers and connecting the masses to
mainstream entrepreneurship needs to be the central economic policy goal of
nation states in pursuit of 'inclusive development' or 'inclusive growth'. A robust
competition policy tends to fulfil these goals, as this chapter argues and explains.
CUTS, a major international NGO representing consumer interests, has been
successfully advocating the need for competition law and policy in many developing
and emerging countries, and has also been involved closely in designing some of
these regimes, including in India. The chapter draws lessons from CUTS's wealth of
experience on competition policy diffusion and highlights the importance of promoting competition policy reforms for the benefit of ordinary people in the developing world and the role that consumer and citizen-oriented NGOs may play in this
regard.

Mor Bakhoum's contribution aims to provide an overview of the interface
between competition law and development, focusing on telecommunications,
a sector of crucial importance for growth and development. His chapter discusses
how to make competition law 'development-friendly', and adapt to the context,
needs and aspirations of developing jurisdictions. With a focus on sub-Saharan

Africa, Bakhoum explores how building competitive telecommunication markets in sub-Saharan Africa can contribute to development.

Simon Roberts's contribution focuses on East and Southern Africa. It discusses the transfer of US and EU models of competition law in these jurisdictions, and the way they have attempted to domesticate them. Roberts notes that '[t]he challenge is to craft a market-oriented approach to economic development which takes into account the real characteristics of these economies' and that high levels of inequality forms part of the economic context in these jurisdictions. Roberts argues for the need to articulate an agenda which incorporates competition and inclusive growth, in particular when competition law institutions are young, have weak capacity and need to garner support. His chapter draws on a range of research undertaken in recent years in East and Southern Africa to consider the nature and extent of competition in practice, and the role, if any, played by competition law and policy. It includes a number of case studies from commodities, such as cement and fertilizers, to competition enforcement in innovative markets for services in telecommunications and finance ('mobile money'). The chapter offers important reflections on the role of barriers to entry and on the need to preserve market access, identifying the main elements of a forward-looking agenda for competition law in developing countries.

The second challenge which confronts modern competition law is to curtail economic power, particularly taking into account the various ways economic power may be leveraged in political or cultural power, eventually affecting the democratic process.

In that regard, Alan Fels's contribution seeks to provide a legal and political account of a major controversy over proposed legislative change in the Australian abuse of dominance law, to illustrate how efficiency and equity considerations have influenced the shaping of the law. The chapter refers to some important legislative changes that have been triggered as a by-product of the inability of governments to resolve directly controversies regarding the abuse of dominance law. It then turns to an economic and legal analysis of the proposed law before returning to the political side to describe the political pressures that different parties applied to support or oppose the change and of the path that was followed on the way to a political outcome. This is a fascinating case study on the interaction of politics with competition law, of great interest for all jurisdictions.

Ariel Ezrachi and Maurice Stucke provide insights into the future struggles of antitrust against power by focusing on the role of antitrust enforcement against market power in the digital age. The rise of digital personal assistants has already changed the way we shop, interact and surf the web. Technological developments and artificial intelligence are likely to further accelerate this trend. Indeed, all of the leading online platforms are currently investing in this technology. Apple's Siri, Amazon's Alexa, Facebook's M and Google Assistant can quickly provide us with information, if we so desire, and anticipate and fulfil certain needs and requests.

Ezrachi and Stucke ask whether these digital assistants might also reduce our welfare by limiting competition and transfer consumers' wealth to providers, the perceived efficiency delivered through technology actually reducing welfare and fostering inequality. And, if this is the case, how can competition law safeguard the welfare of consumers while enabling these technological developments?

Josef Drexl's contribution delves into the broader implications of the mono focus of competition law on economic efficiency, and subsequently of ignoring the effects of digital platforms on the democratic process, in particular in times of 'post-truth' politics. Drexl argues that the efficiency approach, as advocated by the Chicago School in particular, only provides a very narrow approach to competition law analysis that relies on consumer preferences. This approach remains especially insufficient for the regulation of firms that provide citizens with politically relevant news and information. In times of digitization, citizens increasingly rely on news disseminated by Internet intermediaries such as Facebook, Twitter or Google for making political decisions. Such firms design their business models and algorithms for selecting the news according to a purely economic aim Yet recent research indicates that dissemination of news through social platforms, in particular, has a negative impact on the democratic process by favouring the dissemination of false factual statements, fake news and unverifiable conspiracy theories within closed communities. This ultimately leads to radicalization and division within society along political and ideological lines. Experience based on the Brexit referendum in the UK and the more recent presidential elections in the US highlights the ability of populist political movements to abuse the business rationale of Internet intermediaries and the functioning of their algorithms in order to win popular votes with their 'post-truth politics'. The chapter relies on competition law principles to discuss future approaches to regulating the market for political ideas at the interface of competition law and media law in the new digital age. Based on constitutional considerations, the chapter rests on the assumption that media markets should not only provide news that responds best to the psychological predispositions and subjective beliefs of the individual citizen, but also provide correct information and diversity of opinion as a basis for making informed democratic decisions.

The third challenge relates to the complexity of opening competition law to concerns broader than economic efficiency, in view of the emphasis on innovation by developed and developing countries' competition law regimes. The two chapters in this section offer different perspectives on this issue.

David Lewis's contribution challenges orthodoxy and argues for a competition policy that addresses poverty and equality, particularly in developing countries. Lewis considers that progressive redistributive effects of competition law policies may rest on their contribution to promoting ease of access to markets, i.e. ensuring that the opportunity to participate in economic activity is not denied to the 'little guy'. However, his chapter explores another neglected dimension of the potential interfaces between two policy fields that are both focused on encouraging and enabling new entry and enhancing firm-level productivity, namely competition law policy and industrial policy. He argues that 'just as competition policy practitioners have embraced the importance of protecting innovation in the North because it is pro-competition, that is to say, because it produces better quality products at lower prices, so too should it protect developing country innovation in the South'. To the extent that promoting innovation usually takes different forms in the South than the 'codified patenting' or intellectual property protection mostly employed in the North, competition law should aim to cater for these broader industrial policy concerns.

Daniel Sokol's chapter addresses antitrust, industrial policy and economic populism. Sokol recognizes that changing economic circumstances have reinvigorated the call for multiple goals in antitrust but argues that such 'clamoring' threatens consumers. His chapter explores why the current paradigm of consumer welfare, one which increases the influence of economic analysis, better serves consumers in terms of insulated antitrust from its worst excesses. He argues that a change in regime would cause a different set of beliefs to take over and that 'a true believer in antitrust (and thus in markets) does not see the role of antitrust as one of regulation but one of enforcement of market mechanisms against distortions by unlawful monopoly power'. Sokol recommends finding a middle ground for enforcement – 'enough intervention in terms of mergers and conduct cases to deter and correct private and public arrangements that undermine competition, but not so much as to displace market competition with regulation'.

Part III of the volume is entitled 'Reconciling Equity and Efficiency: the Challenge of Effective Antitrust Enforcement'. It examines the role and design of competition policy in order to implement this new vision combining efficiency with equity considerations, and explores how the global governance of competition law may cater for these broader concerns.

In Section A, 'Designing Effective Enforcement Systems', a number of contributions engage with the hot topics of the performance of competition law authorities (including the question of its measurement) and of the design of competition law systems.

In the section's first contribution, Albert Foer reminds us that culture often pre-dates and pre-determines the institutional framework of competition law enforcement. Bert Foer engages with the crucial theme of competition law culture and the cultural dimensions of competition law and policy. He notes that culture is often put forward as a factor explaining cross-jurisdictional differences in the way competition law is enforced but has been the least developed of these differentiating factors, though always present. Foer distinguishes between the notion of a competition culture and the cultural dimensions of competition. He offers a critical literature review on works that have addressed these concerns and draws conclusions from this literature on the process of international convergence of competition law rules, taking a sceptical perspective on the degree of convergence that may be achieved.

Moving to the performance of competition authorities in fulfilling their – broader or narrower – tasks, Bill Kovacic imaginatively tackles this complex topic, summarizing his significant contribution to this debate.[23] Kovacic advances a 'Formula One approach to understanding competition law system performance'. In this chapter, the world of motor sport, in particular its more performance-oriented element, Formula One (F1) racing, supplies an analogy that seeks to capture the institutional foundations for successful implementation of competition law commands. His contribution offers a concise and well-thought-out analytical framework for this complex issue, probably providing a word of caution to competition authorities willing to expand the remit of their intervention so as to tackle equity concerns.

Edward Iacobucci and Michael Trebilcock offer a sceptical perspective on claims that there are readily available metrics to gauge the performance of a competition law agency, thus indirectly marginalizing the criticism that broadening the tasks of competition authorities to tackle equality would affect the performance of competition authorities. They argue that even assuming there is a clear objective function for competition law, valid and meaningful measurement of the success of an agency in achieving relevant objectives is very difficult, if not wholly impracticable. Compounding the problem, competition agencies not only vary across jurisdictions in their objectives, but even within a jurisdiction there are often competing, even mutually incompatible, goals for competition policy. Some jurisdictions emphasize pure economic efficiency in assessing certain matters while others take into account a variety of other objectives, including equity. Strength in pursuing one objective may imply weakness in pursuing another, yet that is not an intrinsically objectionable outcome, given the plurality of concerns that often motivate competition law. A different comparative question could focus less on an agency's substantive decisions, and focus instead more on whether the design and practice of a competition agency vindicate important process values. Here too, however, they are sceptical. Assessing institutional design is also problematic: there are a host of process values pointing in different directions on institutional design, and a single optimal structure is unavailable as a conceptual, let alone a practical matter. This analysis implies that there are reasons for caution in comparative assessments of competition agency effectiveness. First, competition laws may have different goals, and process values may vary as well, across jurisdictions, which may lead to locally optimal, even if idiosyncratic substantive decision-making and processes. Second, even if harmonization is not explicitly adopted as a goal of international discussions around institutions, there is a danger that comparative evaluations, as the literature on legal

---

[23] See, in particular, W. E. Kovacic, The Federal Trade Commission at 100: Into Our 2d Century (Jan. 2009); D. A. Hyman and W. E. Kovacic, 'Competition Agency Design: What's on the Menu?' (2012) 8 *Eur. Competition J.* 527; W. E. Kovacic and M. Lopez-Galdos, 'Lifecycles of Competition Systems: Explaining Variation in the Implementation of New Regimes' (2016) 79 *L. & Contemp. Probs.* 85; W. E. Kovacic and D. A. Hyman, 'Consume or Invest? What Do/Should Agency Leaders Maximize?' (2016) 91 *Wash. L. Rev.* 2395.

indicators in international development more generally suggests, will tend to pressure outliers to conform. Iacobucci and Trebilcock conclude that because of the importance of local objectives and choices, conformity is not necessarily desirable in respect of either substantive competition law or institutional design.

The discussion then turns to the issue of the appropriate design of the competition law system. Dan Crane's chapter explores the interaction between public and private enforcement, focusing on the role of private enforcement in view of the conceptualization of this tool as a mechanism to compensate victims of competition law violations. Crane notes that the rise in private antitrust enforcement in many jurisdictions requires extending institutional analysis to comprehend comparisons between private enforcement systems, by taking into account the complex interactions between public and private systems. Thus his chapter proposes a framework for conducting comparative analysis of antitrust systems in view of the rising growth of private enforcement. Crane argues that a realistic assessment of the country-specific practice of private antitrust litigation requires looking beyond the stated objectives and justifications for the practice and into the actual effects of private enforcement on the overall antitrust ecosystem. Drawing on evidence from the United States' important experience in private enforcement, Crane claims that private litigation has important feedback effects on public enforcement, and may, in some contexts, diminish the incidence and efficacy of public enforcement.

Another issue that needs to be tackled in designing federal systems of competition law enforcement is the allocation of responsibilities and duties between the federal and the national levels.

To that end, Daniel Rubinfeld's contribution explores this question from a normative perspective, asking to what extent antitrust enforcement (and regulatory authority more generally) should be centralized and to what extent the authority should be delegated to lower levels of government. Using the EU (following the principle of subsidiarity) and the US (taking off from the state-action exemption doctrine) as prime examples, while borrowing from political science and economics literature, Rubinfeld emphasizes common themes that can be applied worldwide. At the same time, the chapter suggests that local cultures and politics can point to proposed institutions that vary from country to country. In conclusion, Rubinfeld is more sanguine about the prospects for US regulatory federalism (if reformed) and less enthusiastic about the current state of regulatory federalism in the EU.

Giorgio Monti's chapter focuses on the EU, exploring how the latter is attempting to galvanize national competition authorities (NCAs) in the EU system of competition law enforcement. His chapter explores the interaction between the NCAs (including the European Competition Network (ECN)) and the Commission, exploring how one regional group seeks to supplement coordination with regional procedural norms, and the kinds of monitoring mechanisms that may be designed to accompany them. Monti critically examines the steps currently being taken, in particular the 'ECN+' project, which has culminated in a proposed directive to harmonize antitrust procedures across the Member States. He argues that this narrative suffers from a 'major defect': 'it is based on the premise that antitrust enforcement by NCAs is 'regional' in any meaningful sense'. This contrasts with the evidence revealing, according to Monti, that for the most part NCAs operate to address market failures at local level, whereas instances where NCAs apply EU competition law to anticompetitive conduct beyond their borders being 'exceptional and controversial'. Monti draws conclusions on the chances of success of the ECN+ project and makes a number of insightful suggestions about the direction ahead and the appropriate governance structure for competition law enforcement in Europe and the intersection of NCAs with the Commission.

Section B of this part takes a global perspective, focusing on the effective coordination of competition law enforcement, in particular in the context of enforcing competition law to global value chains.

Dennis Davis's chapter delves into the complex issue of extraterritoriality and the question of jurisdiction in competition law. For Davis, globalization holds significant challenges for the competition community, in particular the importance of extending its regulatory gaze beyond the strict confines of national jurisdiction. Starting with a critical analysis of the recent US case law on extraterritoriality, Davis notes that the shifting patterns of production of goods and services which are becoming increasingly transnational require a similar shift from the attempt to employ a generous interpretation of the scope of the Sherman Act to different forms of international regulation, or at least cooperation. He nevertheless laments the failure to develop international regulation and effective international cooperation, noting that developing countries are often unable to protect themselves from the anti-competitive actions of multinational corporations that can detrimentally affect their economies, and that the existing relatively feeble international competition framework works for the benefit of developed economies. Davis argues that competition law should engage with the current mechanisms of global production of goods and services, in particular the development of global value chains. It is on the basis of an understanding of the global production processes that courts must seek to develop the key jurisdictional basis of competition law.

Petros Mavroidis and Damien Neven explore the international governance of competition enforcement both from the trade perspective (the interface between trade regulation and competition), as well as from the antitrust perspective (the external effects that enforcement decisions can have across jurisdictions). Mavroidis and Neven make two simple but powerful observations. First, from the antitrust perspective, they analyse the sources of conflict across jurisdictions, and find that both the deviation from the objective of the protection of consumer welfare and the scope for capture in enforcement are important root causes of conflicts across jurisdictions. They argue that capture or enforcement in favour of domestic business interests remains a concern, so that an international discipline on the enforcement of domestic rules may be desirable, possibly in the context of bilateral free trade agreements. Second, from the trade perspective, they contend that the preservation of market access commitments through competition enforcement should not necessarily be entrusted to competition authorities. They also argue that new issues at the interface between trade regulation and competition enforcement, for instance in the context of global value chains, should be considered by a subset of like-minded members of the WTO.

Finally, starting from the premise that the balance between equity and efficiency in a global context is also reflected in the tension between diversity and unity in the design of competition policy and the achievement of decisional outcome, Damien Gerard attempts to identify various determinants, and discusses the limits of the notion of convergence as the dominant value of international antitrust enforcement discourse. Gerard starts by mapping the achievements of the EU network enforcement systems in terms of convergence since its entry into force in the early 2000s and from there, while acknowledging the peculiarities of the EU system, proposes a taxonomy of convergence factors capable of informing the structuring of international cooperation beyond the EU, while possibly resonating also beyond competition law. In a rare discussion drawing on a wide array of sources, this contribution describes the forces of convergence but also their limits and whether and how they should or may be overcome. At the end, Gerard addresses the question of conflicts from a preventive angle and articulates convergence as a by-product of enforcement cooperation with significant potential to strengthen the efficiency of competition enforcement with the necessary deference for the autonomous understanding of equity in individual jurisdictions.

The volume concludes with an afterword authored by Professor Eleanor Fox who shares with us the tale of her journey into uncovering synergies between equity and efficiency, thereby providing important insights for the achievement of the novel equilibrium currently in formation.

Overall, the book also inaugurates the *Global Competition Law, Economics and Public Policy* series by Cambridge University Press, directed by professors Ioannis Lianos (University College London), Thomas Cheng (University of Hong Kong), Simon Roberts (University of Johannesburg), Maarten Pieter Schinkel (University of Amsterdam) and Maurice Stucke (University of Tennessee). This book series is aimed at one of the most central questions to the study of competition law, competition economics and policy: how law, economics and institutions respond to an increasingly growing global and interconnected competition community. Its ambition is to further develop a global and cosmopolitan perspective in the study of competition law and economics, a vision that will carry forward the work of the pioneers of global competition law scholarship, such as Professor Eleanor Fox.

PART I

Framing the Tension between Equity and Efficiency as a Global Challenge for Competition Policy

The Vision of a Pioneer

Eleanor Fox: Insights from an Outsider

Diane P. Wood

It is a great honor to reflect on the many contributions my dear friend Eleanor Fox has made to the field of competition law. I could not hope to review every original idea she has had over her more than fifty years of engagement with this fascinating area, nor does anyone here need me to do that. Instead, I will attempt to bring together two themes: Eleanor's role as a pioneering woman, known not just for her contributions to competition law but also for her role as mentor and role model to generations of women who followed her; and her relentlessly individual and clear vision of antitrust – a vision sharpened by the fact that she saw through assumptions others were making, asked the hard questions, and kept her mind open to insights both from non-mainstream sources in the United States and from countries around the world that have worked over her professional lifetime to adopt and tailor their own competition laws to their own situations.

It is probably hard for this audience to think of Eleanor as an "outsider," but back when she started her legal career, that was certainly a fair label to use. As of 1963, the year after she started working at Simpson Thatcher & Bartlett in New York,[1] one roster reported that there were 268,782 lawyers in the United States, of which 7,143 (just 2.7 percent) were women.[2] Recall that Harvard Law School did not begin admitting women until 1950;[3] some other schools were ahead of it, but not by much. Supreme Court Justice Ruth Bader Ginsburg graduated first in her class from Columbia Law School in 1959, but she was turned down by every one of the many New York law firms to which she applied.[4] Justice Sandra Day O'Connor had much the same experience on the West Coast.[5]

---

[1] E. Marie Daly, 'Outstanding Women: Eleanor Fox', *Law* 360 (Apr. 5, 2007), www.law360.com/articles/ 22090/outstanding-women-eleanor-fox

[2] J. J. White, 'Women in the Law' (1966–7) 65 *Mich. L. Rev.* 1051, 1051 n. 2 (citing Hankin and Krohnke, *The American Lawyer: 1964 Statistical Report* 29 (1965)).

[3] A. N. Atiya, 'Women Grads Mark 50 Years At Law School', *Harv. Crimson* (May 5, 2003), www .thecrimson.com/article/2003/5/5/women-grads-mark-50-years-at

[4] C. Grant Bowman, 'Women in the Legal Profession' (2009) 61 *Me. L. Rev.* 2, 9.

[5] Ibid.

By 1970, the year in which Eleanor became a partner at the firm, things were starting to improve, but they still had a long way to go.[6] One study reported that the number of women lawyers in 1970 had reached 13,000, representing 4 percent of the profession.[7] The rate of change accelerated during the 1970s, however: by 1980, the number had jumped to 12.4 percent of the profession.[8] During that decade, Eleanor was breaking down one barrier after another. She served on the Executive Committee of the prestigious Association of the Bar of the City of New York from 1976 to 1980 (and then again later in 1989 and 1990); she chaired the Trade Regulation Committee from 1974 to 1977, and she chaired the Antitrust Law Section of the New York State Bar Association from 1978 to 1979. My own experience during the late 1970s, just after I graduated from law school, suggests strongly that Eleanor was usually either the only woman in the room, or one of a very small number.

Some people may have thought this a disadvantage; others might have felt hesitant to make their presence known. But not Eleanor. Instead, returning in 1976 to New York University Law School, from which she had received her law degree in 1961, she became from the start a leading voice in the field of antitrust law – and a voice that refused to follow the chorus from the mid 1970s onward that took a narrow view about both the scope of antitrust law and the risks to competition in the practices the law addresses.[9] Eleanor herself described this trend very well in the preface to the first edition of the book that she and Lawrence A. Sullivan co-authored in 1989, where they had this to say:

> Antitrust law once reflected broad, value-based policy, informed by the enacting Congresses' distrust of bigness and power and their concern for economic opportunity on the merits. But in the mid to late 1970s, the Supreme Court put a cap on the growing body of antitrust constraints, and in the early 1980s, a new Administration turned the old antitrust on its head. In 1981 the Justice Department, taking a leaf from Chicago School economics, proclaimed that the sole role for antitrust is to stop inefficient transactions; and it asserted that few transactions are inefficient because the market is a robust check on inefficient behavior. Government enforcement since 1981 has focused almost entirely on blatant cartelization. [As of 1989], minimal antitrust is still the rule of thumb.[10]

She was, of course, right. In a series of decisions handed down during the 1970s, the Supreme Court was pulling back from a regime in which (1) high market shares were presumptively anticompetitive; (2) a rather long list of practices (at least compared with the law today) were considered per se illegal; and (3) exclusionary practices

---

[6]   Ibid., at 13.
[7]   Ibid., at 15 (citing C. Fuchs Epstein, *Women in Law* 53 (2nd edn, 1993)).
[8]   Ibid.
[9]   Daly, 'Outstanding Women'.
[10] Reprinted in E. Fox, L. A. Sullivan and R. J. R. Peritz, *Cases and Materials on U.S. Antitrust in Global Context* (2nd edn, West, 2004), vii.

were regarded as just as threatening to competition as cartelization. The "new look," heavily influenced by the work of a number of scholars at the University of Chicago Law School (who thus gave their name to this new approach),[11] first showed up at the Court in the 1974 decision in *United States* v. *General Dynamics Corp.*,[12] which rejected the government's challenge to a stock acquisition that greatly increased concentration in the coal industry. Rather than looking at the market shares of the top 2, top 4, and top 10 firms, as had been common, the Court delved more deeply into the economics of the industry. It concluded that the statistical evidence of concentration did not reveal whether the acquisition was likely to have a substantial, deleterious effect on competition, because the key variable was uncommitted reserves.[13] Viewed that way, the acquisition was not problematic, and so the government's case failed.

General Dynamics was followed just a few years later by *Continental T.V., Inc.* v. *GTE Sylvania Inc.*,[14] the famous case that proclaimed that nonprice vertical restraints would no longer be deemed per se illegal, because on balance they may help *interbrand* competition more than they harm *intrabrand* competition. The opinion relies heavily on Chicago School analysis. It was quickly followed by decisions that made it easier for manufacturers to discourage (or perhaps halt altogether) efforts by retailers to sell products at discount prices, through the holdings first in *Monsanto Co.* v. *Spray-Rite Service Corp.*[15] which was a decision that made it harder to show an anticompetitive agreement and second, in *Business Electronics Corp.* v. *Sharp Electronics Corp.*,[16] which adopted the rule that agreements that merely *affect* price – without dictating it – must be evaluated under the rule of reason. Eventually the Court abandoned the per se rule for all vertical restrictions, deciding in *State Oil Co.* v. *Khan* that maximum resale prices must be judged under the rule of reason,[17] and in *Leegin Creative Leather Products, Inc.* v. *PSKS, Inc.*, that the same is true for minimum resale prices (thereby abrogating a rule that had existed for ninety-six years).[18]

And that was not all. At the same time, the Supreme Court handed down decisions that significantly narrowed the scope of antitrust law's prohibitions against exclusionary conduct. Thus, while the decision in *Aspen Skiing Co.* v. *Aspen Highlands Skiing Corp.*,[19] might have led one to think that efforts by a dominant firm to exclude its rival from the market could (still) be reached under section 2 of

---

[11] See generally R. Posner, 'The Chicago School of Antitrust Analysis' (1979) 127 *U. Pa. L. Rev.* 925, 925–6.
[12] 415 US 486 (1974).
[13] Ibid., at 502.
[14] 433 US 36 (1977).
[15] 465 US 752 (1984).
[16] 485 US 717 (1988).
[17] 522 US 3 (1997).
[18] 551 US 877 (2007).
[19] 472 US 585 (1985).

the Sherman Act, it remains unclear after the decision in *Verizon Communications Inc.* v. *Law Offices of Curtis* v. *Trinko, LLP*,[20] whether there is anything left to such ideas as "essential facilities," and the corresponding rule that prohibits (or prohibited?) a monopolist from denying access to such a facility.

I could go on, but the broad outline is clear. Over the course of Eleanor's professional lifetime, antitrust doctrine in the US Supreme Court has come very close to the vision expressed in such books as Robert Bork's *Antitrust Paradox*, first published in 1978, or Richard Posner's *Antitrust Law: An Economic Perspective*, whose first edition came out in 1976. Under this view, antitrust has one and only one goal: consumer welfare.[21] And that term takes its definition from industrial organization economics. If a transaction meets the criteria of Kaldor–Hicks efficiency – that is, if it makes some people better off, and those people in theory can compensate those who are made worse off (assuming that there are such people) – then there is no reason to regulate it.[22] It makes no difference that the disadvantaged group may not in fact receive this compensation; advocates of this view believe that it is enough that the compensation is possible, and they further believe that optimal allocations are more likely to be achieved with unregulated markets (with the narrow exception of those that are cartelized) than with antitrust interventions.

Another critical part of this view relates to Type 1 and Type 2 errors. In antitrust, a Type 1 error would involve the incorrect labeling of something as anticompetitive, when it is in fact either pro-competitive or neutral; a Type 2 error would involve incorrectly assuming that something is benign, when in fact it is anticompetitive. Chicago School antitrust takes the position that Type 1 errors are much worse for the economy than Type 2 errors, and therefore that the hypothesis that something is anticompetitive should be rejected if there is any doubt about the matter.[23] They point out that, over time, markets should correct anticompetitive arrangements: if a monopolist is charging very high prices, new entrants should appear; if a cartel exists, both cheaters and new entrants should discipline it. So, they reason, the costs of erroneously *permitting* an anticompetitive arrangement are constrained by the market. If, however, the regulator erroneously *forbids* something that is actually pro-competitive, then that strategy is off the table permanently and society loses the option of a pro-competitive method of doing business.

Underlying all of these ideas are the familiar simplifying notions of price theory: demand curves will slope downward (i.e., the lower the price, the more people will want of the item); supply curves will slope upward (i.e., the higher the price, the

---

[20]   540 US 398 (2004).
[21]   See Frank H. Easterbrook, 'Predatory Strategies and Counterstrategies' (1981) 48 *U. Chi. L. Rev.* 263, 266 ("The antitrust laws are designed to maximize welfare by protecting competition, not competitors. A practice that injures competitors is thus of no antitrust concern unless it also reduces consumers' welfare").
[22]   See e.g. R. Posner, *Economic Analysis of Law* (5th edn, Kluwer, 1998) (describing Pareto superiority and Kaldor–Hicks efficiency), 14.
[23]   See e.g. F. S. McChesney, '*Easterbrook on Errors*' (2010) 6 *J. Comp. L. & Econ.* 11.

more the supplier will offer); consumers are rational actors who respond predictably to price signals; and producers are rational actors that will strive to maximize profits.[24] These ideas led some commentators to question whether certain practices that many competition laws forbid, such as predatory pricing, should be addressed at all.[25] The logic goes as follows: if Producer A wants to sell its products below cost, then consumers will get a bargain; antitrust law is not there to keep Producer A from shooting itself in the foot; even if Producers B and C are driven from the market by A's low prices, the minute A raises prices back to a remunerative level, new entrants D and E will come in, and so consumers will never be charged anything worse than the competitive price. Only if there is some way to keep D and E out – that is, only if recoupment is impossible – should anyone even think of worrying about predatory pricing. The Supreme Court endorsed this thinking in *Brooke Group Ltd.* v. *Brown & Williamson Tobacco Corp.*[26] Although the Court did not go further, some have argued that because the latter condition occurs so rarely, it may be just as well to dispense altogether with a ban on predatory pricing.[27]

Eleanor Fox never bought any of this. And she didn't, I believe, in part because she turned the potential detriment of her status as the only woman in the room – the outsider – into an asset. Metaphorically speaking, sitting just a bit off to the side, she was able to see the flaws in this oversimplified portrayal of the market.[28] She neither felt the need to use the "rational person" assumptions, nor was she threatened by a more complex view of antitrust and the people and businesses that are its concern. She challenged the view that the Sherman Act was never about anything but economic efficiency, pointing out that this concept overlooked great swaths of the history that led in 1890 to the enactment of that law.[29] It is hard to look at that history and not come to the conclusion that Congress was worried about both the size and the power of the "trusts" that had taken over a host of major industries: oil, steel, electric power, sugar, and so on. It was worried about size – maybe even size alone – because it was listening to consumers, farmers, laborers, and small business owners. It was worried about power and what harm it might inflict on the democratic process itself. Eleanor has repeatedly made these points.

In so doing, she readily acknowledges that an antitrust law that is concerned with a variety of goals – efficiency, fair business practices, and market access – may be messier than a law that focuses on only one of those *desiderata*. Take resale price

---

[24] See Posner, *Economic Analysis*, at 3–4 (describing fundamental principles of economics).

[25] See generally Easterbrook, 'Predatory Strategies'.

[26] 509 US 209 (1993).

[27] See e.g. Easterbrook, 'Predatory Strategies', at 336–7 ("If there is any room in antitrust law for rules of per se legality, one should be created to encompass predatory conduct. The antitrust offense of predation should be forgotten").

[28] See e.g. Eleanor M. Fox, 'The Politics of Law and Economics in Judicial Decision Making: Antitrust as a Window' (1986) 61 *NYU L. Rev.* 554.

[29] Ibid., at 563–4; E. M. Fox, 'The Battle for the Soul of Antitrust' (1987) 75 *Cal L. Rev.* 917; E. M. Fox, 'The Sherman Antitrust Act and the World – Let Freedom Ring' (1991) 59 *Antitrust L.J.* 109.

maintenance: it may be that the manufacturer sincerely believes that it will sell more items if it imposes a floor on the price at which its dealers may sell; it may even be true that some or all dealers will use the "cushion" that the manufacturer has provided them to spruce up their showrooms, hire knowledgeable sales help, and keep convenient hours. But not all dealers will do that, and not all consumers want the "package" of the product and the pre-sale services that the manufacturer has in mind. Those consumers chafe at the loss of the chance to go to a discounter. And, more troubling even to those with a narrower view of antitrust, if all of the dealers of Brand A are charging the same fixed minimum price, there is a risk that prices not only of Brand A will be higher, but that sellers of Brands C and D will feel comfortable hiking prices. Whether that happens will depend on how many brands there are in the market, of course, and how much product differentiation there is. But there is something to be said for a rule that says, essentially, when in doubt do whatever is possible to enhance price competition for the final consumer.

The Supreme Court became fond, during this era, of repeating a phrase that it had coined in *Brown Shoe Co.* v. *United States*:[30] "Taken as a whole, the legislative history illuminates congressional concern with the protection of competition, not competitors."[31] This is more than a little ironic, given the fact that *Brown Shoe* stopped a merger between a company responsible for 4 percent of the nation's shoe manufacturers with a company responsible for less than 2 percent,[32] and there were statements in the opinion bemoaning the increase in vertical integration in that industry, the pernicious trend toward concentration that the Court detected, the foreclosure of independent manufacturers from markets that had been open to them, and the adverse effect of the merger on local control of industry and small businesses (i.e., a whole string of propositions on which the Chicago School frowns).[33] Nevertheless, the Supreme Court borrowed the phrase in the interest of its new vision of antitrust, exemplified by *NYNEX Corp.* v. *Discon, Inc.*,[34] in which the Court held that the rule against group boycotts does not apply to a buyer's decision to buy from one seller rather than another, even if the reason behind the choice is somehow improper.

Throughout this time, Eleanor stood in the forefront of scholars who said, in essence, "Wait a minute!" How can there be competition *without* competitors? Why should we assume, contrary to common experience, that people (consumers and business operators alike) act as economic automatons, responding only to price and other objective signals? What is wrong with using antitrust in a way consistent with its history, to police unfairly exclusionary practices such as boycotts, tying arrangements, customer and territorial restraints, and predatory practices?

[30] 370 US 294 (1962).
[31] Ibid., at 322.
[32] Ibid., at 302–3.
[33] Ibid., at 327–40.
[34] 525 US 128 (1998).

Those were good questions – so good that economic theory itself evolved to embrace them.[35] Game theory began to shed light on why some of the practices that traditional, pre-Chicago antitrust had condemned were at least troublesome enough to subject to rule-of-reason scrutiny. Behavioral economics began to take its place next to industrial organization theories. Empirical evidence, which (as those who remember Nobel Prize-winning economist Ronald Coase will recall) was the bedrock of the original Chicago School, began to be incorporated once again into the models.[36] And, even granting the fact that antitrust law may have gone too far during the 1940s through the early 1970s, the pendulum apparently swung too far in the opposite direction during the 1980s. Throughout those years, Eleanor and her colleagues provided needed perspective. They never lost sight of the need to have a realistic policy that responded to actual market conditions, human foibles, and strategic behavior.

That takes me to the final point I would like to make about Eleanor's contributions to competition law. During the period when courts and enforcers were following the Chicago School, European competition law was developing rapidly, and in some crucial respects, differently. Key among those differences were its approach to dominance and its approach to vertical restraints. Eleanor, always ready for a challenge, was fascinated by this independent look at competition policy, and she became an expert in EU competition law.[37] It was second nature for her to try to understand what, exactly, were the challenges for competition policy in the European setting – comparable in many ways to that in the United States, in terms of economic sophistication and democratic bases, yet quite different in other ways. Should exclusionary practices be assessed differently if six, or twelve, or twenty-eight, distinct sovereigns are joining together to create a single, integrated market? What, if any, relevance to single-firm dominance does the existence of a larger state-owned sector of the economy have? Should the reach of competition law be affected by the enforcement mechanisms that are used – the Commission and the Member States, versus the all-comers approach the United States uses (the Department of Justice, the Federal Trade Commission, the State Attorneys General, private rights of action)?

Over the years, Eleanor's interests have expanded beyond "just" the United States and Europe, and they now encompass the entire world.[38] And, over the years,

---

[35] See e.g. Fox, Sullivan, and Peritz, *Cases and Materials*, at 73–4 (providing history of antitrust economics).

[36] Ibid., at 74.

[37] See e.g. E. M. Fox, 'Monopolization and Dominance in the United States and the European Community: Efficiency Opportunity and Fairness' (1986) 61 *Notre Dame L. Rev.* 981; E. M. Fox, 'Monopolization and Abuse of Dominance: Why Europe Is Different' (2014) 59 *Antitrust Bull.* 129; E. M. Fox, 'The Central European Nations and the EU Waiting Room' (1998) 23 *Brook. J. Int'l. L.* 251; E. M. Fox, 'Vision of Europe: Lessons for the World' (1994) 18 *Fordham L. J.* 379.

[38] See e.g. E. M. Fox, 'An Anti-Monopoly Law for China – Scaling the Walls of Government Restraints' (2009) 75 *Antitrust L.J.* 173; E. M. Fox, 'India: The Long Road to a Full-Function Competition Law'

competition laws have spread like wildfire. The International Competition Network just held its fifteenth annual conference, which was attended by nearly 550 participants from more than eighty jurisdictions.[39] This is an astonishing number for me, and I suspect for Eleanor, too, when we think back to the early 1960s when it was possible to count on the fingers of one hand the number of significant competition regimes around the globe. There are many commonalities among this plethora of jurisdictions, but many important differences. Those variations stem from such factors as the stage of development of the economy, the size of the state sector, the country's GDP, the business culture, and the stated goals of the competition law.

As competition law has spread around the world, the topic of international harmonization has naturally come up over and over again. During the mid 1990s, Eleanor participated in some distinguished groups that proposed possible international antitrust codes, either for adoption under the umbrella of the World Trade Organization, or for adoption as stand-alone instruments. She resisted strongly the idea that it was proper to acquiesce in practices that she regarded as "beggar-thy-neighbor" measures – in particular, the tolerance of export cartels that exists in many national laws (including those of the United States). Only a global authority, she argued, would have the incentive to look at global welfare, and would thus be able to prevent Country A from exacting anticompetitively high prices from the consumers of Country B.[40]

Not many people thought that Eleanor was wrong, as a matter of substance, but in the end too many people (and I was one, I must admit) thought that the time had not yet come for a legally binding global competition code that matches the world trading regime we have had since 1947. Instead, we have the ICN, which works on a voluntary basis with competition authorities and tries to build on the commonalities that exist.[41] My personal view is that it has succeeded well in this task, and that this ground-up approach is the one with the greatest potential to lead in the long run to greater convergence and better cooperation, all to the benefit of consumers everywhere.

I will close where I started. Eleanor has been a leader in both domestic and international competition law. She has the extraordinary ability to see the issues from many sides at the same time – an ability that I believe started when she brought her unique perspective to this field as the only woman in the room, but a woman

(2007) 21 *Antitrust* 72; E. Fox, 'The WTO's First Antitrust Case – Mexican Telecom: A Sleeping Victory for Trade and Competition' (2006) 9 *J. Int'l Econ. L.* 271.

[39] Competition Policy International, *Report on the ICN's 15th Annual Conference* (May 2016), www .competitionpolicyinternational.com/wp-content/uploads/2016/05/ICN-Column-May-Full-1.pdf

[40] See e.g. E. M. Fox, 'Global Problems in a World of National Law' (2000) 34 *New Eng. L. Rev.* 11; E. M. Fox, 'International Antitrust: Against Minimum Rules; for Cosmopolitan Principles' (1998) 43 *Antitrust Bull.* 5; E. M. Fox, 'The End of Antitrust Isolationism: The Vision of One World' (1992) *U. Chi. Legal F.* 221; E. M. Fox, 'Toward World Antitrust and Market Access' (1997) 91 *Am. J. Int'l L.* 1.

[41] International Competition Network, *ICN Factsheet and Key Messages* (Apr. 2009), www .internationalcompetitionnetwork.org/uploads/library/doc608.pdf

who was always willing and able to challenge the conventional wisdom. She puts herself in the shoes of the excluded dealer, of the company that was forced out of business by the dominant firm's predatory practices, of the smaller country trying to establish a sound competition law for the first time, or of the larger country for which this is a new endeavor. This volume, honoring her work, is most fitting, and I am honored to join all of you, as her colleague, her friend, and her admirer.

2

Citizen Fox

The Global Vision of Eleanor Fox

Philip Marsden and Spencer Weber Waller

This chapter will examine the growth of Professor Eleanor Fox's global and cosmopolitan vision for the future of competition policy. Over her illustrious career, Professor Fox's scholarship traces an arc that began with the battle for the soul of US antitrust law as the Chicago School's influence began to dominate the discourse, enforcement policy, and eventually the case law. At the same time, Professor Fox also participated in the vigorous debate over the extraterritorial application of US law to international cartels, monopolies, and mergers.

Perhaps as a result of the changes in US antitrust law, Professor Fox became a prominent voice in analyzing EU competition law and explaining that system to US and international audiences as the influence of the US as the antitrust hegemon began to wane. EU competition law was a natural focus for her scholarship, given its more complete vision of competition law in numerous important ways that fascinated Professor Fox.

In more recent times, Professor Fox has also focused on the proper level of governance for competition policy in a globalized economy. She has focused on issues of gaps, legitimacy, and sufficiency to argue that global problems deserve, and require, global solutions. Depending on the specific issue, she has argued for the use of true international instruments and institutions ranging from international codes, WTO rules for competition policy, cooperation, harmonization, technical assistance, world restatements, as well as other hard law and soft law solutions, to solve the familiar problems of national competition law being used to regulate global markets.

What most distinguishes Professor Fox from most other scholars in the field is her cosmopolitanism,[1] a willingness to look at competition issues through the lens of global welfare not tied to national citizenship. While often controversial, this

---

[1] Cosmopolitan (adj.): "Pertinent or common to the whole world: an issue of cosmopolitan import. Having constituent elements from all over the world or from many different parts of the world. So sophisticated as to be at home in all parts of the world or conversant with many spheres of interest: a cosmopolitan traveler" (www.thefreedictionary.com/cosmopolitan). See generally Kwame Anthony Appiah, *Cosmopolitan: Ethics in a World of Strangers* (Norton, 2006).

perspective has allowed Professor Fox to find creative solutions for historically intractable problems and maintain an unwavering moral compass in addressing competition policy as a means to address poverty, democracy, and economic justice for the have-nots in the global economy. We salute these accomplishments and conclude by speculating on the future and the promise as well as the obstacles for the implementation of Professor Fox's global vision.

2.1 THE BATTLE FOR THE SOUL OF ANTITRUST

As Professor Fox entered academia in the 1970s, she confronted a narrowing United States antitrust law. The discourse of US antitrust law began to elevate a particular type of economic analysis associated with the so-called Chicago School of antitrust which focused a narrow definition of allocative efficiency as the sole goal for antitrust.[2] Over time, this goal gained primacy in the US courts and enforcement agencies over a broader range of factors including history, precedent, fairness, equity, and the facts on the ground in specific cases.

Much of Professor Fox's early scholarship fought back against the assertion that antitrust, was, or should be, solely about consumer welfare as defined as wealth maximization.[3] Her eloquent work on these issues was not opposed to economic analysis, but suspicious of a single strand of neoclassical economics as the master of, rather the servant, of competition policy.

2.2 THE BROADER COMPETITION LAW VISION OF THE EUROPEAN UNION

Perhaps because of the changes and evolution in US antitrust law, Professor Fox became an ambassador for US and global audience for the broader vision of competition law embodied in the law of the European Union. That vision drew upon the ordoliberal tradition that existed in Germany at the time of the drafting the treaty establishing the European Economic Community (EEC) and the need for European competition law to promote the economic integration of the ever-expanding number of Member States.[4]

As a result, there developed a sophisticated body of EU (and EU Member State)[5] competition law that diverged significantly from the narrow vision of the Chicago

---

[2] See e.g. R. A. Bork, *The Antitrust Paradox* (1978); R. A. Posner, *Antitrust an Economic Perspective* (University of Chicago Press, 1976); R. A. Posner, 'The Chicago School of Antitrust Analysis' (1978) 127 *U. Pa. L. Rev.* 925.

[3] E. M. Fox, 'The Battle for the Soul of Antitrust' (1987) 75 *Cal. L. Rev.* 917; E. M. Fox, 'The Modernization of Antitrust: A New Equilibrium' (1981) 66 *Cornell L. Rev.* 1140. See generally R. Pitofsky (ed.), *How the Chicago School Overshot the Mark* (Oxford University Press, 2008).

[4] D. Gerber, *Law and Competition in Twentieth Century Europe: Protecting Prometheus* (Oxford University Press, 1998); A. Fiebig and S. Weber Waller, *Antitrust and American Business Abroad* (Thomson West, 4th edn, 2016), ch. 17.

[5] See generally A. Fiebig, *EU Business Law* (American Bar Association, 2015), 127–291; A. Ezrachi, *EU Competition Law: An Analytical Guide to the Leading Cases* (Hart, 4th edn, 2014).

School in the United States. Prior to the modernization, most agreements had to be notified to the European Commission or carefully drafted to fit within an existing block exemption. In addition, restrictive agreements potentially qualified for exemptions that could be interpreted to permit agreements which harmed competition but promoted other worthy goals of the EU. Vertical agreements were strictly condemned if they included resale price maintenance provisions or absolute territorial allocations.[6]

While the EU interpretation of hard core cartel agreements has somewhat converged with that in the US, many other areas have not. The EU has always had a more expansive view of abuse of dominance including a special responsibility of dominant firms not to harm competitive market conditions.[7] Thus, practices such as predatory pricing, margin squeezes, tying, loyalty rebates, unilateral refusals to deal, and violations of the essential facilities doctrine, which are either lawful, or extremely difficult to prove, in the United States, remain a fertile source of investigation, litigation, and liability in the EU. A wide variety of public restraints of competition by the Member States as well as regional and local governments are expressly unlawful in the EU, but typically immune from liability in the US under the state action doctrine.[8] State aid is also expressly included as part of EU competition law,[9] while at most weakly constrained by the commerce clause of the US Constitution. Similarly, antidumping and other import restraints are part of competition policy writ large, rather than work in tension with the antitrust laws, as is the case in the United States.[10]

On the procedural side, EU competition diverges significantly from the United States. Until modernization, EU competition law was enforced exclusively by the European Commission. Following modernization, EU competition law is enforced by the European Commission, the National Competition Agencies, and the Member State courts through a multilateral and networked approach embodied in the European Competition Network including a notion of subsidiarity.[11] This notion of a coordinated networked approach is unknown in the United States, which relies more heavy on private litigation and an ad hoc allocation of authority between the twin competition agencies of the federal government and the Attorneys General of the fifty states plus territories.[12]

---

[6]   See Ezrachi, *EU Competition Law*, at 162–80 (summarizing key cases).

[7]   See e.g. *Slovak Telecom*, Case COMP/AT.39523 (Oct. 15, 2014), 5 CMLR 3 [2016].

[8]   S. Weber Waller, 'Bringing Globalism Home: Lessons from Antitrust and Beyond' (2000) 32 *Loy. U. Chi. L.J.* 113.

[9]   J. Jorge Piernas López, *The Concept of State Aid Under EU Law: From Internal Market to Competition and Beyond* (Oxford University Press, 2015); A. Santa Maria, *Competition and State Aid: An Analysis of the EU Practice* (Wolters Kluwer, 2nd edn, 2015).

[10]   J. L. Kessler and S. Weber Waller, *International Trade and U.S. Antitrust Law* (Thomson Reuters, 2nd edn, 2016).

[11]   C. Vlachou, *The European Competition Network – Challenges and Perspectives* (European Public Law Organization, 2010).

[12]   See R. Wolfram and S. Weber Waller, 'Contemporary Antitrust Federalism: Cluster Bombs or Rough Justice?', in R. L. Hubbard and P. Jones Harbour (eds.), *Antitrust Law in New York State* (New York State Bar Association, 2nd edn, 2002), 3.

Professor Fox became over time the explainer in chief for these differences and persistent divergence between the two systems. She was the co-author of the first casebook on European Community law for US audiences with her chapters on competition law later expanded into a standalone casebook on EU competition law.[13] Subsequently, she co-authored a separate casebook on global issues in antitrust and competition law which included substantial EU materials.[14] Even her US antitrust law casebook designed for US students included a comparative perspective often drawing on the EU's experience to highlight US antitrust law's failures and successes.[15]

Equally importantly, Professor Fox has been a strong advocate in the US and abroad for the view that the United States was not the sole legitimate voice how to approach competition law and policy. The mere fact that the US had been one of the first important enforcers of competition law did not grant it a monopoly on wisdom or the correct way to approach a particular issue or controversy. Throughout her work, Professor Fox advocated that differing outcomes outside the US should be judged in terms of the laws, procedures, institutions, history, and legal tradition of that jurisdiction, and not merely on whether the case came out differently than it would have in the US Whether the issue was a different approach to merger law as in Boeing–McDonnell Douglas, monopolization–abuse of dominance in Microsoft, and the more recent high-tech investigations of Google and Facebook, Professor Fox was more likely to explain and analyze difference, rather than criticize it.[16]

2.3 THE LIMITS OF LOCAL LAW IN A GLOBAL ECONOMY

The natural evolution for Professor Fox's scholarship led to a keen interest in the limits of local and national competition law in a global economy. The experience of the United States in competition law began after the Civil War with state common law and later state antitrust statutes, both of which proved to be ineffective in regulating anticompetitive conduct for the rapidly emerging national economy.[17] It was only with the passage of the Sherman Act, and the later Clayton and FTC Acts, that there was an effective national system for regulating competition by law in

---

[13] G. A. Bermann, R. J. Goebel, W. J. Davey, and E. M. Fox, *Cases and Materials on European Union Law* (West Academic, 3rd edn, 2010); E. M. Fox, *The Competition Law of the European Union in Comparative Perspective: Cases and Materials* (West Academic, 2009).

[14] E. Fox and D. Crane, *Global Issues in Antitrust and Competition Law* (West Academic, 2010).

[15] E. Fox, *Cases and Materials on U.S. Antitrust in Global Context* (Thomson/West, 3rd edn, 2012).

[16] See e.g. E. M. Fox, 'Monopolization and Abuse of Dominance: Why Europe Is Different' (2014) 59 *Antitrust Bull.* 129; E. M. Fox, 'Microsoft (EC) and Duty to Deal: Exceptionality and the Transatlantic Divide' (spring 2008) 4 *Comp. Pol'y Int'l* 25; E. M. Fox, 'GE/Honeywell: The U.S. Merger that European Stopped – A Story of the Politics of Convergence', in E. M. Fox and D. A. Crane (eds.) *Antitrust Stories* (Foundation Press, 2007), 331.

[17] J. May, 'Antitrust Practice and Procedure in the Formative Era: The Constitutional and Conceptual Reach of State Antitrust Law, 1880–1918' (1987) 135 *U. Pa. L. Rev.* 495.

a truly national economy that transcended the formal jurisdiction and effective control of any one state.

The EU also needed competition law to maintain competition in the growing common market (later the single market) in order to maintain the free movement of goods, services, persons, and capital within the EU, but also to help achieve the single market in the first place. Like the United States, an EU-wide market required an EU-wide competition law and could not be left to the Member States, few of which had any extensive experience with competition law prior to the formation of the EEC in 1957. But EU-level competition law was also a tool to achieve the common market in the first place, in contrast to the United States where a national economy with free movement and few state imposed barriers to internal trade was already largely a reality when US federal antitrust law was enacted.[18]

The EU wrestled for decades with the issue of what was the proper level for competition law and enforcement as between the EU in Brussels and the growing number of Member States until it settled into its present form following the modernization of competition law in 2004.[19] Now, most notifications to the European Commission outside the merger area are a thing of the past. The Commission continues to set a consistent competition policy, develop block exemptions, as well as challenge significant EU and international cartels, important abuse of dominance cases affecting the EU as a whole, and mergers of a Community dimension within the meaning of the EU Merger Regulation. National competition authorities now enforce both Community and their own Member State competition laws and coordinate their investigations and enforcement actions with each other and the European Commission through the European Competition Network.[20]

The issue of what is the proper level to enforce also has a global dimension. Like the early history of the US and the EU, there are often situations where national (or regional bodies like the EU) must use national (or regional) competition law to seek to regulate anticompetitive conduct that is global in nature in terms of the markets, undertakings, and effects involved.[21] The past forty years are a testament to the importance of concepts like extraterritoriality, effects-based jurisdiction, comity, positive comity, cooperation agreements, mutual legal assistance treaties, and dispute resolution mechanisms in helping achieve a measure of success in specific investigations and enforcement actions involving global markets and multinational

---

[18] S. Weber Waller, 'Understanding and Appreciating EC Competition Law' (1992) 61 *Antitrust L.J.* 55–6.

[19] Council Regulation (EC) No. 1/2003 of 16 December 2002 on the implementation of the rules on competition laid down in Articles 81 and 82 of the Treaty, available at http://eur-lex.europa.eu/legal-content/en/ALL/?uri=CELEX:32003R0001

[20] Commission Notice on cooperation within the Network of Competition Authorities (text with EEA relevance), OJ C 101, 27.4.2004, available at http://eur-lex.europa.eu/legal-content/EN/ALL/?uri=CELEX:52004XC0427(02)

[21] Regional authorities also exist in Africa, the Caribbean, and elsewhere to address the separate issue of pooling resources among smaller and developing jurisdictions.

actors.[22] But it has also led to the recognition of the need to consider a global response to competition policy in a globalized economy.

As a result, Professor Fox has devoted a significant portion of her scholarly agenda to the question of what is the proper level of governance for competition policy in the modern global economy. Obviously, much of competition law is, and will remain, inherently local in nature. But at the same time, the world is replete with examples of serious competition problems which transcend national borders including cartels in world markets, export cartels, monopolization/abuse-of-dominance issues in hi-tech markets across the globe, and mergers which affect multiple markets and jurisdictions.

It is a basic tenet of the work of Eleanor Fox that truly global problems deserve global solutions. She has highlighted where national competition law fails even with the most robust cooperation because of issues of gaps, legitimacy, and sufficiency.[23] In articles and speeches too numerous to discuss in detail, she has examined the promise and pitfalls of:

- international codes;[24]
- international principles;[25]
- WTO rules and dispute resolution proceedings;[26]
- increased use of cooperation and networks;[27]
- technical assistance;[28]
- world restatements of the law of competition;[29] and
- other combinations of hard and soft law.

She explores all of these themes with a true cosmopolitan vision that draws on all three elements of our working definition of that term. First, she approaches competition policy in a manner that is pertinent or common to the whole world. Professor Fox often advocates for a competition policy based on true global welfare rather than any single national interest. Second, she uses constituent elements from all over the

---

[22] Fiebig and Waller, *Antitrust and American Business*, chs. 7 and 15.

[23] E. M. Fox, 'Can We Solve the Antitrust Problems of Globalization by Extraterritoriality and Cooperation? Sufficiency and Legitimacy' (2003) 48 *Antitrust Bull.* 355.

[24] Draft International Antitrust Code as a GATT–MTO–Plurilateral Trade Agreement (International Antitrust Code Working Group Proposed Draft 1993), published and released July 10, 1993, 64 Antitrust & Trade Reg. Rep. (BNA) No. 1628 (Aug. 19, 1993) (Special Supp.).

[25] E. M. Fox, 'Against Minimum Rules, for Cosmopolitan Principles' (1998) 43 *Antitrust Bull.* 5; E. M. Fox, 'Toward World Antitrust and Market Access' (1997) 91 *Am. J. Int'l L.* 1.

[26] E. M. Fox, 'Toward World Antitrust'; E. M. Fox, 'The WTO's First Antitrust Case – Mexican Telecoms: A Sleeping Victory for Trade and Competition' (2006) 9 *J. Int'l Econ. L.* 271.

[27] E. M. Fox, 'Antitrust without Borders: From Roots to Codes to Networks', in A. Guzman (ed.), *Cooperation, Comity, and Competition Policy* (Oxford University Press, 2010); E. M. Fox, 'Linked-In: Antitrust and the Virtues of a Virtual Network' (2009) 43 *Int'l Law.* 151.

[28] E. M. Fox, Antitrust and Regulatory Federalism: Races Up, Down, and Sideways, (2000) 75 *N.Y.U. L. Rev.* 1781 (2000).

[29] E. M. Fox, 'Competition Law and the Millennium Round' (1999) 2 *J. Int'l Econ. L.* 665.

world drawing on US, EU, and many other national and regional competition systems as part of her toolkit.

Finally, she is truly at home in all parts of the world and conversant with many spheres of interest – just consider the many voices in this volume and the enormous number of jurisdictions she has assisted over the years. This cosmopolitan competition law vision is permeated with a focus on how to address poverty, democracy, and economic justice in order to convince jurisdictions and international organizations of the value of robust markets carefully tailored to the history, culture, and legal system of each jurisdiction.

2.4 IMPLEMENTING THE (COSMOPOLITAN) VISION

Since the early 1990s, Professor Fox has been working tirelessly to convince antitrust and trade officials that they are taking a parochial view of what are actually global problems, and to address this she has been arguing for cosmopolitan solutions. Professor Fox suggested that all countries – but particularly WTO Members – ensure that their competition authorities consider the effects that business arrangements in their markets have on foreign competitors. To this end, she proposed a 'market access' principle that complements liberal trade, but which is not a trade norm. As this section will display, her conception is drawn from antitrust's own populist roots, which have long evinced a concern about market foreclosure. Professor Fox argued that not remembering and recognizing this itself contributes to the difficulty in moving forward in a constructive trade and competition work program. What is needed, she argued, is a deeper recognition of what she had long seen as antitrust law's evolving flaw.

To Professor Fox, competition authorities have developed an inappropriately narrow focus on the effects that business arrangements have on competition in their own jurisdiction. Such a 'parochial' focus results in 'blindered national vision' where governments are unable or are unwilling to consider effects on foreign interests.[30] Fox is also troubled by the fact that economic 'effects'-based analysis itself can mean that antitrust law, particularly in the United States, ignores potential harms to economic freedom and opportunity. She describes a rule of law that is 'weak' – not in terms of allowing capricious or lax enforcement of robust law – but in setting a higher probative standard, which thereby also means that remedial measures are less likely to be imposed. As she noted:

> In the 1960s, US law was construed to prohibit restraints that foreclosed less well-situated firms from a significant share of the market, even if the exclusion resulted from strong preferences for dealing with one's friends (reciprocity). The United States has abandoned this construction of law in favour of permissive legal principles that value the freedom of firms to impose vertical restraints unilaterally.

---

[30]   Fox, *Cosmopolitan Principles*, at 11–12.

Plaintiffs challenging vertical restraints under US law today must normally prove the restraint will limit output and harm consumers; it is not enough to show that the restraint merely blocks competitors 'unreasonably' . . . Thus, the problems faced by firms and nations that believe themselves excluded from foreign markets by vertical restraints include, in some nations such as the United States, a 'weak' rule of law, in addition to . . . lack of enforcement.[31]

To Professor Fox, the solution is obvious. In both domestic enforcement and international engagement, governments must take more interest in both the unfairness of the exclusion and the effects it has on competitors from other markets. Convincing WTO Members to take that kind of interest does not require a global harmonization project, Professor Fox argued:

[a] world competition system does not require a compendium of world rules for antitrust law. Nor does it require investigation into the minute differences between the antitrust laws of nations or a determination to harmonize the laws or converge them towards any existing model. Rather, it requires a guiding standard (world welfare), and an understanding of how transactions and action – government and private – may have an impact on world trade and competition in welfare reducing ways.[32]

To do this, Fox argues that more attention needs to be paid to the inherent complementarity among the goals of trade policy, competition policy and the WTO:

in matters of artificial restraints that block markets, trade and competition are two sides of one coin. Market-opening competition law is the virtual twin of liberal trade law. It is a complement of liberal trade law. A system facilitating trade may be put into place; nations may be required to keep open their doors to trade; but if commercial restraints can nonetheless block the market because they are not caught by the discipline of the world trading system, the open-market promise fails. Thus, market access competition issues belong in the WTO.[33]

2.4.1 Market-Opening Competition Law

Understanding market access is critical to appreciating Professor Fox's early global vision for competition law. Professor Fox argues that:

[s]ince market access is the trade/antitrust issue of most interest to the world trading systems today, I focus . . . on a market access principle for the world. Such a principle, focused on the trade and competition intersection, would be an

---

[31]   Ibid., at 22–3.
[32]   E. M. Fox and J. A. Ordover, 'Internationalizing Competition Law to Limit Parochial State and Private Action: Moving Towards a Vision of World Welfare' (1996) 24 *Int'l Bus. Lawyer* 458.
[33]   Fox, 'Competition Law and the Millennium Round', at 666.

especially fitting subject for a WTO agreement, which might naturally be called the Agreement on Trade- Related Aspects of Antitrust Measures, or TRAMs.[34]

Such an agreement would be feasible because:

> [n]ations with antitrust systems already have market access principles embedded in their law. The principles usually address ... cartels, vertical exclusionary restraints and monopolistic exclusions. Nations differ, sometimes significantly, as to what is the best formulation of the market access principle ... It is not the difference in the law that produces frictions and trade disputes, [however] it is the perception that a country does not enforce its own law.[35]

Professor Fox points to Europe as the precedent for a TRAMs from learning from 'Europe's Comparative Advantage':[36]

> [T]he European Economic Community faced the same challenge, among others, in the mid-1950s. It addressed, as its most important goal, the task of taking the parochialism out of trade and competition in the internal European market. In the internal market of the European Union, much parochialism has been removed with respect to both public and private restraints.[37]

Professor Fox explained: "The brilliant basic concept was to lift the frontiers that stood as barriers around each of the nation-states, and to assure that neither governments nor private firms could replace them with border restraints, discriminatory measures, or measures of equivalent effect."[38] And that: "Most basic to the competition law of the European Union is the principle prohibiting private restraints that barricade national markets."[39]

Professor Fox recognized that the trade-related aspirations of WTO Members are more modest than the European goal of market integration with its supranational legal mechanisms and institutions. She argues, however, that "this is a difference of no importance to the point that *we need to embrace global thinking.*"[40] To do that, we should search for the political philosophy deep within antitrust itself.

In seeking a vision of liberal antitrust to fit the world view of liberal trade, Professor Fox again turned to the very foundations of antitrust.[41] Professor Fox's international market access principle is designed to modernize and internationalize antitrust by reminding it of its equity based original position. She argues: "Antitrust should serve consumers' interests and should also serve other, established, non-conflicting objectives ... [including the] dispersion of economic power [and] freedom and

---

[34]   Fox, 'Towards World Antitrust', at 3.
[35]   Ibid., at 23.
[36]   Ibid., at 7.
[37]   Ibid., at 1–2.
[38]   Ibid., at 5.
[39]   Ibid., at 7.
[40]   Ibid., at 8.
[41]   Ibid., at 3

opportunity to compete on the merits."[42] For Professor Fox these are the "traditional antitrust values that protect access to markets."[43]

2.4.2 *The Details of the Market Access Principle: No Substantial Unjustified Market Blockage*

While deep-rooted in traditional values, Professor Fox's proposal itself was direct and detailed: "Nations should have and enforce laws prohibiting commercial conduct that unreasonably impairs market access."[44] At the same time, she views this obligation as a flexible one: "[T]hey might agree to the general principle that *there should be no substantial unjustified market blockage by public or private action* (as well as no transactional cartels). Each nation would then be responsible for implementing this principle in its national law."[45]

Along with the responsibility for implementation, Professor Fox also gives jurisdictions the freedom to define their commitment:

> Opponents of a world system argue that nations would find it impossible to agree on a market access principle. This is not a problem under this proposal. Each nation would define for itself what it means by an 'unjustifiable' market access restraint. Simply, it must formulate its law in a credible, non-discriminatory, clear and understandable way.[46]
>
> She suggests three priority trade/competition areas:
>
> Access to markets may be impaired by conduct in one of three categories: (1) abuse of dominance: exclusions by monopoly or dominant firms, (2) cartels with boycotts, and (3) vertical restraints such as exclusive dealing by the few leading firms in high barrier, concentrated markets wherein entry by outsiders is difficult. The laws of virtually all nations that have competition laws cover such restraints.[47]

She notes that her proposal "does not require that all countries adopt full-blown competition laws. Merely they must not allow unreasonable restraints on market access. [However the] most obvious but not only way to do so is by adoption of competition law at least in the three identified areas."[48]

To this end, Fox has recommended that governments make an international commitment to a cosmopolitan approach. As she explained in the *American Journal of International Law*:

> [C]osmopolitanism is the converse of parochialism. It connotes concern for the interests of the entire community without regard to nationality, while recognising

---

42 E. M. Fox, 'The Modernization of Antitrust: A New Equilibrium' (1981) 66 *Cornell L. Rev.* 1140, 1182.
43 Ibid., at 1189.
44 Fox, 'Competition Law and the Millennium Round', at 672.
45 Fox, 'Towards World Antitrust', at 23.
46 Ibid., at 24.
47 Fox, 'Competition Law and the Millennium Round', at 671.
48 Ibid., at n. 16.

the legitimate role for national and provincial governments to act in the interests of their citizens.[49]

Elsewhere she has stated: "The national-only concern of national law is out of step with the reality that even local transactions have global impacts,"[50] and that: "National law enforcement should account for global impacts, not just national impacts."[51]

That would mean we had to have some idea of *how* trade actions should be decided. Here Professor Fox has argued for a cosmopolitan international welfare standard. A national authority, and if needed, a WTO Panel could be "charged to take a *global* rather than a *national* view of each problem, taking into account all harms and benefits wherever they occur."[52]

In this regard, the WTO Secretariat developed a simple formula to decide when a domestic competition policy decision is out of touch with the world view. Such actions would be unlawful if: *"the negative consequences for foreign interests … exceed the benefits to domestic agents.* Only then does the national competition policy give rise to an inefficient allocation of resources from a global point of view."[53]

Accepting that accounting for all the global costs and benefits would be difficult, if not impossible, proponents of a global welfare standard have recognized that rules of thumb and presumptions would be needed. One example came from the WTO Secretariat quoted above that: "a domestic competition policy approach is out of touch with the world view where the negative consequences for foreign interests exceed the benefits to domestic agents."[54]

When he was WTO Deputy Director General, Anwarul Hoda recognised that:

> use of a rule of reason approach at the multilateral level would involve considerations quite different from those arising in national jurisdictions, for example on standards, enforcement and remedies. Thus, if it were decided to employ a rule of reason in any multilateral competition rules, considerable work would be required to adapt this approach to that particular context.[55]

In terms of detail and in substance, the proposals of Professor Fox – and the related suggestions of the WTO Secretariat – proved ahead of their time. They drew some external criticism,[56] but that was not why their further consideration did not

---

[49] Fox, 'Towards World Antitrust', at 2, n. 4.

[50] Fox, *Cosmopolitan Principles*, at 12.

[51] Ibid., at 8.

[52] Fox, 'Towards World Antitrust', at 855–6.

[53] WTO, *Annual Report 1997*, 1 Special Topic: Trade and Competition 55 (1997) (emphasis added).

[54] Ibid.

[55] Comments by A. Hoda, 'Trade, Competition Policy and the World Trade Organization, Global Forum on Competition and Trade Policy Conference', New Delhi, March 17–19, 1997, at 8 (on file with author).

[56] Critiques of the detailed Fox and WTO proposals can be found in Philip Marsden, *A Competition Policy for the WTO* (2003); Daniel K. Tarullo, 'Norms and Institutions in Global Competition Policy'

advance. The overall pursuit of competition rules in global trade fora was derailed more generally, through the failure of the Doha Round and the decision of governments not to pursue the multilateral competition agenda further through the WTO. That agenda did continue however, namely through the International Competition Network,[57] and again, Professor Fox was influential at its inception and with respect to its work programme.

In one of her articles, *Antitrust without Borders: From Roots to Codes to Networks*, Professor Fox reflects on the journey. She notes that: "The lack of traction of world antitrust in the WTO and the rise of networking have focused our thinking on horizontal solutions to world problems."[58]

The focus on a horizontal solution naturally leads one to the work of the International Competition Network as the largest forum for regular horizontal contact between enforcers. At the International Competition Network, front-line officials swap lessons from their enforcement work, and agree on best practices.[59] These are products that are tangible and worthwhile and have benefits in the near-term. In contrast to trade meetings about competition policy, particularly at the WTO, these meetings are demand-led, by competition officials, and thus discussions are focused and pragmatic. It helps that participants are not sitting behind a particular flag, but instead meet as colleagues, in a shared battle against anticompetitive activity ... and in that way, they are far more cosmopolitan form of competition law than ever before.

But Professor Fox has always wanted more, and she is right to focus on *the:* "*One problem that horizontal solutions won't solve: export and world cartels and trade-restrictive state action.*"[60] Here clearly more work is needed; where these restraints depend on state exemption, it's appropriate that state action – WTO or otherwise – be focused to resolve these problems. Of necessity, that work will require the type of cosmopolitan approach that Professor Fox has embodied throughout her distinguished career.

2.5 CONCLUSION

We salute Professor Fox for leading us on such an incredible journey, with such a truly global vision. Professor Fox is renowned as the champion of the cosmopolitan approach, and empath of foreign legal systems. The journey

---

(2000) 94 *Am. J Intl Law* 478. See also American Bar Association, 'Using Antitrust Laws to Enhance Access of U.S. Firms to Foreign Markets' (1995) 29 *Int'l Law* 945.

57 International Competition Network, www.internationalcompetitionnetwork.org

58 E. M. Fox, Fox, 'Antitrust without Borders: From Roots to Codes to Networks' (November 2015) available at http://e15initiative.org/wp-content/uploads/2015/09/E15-Competition-Fox-FINAL.pdf at 8.

59 See P. Lugard (ed.), *The International Competition Network at 10: Origins, Accomplishments and Aspirations* (2011).

60 Fox, 'Antitrust without Borders', at 5.

along such a path will be a long one but is all the more needed in these times of rising economic nationalism, protectionism, and xenophobia. She is a promoter of equity and rivalry and a relentless optimist – and as such we are honored to honor her with this chapter as a small contribution to her accomplishments and inspiration to us all.

PART II

Reconciling Equity and Efficiency

The Challenge of Making Markets Work for People

A

Competition for the People

3

The Poverty of Competition Law

The Short Story [*]

Ioannis Lianos

3.1 INTRODUCTION

For a long time considered a fringe topic, of interest for developing and emergent economies, the question of inequality and poverty has recently taken centre stage in mainstream competition law scholarship in developed countries. Some of this literature deplores the current state of competition law, which has largely ignored this issue, and argues for a different paradigm that would actively engage with economic inequality and its causes. This literature on the goals of competition law does not also usually engage with the issue of the strategies available to address economic inequality concerns. One may adopt the strategy of *removing* the various obstacles identified that generate and support the specific form of inequality of interest and/or the preferred strategy of *compensating* through the transfer of adequate resources the individuals (or groups) affected by inequality, the latter being the strategy preferred by economists because of the separation in welfare economics of issues of efficiency from issues of distributive justice.[1]

While thought-provoking and suggesting a variety of reforms, these studies have not so far offered a coherent theoretical argument and framework explaining why equality, and its various facets, should become a concern for competition law, and how this will interact with the existing economic efficiency- and/or consumer surplus-oriented paradigm of competition law. If one is to take equity concerns seriously, it becomes essential to provide a solid theoretical framework that would engage with the arguments put forward by those defending the status quo. These are essentially three: (1) the need for competition law to develop concepts and measurement tools that justify, from a welfare perspective, the recourse to state intervention in markets, welfare being narrowly

[*] The author would like to thank Fransisco Alves da Costa-Cabral, Justin Lindeboom and Bjorn Lundqvist for their comments on earlier versions of this study, as well as Andrew McLean for useful research assistance and editorial suggestions.
[1] See, for instance, the way this debate is framed in the recent book by M. J. Trebilcock, *Dealing with Losers: The Political Economy of Policy Transitions* (Oxford University Press, 2015).

defined, for methodological and ideological reasons; (2) the availability of other, presumably more effective, institutions than competition law to deal with inequality; and (3) the existence of a trade-off between equality and efficiency, meaning that focusing on equality may harm economic efficiency.

This Chapter mostly engages with the last two arguments.[2] I show how the mainstream paradigm of competition law tackles issues of economic inequality in an indirect and implicit way, distributive justice choices often remaining unacknowledged and almost never addressed upfront. Taking a social contract perspective, and noting the hybrid nature of competition law, which is a tool of economic order, but also a form of social regulation, I argue that issues of distributive justice and economic inequality should take a more visible and significant role in competition law analysis.

The study then turns to the institutional question, examining the various instruments that governments use in order to equalise, and the respective role of more conventional tools against inequality, such as taxation, concluding that the institutional argument against equity concerns in competition law does not stand serious scrutiny. I examine the various instruments that governments use in order to equalise, and the respective role of more conventional tools against inequality, such as taxation. I then delve into the availability of equally effective alternative institutions and compare their advantages and disadvantages to competition law. I critically assess the argument that there is a trade-off between equality and efficiency, and that focusing on equality may harm economic efficiency, which has often led to prioritising economic efficiency concerns at the expense of less equality.

The final part revisits the question of what is to be equalised. Drawing on the idea of 'complex equality', I argue for a fairness-driven competition law whose purpose will be to equalise the structural position of the individual (or collective) agents in the various overlapping social spheres in which they are active, so that economic power is not easily converted to cultural or political power. I will briefly examine the contours of this fairness-driven competition law, hopefully showing that competition law's enrichment with equity concerns is both politically necessary and conceptually appealing.

3.2 COMPETITION LAW FOR REDUCING INEQUALITY: A POPULIST APPROACH?

A number of authors have recently put forward the idea that competition law should aim to reduce inequality, in addition to its more conventional set of

---

[2] A longer study also explores the first one (I. Lianos, 'The Poverty of Competition Law – The Long Story' (CLES Research paper 2/2018, UCL Faculty of Laws).

objectives.[3] This may lead to more aggressive competition law enforcement against the abuse of market power.[4] The consumer welfare standard should be calibrated to prioritise antitrust action that takes into account the distribution of income and wealth and that benefits the middle class and the less advantaged.[5] These authors accept the possibility that 'anticompetitive conduct by the less well-off that extracts wealth from the rich might not be condemned',[6] and argue for antitrust remedies that primarily benefit less advantaged consumers.[7] Conduct may be considered anticompetitive 'if it harms middle- and lower-income consumers, even while benefiting wealthier consumers and shareholders'.[8] Accepting these suggestions would imply the inclusion of an explicit distributional perspective in the enforcement of competition law.[9]

There are various ways this concern may be operationalised. Economic and social equality can be recognised as one of the goals of competition law, along with consumer welfare and efficiency,[10] for instance by forming part of a broader and explicit 'public interest' standard. This would give a higher priority to public interest goals than consumer welfare and efficiency, such standard also applying in non-merger cases.[11] Proponents of this idea call for a greater simplification of antitrust rules, away from the complicated and expensive to implement rule-of-reason approaches, which are perceived as defendant biased. They are also in favour of structural remedies, instead of 'complicated conduct remedies', which would make antitrust agencies more accountable and transparent.[12]

According to these authors, antitrust should aim to tame economic concentration and to distribute economic ownership and control. This will prevent unjust wealth transfers from consumers to firms with market power, and will preserve open markets.[13] In their view, the simplification of antitrust should aim to restore 'a progressive-populist antitrust under the citizen interest standard', breaking with the past lax approaches towards mergers, monopolisation and vertical restraints. This may go as far as challenging the possession of damaging monopoly and oligopoly power by firms through some form of 'no-fault' monopoly or oligopoly doctrine, whenever possessing a monopoly or an oligopoly 'inflicts substantial injury and cannot be justified on operational grounds, such as economies of scale'.[14]

---

[3] See, among others, J. B. Baker and S. C. Salop, 'Antitrust, Competition Policy, and Inequality' (2015) 104 *Georgetown Law Journal* 1, 11; L. Khan and S. Vaheesan, 'Market Power and Inequality: The Antitrust Counterrevolution and Its Discontents' (2017) 11 *Harvard Law and Policy Review* 235, 245.

[4] Baker and Salop, 'Antitrust, Competition Policy, and Inequality', 22–3.

[5] Ibid., 18–20.

[6] Ibid., fn. 61.

[7] Ibid., 20.

[8] Baker and Salop, 'Antitrust, Competition Policy, and Inequality', 24.

[9] See, T. Atkinson, *Inequality: What Can Be Done?* (Harvard University Press, 2015).

[10] Baker and Salop, 'Antitrust, Competition Policy, and Inequality', 25.

[11] Ibid.

[12] L. Khan and S. Vaheesan, 'Market Power and Inequality: The Antitrust Counterrevolution and Its Discontents' (2017) 11 *Harvard Law and Policy Review* 235, 276.

[13] Ibid., 279.

[14] Ibid., 285. These proposals are reminiscent of some suggestions made in the past. On the basis of this declaration of the inability of Section 1 of the Sherman Act to deal with the 'oligopoly problem' and

The emphasis on 'populist' antitrust is understood as a counterpoint to the technocratic consensus built over the last three decades, first in the US, then in the EU and some other jurisdictions, that competition law should rely on the learnings of neoclassical price theory and on economic efficiency considerations, although the extent of influence of the latter varies from jurisdiction to jurisdiction.[15] Technocracy presupposes the systematic integration of scientific (here economic) expertise in policymaking and implementation. In addition to the criticisms, a growing number of competition law scholars have also expressed concern over the apparent dissociation of competition law technocracy from the political sphere, and the resulting 'democratic deficit' that has probably ignited the 'populist' backlash we have observed in recent years.[16]

These different proposals have been criticised, and the debate is still ongoing among the competition law and economics expert community. Although it seems relatively uncontroversial that lack of competition and market power may contribute to inequality, a more fundamental issue consists in understanding whether reduced competition in markets constitutes one of the most significant sources of inequality, or whether it plays a relatively minor role, in which case, it could be argued that one should take care of other, more 'significant causes' of economic inequality. These other causes may relate to inheritance of wealth and human capital inequality, which acts cumulatively along the various generations and may lead to substantial differences in economic power and consequently inequalities in income. These may be exacerbated by the possibility of those possessing capital to use these assets as collateral in order to obtain loans on financial markets, something that is not possible for those that do not hold capital (property, tangible and intangible assets), and who exclusively rely on their labour, which cannot be used as collateral.[17]

As valid as these concerns may appear, it could be argued that the consumer welfare approach prevailing in most competition law systems around the world already takes into account some of these distributive justice concerns. But, is this the case?

the difficulties of expanding the scope of both Sections 5 of the FTC Act and 2 of the Sherman Act, the White House Task Force on Antitrust Policy (the *Neal Report* of 1968), and the Industrial Reorganization Act proposed by Senator Philip Hart in 1972 suggested the targeted breakup of tightly oligopolistic industries, a prospect that was heavily opposed by antitrust conservatives, influenced by the Chicago school of antitrust economics, whose intellectual influence began to rise in the 1970s (P. C. Neal, W. F. Baxter, R. H. Bork and C. H. Fulda, 'Report of the White House Task Force on Antitrust Policy' (1968) 2 *Antitrust Law and Economics Review* 11; S. 3832, 92nd Congress, 2nd Session (1972)).

[15] This could be considered as the essence of the 'economic approach' in competition law. For a discussion of the view of antitrust as technocracy, see D. A. Crane, 'Technocracy and Antitrust' (2009) 86 *Texas Law Review* 1159.

[16] H First and S Weber Waller, 'Antitrust's Democracy Deficit' (2013) 81(5) *Fordham Law Review* 2543.

[17] For a discussion of this distinction between capital and labour as a contributing factor to inequality, see G. M. Hodgson, 'How Capitalism Actually Generates More Inequality'; G.M. Hodgson, Conceptualizing capitalism: A summary, (2016) 20(1) *Competition & Change*, 37 (Evonomics), available at http://evonomics.com/how-capitalism-actually-generates-more-inequality

3.3 THE CONSUMER WELFARE APPROACH AND DISTRIBUTIVE JUSTICE CONCERNS

In its simplest, the case for intervention against market power is based on an understanding that a substantial position of market power forms the classic case of market failure.[18] Market failure is a general term describing situations in which market outcomes are not Pareto efficient. Pareto efficiency occurs when resources are so allocated that it is not possible to make anyone better off without making someone else worse off. This is an abstract concept, which is grounded on the theoretical construct of general equilibrium, which looks at the economy in its entirety, that is, where all markets are considered together. In practice, though, the case against monopoly (as the archetypal example of market failure due to market power) is based on partial equilibrium analysis, which looks at only one market at a time, characterised by its demand and supply curves.[19] In a nutshell, to focus on a single market rests on the assumption that the levels of income and the prices of both substitute and complement products are fixed. Otherwise, an increase in income levels would shift the demand schedule outwards.[20]

By definition, this assumption does not consider the implications of a change of prices of substitute or complement products in a market on income levels. This is a quite heroic assumption to the extent that each market is analysed independently of others and interdependencies between prices in one market and income levels in another are usually not taken into account. Although the partial equilibrium model may be useful for analysing distributional consequences within the same relevant market, it ignores distributional implications in the other parts of the economy. Although from the point of view of economic efficiency, this simple summary of a complex system may provide sufficient information when analysing the effects of a price change on a specific market, from the point of view of equality, it is less so, to the extent that the analysis in this case would be to analyse the distribution of wealth among the people of a community, by definition active in multiple markets, as consumers, workers, shareholders, etc. But this is the price to pay for the benefits of the simplicity of the model and the capacity to draw inferences from it.

Consequently, the distributional implications of an anti-competitive activity within a relevant market are the bread and butter of competition law. The trigger for competition law enforcement is (likely) changes to consumer surplus caused by an increase in price/restriction in output due to the exploitation of market power (or,

---

[18] Part of the discussion in this section and the following one draws on I. Lianos, V. Korah with P. Siciliani, *Competition Law: Analysis, Cases and Materials* (Oxford University Press, 2019).

[19] See, for a discussion, G. J., Werden, *Antitrust's Rule of Reason: Only Competition Matters* (US Department of Justice – Antitrust Division, 2013).

[20] The same holds for a reduction in the price of complement products (which correspond to a discount in the price for the combination of products); whereas a reduction in the price of substitute products would shift the demand schedule inwards (since consumer would demand a similar price reduction to keep purchasing the product sold).

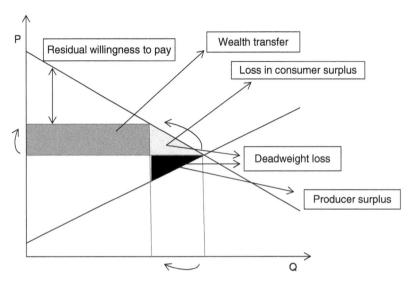

FIGURE 3.1 Market power and efficiency

more concretely, the likelihood that an increase in market power will lead to its exploitation). This is basically treated as a proxy for consumer welfare, although the exact definition of this term is a matter of controversy.[21]

Consumer surplus can be graphically depicted as the area under the downward sloping demand curve but above the price charged (i.e. the residual consumer willingness to pay) (see Figure 3.1). Total surplus is the sum of consumer and producer surplus, the latter roughly corresponding to the accounting concept of operating profit margin, so that changes in producer surplus should equate to changes in profits.

Usually, looking at changes in total or consumer surplus makes no difference in practice, since both tend to move in the same direction, as graphically captured by the deadweight loss, which is the loss of consumer and producer surplus due to a restriction in output caused by an increase in price, and stands to signify how allocative efficiency has worsened due to the exploitation of market power. As put by Werden '[a] nything enlarging the metaphorical pie offers a potential Pareto improvement because it is possible to make at least one individual better off while no one is worse off'.[22]

In this sense, the case against the exploitation of substantial market power, if one takes an economic efficiency perspective, is not linked to the transfer of wealth from

---

[21]   One may, for instance, refer to the use of the term 'consumer welfare' by R. H. Bork, *The Antitrust Paradox: A Policy at War with Itself* (Free Press, 1978), 66, advancing a 'consumer welfare prescription' for US antitrust law, but basically confusing this concept with allocative efficiency (loss of total surplus), as he conceived 'consumer welfare' as an efficiency and not a distributive justice goal. For a discussion, see K. Heyer, 'Consumer Welfare and the Legacy of Robert Bork' (2014) 57(S3) *Journal of Law and Economics* S19.

[22]   Werden, *Antitrust's Rule of Reason*, 28.

consumer to producers over those (infra-marginal) units of output still sold (i.e. the rectangle in the graph above, also called wealth transfer), but merely on the lost transactions which could have taken place under a more competitive scenario (i.e. the deadweight loss).[23] In any case, for operational purposes the focus is on consumer harm, as captured by the (likelihood of) higher prices and lower quantity; bearing in mind that in practice hardly anyone in the field of enforcement ever actually attempts to measure/estimate actual changes in either total or consumer welfare.[24]

Beside allocative efficiency, it is often argued that a competitive equilibrium will also maximise productive efficiency, where output is produced with the least amount of resources, given the current set of production technologies – i.e. demand is served by the most efficient firms. This is not, however, always the case, in the sense that there are market configurations where a trade-off between allocative and productive efficiencies triggered by an increase in a position of substantial market power might emerge. Oliver Williamson put forward the possibility of a trade-off between allocative inefficiency and productive efficiency, coming to the conclusion that small cost savings may offset relatively larger price increases, thus entailing a more permissive standard for antitrust enforcement.[25] However, his conclusions were reliant on strong assumptions, such as that the market configuration before the increase in market power was competitive; whereas if firms had already some degree of market power (so that prices were already above costs) total welfare would most likely be reduced, i.e. alongside consumer welfare.[26]

The Williamsonian trade-off between productive and allocative efficiency also takes place within a static framework, that is holding technology and the product space fixed. In reality, firms compete also through innovation, which could either be process oriented (i.e. increasing productive efficiency) or product oriented (improving the variety and/or quality of their offer). Under these circumstances, the trade-off is not as much between productive and allocative efficiency, but between dynamic and allocative efficiency, the former, more elusive, concept capturing the idea that product innovation, where firms compete on quality (horizontal and vertical)

---

[23] The irrelevance of distributional concerns is normally justified with reference to the 'compensation principle' (also called the Kaldor–Hicks efficiency criterion, or potential Pareto improvement) which posits that, if gainers can compensate losers and still be better off, the change observed in the partial equilibrium analysis is desirable. That is to say, even if the compensation never actually takes place, it is down to the political system to take care of the redistribution of the 'pie' (the separability thesis).

[24] There are some examples of competition authorities commissioning studies into the effects of their past decision, thus basically assessing whether their intervention (or lack thereof) has increased consumer surplus. For an overview, see, OECD, *Impact Evaluation of Merger Decisions* (2011) available at www.oecd.org/daf/competition/Impactevaluationofmergerdecisions2011.pdf

[25] O. E. Williamson, 'Economies as an Antitrust Defense: Welfare Tradeoffs' (1968) 58 *American Economic Review*, 18.

[26] M. D. Whinston, 'Antitrust Policy Towards Horizontal Mergers', in *Handbook of Industrial Organization* (Elsevier, 2007), vol. III, ch. 36, 2374.

attributes, as opposed to price/quantity in a static fashion, is equally important for the maximisation of social welfare in the long run.

Traditionally, the analysis of market power, and the corresponding trade-offs outlined above, focus on economic efficiency and do not explicitly deal with distributional issues. The case against monopoly is motivated by the desire to correct for the inefficiency caused by lost (marginal) transactions (or volume effect) – the deadweight loss – rather than the implicit wealth transfer from consumers to producers over (infra-marginal) transactions. Moreover, reliance on firms' profitability as a guide for enforcement is problematic in light of the difficulty to tell whether high profits are the results of superior efficiency/quality, or the outcome of anticompetitive entry and expansion barriers. Focusing on the source of the superior profits of the firms, superior efficiency/quality or anticompetitive strategies, indicates some form of 'moral' judgement on the worthiness of curative action, which may be motivated by the idea that competition law should promote competition 'on the merits', and that a successful competitor should not be turned away when he wins. It may also result from a more Schumpeterian idea that superior profits may lead to an innovation race that would be overall welfare enhancing (in the sense that technological progress will spur an increase of total surplus).

However, it is possible to build a broader narrative for intervention, on the basis of some wider conception of 'consumer welfare' or 'consumer harm'. The concept of 'consumer harm' has been used to promote the view that competition law takes into account only the interests of a group, consumers, and not those of other groups of actors in the economy (e.g. managers, shareholders, employees). From this perspective, the various expressions of consumer harm employed in competition law (i.e. consumer welfare, consumer harm, consumer choice) may be linked, to varying degrees, to the principle of distributive justice. Certainly, the concept of distributive justice has multiple dimensions and its meaning has evolved through time,[27] but it is possible to define it as referring to the morally required distribution of shares of resources among members of a given group, either because of their membership to that group or in accordance with some measure of entitlement which applies to them in virtue of their membership. This is understood dynamically, that is across various situations in the specific jurisdiction. Rights and duties in distributive justice are thus 'agent-general', as they relate to a specific category of actors or group.

There may be various theoretical justifications for an approach that would favour consumers, if one starts from the hypothesis that there is a state of inequality in the structural position of the group of 'consumers' vis-à-vis other groups in society. One could argue for a public choice/political economy view based on the relative weakness of consumers' lobbying compared to firms' or workers' lobbying,[28] to the extent that their heterogeneity and their great numbers make collective action in

---

[27] See, S. Fleischacker, *A Short History of Distributive Justice* (Harvard University Press, 2005).
[28] See D. Neven and L.-Hendrik Röller, 'Consumer Surplus vs. Welfare Standard in a Political Economy Model of Merger Control' (2005) 23 *International Journal of Industrial Organization* 829.

their interests more difficult to organise. Competition law may also have been designed to offer an institutional bias in favour of consumers,[29] to the extent that other areas of law prioritise the interest of other societal groups (e.g. labour law–the interest of workers, company law–the interest of shareholders, intellectual property law the–interest of inventors).

One may also take a social contract perspective, such as that put forward by John Rawls[30] to argue for the protection of consumers, rather than other groups that may be affected by a restriction of competition.

According to Rawls's first principle of social justice, each person was recognised as having an equal right to the most extensive liberties compatible with similar liberties for all, a principle to be inscribed in the political constitution. Rawls's second principle of social justice advances that social and economic inequalities are to satisfy two conditions: first, they are to be attached to offices and positions open to all under conditions of fair equality of opportunity; and, second, they are to be to the greatest benefit of the least-advantaged members of society (the difference principle or maximin).[31] His justification of this principle of justice makes use of a thought experiment, a hypothetical situation called the 'original position', where individuals (an impartial observer) choose the basic principles of the society behind a 'veil of ignorance', that is without knowing their own position in the resulting social order, as well as being ignorant of their personal identities, individual social standing and chances in life.[32] The original position thought experiment relies on several assumptions. First, Rawls assumes that people are self-interested and make choices in order to maximise the primary goods they would use for carrying out their life plan, without however having any knowledge as to the distribution of endowments in society. Second, Rawls assumes that people are extremely risk averse, hence their choice, at the original position, to promote the situation of the least advantaged group.

Under the difference principle, Rawls favours the establishment of institutions that would maximise the improvement of the 'least-advantaged' group in society, by enabling these individuals to exercise control of wealth and other economic resources. This avoids Rawls the need to make any interpersonal comparisons of utility, between rich and poor persons, as what counts is the welfare of the least well-off person. By 'least advantaged' group Rawls refers to 'those belonging to the income class with the lowest expectations'.[33] Although the advantaged may deserve their

---

[29] J. Farell and M. Katz, 'The Economics of Welfare Standards in Antitrust' (2006) 2(2) *Competition Policy International*.

[30] See, most notably, J. Rawls, A *Theory of Justice* (Harvard University Press, 1999, first pub. 1971).

[31] Ibid., 63–73.

[32] Rawls's impartial observer arrives at rational decisions under conditions of uncertainty. In contrast, Harsanyi's impartial observer makes decisions under conditions of risk and therefore may take into account the frequencies of different income levels. See, J. Harsanyi, 'Cardinal welfare, individualistic ethics and interpersonal comparisons of utility', (1955) 63 Jourrnal of Political Economy 309.

[33] J. Rawls, *Justice as Fairness: A Restatement* (Harvard University Press, 2001), 59.

greater share of surplus because of their greater contribution to production, it is important to also aim to improve the 'least advantaged group' in society to enhance their active participation in the communal deliberative life of the community.[34] Rawls also recognises the role of 'reflective equilibrium' which enables a deliberative process under a coherence account of justification that may adjust the initial decision of general justice principles, that is, the current set of beliefs deduced from the hypothetical thought experiment of the original position, with a process of reflective deliberation incorporating a wide range of diverse moral commitments into a coherent moral system in which all moral beliefs are consistent and mutually supporting.

Would adopting a Rawlsian perspective that incorporates an equality concern, in the sense of a maximin social welfare function, imply the choice of a consumer welfare approach? Hence, the category of 'final consumer' may be considered as the 'least advantaged' category, whose interests an impartial observer may opt to protect, when designing the desirable social order behind a veil of ignorance.

This may provide a theoretical justification for a distributive justice principle that would promote the interest of final consumers in competition law. The same principle may justify weighing more the effects of an anticompetitive conduct on low-income categories of final consumers, as opposed to efficiency gains passed on to a wealthier category of final consumers or suppliers, by integrating some distributional weights, on the assumption that it is more likely that corporate shareholding, either directly, or indirectly through pension funds, is more widespread for the rich than for the poor.[35]

---

[34] Hence, this is independent of their eventual contribution to the productive process (G. Warnke, *Justice and Interpretation* (Polity, 1992) 10), although as Rawls remarked 'it seems impossible to avoid a certain arbitrariness' in defining the category (*Theory of Justice*, 98). In more recent work Rawls defined the 'least advantaged' in relation to the share they have of primary goods, noting also (*Justice as Fairness*, 57–61) that 'the least advantaged is not a rigid designator'. However, even if one takes the view that Rawls requires some form of participation in the productive process for the 'least advantaged' category, it may easily be argued that in the digital economy consumers participate in the production process by enabling their data to be harvested by digital platforms and then used as input in the input–output process that ends up with the monetisation of 'big data' in product or financial markets.

[35] On the use of distributional weights in competition law, see *Superior Propane*, where the Canadian Bureau of Competition when considering the possible trade-off between efficiencies and likely anticompetitive effects, took into account, with regard to the latter, not only the loss in allocative efficiency but also the socially adverse portion of the wealth transfer from lower-income residents (the consumers) to bulk propane retailers (the suppliers), thus adhering to a 'balancing weights' approach (Federal Court of Appeal, *Canada (Commissioner of Competition)* v. *Superior Propane Inc. and ICG Propane Inc.*, [2001] 3 FC 185, paras. 139–40; *Canada (Commissioner of Competition)* v. *Superior Propane Inc.* ('Propane'), Competition Tribunal redetermination (2002), paras. 47–57; upheld by Federal Court of Appeal, *Canada (Comm'r)* v. *Superior Propane Inc. and ICG Propane Inc.*, [2003] FC 529). For discussion, see R. O. Zerbe and S. Knott, 'An Economic Justification for a Price Standard in Merger Policy: The Merger of Superior Propane and ICG Propane' (2004) 21 *Research in Law and Economics* 409.

If one refers to the criterion of income, in order to define the 'least advantaged' category, it will not necessarily follow that competition law should protect consumers, as opposed to shareholders or employees. In some circumstances (e.g. a luxury good market), final consumers may have a higher, on average, income than the suppliers of these goods, in particular if the latter are small and medium firms.[36] However, in most cases, this does not occur. Alternatively, it may be argued that final consumers are the 'least advantaged' group if one focuses on the competitive process, as they may be exploited by intermediary consumers (e.g. retailers) or suppliers, without having the possibility of passing on these losses to anyone else in the value chain (unless, for example, they are also suppliers in other relevant markets). All market actors are, to a certain extent, final consumers, while not all of them are necessarily suppliers, competition law being non-applicable to employment relations. This would suggest that competition law should aim to protect final consumers, but not necessarily intermediary consumers.

Notwithstanding this indirect link between competition law and distributive justice it may be argued that competition law does not address inequality directly, to the extent that it intervenes only when there is market distortion following the exercise of market or economic power; hence, there is already some indication of a possible reduction in economic efficiency.

3.4 IS THERE A DIRECT LINK BETWEEN COMPETITION LAW AND INEQUALITY?

The first issue one needs to determine is whether market distortions and the exercise of market power constitute the main cause for economic inequality. Many causes could explain the recent rise in poverty and inequality: the globalisation of production, the erosion of collective bargaining systems, the continued drop in real wage values, tax evasion or unfair tax systems. However, market power may be a significant source of both inefficiency *and* inequality. Joseph Stiglitz notes that 'today's markets are characterised by the persistence of high monopoly profits',[37] rejecting Joseph Schumpeter's view that monopolists would only be temporary. He also argues that 'policies aimed at reducing market power can accordingly play some role in the reduction of inequality', although he remains

---

[36] Although it has been convincingly argued that this holds only in very few situations and that, in most cases, '[t]he returns from market power go disproportionately to the wealthy – increases in producer surplus from the exercise of market power accrue primarily to shareholders and the top executives, who are wealthier on average than the median consumer', as highlighted by Baker and Salop, 'Antitrust, Competition Policy, and Inequality', 11–12.

[37] J. Stiglitz, 'Monopoly's New Era' (2016) available at www.project-syndicate.org/commentary/high-monopoly-profits-persist-in-markets-by-joseph-e–stiglitz-2016–05

careful of setting this as an explicit aim of competition law.[38] Other economists have been equally vocal on the need for a robust competition law intervention against economic inequality. Tony Atkinson has suggested the integration of explicitly distributional dimension into competition policy, among some of his proposals for limiting the growing inequality.[39] A recent report of the Council of Economic Advisers to the White House published in April 2016, tracks the rise of the concentration of various industries in the US, and notes that the 'majority of industries have seen increases in the revenue share enjoyed by the 50 largest firms between 1997 and 2012'.[40] Is increasing economic concentration leading to higher degrees of inequality of wealth? This may be a difficult question to answer in view of the overall tendency of wealth concentration that has been observed during the twentieth century and at least part of the nineteenth century,[41] and according to more recent studies, apparently since the fourteenth century,[42] although one should note the various measurement and data-related difficulties for such research endeavours.

There might, however, exist a link between the effects of concentration and the unequal distribution of wealth. In the age of 'secular stagnation'[43] and intense financialisation, when return to capital exceeds economic growth, rentiers or senior executives, which form the bulk of the richest 1 per cent of the population, may

---

[38] J. Stiglitz, 'Towards a Broader View of Competition Policy', in T. Bonakele, E. Fox and L. McNube (eds.), *Competition Policy for the New Era – Insights from the BRICS Countries* (Oxford University Press, 2017), 4, 15; J. Stiglitz, N. Abernathy, A. Hersh, S. Holmberg and M. Konczal, *Rewriting the Rules of the American Economy: An Agenda for Growth and Shared Prosperity* (Norton (Roosevelt Institute), May 2015, www.rewritetherules.org).

[39] Atkinson, *Inequality*, 126–7 ('competition policy should embody explicit distributional concerns').

[40] White House CEA, 'Benefits of Competition and Indicators of Market Power' (April 2016), available at www.whitehouse.gov/sites/default/files/page/files/20160414_cea_competition_issue_brief.pdf ; G. Grullon, Y. Larkin and R. Michaely, 'Are U.S. Industries Becoming More Concentrated?' (31 August 2017), available at https://ssrn.com/abstract=2612047

[41] See, for instance, F. Alvaredo, A. B. Atkinson, T. Piketty and E. Saez, 'The Top 1 Percent in International and Historical Perspective' (2013) 27(3) *Journal of Economic Perspectives* 3–20; A. Atkinson, T. Piketty and E. Saez, 'Top Incomes in the Long Run of History' (2011) 49(1) *Journal of Economic Literature* 3; T. Piketty, G. Postel-Vinay and J.-L. Rosenthal, 'Wealth Concentration in a Developing Economy: Paris and France, 1807–1994' (2006) 96(1) *American Economic Review* 236; J. Roine and D. Waldenström, 'Long Run Trends in the Distribution of Income and Wealth', in A. Atkinson and F. Bourguignon (eds.), *Handbook of Income Distribution* (North-Holland, 2015), vol. II, 469.

[42] G. Alfani, 'Economic Inequality in Northwestern Italy: A Long-Term View (Fourteenth to Eighteenth Centuries)' (2015) 75(4) *Journal of Economic History* 1058; G. Alfani, 'The Rich in Historical Perspective. Evidence for Preindustrial Europe (ca. 1300–1800)' (2017) 11(3) *Cliometrica* 321.

[43] L. Summers, 'The Age of Secular Stagnation: What It Is and What to Do About It', *Foreign Affairs* (17 February 2016) (noting the imbalance between excessive savings and investment, pulling down interest rates, savings tending to flow into existing assets, thus causing asset price inflation and rising economic inequality).

see their share of total wealth increase. One may also rely on empirical evidence linking higher concentration following mergers to higher prices,[44] and evidence showing that in 'winner-take-most' competition, where 'superstar firms' command growing market shares and become highly profitable, one may observe a larger decline in labour's share.[45] This has obviously an impact on economic inequality.

A recent paper of the OECD 'Market Power and Wealth Distribution' shows a substantial impact of market power on wealth inequality.[46] According to the study which relies in terms of methodology on some work previously completed by Comanor and Smiley in 1975,[47] market power may account for a substantial amount of wealth and income inequality.[48] The report found that the increased margins charged to customers as a result of market power will disproportionately harm the poor who will pay more for goods without receiving a counterbalancing share of increased profits as they are not usually shareholders, while the wealthy benefit more from higher profits, due to their generally higher ownership of the stream of corporate profits and capital gains. This study only explored eight developed jurisdictions, thus showcasing the need for equivalent studies to be performed in the context of emergent/developing countries.

Tackling market power in order to improve the position of consumers is therefore good for inequality given that lower prices (or, better still, higher quality/price ratios) improve the purchasing power of disposable income and consequently benefit the poorest quintile, in particular if this leads to lower prices for the goods/items they usually purchase. Moreover, where high profits are siphoned off by corporate elites (i.e. rather than returned to dispersed shareholders), the concern might be that the resulting concentration of income (and, over time, accumulated wealth) is deployed to lobby against redistribution fiscal policies aimed at addressing economic inequality. From a macroeconomic perspective, the concern may be that high profits induced by anticompetitive entry and expansion barriers are not reinvested. The resulting low levels of corporate investments would not only reduce aggregate demand, but also suppress productivity growth, which would ultimately constrain

---

[44] See J. Kwoka, *Mergers, Merger Control, and Remedies* (MIT Press, 2014); J. Kwoka, 'Does Merger Control Work? A Retrospective on U.S. Enforcement Actions and Merger Outcomes' (2013) 78(3) *Antitrust Law Journal* 619.

[45] D. Autor, D. Dorn, L. Lawrence, F. Katz, C. Patterson and J. Van Reenen, 'Concentrating on the Fall of the Labor Share' (2017) 107(5) *American Economic Review* 180.

[46] OECD, *Market Power and Wealth Distribution*, DAF/COMP(2015)10, available at www.oecd.org/officialdocuments/publicdisplaydocumentpdf/?cote=DAF/COMP(2015)10&docLanguage=En

[47] W. S. Comanor and R. H. Smiley, 'Monopoly and the Distribution of Wealth' [1975]89(2) *Quarterly Journal of Economics* 177.

[48] See A. K. Dutt, 'Stagnation, Income Distribution and Monopoly Power' (1984) 8 *Cambridge Journal of Economics* 25 (on a model constructed to depict the Indian economy arguing that reducing monopoly power may have positive effects on both economic growth and income distribution).

wage growth.[49] Shareholders and senior executive managers benefit from returns to capital, and constitute eventually the primary group to gain from market power and monopoly rents. Their share in the total income and wealth increases, in comparison to other groups in society, as returns to capital exceed the rate growth of output and income (wages).[50] It is possible that in the long run, the situation of the largest part of the population (wage workers, small and medium firms shareholders and the unemployed following the exclusion from the market of 'inefficient' firms and economic sectors) will see their income and/or share of wealth stagnate or decrease, while the most affluent parts of the population will benefit from a phenomenal increase of wealth, as this has been documented, at least since the 1970s.[51] Inequality may rise even if the lowest quintiles may also benefit from some additional growth, and the absolute level of poverty reduced. The issue here may be 'relative' and 'subjective poverty', and inequality, rather than 'absolute poverty'.[52] Under these circumstances, aggressive antitrust enforcement ought to be welcome from a distributional perspective as well.

Would this argument hold if one moves to a general equilibrium-plus approach and takes into account income effects in other markets on which the specific agents are present in one way or another (as consumers, senior executives, shareholders, workers)? Some have argued that, at least in the developed world, all consumers are also owners of businesses, and hence they could benefit from monopolistic price increases.[53] Professor Crane has expressed doubts as to the possibility of performing the complex analysis that would be required for an explicitly distributive competition law, as competition authorities would need information about a large number of factors, such as 'the relative wealth of producers and consumers, overcharge pass-on rates, the effects of market power on employees of the firm, the distribution of

---

49   'Too Much of a Good Thing – Profits Are Too High. America Needs a Giant Dose of Competition', *The Economist*, 26 May 2016, available at www.economist.com/news/briefing/21695385-profits-are-too-high-america-needs-giant-dose-competition-too-much-good-thing

50   See the analysis in J. Furman and O. Orszag, 'A Firm-Level Perspective on the Role of Rents in the Rise in Inequality' (16 October 2015), available at https://obamawhitehouse.archives.gov/sites/default/files/page/files/20151016_firm_level_perspective_on_role_of_rents_in_inequality.pdf citing also the work of J. Stiglitz, *The Price of Inequality: How Today's Divided Society Endangers Our Future* (Norton, 2012).

51   See M. Ravallion, *The Economics of Poverty – History, Measurement and Policy* (Oxford University Press, 2016), 102–5; F. Bourguignon, 'World Changes in Inequality: An Overview of Facts, Causes, Consequences and Policies' (Bank of International Settlements, August 2017) 17–21 (noting the common forces behind the rising trend observed over the two or three last decades in a sizeable number of countries with regard to inequality but also observing that some country-specific factors have been at play).

52   Ravallion, *Economics of Poverty*, 106–10.

53   The argument was first made by Bork, *Antitrust Paradox*, 110 when criticising Oliver Williamson's trade-off. See also D. Crane, 'Antitrust and Wealth Inequality' (2016) 101(5) *Cornell Law Review* 1171, 1186 (noting that '[s]hareholding is far from an exclusively upper class vocation' and also arguing (ibid., 1192) that the argument that 'senior managers are the primary beneficiaries of anticompetitive market structures is weak, at best'. Crane argues instead that 'increases in market power yield higher wages for blue-collar employees').

rents between managers and shareholders, the progressive or regressive effects of antitrust violations where government entities are the purchasers, and the distribution of rents among classes of managers'.[54]

Such concerns should obviously be watered down if one takes into account developing and emerging economies, where a few local conglomerates or global multinationals control the economy, there is lack of capital for new entrepreneurs and labour mobility is quite limited.[55] There is significant empirical literature on the welfare losses resulting from monopoly power for the poorest parts of the population,[56] and on the benefits of competition for taming corrupt elites that want to take advantage of the liberalisation process.[57]

Furthermore, it has also been claimed that an 'undifferentiated increase in antitrust enforcement – actions to augment and strengthen enforcement as a general matter' may also produce regressive effects as it can block voluntary action by private firms pursuing wealth redistribution goals.[58] There are indeed circumstances where the relationship between policies aimed at promoting competition and economic inequality is not straightforward. Low levels of corporate investment may result from excessive capacity spurring cut-throat price competition. This can be particularly the case where competition takes place on a global scale and the bargaining power of the local workforce is greatly undermined (e.g. steel production). Similar dynamics can take place where the mobile factor of production is not capital (i.e. with employers threatening to relocate where the cost of labour is lower) but labour itself, thanks to immigration at all skill levels, from seasonal or construction workers to knowledge-economy professionals. Under these circumstances, the common belief is that only firms' top executives can emerge as winners from these ultra-competitive labour markets, whereas the rest of us (i.e. the 99.9 per cent) feel the pressure. These concerns may prompt protectionist calls for state intervention aimed at restricting competition, with the result that both productive and allocative efficiency would suffer. That is to say, policies that may cause economic inefficiencies may be called upon to address economic inequality.

---

[54] Crane, 'Antitrust and Wealth Inequality', 1174.

[55] This point is conceded by D. A. Crane, 'Is More Antitrust the Answer to Wealth Inequality?' (winter 2015–16) *Regulation* 18, 19.

[56] See, for instance, G. Porto, N. Depetris Chauvin and M. Olarreaga, *Supply Chains in Export Agriculture, Competition, and Poverty in sub-Saharan Africa* (World Bank and CEPR, 2011) (exploring a number of case studies in Africa with regard to cotton, coffee, tobacco and cocoa); J. Argent and T. Begazo, 'Competition in Kenyan Markets and Its Impact on Income and Poverty: A Case Study on Sugar and Maize' (World Bank Policy Research Working Group 7179, January 2015); and the examples included in World Bank and OECD, *A Step Ahead: Competition Policy for Shared Prosperity and Inclusive Growth. Trade and Development* (World Bank, 2017).

[57] See, for instance, A. Banerjee, R. Hanna, J. Kyle, B. A. Olken and S. Sumarto, 'The Role of Competition in Effective Outsourcing: Subsidized Food Distribution in Indonesia' (March 2017), available at www.povertyactionlab.org/sites/default/files/publications/553_The-role-of-Competition_in-Effective-Outsourcing_March2017.pdf (regarding outsourcing of food-delivery services).

[58] D. Crane, 'Antitrust and Wealth Inequality' (2016) 101(5) *Cornell Law Review* 1171, 1175.

One should also integrate in this analysis dynamic efficiency concerns that are increasingly at play in competition law enforcement. It is often argued that hyper-competitive rivalry is the norm in digital industries subject to 'winners-take-all' competitive dynamics, where a position of super-dominance is the market outcome of strategies based on very aggressive pricing and/or relentless product and process innovation. On the one hand, competition 'for' (rather than 'in') the market means that consumers benefit greatly from lower prices, more convenient mode of consumption and strong innovation. On the other hand, 'winner-takes-all' dynamics raise concerns about excessive economic (and, thus, political) power concentrated in very few massive corporations, to the benefit of a new breed of corporate elites consisting of technical (rather than finance) experts. The picture is made gloomier by the concern that these high-tech giants are the driving force behind automation, which threatens to further weaken the employment prospects of future generations and therefore could have important distributional consequences for a large part of the population. In summary, this would be a world where economic scarcity is no longer the foundation of the market-driven allocation mechanisms underpinning modern capitalistic societies, and where policies aimed at promoting competition in the pursuit of (allocative, productive and dynamic) efficiency could be seen as self-defeating. In contrast, an approach focusing on equality of opportunity for small local entrepreneurs to prosper and achieve a larger scale may become more appealing, despite the possibility of economic inefficiencies.

3.5 IS COMPETITION LAW THE MOST ADEQUATE TOOL AGAINST ECONOMIC INEQUALITY?

The implicit assumption for those criticising competition law intervention aiming to reduce the occurrence of inequality, is that the tax system is a more efficient way of engaging in redistribution than the regulatory system, or a specific facet of the latter, such as competition law.[59] However, one may reverse the order of these arguments and suggest instead that it is *only* if the question of fair and equitable income distribution is addressed by the political system that it may be legitimate for competition law to focus exclusively on economic efficiency.

It is therefore important to take into account the institutional framework for equality-focused state action, such as progressive taxation in the specific jurisdiction, before arriving at any conclusion as to the superiority of other mechanisms of redistribution, such as taxation. The inability of the EU to employ fiscal instruments

---

[59]   This is related to the discussion over the comparison between taxation by regulation and direct taxation, the latter being considered more efficient, *under* very specific conditions (A. Atkinson and J. Stiglitz, 'The Design of Tax Structure: Direct versus Indirect Taxation' (1976) 6 *Journal of Public Economics* 55–75), or more generally the relative efficiency of the income tax system vis-à-vis the legal system in general for redistributing income (L. Kaplow and S. Shavell, 'Why the Legal System Is Less Efficient than the Income Tax in Redistributive Income' (1994) 23 *Journal of Legal Studies* 667).

to systematically redistribute wealth across the Union should therefore be a relevant fact. EU Member States differ greatly in their levels of wealth. McDonnell and Faber note that powerful firms are not randomly distributed across Europe, and hence 'producer surplus is likely to accrue primarily to the most powerful and wealthy EU members, increasing existing wealth disparities at the margins'.[60] Efficient rules that would focus only on total surplus with no attention to the allocation of that surplus between producers and consumers (which is excluded by efficiency analysis as a distributive justice issue) will tend to pump wealth in the 'wrong' direction.[61] In the absence of adequate resources and EU competence to mitigate these distributional consequences across the Union (in view of the absence of an EU corporate income tax and the low wealth transfer from rich to poor Member States (assuming that the qualification of 'rich' and 'poor' states represents average disposable income for consumers)), there may be a less strong argument for separating efficiency, allegedly the domain of competition law, and equality, which should be dealt with by another instrument, such as taxation, in the EU than in jurisdictions, such as the United States, which possess the adequate fiscal instruments to pursue redistribution at the federal level.

More generally, it is questionable that redistributive policies implemented through the taxation system could be considered as a superior option to integrating redistributive concerns in competition law. The claim that the tax system is superior to competition law in redistributing income relies on the idea that the economic system is designed in such a way that it would be possible to eliminate disparities of economic power that lead to wealth and income inequality by introducing changes in the tax schedule to improve the position of the weaker parties. An extreme scenario would be to consider that taxing monopoly profits will be a superior option than implementing competition law remedies with the aim of addressing the monopoly problem. Taxing monopoly profits may not always be a good idea, in view of the subsequent wealth transfers this may entail (as firms may pass on these taxes to consumers). Nor does it deal with the underlying imbalances of economic/bargaining power between the economic actors, which have been at the source of inequality. What it does, as Emmanuel Voyiakis rightly notes in a different context, is to 'increase consumers' *purchasing* power, leaving their bargaining position unchanged'.[62]

The differential of economic power is converted to an imbalance in the 'structural position' of the least advantaged, for instance the poorer consumers, vis-à-vis those with a stronger structural position, the well-off in the specific context, i.e. a firm in a dominant position.[63] Indeed, having additional resources, through the wealth

---

[60] B. McDonnell and D. A. Farber, 'Are Efficient Antitrust Rules Always Optimal?' (2003 Fall) *Antitrust Bulletin* 807–35, 825.

[61] Ibid.

[62] E. Voyiakis, *Private Law and the Value of Choice* (Hart, 2017), 195.

[63] On the concept of structural position, see A. J. Julius, 'Basic Structure and the Value of Equality' (2003) 31 *Philosophy and Public Affairs* 321.

distribution effect of taxation, would not put consumers in a better bargaining position, insofar as they would still occupy the structural position that led to their structural weakness in the first place, in essence the lack of a next best alternative in a monopolised market.[64] To the extent that such structural weakness is to continue, the maintenance of the wealth transfer mechanism, necessary for the transaction to be considered 'fair', would require consumers to resort to some bargaining power in the overlapping game of the political sphere. However, to the extent that economic power may be converted to political power, one may doubt that such a structural position equaliser would operate effectively.

More fundamentally, Voyiakis asks what makes us think that consumers or citizens will have 'a general reason to favor increases in their purchasing power over protections against the use of businesses' superior bargaining power'?[65] Surely, purchasing more and cheaper products is an option that any consumer has reason to value, but, as Voyiakis rightly observes with regard to private law, but this is also relevant in our context, it is not always in the consumers' general reasonable interest to favour rules that value increases in purchasing power rather than preferring competition law enforcement that would leave their structural position less exposed.[66] This is true, in particular, if one takes into account the risk that structural unbalances will not be corrected by effective wealth transfers in the future, in case the economic bargaining power of the dominant undertakings, for instance, is leveraged to political bargaining power that may oppose progressive taxation.

It therefore seems that the argument often made that taxation will be a superior system of wealth redistribution than regulation or competition law, takes a quite narrow perspective. First, it ignores the institutional framework, which might be different in each jurisdiction, and the likelihood that redistribution through taxation may not be a realistic option in the specific political or economic context. Second, it assumes that consumers, or the least advantaged category, will prefer an increase in their purchasing power following the implementation of a system of progressive taxation, which nevertheless will deal only superficially with the problem of the structural weakness of their position vis-à-vis the monopoly, to the implementation of competition law with the aim of taming, or eventually eradicating, the main source of the unequal outcomes in this case, the imbalance of structural positions between the consumers and the monopoly.

Similar arguments have been made with regard to the possibility of satisfying equity concerns through other instruments of state intervention than competition

---

[64] Voyiakis, *Private Law*, 196.

[65] Ibid.

[66] E. Voyiakis, 'Contract Law and Reasons of Social Justice' (2012) 25 *Canadian Journal of Law and Jurisprudence* 393. A similar conclusion may be reached if one takes the no-envy approach to determining what is a fair allocation of resources (see our analysis below). As Ayal rightly notes, '[e]nvy of consumers (or other producers, unable to enter the lucrative market) granted, it is aimed not at the profit itself, but at the superior position granted to the monopolist pre-existing market imperfections' (A. Ayal, *Fairness in Antitrust* (Hart, 2014), 179).

law, for instance economic regulation. It has been argued that competition law should focus on economic efficiency and the interrelated concept of consumer surplus, leaving to regulation the task of addressing equity concerns.[67] This position rests on the following implicit assumptions: (1) economic regulation is available in the specific economic sector; (2) economic regulators offer a superior institutional mechanism to competition authorities to take into account fairness concerns; (3) economic regulation can take sufficiently into account equity concerns so that there is no need for additional intervention by competition law; (4) there is some form of allocation of tasks between economic regulators and competition authorities, the latter focusing on making markets work better for people, only from a (narrow) economic efficiency perspective, while the former is perceived as a tool whose purpose is to replace the price signalling role of the market,[68] through price regulation, or to 'correct' the market outcome, markets, as a form of social organisation, failing in this case to satisfy social welfare.

In my view, these assumptions and the position of these authors reflect a theoretical confusion and conceptual misunderstandings. First, economic regulation is not always available, and for good reason! In most cases markets work relatively well for social welfare and there is no need for the state to step in in cases of market failure. Our analysis puts forward the idea that in monopolistic and concentrated markets, market failure may take different forms to the traditional output, price or innovation effects, and may negatively affect the type of equality cherished by the specific social contract.[69] These equality effects may be taken into account by economic regulation, but in case they have not, and this is clear if the sector is unregulated, then there is no reason for competition law to ignore these concerns. To the extent that opportunities for regulation are often limited, and the regulatory process burdensome, competition law may be a cheaper institutional alternative to take into account these equity concerns.

Second, it is possible that regulation may take sufficiently into account fairness concerns. However, it is not clear that this will be done in the most efficient (i.e., less wasteful) way. Regulation may be quite intrusive to economic freedom and free markets. It is more prone to capture than competition law (which is applied horizontally to all sectors and thus raises lower risks of capture), and includes, in most cases, of a less advanced arsenal of 'smart' regulatory technologies than competition law, either in targeting intervention, or in remedying the market problem identified. For instance, competition does not impose similar duties on dominant firms and firms without market power, and its application rests on a careful consideration of the specific economic and legal context on a case-by-case

---

[67] See Chapter 13 in this volume.
[68] This is the classic perception of the price system by F. A. Hayek, 'The Use of Knowledge in Society' (1945) 35(4) *American Economic Review* 519.
[69] That could be equality of income, wealth, gender equality, or as I argue in this study complex equality.

basis, or on the development of standards of intervention for specific types of practices, following some economic analysis. Competition law can be both backward-looking and forward-looking, and relies on a minimal, almost architectural, intervention on incentives so that markets operate smoothly. Economic regulation is sector specific and thus more prone to the risk of capture. It is often only forward-looking and enables less targeting as it is usually framed in a way that casts a wide net even over conduct adopted by non-dominant firms. It also relies on the idea that market incentives do not suffice to promote the social good. Hence, because of its flexibility, the competition law tool may be a superior institutional alternative to regulation in reconciling economic efficiency and equity concerns, while still largely relying on the market system.

Third, even if regulation takes into account fairness concerns, competition law may still intervene in order to ensure that the regulatory option chosen is proportional to the market problem identified.[70] To the extent that fairness-related regulation is often national, in view of the lack of a broader EU competence in the social sphere, EU competition law may ensure that regulation will not negatively affect, also from a fairness perspective, the population of other Member States. However, the different nature of the relation between the federal and the state levels in the US may justify a different approach.

Fourth, the separation of tasks between regulators, who are presumably interested in fairness, and competition authorities, which are exclusively preoccupied with economic efficiency, is both descriptively wrong and normatively self-defeating. Regulators take into account both economic efficiency and fairness concerns. In many jurisdictions, they can implement competition law and may impose competition law remedies, in addition to regulatory ones.[71] Their mission statement often includes extensive duties to promote competition, as well as to preserve the public interest. Competition law may intervene in order to establish the structural conditions that will make markets work for the benefit of the people, eventually also integrating in the competition analysis broader public interest concerns that go beyond the usual focus on price and output. Competitive and contestable markets may provide sufficient opportunities for 'voice' and participation of all affected

---

[70] EU competition law accepts the cumulative application of competition law and economic regulation. *Ex ante* regulation by a national regulatory authority does not prevent the *ex post* intervention on the basis of EU competition rules. See Case C-280/08 *Deutsche Telekom AG* v. *Commission* [2010] ECR I-9555; Case C-295/12, *Telefónica SA and Telefónica de España SAU* v. *Commission*, ECLI:EU: C:2014:2062. For a more detailed analysis, see G. Monti, 'Managing the Intersection of Utilities Regulation and EC Competition Law' (2008) 4(2) *Competition Law Review* 123; J. Tapia and D. Mantzari, 'The Regulation/Competition Interaction', in I. Lianos and D. Geradin (eds.), *Handbook on European Competition Law – Substantive Aspects* (Edward-Elgar, 2013), 588. Concerning UK competition law, see G. Monti, 'Utilities Regulators and the Competition Act 1998', in B. Rodger (ed.), *Ten Years of UK Competition Law Reform* (Dundee University Press, 2010), 139.

[71] See, for instance, the model followed in the UK, where the UK legislator has chosen a regime of concurrent jurisdiction with regard to the application of EU and national competition law by sector-specific regulators in their area of competence.

interests,[72] their outcome being judged fair to the extent that adjustments are made to ensure that the problems of missing markets and asymmetrical bargaining power are neutralised. It is only if reliance on markets fails to achieve fair *and* efficient outcomes that governments should turn to economic regulation. By not giving a chance to the institution of markets, following competition law intervention and adjustment, to prove that they can deliver fair outcomes, and by bypassing markets altogether in favour of regulation, such proposals would yield results that are counter to those anticipated by their proponents.

3.6 EQUITY AND EFFICIENCY: IS THERE A TRADE-OFF?

The opposition to an increasing role for equity concerns in competition law is often motivated by the perception that such inclusion will necessarily lead to the demise of economic efficiency as the main principle guiding the 'soul' of competition law. The literature on the 'goals of competition law', initiated during and after the Chicago school revolution conceptualises efficiency and fairness as antagonistic to each other. By doing this, it promotes a conceptualisation of their relation as a pair of 'binaries', in the way Derrida understood this term, that is, a pair of related concepts opposite in meaning, but also, as he explains, an opposition that remains profoundly arbitrary and unstable.[73] I believe that the disputes we may have over the way the principle of justice is implemented in competition law, reflect differences not only over what the political and legal culture of our societies entails, with regard to the level of acceptable economic power to be exercised in markets or the 'normal' level of economic inequality that a markets-based society could aspire to,[74] but also differences over which institutional arrangements could better implement such 'consensus' over levels of acceptable economic power and/or 'normal inequality'.[75] This section challenges the conceptualisation of equity and efficiency as separate spheres that are in an antagonistic relation to one other, requiring from the decision-maker some trade-off exercise. In section 3.6.1, I explain why conceiving their interaction as a static trade-off might not reflect the true nature of their relation. In section 3.6.2, I also question the possibility of a dynamic trade-off between equity and innovation.

---

[72] See, for instance, the 'participation-centred' approach of N. Komesar, *Imperfect Alternatives: Choosing Institutions in Law, Economics and Public Policy* (University of Chicago Press, 1997).

[73] J. Derrida, *Margins of Philosophy* (Harvester Wheatsheaf, 1982) 195.

[74] See, for instance. F. Bourguignon, *The Globalization of Inequality* (Princeton University Press, 2015), 163 referring to 'normal' level of economic inequality as the conditions 'prior to the last two or three decades'.

[75] As I have explained in a different study, exploring the question of the goals of competition law should be preceded by examining the question of institutional choice and comparative institutional analysis. See I. Lianos, 'Some Reflections on the Question of the Goals of EU Competition Law', in I. Lianos and D. Geradin, *Handbook on European Competition Law: Substantive Aspects* (Edward Elgar, 2013) 1 (also available at the SSRN).

3.6.1 *Equity and Efficiency: Separate Spheres and the Static Trade-off Position*

People enter into cooperation with other people to the extent that this cooperation may produce a joint surplus that would not be possible absent that cooperation. Assuming that individuals have the incentive to cooperate with others, and consequently limit their freedom of action to a certain extent, in order to increase their welfare through cooperation, this joint surplus will be 'the difference between the benefits (net of direct costs) each gains from the joint activity and the benefits each would receive in their next best alternative'.[76] Each participant in a joint project should therefore receive benefits at least as great as in their next best alternative, to maintain their incentive to participate in the joint project (the so called participation constraint).[77] As long as the 'participation constraints' of all participants to the cooperative project are satisfied, the question of distribution is settled in an economically efficient way.[78] What matters is not the distributive outcome as such, for instance that each participant enjoys an equal share of the joint profit, but the fact that each participant has been able to get a payoff equivalent to their next best alternative. Absent this rent from the joint surplus collected by the participants, these will have no incentive to enter into the joint activity at the first place. It is possible to imagine that a single participant could gain the most important part of the joint profit if, for instance, he makes take-it or leave-it offers to the rest of the participants that are only 'barely superior to their next best alternatives'.[79]

If one focuses on efficiency in consumption, the resulting allocation will be Pareto efficient as the joint surplus is net of the participants' next best alternatives, the surplus being allocated in such a way that it would not be possible by any reallocation to make people better off without making anybody else worse off.[80] In practice, applying such a criterion may be quite rare, as in most situations some of the participants might be incurring losses from what would have been their next best alternative, for instance had there not been a move from one state of the economy to another. Economists have put forward the potential Pareto improvement criterion (or Kaldor–Hicks efficiency), which advances that if the magnitude of the gains from moving from one state of the economy to another is greater than the magnitude of the losses, then social welfare is increased by making the move even, if no actual compensation is made.[81] According to Kaldor–Hicks efficiency, an outcome is efficient if those that are made better off can, *potentially*, compensate those that were made worse off, with the resulting outcome still being Pareto-optimal. The

---

[76] S. Bowles, *Microeconomics – Behavior, Institutions, and Evolution* (Princeton University Press, 2004), 168

[77] Ibid., 171.

[78] Ibid.

[79] Ibid.

[80] Ibid.

[81] J. R. Hicks, 'The Foundations of Welfare Economics' (1939) 49(196) *Economic Journal* 696; N. Kaldor, 'Welfare Propositions in Economics and Interpersonal Comparisons of Utility' (1939) 49 (145) *Economic Journal* 549.

winners should, in theory, be able to compensate the losers, but there is no requirement that compensation should be effectively paid.

It is true that this outcome may not be considered fair to the extent that it leads to
an unequal allocation of the joint profit, should one consider that fairness requires
that the joint surplus produced be allocated equally between the participants.
However, fairness, in the form of equality of outcomes in the allocation of the
surplus, is not a concern for welfare economics, which simply focuses on the size
of the pie, rather than the way the pie is distributed for consumption. Welfare
economic analysis carefully separates questions of efficiency from questions of
distributive justice. This separation is explained by a number of crucial assumptions.

The first is what has been called 'the Second Fundamental Theorem of Welfare
Economics', according to which if one assumes that all individuals and producers
are selfish price takers, then almost any Pareto-optimal equilibrium can be supported via the competitive mechanism, provided appropriate lump-sum taxes and
transfers are imposed on individuals and firms.[82] The main idea is that in the long
run the competitive process will eliminate any benefit from the joint surplus that is
higher than the participation constraints of each of the participants. This further
assumes that 'only competitive equilibrium transactions take place', a quite heroic
assumption which, in the best-case scenario, only holds in the very long term.[83] The
theorem also implies that if a particular state of the economy is judged to be
desirable, it may be achieved through lump-sum transfers, for instance progressive
taxation and the welfare state. This separates issues of efficiency from issues of
distributive justice, but for the reasons we explained above, this may not necessarily
take place.

A second assumption is that allocational outcomes may not affect distributional
outcomes, which is also quite unlikely, as the existing allocation of resources
determines the next best alternative for each of the participants and consequently
the distribution of the joint surplus. Hence, the second welfare theorem of economics denotes a status quo bias for the existing allocation of resources, which is deemed
to be efficient. However, the existing resource allocation may be the product of an
unjust initial distribution of income that may contravene principles of social justice,
as these are defined by non-utilitarian theories of justice.

Conversely, conflicts relating to the fair distribution of rents may contribute to
inefficiency, to the extent that resources may be spent on advancing distributional
claims and rent-seeking that deviates resources away from productive activities.[84]
Participants may also be driven in their selection for technologies and the organisation of their activity to activities that increase their share of the joint surplus, rather
than to those increasing the size of the joint surplus. Finally, it is possible that joint-

---

[82] M. Blaug, 'The Fundamental Theorems of Modern Welfare Economics, Historically Contemplated'
(2007) 39(2) *History of Political Economy* 185.

[83] Bowles, *Microeconomics*, 172.

[84] Ibid.

surplus-generating activities may be blocked following intense conflicts over the distribution of the joint surplus and 'bargaining breakdowns leading to foregone mutual beneficial opportunities'.[85]

Modern economics recognise that most markets are characterised by externalities, imperfect competition and generally market failures. Most of the time, curative action undertaken in order to 'correct' these market failures, with the aim of establishing the conditions of the first theorem of welfare economics, will not succeed in bringing in a Pareto-efficient outcome, the best-case scenario being a Kaldor–Hicks-efficient outcome. Hence, the situation will often call upon the application of the second welfare theorem and wealth transfers. But this leads to an indirect effect flowing from this conceptualisation of efficiency and fairness/ equality as two separate realms: the idea that their logic may not always be convergent and that, at some level, pursuing economic efficiency may come at the price of less equality. Hence, in this view, society should face a trade-off between equality and efficiency.

Assuming that there is a trade-off, and that the domain of this trade-off is quite large (if one takes the view that the situations in which the logic of efficiency and equality are not convergent constitute the majority of cases), the question is how this trade-off should be made, and by whom. The separability thesis assumes that issues of efficiency should always come first, in which case I can think of two possible approaches. One approach would be to leave the decision over the appropriate trade-off to the political realm, and its own mechanisms of resolving conflicts between policy values, economics-driven competition law only focusing on the generation of efficient outcomes, rather than on the generation of fair outcomes, the appropriate level of fairness vis-à-vis the appropriate level of efficiency (the trade-off) being a value-laden judgement that unelected officials should not be authorised to make in a democratic society.[86] However, this approach ignores the distributional implications of relying solely on an economic efficiency criterion, something we have highlighted above (as the fact that efficiency and equality are conceived as separate does not exclude that there may be some form of interaction between the two, producing effects across the two separate realms). Nor does it explain why the same argument against decisions being made by unelected officials cannot also be opposed to decisions made solely under the guise of the first fundamental principle of welfare economics, to the extent that the choice of economic efficiency inevitably produces distributional implications. Another approach would be for an economics-driven competition adjudicator to explore the social implications of the choice of

---

[85] Ibid., 173.

[86] The separability between questions of economic efficiency and issues of distribution has been criticised by L. Robbins who advanced the view that there is a distinction between normative and positive economics but that economists should avoid value-laden policy recommendations, without making explicit their normative predispositions (' Economics and Political Economy' (1981) 71 *American Economic Review* 1).

different examples of trade-offs between efficiency and equality, on the basis of the dominant cultural norms prevailing in the specific political community (by elaborating, for instance, a sort of culture-dependent social welfare function).

But, these are not the only options on the table. One may conceive that the relation between efficiency and equality is not divergent, but mostly, or almost always, convergent, thus starting from a different premise. In order to illustrate with some examples how these different conceptions of the relation between equality and efficiency play out in economic scholarship, I will compare two different visions of this interaction.

The first view is that of economist Arthur Okun, who in his influential book *Equality and Efficiency – The Big Tradeoff*, published in 1975, set, to a large extent the consensus view in economics and public policy, for the next three to four decades.[87] While accepting that in some cases efficiency and equality have convergent logics, Okun focused on situations where society 'deliberately' opted for equality, by establishing entitlements and rights, noting that this choice could compromise efficiency, which he views as intrinsically related to the existence of markets.[88] This theoretical conception of market-free space of rights notwithstanding, Okun recognises that, in reality, 'the marketplace transgresses on virtually every right',[89] giving the example of the disadvantaged position of the poor with regard to equality before the law, the link between money and political power (in particular campaign financing, lobbying), the fact that the transgression of equal political rights often leads to consumer harm. With regard to the 'corrective strategy' that needs to be developed, he disfavours 'general efforts to curb bigness and wealth', although he notes that limiting the scope of economic activity and markets controlled by the 'plutocrats' (in particular conglomerate mergers) can help a little.[90] Instead, he opts for 'specific aids and sanctions', which will not bring 'complete equality', but might correct serious transgressions of money 'on the domain of rights'.[91] Okun considers both equality of income/wealth and equality of opportunity, which, he notes may lead to greater equality of income, but also constitutes 'a value in itself'.[92] Okun starts from the premise that equality and efficiency are equally valued, and 'in places where they conflict', 'any sacrifice of either has to be justified as a necessary means of obtaining more of the other (or possibly of some other valued social end)'.[93] He does not examine the latter option but focuses on the bilateral relation between efficiency and equality, and to which of the two values the decision-maker should give priority. His position is that in performing this trade-off (balancing) of these conflicting values, 'the social constitution should not seek to

---

[87] A. M. Okun, *Equality and Efficiency – The Big Tradeoff* (Brookings Institution, 1975, repub. 2015).
[88] Ibid., 5.
[89] Ibid., 22.
[90] Ibid., 30.
[91] Ibid., 31.
[92] Ibid., 83–4.
[93] Ibid., 88.

settle forever the precise weighting of inequality', but should instead weight equality heavily, and rely on the democratic process to 'select reasonable weights on specific issues as they arise'.[94]

One may contrast this view with that of British economist Ken Binmore who understands the relation between equality and efficiency as complementary, rather that antagonistic, both being considered as necessary conditions for the emergence of a social contract that would bring together different people by promoting a common set of understandings allowing them to coordinate their efforts, or, in other words, 'coordinate on a particular equilibrium of the game of life that we play together'.[95] Binmore takes an 'evolutionary approach to social contract theory', advancing three levels of priority for a social contract to be 'internally stable', that is to be maintained without the need for a specific external enforcement agency: first, it should be stable, the social contract not needing any 'glue' but holding together by coordinating human behaviour on an equilibrium in the game of life.[96] In my opinion, although this may slightly misrepresent Binmore's position, that stability can be compared to the criterion of 'systemic resilience', which I will explain in more detail in section 3.8.[97] The second priority of a social contract is efficiency, as each society competes with the social contacts in other societies and being efficient, or in other words avoiding waste, enables the specific society to compete successfully with other social groups in the game of life. The third priority for the social contract to hold together is fairness. This is a particularly important principle, as there may be various efficient equilibria available as possible social contracts, thus making it necessary for society to select one of these on which to coordinate.[98]

For Binmore, fairness norms provide an 'informal equilibrium selection device' in the repeated game of life and the necessary coordination of collective decisions in society.[99] Not any efficient outcome will be considered as socially optimal. Only the efficient outcome that is also fair in the specific society and context. What counts as fair depends on the specific culture, fairness norms differing in different times and places, but also on the 'deep structure' of 'universal principles of justice', devised with the assistance of the mechanism of interpersonal comparison effectuated at a hypothetical original position under the veil of ignorance, a method employed by John Rawls and John Harsanyi, although with different results in each case.[100] Binmore laments that '[m]odern economic textbooks usually have little to say

---

[94]   Ibid., 94.

[95]   K. Binmore, *Natural Justice* (Oxford University Press 2005) 3–14, 4.

[96]   Ibid., 4–5

[97]   Binmore notes that utilitarianism fails to recognise the first priority of stability (ibid., 189).

[98]   Ibid., 14. Again Binmore considers that a utilitarian distribution 'will be in difficulty' at this third level of priority (ibid., 189).

[99]   Ibid., 197.

[100] Ibid. 15–17. The first one advanced that the application of such interpersonal comparison using the device of the original position will lead to an egalitarian distribution of goods and services, while the second argued that the use of this device will lead to a utilitarian distribution.

about fairness' and criticises the 'myth' that 'there is a necessary trade-off between equity and efficiency'; he also notes that neoclassical price economists 'mostly brush the problem of distribution under the carpet altogether by defining any efficient outcome to be socially optimal', and thus rejecting any possibility that a particular efficient outcome is unfair.[101] He expresses discontent with the one equilibrium models used in economics, such as the neoclassical ideal of a perfectly competitive market, which explain why there is no role for fairness in these models.[102] He remarks that we may need to select from a wide variety of efficient Nash equilibria and fairness norms will constitute the backbone of the selection process effectuated in the hypothetical original position. He criticises the 'schizophrenia' of micro economics to reject interpersonal comparisons of utility, and its narrow focus on 'economic surplus', simply because 'maximizing economic surplus is what happens when a perfectly competitive market operates without constraint.'[103] According to Binmore, this 'dishonest argument makes the operation of the market seem socially optimal only by slipping in the assumption that each extra dollar is equally valuable no matter to whom it is assigned', although most of us would rather spend a tax dollar on 'relieving the suffering of the poor and needy rather than providing tax breaks for the rich and powerful'.[104] Binmore believes that fairness norms evolved out of the need to select from multiple efficient equilibria, therefore finding the idea that some trade-off between equity and efficiency is necessary as making 'no sense at all'.[105]

One may argue instead for an 'envy' criterion in which a single efficient equilibrium will be deemed fair if nobody would envy the bundle of commodities assigned to someone else, or in other words that people at any given time will, at least weakly, prefer their own bundle of commodities to all others.[106] Although Binmore finds that this would be 'a lot more respectable' than arguing for a trade-off between efficiency and fairness, he finds that the no-envy criterion is unsatisfactory, because it only focuses on the assignment of bundles of goods/possessions and their subjective valuation and overlooks the fact that when interpersonal comparisons are made one may focus on empathetic preferences, each person imagining herself/himself in

---

[101]   Ibid., 66.
[102]   Ibid., 66–7.
[103]   Ibid., 116.
[104]   Ibid.
[105]   Ibid.
[106]   An allocation is deemed fair if none envies the bundle of commodities another has. See H. Varian, 'Equity, Envy and Efficiency' (1974) 9 *Journal of Economic Theory* 63; A. Feldman and A. Kirman, 'Fairness and Envy (1974) 64 *American Economic Review* 995; H. Varian, Dworkin on Equality of Resources' (1985) 1 *Economics and Philosophy* 110; C. Arnsperger, 'Envy-Freeness and Distributive Justice' (1994) 8 *Journal of Economic Surveys* 155. For an application of this approach in competition law, see the excellent analysis provided by Ayal, *Fairness in Antitrust*, 164–81. The no-envy criterion may provide a proxy for welfare without necessarily proceeding to an interpersonal comparison of utility as it simply enables each person to make a choice about her/his preferred bundle of commodities. 'Comparisons are thus *within* and according to subjective valuations, and not *across* individuals' (ibid., 168, emphasis in source).

another person's shoes. Binmore provides the example of an interpersonal comparison between a person who is poor with another who is rich but suffers from clinical depression, to show the futility of the no-envy argument so long as this only focuses on the possession of bundles of commodities.

Binmore's conceptualisation of fairness norms relies on the 'mental machinery' of 'empathetic preferences', that is the ability of humans to imagine themselves into the position of other human beings, without necessarily that meaning that they feel any concern for others' welfare.[107] In a repeated game, the expression of individual's empathetic preferences will lead to the emergence of an 'empathy equilibrium' which would encapsulate the choice of a standard of interpersonal comparison in use in the specific society when the evolutionary game reaches a Nash equilibrium.[108]

The approach put forward by Binmore emphasises the futility of the trade-off between efficiency and fairness, both values being important for the stability of the social contract. Fairness norms enable the selection of one among many efficient equilibria that would maximise the chances of the specific social contract to survive and be internally stable without the presence of an omnipotent external enforcement agency.[109] This is critical if a new technology, innovation or environmental change unexpectedly expands or reduces the available set of efficient equilibria to be selected. Demands for a fair distribution of the surplus will in this case be particularly strong, making it necessary to rely on some fairness norms on the basis of an egalitarian bargaining solution, as this is framed by the past history, culture and values of the society in question. In the long term, a market mechanism may erode the moral values of the society in question, but social systems 'take time to find their way to an equilibrium', while 'fairness evolved to provide *short-run* resolutions to the equilibrium selection problem'.[110] Although Binmore recognises some limits in his approach, this work shows the weak theoretical foundations of the trade-off conception of the relation between efficiency and fairness and the importance of taking care of even short-run inequality effects.

3.6.2 *Equity and Innovation: the Dynamic Trade-Off Position*

The trade-off conception of the relation between efficiency and equity/fairness has also been quite influential in envisioning their interaction in a dynamic or evolutionary perspective. In this case, the trade-off is not set in present terms but relates to the view that pursuing equality may affect innovation.

---

[107]   He distinguishes empathetic preferences from sympathetic preferences, which concern the individual's personal preference to sympathise with another human being (Binmore, *Natural Justice*, 114–15).

[108]   Ibid., 126.

[109]   Ibid., 170–5.

[110]   Ibid., 184.

Drawing on the work of Austrian economist Joseph Schumpeter,[111] some literature distinguishes between firms that 'deliberately strive to be leaders in technological innovations' and those that 'attempt to keep up by imitating the successes of the leaders'.[112] Competition is not static but dynamic, and thus leads to a process of continuing disequilibrium fundamentally different from the static price competition depicted by neoclassical price theory with winners and losers. The market is considered as 'a device for conducting and evaluating experiments in economic behavior and organization', leading to the elimination of the less innovative firms and tipping the market to the innovation leaders. The market structure thus evolves to one involving large firms with considerable degree of market power, but this is 'the price that society must pay for rapid technological advance' as these firms have the 'capability advantages' in terms of risks spreading, economies of scale in R&D, financial resources for taking care of the sunk costs of the research, as well as the 'appropriability advantages' for better protecting their innovations through IP rights.[113]

In essence, the argument is that the static costs of a concentrated market structure and the exercise of market power may lead to welfare losses because of output restriction (and higher prices). However, these losses may be traded-off by a faster rate of growth of productivity because of investments in innovation and pushing even further the production possibility frontier of the specific economy. More importantly, product innovation benefits to consumers in the long run. Figure 3.2 is an attempt to portray the positive welfare implication of Schumpeterian competition long-term.[114]

Here, it is the demand schedule that is shifted outwards to the right as a result of product innovation. This demand shift reflects the fact that consumers have higher willingness to pay for the new generation of products which, therefore, supplants the current generation. Let's assume first that the latter, however, was produced under competitive conditions (i.e. the product life cycle reached the maturity stage of commoditisation). Similarly to the previous trade-off between productive and allocative efficiency, the assessment of the net impact in terms of total welfare requires the balancing between the anticompetitive deadweight-loss triangle and the procompetitive quadrilateral shaped area.

In this case, however, rather than being entirely appropriated by the dominant firm in the form of higher producer surplus, the procompetitive effect is mostly beneficial to consumer, thanks to higher consumer surplus. This is even more the

---

[111]   J. Schumpeter, *Capitalism, Socialism and Democracy* (Harper & Row, 1942) 84 ('[C]ompetition from the new commodity, the new technology, the new source of supply, the new organization … competition which commands a decisive cost or quality advantage and which strikes not at the margins of the profits and outputs of the existing firms but at their very foundations and their very lives').

[112]   R. N. Nelson and S. G. Winter, *An Evolutionary Theory of Economic Change* (Harvard University Press, 1982), 275.

[113]   Ibid., 278.

[114]   The next two paragraphs draw on Lianos et al., *Competition Law*.

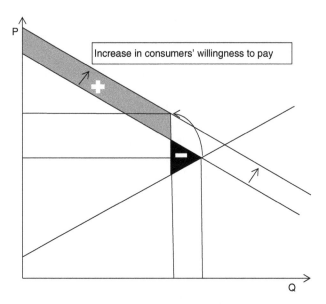

FIGURE 3.2 Dynamic efficiency and the Schumpeterian trade-off

case where the sellers of the displaced product had market power (i.e. as in the sequence of monopolist), so that allocative efficiency was already not being max-imised. Under these circumstances, the disruption due to dynamic competition would be unambiguously beneficial for consumers.

These approaches put forward the need to protect the incentives of large firms to innovate, on the assumption that these will invest their profits in R&D. However, there are various problems with this assumption. First, as it is recognised even by authors advocating a dynamic competition approach, the Schumpeterian trade-off may be different from industry to industry; in particular, in an industry marked by cumulative innovation, 'a more sheltered competitive environment, with its asso-ciated higher mark-ups, does lead to more rapid productivity growth'.[115] Second, one may take with a grain of salt the argument made sometimes that the reduction of the profits of large firms following competition law enforcement, immediately and to a similar extent, affects their incentives to fund R&D. Indeed, recent studies show that, for instance in the pharma sector, companies do not invest the majority of their profits in R&D, but prefer instead to buy their own shares to provide higher revenues

---

[115]   Nelson and Winter, *Evolutionary Theory of Economic Change*, 350. The same authors remark that 'Schumpeterian competition selects both on inventions and on firms, and moulds market structure as well as the flow of technology. But it also proceeds in part through conscious social policy. Thus, for example, antitrust laws were put in place to prevent or retard the growth of concentration.' The authors raise the possibility that an industry dominated by a large firm that has 'lost its innovative prowess' and by imitating competitors, barricades the industry 'from the entry and growth of small innovators', in particular in sectors where experience counts.

to their management and shareholders.[116] Other studies have shown that a lot of R&D in this sector is publicly funded, state resources funding the riskier parts of the pharma R&D effort, and that the rate of innovation has fallen with few new drugs being brought into the market, as a result of reduction of the part of profits spent on R&D and the prevalence of the share-buybacks practice.[117] Companies prefer to retain earnings and distribute them to shareholders and the management leading to an increase of conspicuous consumption (and reinforcing asset bubbles),[118] rather than invest them in R&D.[119] Investments in R&D are increasingly concentrated in a few sectors across most of the mature economies.[120] Firms may also employ cash hoarding as a defensive tool in order to protect their current stock of technology, and not in order to invest in new technologies. Statistics show that business investment has steadily declined since the late 1970s, if measured as a share of GDP.[121]

Companies may also prefer to buy potential competitors rather than compete on innovation with them, as this is indicated by a considerable increase of M&A transactions in recent years. The concept of research has also changed – a lot of money is actually spent on product adaptation, design and development, copying a feature or add-on from another product or adjusting the product stock to local demands, the D, and little is spent to the R.[122] Growth in real investment on R&D is declining, the US National Science Foundation reporting that its measure of R&D intensity has flatlined since 1995.[123] Many companies have reacted to problems with their R&D strategy by outsourcing R&D to smaller firms that can take bigger

---

[116] W. Lazonick, 'Profits without Prosperity' (2014) 92(9) *Harvard Business Review* 46.

[117] M. Mazzucato, *The Entrepreneurial State: Debunking Public vs. Private Sector Myths* (Anthem Press, 2013).

[118] On 'conspicuous consumption', see T. Veblen, *The Treaty of the Leisure Class* (1st edn 1899, Pennsylvania State University Press, 2003).

[119] See, for instance, some recent research on big pharma: Lazonick, 'Profits without prosperity', 46–55; W. Lazonick and M. Mazzucato, 'The Risk–Reward Nexus in the Innovation–Inequality Relationship: Who Takes the Risks? Who Gets the Rewards?' (2013) 22(4) *Industrial and Corporate Change* 1093–1128; P. Gleadle et al., 'Restructuring and Innovation in Pharmaceuticals and Biotechs: The Impact of Financialisation' (2014) 25 *Critical Perspectives on Accounting* 67–77. At a broader level, it can also be seen how financialisation alters a firm's incentives away from investment and in favour of short-term shareholder's return (O. Orhangazi, 'Financialization and Capital Accumulation in the Nonfinancial Corporate Sector: A Theoretical and Empirical Investigation on the US Economy, 1973–2004' (2007) MPRA Paper No. 7724, available at: https://mpra.ub.uni-muenchen.de/7724); M. Mazzucato, 'Financing Innovation: Creative Destruction vs. Destructive Creation' (2013) 22(4) *Industrial and Corporate Change* 851–67.

[120] See for example G. Clark, 'Winter Is Coming: Robert Gordon and the Future of Economic Growth' (2016) 106(5) *American Economic Review: Papers and Proceedings* 68–71.

[121] Ibid., 29.

[122] F. Erixon and B. Weigel, *The Innovation Illusion* (Yale University Press, 2016), 33.

[123] Ibid., 34, noting that 'R&D intensity, measured as the share of industry-level R&D expenditure to sales, increased in the seed sector from 11.0% in 1994 to 15.0% in 2000 before falling back to 10.5% in 2009'.

risks.[124] Once the R&D investments have begun to mature into innovative products, large companies have acquired them and integrated them into their global value chains.[125] This may affect the innovation and entrepreneurial ethos and consequently the trade-off to be made, should one take stock of the fact that a lower percentage of profits will be invested in innovation in view of the lower profitability of R&D research.[126] In the absence of some assurance that large firms will invest their profits to promote innovation and increase the production possibility frontier, rather than in other activities, the Schumpeterian trade-off may not justify the sacrifice of allocative efficiency incurred and the resulting inequality, just because of the promise of some future innovation gain.

Challenging the idea that there is a trade-off between efficiency/innovation and equality brings forward the need to reconceptualise competition law integrating a fairness/equity perspective.

3.7 A FAIRNESS-DRIVEN COMPETITION LAW: COMPETITION LAW FOR COMPLEX EQUALITY

An important feature of the recent focus on economic inequality is the perception that the concentration of economic power and rampant economic inequality is affecting other spheres of social activity that are not usually related to the market, such as politics and academia. There is a widespread perception in public opinion and commentators, that a small group of concentrated interests have rigged the political process undermining democracy, or more generally the autonomy of the political and cultural order vis-à-vis the economic order. There are studies documenting how corporate lobbying is directly related to firm size.[127] The highest echelons of business and multinational companies benefit from tax cuts, special tax regimes or practice elaborate forms of tax evasion at the same time as austerity policies, salary cuts and taxes rise for the least well off and the middle class.[128] Some have put forward the view that the rising economic concentration may be explained

---

[124]   See, for instance, P. Gleadle et al., 'Restructuring and Innovation in Pharmaceuticals and Biotechs: The Impact of Financialisation' (2014) 25 *Critical Perspectives on Accounting* 67–77

[125]   Comanor and Scherer point out how M&A may have been used as a safety net for companies against the uncertain prospects of innovation projects or to acquire synergies in R&D (W. S. Comanor and F. M. Scherer, 'Mergers and Innovation in the Pharmaceutical Industry' (2013) 32 *Journal of Health Economics* 106–13. Similar analyses can also be found in Gleadle et al., 'Restructuring and Innovation', 67–77.

[126]   See Gleadle et al., 'Restructuring and Innovation', 67–77.

[127]   M. D. Hill, G. W. Kelly and R. A. Van Ness, 'Determinants and Effects of Corporate Lobbying' (2013) 42(4) *Financial Management* 931.

[128]   See T. Cavero and K. Poinasamy, 'A Cautionary Tale: The True Cost of Austerity and Inequality in Europe' (2013) 174 *Oxfam Briefing Paper*; European Network on Debt and Development (Eurodad), 'Tax Games: The Race to the Bottom' (2017) *Eurodad Tax Justice Report*; J. Portes and H. Reed, 'Distributional Results for the Impact of Tax and Welfare Reforms between 2010–17, Modelled in the 2021/22 Tax Year: Interim Findings' (2017) *Equality and Human Rights Commission Research Report*.

by a 'Medici vicious circle', 'where money is used to get political power and political power is used to make money': the more firms have market power, the more they have 'both the ability and the need to gain political power'.[129]

The concern over inequality and the corresponding quest for equality should not only be interpreted as a quest for an equal part of resources (as egalitarians would claim) or for improvements in available income for the worse off (as prioritarians would ask), but a quest for equal status at the political realm, and for equal consideration in all other realms of social action. Indeed, the connection between the 'spheres' of politics and markets show, as Michal Walzer wrote, that 'the idea of distributive justice has as much to do with being and doing as with having, as much to do with production, and with consumption, as much to do with identity and status as with land, capital, or personal possessions'.[130]

For Walzer, there has never been a single criterion or a single set of interconnected criteria, for all distributions, 'for no such criterion can possibly match the diversity of social goods'.[131] He puts forward three 'distributive principles': desert, free exchange and need.[132] These rely on a diverse set of criteria, such as merit, qualifications, birth, friendships, loyalty, democratic decision, each having a place, along with many others, and possibly uneasily coexisting with them. Starting from the assumption that society is structured along different 'spheres of justice', he claims that '[t]he principles of justice are themselves pluralistic in form', as different 'social goods' ought to be distributed for different reasons, in accordance to different distributive procedures, by different agents and criteria.[133] All goods are 'social goods' in the sense that they have 'shared meanings because conception and creation are social processes'.[134] That also means that 'goods may have different meanings in different societies'.[135] They can also be 'historical in character, and so distributions, and just and unjust distributions, change over time'.[136] This society- and time-specific definition of 'distributive justice' (or fairness) has also been important in Binmore's work, as we have previously exposed. Walzer finds that the distinctness of these various social meanings should have implications on the way the various criteria of distribution should operate.[137] For

---

[129] L. Zingales, 'Towards a Political Theory of the Firm', NBER Working Paper No. 23593 (July 2017). Of course, other (cumulative or alternative) explanations for market concentration have been put forward. For a comparative discussion of various causes, see J. E. Bessen, 'Accounting for Rising Corporate Profits: Intangibles or Regulatory Rents?' (9 November 2016). Boston University School of Law, Law and Economics Research Paper No. 16-18. Available at SSRN: https://ssrn.com/abstract=2778641

[130] M. Walzer, *Spheres of Justice: A Defense of Pluralism and Equality* (Basic Books, 1983) 3.

[131] Ibid., 21.

[132] Ibid., 21–6.

[133] Ibid., 3.

[134] Ibid., 7.

[135] Ibid.

[136] Ibid., 9.

[137] Ibid., 10.

him, 'distributions must be autonomous', as every social good or set of goods should be perceived as 'a distributive sphere within which only certain criteria and arrangements are appropriate'.[138]

Recognising the existence of separate spheres of justice with autonomous distributions also makes Walzer distinguish between 'dominance' and 'monopoly'. Monopoly refers to the situations where a specific social good is monopolized, for instance for scarcity reasons (e.g. water in the desert).[139] Dominance is a more complex concept, as it refers to the control of a social good, whose control commands wide range of other goods, presumably in other spheres of social activity.[140] For instance, economic power may lead to political and cultural power, not only in the sense that it will generate some form of resource dependence, measured by the ability to raise prices profitably on a relevant market, or the ability to exercise superior bargaining power, in the specific social sphere (monopoly), but also because it will influence the options available for each individual agent in other *spheres* of social activity. Dominance will therefore challenge the autonomous distribution criteria applying in the various distributive spheres. In other words, the claim for autonomous distribution criteria for each sphere of justice is meant to challenge the dominance of a social good, rather than just deal with situations of monopoly.

Preserving the boundaries of these 'spheres of justice' becomes a possible strategy if one is to respect the process through which the members of the community develop a diversity of criteria mirroring the diversity of the social goods. Focusing on 'simple equality' implies a claim that the monopolised good should be redistributed so that it can be equally or at least more widely shared. This may result in 'continuous state intervention to break up or constrain incipient monopolies and to repress new forms of dominance'.[141] Hence, once inequalities of wealth or income are dealt with through state intervention, different forms of inequality emerge, leading to new forms of dominance and therefore sites of competition. Indeed, as Walzer notes, 'state power itself will become the central object of competitive struggles'.[142] In particular if 'the state is weak to cope with re-emerging monopolies in society at large', groups attempting to monopolize the state and then to use it in order to consolidate their control of other social goods.[143]

---

[138] Ibid. He further explains: '[t]here is no single set of primary or basic goods conceivable across all moral and material worlds – or, any such set would have to be conceived in terms so abstract that they would be of little use in thinking about particular distributions. Even the range of necessities, if we take into account moral as well as physical necessities, is very wide, and the rank orderings are very different' and things become even more complex 'as we pass from necessities to opportunities, powers, reputations, and so on' (ibid., 8).

[139] Ibid.

[140] Ibid., 11 ('possess that own, and the others come in train').

[141] Ibid., 15.

[142] Ibid.

[143] Ibid., 16.

The process will end up in a recurrent circle where political power will be mobilised to check monopoly, for instance undertakings with significant economic or market power, but then once the monopoly of money is challenged, political power itself will need to be checked, the process opening opportunities to 'strategically placed' actors to use political power in order to 'seize and exploit important social goods' ('tyranny').[144] There are incentives for adopting such strategy, as power is a 'special sort of good', in the sense that it also operates as a 'regulative agency' 'defending the boundaries of all the distributive spheres, including its own', but may also 'invade the different spheres' and 'override' their social meanings.[145] This problem of recurrent circles of monopoly followed by dominance derives, in Walzer's opinion, from 'treating monopoly, and not dominance, as the central issue in distributive justice'.[146]

'Complex equality' takes a different perspective. It aims to narrow the range within which particular goods are convertible and to vindicate the autonomy of distributive spheres. Specific social goods may be monopolised, but with no particular good being 'generally convertible'.[147] State intervention will not therefore be continuous in this case, and this will reduce the likelihood that the state, and political power, may become the site of competitive struggle, with the aim to capture the state and convert, for instance, political power to economic power. According to Walzer, in a complex egalitarian society, '[t]hough there will be many small inequalities, inequality will not be multiplied through the conversion process and expanded across different social goods, because of the autonomy of distributions and the possibility of more particularized and diffused forms of social conflict'.[148] No citizen's standing in one sphere or with regard to one social good can be undercut by his standing in some other sphere, with regard to some other good. 'Pervasive equality' would just be maintained by avoiding situations of dominance. It will be promoted by an 'open-ended distributive principle' that would respect the autonomy of the different distributive spheres: '[n]o social good x should be distributed to men and women who possess some other good x merely because they possess y and without regard to the meaning of x'.[149]

How could Walzer's theoretical framework be of relevance for competition law? The decline of complex equality may explain the emergence of populist movements in Europe and the United States, as they criticise liberalism and capitalism, and challenge the value of expertise, considered as biased and rigged by economic interests, rather than an independent source of knowledge.[150] Proponents of

---

[144] Ibid., 14.
[145] Ibid., 16.
[146] Ibid.
[147] Ibid., 17.
[148] Ibid.
[149] Ibid., 20.
[150] EU Monitor, 'A Profile of Europe's Populist Parties: Structures, Strengths, Potential' (28 April 2015), available at www.dbresearch.com/PROD/RPS_EN-PROD/PROD0000000000441777/ A_profile_of_Europe's_populist_parties%3A_Structures.PDF; Euromonitor, 'Deutsche Bank

populism criticise the effort of promoting technocratic government instead of political antagonism as the main procedure for policymaking.[151] For the populist project, social antagonisms are not to be tamed by 'deliberative democracy' leading to an elaborate process of consensus-building managed by independent technocrats. They are instead transformed to an ambitious and enthusiastic 'agonistic confrontation' between hegemonic projects.[152] The type of 'expertise' that may be required for the completion of the populist project is also different and relates to the ability of social mobilization in order to constitute the 'people' (be that workers, farmers or in the more recent versions of populism, consumers[153] or even entrepreneurs).[154] It is not linked to the traditional conception of expertise, which relates to a body of technical knowledge, most usually a codified body of knowledge in the context of an academic discipline. By adopting the single narrative of the antagonistic struggle of competing hegemonic projects, populism blurs the boundaries between the different 'spheres of justice' and ignores the complex interplay of various 'orders of worth' functioning according to different tests of justification.[155]

In the competition law field, the competing hegemonic projects would be the 'left-wing' now consumer-focused populist movement versus the 'right-wing' entrepreneurs-focused populist movement, which glorifies monopolies on the basis of a distorted conception of innovation and technological progress on the blind belief that business leaders will be only motivated by the common good. In contrast to the populist approach, an approach relying on the complex equality principle will not view societies as a single order to be dominated by a hegemonic project winning a political 'agon', but an interweaving of multiple orders, a compromise on the basis of the 'common good' eventually developing in order to settle the conflict among the actors with a variable degree of legitimacy. But, crucially, this compromise is fragile, as attempts to determine the common good are bound to reignite the conflict, eventually leading to a different compromise. In contrast to a narrow technocratic approach, which would rely, in the neoliberal tradition, on the market as the unique site of '*veridiction*-falsification' for the action of the various agents (firms, government),[156] an approach inspired by complex equality will be open to a variety of

      Research, Who Is Afraid of Populists?' (23 March 2017), available at www.dbresearch.com/PROD/
      RPS_EN-PROD/PROD000000000041789/Who_is_afraid_of_populists%3F.pdf
[151] They argue for 'agonistic politics' and 'agonistic democracy'. C. Mouffe, *On The Political* (Routledge,
      2005); C. Mouffe, 'Agonistic Democracy and Radical Politics', *Pavilion*, available at pavilionmaga
      zine.org/chantal-mouffe-agonistic-democracy-and-radical-politics
[152] E. Laclau and C. Mouffe, *Hegemony and Socialist Strategy – Towards a Radical Democratic Politics*
      (2nd edn, Verso, 1985); E. Laclau, *On Populist Reason* (Verso, 2005).
[153] S. Vaheesan, 'The Evolving Populisms of Antitrust' (2013) 93(2) *Nebraska Law Review* (Article 4).
[154] See B. Orbach, 'Antitrust Populism' (2017) 14(1) *NYU Journal of Law and Business* 1 (detailing the
      emergence of the 'anti-bigness' and the 'anti-enforcement' populisms in US antitrust law).
[155] L. Boltansky and L. Thévenot, *On Justification: The Economies of Worth* (Princeton University Press,
      2006).
[156] M. Foucault, *The Birth of Biopolitics – Lectures at the Collège de France 1978–1979* (Palgrave
      Macmillan, 2010), 32 (noting that 'inasmuch as prices are determined in accordance with the natural

criteria, respecting the autonomy of these different 'spheres' of social activity and the multiple values they cater for.

What would be the place of a competition law relying on economic, or more broadly, social science expertise, in an era of populism? Is the re-emergence of populist antitrust the only way ahead if competition law is to maintain its legitimacy in a political context characterised by a deep suspicion towards technocracy, in particular economic expertise, and the view that competition authorities, have not acted to prevent the rise in economic concentration and inequality in recent years? Or, is antitrust moving to institutional oblivion, soon to be replaced by direct forms of regulation, or regulation through public ownership, with the alleged aim of 'moralising' economic activity, but, in reality, to subject it to the dictates of political power? If the idea of complex equality is to be taken seriously in competition law, one needs to be equally concerned with the tendency of economic power to expand into the realm of politics, as well as with the tendency of political power, becoming dominant as the sphere of politics is slowly transcending all other 'spheres of justice', to convert itself to economic power, suppressing market freedoms.

To provide an example, 'complex equality' concerns may influence the competition law principles applying to digital platforms that have become the central nervous system of modern capitalist value generation. Some jurisdictions, like the EU, have been quite concerned by the transformation of these digital platforms to important gatekeepers for various economic activities in the digital economy,[157] and of their ability to leverage their economic power (resulting from the control of resources such as big data, advanced algorithms and artificial intelligence, on which the new model of economic production depends) in various domains of activity, including the capture of an even higher percentage of the total surplus value of the respective value chain.[158] Algorithmic firms may harvest immense technological and ultimately economic power differential vis-à-vis their non-algorithmic rivals. Would domain expertise enable these firms to resist the technological prowess of digital platforms, and what could be the appropriate role for competition law in this context? Should competition law be enforced when digital platforms adopt

mechanisms of the market they constitute a standard of truth which enables us to discern which governmental [but one can also add firm] practices are correct and which are erroneous', the 'natural' mechanisms of the market being the invisible hand of Adam Smith and its intellectual progeny (including 'perfect competition').

[157] See EU Communication on digital platforms of 25 May 2016 (COM(2016)288 final) 12, noting that '[a]s online platforms play an increasing role in the economy, the terms of access to online platforms can be an important factor for online and offline companies. For SMEs and micro-enterprises, some online platforms constitute important, sometimes the main, entry points to certain markets and data.'

[158] This explains the recent focus of competition authorities in Europe on leveraging practices, with the aim to ensure the 'equality of opportunity' of economic operators (European Commission, Case AT 39.740 – Google Search, paras. 332 and 334), as well as recent ideas to regulate from a fairness perspective platform to business relations (Inception Impact Assessment, Fairness in Platform to Business Relation, Ares(2017)5222469, available at https://ec.europa.eu/info/law/better-regulation/initiatives/ares-2017-5222469_en).

exclusionary practices that may stifle the capacity of non-algorithmic firms to innovate or to develop independent technological capabilities, and thus to limit their technological dependence on them, but by doing so improve their own efficiency? Control of (personal) data by these digital platforms may also affect privacy,[159] but also more generally the democratic process.[160] This could lead to the emergence of an entrenched dominant position or oligopolistic market structure over an essential social good (information) for the proper functioning of democratic debate and providing important economic (and political/cultural) power to the 'big five'.[161] Should competition law also address these concerns? The answers to these questions may vary between different competition law systems.

3.8 THE NECESSARY AND LONG-AWAITED ENRICHMENT OF COMPETITION LAW

The concrete implications of a fairness-driven competition law for the various areas of competition law doctrine are explored in a different study.[162] However, I would like to briefly describe the main changes that, in my opinion, the shift towards fairness entails for competition law. The approach undertaken may vary from jurisdiction to jurisdiction and will largely depend on the hermeneutic conversation that will take place within *each* legal and political system, and the subsequent accommodation of conflicting narratives regarding the relation between the state and the market, or more generally an atomist versus a more social view of human-kind's dependence on society to realise the 'human good'.[163]

It is clear that issues of distributive justice and fairness are essential and any effort to sweep them under the carpet to avoid this inconvenient discussion, as unfortunately has been the case in the last thirty years in competition law doctrine, is not only futile, as fairness concerns may return with some vengeance, but also wrong from moral and social theory perspectives. The implementation of fairness concerns

---

[159] See European Data Protection Supervisor, 'Privacy and Competitiveness in the Age of Big Data: The Interplay between Data Protection, Competition Law and Consumer Protection in the Digital Economy' (March 2014); Autorité de la Concurrence and Bundeskartellamt, 'Competition Law and Data' (16 May 2016); US FTC, 'Big Data – A Tool for Inclusion or Exclusion?' (January 2016). Some public authorities have also looked to these questions when exploring the changes brought by platform competition (European Commission, 'Online Platforms and the Digital Single Market Opportunities and Challenges for Europe', COM/2016/0288 final; House of Lords, 'Online Platforms and the Digital Single Market', HL Paper 129 (2016); OECD, 'Big Data: Bringing Competition Policy to the Digital Era', DAF/COMP(2016)14).

[160] See, for instance, the debate about 'fake news' as being an 'antitrust problem' (S. Hubbard, 'Fake News Is A Real Antitrust Problem' (2017) *Competition Policy International*; S. P. Sacher and J. M. Jun, 'Fake News Is Not an Antitrust Problem' (2017) *Antitrust Chronicle*).

[161] These are Alphabet, Amazon, Apple, Facebook, Microsoft.

[162] I. Lianos, 'Implementing Fairness in EU Competition Law' (forth. Research Paper 4/2019).

[163] C. Taylor, 'The Nature and Scope of Distributive Justice', in *Human Agency and Language – Philosophical Papers* (Cambridge University Press, 1985), 289 (distinguishing the atomist view of Locke and more recently Nozick to the social view of Aristotle and more recently Rawls and Walzer).

requires from competition law enforcers delicate and difficult hermeneutical choices with regard to the principles and values of justice as fairness to be read in the competition law legislation and jurisprudence, in a way that would guarantee the coherence of the specific legal and political system.

According to some, the return to 'populist' antitrust may provide an adequate response to the current rise of inequalities, in particular those generated by the prevalence of the network effects and 'winner takes all' dynamics of the digital economy,[164] at least as long as the existence of market concentration, market power and declining labour share, may be considered among the principal causes of these inequalities. What this means for the area of competition law has been spelled out in various publications of the 'new Brandeis movement',[165] essentially a hermeneutical standpoint that claims to offer a thicker and more genuine meaning to the antitrust law enterprise, arguably in a closer connection to its historical and cultural roots.

These perspectives should not be dismissed out of hand, for the simple reason that they spoil the 'consensus' arrived at in recent decades between the right and the left on the standard of consumer welfare. First, it is not clear what this consensus exactly entails in practice, as consumer welfare or consumer harm, even if it provides a general hermeneutical principle, is notoriously vague, from an operational perspective, and as some prominent authors explain, does not even constitute an element of a competition law offence that 'must be proved independently of the law violation'.[166] Second, there cannot be any 'end of history' moment in competition law scholarship and jurisprudence. The 'overlapping consensus', to use Rawls's term, may change and the legal interpreter should be careful to integrate the important technological and socio-economic transformations unveiling, and to address the various arguments put forward by the different hermeneutical communities of competition law. Third, although antitrust/competition law has historically focused on situations of economic coercion and restriction of competitive rivalry in markets, with the aim of taming the risk of private government, economic power may crystallise in various insidious forms, taking advantage of recent advances in science (e.g. psychology, behavioural economics, business strategy) to frame preferences and influence/nudge individual decision-making. Fourth, competition law takes place in various fields, not only on product markets, but also on financial markets and future markets for innovation, more so as market participants and market experts offer new imaginative market devices to respond to this growing demand for futurity.

---

[164] L. Khan and S. Vaheesan, 'Market Power and Inequality: The Antitrust Counterrevolution and Its Discontents (2017) 11 *Harvard Law and Policy Review* 235.

[165] L. Khan, 'The New Brandeis Movement: America's Antimonopoly Debate' (2018) 9(3) *Journal of Competition Law and Practice* 131.

[166] I refer here to no other than R. Bork who observes that: '[c]onsumer harm is not an element of a Sherman Act offense that must be proved independently of the law violation. Antitrust conclusively *presumes* consumer harm when unlawful behaviour is shown' (R. Bork, 'Trust the Trustbusters: Why Conservatives Are Wrong about Antitrust', in *A Time To Speak* (ISI Books, 2008) 476.

What could be the practical implications for competition law of the concerns raised by the populists? These concerns may not necessarily be addressed through more aggressive competition law intervention in markets. Antitrust 'conservatives'[167] may find comfort with approaches suggesting the expansion of markets and the reconceptualisation of property rights,[168] in order to deal with the complete markets assumption problem that has always bedevilled equilibrium analysis in economics.[169] Other approaches emphasising the role of countervailing bargaining power (of final consumers or other market participants) in order to neutralise economic power and its various sources have also been put forward.[170] However, in my view, such approaches may offer, at best, partial solutions to the concentration of economic power, and to its conversion to inequality, in other spheres of justice.

Some more active and vigilant competition law enforcement may therefore be needed. This involves focusing again on economic concentration as such. A complex equality-driven competition law will view more critically merger activity and the common shareholding of major corporations, which may produce anticompetitive effects across different economic sectors,[171] in view of the financialisation process of the global economy.[172]

---

[167] By this expression I mean those that fear more type I errors (over-enforcement) than type II errors (under-enforcement).

[168] See, for instance, the recent book by E. Posner and E. G. Weyl, *Radical Markets Uprooting Capitalism and Democracy for a Just Society* (Princeton University Press, 2018) (suggesting a greater use of Harberger taxes and the end of the monopoly paradigm of property rights perceived as a right to exclude).

[169] The assumption that consumers may access a full set of insurance contracts and thus be protected against any possible idiosyncratic risk that may affect their individual consumption (e.g. loss of job, accident, stock market boom or bust) deals with the inherent uncertainty of a market system, contingent consumption claims being settled before uncertainty is revealed, and enables economists to assume that individual behaviour coincides with aggregate behaviour, thus greatly simplifying economic analysis and consequently the lessons that may be drawn for both individual and aggregate analysis just by studying either indifferently. For a critical discussion, see T. Jappelli and L. Pistaferri, 'Complete Markets', in T. Jappelli and L. Pistaferri, *The Economics of Consumption: Theory and Evidence* (Oxford University Press, 2017), 46.

[170] See, for instance, M. S. Gal and N. Elkin-Koren, 'Algorithmic Consumers' (2017) 30(2) *Harvard Journal of Law and Technology* 309 (advancing the possibility of consumers to turn also algorithmic and thus tame the technological power of algorithmic firms); I. Arrieta Ibarra, L. Goff, D. Jimenez Hernandez, J. Lanier and E. Glen Weyl, 'Should We Treat Data as Labor? Moving Beyond "Free"' (2017) 1(1) *American Economic Association Papers and Proceedings*, available at https://papers.ssrn.com/sol3/papers.cfm?abstract_id=3093683 (arguing for providing search engines' users the possibility of resorting to collective bargaining with digital platforms).

[171] J. Azar, M. C. Schmalz and I. Tecu, 'Anti-Competitive Effects of Common Ownership' (15 March 2017) *Journal of Finance*. Available at SSRN: https://ssrn.com/abstract=2427345 or http://dx.doi.org/10.2139/ssrn.2427345; J. Azar, R. Raina and M. C. Schmalz, 'Ultimate Ownership and Bank Competition' (23 July 2016). Available at SSRN: https://ssrn.com/abstract=2710252 or http://dx.doi.org/10.2139/ssrn.2710252

[172] J. Montgomerie and K. Williams, 'Financialised Capitalism: After the Crisis and Beyond Neoliberalism' (2009) 13(2) *Competition and Change* 99–107. For a historical and explanatory analysis of the concept financialisation, with regard to profitability, shareholder value and shifted

A complex equality-driven competition law may also take a wider perspective on economic power, not just focusing on 'market power',[173] but considering all sources of power, rehabilitating concepts such as relational market power or superior bargaining power. This may provide grounds for action in order to avoid the quasi-totality of the total surplus of global value chains being appropriated by 'lead' companies, while leaving a number of market players without proper compensation for their efforts and contributions, when this has negative effects on innovation, productivity as well as long-term consumer interest.[174] We should not forget that the main benefit of markets is to reward productivity. This ensures their resilience as a mechanism of social organisation.

We may also have to focus on consumer *well-being* in markets where this makes sense from a complex equality perspective, where we know that most of the consumers (or people), affected will be among the lower-income strata, or that monopolistic control of the specific social good may lead to the emergence of dominance that can be converted and extended more easily in other markets and other social spheres (outside market exchange). We may want to take a broader perspective, for instance by considering broader public interests that would preserve fairness and social stability, even if this is at the price of some reduction in economic efficiency. This could include effects on employment and the interests of workers and the unemployed, the protection of privacy, the democratic process and media pluralism, or environmental concerns, to the extent that these effects result from restrictions of competition, systemic resilience becoming the driving force of competition law.[175]

New tools may also be added to the competition law toolkit box. It is clear that market definition with its emphasis on price competition may fail to represent the various forms of competitive interaction that take place in the digital economy, and the various other values than lower prices that may animate public policy in specific markets. By focusing on 'horizontal competition', that is the competition from existing firms in a specific relevant market, market definition also ignores 'vertical competition', competition from suppliers upstream or customers downstream, in different segments of the industry, that may represent more meaningful constraints

---

incentives on innovation, see N. van der Zwan, 'State of the Art: Making Sense of Financialisation' (2014) 12 *Socio-Economic Review* 99–129.

[173] See also the proposals of A. Ayal, 'The Market for Bigness: Economic Power and Competition Agencies' Duty to Curtail It' (2013) 1(2) *Journal of Antitrust Enforcement* 221.

[174] I. Lianos and C. Lombardi, 'Superior Bargaining Power and the Global Food Value Chain: The Wuthering Heights of Holistic Competition Law?' (2016) 1 *Concurrences* 22; I. Lianos, 'Global Food Value Chains and Competition Law – BRICS Draft Report' (1 January 2018). Available at SSRN: https://ssrn.com/abstract=3076160

[175] See I. Lianos, 'Polycentric Competition Law' (2018) *Current Legal Problems* 1. For instance, it can be argued that these concerns should be integrated in the competition law analysis in EU law, in view of the social and economic rights included in the Charter and the broader horizontal clauses in the EU Treaties, such as Article 9 TFEU. For a discussion, see I. Lianos, 'Legal Hermeneutics and Competition Law' (CLES Research Paper 5/2019).

to the economic power of dominant companies, in particular in the digital economy.[176]

Vertical competition may also play a more significant role in competition law if the analysis shifts from solely focusing on the generation of even higher surplus value to understanding the allocation of the total surplus value that is generated in the context of a value chain. To the extent that fairness and guaranteeing complex equality become important objectives of competition law, the distribution of the total surplus value may become an important concern. Restrictions to vertical competition may also affect productivity and provide 'superstar' large digital platforms the possibility to pull away from competition and enjoy tremendous levels of profitability, without these accumulated profits being used for productive investments. The conceptual tool of value chain (or global value chain) may offer an excellent mapping tool that could be further used in competition law. Market studies and enquiries may also provide a more complete picture of economic power and of the competitive interactions in an industry, eventually offering further opportunities for better targeting competition law enforcement or for using ad hoc remedies.

The realisation is that for societies to stay stable, they need to stand on two legs: economic efficiency but also fairness, may call for a limited redesign of competition law. This should not only be focusing on efficiency (and consumer surplus or welfare), but also on guaranteeing complex equality. This 'complex equality-driven' competition law may opt for some of the reforms suggested above by the proponents of 'populist' antitrust. However, to the difference of the views put forward by the populists, the boundaries of competition law enforcement should also be clear and limiting principles to state intervention developed in order to avoid the dominance of politics over the marketplace, considered as a separate sphere of justice. Accepting that some degree of inequality of resources may be the consequence of the operation of the various criteria adopted by the different spheres of justice (in the marketplace, competition on the merits), and that promoting equality of opportunities needs to stand on well-designed standards that provide equal consideration to the various interests affected (including the rights of the monopolists and oligopolists)[177] constitute some of the necessary steps ensuring that competition law furthers complex equality and systemic resilience.

Competition law cannot be transformed again to being just a tool of social regulation. In contrast to the period of antitrust populism that followed the Bretton Woods agreements,[178] free circulation of capital globally constitutes one

---

[176]   For a more in-depth analysis of the role of 'vertical competition' in the digital economy, see I. Lianos, 'Digital Value Chains and Competition Law' (CLES Research Paper 1/2019).

[177]   For an interesting argument in favour of considering also the rights of the monopolists, see Ayal, *Fairness in Antitrust*, 122–43.

[178]   The international economic system resulting from the Bretton Woods included capital controls for the first time at a broad basis to guarantee financial stability after the Second World War. These

of the building blocks of modern financial capitalism, thus intensifying competition between capitals for the most profitable investment.[179] Hence, as long as the free flow of capital remains an essential element of the global capitalist system, competition law should also accommodate economic policy concerns, such as attracting foreign direct and indirect investments as well as promoting productivity.

Competition law may not reverse the trend towards economic inequality.[180] However, in view of the difficulty of the traditional tools of the welfare state to deal with some of the causes of economic inequality, in particular monopoly power, and the fact that social expenses have reached a plateau in some jurisdictions, competition law may fulfil a quite important role in the struggle against economic inequality. From this perspective, the systemic resilience of the social contract may offer a high-end goal that would accommodate both efficiency and fairness concerns. Under these limitations, competition law should provide the necessary balancing force to populism and may become an important tool in promoting complex equality. The choice appears therefore to be broader than the dilemma between the return of 'populist' antitrust and a competition law marginalised in an era of 'populism'.

restrictions were gradually taken away after the collapse of the Bretton Woods system in the early 1970s. However, the Asian crisis of 1997 and the most recent 2008 financial crisis brought back the view that capital controls are not just a tool to mitigate financial crises, but can become a regular monetary policy tool, even if there is no crisis (IMF, 'Strengthening the International Monetary System – A Stocktaking' (22 February 2016), available at www.imf.org/external/np/pp/eng/2016/022216b.pdf).

[179] This of course creates constraints for national governments with regard to adopting more 'aggressive' competition law enforcement, although the size of their market, and not just the rates of return on capital, could also play some role in the decision of global capital to flee elsewhere, should competition law enforcement significantly halve its returns on investment.

[180] This has been in operation for thousands of years, and temporarily interrupted only because of the impact of the 'four horsemen': war, revolution, systemic collapse and pandemics (W. Scheidel, *The Great Leveler* (Princeton University Press, 2017), 443, observing the 'common root' of these in the 'massive and violent disruptions of the established order', and noting that 'the periodic compressions of inequality brought about by mass mobilization dwarfed any known instances of equalization by entirely peaceful means'. However, the standards of equality to which one may aspire to return to may not be those of the forager societies prior to the Holocene!).

4

The Social Contract at the Basis of Competition Law

Should We Recalibrate Competition Law to Limit Inequality?

Michal S. Gal

4.1 INTRODUCTION

The social contract is a voluntary agreement among individuals by which organized society comes into being and is vested with its rights. While the social contract is a metaphor, the idea at its basis has great value, as it serves to conceptualize the relationship between the state and its citizens, as well as among citizens, and it creates the basis for the legitimacy of state action. Indeed, this enormously influential metaphor has served as the basis for one of the most dominant theories of moral and political theory of modern history.

The idea of a social contract appears in the writings of Socrates, and was developed in the modern era by philosophers such as Thomas Hobbes, John Locke, Jean-Jacques Rousseau, John Rawls, David Gauthier, and others.[1] While each philosopher suggested a somewhat different basis for the social contract, their theories all share several common traits: men voluntarily choose to submit to the authority of a state; they do so in order to be able to live in a civil society, which is conducive to their own interests; the state, once formed, is directed toward the common good, understood, and agreed to collectively. Most philosophers also agree that mutual security and the protection of social and individual welfare stand at the basis of the social contract.

Competition law, like any other form of governmental regulation, is part of the social contract. In market-based economies it constitutes an important element of the socio-economic portion of this contract, which is focused on increasing total and individual welfare. It does so by ensuring that, where possible, privately erected artificial barriers to competition are prohibited. To be sure, the conceptions of total

Many thanks to Bill Kovacic, as well as participants at the Symposium in honor of Eleanor Fox in Brussels, for most helpful discussions on the subject, and many thanks to Ioannis Lianos for excellent comments on an earlier draft. All omissions and errors remain the author's.

[1]   See e.g. Celeste Friend, 'Social Contract,' *Internet Encyclopedia of Philosophy* www.iep.utm.edu/soc-cont

and individual welfare may differ even among market economies. For example, jurisdictions may give different weight to total over individual welfare in the short run, or they may value dynamic efficiency more than allocative efficiency. They may also give more value to considerations of equal access into markets over lower prices.[2] Yet such economies all share a core assumption that the total and individual welfare of members of society (rather than, for example, a dictator), stands at the basis of the social contract.

Accordingly, for the social contract to work well, at a minimum its conditions should ensure that total welfare will be increased, at least in the long run. Indeed, competition law is based on the assumption that competition can reduce prices and increase all types of efficiency, including allocative, productive, and dynamic efficiency. The protection of competition also serves non-economic goals such as dispersing power and opportunity, reducing socially harmful political effects, and supporting democracy and freedom of speech.[3]

Furthermore, the social contract should ensure that individual welfare is also increased, at least in the long run. It is assumed that competition law does so in several cumulative ways. Most basically, consumers enjoy better and cheaper products and services, thereby increasing their ability to better fulfill their individual preferences.[4] Of no less importance, Competition can positively affect social mobility and equality of opportunity of members of society. By lowering artificial barriers to entry, potential competitors will be able to enter or expand in the market, compete on merit, enjoy (at least partially) the fruits of their success. Indeed, social mobility is a likely and expected outcome of competition. This is due to the fact that people with good ideas or good managerial skills do not necessarily come from any particular part of society. Moreover, those from lower socio-economic classes often have a stronger motivation to succeed economically and climb up the ladder, thereby leading them to invest more effort in the market game than those who treat their economic benefits as natural.

Of course, competition is not a panacea; it does not work well where significant market failures exist, such as information asymmetries, natural monopolies, negative externalities, free riding, or collective action problems. Furthermore, competition does not attempt to solve all welfare issues. Rather, it is part of a broader set of governmental instruments designed – at least in theory – to collectively meet the goals of the social contract. To give one example, education and retraining

---

[2] See e.g. D. L. Waked, 'Antitrust Goals in Developing Countries: Policy Alternatives and Normative Choices' (2014) 38 *Seattle U. L. Rev.* 945; A. Ezrachi, 'Sponge' (2017) 5(1) *Journal of Antitrust Enforcement* 49.

[3] A vast literature exists on the goals of competition law. For a good analysis of the different goals adopted by competition law See e.g. Waked, 'Antitrust Goals'; Daniel Zimmer (ed.), *The Goals of Competition Law* (Edgar Elgar, 2012).

[4] Observe, however, the consumers' preferences may change with the change of options in the market, and the ability of their reference group to consume similar products, thereby not necessarily significantly increasing their feeling of well-being for a long time.

programs, that increase entry and mobility in the market, are essential parts of a social contract aimed at increasing total and individual welfare in the long run.

Unfortunately, it seems that at least in some economies the socio-economic social contract is not working well in practice. Recent years have envisaged an increased rate of dissatisfaction with market economies. A growing number of citizens believe that the promises of the competition-based market system, which form an important part of the implicit social contract, are not fulfilled and that capitalistic markets are no longer working in their favor. Indeed, statistics indicate that social mobility is low; that wealth is aggregated disproportionately in the hands of the already well-off;[5] that wealth inequality keeps rising;[6] that several large firms dominate the digital economy, thereby blocking at least some of the promises that technological changes were thought to bring about; that technological changes such as robotics create significant disruption effects and have negative implications on the labor market; or that education and social security do not create viable solutions for workers in order to ensure that wide geographic areas or demographic groups are not significantly and irreparably harmed. In the US and the European Union, for example, the economic prospects of young people are, for the first time in several decades, grimmer than those of their parents.

This, in turn, creates social unrest and a degree of distrust in the market system which, in turn, reduces the ability of markets and societies to function well.[7] This unrest has led, inter alia, to social protests, such as the Israeli so-called "Cottage Protest," referring to the increase in price of cottage cheese, and the US movement "We are the 99%," whose name indicates the fact that a large part of the wealth is concentrated in the hands of the few, pointing to the significant and growing inequality in the distribution of economic resources.[8] The Arab Spring was also, at least partially, based on the upheaval of the underprivileged against inequality in sharing the gains from trade. The recent elections in the US have also brought to the forefront questions of whether capitalism and liberalism, the way they are currently practiced, indeed further the interests all members of society, or whether they serve only some parts of society. All these protests share a common belief that the dogma of open markets and free trade is, in practice, working well for the elites, but not for the masses.[9]

---

[5] See e.g. A. B. Atkinson, T. Piketty, and E. Saez, 'Top Incomes in the Long Run of History' (2011) 49 J. Econ. Lit. 3, 8 (focusing on US markets); OECD, 'Are We Growing Unequal?' (2008) 7, www.oecd.org/dataoecd/48/56/41494435.pdf; T. Piketty, *Capital in the Twenty-First Century* (Harvard University Press 2014).

[6] OECD, *Divided We Stand: Why Inequality Keeps Rising* (2011), www.oecd.org/els/socialpoliciesand data/49170253.pdf.

[7] See e.g. J. Stiglitz, *The Price of Inequality: How Today's Divided Society Endangers Our Future* (Norton, 2012).

[8] See statistics cited in J. B. Baker and S. Salop, 'Antitrust, Competition Policy, and Inequality' (2015) 104 Geo. L. J 1.

[9] For a similar conclusion on the global scale see, e.g. Dani Rodrik, *The Globalization Paradox: Democracy and the Future of the World Economy* (Norton, 2011).

These developments require us to examine the social contract from which state regulation acquires its legitimacy and determine whether its instruments should be changed, to meet these new challenges. In particular, this short chapter focuses on whether equality and inclusive growth goals should play a more pronounced role in competition law. Some leading scholars, spearheaded by Eleanor Fox, argue for the inclusion of such goals in developing countries. This chapter explores whether these goals should also be given more weight in developed jurisdictions as well, and, if so, how. As noted, competition law is only part of the regulatory toolbox which affects socio-economic conditions. Yet because it is the basic instrument that regulates competition in most markets, the time is ripe to ask whether its current form indeed serves the social contract.

To do so, I first explore the connection between the social contract and inequality. I then explore the interrelation between competition law and inequality, exposing the duality and the dilemma which it creates, which go to the basis of competition law. I also analyze the assumptions that competition law is based upon, and the way they are met in the real world. The last part suggests some ways in which competition law can incorporate some measures designed to reduce inequality, without significantly changing its focus.

4.2 THE SOCIAL CONTRACT AND INEQUALITY[10]

Is equality part of the social contract, and, if so, what weight should be given to it when it clashes with other values? Interestingly, equality plays different roles in the writings of social contract theorists. According to Rousseau, inequality stood at the basis of the formation of the social contract: the invention of property strengthened the initial conditions of inequality in the state of nature. It therefore was in the interest of those who had property to create a state that would protect them from those who did not possess property but might have been able to acquire it by force. So, while the social contract purported to guarantee equality and protection for all, its true purpose was to fossilize the very inequalities that private property has produced. Rousseau then argued for a normative social contract, which is meant to respond to and remedy these social and moral ills, and determine how we ought to live.[11] It is this normative social contract that I wish to focus upon.

With regard to the content of a normative (hypothetical) social contract, all modern philosophers assume that the state is formed when free and equal persons come together and agree to create a new collective body, directed to the good of all. As such, it should not serve the interests of one group over another. Therefore,

---

[10]   This part is partly based on Friend, 'Social Contract'. Other contractualist perspectives on inequality also exist. See e.g. T. M. Scanlon, *What We Owe to Each Other* (Harvard University Press, 1998).

[11]   J.-J. Rousseau, *The Basic Political Writings*, trans. Donald A. Cress (Hackett, 1987).

inherent inequality could not form part of the social contract. Otherwise, those suffering from such inequality would not have agreed to join the collective.

This idea is embodied, in its most famous form, in Rawls's A *Theory of Justice*,[12] in which he argues that the moral and political content of the social contract is discovered via impartiality. He suggests the use of a symbolic veil of ignorance, behind which each person is denied any particular knowledge of one's circumstances, such as one's gender, race, particular talents or disabilities, social status, or preferences. Persons are also assumed to be rational and disinterested in one another's well-being. These are the conditions under which, Rawls argues, one can choose principles for a just society, on which the social contract can be based. Because no one has any particular knowledge that could be used to develop principles that favor his or her own particular circumstances, the principles chosen from such a perspective are necessarily just.

Rawls argues for two principles of justice that would emerge in such a situation, which determine the distribution of both civil liberties and social and economic goods. The first principle states that each person in a society is to have as much basic liberty as possible, as long as everyone is granted the same liberties. The second principle (known as the difference principle or the maximin principle) states that while social and economic inequalities can be just, such inequalities must be to the advantage of everyone. This means, in Rawls's view, that economic inequalities are only justified when the least advantaged member of society is better off than she would be under alternative arrangements. Rawls also emphasizes that a just distribution should be based on real fair equality of opportunity, and that this principle has precedence over the maximin principle. Observe that these principles do not necessarily lead to a situation in which citizens are equal, either in each point in time or in the end state. Rather, short-term inequality might be justified in order to serve long-term justice.[13] Nonetheless, distributional effects are put under a magnifying lens: it matters not only which general groups benefit from the action, but rather if weaker individuals also benefit.

Rawls's conception of a just social contract can, however, be questioned.[14] Some have argued that the rules chosen behind a veil of ignorance depend on the level of risk aversion of the individuals determining the contract, and the rules by which the contract is set. Should most individuals be risk neutral or have a low level of risk aversion, and the gains to the total welfare pie would be large as a result of inequality, we might envisage a social contract which does not necessarily embody the maximin principle in its strictest form, but rather embodies a rule which maximizes the average welfare while ensuring some minimum standard of welfare to all. Also, much depends on the normative values at the basis of each society. Furthermore,

---

[12]   J. Rawls, A *Theory of Justice* (Harvard University Press 1971, rev. edn, 2000).
[13]   Ibid., 122–3.
[14]   For some of the criticism on Rawls's work See e.g. the sources cited in the following discussion as well as G. A. Cohen, *If You're an Egalitarian, How Come You're So Rich?* (Harvard University Press, 2000).

Rawls does not look at the conditions which have led to a situation in which the individual is less well off. Yet we may wish to treat differently one who was born with a low income and one who lost his wealth due to laziness. Other theorists question the incentives which the Rawlsian contract create: whether it creates incentives for individuals to contribute to society in a way which will maximize the total welfare pie, so that it could then be distributed among members of society.

Of course, the Rawlsian ideal of a just society is not the only one possible. Others put more emphasis on different values at the basis for the legitimacy of the state. One such theory is libertarianism, which gives liberty precedence over other values, including equality.[15] Robert Nozick, a leading scholar in this school of thought, views the role of the state as one respecting citizens' individual liberties, mainly property rights, rather than ensuring a just distribution of means. Accordingly, such liberties should not be sacrificed, without the individuals' consent, in order to achieve broader social goals, including distributive justice. This night-watchman state, which completely disregards distribution concerns as such, was not adopted by any state in this strict form. Criticisms of this view focus, inter alia, on the fact that it is assumed that current property rights are based on a just distribution, and that it fails to recognize the fact that property rights, in themselves, limit the liberties of others.[16]

Other leading theories of justice include, inter alia, utilitarianism[17] and the capabilities approach.[18] Utilitarianism emphasizes the maximization of utility, regardless of its distribution among individuals. Inequality should be remedied only if it harms overall utility. The capabilities approach is based on two core normative claims: the freedom to achieve well-being is of primary moral importance, and freedom to achieve well-being is to be understood in terms of people's capabilities, that is, their real opportunities to do and be what they have reason to value. To enable every person to enjoy his right to well-being, at least at a minimum level, distribution should relate not only to the resource which is redistributed (as suggested by liberals such as Rawls), but also to each individual's basic capabilities to use this resource to further his goals. Nobel laureate Amartya Sen emphasizes that this focus is the only way to ensure real equality between individuals to achieve their goals.[19] Martha Nussbaum argues that the capabilities approach remedies a basic

---

[15] See e.g. R. Nozick, *Anarchy, State and Utopia* (Basic Books, 1971).

[16] For criticism of libertarianism See e.g. J. Paul (ed.) *Reading Nozick: Essays on Anarchy, State and Utopia* (Rowman & Littlefield, 1981); W. Kymlicka, *Contemporary Political Philosophy – An Introduction* (Oxford University Press, 2000); G. A. Cohen, 'Capitalism, Freedom and the Proletariat', in David Miller (ed.), *Liberty* (Oxford University Press, 1991).

[17] See e.g. J. Bentham, *An Introduction to the Principles of Morals and Legislation* (Clarendon Press, 1907).

[18] A. Sen, *Choice, Welfare and Measurement* (Basil Blackwell, 1982); *Development as Freedom* (Knopf 1999); *The Idea of Justice* (Harvard University Press, 2009); M. Nussbaum, *Women and Human Development: The Capabilities Approach* (Cambridge University Press, 2000); *Frontiers of Justice: Disability, Nationality, Species Membership* (Harvard University Press, 2006).

[19] Ibid.

flaw in many modern conceptions of a social contract, which envisage a negotiation between rational and physically and mentally sound individuals, not taking into account those that do not belong to this group. Critics of the capabilities approach emphasize, inter alia, the difficulties in comparing the capabilities of different individuals.[20]

Despite this plethora of theories relating to the goals of the social contract at the basis of the state, it can be argued that, at least in most western societies, equality should serve as a basic guiding principle of the social contract.[21] At a minimum, inequality should only be accepted if its benefits to the common good significantly outweigh the harm it causes to (some) individuals, and even those individuals enjoy benefits from the overall regulatory scheme, to make their position Pareto-optimal in the long run, relative to a different set of rules governing and regulating society. The following analysis takes this minimum as a basis for the analysis.

Inequality in the marketplace has two main facets: inequality of opportunity to enter and expand in the market (suppliers), to take advantage of what it can offer (consumers); and inequality of wealth, which affects the ability to act both as suppliers and as consumers. Inequality of opportunity may clash with the social contract in at least three ways. First, it does not justly disperse the opportunities for participating in and enjoying the benefits of the marketplace, as it allows some to enjoy a comparative advantage over others. Put differently, it severs or weakens the connection between one's contribution to the marketplace and one's reward. Second, it may clash with the economic goal of increasing the total welfare pie, for the benefit of all, which could then be distributed among members of society. As economic studies have shown, inequality reduces overall economic growth by preventing or limiting the ability of some parts of society to contribute to the marketplace. Third, and relatedly, inequality of opportunity has not only economic consequences but also psychological ones. As psychologists and others have shown, one's satisfaction and motivation to take part in an action is based not only on what one has in absolute terms, but, even more importantly, on the opportunities others have relative to himself. Indeed, we do not live as separate individuals but rather interactions and comparisons form an integral part of our well-being. Accordingly, inequality of opportunity further harms the economic goal of individual and societal welfare by creating social unrest which can shake the foundations of society.

Observe, however, that while equality of opportunity in the long run can be viewed as a foundational legitimizing principle of many western societies, this does not imply a complete equality of opportunity at any point in time. Rather, much depends on the conditions which have led to such inequality. To illustrate,

---

[20]   See e.g. M. Nussbaum and A. Sen (eds.), *The Quality of Life* (Clarendon Press, 1993).

[21]   For a similar argument, see Piketty, *Capital in the Twenty-First Century*, 571 (unchecked and growing inequality is "potentially threatening to democratic societies and to the values of social justice on which they are based"); Baker and Salop, Antitrust, Competition Policy, and Inequality', 24.

a comparative advantage which is a result of hard work and effort, as such, should not be viewed as a manifestation of unequal opportunity.

Inequality of wealth raises more difficult questions. When it results from inequality of opportunity, it is deemed to be unjust and unjustified. Yet inequality of wealth can also result from other factors, such as talent and motivation. Their acceptance as a basis for inequality of wealth depends, inter alia, on the normative concepts and assumptions at the basis of the social contract. In communist economies inequality of wealth is generally unacceptable, while in market economies it is treated, at least to some extent, as an inherent and even important part of the social contract, as elaborated below.

Of course, reality is much more complicated than this idealized conceptualization of a contract struck between members of society. The idea that citizens are free to choose a society which adheres to their normative values, by moving between states, can easily be questioned. So can the idea that the state is a benevolent actor, which strives to fulfill its goals for the welfare of all, free of political influences that serve specific groups at the expense of the general public. Therefore, the social contract is an abstract notion, not to be found in the real world in its pure form. Yet the legitimacy of state action is dependent, in many citizens' eyes, on such action serving at least some basic normative principles that further the common and individual good. In such an environment, extreme and long-term inequality can have a significant destabilizing force. Accordingly, this chapter suggests examining the current application of competition law in light of this social contract.

4.3 COMPETITION LAW AND INEQUALITY: THE BASIC DILEMMA

I now turn to examine the role inequality plays in competition law. This requires us to go to the heart of the goals and values at the basis of this regulatory tool. As elaborated below, competition law has an intricate and dual relationship with inequality, which creates a basic tension.[22]

In most jurisdictions competition law is applied in a manner in which inequality considerations are dealt with only indirectly. Nonetheless, competition law's inherent characteristics reduce inequality – of both opportunity and wealth – in several ways. First, by lowering artificial entry barriers into the market, competition law increases equality of opportunity by way of allowing more people to enter the market and compete or expand in it based on merit. Second, by lowering prices and increasing quality, it enables more consumers to enjoy the benefits that the market can bring and it reduces inequality of wealth. Third, by reducing the ability of market players to enjoy non-merit-based market power, both types of inequalities are

---

[22] See also P. Mehta, 'Preface', in Pradeep Mehta and Taimoon Stewart (eds.), *Should Competition Policy and Law Be Blind to Equity: The Debate* (CUTS, 2013).

reduced. This is because market power might have been translated into political power and influence, thereby creating political economy effects that enable strong groups to enjoy a disproportional part of the welfare pie.

At the same time, competition law naturally furthers inequality of wealth, at least in the short run. The very concept of competition encapsulates the idea of winners and losers; of Darwinian forces that shape the marketplace based on consumers' preferences and technological abilities, regardless of the effort invested by each supplier or his non-market-rewarded traits. In extreme cases, just like in the Abba song, "[t]he winner takes it all." Accordingly, competition naturally results is an inherent inequality of wealth between suppliers. Should the winning suppliers enjoy significant market power, this can also lead to wealth inequalities between suppliers and consumers.

Yet this resulting wealth inequality, it is believed, is what drives competition in the first place. It is part of the engine and driver behind competition. The US Supreme Court's famous dictum in *Trinko* emphasizes this point: "[t]he opportunity to charge monopoly prices – at least for a short period – is what attracts 'business acumen' in the first place; it induces risk taking that produces innovation and economic growth."[23] Add to it the fact that people's motivation to invest time and effort are often driven by their comparison to their peers, and it becomes clear that inequality plays an important role in bringing about the benefits that competition has to offer. Furthermore, where equality of opportunity exists and entry barriers into the market are low, inequality of wealth is deemed to reflect the comparative efforts of individuals. This is because success in the market game is affected, inter alia, by the motivations of individual to use their comparative advantages in order to create better products and services. Accordingly, inequality of wealth is often treated as an inherent and even important aspect of competition, which, while creating harmful static short-run effects, is necessary to create the more important long-term dynamic effects that, as Nobel laureate Robert Solow and others have shown, are the main drivers of welfare in western societies.[24] It is an "inherent bad" of market societies.

Inequality of wealth, however, is assumed to be short-term with regard to each and every supplier. Competition is seen as a dynamic process, in which those that currently possess market power can be replaced by newcomers into the market. Therefore, most competition laws do not place significant weight on issues of the short-term distribution of the benefits from trade.[25] Moreover, it is generally believed that most markets will be competitive once artificial entry barriers are eliminated, and thus inequality will be minimized by the market's invisible hand. The common

---

[23]   *Verizon Communications Inc.* v. *Law Offices of Curtis V. Trinko, LLP*, 540 US 398, 407 (2004).

[24]   R. M. Solow, 'A Contribution to the Theory of Economic Growth' (1956) 70 *Q. J. Econ.* 65; R. M. Solow, 'Technical Change and Aggregate Production Function' (1957) 39 *Rev. Econ. & Stat.* 312.

[25]   For a discussion of such considerations in the context of developing jurisdictions See e.g. M. S. Gal and E. Fox, 'Drafting Competition Law for Developing Jurisdictions: Learning from Experience' in M. Gal et al. (eds.) *Competition Law for Developing Jurisdictions* (Edgar Elgar, 2014).

view that inequality of better addressed by other regulatory tools also contributes to this policy.[26]

The increased reliance on the market's invisible hand, which does not deal directly with inequality issues, also follows libertarian ideals: reducing regulatory interference in the market to the minimum necessary, and allowing private forces to take their course. Inequality of wealth which results from competition on the merit can also be justified, at least to some extent, by other theories as well, including utilitarianism and some libertarian approaches. The question then becomes at what point does inequality of wealth stop furthering the social contract that lies at their basis.

4.4 FURTHERING EQUALITY IN DEVELOPING JURISDICTIONS

The goal of inclusive growth – reducing inequality in the distribution of benefits created in the marketplace through competition law – has been advocated for developing jurisdictions. Professor Eleanor Fox has been a leading voice in arguing that fighting long-term and entrenched inequality should be one of the main goals of competition law in developing countries. According to her thoughtful and thought-provoking scholarship, the goal of maximizing welfare should be understood as "inclusive welfare": building a ladder of mobility from the lowest rung up in order to enable mobility, incentivize entrepreneurship, and stimulate innovation.[27] In our joint paper on competition law for developing jurisdictions, Professor Fox and I have argued for sensitiveness with regard to where the benefits from trade fall.[28]

What are the reasons that lie at the basis of such suggestions? First, it satisfies a need for legitimacy. The safeguarding of economic opportunity and the distribution of benefits may be so important to legitimacy that a distribution-blind law may not take root. This is especially important in those developing economies in which a distribution-blind welfare approach might prevent societal acceptance and disintegrate the social fabric because it would strengthen or maintain existing wealth disparities, especially where it parallels a racial divide. As Chua has argued, the overlapping of class and ethnicity characteristics, which characterize many developing economies, mandate that the distributional effects of a market economy be taken into account. Otherwise, this may create instability, which could convert into an engine of potentially catastrophic ethnonationalism.[29] Indeed, in a recent

---

[26] See discussion in section 4.5.4.

[27] E. M. Fox, 'Economic Development, Poverty, and Antitrust: The Other Path' (2007) 13 *SW. J. L. & Trade in the Americas* 211, 220; E. M. Fox, 'Equality, Discrimination and Competition Law: Lessons from and for South Africa and Indonesia' (2000) 41 *Harv. Int'L L. J.* 579, 593. For a discussion of such goals, see also Waked, 'Antitrust Goals'.

[28] Gal and Fox, 'Drafting Competition Law'.

[29] A. Chua, 'Markets, Democracy and Ethnicity: Towards a New Paradigm for Law and Development' (1998) 108 *Yale Law Journal* 1; AL Chua, 'The Paradox of Free Market Democracy: Rethinking Development Policy' (2000) 41 *Harvard International Law Journal* 287.

OECD roundtable on competition and poverty reduction, delegates of competition authorities in developing jurisdictions argued that "the political credibility of the competition policy authorities depends to a large extent on how they are seen as contributing to poverty reduction and employment creation. It would be risky for them to state that their only target is combating harm to competition by producers, and that the impact of their efforts on poverty or inequality is irrelevant."[30]

Second, opportunity only to the already powerful means that the country is not making efficient use of the talents and potential contributions of large segments of its population.[31] Indeed, the current literature on development and growth stresses the importance of inclusive growth.[32] It suggests that developing countries need to give weight not just to efficiency defined as increased aggregate wealth – but efficiency defined also in terms of enabling the masses of people to participate on their merits in the economic enterprise. Observe that this goal also requires that consumer welfare be taken apart, to determine which classes of consumers are benefiting from the economy.

Third, Fox argues, "antitrust for developing countries must be seen in a larger context. The canvas includes the dire economic conditions of developing countries … Developing countries often see free-market rhetoric and aggregate wealth or welfare goals as inappropriate to their context because of the tendency of free-market policies to disproportionately advantage the already advantaged in every game played."[33]

The importance of inclusive growth was also recognized by the Spence (World Bank) Growth Report, which concluded that "not only does growth critically matter, but inclusive growth critically matters. Distribution counts. And distribution of wealth and, more important for our purposes, of opportunity and chance for mobility was [and is] deeply skewed.[34]

4.5 THE DILEMMA: INCLUSIVE GROWTH GOALS IN DEVELOPED JURISDICTIONS

Let us now explore the limits – rather than the limitations – of the suggestion for inclusive growth as part of competition law. In particular, should its justifications be

---

[30]   OECD, 'Are We Growing Unequal?', 7.
[31]   T. Indig and M. S. Gal, 'Lifting the Veil: Rethinking the Classification of Developing Economies for Competition Law and Policy', in M. S. Gal et al. (eds.), *The Unique Characteristics of Developing Jurisdictions and Their Effects on Competition Law* (Edward Elgar, 2015).
[32]   See e.g. World Bank, *Growth Report: Strategies for Sustained Growth and Inclusive Development* (2008), http://web.worldbank.org/WBSITE/EXTERNAL/EXTABOUTUS/ORGANIZATION/EXTPREMNET/o,,contentMDK:23225680~pagePK:64159605~piPK:64157667~theSitePK:489961,00 .html. See also D. Acemoglu and J. A. Robinson, *Why Nations Fail: The Origins of Power, Prosperity and Poverty* (Crown Publishers, 2010).
[33]   Equality (n 27).
[34]   See Commission on Growth and Development, *The Growth Report: Strategies for Sustained Growth and Inclusive Development* (2008) http://cgd.s3.amazonaws.com/GrowthReportComplete.pdf

taken one step further and apply to at least some developed jurisdictions. The time is ripe for such an exploration, given global dissatisfaction with at least some aspects of capitalism and market liberalism.

To answer this question, we need to look deeper into the assumptions that generally lead developed countries not to include reduction of inequality and inclusive growth as a direct goal of competition law, but rather to treat them as indirect – yet important – results of competition. Accordingly, this chapter sheds light on four basic assumptions that, I believe, stand and the basis of the existing status quo of many competition laws in developed economies:

1. All market players have relatively equal opportunity to enter and to expand in the market, to be used based on their personal skills and motivations.
2. Once we deal effectively with artificial entry barriers, the market's invisible hand will reduce most instances of inequality.
3. The remaining inequality is an inherent and important part of the competitive process that serves to increase the total welfare pie.
4. Even if equality is an important goal that should be given priority over total welfare in at least in some circumstances, competition law is not the correct tool to limit it.

Below we analyze each of these assumptions.

4.5.1 *Equality of Opportunity*

With regard to equality of opportunity, the assumption on which competition law is based in developed jurisdictions is that people have relatively equal opportunities for access and expansion in the market. While it is acknowledged that people possess different skills and resources, it is assumed that the state's efforts in creating and maintaining a reasonable educatory system, and an environment with well-functioning market institutions and due process, create an enabling environment for at least most people to take advantage of market opportunities. For example, a well-functioning market can provide sufficient funding opportunities for good ideas for those potential entrants that do not possess personal funds.

Why is this assumption important? Because it supposes that participation and success in the market are dependent, mostly, on the motivations of people to invest in the market game. It also supposes that all citizens are given a relatively equal shot at the market game. Moreover, it supports at least one form of social justice: those who contribute most to society because they create new and better widgets, get a larger share of the welfare pie, which indicates their contribution to overall welfare.

But is there real equality of opportunity in developed jurisdictions? As the statistics cited above indicate, at least in some economies the answer is negative. Successful entrepreneurship in many markets – even more pronounced in today's technologically advanced world – requires inputs that the market does not or cannot easily provide to all potential entrants, and that states often fail to provide at an adequate level. These include, inter alia, high levels of education (which provide necessary skills for the marketplace including adaptability to new environments) and social connections to other, successful, market players. Inequality in such inputs can lead to large discrepancies in access and expansion opportunities.

Another challenge to equality of opportunity it created by competition itself. In some markets, fierce competition exists over entry spots, which creates advantages to those with existing funds. For example, competition has led to a situation in which in some markets interns work for free. Accordingly, only people with funds can afford to work as interns, and without the experience you will generally not be hired. So, the ability to enter the profession is dependent on more than skill.

Add to this political economy influences: in many developed economies policies backed by captured politicians and regulators sometimes benefit the few which have a stronghold on the market.[35] In such an environment, even investments in costly higher education do not provide the key to unlocking the door of success.

Indeed, statistics show that social mobility in many developing economies is low. If the market system truly created equality of opportunity, then social mobility should have been at a much higher level. So even according to the free market paradigm, something has gone wrong and the current system cannot be assumed to provide equal opportunity to all market participants.

4.5.2 *The Market Will Reduce Most Instances of Inequality in the Long Run*

The second assumption is that once we deal effectively with artificial entry barriers, the market's invisible hand will reduce most instances of inequality, at least in the long run.

Undoubtedly, limiting artificial entry barriers into markets – the main task that competition law seeks to perform – can increase equality. However, as elaborated above,[36] inequality of wealth is an integral part of the market system, at least in the short and medium run.

Furthermore, while the above assumption may be true in a jurisdiction in which all, or most, markets enjoy conditions of perfect or at least workable competition, it is not true once market failures are taken into account. Rather, market failures such as asymmetric information, collective action problems, or political economy influences may create conditions of significant inequality that may not be easily eroded. In such instances, competition law is a limited tool. Moreover, one of the major tools that competition law has to offer – merger law – generally applies only to firms that already possess significant market power or are likely to possess such power as a result

---

[35] Fox provides such an example ('Equality', 112–13).
[36] Section 4.2.

of the merger. When the door to proving such market power is based solely on turnover rates, merger law does not capture under its wings instances in which transactions can create significant market power in new markets, power that might not be easily eroded afterwards.[37]

Exogenous factors have further increased inequality of wealth on both national as well as international level. The main factor is globalization and the internationalization of trade, which strengthen competition over the locus of businesses, based on their relative comparative advantages. This is due, in part, to the lowering of transportation and transaction costs that enable distant producers to become potential suppliers. Another exogenous factor involves technological changes such as the increased use of robotics and computerized systems to perform many actions, thereby reducing the need for many kinds of human interventions in production or supply processes. This factor also increases the difficulty involved in supplying a safety net in the form of retraining, especially where the need for middle-class workers is significantly shrinking and the education system is not designed to enable most workers to perform technologically advanced jobs. The combined effect of these factors has led to a troubling situation in which it is much more difficult nowadays to be gainfully employed. Indeed, studies show that the current generation is not likely to be better off economically than its parents. Jobless citizens are subject to a myriad of negative effects. These include adverse economic, psychological, and health-related effects, mistrust in the capitalistic market system, and lower buying power that directly affects the level of dynamic efficiency in markets. Often the harm is not limited to individuals, but also affects local communities that have lost their comparative advantages. Observe that while most developed jurisdictions do not suffer from large economic discrepancies between different ethnic groups, social unrest can be created based on inequality between different socio-economic groups (e.g. blue collar vs white collar), which are exacerbated as a result of globalization and technological changes. When the market does not offer viable alternatives for such workers, a sole focus on lower prices or higher-quality products may seem to some to be misguided.

Inequality of wealth can be further increased by discrepancies between consumers, which are not equally equipped to take advantage of potential market opportunities. To make optimal decisions, consumers need to be able to compare options and choose the one which best serves them. Digital literacy is an important factor, as is access to information and comparison tools (such as telecommunication networks and computers) that enable better comparisons, and transportation infrastructure (such as roads and trains) that enlarge the scope of potential suppliers. Inequality of opportunity of consumers to take advantage of market opportunities is especially pronounced when these consumers are also suppliers.

---

[37] Some jurisdictions have started to look into such issues.

4.5.3 *Inequality Is Inherent to Competition*

Indeed, there can be no doubt that inequality of wealth is an inherent and important part of the competitive process that serves to increase the total welfare pie. Yet it is a matter of degree and of causes. If inequality results from unequal opportunities to participate in the market or take advantage of its offers, then it might be viewed as unjust. Furthermore, much depends on the degree of inequality created by market interactions.

4.5.4 *Competition Law Is Not the Correct Tool*

The fourth assumption on which competition law is based is that even if equality should take precedence in some cases, competition law is not the correct tool to further it. More efficient tools might include, inter alia, tax, social security, support of small and medium businesses, education, requirements for foreign direct investment and creating a better infrastructure for commerce.[38] These tools can, at least theoretically, rebalance the social contract by augmenting and complementing competition law.

While these tools are important, most have inherent limitations that should be recognized. Education, for example, is very long term; social security suffers from psychological limitations, because its recipients might feel that they are left out of the market and are dependent on the government instead of on their own efforts; and political effects shape at least some of these tools so that they are not applied efficiently. Furthermore, as elaborated in Chapter 5, competition law can be shaped, at least in its margins, to take distributive and inequality concerns into account.

It is noteworthy that an important difference exists between artificial entry barriers (such as those that result from political economy effects) and natural barriers (such as those that result from lower labor or transportation costs elsewhere) that affect comparative advantages. While the first may potentially be reduced by competition or competition law (but not always), the second cannot. In fact, some types of natural entry barriers are taken as a given in all governmental policies.

These assumptions, taken together, challenge the way that the free market and libertarian ideals are currently applied. One of the main arguments is that the social contract is not working well. It promised equal opportunity for all to participate in markets; it promised that if people invest in doing their best (e.g. spend time and resources on higher education), then most will have a good chance to recover their investment and lead a comfortable life; and that the combined efforts of individuals

---

[38] For an argument for the superiority of these tools for distributive goals, see e.g. L. Kaplow, 'On the Choice of Welfare Standards in Competition Law', 2 http://papers.ssrn.com/sol3/papers.cfm? abstractid=1873432; *contra* I. Lianos, 'Some Reflections on the Question of the Goals of EU Competition Law', in I. Lianos and D. Geradin (eds.,) *Handbook on European Competition Law* (Edgar Elgar, 2013), 1.

who act in such a way will further public welfare. These promises have not been fulfilled, at least for some segments of the population. The increased disbelief in the market system as it is currently applied is troubling, because for the market system to operate, people must believe in its mechanism. Such trust, in turn, legitimizes the economic system and creates stability. Cynicism, on the other hand, creates unrest and might disintegrate the social fabric of societies. It also reduces the number of people who can and are willing to contribute to the market game.

Accordingly, section 4.6 suggests examining the current application of competition law in light of this failure of the social contract. This point of view emphasizes the links between efficiency and distribution as well as between profitability and sustainability, which can reinforce each other.[39]

4.6 THE ROLE OF COMPETITION LAW IN LIMITING INEQUALITY

While education and infrastructure might be more important tools in increasing equality in the long run, some changes in competition law might also be justified as part of an overall societal effort to reinstate a stable social contract which is based on a belief in the market as a source of welfare. While these changes need not be extreme, they can nonetheless play a significant part in meeting the goals of the social contract.

4.6.1 When Fine-tuning Might Be Required

Before we delve into some suggestions, it is important to observe that competition law in developed jurisdictions already includes some focus on distributive effects. Most importantly, most competition laws further the goal of consumer welfare, rather than supplier or total welfare.[40] Even Canada has moved from a pure total welfare approach toward a more nuanced one, which looks at where the benefits from the trade fall. The EU has gone a bit further, requiring that restrictive agreements be allowed only if consumers enjoy a "fair share" of the benefits from the joint venture; and that monopolists not be allowed to charge "excessive prices," even if they result from competition on the merit.[41] Yet all these laws aggregate consumers into one group, not attempting to look further at the effects on different classes or types of consumers that are affected by the conduct or the transaction. As Farrell and Katz have observed, "rich and poor consumers may be differentially affected by an

---

[39] See also M. E Stucke, 'Occupy Wall Street and Antitrust' (2012) 85 *Southern Cal. L Rev. Postscript* 33, 50; M. E. Porter and M. R. Kramer, 'Creating Shared Value: How to Reinvent Capitalism and Unleash a Wave of Innovation and Growth' (2011) *Harvard Business Review* 77.

[40] See e.g. K. J. Cseres, 'The Controversies of the Consumer Welfare Standard' (2007) *Competition Law Review* 121, 122.

[41] Articles 101–102 of the Treaty on the Functioning of the European Union.

antitrust decision; distributional concerns would suggest weighing the impact on the poor more heavily, but a consumer surplus standard insists that they count equally."[42]

To strengthen the belief in the social contract at the basis of competition law, a fine-tuning of the system might be required: giving more thought and weight to where profits accrue. Not only whether consumers or producers, as two distinct groups, are affected, but also which subgroups are affected, and the importance of the transaction to their welfare as well as to total welfare. This requires going beyond simple legal assumptions, taking the position that differences between subgroups should not be ignored, and accommodating the special characteristics and needs of some subgroup over others.[43] Recognizing such differences can create an opportunity for correcting some of the ills of the current system. Yet it must be done carefully, to ensure that the social contract is indeed fulfilled.

Let me give four examples of cases where the above suggestion may be relevant. I do not argue that these examples should necessarily affect the content and application of competition law. To determine whether such a change is justified, we need to engage in a deeper analysis which is beyond the scope of this short chapter. Such an analysis must take into account, inter alia, the effects of more complicated and nuanced rules on enforcement costs and on the conduct of market players and enforcers. Such an analysis will also need to determine whether the competition authority is the right locus to engage in more nuanced social analysis, in light of the tools at its disposal as well as its democratic mandate and its level of susceptibility to political influences. Nonetheless, the examples illustrate instances in which in it worth considering performing such an analysis.

The first example involves a case in which the relevant transaction makes all consumers[44] and suppliers better off or at least does not harm their welfare with regard to the specific transaction, so that the condition of Pareto optimality is met, that is, no other distribution of benefits from the transaction could make at least one person better off without making someone else worse off. On its face, this transaction should be allowed and indeed will be allowed in most – if not all – developed jurisdictions around the world. Yet this analysis disregards existing discrepancies in society and treats all consumers as equal. Let us assume that indeed all consumers are better off, but some – the more wealthy ones – are much better off than the poor ones. Such a transaction will increase existing wealth discrepancies in society,

---

[42] J. Farrell and M. L. Katz, 'The Economics of Welfare Standards in Antitrust' (2006) *Competition Policy International* 1.

[43] It should not be automatically assumed that competition law offenses necessarily harm the poor and enrich the rich. For such an exposition, see D. A. Crane, 'Antitrust and Wealth Inequality' (2015) 101 *Cornell Law Review*.

[44] For simplicity, I refer to consumers. Yet in some cases the relevant group might be workers or even shareholders such as pension funds of middle-class workers. Whether policymakers wish to capture and differentiate such groups is a policy question subject to the same decision-theory considerations noted above.

thereby potentially making the overall position of the weaker members of society worse off. Observe that this example does not fulfill the maximin principle suggested by Rawls as a basis for a just social contract

The second example adds additional sets of considerations, such as the agency's limited resources. Consider, for example, a case which is Pareto-optimal to all consumers when focusing only on the effects of the specific transaction. Yet this time only a distinct subgroup of consumers benefit from the transaction. Other subgroups of consumers are not affected by it because they do not consume the relevant product or service. This can be illustrated by two extreme examples: lowering the costs of luxury cars would only affect the wealthier members of society; and lowering the costs of cheap furniture would mainly affect the weaker members of society. Once we look more carefully at which subgroup of consumers is affected, it is clear that in a world of scarce enforcement resources, the second case may serve societal needs and the social contract better.[45] Indeed, in choosing between the two cases, using scarce enforcement resources to follow the second one may be Pareto-optimal to all members of society in the long run.

The third example involves a case in which not all consumers are better off. Rather, some subgroup(s) of consumers are better off, and some are worse off. Under the competition laws of most developed jurisdictions, such a transaction would not be allowed. Yet despite the fact that the condition of Pareto optimality is not met in the specific transaction, it might be met in the long run, if the transaction significantly benefits the weaker members of society while only marginally harming the wealthy ones. It might also serve Kaldor–Hicks efficiency, whereby overall welfare is increased. Kaldor–Hicks requires that the overall benefits to those that are made better off could in theory compensate those that are made worse off.

So far we have disregarded suppliers. Indeed, the competition laws of most developed jurisdictions generally use consumer welfare as a proxy for total welfare, thereby disregarding effects on suppliers. Moreover, even when such a focus is added, as in Canada, the analysis does not take apart the effects of suppliers on other groups in society, most importantly the suppliers' workers or the workers of other market players which interact with them. As noted above, this is partly based on two assumptions: (a) that while the supplier might need to leave the market, most of its workers will not leave the job market since they could relatively easily switch jobs; and (b) even if they cannot find jobs easily on their own, other governmental instruments, such as retraining programs, provide relatively efficient instruments designed to assist workers in finding new jobs. As elaborated above, in reality these assumptions are often problematic, and several factors combine to make the realization of these goals much more difficult than in previous decades. Such an environment crystalizes issues of inclusive growth and significant economic inequality in

---

45 One caveat exists once we add the globalization dimensions: if the wealthier ones have other options and are likely to move to other jurisdictions if prices for luxury goods are much higher than elsewhere.

the gains from trade. Accordingly, society must ask whether it would better serve its social contract to focus solely on lowering prices and potentially increasing quality, even marginally, at the expense of losing jobs, or whether a more delicate balance should be struck which gives more weight to the interests of society in its citizens as workers.

4.6.2 *Some Suggestions*

Even if one believes that the social contract is better served by giving weight to equality and inclusive growth considerations, the question remains whether competition law is necessarily the best tool to achieve these goals. Competition law suffers from some significant inherent limitations. It has a limited number of instruments at its disposal, that mainly include fines and prohibitions, rather than tools that allow for transfer payments between different groups of society; it does not have the information or the ability to see the larger picture, of all the tools available to the state to remedy a problem and the state's overall interests in remedying it; it does not have the democratic mandate to engage in such balancing exercises, which involve public interest considerations that go beyond pure competition concerns.

In light of these limitations, this section suggests several ways in which competition law can better serve the social contract, without significantly changing its focus and the tools at its disposal, yet introducing a more nuanced distributional dimension into it.[46] As noted above, more significant changes, while possibly justified, require a deeper analysis based on decision theory considerations, balancing between benefits and costs in light of realistic options.[47]

The above considerations should *affect the choice of cases*, especially where enforcement resources are scarce.[48] The authority should consider focusing on market access issues which affect the ability of the weaker parts of society to take part and participate in the market on a larger scale than their current conditions allow them. It should also consider giving priority to cases which increase consumer welfare of the weaker groups in society. To use the above example, lowering entry barriers in the market for lucrative cars should be given a lower priority than in the market for cheap furniture.

Moreover, competition law enforcers should attempt to *unpack the aggregatory group of consumers*, where it is likely to significantly increase social welfare.[49]

---

[46] See also J. F. Brodley, 'The Economic Goals of Antitrust: Efficiency, Consumer Welfare and Technological Progress' (1987) 62 NYU *Law Review* 1020("[a]ntitrust law has always permitted some degree of social conduct that is not in the immediate interest of consumers in order to sustain innovation and production efficiencies"); M. E. Porter, 'Competition and Antitrust: Towards a Productivity-based Approach to Evaluating Mergers and Joint Ventures' (2001) 46 *Antitrust Bulletin* 919, 933.

[47] For a suggestion that goes further, arguing that competition law should take into account distributional concerns, see A. B. Atkinson, *Inequality: What Can Be Done?* (Harvard University Press, 2015).

[48] For a similar suggestion, see Baker and Salop, Antitrust, Competition Policy, and Inequality'.

[49] For such an example See e.g. South African Competition Act, Act No. 89 of 1998, ch. 1, para. 2(f).

In relevant cases, Kaldor–Hicks optimality should be preferred to Pareto optimality. To reduce uncertainty, however, the authority should develop tools that clearly spell out the balance to be sought, and only divert from the aggregatory analysis where a more nuanced analysis is likely to bring about significant benefits to social welfare. Transparency is an essential element of this analysis, to limit political pressures and to increase awareness of the considerations taken into account.

Furthermore, even if competition law is not the best instrument for furthering the social interest in securing jobs for workers for the long-term benefit of society, we still need to ensure that the application of competition law *does not inhibit the application of other policies* which are aimed at furthering reinforcing goals. Most importantly, it must be ensured that competition law does not create a de jure or de facto veto power to competition law considerations, where it is in the public interest that they be balanced with other considerations. Israel provides an illustrative example. Offers to buy a large bankrupt firm must receive both the approval of the Bankruptcy Court and the Competition Authority. Under Israeli merger law, the Authority can only take into account competition law considerations.[50] Wider considerations can only be taken into account, if at all, by the Competition Tribunal, in a lengthy process. This creates a de facto veto power for the Authority to block mergers with bankrupt firms that significantly harm competition, even if wider public interest considerations would have led to a different result.

In addition, the Competition Authority's *advocacy role* can play an important double role in augmenting and strengthening the social contract. It should be used to advocate the adoption of governmental policies that further the social contract by complementing competition law. These may include, inter alia, increasing possibilities for market entry, relocation and retraining programs for workers, and incentives for creating jobs in unemployment-ridden areas. They should also include tools that create an equitable system of social redistribution, both in the short and in the long run.

Relatedly, in those cases in which the straightforward application of competition laws harms the furtherance of equality and social justice, competition law may need to be calibrated to do so. Crane offense an eye-opening example with regard to the application of competition law rules to limit subsidization of the less profitable women's sports teams, which could limit the furtherance of such sports teams.[51]

The Competition Authority should also use its advocacy role to explain to the non-competition-law-educated wide public the logic behinds the choice of its actions, to strengthen their understanding of the market system and in the authority's choices. This is especially important where the positive effects of its actions could only be observed in the long run; or where the legal tools are inherently limited and citizens might get the

---

[50] Israeli Competition Law 1988, s. 21.
[51] Crane, 'Antitrust and Wealth Inequality', 4.

impression that the system is not working for them. Such advocacy can strengthen the trust that the actions taken are indeed in line with the social contract.

Merger policy should also be changed so it would capture more firms that create significant economic power. As Maurice Stucke suggests, it should be expanded to ensure that concentration without offsetting benefits is arrested in its incipiency.[52] Also, antitrust agencies and courts should be careful not to focus solely on static price competition and productive efficiencies.[53]

Finally, as suggested by David Lewis,[54] the tool of *market inquiries*, used by a growing number of jurisdictions around the world, enables competition authorities to point out public restraints that strengthen or maintain elite dominance. This is because it grants them formal powers that extend beyond the traditional powers of enforcement.[55]

4.7 CONCLUSION

Significant and persistent inequality in favor of specific social groups creates a major challenge to the existing social contract, or at least to the way we apply it in practice. This has led to social tensions, unrest, and protests around the world. It is thus time to question whether our tools must be changed to enable a better furtherance of the goals of this contract.

As this short chapter has showed, the challenges to the social contract, as it is currently applied, go to the heart of the goals at the basis of competition law. They require that the goals of competition law be broadened, in appropriate cases, to include distributional effects. Indeed, suggestions with regard to inclusive growth are relevant, at least partially, to developed countries and not just to developing ones.

It should nonetheless be stressed that in order for inequality to be reduced, competition law should be one of several tools harnessed for advancing equality and inclusiveness. Loading the delicate task of changing the current socio-economic fabric on competition law alone might be highly problematic and negatively affect the ability of competition law to achieve its other goals.

---

[52] Stucke, 'Occupy Wall Street and Antitrust'.
[53] Ibid.
[54] David Lewis as cited in Mehta (Mehta and Stewart, *Competition Policy*).
[55] See, e.g. T. Indig and M. S. Gal, 'New Powers, 'New Vulnerability? A Critical Analysis of Market Inquiries', in Fabiana DiPorto and Josef Drexl (eds.) *Competition Law as Regulation* (Edward Elgar, 2015), 89; OECD Directorate for Financial and Enterprise Affairs Competition Committee, *Policy Roundtables: Market Studies* (OECD 2008).

5

Oligarchies, Competition, and Development

Abel M. Mateus

5.1 INTRODUCTION

Economies with non-inclusive institutions have serious limitations to competition policy. These are the result of having markets with high levels of concentration and high barriers to entry. These might be regulatory, bureaucratic, access to credit, or simply informal. There are sectors and/or activities that are reserved to certain groups, showing the persistence of wealth accumulation. These groups are connected with political and economic power either through economic and financial networks, family, or social ties. In the literature, they are considered connected groups or families and they have vested interests for preserving their monopoly status.

But what is important for economics and development is not the existence of economic elites. The stratification of society occurs both in high growth (GDP) or declining nations. The problem occurs when there are no contestable markets and no opportunities for the outsiders to challenge the incumbents' status, and when incumbents use all means legal and illegal to retain their privileges. The US gilded period in the second half of the nineteenth up to the second decade of the twentieth century is a paradigm in the move from non-contestable structures to starting the process for contestability.

There has been a rise in the share of world billionaires of emerging markets. This share has increased from 20 percent in 2004 to 43 percent in 2014.[1] From large pharma groups in India to large manufacturing groups in China or Turkey, these groups have taken center stage in global trade. But these are not the groups that concern us in this chapter. Crony capitalism associates concentration with protectionism. Only groups that are in non-tradables or sectors with substantial barriers to

I would like to thank Sergey Guriev for extensive discussions on the subject that led to significant extensions of the chapter, although any errors and opinions are of my own responsibility.

[1] C. Freund, 'Rich People Poor Countries: The Rise of Emerging-Market Tycoons and Their Mega Firms' (Peterson Institute for International Economics, 2016).

entry either due to natural factors (e.g. natural resources) or due to regulatory or state privileges (e.g. licensing), and thus protected from global or national competition usually lead to the phenomenon of the control of the state by economic groups that aim to perpetuate those barriers. Another problem is the contestability of ownership of those groups by market processes like takeovers or opening capital through stock markets. These processes allow the replacement by most efficient management. There are good economic reasons for large firms to play an important role in the development process: technological know-how, special ability of entrepreneurs, need of large sunk costs and access to capital, synergies in market access or production networks, as Freund documents.[2] And, as Foster et al.[3] have shown firm dynamics are essential to development, as resources move from low to high productivity firms, which explains a large part of productivity growth.

Several economists maintain that to build a market economy with a democratic regime, the capitalist way requires a preliminary phase of state capitalism or what Schumpeter calls "captains of the industry."[4] The reason is the scarcity of entrepreneurship and management skills-cum-coordination problems (à la Rosenstein-Rodan)[5] coupled with the scarcity of savings. The work of Freund,[6] documents the importance of large firms in the most dynamic emerging economies in the last two decades. The natural distribution of firms will lead toward a few large firms leading productivity and economic growth. But we should not extrapolate to the overall statistical distribution: there might be a large section of middle-sized firms in the statistical distribution, leading to a lower level of skewness. In fact, empirical and theoretical evidence has shown that there is a negative correlation between wealth and income concentration and development.[7]

Some nations after the Second World War moved toward filling this gap by way of public enterprises. But the problem with state enterprises is that it is at least questionable whether bureaucrats make better entrepreneurs, the problem of incentives is very serious and the lack of well-functioning markets poses serious information and efficiency problems. In fact, in the 1960s and 1970s, both the developed and the developing world was full of inefficient public enterprises. Consequently, a relatively high concentration of wealth at the beginning of the development

---

[2] Ibid.

[3] L. Foster, J. Haltiwanger, and C. Krizan, 'Aggregate Productivity Growth: Lessons from Microeconomic Evidence', in C. Huten, E. Dean, and M. Harper (eds.), *New Developments in Productivity Growth* (University of Chicago Press, 2001).

[4] J. Schumpeter, *Capitalism, Socialism and Democracy* (Routledge, 1945).

[5] P. Rosenstein-Rodan, 'Problems of Industrialization of Eastern and South- Eastern Europe' (1943) 54 (210–11) *Economic Journal* 202–11.

[6] Freund, 'Rich People Poor Countries'.

[7] J. Ostry, A. Berg and C. Tsangaridis, 'Redistribution, Inequality and Growth'. IMD Discussion Note SDN 14/02 (2012). A consensus is emerging in the growth literature that inequality can undermine progress in health and education, cause investment-reducing political and economic instability, and undercut the social consensus required to adjust in the face of major shocks, and thus that it tends to reduce the pace and durability of growth.

process may be inevitable. The problem is if the political and regulatory environment keeps the level-playing field for new versus established entrepreneurs and if competitive markets keep the pressure on existing firms to be efficient and innovate. The case of Turkey versus Egypt contrasts these two paths, as we are going to document in this chapter.

Development is blocked when businesses do not invest and innovate continuously and elites are not continuously renovated with new talent and expertise. The low levels of investment and low increase in productivity of the factors of production and technological progress leads to low GDP growth, aggravated by unequal income and wealth distributions. It is this dynamic process that leads to stagnation. And when aspirations are not satisfied, poverty soon leads to an explosive situation and social conflicts.

The theme of "crony capitalism" attracted attention in the aftermath of the Asian financial crisis of 1997, especially with cases like Indonesia. Stephan Haber[8] posits that crony capitalism arises to solve the commitment problem of the government (e.g. of no expropriation), when there is no limited government (i.e. state with balanced powers and rule of law). It is like an implicit contract between the government and the economic elite that allows rent-seeking in exchange for support to the political regime.[9]

Eleanor Fox[10] was one of the first competition specialists to call attention to the problem: "developing countries (have) much weaker markets and much larger problems of abuses by state monopolies and government-privileged dominant firms (cronies)," which makes transposing competition law and policy from developed to developing countries rather difficult.

The question of the formation of authoritarian states or oligarchies versus democracies has not yet attracted enough research among political economists to provide a convincing explanation. History shows that democracy is a relatively recent phenomenon, except for some episodes like the Athenian state.[11] The norm is some form of authoritarian state, so the difficult question is to explain why democracy arises. Acemoglu and Robinson[12] make an important contribution by building a game between an elite that detains political power and the citizens that prefer democracy. Transitions to democracy may happen when disfranchised citizens gain

[8] In S. Haber (ed.), *Crony Capitalism and Economic Growth in Latin America* (Hoover Press, 2002).

[9] Latin America has also experienced a number of historical experiences of crony capitalism, namely the Mexican Porfirio Diaz dictatorship of 1876–1910, and Brazil in the nineteen century.

[10] Introduction to vol. II in E. Fox and A. Mateus, *Economic Development: The Critical Role of Competition Policy and Law* (Elgar, 2011).

[11] Although this was a very different type of democracy, by modern standards, with more than two-thirds of the population either without the right to participate in the political life (women, foreign born) and with an underclass of citizens (slaves).

[12] D. Acemoglu and J. Robinson, 'A Theory of Political Transitions' (2001) 91(4) *American Economic Review* 938–63; D. Acemoglu and J. Robinson, *Economic Origins of Dictatorship and Democracy* (Cambridge University Press, 2006); D. Acemoglu, 'Oligarchic versus Democratic Societies' (2008) 6 (1) *Journal of the European Economic Association* 1–44.

temporary political power in social disorder or revolutions, so the elite to avoid major losses extends them a free vote and periodic elections, free media-cum-institutionalized redistribution. An oligarchy protects property rights but erects barriers to entry; a democracy avoids barriers to entry and redistributes income using taxes. However, there is still much to explain about why social disorder and revolutions occur, and to what extent the threat tilts the level-playing field toward the majority. Will modernization do the trick? Does the structure of the economy like predominance of natural resources make a difference? We will explore some of these questions.

Furthermore, one type of authoritarian regime is the predatory (as opposed to developmental) state as studied by Robinson.[13] We are particularly interested in the way that these states arise. This author points to the high level of rents from investment accruing to the elite (level of encompassing),[14] the low-income level and unequal distribution as the main causes. Factor endowments is also important; thus, a resource-rich country will have more probability of evolving toward a predatory state. These governments do not pursue economic development policies because they may change the distribution of political power, e.g. providing public goods, such as education or infrastructure will increase the ability of citizens to contest elite control by collective action.

New data and research is now being done to corroborate the importance of competition policy to development and even to peace and social stability. We will consider some of this research to highlight the importance of competition policy and its crucial role for development. This chapter studies the political economy of competition policy in developing countries, focusing on the Middle East and North Africa. The Arab uprising of 2011, known as the Arab Spring is a case in point. While there are similarities among this group of countries, there are also important differences. We are going to contrast the cases of Egypt and Turkey: why Egypt blocked the development while Turkey succeeded, mainly after the serious financial crisis of the beginning of the twenty-first century[15]

The chapter starts by characterizing the main differences and similarities between Turkey and Egypt in terms of competition policy. Section 5.2 computes an index of concentration-cum-protectionism, also known as an index of crony capitalism, which shows that Egypt has had a much higher level of concentration with lack of competition coupled with institutional fragility than Turkey.[16] Section 5.3 discusses the reforms and processes that may be required to reduce the level of crony

---

[13]   J. Robinson, 'When Is a State Predatory?' (CESifo Working Paper no. 178, 1999).

[14]   This depends on the initial distribution of endowments.

[15]   Egypt was part of the Ottoman Empire with the epicenter in modern Turkey, since 1517, when the Ottomans seized power from the Mamluk sultanate, and separated definitively from that Empire in 1914 with its dissolution. The main historical difference between the two nations was the imposition of secular rule by Ataturk on young Turkey.

[16]   Our analysis stops in 2015. The coup that took place in 2016 in Turkey poses a challenge to democracy and competition policy, but it is still very early to make an evaluation of its impact.

capitalism, based on theoretical models and historical experience, while section 5.6 concludes. We want to underline that most of this research crosses economics, politics, and other fields of social sciences and is still in its infancy.

5.2 POLITICAL ECONOMY OF COMPETITION: CASE STUDIES OF EGYPT AND TURKEY

Acemoglu and Robinson[17] as well as others describe extensively exploitative institutions, where the economic surplus is appropriated by a small elite which does not reinvest it or reinvests with low returns, leading to stagnation or decay of economic growth. This is characteristic of a number of natural resource-rich economies, where a political group appropriates the rights of exploitation of those resources and uses them mostly for their own enrichment, but is also the case of other developing economies where a political group appropriates the rights of a large section of the economy, monopolizes it and closes off the opportunities for a large section of the population.

This phenomenon has been known in the economic literature as rent-seeking, when an economic group uses a regulation to block entry or puts tariffs or non-tariff barriers to increase prices and profits for their own benefit and in detriment to consumers and the firms that use inputs from the protected sector.[18] In political science, economies characterized by this type of structures and where political power is also concentrated and cater to these vested interests are called "crony societies." Concentration of political power is a result and reinforces economic concentration. Most of the times these societies are also highly corrupt, either because government agents take bribes, or because politicians, entrepreneurs, and managers trade favors and economic benefits.

It is important to clarify what we define as competition policy. It is building the market infrastructure for the rivalry process to take hold, and correct the market failure of monopolization by incumbent firms. Especially in developing countries it includes: (1) external trade policy with low levels of protection leading to continuous pressure of foreign competition; (2) maintain arm's length between state and private sector in order to level the playing field in economic policies; (3) maintaining or building a vibrant private sector through privatization and good corporate governance; (4) policies to build and maintain an efficient price mechanism; (5) a system of independent regulatory authorities to suppress market failures for technical regulation; (6) open and competitive procurement policies; and (7) antitrust law and enforcement. It is obvious that these policies require an environment of rule of law and inclusive institutions without corruption.

---

[17] D. Acemoglu and J. Robinson, *Why Nations Fail: The Origins of Power, Prosperity and Poverty* (Crown Business, 2012).

[18] See K. Murphy, A. Shleifer, and A. Vishny. 'Why Is Rent-seeking So Costly to Growth?' (1993) 83(2) *American Economic Review* 409–14.

It is obvious that in these economies, most of the time also under a politically authoritarian regime, competition policy, and much less competition law, has no place in the panoply of policies or constitutional law of that government.[19] How can antitrust challenge the interests of those major economic groups that control the state when they abuse their dominant positions? And the law does not usually allow "structural solutions," like the breakups of the oil and steel conglomerates at the beginning of the twentieth century in the USA. Guriev and Rachinsky[20] go even further: they dispute that antitrust can change anything of the oligarchy in Russia, since a few monopolies are in export industries competing in the world market with a low share at the world level.[21]

In these countries, policies are geared toward creating advantages for incumbent elites, rents are generated for business and political elites and special interests are insulated from competitive pressures of domestic and foreign markets: policy choices are endogenous to political interests.

But these institutional weaknesses in developing countries play ironically against the interests of the population at large. In fact, the effectiveness of the state – in market interventions or insulation from private interests – hinges on state capacity. And it is this same state that is dominated by the vested interests.

This circularity is characteristic of a two-level equilibrium: one good and the other bad. In the good equilibrium the high state capacity is able to intervene in the public interest and provide high levels of welfare, reinforcing its reputation and respect by the people. In the bad equilibrium, the weaknesses of the state are used to the advantage of the dominant economic groups which employ the state as an instrument to preserve its political and economic power.

This is the case of the Arab development model, especially its inability to support an independent and competitive private sector that has characterized several Middle East and North African states and led to several uprisings.

Based on a distorted legacy of intervention and distribution, this development model is structurally incapable of reconciling aspirations with economic opportunities. The contradictions associated with this development model are particularly apparent in the region's labor-abundant economies, where a shrinking resource envelope has led to an erosion of the social contract, resulting in a scaling back of public employment and welfare services. Worryingly, the space vacated by a shrinking state has not been filled by a vibrant private sector.[22]

[19]   See A. Mateus, 'What Competition Law Regime?', in D. Sokol, T. Cheng, and I. Lianos (eds.), *Competition Law and Development* (Stanford University Press, 2013), 115.

[20]   S. Guriev and A. Rachinsky, 'The Role of Oligarchs in Russian Capitalism' (2005) 19(1) *Journal of Economic Perspectives* 131–50.

[21]   "Instead, it is more important that Russian competition policy assure the level ground field for all owners without regard to their size and political influence – so-called 'political antitrust'" (ibid., 138).

[22]   A. Malik and B. Awadallah, 'The Economics of the Arab Spring' (May 2013) 45 *World Development* 296.

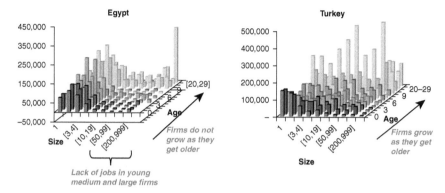

FIGURE 5.1 Lack of growing SMEs that could potentially challenge large firms in Egypt
Sources: Malik and Awadallah, 'Economics of the Arab Spring'; A. Malik, 'Political Economy of Arab Uprisings', *New Palgrave Dictionary of Economics* (Palgrave, 2015)

Why was there an underdeveloped private sector? In much of the Arab world the private sector acts as an appendage of the state. Businesses tend to survive either when they are too close to the state, such as crony capitalists, or too far, which is the case with informal firms. Figure 5.1 illustrates the composition of small and medium enterprises (SMEs) in Egypt and Turkey for 2011. It shows that while in Turkey there is a significant number of enterprises that populate all the firm sizes categories, in Egypt microenterprises predominate. Even more interesting, the rate of SMEs that survive and prosper after several years is significant in Turkey but very low in Egypt.[23]

Figure 5.2 also shows how small the formal private sector is in Egypt. In a nation of 80 million there are only around 3.2 million employed in this sector.

As Malik recognizes, traditional policy reform will not work.[24] Relieving greater competitive space for the private sector requires a *political concession* that grants autonomy to independent businesses and relaxes barriers to trade.

The firms that occupy activities protected by the government are called politically connected or simply connected firms (CFs), and the rest are called non-connected firms (NCFs). CF are disproportionally present in sectors that are closed to foreign direct investment (FDI) and which require licensing, they are usually dominant firms, and exclusionary mechanisms increase once they entered the sector. It is a fallacy to consider that CFs have high returns on their investments, simply because these entrepreneurs are usually risk averse and the effort to excel from competition is lacking. CFs may not have higher returns than NCFs, due to larger inefficiencies that compensate for higher barriers to entry.

[23] The problem of the missing middle in the distribution of enterprises by size was raised by Tybout a long time ago, but there have been contradictory explanations, from just statistical artifact to barriers to entry in the tradition of de Soto.

[24] Therefore, international financial organizations have generally failed in their policy advice. No government will take measures against their own personal interests.

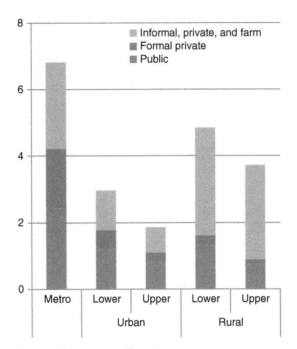

FIGURE 5.2 Employment by sector (millions)
Source: World Bank, 'Egypt: Promoting Poverty Reduction and Shared Prosperity, a Systematic Country Diagnostic' (P151429, 2015)

Egypt and Turkey are both Arab states, where the military sector is an important part of the economy (estimates between 10 and 30 percent of GDP), and where large conglomerates belong to dozens of families that are connected to political power. Research undertaken at Harvard and Oxford is now coming out, collecting statistics of these firms. Tables 5.1(a) and 5.1(b) give the data for Egypt.

From the Tables above (5.1(a) an 5.1(b) it is evident that CFs are important in the real estate and services sectors, as tourism is a major sector in Egypt.[25] In Table 5.1 (b), the NDP (National Democratic Party)-connected firms of Mubarak's regime are distinguished from Islamist firms (of which five are also connected with the political party) and the military. The data reveals the large presence of the military in manufacturing and transport.[26]

[25] Two iconic cases, in court in 2013, illustrate the methods used. The first is of Mr. Ahmad Ezz who had steel factories dominating 65 percent of the Egyptian market. He was accused of acquiring the largest public steel corporation at artificially low price, to practice excess profits, to obtain protection from imports and lobbied Parliament to water down antitrust legislation. A prominent member of the National Democratic Party (Mubarak's party), he was the head of the Committee that oversaw the Competition Commission. The other case concerns Mr. Ahmed Al-Maghrabi, owner of Palm Hill, who used his position as Minister of Housing to acquire vast tracts of land from the state at low prices.

[26] The large presence of the military in the productive economy was encouraged by the US military assistance during the cold war in Latin America and countries in the MENA region, in particular.

TABLE 5.1(A) *Number of firms per sector for CFs and NCFs*

Sector	Services	Metals	Primary	Wholesale	Real estate	Chemicals	Textile
NCF	19	7	5	2	25	4	13
CF	6	2	0	0	6	0	3

Sector	Food	Banks	Hotels	Transportation	Machinery	Publishing	Financial Services	Total
NCF	8	4	3	1	1	1	1	94
CF	3	0	1	1	0	0	0	22

Source: H. Chekir and I. Diwan, 'Crony Capitalism in Egypt', mimeo (Harvard Kennedy School, 2013)

TABLE 5.1(B) *Firm connections by sector*

	NDP	Military	Islamic	Non-connected	All
Agriculture	0	0	0	8	8
Construction	3	0	0	7	10
Consumer goods	0	1	0	3	4
Education	0	0	0	2	2
Financial services	4	0	5	23	31
Food and beverages	2	8	1	10	20
Healthcare	1	4	0	6	11
Industrial manufacturing	3	10	1	23	37
Leisure and tourism	1	1	0	7	9
Media	0	1	0	0	1
Mining and metals	2	2	0	3	7
Oil and gas	0	2	0	2	4
Real estate	4	0	4	18	23
Services	0	0	0	1	1
Telecommunications	1	0	2	0	3
Transport	1	4	0	1	6
Total	22	33	13	114	177

Notes: The table shows the number of NDP-connected, military-connected, Islamic, non-connected, and all firms in each of the 16 sectors of the economy. There is no overlap between NDP-, military-, and non-connected firms. Among the 13 Islamic firms, 5 are connected to NDP and the other 8 are connected to neither the NDP nor the military. Definitions of sectors are taken from zawya. *Source*: D. Acemoglu, D. T. Hassan, and A. Tahoun, 'The Power of the Street: Evidence from the Arab Spring' (2018) 31(1) The *Review of Financial Studies*, doi:10.1093/rfs/hhx086

Favoritism in public procurement and privatizations as well as watering down antitrust was recurrent. The government of Egypt made a gesture of liberalizing import tariffs by reducing drastically the average tariff in 2007, responding to domestic and international pressures, and following the Association Treaty with the EU. However, a study by Malik[27] has shown that the reduction of tariffs was more than compensated by an increase in non-tariff barriers (Figure 5.3). Moreover, these non-tariff barriers, from sanitary regulations to other types of regulations, benefited disproportionally the sectors where CFs are dominant.

Egypt scores poorly on governance, institutions, and regulatory framework. It ranks in the bottom tier of countries in terms of the effective enforcement of government regulations, it is the MENA (Middle East and North Africa) country with the largest gap between the quality of rules and regulations on paper and their effective enforcement in practice. And the due process in administration

---

[27] Malik, 'Political Economy of Arab Uprisings'.

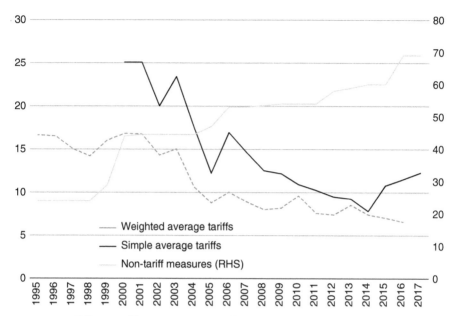

FIGURE 5.3 Falling tariffs, growing non-tariff protection in Egypt
Sources: World Bank database; WTO, Trade Policy Review, report by the Secretariat (Egypt, January 16, 2018); Malik, 'Political Economy of Arab Uprisings'

proceedings, and enforcement of taxes and customs regulations shows opaque procedures and arbitrariness in public decisions, opening the way for corruption and cronyism.[28]

We will now try to characterize countries according to their degree of concentration-cum-protectionism that may lead to states with declining growth.

5.3 THE CONCENTRATION-CUM-PROTECTIONISM INDEX (CPI)

In order to define a composite index of concentration and protectionism (Table 5.2), let us start by defining the sectors in the private sector that are either protected from external competition (non-tradables) or subject to entry regulation or dependent from natural resources. These are sectors that are usually prone to rent-seeking: oil and gas, real estate and construction, banking, infrastructure, casinos, mining, ports, airports, and telecoms. We obtain a measure of concentration in these sectors by estimating the wealth of billionaires[29] generated in these sectors as a proportion of GDP.[30] A better estimate would be an aggregate concentration ratio for the protected sectors, but it would imply obtaining not only market shares, but also direct and indirect

---

[28] See World Bank, for indicators.
[29] The data is taken from the database of the Forbes magazines.
[30] This is like the index of crony capitalism published by *The Economist* in March 14, 2014, table 2, column A, which presents those estimates for 2015.

TABLE 5.2 *CPI and institutional weakness (2015)*

	A	B	C
Ukraine	17.0	32	541
Russia	18.0	24	440
Philippines	14.9	20	292
Mexico	10.0	27	265
Egypt	6.5	21	187
Brazil	5.0	29	143
Argentina	3.5	37	128
Malaysia	17.9	6	101
India	5.0	16	80
Indonesia	4.5	16	70
Portugal	4.9	12	60
Turkey	2.8	19	53
Thailand	2.4	21	50
South Africa	3.2	12	38
Poland	1.9	16	30
United States	2.2	8	18
Korea	0.7	18	13
France	1.3	9	11
Britain	2.6	3	9
Japan	0.9	3	3
Germany	0.5	5	2

A = protected Sectors With Private
    billionaires
B = Institutional weakness index (WEF),
    higher is weaker
C = CPI is equal to AXB

Source: author's estimates

connections between firms owned by the same person or family, which are not easily available. Russia, Ukraine, and Malaysia are the countries with the highest indices of crony capitalism. The most developed countries have the lowest. However, we think that the worst in terms of potential impact on welfare of a country is a combination of high concentration with weak institutions, because of the capture of state institutions by these groups. We take the measure of "Institutions" from the World Competitiveness Report published by the World Economic Forum and rescale it to be consistent with column A. This index is presented in column B. Then in column C we combine both indices using a simple multiplication to obtain the CPI. Once again Russia and Ukraine are the worst,[31] followed by Philippines and Mexico.

[31] We obtained even higher indices for some countries like Angola, but there are no reliable indicators for A and B.

It is important to point out that the table only considers a sample of developing countries for which data on wealth is available. The countries with the lowest level of crony capitalism are France, Britain, Japan, and Germany. Surprisingly Korea also comes with a low index, despite the chaebols, because these conglomerates are mainly in the tradable sector, exposed to foreign competition. However, Korea has a lower institutional strength index than the other developed countries.

A measure of GDP for developing countries in this case may not be appropriate, because of the large extension of the informal sector. Thus Table 5.3 presents for column A, the ratio of Table 5.2 divided by one minus the percentage of informal employment[32] in the non-agricultural sectors.

Comparing Tables 5.2 and 5.3, countries with large informal sectors now see an increase in their CPI, notably Philippines becomes the country with the highest index, and India and Indonesia also rise up the scale.

Of a particular importance for this chapter, Egypt has in Table 5.3 an index of crony capitalism that is about five times higher than that of Turkey, despite the fact that Turkey has 30 of the 500 billionaires estimated by Forbes. Istanbul is the fourth highest city in the world in number of billionaires.

Figure 5.4 plots the CPI of Table 5.2 against a measure of economic success which is equal to the average annual growth rate in the 1990–2014 period of the GDP per

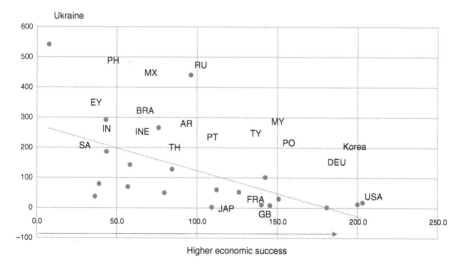

FIGURE 5.4 CPI and economic success
Source: author's estimates

---

[32] We used the data published by the ILO in its database.

TABLE 5.3 *CPI and institutional weakness (2015)(corrected by the level of informal sector)*

	A	B	C
Philippines	45.2	20	884
Ukraine	18.8	32	597
Russia	21.9	24	536
Mexico	15.5	27	412
Egypt	12.3	21	264
India	15.4	16	245
Indonesia	12.8	16	245
Brazil	15.4	16	199
Argentina	4.9	37	180
Malaysia	23.2	6	131
Portugal	4.9	12	60
Turkey	2.8	19	53
Thailand	2.4	21	50
South Africa	3.9	12	46
Poland	1.9	16	30
United States	2.2	8	18
Korea	0.7	18	13
France	1.3	9	11
Britain	2.6	3	9
Japan	0.9	3	3
Germany	0.5	5	2

Source: author's estimates

TABLE 5.4 *Infrastructure PPPs (US$ millions)*[1]

	2012	2013	2014	2015	2016[2]
Airports	347	530		1,607	470
Road transport	1,000	2,500	5,700	2,325	10,000
Ports		2,561		300	
Health			718	3,020	1,677
Total	1,347	5,591	6,418	7,252	11,147

[1] *Source:* http://infrapppworld.com/pipeline-html/projects-in-turkey
[2] First four months.

capita in PPP (purchasing power parity) (US$) times the level of this variable in 2014. There is clearly a negative relation between these two variables. Ukraine and Russia are clearly outliers, with a CPI much higher than the level of GDP, as is Philippines and Mexico.

In contrast, South Africa has a CPI below what is expected. If we scale up due to the informal sector India and Indonesia approach the straight line. It is important to remember that Indonesia was the paradigm of crony capitalism when the Asian financial crisis of 1997 exploded.

Next we study the cases of Turkey and Egypt to illustrate the causes and effects of different competition policy regimes largely as a result of different levels of concentration-cum-protectionism.

5.4 WHY TURKEY WAS MORE SUCCESSFUL COMPARED WITH EGYPT?

Egypt and Turkey both had the same income per capita in the early 1990s, measured in PPP (Figure 5.5), but by 2014 Turkey had almost double the income of Egypt. What explains the success of Turkey and the slower growth of Egypt? Both are countries with a deep Islamic background, and both belonged to the Ottoman Empire[33] but the development and political models were quite different after the dissolution of the Empire in 1914. First, the regime roots are diverse. Egypt had the military and socialist regime of Nasser (after the Suez conflict) followed by Sadat that only "opened up" to the private sector, for Mubarak to allow a private sector to form in the shadow of the military state. Turkey was always closer to Europe and rooted in the "secular revolution" of Ataturk; it maintained a more pragmatic market-oriented policy. The military in this case have also intervened in situations of social crisis but to preserve the heritage of Ataturk, keeping a hands-off approach to economic policies.

Turkey is a typical case of the success of the three-pronged approach proposed by a number of economists in the 1980s: (1) trade liberalization and integrating its economy in the global economy; (2) privatization and enhancement of the role of the private sector; and (3) macroeconomic stability by price stability and fiscal sustainability. To this economic dimension must be added the build-up of a democratic state with political and social stability as well as inclusive institutions. The Turkish experience shows the importance of proactive social policies by providing equal access to health and education to the populations and support to SMEs as a way to promote equity.[34]

Turkey already had experience of a democratic regime with a multiparty system after 1950. The economic strategy of the 1960s and 1970s was based on import substitution and public enterprises, but never led to a socialist regime. GDP grew

---

[33] After the Napoleonic invasion Egypt became an autonomous state but soon was to become a protectorate of the Ottoman Empire.

[34] The Turkish case follows, in a certain way, the so-called modified Washington Consensus, as expounded by D. Rodrik ('Goodbye Washington Consensus, Hello Washington Confusion?', mimeo, Harvard University, 2006), paying more attention to an equitable access to public goods. However, most of the rise in the middle class and reduction in poverty was due to economic growth, which lifted all social classes.

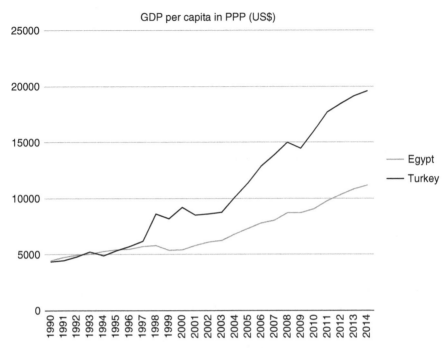

FIGURE 5.5 GDP per capita in PPP (Egypt–Turkey)
Source: World Bank database

at high and stable rates, but the strategy had run out by the end of the 1970s. The share of state-owned enterprises (SOEs) in manufacturing employment and value added exceeded 35 and 40 percent, respectively, in the late 1970s (paper, chemicals, cement, iron and steel, certain types of machinery and equipment). A new policy regime was introduced by PM Turgut Ozal who took office in 1983, based on export promotion policy, first using export subsidies and afterwards tariff cuts. The output-weighted average nominal tariff rate for the manufacturing industry that stood at 75.8% in 1983 declined to 40% in 1990 and to 20.7% in 1994, and the number of imports subject to authorization was reduced from 46% in 1986 to 6% in 1988. Quantitative restrictions were completely phased out by 1990. Turkey formed free trade areas with the European Free Trade Association (EFTA) in 1992 and then with the prospective European Union (EU) candidate countries in Central and Eastern Europe since joining the customs union. Labor and resource-intensive sectors were the first to respond to these measures, and total volume of exports (in US$) increased more than fourfold from 1980 to 1989.

Further trade liberalization took place with the formation of a customs union with the EU in January 1996. Based on the customs union decision, Turkey abolished all trade barriers in the manufacturing sector vis-à-vis the EU, and it has considerably reduced barriers against third countries by adopting the EU's common external tariff. Turkey has also gradually taken on an array of EU preferential trading relationships, such as the Euro-Mediterranean partnership and Generalized System of Preferences (GSP). The average annual growth rate of the value of exports (in US$) was about 25 percent in the period 2001–6 with two leading sectors: automobiles and consumer electronics.[35]

The response to the trade liberalization policy was substantial. Import penetration increased from 17 to more than 22 percent in 1983 to 1988 and the exports–sales ratio from 12 to 19 percent.[36] Studies done with a large sample of manufacturing plants for the 1986–96 period, using the Olley–Pakes methodology, showed productivity gains in import-substituting industries of 8 percent per year, and substantial within-plant productivity increases in export industries. Trade liberalization reduced the price–cost margins in the private sector, but did not have the same impact in oligopolistic markets, which shows that trade liberalization is not enough to increase competition in concentrated markets.[37]

Turkey began its privatization initiative in 1984 when the government commissioned an official report to evaluate the state of the economy and the benefits of undergoing a privatization effort. Since 1985, state shares in 188 SOEs have been privatized. The first privatization was the sale of Teletas in 1988, a very profitable company in the telecommunications industry, that took place in a public offering with a set price on the Istanbul stock exchange. From 1991 to 1997 the leading sectors privatized in Turkey were the cement industry, the iron and steel industries, airport and ground services, aircraft tires, public banks, and energy. From 1984 to 1997 the total revenues from privatization was US$3.6 billion. Due to legal challenges to some of the privatizations, a new law was enacted in 1994 that created a political body headed by the prime minister and an administrative body to execute the privatization. The Competition Authority, created the same year, was given the power to clear privatizations from the perspective of competition law. A list of public enterprises candidates for privatization was created. In 1999 the program yielded US$1.0 billion and in 2000 US$2.7 billion. But the largest program was carried in 2005 and 2006 with a revenue of US$16.2 billion. In 2008 the final privatization of Petkim, a large petrochemical group, was completed for US$2 billion as well as another public offering of shares in Turkish Telecom. A push to privatize parts of the Turkish infrastructure culminated in the 2009 announcement that Turkey would

[35] The following brands have built plants: Ford (2001), Toyota (1994), Hyundai (1997), and Honda (1995). In 2000, they had 50,000 workers. Turkey also has a thriving car parts industry (including producers Bosch, Valeo, Delphi Packard, and Mannesmann Sachs) well integrated in world production chains. In consumer electronics, it produced more than 20 million television sets. Both industries have a much higher productivity than the rest of manufacturing. It has benefited from lower unit labor costs than the EU.

[36] C. Yalcin, 'Price–Cost Margins and Trade Liberalization in Turkish Manufacturing Industry: A Panel Data Analysis', mimeo (2000).

[37] S. Osler and K. Yilmaz, 'Productivity Response to Reduction in Trade Barriers: Evidence from Turkish Manufacturing Plants', mimeo (2007).

sell its twenty electricity distribution networks under a plan to boost investment in electricity production, and several ports.

Along with the growth of the privatization initiative in the early 2000s, Turkey also launched with the help of the World Bank a social support initiative to help affected workers. This initiative, called the Privatization Social Support Program, ran from 2001 to 2005 and was financed with US$250 million of World Bank loans. The program created two major channels for helping the Turkish workforce: a job-loss compensation initiative and a labor redeployment service. The objective of the job-loss compensation program was to improve the temporary negative social and economic impact of lost jobs, which was a result of the privatization of SOEs. It helped about 17,000 workers. This component financed initial severance and ongoing unemployment payments, as regulated by law, to workers displaced due to the privatization of SEEs. Along with severance pay and forced retirement, the Turkish government also set up temporary employment programs for affected work-ers. The program was run by the Turkish Employment Agency (ISKUR) responsible for aiding unemployed workers, which aided about 27,000 workers, and the Small and Medium Industry Development Agency (KOSGEB) which retrained 34,000 workers, and also served as an incubator for new business formation, helping to create 533 new businesses.[38]

Turkey has also been at the forefront of public–private partnerships. The BOT law of 1994 was the framework for most of these operations. They have benefited mainly the transport (two bridges over the Bosphorus and a tunnel in the same channel, several motorways, ports, and airports), energy (one-quarter of the installed capacity in electricity) and health sectors (new regional hospitals). In the 2012–16 period there were PPPs in infrastructure amounting to US$31.7 billion.

The third essential policy for development was macroeconomic stability. In the 1980s and 1990s Turkey went through repeated economic crises with lack of fiscal discipline and monetary financing of the deficit which caused high inflation and foreign currency crisis.

Since the crisis of 2001, with large support loans from the IMF and World Bank, the country undertook important reforms. An independent Central Bank was cre-ated with a floating exchange rate regime. Insolvent banks were liquidated, energy and telecommunication markets were liberalized, financial control over state enter-prises and state banks was strengthened, and regulation was introduced in telecoms and energy. FDI increased substantially from around US$1 billion in the 1990s to an annual average of US$15 billion in 2007 to 2012.

Turkey's economy has been boosted by the rise of a new class of export-oriented entrepreneurs known as the 'Anatolian Tigers,' nurtured by business networking through Islamic social networks and return migration from Germany. Starting with

---

[38]   The issue of compensating the losers is well treated in M. Trebilcock, Dealing with Losers: The Public Economy of Policy Transitions (Oxford University Press, 2015).

family-owned small and SMEs, they unleashed an industrial renaissance in various Anatolian cities in the country's Asian heartland, notably in Balıkesir, Denizli, Gaziantep, Kayseri, and Konya. In the 2000s there was a significant shift in Turkey's political economy, with the reemergence of an extended period of one-party government. In fact, one of the weakest points of the Turkish democracy is the lack of within-party competition.[39] Another important movement was the declining role of the military and the growing political voice of the Anatolian conservative lower and middle class – the main constituency of the ruling AK party. The increasing urban middle class demanded and rewarded the government with the improvement in public services and infrastructure. And the pro-market and pro-reform domestic policy consensus was further enhanced and anchored by the EU accession process. In terms of institutional development, Turkey had a perception corruption index of Transparency International of 50 (53rd place) while Egypt had a score of 32 (114th place) in 2013.

The fourth element essential to understanding the success of Turkey is the integration in the geographic region of Europe and EU to the West, as well as to Middle East, Caucasus, and Central Asia. In fact, the commodities boom and strong growth of these regions, in countries like Kazakhstan and Azerbaijan offered oppor-tunities for Turkish exports of construction, capital, and consumer goods which the dynamic entrepreneurs took advantage of. Even the situation of war in Iraq and the sanctions to Iran presented huge opportunities that Turkey took advantage of. In 2014 Turkey was a much more open economy than Egypt (exports of goods and services over GDP are 27.7 percent versus 14.4 percent).

But several economic problems remain: (1) rising levels of indebtedness: the ratio of household liabilities to disposable income has grown from 4.7 per cent in 2002 to 50.6 per cent in 2012; at 51 per cent of GDP, Turkey's net external debt is among the highest for emerging markets, driven mainly by a surge of private sector borrowing. The average debt-to-equity ratio of the largest 500 firms in Turkey was 120 per cent in 2010 and 141 per cent in 2011, compared with roughly 50 per cent in the United States and 70 per cent in Europe in 2011; (2) the structural current account deficit that reflects the deficit in domestic savings, or in other words, the fact that productive capacity does not keep pace with the rise in domestic demand; (3) the level of technological sophistication is still relatively low–intermediate,[40] both in terms of sophistication of

---

[39] The current political party law gives all the power to the party headquarters, the party leadership controls the channels through which the party rank and file can replace the leaders/cadres that are proven to be unsuccessful. As a result, the rank and file has very little chance of removing the leadership. The party headquarters can annul the local chambers of the party and appoint new members. Consequently, in the Turkish political system, political parties become nothing more than the fiefdoms of the party leaders and their immediate supporters. Those members who oppose the leadership, on the other hand, stand no chance of survival within the party.

[40] One of the least-known aspects of the recent Turkish external trade policy is the use of quantitative restrictions to lower competition from China, other emerging markets, and even the EU (K. Karacaovali, 'Turkey: Temporary Trade Barriers as Resistance to Trade Liberalization with the European Union?', mimeo (2011)).

exports[41] and the level of complexity of the economy. It is specialized in low-wage industries, and high-tech exports only represent 2 percent of the total;[42] and (4) the intermediate–low level of human capital, coupled with discrimination against women.[43]

The high growth experienced by Turkey translated into a substantial improvement in the economic situation of the lower and middle classes of the country. Figure 5.6 shows that from 1993 to 2010 the middle class expanded from 18 to 42 percent, although at a lower level than Malaysia and Chile (47 percent).[44]

What makes Turkey's experience interesting is that improvements in the income of the poor have not resulted from changes in the distribution of income as for instance in Latin America.[45] Instead, they reflect rising labor market earnings across the distribution, and public investment in the expansion of health, education, and municipal infrastructure, as well as the strengthening of Turkey's social security arrangements. The Human Development Index for Turkey was .761 in 2014 (71st position) compared with .742 in 2000 (85th position). In contrast, Egypt increased from .642 in 2000 (115th) to .69 in 2014 (108th position), but is in a much lower position. The enrollment ratio at tertiary level of education in Turkey is almost triple that of Egypt: 79 percent, against 30 percent in 2013.[46]

Turning now to Egypt. The economic and social situation in Egypt was not only fragile in the 2000s but it deteriorated dramatically on the eve of the uprising that toppled Mubarak. Dang and Ianchovichina[47] carried out an interesting data analysis for the countries of the Arab Spring. Figure 5.7 and Table 5.5 report their estimates around 2010. They show that Jordan, Tunisia, and Turkey had the lowest poverty and vulnerability rates, and Egypt and Yemen the highest. The poverty ratio of Egypt is about nine times higher than that of Turkey, and the middle class about ten times lower. These indicators are the most striking, showing how much Egypt has fallen behind Turkey.

Even more interesting is the evolution of these economic classes in the period before and around the Arab Spring: from the beginning to the end of the 2000s

[41] See R. Anand, S. Mishra, and N. Spatafora, 'Structural Transformation and the Sophistication of Production' (IMF Working Paper, WP/12/59, 2012); R. Hausmann, C. Hidalgo, and collaborators, 'Atlas of Economic Complexity: Mapping Paths of Prosperity, Centre for International Development', Harvard University, 2011. In their atlas, Turkey comes in at 43rd place, behind China, Malaysia, and Thailand. Egypt comes much lower, at 63th position, just above Vietnam and Guatemala.

[42] World Bank database: http://data.worldbank.org/indicator/TX.VAL.TECH.MF.ZS?page=1

[43] In mathematical, reading, and scientific skills Turkey stands 32nd among 34 OECD members and 40 percent of Turkish 15-year-old students do not achieve a basic level of competence in mathematical literacy.

[44] Middle class is defined as the share of population with an income per capita of at least US$10 per day, in PPP.

[45] See J. Azevedo and A. Atamanov, 'Pathways to the Middle Class in Turkey' (World Bank WP 6834, 2014).

[46] World Bank database.

[47] H. Dang and E. Ianchovichina. 'Welfare Dynamics with Synthetic Panels: The Case of the Arab World in Transition' (World Bank Policy Research Working Paper No. 7595, 2016)).

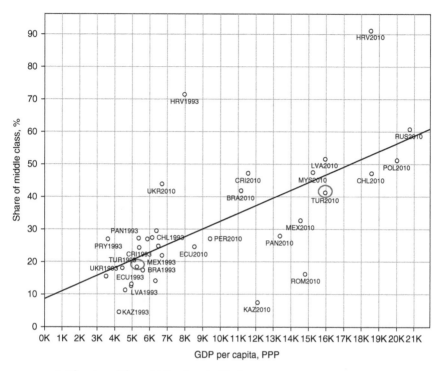

FIGURE 5.6 The rise of the middle class in Turkey
Source: J. Azevedo and A. Atamanov, 'Pathways to the Middle Class in Turkey' (World Bank WP 6834, 2014)

decade. Figure 5.7 shows a strong decrease in the middle class in Egypt and Yemen and an improvement in Tunisia and Syria. In Egypt, the bottom 40% income class of the population increased by 38% along that decade and the next 40% class decreased by 13%. Subjective well-being measures based in polls also show a deterioration along the decade, which certainly paved the way for the discontent that exploded in people's revolt in these countries.

The analysis of the World Bank in the diagnostics of the Egyptian situation,[48] preoccupied with political economy issues, includes for the first time a detailed assessment of the institutional issues, with particular attention to governance and regulatory systems. However, there is no analysis of the type we address in this chapter, mainly regarding the economic and political groups and their interconnections.

It is particularly interesting what kind of policies are suggested to solve the governance issues in Egypt. Several examples of growth strategies are cited like Korea and Turkey, but only a change in the structure of incentives is recommended,

[48] World Bank, 'Egypt'.

TABLE 5.5 *Income classes around 2010*

	Poor	Vulnerable	Middle class	Poverty rates
Palestine	0.7	19.1	80.1	0.6
Tunisia	4.9	31.3	63.8	4.5
Jordan	2.4	46.9	50.7	1.2
Syria	8.4	52.2	39.4	8.4
Egypt	29.2	61.0	9.8	27.4
Yemen	55.8	36.2	8.0	37.3
Morocco	15.5	52.4	32.1	15.5
Turkey	5.0	22.0	73.0	3.1

Note: Poverty line at US$2/day; vulnerability line at US$4.9/day.
Sources: H. Dang and E. Ianchovichina, 'Welfare Dynamics with Synthetic Panels: The Case of the Arab World in Transition' (World Bank Policy Research Working Paper No. 7595, 2016); author's estimations

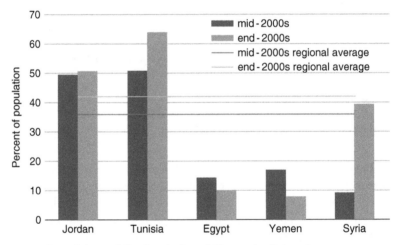

FIGURE 5.7 Size of the middle class (vulnerability method) (2010)
Source: Based on data in H. Dang and E. Ianchovichina, 'Welfare Dynamics with Synthetic Panels: The Case of the Arab World in Transition' (World Bank Policy Research Working Paper No. 7595, 2016)

like better procurement and merit-based management in the public sector.[49] First, it is very difficult to see who is going to formulate and take decision on these

---

[49] "Egypt's poor performance ... over the past thirty years is largely rooted in weak public governance, making this a crucial and urgent area for reform. The public sector in Egypt needs to be more transparent and accountable, public procurement and financial management procedures need to be strengthened, and hiring and promotion need to be merit-based. This would create positive incentives for regulators, bureaucrats, and other public servants, improving the quality of public service delivery and creating a predictable and equitable regulatory environment" (ibid., p. xi).

policies. Second, there is the question of implementation. And even if they are implemented, it is difficult to accept that these minor reforms are going to do the "trick."

5.5 ARE THERE WAYS TO REFORM CRONY CAPITALIST SOCIETIES?

Reforming an economy under crony capitalism is not a simple matter. Acemoglu and Robinson in 2016 develop some of the insights of their bestseller of 2012[50] by looking at case studies of how inclusive political institutions emerge. They define these institutions by a balanced outcome of state capacity and broad distribution of political power. State capacity is defined by a bureaucracy capable of ensuring property rights, rule of law, and implementing a redistributive system of taxation. An equitable and universal distribution of political power empowers citizens with free and periodic elections, free media, and low barriers to entry. They use the case of the reforms of Solon and Cleisthenes in Athens during the sixth century BC, and the reforms of Tudor England in the seventeenth century to illustrate a set of social norms and informal institutions that led to state building and modernization through the rise of a middle class. The same could be said of the northern Italian states, especially when contrasted with south Italy. But the characterization of these norms and institutions are still quite incipient. One other major observation is that modern democracy, with three branches of state with separation powers and regulatory state, is a recent phenomenon that cannot be compared with ancient political regimes.

The modernization theory has guided the work of several international institutions like the EBRD. Its approach is that building a large middle class by encouraging SMEs and lowering barriers to entry would pave the way toward democracy. But the political side of transition is also important like ensuring free and periodic elections and free media as well as the other elements of inclusion are important. Also, part of the process is building the regulatory framework for a competitive economy. In fact, Acemoglu and al.[51] had already questioned a narrow interpretation of modernization by showing that controlling for historical factors by including fixed country effects removes the correlation between income and democracy, as well as the correlation between income and the likelihood of transitions to and from democratic regimes. Most of their work is inspired by the idea that some critical events during critical historical junctures can lead to divergent political–economic development paths, some leading to prosperity and democracy, others to relative

---

[50] D. Acemoglu and J. Robinson, 'Paths to Inclusive Political Institutions' (January 19, 2016), available at https://economics.mit.edu/files/11338; D. Acemoglu and J. Robinson, *Why Nations Fail: The Origins of Power, Prosperity and Poverty* (Crown Business, 2012).

[51] D. Acemoglu, S. Johnson, and J. Robinson, 'Revaluating the Modernization Hypothesis', mimeo (2007).

poverty and non-democracy. The problem is how to characterize these events and why did they occur?

Acemoglu also tackles the issue of dynamics in political regimes.[52] He suggests that oligarchies may be the most efficient regime when a small number of entrepreneurs are the most productive – and we add, as above, need of technological know-how, special ability of entrepreneurs, need of large sunk costs and access to capital, synergies in market access or production networks scarcity of savings. In his model, redistributive taxes would also be highly distortionary. How would this regime would evolve toward a democracy? As comparative advantage changes, incumbents lose their place in the productivity chain, not only in terms of lifetime of dynasties of oligarchs, but also because of intersectoral comparative advantage. The economy starts to lag and growth may come to halt, as barriers to entry preclude the new opportunities to be exploited, and the move toward democracy gains ground. This pattern has taken place in several Arab countries as well as in Eastern European and Central Asian countries.

Deep economic and financial crises are considered by A. Tornell, using the case of Mexico in the 1980s and 1990s, caused by cronyism itself, as the cause (or occasion) of major reforms.[53] As some groups relinquish privileges to prevent other groups harming them even more, as conflicts among groups arise due to the crisis. However, this seems more like a trading of benefits and costs among members of the elite than a relinquishing of rights by the whole elite, which could arise like in some historical contexts when the elite relinquishes power to the rest of the population to avoid, for example, a revolution.[54]

Guriev and Sonin study the dynamics between a group of oligarchs and a dictator.[55] The oligarchs, once in power want protection of property rights and would like to choose a strong dictator, but the problem is that this dictator could exercise its power and expropriate one or several oligarchs. Thus, the most likely equilibrium is a choice of a weak dictator with the continuation of rent-seeking, which reduces the efficiency of the economy

One of the most interesting case studies regarding the transformation of crony capitalism to a modern democracy is the passage of the gilded era of the "robber barons" in the second half of the nineteenth century to the progressive era usually situated from 1890 to 1918 up to the New Deal, in the USA. The first was characterized by large monopolies trusts in manufacturing, transport, banking, and other sectors; these vested interests largely controlled the judiciary, there were no regulations, there was rampant corruption, and large segments of the government were captured by these interests.

---

[52] Acemoglu, 'Oligarchic versus Democratic Societies'.
[53] A. Tornell, 'Economic Crisis and Reforms in Mexico', in Haber (ed.), *Crony Capitalism*, 127.
[54] This is the case of England when, e.g., it extended voting rights to several groups of citizens.
[55] S. Guriev and K. Sonin. 'Dictators and Oligarchs: A Dynamic Theory of Contested Property Rights' (2009) 93 *Journal of Public Economics*, 1–13.

The enactment of the Sherman Act in 1890, the first antitrust law, marked a turning point in the history of the USA, as a response of small farmers and food industries to the trusts of railways. It remained dormant for about a decade but was then used to break some of the trusts and more important to prevent further monopolization of the economy. The second important reform was the rise of regulatory state[56] with the introduction of the Interstate Commerce Act in 1887 that substituted private litigation by regulation. This was important because it ended the subversion of the judicial system by power and wealth. The third reform was the development of tort law. The fourth was the introduction of the independence of the judiciary vis-à-vis the political system and the recall of judges.

A major role in progressivism was played by muckrakers, using the freedom of the press, to expose corruption and cronyism. Hofstadter[57] describes them as enemies of trusts, unions, and political machines. They expressed the need for entrepreneurship, individualism, and moral responsibility, rather than economic (or other) organizations.

Besides the reform of judiciary, law, and the role of the freedom of the press, free and periodic elections also played a major role, as reformers like Woodrow Wilson got elected to the presidency. Other reforms in the political system, like direct election of senators, use of voters' referendums to decide on local issues, and the growth of the state in general with larger fiscal capacity also played a role. The impact of these reforms on wealth inequality is evidenced by Figure 5.8. Even discounting the impact of the two great wars that always have a strong redistributive effect, there was a strong decrease in the top 1 percent and 10 percent group of wealthiest individuals.

Competition law was introduced in Turkey in 1995, starting operations in 1997, as a result of the custom union agreement with the EU that established the Turkish Competition Authority as an autonomous antitrust enforcement agency, with a Board to resolve cases and set policy.[58] The law was widely modelled on EU competition law and the Authority enjoys a reasonable level of independence. The Authority has established a good reputation as an effective and well-administered agency, with an important role in furthering competition policy and consumer-welfare-based market mechanisms. However, its activities have been restricted by the lack of recognition of antitrust matters by the judicial system and some sectors of the government. In terms of substantive law, it is not able to intervene in cases of state monopolies or in firms with state privileges and powers that enable them to undertake anticompetitive behavior,[59] intervene in bank mergers and on any form of state aid.[60] Landmark

---

[56] E. Glaeser and A. Shleifer, 'The Rise of the Regulatory State' (2003) 41(2) *Journal of Economic Literature* 401–25.

[57] R. Hofstadter, *The Age of Reform* (Random House, 1955).

[58] For a review of the activities of this agency, see J. Shaffer, 'Competition Law and Policy in Turkey' (2006) 8(2) *OECD Journal of Competition Law and Policy* 177–251.

[59] Notwithstanding, the Authority has not refrained from acting in two cases where the decisions were taken autonomously by the state firms, despite the law.

[60] In Mateus, 'What Competition Law Regime?', Turkey is classified in 36th position in terms of competition law enforcement, and Egypt in 71st, in a sample of 101 countries.

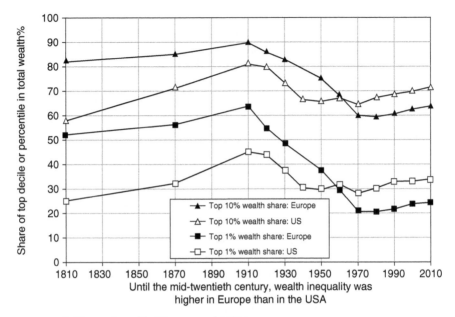

FIGURE 5.8 Share of wealth (Europe and USA)
Source: T. Pikettty, *Capital in the 21st Century* (Harvard University Press, 2014)

cases have been the fines applied to cement cartels, and abuse of dominance by the
telecom incumbent for preventing access to essential facilities. The Authority has also
the power to block privatizations. Its intervention in the telecom case led to the breakup of the telecom monopoly, with the state still retaining the cable and satellite
branches. On balance, the Turkish Competition Authority has established itself as
a reputable independent agency and contributed to the establishment of a more
competitive environment is certain markets.

The Egyptian competition law regime was established in 2005 by the Egyptian
Law no. 3, on Protection of Competition and the Prohibition of Monopolistic
Practices which also created the Egyptian Competition Authority. The law was
under discussion for ten years and faced opposition from major economic groups.
It was passed only after the Euro-Mediterranean treaty.[61] Merger rules have been
shaped by COMESA. Its effectiveness was limited by the fact that up to 2008 fines
were capped at low levels, and up to 2014 antitrust cases could only be referred to
courts by the competent minister (Minister of Trade and Industry). Besides, it could
not intervene against state monopolies or in markets with prices fixed by the state.[62]
In the case of Egypt, where a strong and independent competition authority could

[61] H. Ghaly, 'Competition Law and Policy in Developing Countries: The Case of the Egyptian Steel
      Monopoly', mimeo (American University in Cairo, 2011).
[62] On the enforcement practice of the Egyptian Authority, see M. ElFar, 'Enforcement Policy of the
      Egyptian Competition Law: Vertical Relations' (2014) 35(5) *ECLRev.* 209–15. The paper refers to an

play a major role in furthering a more competitive economy, it is clear that it does not have the support of key branches of the government to make sufficient inroads in the noncompetitive markets.

5.6 CONCLUSIONS AND FURTHER RESEARCH

It is easy to sketch a model retaining the basic fixtures of a country where crony capitalism blocks growth and development. First, it must be assumed that good entrepreneurial and management resources are extremely scarce, especially in a developing country. Second, we must specify the engine of growth. Growth requires continuous investment in physical and human capital as well as innovation and technological progress. However, the intensity and extensive domain of this process depends on having competitive and efficient markets. We should distinguish two sectors: tradables and non-tradables. Now, the non-tradables sector has a low level of competition due to regulations and/or entry barriers that reserve those sectors to incumbents, these are the sectors more affected by the connected firms. The tradables will also have a low level of competition because governments maintain high levels of protection from foreign competition, either through tariffs or non-tariff barriers, protecting in this way also connected firms.

There is no new entry and no contestability. Where is investment going to occur? Mainly in protected sectors. However, the impact on the overall economy may be rather by the small domestic market. The size of the market may also be affected by income inequality. The lack of pressure to improve productivity, due to natural or legal protectionism also lowers the macroeconomic impact on productivity Another factor that reduces growth is the fact that credit is mainly allocated to these protected sectors, because of low risk.[63] Finally, the rest of the population is squeezed out to the informal sector, or survives in small firms in the non-protected formal sectors. The model generates a stagnant or low-growth economy, which can be further restrained by demographic growth.

There are two interesting questions that can be posed. First, why does an economy or society fall into a situation of high concentration-cum-protection? Second: how can such an economy escape from this situation? The high level of concentration is

interesting case, known as the *Steel* case, of a vertical agreement of exclusivity by a dominant steel producer. The Authority did not find an infringement because lack of effects (the agreement affected only 8% percent of the relevant market). However, after the events of 2011, the Prosecutor's Office received a complaint stating that the ECA's decision was biased in favor of a main political figure from that ousted regime, who was also the chairman of this dominant undertaking. Therefore, the prosecution started an investigation of the case, and the Economic Criminal High Court and Court of Appeal, which delivered a landmark decision, based on a per se rule, imposed a fine of US$14.5 million.

[63] EBRD, *Transition Report, 2016–2017*, ch. IV gives the results of a survey on financial inclusion in all EBRD countries. The level of financial inclusion in Egypt is one of the lowest among EBRD members. It also shows that micro enterprises do not even apply for bank credit because they are discouraged.

usually the result of a historical process that had its roots in colonialism, a feudalistic society or some foreign power that dominated the country. But the proximate causes should be more refined, and we have to rely on political economy, political science, and other social sciences to give an explanation. In Egypt, the proximate causes seem to be the military regime after the Suez war, socialism, and the rentier society created with the windfall created by the oil price booms in aid from Arab states and USA, as well as from revenues from emigration.[64] In Turkey, the role of Ataturk and the multiparty democracy of the 1940s and 1950s, despite the incipient democracy, avoided an authoritarian regime. The larger resource and human base was also crucial to explain the lower concentration of economic and political power. But despite these observations, this is an issue that needs further research if some general theories are going to emerge.[65]

The question of how such an economy can escape from a situation of crony capitalism is also very important but intriguing. It would be natural to ask next: how can the country reduce wealth concentration? This has happened in several countries through revolutions or after wars.[66] Otherwise only a gradual transformation using antitrust, regulatory, and fiscal policies, with strengthening institutions and the balancing of the three branches of the state reflecting a more mature democracy, can peacefully lead each country to a more open, equitable, and inclusive society, as the USA experience shows from the gilded era of the last half of the eighteenth century to the regulated state of the first half of the twentieth century. The experience of the path followed by Turkey, in contrast with Egypt, could also point the way for the Arab countries' reform and growth in the long term.

---

[64] H. El Beblawi, 'Economic Growth in Egypt: Impediments and Constraints (1974–2004)' (World Bank Commission on Growth and Development WP 14, 2008).

[65] The work of Acemoglu in this field is very important.

[66] Korea after the Japanese were thrown out of the country, or after General McArthur in Japan. More recently, in Portugal after the 1974 revolution. However, the Arab uprisings have not yet produced any transition toward a more equitable society with less concentration of wealth, with Tunisia perhaps being the most encouraging case.

6

Promoting Competition Reforms for the Benefit of Ordinary People

Pradeep S. Mehta

6.1 INTRODUCTION

'End poverty in all its forms everywhere' is the first goal of the Sustainable Development Goals[1] (SDGs) agreed by the international community to be achieved by the year 2030. Various barriers – economic, political and social – which have blocked the access to resources and opportunities for a huge portion of the population, have been major contributors to continuing global poverty. Removing those barriers and connecting the masses to mainstream entrepreneurship needs to be the central economic policy goal of nation states in pursuit of 'inclusive development' or 'inclusive growth' – which in the terms of SDGs has been described in Goal 8 as 'promote sustained, inclusive and sustainable economic growth, full and productive employment and decent work for all'. A robust competition policy tends to fulfil these goals, as this chapter argues and explains.

Competition policy is essentially a commitment by government to promote competition in all sectors of the economy. This entails a thorough process of scanning of economic elements of key policies and legislation in order to assess their impact on competition in the market. Competition law, in general, is needed to curb market malpractices having anti-competitive effects. While competition policy is an *ex ante* tool to promote competition, competition law gives an *ex post* mechanism to deal with anti-competitive practices, behaviour and effects in a market.

While competition agencies are empowered and equipped to take actions against anti-competitive practices by market players, in most countries these agencies can only advise governments on distorting policies and their effects. In order to evolve well-functioning markets, it is necessary to identify such competition-distorting policies and highlight how they affect consumers and/or producers.

---

[1] https://sustainabledevelopment.un.org/sdgs

Competition distortion denotes a situation in which companies (both public and private) do not compete under equal conditions. Some of them are placed in an advantageous position as a result of government policies, regulations or praxis. Inappropriate regulations and policies by national, state and local governments can cause such market failures. It promotes inefficiency in the market, as under-performing firms are not compelled to improve their performance. Such sectors are often characterised by a sluggish growth rate.

If countries eliminated such policies that distort competition in markets, they could grow rapidly. An example is the Indian automotive sector, which is one of the fastest-growing sectors in the country. This was a result of the government decision to abandon many of the limits on foreign investment in the automotive industry over the last decade or so. Quite remarkably, India is also exporting automobiles overseas. This is something that was unthinkable earlier.

In Kenya, the Sugar Act prevented the establishment of a sugar mill within a 40-km radius of an existing one. This prevented establishment of sugar mills in the country, and sugar farmers had to spend considerable time and money on transport-ing their stock. The government of Kenya realised this over time, and issued licences for the establishment of a new sugar mill (Butali Sugar) in 2012, which brought smiles to many farmers in the Kakamega area of western Kenya. Similarly, when competition was introduced in generic drugs in South Africa, prices for antiretro-viral drugs fell by up to 88 per cent since 2003 and access increased from 20,000 to 155,000 units.

A report by the Australian Productivity Commission quantifies the expected benefits from competition reforms as an annual gain in real GDP of 5.5 per cent, consumer gains by AU$9bn.[2] In addition, a 2007 World Bank Study found that the world's poorest countries tend to have low levels of competition in domestic markets and a high degree of market dominance.[3] Furthermore, a 2005 European Central Bank paper shows a robust and significant negative link between competition and inflation both at aggregate and sectoral levels.[4]

In the book *The Power of Productivity*, author William Lewis emphasises the need for lesser developed countries to have a robust competition regime.[5] In doing so, he dispels the commonly held myth that competition policy and law are tools for the rich alone. He argues that if such countries could eliminate the policies that distort competition, they could grow rapidly. As the 2001 Nobel Prize winner Joseph Stiglitz has rightly concluded in an article that 'Strong competition policy is not just a luxury

---

[2]   DAF/COMP/GF/WD(2013)9, p. 1.

[3]   R. S. Khemani, *Competition Policy and Promotion of Investment, Economic Growth and Poverty Alleviation in Least Developed Countries* (Occasional Paper 19, FIAS, World Bank (2007), p. 3).

[4]   M. Przybyla and M. Roma, *Does Product Market Competition Reduce Inflation?* (Working Paper Series No. 453, European Central Bank (2005), p. 4).

[5]   William W. Lewis, *The Power of Productivity: Wealth, Poverty, and the Threat to Global Stability* (University of Chicago Press, 2004).

to be enjoyed by rich countries, but a real necessity for those striving to create democratic market economies.'[6]

Professor Eleanor Fox noted about competition policy that: 'There is no such thing as competition law for the rich (well off; enabled) and competition law for the poor.'[7] She further goes on to explain that competition is not only about the focus on competition law and enforcement priorities on products and services, critical to low-income groups. Competition is in fact:

> a market system with handful of sister systems and efforts, the success of each being a necessary condition for enabling the disempowered. This includes education, health care, infrastructure, job opportunities, and availability of capital for good ideas, all in a context of good governance, and that must include absence of pervasive corruption. The house of opportunity, participation, and ultimately growth is built one small brick at a time. The entire system, if it pulls together, can improve the lot of the half of the world living in poverty. All of the efforts together can help to close the gap.[8]

CUTS International[9] has been carrying forward this baton of competition advocacy through its various initiatives and interventions, since it was established in 1983. This line of the work was intensified after the developing world adopted economic reforms in the early 1990s and globalisation was hastened with the arrival of the World Trade Organization (WTO) in 1995. It was realised that liberalisation and deregulation only buttressed the need for good market regulatory institutions, without which the gains of liberalisation would not accrue to people, for whom it was designed. In due course two specialised CUTS Centres were established, first in 1996 to deal with international trade issues and second in 2003 to look into competition, investment and regulatory issues – Centre for International Trade, Economics and Environment (CITEE) and the Centre for Competition, Investment and Economic Regulation (CCIER).

CUTS has had successfully advocated the need for competition policy and law in many countries, and had also been involved closely in designing some of such regimes, including India. Through various study projects CUTS has also been evaluating regulations in key sectors (having larger public interface) from the competition perspective in India and other developing countries. It has implemented various cross-country projects on competition and regulatory issues. In addition, CUTS has been closely working with key international organisations like the WTO, United Nations Conference on Trade and Development (UNCTAD), Organisation for Economic Co-operation and Development (OECD) on trade, competition and related issues.

---

[6] J. Stiglitz, 'Competing over Competition Policy' (2001) www.project-syndicate.org/commentary/com peting-over-competition-policy (accessed 28 July 2017).
[7] DAF/COMP/GF(2013)4, p 2.
[8] Ibid., pp. 2–3.
[9] www.cuts-international.org

This chapter generally draws lessons from the CUTS wealth of experience on the competition policy dispensation. It highlights the importance of having competition policy reform for the benefit of ordinary people in the developing world.

6.2 COMPETITION POLICY REFORM: PRINCIPLES AND PROCESSES

Competition in a market cannot be achieved automatically: it needs to be nurtured. This is particularly true for countries that have recently started promoting private participation in their economies. Given the background of considerable government intervention in these markets, sectoral policies were traditionally developed such that it favoured the incumbent government player, the so-called state-owned enterprise (SOE). Competition policy would seek to rectify biasness in such policies.

In addition, the liberalisation process is often accompanied by exploitative practices resorted to by large firms. An effective competition law curbs such exploitative practices and disciplines market players, thereby protecting the interest of both the country's economy and also consumers. Large firms also tend to exploit the nefarious politics–business nexus to obtain favourable policies, which can go against small market players. A competition policy approach would discourage such trends.

The review and refining process of competition-distorting policies and practices is termed competition policy reform, or simply competition reform, which is an aggregate of the following three components:[10]

- Policies: enabling government policies (including legislation, programmes, etc.) designed to facilitate a level playing field (fair competition) in a sector.
- Regulation: a well-designed regulatory framework with an adequately resourced regulatory agency that promotes healthy development of the sector and aims to promote competition in it.
- Competition regime: presence of competition law with effective enforcement mechanisms to curb anti-competitive practices.

In essence, competition reform is infusing competition principles in policies and practices. For instance, the guiding review and reform principles in the Australian National Competition Policy were that: (1) the legislation should not restrict competition unless the benefits of the restriction to the community as a whole outweighed the costs; (2) the objectives of the legislation can only be achieved by restricting competition; and (3) legislation that restricts competition is consistent with the guiding review and reform principle.[11]

---

[10] *Framework for Competition Reforms: A Practitioners' Guidebook* (CUTS International, 2015), p. 5; www.cuts-ccier.org/crew/pdf/FCR_Practitioners_Guidebook.pdf (accessed 28 July 2017)

[11] Competition Principles Agreement – 11 April 1995 (as amended to 13 April 2007).

The main targets of competition reform are policies and practices that:[12]

- Distort the level playing field between competitors
  - Does the policy discriminate between the SOEs and private players? Does it distort competitive neutrality?
- Create entry barriers
  - Does the policy limit foreign players into domestic markets?
  - Are procedures and rules time bound, transparent, fair and non-discriminatory? Are the licensing and authorisation conditions imposed for starting business too onerous or arbitrary?
  - Does the standard set for product quality provide unfair advantage to some suppliers over others?
  - Is there a grandfather clause that treats incumbent firms differently from new ones in a manner that raises costs of production of the new players and creates entry barriers?
  - Does the policy deny third-party access to essential facilities?
  - Does the policy create geographical barriers?
- Limit free and fair market process
  - Does policy limit the free flow of goods and services?
- Promote monopolies and their abuse
  - Does the policy encourage the exchange between suppliers, or publication, of information on prices, costs, sales or outputs?
  - Does it grant exclusive rights for a supplier to provide goods or services?
  - Does it allow for firms to use incumbency advantage to create strategic entry barriers for new players?
- Limit the scope to introduce new products or supply existing products in new ways
  - Is there a restriction on the product that can be supplied?
  - Is there a restriction on the production process used or means of supply?
- Are driven by vested interests promoted by government
  - Is the government enjoying benefits from opposing reforms?
  - Is the government sharing high profits through taxes, etc. that dominant players may be able to make if they are allowed to maintain such position in the absence of competition in the market?
- Limit institutional independence
- Do not effectively prevent anticompetitive conduct

The process of competition reform, generally, involves the following steps:[13]

---

[12] Adapted from CUTS' *Competition Impact Assessment Toolkit* (CUTS International, 2014), p. 15; www.cuts-ccier.org/Compeg/pdf/CUTS_Competition_Impact_Assessment_Toolkit-A_Framework_to_Assess_Competition_Distortions_Induced_by_Government_Policies_in_the_Developing_World.pdf

[13] Ibid., p. 31.

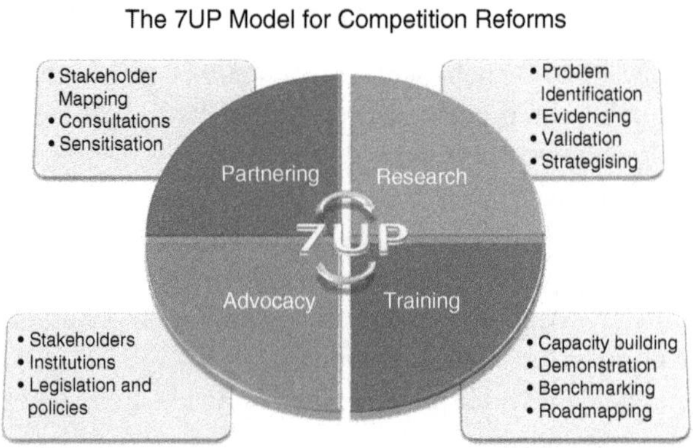

The 7UP Model for Competition Reforms

FIGURE 6.1 Model for competition reforms

- Sector selection for competition analysis. The priority of the sector is generally ascertained by taking into account: (a) its importance to the economy; (b) its importance to consumers; (c) having history of anti-competitive conduct allegations; (d) opposition from vested interest to reforms; (e) pattern of high market concentration, etc.
- Determining the relevant market and competitors. Both relevant geographic market and relevant product market is determined based on several factors
- Ascertaining: (a) level of concentration in the relevant market; (b) presence of entry barriers; (c) countervailing power by buyer
- Examining policies, legislation, rules, regulations dealing with the chosen sector in light of above-stated competition principles
- Formulating agenda for competition advocacy in the sector
- Competition advocacy

However, it is not easy to successfully advocate competition policy reform, mainly due to political–economy issues. Therefore, some of these changes will need considerable push from the ground to fructify, consequently making it important to involve civil society, academia and media in such processes. CUTS International has had visible success in this regard, using the 7UP Model for Competition Reforms (see Figure 6.1).

One of the ways to enhance acceptance for competition reform is to present it along with evidence of consumer welfare and producer welfare, which could be brought in by such reform. Consumer welfare can be shown by using indicators like: access to goods and services; assurance of quality goods and services; better choice to consumers; competitive price; time saving.[14]

---

[14]   CUTS International, *Framework for Competition Reforms*, p. 6.

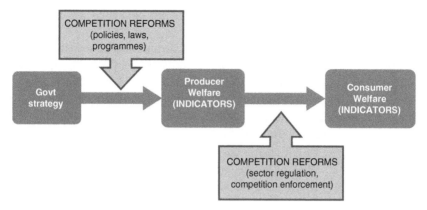

FIGURE 6.2 Competition reforms and welfare continuum
Source: CREW, 'Competition Reforms in Key Markets for Enhancing Social & Economic Welfare in Developing Countries Undertaken in Four Countries: Ghana, India, the Philippines and Zambia' (www.cuts-ccier.org/CREW Project Synthesis Report)

Similarly, producer welfare can be mapped by using indicators like: access to essential services and inputs like labour, capital, technology, communication infrastructure, essential facilities, raw materials; ease of entry and exit in the market; level playing field for all firms; growth-enabling conditions in the market, for instance, absence of regulation that may restrict growth of firms such as production quotas; potential to attract investment; potential to save operating, legal and other administrative costs due to efficiency in both input and output market.[15]

In sum, a pro-competitive government policy in market can help producers/businesses enter a market easily and operate efficiently deriving certain benefits. Consumers in turn benefit from enhanced competition in the market. This is further explained in the flow chart in Figure 6.2.

6.3 COMPETITION REFORMS AND PUBLIC WELFARE: ILLUSTRATIONS

6.3.1 *Mauritius Milk Powder Crisis*

Mauritius had to rely on powdered milk to meet their and their children's nutritional demand as fresh milk was unavailable in the country prior to 2006. The powdered milk market was dominated by a handful of players. One of them enjoying 60 per cent of the market share (clearly a dominant position) decided to raise the price of the product abruptly. The price rose to a peak of Mauritius rupees (MUR)

---

[15] Ibid.

190/kg during the period 2004–6. The company was enjoying a profit margin of nearly 41 per cent in the retail market, then.

At this point, as a result of CUTS project on competition policy and law issues (7Up3 project) the level of awareness and understanding on competition issues in the country had improved considerably. The impact of anti-competitive practices on consumers' daily lives was being discussed in public platforms/media, etc. This was largely due to the outreach made possible by the advocacy partner of CUTS for the 7Up3 project in Mauritius, Institute for Consumer Protection (ICP). Pursued by continuous lobbying by ICP, the government eventually intervened in the market and fixed the margin of profit for the sector. This led to a decrease in price, which later stabilised at MUR 90–120/kg across the country.

6.3.2 *High Banking Fees in Namibia*

The Namibian Consumer Association (NCA) led a campaign in 2006–7 pointing out how Namibian banks were charging customers high service charges/bank fees. This campaign of NCA (the only consumer organisation in Namibia) was strengthened by research undertaken by Namibia Economic Policy Research Unit (NEPRU), a premier think tank in the country which provided the evidence to substantiate NCA's claim. A large number of Namibians (nearly 45 per cent) remained unbanked owing to such high charges which made banking unaffordable for the ordinary Namibians.

NEPRU had been implementing a project in cooperation with CUTS (7Up3) in Namibia over this period and highlighted a low level of competition in retail banking (as one of the factors) contributing to high bank charges in the country (especially among the four leading banks). It was also reported that often the banks were not very clear and/or transparent about these charges. So a large number of ordinary Namibians (using the facility of these banks) were being adversely affected by these practices.

As a result of evidence provided by NEPRU and the constant lobbying by NCA, the matter reached the Parliamentary Standing Committee on Economics, Natural Resources and Public Administration of Namibia. The Committee recommended that all banks become more transparent while dealing with their customers and to state their charges upfront while servicing them.

6.3.3 *Small Business in Zambia*

A CUTS project earlier in 2000–2 (7Up1)[16] noted with concern that the competition authority of Zambia was engaged mainly with big business and did not look at the problems of small businesses. The Zambia Competition Commission (ZCC)

---

[16]   www.cuts-ccier.org/7Up1

personnel felt that their law restricted it to act on business malpractices that had significant impact on the economy. This point was debated on during the meeting of the National Reference Group (NRG), formed for project implementation. The purpose of the meeting was to come up with recommendations, which the project would seek to have addressed by influencing the relevant stakeholders.

The NRG members recommended that 'ZCC should address the concerns of small-scale sector'. ZCC was represented in the meeting and agreed to take the issue forward. Following the project, there was a noticeable change in approach of ZCC towards the small scale sector. Examples include ZCC directing a monopoly retailer (Shoprite of South Africa) to purchase farm produce from the small-scale farmers rather than importing and ZCC holding discussions with the multinationals in the tobacco, cotton and poultry sectors to stop abusive practices against small-scale farmers.

6.3.4 ZCC on Contract Farming

In 2005, ZCC saw a report in a local newspaper, *The Post*, where women farmers in Katete were calling for a review of farming contracts as they were being abused by the dominant firms. Two multinationals (Dunavat and Cargill Cotton) were dominating the market with a CR2 of 83.49 per cent and abused the outgrower scheme by charging high input prices and paying a low final price.

Before ZCC's intervention, they paid a price of ZK850/kg for grade-A cotton while charging the input prices at ZK40,000/pack. While investigations were still underway, Dunavat indicated that they were now reducing input prices to ZK36,000 while increasing the planting price to ZK1,000/kg. Cargill also decreased input price for the 2006 season by 28 per cent and increased the buying price to ZK1, 120/kg. According to Cargill's estimates, the changes gave an average farmer an additional net income increment of 75 per cent compared to the previous year. One can well imagine the huge multiplier effects of these systemic changes on poor people and particularly their livelihoods.

6.3.5 Zambia Miller Subsidy Programme

The Zambian miller subsidy regime programme for maize, the staple food, was introduced between September 2011 and March 2012. Government sold maize to millers at subsidised rates, with the expectation being that the cost of the final product, maize meal, would also become lower for the poor consumers to afford. However, there was no apparent downward price movement in response to the subsidy, as it was established that the mill-to-retail marketing margins (difference between the wholesale maize price and retail maize meal price) actually increased significantly by about 55 per cent during the subsidy period.

This implies that the benefit of the subsidy was only enjoyed by the millers at the expense of the consumers. This failure can be attributed to collusive behaviour among the millers, which helped cushion fears of being undercut by rivals in price setting. In addition, only a number of millers were able to benefit, which also enhanced collusion possibilities due to a small number of players involved.

Similarly, the noble intentions of the Zambian government's Farmer Input Support Programme (FISP) were thwarted by collusive practices by fertiliser suppliers. Two companies, Nyiombo and Omnia, became the main winners of the fertiliser tenders and allegations of inflating fertiliser costs through cartelised behaviour soon followed.

6.3.6 Competition Reform in the Zambian Sugar Industry

As a policy, all sugar for household consumption in Zambia has to be fortified with vitamin A in specified quantities. This fortification requirement was introduced in response to a serious vitamin A deficiency that had been noticed in Zambia when compared to other countries in the region. However, the requirement was introduced at a time when there was only one sugar producer – Zambia Sugar plc.

The firm forced government to give an undertaking that they would be willing to participate in the fortification process only if the government gave an undertaking to introduce legislation barring any importation of sugar into Zambia. This virtually killed off any competition. Currently, importation of sugar can only be done by the milling companies (there are now three millers, with the other millers entering the market after the fortification policy was already operational). However, the disparities that currently exist between the sugar prices in Zambia and its neighbouring countries are too high to be attributed to the fortification costs. Thus, while the government was able to enhance vitamin A among the Zambians, this was achieved at a cost – excessive price due to abuse of dominance.

6.3.7 Pontianak Orange Market of Indonesia

Tebas District, Sambas Municipality in West Kalimantan Province was one of the wealthiest districts in Indonesia. The agriculture sector, especially the Pontianak Orange, contributed about rupiah 1.5bn to the local government treasury, a big amount of money until the rupiah devaluated due to a monetary crisis. Due to its high-quality Pontianak Orange hardly had competitors, and thus dominated the market.

In 1991, the central government decided to take over the trade of these oranges, and issued regulations that required all harvested oranges should be channelled through a company called Bina Citra Mandiri (BCM). This company, rather than being a state-owned company, belonged to a close family member of the president. Farmers or merchants who tried to sell directly in the open market could be charged for smuggling and put into jail. Besides, BCM also regulated the price and quotas in distribution. Farmers and merchants were allowed to sell 10 per cent of the harvest in the market, while the remaining 90 per cent was to be sold to BCM.

This monopsonistic system resulted in a great loss for farmers. Consequently, they decided to stop harvesting their orange crop, because it was unremunerative. By not harvesting the oranges, the rotting crop led to virus infection. Within a very short time, 7.6 million trees located in 19,000 hectares had to be cut down in order to curb the disease. Later, the Ministry of Agriculture and the National University of Tanjungpura Pontianak had to work hard to recover from the situation. It took some time before the team could even gain support from the farmers who had experienced such a trauma.

6.3.8 Learnings under the CREW Project

In 2015, CUTS completed the implementation of a two-year project entitled, 'Competition Reforms in Key Markets for Enhancing Social and Economic Welfare in Developing Countries', referred to as the CREW project. The project was implemented in four countries; Ghana, India, the Philippines and Zambia. The CREW project looked through the lens depicted in Figure 6.2 into two key sectors – staple food and bus transport.

It was found that even after the allocation of resources, the commodities and/or services thus provided are either overcharged or are of substandard quality. The ordinary consumers, especially the poor, are disadvantaged in such a scenario as they struggle to balance their small budgets. In pursuit of providing essential services to the consumers and assured income to the producer, the creation of state-led monopolies virtually block entry of new players and innovation. A competition reform imperative would advise in such situations to gradually introduce competition in the market and levelling the playing field between SOEs and private players, accompanied by sound and effective independent regulation.

In Zambia, for example, many sectors were liberalised in the early 1991 including the bus transport sector. The deregulation of the sector and the accompanying measures introduced by the Zambian government, such as tax concessions on import of buses, reduction in the time required to obtain bus licenses and improved access to infrastructure (bus stops and stations) have had a positive impact on the entry of new service providers (private sector) and thereby, competition in the sector.

However, even though the access to bus services has increased for the consumers (or passengers), deregulation of Zambia's transport sector and the resultant increase in competition has not been able to generate significant benefits in terms of intra-city bus transport quality as well as (increasing) fares. This is mostly due to the fact that the transport operators have been able to find a way of manipulating the regulatory system to their advantage, especially through the fare setting system that is skewed in their favour. The absence of a route allocation system for intra-city transport has also seen the consumer being less prioritised. Thus there is a missing link (absence of right regulation) in the continuum, somewhere between service providers and consumer welfare.

However, in Ghana, despite the existence of the publicly owned Metro Mass Transit (MMT) bus service (owned by the government and run on a public–private partnership model), no barriers were imposed by government to protect MMT from competition. The private sector has been able to gain a lot of consumer patronage despite the higher fares they charge due to better quality of services being provided by them. Thus consumers now have improved choice – either to opt for quality and pay a higher fare or for low fare and poor quality of the MMT. This implies that competition oriented reforms have been able to have an associated welfare enhancing mechanism.

Another example on benefits from competition-oriented reforms is from the seed sector in the state of Bihar in India, which seems to validate the continuum presented in Figure 6.2. Enabling state government policy and strategy in the agriculture sector helped entry and establishment of private sector seed companies in the state. The state government provided the framework for these players to operate and encouraged them to develop strong distribution networks. The Bihar state government also ensured that these players were able to operate effectively and help the farmers (as consumers) obtain good quality seeds at low price. Overall, usage of good quality certified seeds by the farmers in the state led to better yields in many cases.

Furthermore, the infrastructure sector is a good example of overarching impacts. The World Bank (in 2002) noted that 'improvements in infrastructure services can help promote competition in other markets, and there is evidence that infrastructure has a positive impact on growth and poverty reduction'.[17] CUTS's experience corroborates this fact, that underdeveloped infrastructure is deterrence in private sector participation leading to issues of accessibility and high prices to both consumers and producers. For example, in the state of Bihar, even though the state government removed the policy barriers to allow private sector participation in the agricultural sector, including procurement of agriculture produce, the less developed infrastructure is resulting in lesser realisation of desired gains that could have accrued to farmers and consumers.

Lower-income group consumers have to spend a greater part of their income on goods and services, and therefore high prices arising from anti-competitive practices will have a greater impact on them than on other segments of society. An important approach to poverty reduction is to empower the poor, provide them with productive employment and increase their access to land, capital and other productive resources. But this approach cannot be successful unless these people are linked

---

[17] World Bank, *Building Institutions for Markets – World Development Report* 2002 (IBRD/OUP, 2002), 166.

to the markets and markets are made to work for the benefit of the poor. This would open economic vistas for them, providing them with economic empowerment and freedom that is so crucial for their survival and well-being.

For example in Ghana a liberalised procurement market led to the emergence of private women traders (referred popularly to as market queens) involved with the procurement of various crops in the national and the regional markets. The wholesale market is dominated by the market queens who procure maize from the rural farmers using their network on the ground (village assemblers) and supply to the market. There is a certain level of contestability among these market queens, since each of them are constantly working towards strengthening their own distribution networks, improving access to capital and establishing strong ties with various market participants. However, there seems to be some coordinated behaviour among the market queens that can qualify as abuse of their dominance.

The market of agricultural producers is often considered to be an example of a perfectly competitive market. However for consumers the experience is different. Farmers do not reach the consumers directly and there is a chain of intermediaries. Unfortunately, these sets of intermediaries do not always work in a competitive manner. Thus, the final consumers of agricultural products do not get the advantage of a competitive market. Hence a huge gap exists between the prices the consumers pay and the prices the primary producers receive.

This kind of a situation is not restricted to some particular countries, but has become a global feature. These intermediaries abuse their monopolistic dominance in the market for final products while in the markets for primary products they abuse their monopsonistic dominance. Apart from adversely impacting the final consumers, they also have a negative impact on the farmers who draw their livelihood directly from agriculture. Thus a competition reform, with producer welfare and consumer welfare approach (CREW Model), particularly in agriculture sector, is a necessity for international community, in general, and developing countries, in particular.

6.4 CONCLUSION

It can indeed be demonstrated that there is a direct linkage between competition policy and some SDGs – reflecting the importance of competition policy as a strategy for the attainment of such SDGs. The five transformative shifts of the SDGs Agenda (namely: (1) leave no one behind; (2) put sustainable development at the core; (3) transform economies for jobs and inclusive growth; (4) build peace and effective, open and accountable institutions for all; and (5) forge a new global partnership) also resonate well with the following five objectives of competition policy and law (as per the UN Set on Competition):

- to ensure that restrictive business practices do not impede or negate the realisation of benefits that should arise from the liberalisation of tariff and non-tariff barriers affecting world trade, particularly those affecting the trade and development of developing countries;
- to attain greater efficiency in international trade and development, particularly that of developing countries, in accordance with national aims of economic and social development and existing economic structures, such as through (a) the creation, encouragement and protection of competition; (b) control of the concentration of capital and/or economic power; (c) encouragement of innovation;
- to protect and promote social welfare in general and, in particular, the interests of consumers in both developed and developing countries;
- to eliminate the disadvantages to trade and development which may result from the restrictive business practices of transnational corporations or other enterprises, and thus help to maximise benefits to international trade and particularly the trade and development of developing countries;
- to provide a set of multilaterally agreed equitable principles and rules for the control of restrictive business practices for adoption at the international level and thereby to facilitate the adoption and strengthening of laws and policies in this area at the national and regional levels.

The best way to achieve these transformative shifts is to have empowered citizens, the consumers. If consumers are better empowered to exercise their rights and discharge their responsibilities as per the United Nations Guidelines for Consumer Protection, 1985[18] and with effective laws, regulations and institutions in place, then these transformative shifts are attainable.[19]

Many times the policies, especially the trade policies, are at the extreme ends of the spectrum – either they are more beneficial for international firms to operate in domestic markets or they are protectionist enough leading to inefficiencies, crowding out of competition and economic losses. A balanced approach therefore is needed to design policy provisions, including competition law/policy and sectorial policies.

The following are policy pointers emerging from the experience of CUTS's work:

- Regulatory safeguards are an important factor to ensure that benefits of trade/economic liberalisation can be derived fully by the people/country. Absence of such safeguards might see the reforms being used as an opportunity by private players to exploit the market.

---

[18]   As revised and adopted by the UN General Assembly in Resolution 70/186 of 22 December 2015; http://unctad.org/en/PublicationsLibrary/ditccplpmisc2016d1_en.pdf (accessed 28 July 2017)

[19]   CUTS International, 'Strategic Business Plan 2014–18', pp. 8–9; www.cuts-international.org/pdf/CUTS_Strategic_Business_Plan-2014–2018.pdf

- The competition regulation should extend to SOEs or state monopolies too. More often than not, these SOEs are economically inefficient and with no incentive to innovate (owing to state support), amass huge economic losses. Including these SOEs in the purview of competition laws may help in managing these monopolies.
- Evidence suggests that the exemptions done in some sectors like agriculture (by way of subsidies) should be minimum and well targeted. This calls for strengthening government capacity to ensure that they are able to carry out targeted subsidy programmes, effectively.
- Proper redressal mechanism to ensure anti-competitive injustice incurred by the poor should be available. Most of the times, the poor are left at a disadvantage as justice for the poor in such scenarios is wrought with political economy issues, thereby disfavouring the poor population.
- Last but not the least, there is a need for active advocacy against 'state interventions' and 'abuse of dominance' that lead to anti-competitive environment. Civil societies can play a major role in taking up this mantle. Additionally, civil societies can also advocate global good practices to ensure that the domestic markets are well functioning.

In conclusion, the words of Dr Mukhisa Kituyi, Secretary General, UNCTAD would be quite relevant, when he observed:

It is widely acknowledged that sustainable and inclusive economic growth requires higher levels of economic productivity through diversification, technology upgrading and innovation. Appropriate industrial and trade policies are necessary but not sufficient to achieve this. There remains a need for complementary and coherent policies that ensure countries benefits from free trade. Competition policy is one of these policies, which governments need to develop and implement in order to achieve the goals of the 2030 Agenda.[20]

---

[20] CUTS International, 'Pursuing Competition and Regulatory Reforms for Achieving Sustainable Development Goals' (CUTS International, 2015).

7

Competition (Law) and Access to Telecommunications Technologies in Sub-Saharan Africa

Mor Bakhoum

7.1 INTRODUCTION

In the context of the emerging so-called "international standards"[1] in competition law, the emerging scholarship on development and competition law is a cautionary tale against blindly adopting competition law standards that do not take into account the needs, goals, and concerns of developing and emerging markets. More than just a word of caution, the scholarship on developing countries outlines a new perspective, a new orientation of competition law and policy, which integrates equity and development concerns – in complement to and in harmony with efficiency – as the objectives of competition law. New concepts such as "pro-poorer competition law," "pro-development competition law," "efficient inclusive growth," and "sustainable economic growth"[2] interface competition and development. Such orientation sets forth the foundations of the emergence of a new language in competition law,[3] a language of development and inclusiveness of a competition policy which takes

---

[1] This is especially the case with the work of the ICN which aims at reducing the substantive and enforcement gaps in competition authorities. The question has been raised as to whether such approach takes into account the needs of developing countries to develop their own standards in competition law which take into account their context. For discussion, see Eleanor M. Fox, 'Linked-in: Antitrust and the Virtues of a Virtual Network', in Paul Lugard (ed.), *The International Competition Network at Ten* (Intersentia, 2011) see esp. 213ff.; David Lewis, 'Some Reflections on the ICN', ibid., 205–16; more information about the ICN is available at www.internationalcompetitionnetwork.org

[2] See some of Eleanor Fox's writing on this perspective: 'Competition, Development and Regional Integration: In Search of a Competition Law Fit for Developing Countries', in Josef Drexl et al. (eds.), *Competition Policy and Regional Integration in Developing Countries* (Edward Elgar, 2012) 273–90; Eleanor M. Fox and Michal S. Gal, 'Drafting Competition Law for Developing Jurisdictions: Learning from Experience', in Michal S. Gal et al. (eds.), *The Economic Characteristics of Developing Jurisdictions: Their Implications for Competition Law* (Edward Elgar, 2015).

[3] Discussing the emergence of such language in competition law, see Mor Bakhoum, 'A Dual Language in Modern Competition Law? Efficiency Approach versus Development Approach and Implication for Developing Countries' (2011) 34(3) *World Competition* 495; Fox and Gal, 'Drafting Competition Law.'

into account the specific context of developing countries and the need to make their "markets work for people."[4]

Approaching competition law as a development tool with equity goals which do not solely rely on economic theory as the main tool[5] for dealing with restrictions of competition raises questions from a conceptual as well as enforcement perspective. Is there a development-friendly competition law? What are the features of a development-friendly competition law? Does a development-friendly competition law depart from the "traditional" competition law approach and its tools? Is there a need to conceptualize a "new approach" to competition law in order for it to be development-friendly? Could/should a development-friendly competition law be worked out within the boundaries of competition law?

An emerging scholarship on competition law in developing countries defines the perspectives of competition law and policy for developing jurisdictions by relying primarily on the traditional tools and methods of competition law. It does not advocate reinventing the wheel or conceptualizing a new competition law fit for developing countries. Using the known competition law methods and tools, much can be done within the boundaries of competition law in order to accommodate development concerns. Such an approach requires a different perspective when drafting a competition law. It also requires an *imaginative* application of competition law. In order to integrate development concerns within the realm of competition law, the boundaries of competition law can be stretched while simultaneously (and that is a challenge) giving deference to the core principles of competition law.

This contribution gives a very brief overview of the interface between competition law and development. It discusses how to make competition law "development-friendly" and adapted to the context, needs, and aspirations of developing jurisdictions. Building on such an approach and as an illustration thereof, the competition-related issues in the telecommunications sector, with a focus on sub-Saharan Africa, will be discussed. The question of how building competitive telecommunications markets in sub-Saharan Africa can contribute to development will then be addressed. The scholarship discussing the interfaces between competition law and policy and development focuses mainly on enforcing competition law in sectors considered as basic needs.[6] Studies which take a close look at the interface between access to telecommunications technologies, growth, and development are rare.[7] In a recent

---

[4] Eleanor M. Fox, 'Making Markets Work for People, as a Post-Millennium Development Goal', at http://unctad.org/meetings/en/Contribution/CCPB_7RC2015_HLRTCompSusDev_Fox_en.pdf

[5] On the discussion on the issue of how to reconcile economic goals with equity goals, see also Fox and Gal, 'Drafting Competition Law.'

[6] Simon Evenett argues that competition authorities in developing countries should focus their enforcement efforts on sectors where the consumers spend much of their income such as sectors of basic needs ('Competition Law and the Economic Characteristics of Developing Countries', in Gal et al. (eds.), *Economic Characteristics of Developing Jurisdictions*, 15).

[7] See, for instance, Javier Tapia and Simon Roberts, 'Abuse of Dominance in Developing Countries: A View from the South, with an Eye on Telecommunication', in Gal et al. (eds.), *Economic*

study on competition-related issues in sub-Saharan Africa, the World Bank, in collaboration with the African Competition Forum (ACF),[8] discussed the competition-related issues in the telecommunications sector in sub-Saharan Africa. This chapter will build on the findings of this report and address the following questions: how can access to telecommunications technologies help stimulate growth and development? How can access to technologies foster entrepreneurship and the creation of new business models for the benefit of the consumers? Access to financial services for the people active in the informal economy is a prime example of how access to telecommunications technologies benefits consumers. What are the competition-related issues identified in the telecommunications sector in sub-Saharan Africa? How should one balance opening up the telecommunications sector to competition and regulating the sector? Which approach is more efficient and beneficial?

Section 7.2 discusses briefly the formulation of a development-sympathetic competition law and policy. Section 7.3 deals with access to telecommunications technologies, growth, and development in sub-Saharan Africa. Section 7.4 discusses competition in the telecommunications sectors in sub-Saharan Africa. Relying on the findings of the World Bank study, this section explains the main competition-related issues in the telecommunications sector. Building on that, section 7.5 discusses whether competition law and/or regulation are appropriate tools for dealing with restrictions of competition in the telecommunications sector.

7.2 THE FORMULATION OF A PRO-DEVELOPMENT COMPETITION LAW: CONTOURS OF A DEVELOPMENT SYMPATHETIC COMPETITION POLICY

Three points will be discussed in order to illustrate the approach to development-friendly competition: first, the relationship between markets and competition law; second, development and the goals of competition law; third, competition law and substantive law.

7.2.1 *"Development-Friendly" Competition Law and Markets*

Markets are important for development.[9] Competitive markets constitute the basis for economic development. The very basic goal of competition law should be to make

---

    Characteristics of Developing Jurisdictions, 357ff.; see also a recent study on key sector in Africa, Simon Robert (ed.), *Competition in Africa: Insights from Key Industries* (HSRC Press, 2016). The study looked at sectors such as the cement industry, the agricultural sector with a focus on the sugar industry, the ago-processing industry, and the fertilizer industry.

[8] See, on the ACF www.africancompetitionforum.org

[9] The well-functioning of the market should not be distorted in order to take into account equity considerations (see for this approach, Fox, 'Competition, Development and Regional Integration', 273–90).

markets work for the good of people in general.[10] However, what kind of market is beneficial for development?[11] Markets should be open and competitive. But, more importantly, markets should be inclusive by drawing people and businesses into the economic channels. To this end, competition law should help remove entry barriers, ensure mobility, and promote competition on the merits. Competition law should empower people to do what they can do by themselves.[12] Only competitive markets which are inclusive could help achieve this objective. This approach to markets and competition law not only helps the final consumers in developing countries, but more importantly also the small business entrepreneur. The need to build inclusive markets is getting more traction in the work of the World Bank.[13]

7.2.2 *"Development-Friendly" Competition Law and Goals*

What should be the goals of competition law in developing countries? Which competition law goal(s) are more sympathetic to development? These questions have raised a great deal of controversies in the scholarship dealing with competition law in developing countries.[14] Efficiency is a very important objective for developing countries. Efficiency should not be rejected as a core goal of completion law for the sake of promoting development. Nevertheless, a development-sympathetic competition law should be inclusive and equitable.[15] Efficiency *could* and *should* accommodate inclusiveness of markets players which are able to compete on the merits. Protecting, for instance, the competitiveness of the small and medium-sized enterprises (SMEs) is pro-competitive. It is in line with efficiency. Competition law should not protect small and inefficient companies which are not able to compete on merit. As one contended: "protecting small firms from competition itself is anti-antitrust."[16]

---

[10] Fox, 'Making Markets Work.'

[11] Fox engages in this discussion on the concept (approach) of markets which is more suitable to development. She contrasts the Washington Consensus approach with the Spence approach and concludes that the approach of market which favor inclusiveness is more suitable to the characteristics and goals of developing countries ('Competition, Development and Regional Integration').

[12] This is in line with the social function of competition law which also aims at empowering people ('Competition, Development and Regional Integration', 275).

[13] World Bank, *Growth Report: Strategies for Sustained Growth and Inclusive Development* (2008) https://openknowledge.worldbank.org/bitstream/handle/10986/6507/449860pub0box31010officialou seoonly1.pdf; the report stresses that inclusive growth is critically important for development.

[14] On a discussion of the goals of competition law from the standpoint of developing countries, see Fox and Gal, 'Drafting Competition Law', 323–9; see Bakhoum, 'Dual Language in Modern Competition Law?'; Josef Drexl, 'Consumer Welfare and Consumer Harm: Adjusting Competition Law and Policies to the Needs of Developing Jurisdictions', in Gal et al. (eds.), *Economic Characteristics* of *Developing Jurisdictions*, 265–95.

[15] This approach is in line with Fox's argument on how competition law should be approached in developing jurisdictions.

[16] Fox and Gal, 'Drafting Competition Law', 328.

The discussion on the goals of competition law in developing countries entails a common misperception that including equity goals[17] in competition law will lead to the sheltering of small and inefficient firms from competition. Making markets inclusive and protecting the competitiveness of the small (efficient) players are in line with the core principles of competition law which aim to open up the market by protecting the freedom to compete of every single market player, big or small. Equity and inclusiveness are not in opposition to efficiency as an economic concept. The two concepts can be aligned and be reconciled when designing and enforcing a competition law. The objective of "efficient, inclusive development" sums up the idea that efficiency can be inclusive, while also fostering development.[18]

7.2.3 *"Development-Friendly" Competition Law and Substantive Law*

How can substantive competition rules be designed and applied in a pro-poor, pro-development, pro-inclusive perspective without hindering efficiency? This is a complex balancing. The rules on dominance are particularly important when creating inclusive markets. They can deal with concentration of power and open up business opportunities for many. As contented: "availability of the abuse of dominance prohibition is one of the most important weapons in the antitrust arsenal of developing countries to open up closed markets and thus help make markets work where they have never worked before."[19]

How to apply rules on dominance is a question of perspective. The US has a permissive approach toward dominance. Contrary to the US approach, developing countries should worry about false negatives, given that "dominant firms have for too long been protected from the forces of competition and that people/firms with no power have often been excluded from entering markets and competing on the merits."[20] Developing countries may need a stricter approach to dominance. The US approach to predatory pricing and excessive pricing might not be suitable for developing countries. Here, again, applying the rules on dominance, while keeping in mind the perspective of opening up the market, can yield positive results. How to approach dominance in the telecommunications sector is very important.

Let us now turn to the telecommunications sector and see how the interface between competition law and development is relevant in that sector.

---

[17] Fox distinguishes between equity/economic goals (such as protecting small and middle-sized businesses from abuse; safeguarding economic opportunities for all) and equity/non-economic goals (such as protecting small players per se; protecting jobs; promoting the nation's industries).

[18] On this aspect, see Bakhoum, 'Dual Language in Modern Competition Law?'; Fox and Gal argue in the same vein. They contend: "developing countries also need to give weight to an equity/economic goal of inclusiveness; not just efficiency defined as increased aggregate wealth, but efficiency also defined in terms of enabling the masses of people to participate on their merits in the economic enterprise" ('Drafting Competition Law', 328).

[19] Bakhoum, 'Dual Language'.

[20] Ibid.

7.3 ACCESS TO TELECOMMUNICATIONS TECHNOLOGIES, GROWTH, AND DEVELOPMENT

The development of the telecommunications sector in sub-Saharan Africa and its potential in contributing to growth are discussed in this section. The issue of access technology has mainly been dealt with from the perspective of intellectual property rights (IPRs). It has been argued that the IP-related flexibilities are a tool that developing countries can use in order to foster transfer of technology from developed countries. This approach is mainly advocated by using the flexibilities within the TRIPS agreement in order to foster technology transfer.[21] Access to technology through technology transfer is a key approach embodied in the TRIPS agreement.

A more recent approach to the interface between IP and competition law emphasizes the prominent role that competition law should play in fostering not only access to technology, but also innovation.[22] As illustrated by EU case law, such as *Magill*, *IMS Health*, and *Microsoft*, competition law may be used as an innovation instrument. From the perspective of developing countries, access to technology can be fostered by designing and applying competition rules to IP-related restrictions of competition. This can be illustrated in the telecommunications sector.

Although not fully developed by Prof. Fox in her scholarship, she nevertheless recognizes the importance of access to modern technology, including telecommunications technology for developing countries. She states in this regard:

> Much of modern technology including that used in computers, smart phones and other mobile phones incorporates intellectual property. Access to information and communication technologies is critical; it means access to business opportunity, at home and in the world. There is growing literature and experience on how *mobile phone technology enables market information flows and financial transactions of cottage industries and isolated entrepreneurs*, such as fishermen getting on-the-spot information as to where they can sell their catches, and *migrant wage earners needing to transfer money to their families simply and fast, which they now do through M-Peas. Keeping modern technology within the reach of competition and competition law is a critical pro-poor policy.*[23] [emphasis added]

Access to telecommunications technology is pro-poor. The crucial point of the analysis in this section will be the question of how competition law can help foster access to telecommunications technology and thereby promote growth and development.

---

[21]   On this aspect, see Mor Bakhoum and Beatriz Conde, 'TRIPS and Competition Policy: From Transfer of Technology to Innovation Policy', in Hanns Ullrich et al. (eds.), *TRIPS Plus 20: From Trade Rules to Market Principles* (Springer, 2015) 529–60.

[22]   ibid.

[23]   E. Fox, *Competition and Poverty Reduction*, OECD Global Forum on Competition (DAF/COMP/GF(2013) 4), para. 28.

7.3.1 *Progressive Development of the Telecommunications Market*

The telecommunications sector has witnessed an exponential development in sub-Saharan Africa over the past two decades. The current level and scope of access to mobile and internet services is in contrast with the situation in the 1990s, when the sector was characterized by limited access to telecommunications services, poor services, and monopolies. Mobile network has progressively replaced fixed network making mobile communication technologies more accessible. The progressive opening of the telecommunications sector in sub-Saharan Africa in the course of the 1990s is not an isolated phenomenon. It is rather part of a larger process of liberalizing key economic sectors which used to be controlled by the respective States. The wave of macroeconomic reforms in the form of structural adjustment programs initiated by lending institutions (IMF and World Bank) in sub-Saharan Africa did not spare the telecommunications sector. The negotiations which were initiated during the Uruguay Round and led to the WTO also concerned the opening up of telecommunications markets in developing countries and allowing more FDI[24] into the sector. Developed countries, especially the United States, pushed for more access to the telecommunications markets of developing countries.

However, it was not until 1996 that principles on the access to telecommunications markets were agreed upon at the WTO. Such principles were laid down in a reference paper[25] which put forward safeguards for market access and fair competition of new entrants in the telecommunications market. Those principles were especially important in the process of opening up the telecommunications market of developing countries which used to be dominated by monopoly operators.[26] It was observed that with more competition and increasing access of international companies in the sector, there was improvement in the access and quality of telecommunications services. Despite the presence of state-owned companies in the telecommunications sector in Africa, the market is still dominated by multinational companies.[27] Yet, state involvement and the control of key segments of the telecommunications sectors by means of regulation measures are still present in many

---

[24] For discussion of the evolution of the telecommunication services in the WTO, see Marco Bronckers and Pierre Larouche, 'A Review of the WTO Regime for Telecommunication Services', in Kern Alexander and Mads Andenas (eds.), *The World Trade Organization and Trade in Services* (Brill, 2007), 319–79.

[25] World Trade Organization, reference paper, at: www.wto.org/english/tratop_e/serv_e/telecom_e/ tel23_e.htm; principles agreed on relate to: competitive safeguards, interconnection, universal service, allocation, and use of scarce resources. For discussion of the core principle of the reference paper, see Bronckers and Larouche, 'Review of the WTO Regime', 330–47; Boutheina Guermazi, exploring the reference paper on regulatory principles, at: www.wto.org/english/tratop_e/serv_e/telecom_e/work shop_dec04_e/guermazi_referencepaper.doc

[26] World Trade Organization, reference paper, at: www.wto.org/english/tratop_e/serv_e/telecom_e/ tel23_e.htm, 331.

[27] See Rachel Alemu, *Promoting Competition in the Telecommunication Markets of sub-Saharan Countries through Liberalization: An Analysis of the Regulatory Framework in Uganda* (Springer, 2018).

African countries. For instance, access to the markets for mobile and internet services is subject to obtaining a license from the state. Access to spectrum is strongly regulated. States still hold interest in the sectors through state-owned enterprises. As a result, the telecommunications sector in sub-Saharan Africa swings back and forth between an increasing openness and a strong regulatory framework. This has far-reaching implications in the process of creating competitive markets in the telecommunications sector.

7.3.2 *Access to Telecommunications Technologies, Entrepreneurship, and Growth*

The development of the telecommunications market in sub-Saharan Africa is of course a very welcome development. Access to telecommunications technologies is key to development. This is especially true in the area of the digital economy where telecommunications technologies such as internet and mobile communication play a key role. Positive links have been observed between access to telecommunications technologies, productivity, and growth.[28] Mobile network plays an increasing role in facilitating access to telephone and internet services. As shown in Figure 7.1, mobile market penetration rate in sub-Saharan Africa reached 80 percent between 2000 and 2008. This highlights the exponential development of the mobile market.

A recent World Bank study found that a 10 percent mobile phone penetration in developing countries would lead to a 4.2 percent increase in productivity.[29] There is a significant potential for mobile broadband to become a driver of sustainable economic growth and job creation in Africa.[30] In addition to helping to boost productivity, new business models are being created based on the telecommunications services. Hence, mobile telecommunications services have a positive impact on both consumers and businesses.[31] This is especially true in the financial services. Access to financial services is a challenge for consumers and small businesses in sub-Saharan Africa.

The share of mobile money account holder in sub-Saharan Africa is higher than in the rest of the world as shown in Figure 7.2.

Thus, for the benefit of the consumers and small businesses, there is a need to make access to financial services more accessible. Access to mobile technology is making access to financial services easier for the consumers. A success story that has been praised and which attracted lot of attention is the M-Peas payment system

---

[28] See Hopestone Kayiska Chavula, 'Telecommunications Development and economic growth in Africa' (2013) 19(1) *Information Technology for Development* 5.

[29] World Bank Group, 'Breaking Down Barriers: Unlocking Africa's Potential through Vigorous Competition Policy' (2016) 90, at: http://documents.worldbank.org/curated/en/243171467232051787/Breaking-down-barriers-unlocking-Africas-potential-through-vigorous-competition-policy

[30] Ibid., 92.

[31] Ibid.

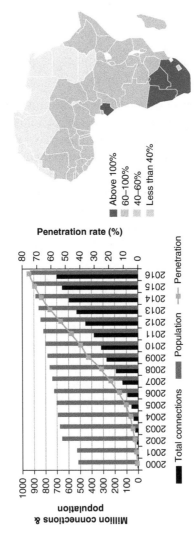

FIGURE 7.1 Mobile market penetration rate in sub-Saharan Africa
Source: Wireless Intelligence

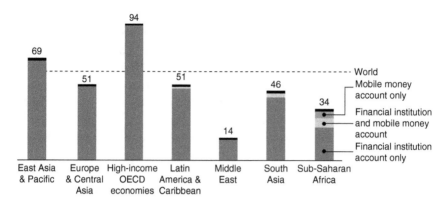

FIGURE 7.2 Sub-Saharan Africa has world's largest share of mobile money accounts adults with an account (%), 2014
Source: Global Findex database

developed by Vodacom in Kenya.[32] M-Peas subscribers can, by using their cell phone, deposit money in their account as well as send and receive money; they are thus able to make financial transactions without the need to have a traditional bank account with a financial institution.[33] This business model not only allows many to have access to financial transactions, but also increases competition for established financial institutions.[34] The success of such business model is guaranteed by access to mobile telecommunications technologies. In the M-Peas case, the support provided by financial regulators during the initial stage, especially by the Central Bank of Kenya, was key to the success.[35]

This business model is beneficial to both entrepreneurs and consumers. For consumers, mobile banking allows access to financial transactions at lower costs,

[32] See, on the development of the M-Pesa, Nick Hughes and Susie Lonie, 'M-PESA: Mobile Money for the "Unbanked" Turning Cellphones into 24-Hours Tellers in Kenya' (winter–spring 2007) 2 *Innovations* 63.

[33] See Marion Mbogo, 'The Impact of Mobile Payments on the Success and Growth of Micro-Business: The Case of M-Pesa in Kenya' (2010) 2(1) *Journal of Language, Technology & Entrepreneurship in Africa* 182; the study stresses that "Micro-business enterprises in the developing world are increasingly deploying the use of mobile payments to enhance the quality of their services and increase growth." Convenience of the service, its accessibility, cost, and security features are among factors which encourage small businesses to use the service.

[34] See Amine Mansour, 'How Can Competition Law Enforcement in the Digital Economy Help in the Fight Against Poverty?', https://developingworldantitrust.com/2016/05/20/how-can-competition-law-enforcement-in-the-digital-economy-help-in-the-fight-against-poverty

[35] As pointed out, the regulatory authorities, especially the Central Bank of Kenya, give to Safaricom the leeway to design the service in a manner that fits the markets and the consumers, while putting safeguards aimed at protecting consumers. For instance all funds of the consumers have to be deposited in a regulated financial institution and the security features of the platform have been reviewed (Ignacio Mas and Dan Radcliffe, 'Mobile Payments Go Viral: M-Pesa in Kenya' (March 2010) 10–11, http://siteresources.worldbank.org/africaext/resources/258643–1271798012256/m-pesa_ke nya.pdf).

while for small entrepreneurs it helps to get access to relevant information about markets. Mobile banking is constantly increasing in sub-Saharan Africa as is the success of M-Peas. In West Africa, Orange has developed "orange money" with the same services as M-Peas. Tigo, the mobile branch of Millicom, has Tigo cash. Consumers with mobile money accounts are able to store money in their account, send and receive money, pay their bills by phone, and make various financial transactions. For the final consumers, access to those services is easy. It does not require a financial background check or opening a formal bank account. One only needs a phone a number.

A similar transfer service which is very popular and which competes with the traditional money transfer is "Wari."[36] Wari was established in Senegal and it is now present in many sub-Saharan Africa countries. Given the simplicity and convenience of the services, Wari is used far more frequently for money transfer than, for instance, Western Union or MoneyGram. It is a strong competitor to the more established international money transfer companies. The fact that there is a Wari shop on every street corner[37] makes the services very accessible to consumers and explains its success. Wari is developed and owned by local entrepreneurs and it is now present in more than one hundred countries. Mobile technology is also at the center of the service. Both the sender and the receiver need a cell phone in order to complete the transaction.

It has recently concluded a collaboration agreement with MasterCard in order to expand and offer more secured financial services to its customers.[38] Wari's CEO stated at the signing of the agreement:

> The partnership with Mastercard will provide us with the ability to boost digital payment acceptance in the markets that we operate. With the Mastercard experience in securing payments across the world, customers can rest assured that their payment, whether done by card or mobile, will be secure. This alliance reinforces our commitment to provide to our partners and users, access to easy to use digital solutions. The alliance between Wari and Mastercard is an important milestone in making financial inclusion a reality for all Africans.[39]

Wari is an interesting case on how fast the financial services supported by the telecommunications services in developing in Africa. Wari is founded in Senegal by a local entrepreneur. Its success and reach go far beyond Senegal financial services, and are becoming an important part of the business strategy of mobile phone operators.

Business models based on telecommunications technologies are developing at a very fast speed for the benefit of the consumers in developed countries. It is

---

[36] See www.wari.com; Wari offers different services, including sending and receiving money, paying bills, etc., which are very popular and largely used by the population.

[37] Wari claim to have more than 500,000 outlets worldwide (ibid.).

[38] www.itnewsafrica.com/2016/12/wari-and-mastercard-to-deliver-smart-digital-payment-solutions

[39] ibid.

interesting to notice a close link between telecommunications services, especially mobile technologies, and financial services. Financial services are increasingly based on mobile technologies. Mobile banking and mobile money transfer are becoming common in sub-Saharan Africa. This development has great potential for countries which witness an increase in the development of mobile technologies. An increased closeness has been noticed between the mobile service market and the financial services markets. A strategic move has recently been made by the acquisition of Wari of a mobile phone company. A high-profile transaction in Senegal with the acquisition of a money transfer service company, Wari of a mobile phone service provider Tigo is a sign of a stronger bond between financial services and telecommunications technologies, in particular mobile phone services.

7.4 DEVELOPMENT OF THE TELECOMMUNICATIONS SECTOR IN SUB-SAHARAN AFRICA

Sub-Saharan Africa countries have undergone a tremendous development in telecommunications services, internet, and the mobile markets. A recent report of the World Bank group estimates that Africa has experienced the fastest growth worldwide in telecommunications services.[40] There has been a steady increase in the penetration of the mobile technology, and revenues from mobile services have reached approximately 3 percent of GDP. Internet access through mobile technologies also increases very rapidly, thereby giving internet access to a large part of the population.[41] The World Bank Group estimates that by 2025, internet access impact could account for 10 percent of the GDP compared to 1 percent in 2013.[42]

Despite the steady development in the telecommunications services in Africa, the quality of the services remains poor, and the affordability of telecommunications services is still an issue. Sub-Saharan Africa countries have the highest prices for mobile and fixed broadband services, and an average mobile phone owner spends 3 percent of his monthly income on mobile services.[43] The realization of the potential benefits of telecommunications services for consumers and businesses may be hindered by market failures obstructing access. The structure of the telecommunications markets and lack of competitiveness therein may explain the high prices of telecommunications services in sub-Saharan Africa. Making telecommunications markets more competitive may be a solution to making telecommunications services accessible at affordable prices. A better understanding of the market

[40] World Bank Group, 'Breaking Down Barriers', 91.
[41] Ibid.
[42] Ibid.
[43] Ibid., 90.

dynamic in the telecommunications sector would help formulate policies which make the markets more competitive.

7.5 COMPETITION IN THE TELECOMMUNICATIONS MARKET

This section builds on the findings of the Word Bank report on the characteristics of the telecommunications markets in Africa. The report explains the market structures and the competition dynamics. Key elements of the report will be explained. This constitutes the basis of our core analysis which discusses the issues of regulation and competition as two approaches to combine in order to build competitive markets.

The following features can be identified as characterizing the market of telecommunications market in Africa.

7.5.1 *Structural Characteristics of the Telecommunications Market*

7.5.1.1 The Input Market: High Investment Costs and Scarcity of Resources

High fixed costs for new entrants and the need to achieve economies of scale characterize the investment in the telecommunications sector, especially in the fixed phone services. Incumbents that have invested in building the infrastructure for which they enjoy a dominant position may be reluctant to grant access to new incumbents wishing to enter the market. This is especially relevant for land-line phone and broadband internet. Access to the infrastructure of the incumbent, which can be analyzed as an essential facility, would be crucial for potential competitors in order to enter the market and offer competing services. The owner of the infrastructure, which could be considered a dominant wholesaler, may limit access to its infrastructure, prevent new entrants, and thereby limit competition. How to regulate access to telecommunications infrastructures is therefore an essential point that competition and regulatory authorities have to deal with. However, in the context of sub-Saharan Africa the progressive development of mobile networks to replace fixed networks makes the issue of access to facility less of a problem.

Whether a competition approach or an intervening regulatory approach is more appropriate in order to foster access to essential telecommunications infrastructure is relevant from a policy perspective. This is especially true since it is not economically sound that each new entrant builds its own infrastructure. Although wireless technology may temper the need to access to infrastructures, access problem to infrastructure is still an issue in Africa.[44]

Similarly, access to input market and scarcity of resources characterize the mobile telecommunications market. The most problematic issue in the mobile

---

[44]   Ibid., 93.

telecommunications industry is how to efficiently allocate limited spectrum. Limited availability of spectrum is a structural barrier to entry in the mobile telecommunications services. The way spectrum is assigned impacts competition in the whole sale and retail market of telecommunications services. As pointed out, "given that spectrum is an inherently scarce resource, how it is managed can set the competition dynamics of the market; sector regulators must therefore establish and administer spectrum policy to achieve maximum competition benefits."[45] From a policy perspective, it is very relevant to identify what criteria should be considered when assigning spectrum and which obligations should fulfill the beneficiary of the spectrum. Whether to assign spectrum on a competition basis or on a discretionary basis is a policy question which should be decided from a policy perspective, taking into account the need to create competitive markets for the benefit of the consumers. Building new infrastructure in the telecommunications sector requires substantial investment and the returns on investments and economies of scale are only possible in a long-term perspective. Promoting competition on infrastructure might lead to lower cost and lower prices. However, it may affect economies of scale and thereby negatively impact investment incentives. Hence, markets of infrastructure might not be able to support too many competitors in order to produce economies of scale. Regulators should take these aspects into account when regulating the input markets. The input market should be open enough and competitive enough to allow new entrants. Further, in order to achieve economies of scale and ensure return on investment, the input markets should not accommodate more competitors than necessary.

7.5.1.2 Market Concentration and Network Effects

The telecommunications sector is also characterized by natural monopolies and high levels of concentration which, in turn, may lead to network effects in the retail segments of the market. In contrast with the high investment required to build telecommunications infrastructures, especially for fixed networks, mobile networks require less investment and are easier to replicate. As a consequence, entry into the mobile industry is highly regulated. The issuing of a license by the competent authorities, which comes with a number of obligations, is often required in order to operate. Regulation therefore plays a relevant role and shapes the market structure of the mobile industry. This is done through both a licensing system and a system of allocation and assignment of spectrum.[46] The tight regulatory control of entry leads to the existence of a limited number of players in the sectors, and thereby to monopoly or oligopoly situations.

---

[45] Ibid., 95.
[46] Ibid.

Hence, the trend in the mobile industry is to have between two to five operators.[47] Such market structure with high levels of concentration may lead to anticompetitive issues. Hence, concentrated markets with a limited number of players may lead to abuses of unilateral market power. Issues of access to a given network, especially for small operators, as well as interconnection and network effects can also be a problem. An operator with significant market power can, for instance, restrict access on its network in order to protect and reinforce its market power. The dominant operator may restrict interconnection, set high prices for termination rates and put restrictions on the quantity and quality of information required by its competitors. This issue is especially true with regard to pricing of on-net and off-net calls. Pricing of termination rates may lead to reinforcement of unilateral market power of the dominant operator. Regulation can help address this issue and help avoid market failures.

7.5.2 *Competition-Related Issues That Affect the Telecommunications Market*

A number of relevant findings have been made by the recent World Bank report on the main factors that characterize the mobile market in Africa which affect the competition dynamic. I am going to summarize them as information, as they are relevant to understanding the competition-related issues in the mobile market. They also provide relevant background information on the policy question of whether regulation and/or competition is more suitable in the mobile market.

7.5.2.1 Finding 1: Concentrated Markets and High Presence of Pan-Regional Economic Groups

The WBG report finds that the mobile market in Africa is highly concentrated and pan-regional groups dominate the sector. A result of the report is that "in 2015, mobile markets in Africa included seven monopolies, 11 duopolies and 20 economies with three competitors, and 19 with at least four suppliers."[48] The high market concentration confirms the highly regulated character of the mobile industry with limited competition on the input market. The same players compete on the main mobile markets in Africa. Five pan-regional groups (Orange, MTN group, Bharti Airtel, Etisalat Group, Vodafone/Vodacom) are present in forty-two economies. Taken together, they concentrate 64 percent of total connections in Africa. Those groups, according to the report, "are becoming more symmetric over time, while holding their total Africa share constant."[49] This determinant of the mobile market is not specific to the mobile sector in Africa. From an international perspective, entry into the mobile market is also regulated and not more than five operators compete in

---

[47] Ibid.
[48] Ibid., 100.
[49] Ibid., 103.

a country. The presence of regional groups could positively impact the creation of cross-border networks that connect neighboring countries.[50] It may, at the same time, threaten competition at the national level, especially for national mobile operators.[51]

7.5.2.2 Finding 2: Multimarket Contacts between Suppliers

As a consequence of the oligopoly situation in the mobile market and the asymmetric presence of the pan-regional groups, the report finds that "there is significant multimarket contact between the five largest telecommunications groups across Africa." This finding raises the issue of potential anticompetitive practices among the five dominant pan-regional groups. It also highlights the need to address the competition-related issues in the telecommunications sector from a regional perspective. In this regard, the report stresses the importance of a regional perspective: "There is a need for regional coordination to address the potential anticompetitive effects of the multimarket telecommunications sector. These include tacit coordination across the region and unilateral practices conducted by the same group in different countries."[52]

Dealing with potential anticompetitive issues can be done better at the regional level and by a regional competition authority. The regulatory dimension should also be dealt with, while taking into account the market power and the presence of the group at the regional level, especially if the group operates in a regional market under the principle of free movement of goods. For instance, when allocating a new spectrum, the market share of the group at the regional level should be considered. This would allow the regulatory authority to control the market power of the company and encourage the entry of competing actors.

7.5.2.3 Finding 3: Lack of Use of Competitive Mechanisms for Spectrum Assignment

The way spectrum is assiged may impact the structure of the mobile market. The report shows that assignments of new spectrum in Africa are not made with the use of pro-competitive mechanisms. Countries use different methods for assigning spectrum. The report concludes that "there is a need to adopt an approach to spectrum pricing and assignment that incentivizes efficient use of scare public resources, for instance through auction and other competitive selection methods."[53] How assignment of spectrum should be regulated will be dealt with in the following section.

---

[50] Alemu, *Promoting Competition.*
[51] Ibid.
[52] World Bank Group, 'Breaking Down Barriers', 106.
[53] Ibid., 107.

7.5.2.4 Finding 4: State Participation in the Provision of Mobile Services

The mobile sector is highly regulated. States still play an important role, despite the move toward injecting more private investment in the sector. States can be market actors through state-owned mobile companies. States also influence the market structure and competition through allocation of spectrum and the regulation of termination rates. Inefficient regulation of termination rates or uncompetitive allocation of spectrum could lead to market failures and thereby negatively impact the final consumer. Hence, while regulation may foster competition in the mobile sector, inefficient regulation may hinder the creation of competitive markets. Various government regulations may restrict competition in the mobile markets. For instance, inefficient spectrum regulation or inadequate regulation of termination rates may negatively impact competition on the market.

7.6 COMPETITION IN THE TELECOMMUNICATIONS (MOBILE) SECTOR: BETWEEN COMPETITION AND REGULATION

Two regulatory approaches coexist in the mobile sector. They are complementary legal tools that make the mobile market open and competitive. The input market is highly regulated by the government control which authorizes the entry of new competitors. Competition on the downstream market is policed by competition authorities applying "traditional" competition law tools in order to protect competition for the benefit of consumers. Government's *ex ante* regulatory intervention on the input market in the mobile sector may have ambivalent effects on competition. While regulation may produce efficient outcomes, in terms of economy of scale, it may also affect competition. Regulating a liberalized market might sound contradictory. However, the telecommunications sector exhibits characteristics which requires a balance between regulation and competition it order to avoid market failures and foster competition.

Two aspects will be discussed in order to illustrate the ambivalent effects of regulation in the mobile markets: the *ex ante* regulation of the input market and the *ex post* regulation of termination rates. But, first, a brief overview of the characteristics of the telecommunications sector that command the regulation of the market.

7.6.1 *Regulation, and the Characteristics of the Telecommunications Sector*

The telecommunications sector exhibits specific characteristics that command combining regulation with openness to competition in order to make the market open and competitive. The telecommunications sector is characterized by natural monopolies, network externalities and high switching costs which command regulatory interventions in order to avoid potential abuses of market power.[54]

---

[54] See Alemu, *Promoting Competition.*

The telecom sector was deemed to be a natural monopoly which used to be exercised by the state before its progressive opening to competition. Although the sector was progressively opened to competition, entry into the market is still subject to regulatory measures. Entry into the sector is still legislation based. This entry restriction, from an economic point of view, is justified by the need to create economies of scale, as the sector may only support a limited number of competitors. While there is a progressive opening to competition, scarcity of resources (scarcity of spectrum) in the input market requires an efficient allocation of spectrum.

From a regulatory perspective, there is a need to balance competition with necessity to ensure return on investments. Additional public policy concerns such as the need to ensure universal access to telecommunications technologies require regulatory intervention. Network effects which give a competitive edge to the incumbent are another characteristic of the telecommunications sector that requires regulatory intervention.[55] Absent regulatory intervention, for instance mandatory interconnection, incumbents would exercise their market power by refusing inter-connection. As a consequence, new entrants would not be able to effectively enter the market. As we shall see, termination rates should also be regulated. Switching costs[56] may be very high absent regulatory measures that make the costumers switch very easily. High switching costs create network effects and reduce the dynamism of the market. Firms would not innovate and consumers would not easily switch to another operator. Regulatory measures that allow consumer to easily switch would foster price competition and competition in innovation among operators.

7.6.2 Ex ante *Regulation of Input Market: Allocation of Spectrum, Access, and Interconnection*

The way spectrum is allocated and managed by regulatory bodies, for instance, may affect the structure of the markets and competition. Spectrum allocation is of paramount importance in the input market in the mobile sector. Its inefficient allocation may affect competition. Inefficient spectrum allocation favoring the incumbent which already had a dominant position in the mobile sector may affect competition by reinforcing the incumbent's dominant position. Spectrum alloca-tion rules which favors the already dominant incumbent and lack of regulation of trading and leasing of spectrum may reinforce dominance and lead to market foreclosure for new competitors.[57]

When imposing conditions in telecom licensing or concession, the need to ensure full access to telecommunications services should be balanced with the need to make the investment profitable for the mobile companies. Rules that impose geographical coverage, especially in areas which are not dense enough to be

---

[55]   Ibid.
[56]   Ibid.
[57]   World Bank Group, 'Breaking Down Barriers', 107.

profitable for the company, may have the effect of limiting entry of new competitors. In such situations, it would be advisable to create incentives for the company in order to ensure full coverage of areas which are not dense in term of population and attractive.

Allocation of spectrum is regulated according to different models. While some countries allow full competition, others allocate spectrum on a discriminatory basis. As pointed out:

> in many countries, spectrum is assigned administratively to operators that already in the market or to the largest or state operator, as in Cameroon and Rwanda. Tenders in mobile markets are sometimes designated without considering competition implications. There is a need to protect consumers against accumulation of spectrum and to provide for safeguards against concentration of spectrum in the hand of a few players, while considering efficient use of spectrum.[58]

In Kenya, the most efficient band has been assigned to the already dominant operator. Likewise, in Senegal the license for 4G is assigned to the dominant operator Orange, giving it a first-mover advantage.

It seems that spectrum allocation models used in sub-Saharan Africa are not competitive. The World Bank report concludes that there is a lack of use of competition mechanisms when allocating spectrum in Africa. So far, Nigeria is the only country in Africa which has used spectrum auctions when assigning new spectrum.[59] Using pro-competitive mechanisms when allocating new spectrum, such as spectrum auctions, would lead to efficient and pro-competitive results.

Access to and interconnection of different networks is key to the well-functioning of the market in the mobile sector. Mutual access to the networks of competitors should also be regulated in order to avoid market failures which could affect the consumers. Mutual access to network of competing operators should be designed in a way that they are non-discriminatory and cost-oriented fees. Conditions of access should be spelled out clearly by designing and implementing an effective access policy. The issue of access and interconnection is closely linked to how termination rates are regulated.

7.6.3 Ex post *Regulation: Termination Rates and Competition*

Regulation of termination rates between different mobile companies has implications on competition on the mobile markets. Its efficient regulation may allow access and interconnection between consumers in different operators at an affordable price. Given the monopoly each operation enjoys in its network and the bottleneck it creates for other operators wishing to access the networks, it is crucial that termination rates are regulated in order to avoid market failures. Without such a regulation, mobile operators may charge high termination rates, which, consequently, limit

---

[58]   ibid.
[59]   The remaining countries use a first-come, first-served basis to allocate new spectrum.

interconnection as well as the access to competing networks. Due to the high termination rates, the final consumer may decide to stay with the dominant operator. This may lead to club or network effects with consumers choosing to stay with the dominant operator. Undue price asymmetry and price discrimination between on-net and off-net calls may lead to the consumer's de facto entrapment in the mobile operator which offers the best rates for on-net calls. A dominant operator may, for instance, offer very cheap rates for on-net calls and charge high rates for off-net calls. In the absence of regulation of termination rates, a consumer is likely to stay on net. Moreover, consumers could also shift to the dominant operator which offers cheaper rates, thereby reinforcing its dominant position. It is therefore important to regulate termination rates not only in order to ensure interconnections between different networks, but also in order to avoid compromising the market structure through the reinforcement of the dominant position of the already dominant operator. Hence, price discrimination resulting from the lack of regulation of termination rates between mobile operators may have the effect of inciting mobile operators to call the sub-scribers of the same operators and have consumer to switch to the bigger operator in order to benefit from the cheaper prices of the dominant network. Switching to the bigger operator may lead to foreclosure effects on the smaller operators.

Inefficient regulation of termination rates is an issue in the mobile sector in Africa. High termination rates may also prompt consumer to have a SIM card for each operator, which they use when making calls on the respective network. The phenomenon of multiple SIM card ownership is widespread in Africa. It may even explain the high penetration rate of prepaid services in the mobile sector in Africa. The phenomenon of multiple SIM card ownership may be the result of high termination rates in Africa. Hence, high termination rates are still very common in Africa, compared to OECD countries.[60]

A regulatory approach of fixing termination rates which protect competition and the final consumers against high termination rates is necessary. A regulatory intervention which would decrease high termination rates and allow for more interconnection and competition between operators is particularly necessary in Africa in order to maximize the benefits of the high rates of penetration in the mobile sector.

7.7 THE INSTITUTIONAL DIMENSION

Questions arise as to which aspects are better dealt with by competition authorities and which should be dealt with by regulatory authorities. Regulatory authorities are created in different sectors. They coexist with competition authorities. While the competences of the competition authorities are general, the regulatory authorities have their attribution limited to specific issues in their sector. In the telecoms sector, the electricity sector, and the banking sector, regulators are created with the aim of

[60] World Bank Group, 'Breaking Down Barriers', 110.

overseeing specific aspects of the industry. Public policy objectives, in addition to protecting competition, justify such an approach.

Competition law authorities should deal with practices affecting the market. Regulatory authorities should deal with aspects such as interconnection obligations, quality requirement, and setting termination rates.

Also, competition authorities might need to closely collaborate with regulatory authorities when dealing with anticompetitive practices in the telecommunications sector. Some countries have taken this approach while other recognize the regulatory authority with the competence to deal with anticompetitive practices in the telecommunications sector. Although one could argue that such an approach promotes specialization since the regulatory authority is more familiar with the competition-related issues of its own sector, it is not unlimited. The regulator is not an enforcer with general power such as the competition authority. It does not necessarily have the competence to deal with anticompetitive practices in the sector, taking into account the actual impact in the sector. Competing enforcement powers of two competition authorities is also an issue.

A more efficient approach is to recognize the competition authority with the competence to deal with anticompetitive practices in the telecommunications sector and establish collaboration mechanism between the two authorities.

7.8 CONCLUSION

The development of the telecommunications services, especially the access to mobile communication and internet, is a welcomed in sub-Saharan Africa. It has allowed the emergence of new business models for the benefit of consumers. Access to mobile banking services and access to information are more democratic. In addition to inefficient regulation, anticompetitive practices may affect the well-functioning of the market. Market power on the upstream market due to anticompetitive allocation of spectrum may, for instance, affect competition in the downstream market and thereby affect the final consumers.

The potential of the telecommunications sector to contribute to growth can only be materialized with balanced combination of regulation and openness to competition. While it is important to regulate some aspects such as spectrum allocation, interconnection, and termination rates, it is crucial to police potential anticompetitive practices. In this regard, the regional dimension is of paramount importance. The telecommunications sector is dominated by pan-regional multinational companies which are present in different national markets. Taking a regional approach when regulating the sector and policing anticompetitive practices is therefore very important. The emergence of functioning regional trade agreements with a regional competition law framework is a welcome development in this regard. Regional competition authorities should pay more attention to the telecommunications sector.

8

Competition Law Prescriptions and Competitive Outcomes

Insights from Southern and East Africa

Simon Roberts

8.1 INTRODUCTION

Competition law has been vigorously promoted around the world with the adoption of competition laws being much remarked upon. There have been important debates, led by Eleanor Fox, on different models and possible convergence.[1] In East and Southern Africa, most countries have adopted competition laws in the past twenty years. There has also been a push to adopt guidelines for merger evaluation, restrictive practices (including cartels) and abuse of dominance. These have generally been done by 'international experts' and provide a picture of broad convergence on paper, albeit with the playing out of USA and EU differences, depending on the funding and the expert.

However, there has been relatively little comparative analysis of the interplay of policies and competition in practice as compared with the establishment of institutions and adoption of guidelines. Indeed, the latter have often been seen as outcomes in their own right. This chapter seeks to understand how competitive markets evolve and the challenges for competition authorities in nurturing this evolution.

There is a broad consensus that we want to foster competition which is based on investing in productive capacity and creating products responsive to consumers' preferences. We want markets which are open to participants and reward effort and creativity, while recognising that economies of scale and scope, and the size and duration of investments required for research and development, mean large firms are critical to economies. What is the role for competition law here?

In enforcement, we seek to distinguish beneficial from harmful conduct, with the laws specifying how these effects should be distinguished in only the broadest terms. The tests aim to weigh the probability and costs of type 1 and type 2 errors, where type 1 errors are false positives (finding harm where there is none), and type 2 errors are

---

[1] See, for example, E. Fox, 'Competition, Development and Regional Integration: In Search of a Competition Law Fit for Developing Countries', in J. Drexl et al. (eds.), *Competition Policy and Regional Integration in Developing Countries* (Edward Elgar, 2012).

the failure to identify, sanction and deter harmful conduct where it *is* taking place. It is trite to observe that the probability and costs of these errors vary with country conditions. For example, higher barriers to entry mean the costs of under-enforcement are higher. The obvious implication is that countries should not necessarily have the same standards and onus in applying even identical legal provisions. In this context, the USA and the EU are far outliers in terms of their market characteristics being, by comparison with almost all other jurisdictions, incredibly large markets. They are outliers in many other ways also, such as in the history of their institutions and development of their laws. For example, the mandatory treble damages in the USA has very substantial implications for the balancing of possible under and over enforcement.

Most developing countries have, however, faced a transplant of laws, no matter what has been done to 'localise' them in appearance. It is natural to draw on experience from other places. The challenge is to craft a market-oriented approach to economic development which takes into account the real characteristics of these economies.

For African economies with which I am concerned here, these characteristics include the high levels of inequality along with the rapid growth since around the year 2000.

It is important to articulate and give effect to competitive markets which support the building of local productive capacities and wider participation. If this cannot be done then competition law and the authorities will be sidelined. They will risk being viewed as irrelevant, something put in place simply to keep donors happy while the policy action happens elsewhere. Alternatively, the rules may simply be bypassed through corruption to skew market outcomes and secure opportunities.[2]

This chapter draws on a range of research done in recent years in East and Southern Africa to consider the nature and extent of competition in practice, and the role, if any, played by competition law and policy. It starts with analysis of two commodities, cement and fertiliser, which can be considered the 'bread and butter' of competition enforcement. These are relatively homogeneous products with concentrated markets and high incentives for firms to collude. Indeed, cartels in Southern Africa in cement and fertiliser have been uncovered by competition authorities. Second, I draw on work at the other end of the spectrum in innovative markets for services in telecommunications and finance described under the heading of mobile money. East Africa, specifically Kenya and Tanzania, are global leaders in the development of these services. Network effects favour the first-mover implying it can become dominant and wield substantial market power. Third, I reflect on work relating to barriers to entry in South Africa. The chapter draws

---

[2] This is arguably what has been happening in South Africa. See Public Protector of South Africa, *State of Capture* (2016).

on the insights from these three areas to identify the main elements of a forward-looking agenda.

8.2 COMPETITION IN COMMODITIES: FERTILISER AND CEMENT

Fertiliser and cement are important commodities in their own right. Fertiliser is the main input for commercial agriculture, and cement is critical for the expansion of housing and infrastructure. These sectors are central to most African countries' growth. The nature of competition issues in these markets point to important challenges for competition law enforcement in African countries.

8.2.1 Fertiliser[3]

There are three main plant nutrients provided by fertilisers, namely nitrogen, potassium (in the form of potash) and phosphate. A few main forms of fertiliser dominate world trade and production. Nitrogenous fertilisers are the most important with the main product being urea. This is produced in large, energy-intensive industrial plants. Other ammonia-based nitrogenous fertilisers also require cheap energy and large-scale production such as calcium ammonium nitrate and diammonium phosphate (DAP). These are normally produced where there are sources of natural gas. Phosphate and potash are mineral products with production depending on the naturally occurring endowment.

The only substantial producer of fertiliser in Southern and East Africa is South Africa. It is a producer of both ammonium nitrate-based fertilisers and phosphate fertiliser.[4] It is still a large net importer of nitrogenous fertilisers, mainly in the form of urea. The market demand in Southern and East African countries is thus met largely by importers. On the face of it, this means that barriers to the entry of new (import) suppliers should be low. However, the scale required for economic shipping, and the logistics and transport infrastructure for local distribution, mean that in practice there are only a few major suppliers in each country. Markets may still be contestable, where a deviation from cost-reflective prices will see a new entrant readily able to take advantage of the opportunity presented.

In practice, it appears as if outcomes have been far from competitive. And, the high prices of fertiliser, and its importance for agricultural production, have led

---

[3] This section draws primarily from P. Ncube, S. Roberts and T. Vilakazi, 'Study of Competition in the Road Freight Sector in the SADC Region – Case Study of Fertilizer Transport and Trading in Zambia, Tanzania and Malawi', CCRED Working Paper 3/2015; P. Ncube, S. Roberts and T. Vilakazi, 'Regulation and Rivalry in Transport and Supply in the Fertilizer Industry in Malawi, Tanzania and Zambia', in S. Roberts (ed.), *Competition in Africa* (HSRC Press, 2016).

[4] Minjingu in Kenya is a small producer of phosphate fertiliser. Other producers of fertilisers are blenders from imported fertiliser components rather than manufacturers.

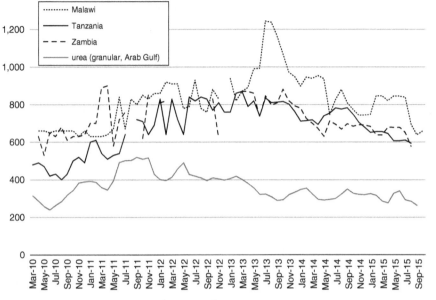

FIGURE 8.1 Urea prices (average $/ton retail across countries)
Source: Amitsa and World Bank

governments and donors to subsidise fertiliser supply through an array of programmes.

Fertiliser has cost substantially more in African countries than benchmark world prices.[5] Here we reflect the prices for the nitrogenous fertiliser product of urea on a free-on-board (fob) basis in the Arab Gulf with the average retail prices in Malawi, Zambia and Tanzania (Figure 8.1).[6] The Arab Gulf prices are most relevant for actual supplies to these countries through the ports of Dar es Salaam (in Tanzania) and Durban (in South Africa), however, the prices are similar to those quoted for shipments from the Black Sea and from the USA, prices which are available to farmers in Eastern Europe and North America, with overland transport costs added.

In 2010, prices in Tanzania were around $100/t more than in the Arab Gulf, while prices in Malawi and Zambia were around $200/t to $300/t more, or roughly double the fob prices. From 2011 the gap increased substantially although the direct costs of sea and land transport have not increased. It appears as if the increase in prices initially tracked international prices, but when international prices came down, the local prices remained at higher levels. It meant that in 2012 through to 2014 prices in all three countries were around $400/t more than the fob prices and, in the case of Malawi, for some of the time prices were substantially higher.

---

[5] World Bank, *Boosting Competition in African Markets* (World Bank, 2016).
[6] A very similar picture is given by diammonium phosphate (DAP) prices. Urea and DAP are the two most important products in these countries.

Are the prices the result of uncompetitive markets? Almost certainly. Are they the result of anticompetitive conduct? Not necessarily so.

As a landlocked importing country, prices in Zambia would be expected to be higher than coastal countries such as Tanzania, and similar to prices in its neighbour, Malawi. This is what is observed in 2010. In the later years, however, we see prices in Zambia which are in line with, or lower, than those in Tanzania. There has been cartel conduct which was uncovered in Zambia in 2012.[7] The lower prices in 2014 and 2015 are also a result of a new entrant and changes in the procurement processes to supply the government's farmer support programme. Prices in Zambia, however, remained around $300/t higher than the international benchmark in 2015.

Against the Zambian prices, those in Malawi and Tanzania certainly do not seem competitive but no cartel conduct has been identified. A competitive cost build-up suggests that in 2014 sea freight should have been no more than $50/t with offloading, port charges, storage, bagging and an importer margin adding another $80/t at most.[8] This means that the cost price ex-warehouse for bagged fertiliser should have been around $130/t above the fob price. Inland transport to important agricultural producing areas were estimated at $50/t while retailer margins and other costs should at most contribute another $110/t meaning a retail price of some $160/t above the ex-warehouse price.[9] This took into account actual costs of transport, given the existing inefficiencies, as well as reported margins. Observed prices in Tanzania were some $100-$150/t (around 20 per cent) higher than the price calculated from cost and margin build-ups.

A number of factors underpin the higher prices in Tanzania. A combination of restrictions on transport, storage and trading have supported incumbents. In addition, the fertiliser subsidy programme had been increased in value to provide an effective floor price above the competitive price level. In terms of the overall market, a few large firms dominate fertiliser supply in Tanzania, led by Yara. Control of offloading and bagging facilities at the port are critical also. High levels of concentration have gone along with high prices and margins in fertiliser trading after accounting for transport costs.

In Malawi fertiliser prices have been approximately $200/ton higher than in Zambia, which can be explained by a combination of factors, including high domestic transport rates and fertiliser price distortions caused by the subsidy programme. Domestic transport rates in Malawi are between $0.13 and $0.14 per ton per kilometre, around double what rates should be.[10] Part of this is due to higher costs

7 www.zambia-weekly.com/media/zambia_weekly_2013_-_wk_38.pdf. See also Competition and Consumer Protection Commission (CCPC) of Zambia, *Competition and Consumer Protection News* (April–June 2013) 6.
8 Ncube et al., 'Study of Competition'; Ncube et al., 'Regulation and Rivalry'.
9 Ncube et al., 'Study of Competition', table 5.
10 T. Vilakazi and A. Paelo, 'Understanding Intra-Regional Transport: Competition in Road Transportation between Malawi, Mozambique, South Africa, Zambia, and Zimbabwe', UNU-WIDER Working Paper 2017/46.

and the substantial lack of return loads within Malawi. It also appears that local associations have a strong hold over transport in the country.

The uncompetitive markets are therefore due to a combination of factors. While anticompetitive conduct is likely to be part of the picture it is not clear how effective enforcement by national authorities can be. In addition to the cartel identified in Zambia, two further cartels which impacted on these countries highlight the challenges. The South African Competition Commission uncovered a cartel in nitrogenous fertiliser between Sasol, Omnia and Yara which ran until the mid 2000s.[11] Various bodies were used by market participants to coordinate the sharing of information which had the effect of increasing transparency and the ability to monitor competitor behaviour (and possible deviations from the arrangement) in the market. These bodies included the Nitrogen Balance Committee (NBC), the Import Planning Committee (IPC), the Export Club and Fertiliser Society of South Africa of which the main members were the primary fertiliser companies.[12] By monitoring domestic market shares, as well as exports and imports of products, members could track market shares and the behaviour of competitors given the highly concentrated nature of the market. It is also important to note that there was an agreement on how list prices would be determined, through adding on agreed costs to the international benchmark prices to get local prices in different regions. It is highly likely that the arrangements affected other countries in Southern Africa , although it is difficult to see how their national authorities could have addressed them.

Fertiliser prices in African countries have also been affected by global arrangements in potash and phosphates, which are important alongside nitrogenous fertilisers such as urea. The arrangements include two export cartels which dominate the world potash market.[13] Between them, Canada and Russia account for 80 per cent of global potash reserves, with the three largest North American potash producers operating in the Canpotex joint marketing organisation and the three largest Russian and Belarusian potash producers in the BPC joint venture. Mark-ups from the international collusion in potash supply have been estimated for 2008 to 2012 at around 50 per cent to 63 per cent.[14]

[11]   G. Makhaya and S. Roberts, 'Expectations and outcomes – Considering Competition and Corporate Power in South Africa Under Democracy', *Review of African Political Economy* (2013) 138 556–71. The consent and settlement agreement between the Competition Commission and Sasol Chemical Industries Ltd relating to the cartel conduct was confirmed by the Competition Tribunal in June 2009.

[12]   See R. Das Nair and L. Mncube, 'The Role of Information Exchange in Facilitating Collusion: Insights from Selected Cases', in K. Moodaliyar and S. Roberts (eds.), *The Development of Competition Law and Economics in South Africa* (HSRC Press, 2012).

[13]   World Bank, *Boosting Competition*.

[14]   F. Jenny, 'Export Cartels in Primary Products: The Potash Case in Perspective', in S. Evenett and F. Jenny (eds.), *Trade, Competition and the Pricing of Commodities* (CEPR, 2012); H. Gnutzmann and P. Spiewanowski, 'Did the Fertilizer Cartel Cause the Food Crisis?', Beitrage zur Jahrestagung des Vereins fur Socialpolitik 2016: Demographischer Wandel – Session: International Trade and Development, No. A19-V2.

In phosphates, PhosChem is a USA Webb-Pomerene export cartel whose members include PotashCorp and Mosaic which are also members of Canpotex.[15] The other major source of phosphate fertiliser is OCP of Morocco which is a government-owned monopoly over phosphate mining in that country. Over three-quarters of global reserves of phosphate rock are located in Morocco and the Western Sahara.

8.2.2 *Cement*

Cement is the product perhaps most often associated with cartel conduct around the world. In Southern and East Africa, as in developing countries more generally, the local producers are affiliated with or are subsidiaries of large multinationals, of which the most significant are Lafarge and Holcim (now merged), and Heidelberg Cement. These companies have a history of collusive arrangements between them in several country markets globally.[16] These firms also have multi-market contacts across many countries in Africa.[17]

Very different ex-factory prices have been observed in a six-country study across Botswana, Kenya, Namibia, South Africa, Tanzania and Zambia over the period 2004 to 2012.[18] In countries in the Southern African Customs Union (SACU) there had been a cartel prosecuted in South Africa of the four producers which had operated through the industry association until 2009. In the East African Community (which includes Kenya and Tanzania) there is a similar association, the East African Cement Producers Association. Prices in Zambia were the highest of all the countries and had a single dominant firm, Lafarge, until 2015.

In 2015 and 2016 prices came down in all of the countries as new entrants brought more competitively priced product to market. The most important entrant with plants across several countries including South Africa, Zambia and Tanzania is Dangote Cement. In Kenya, there have been several entrants since 2011, including National Cement and Savannah Cement. In Namibia, Ohorongo entered soon after the ending of the SACU cartel, starting operations in 2010. The entrants reduced prices to around $5.50/bag in Kenya in 2015, a reduction of $2.50 or 30 per cent.[19] The entry of Dangote in Zambia saw prices falling to below $6 in 2015, 40 per cent lower than the prevailing levels in 2009 to 2012. In South Africa prices reduced to $4.50 with the starting of supplies by Sephaku Cement (in which Dangote is the

[15] World Bank, *Boosting Competition*.
[16] J. M. Connor, 'Price-Fixing Overcharges: Revised 3rd edition', Working Paper (2014).
[17] World Bank, *Boosting Competition*.
[18] As in figure 2 from T. Amunkete et al., 'Regional Cartels and Competition in the Cement Industry across Botswana, Kenya, Namibia, South Africa, Tanzania and Zambia', in S. Roberts (ed.), *Competition in Africa* (HSRC Press, 2016).
[19] www.businessdailyafrica.com/Cement-and-steel-manufacturers-cut-retail-prices/-/539546/2631942/-/foyrcs/-/index.html

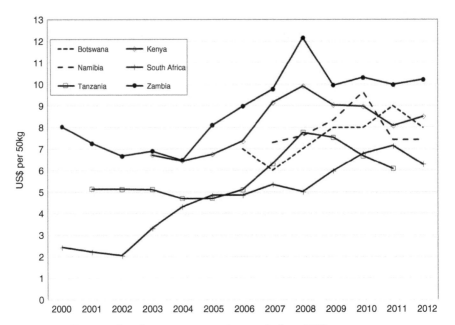

FIGURE 8.2 Estimated ex-factory cement prices, 50 kg bag, US$
Sources: as in T. Amunkete et al., 'Regional Cartels and Competition in the Cement Industry across Botswana, Kenya, Namibia, South Africa, Tanzania and Zambia', in S. Roberts (ed.), *Competition in Africa* (HSRC Press, 2016). Averages computed by researchers from data obtained from companies and national statistics. Note: Kenya and Tanzania data from respective National Bureau of Statistics (per tonne prices converted to per 50 kg and thus exclude bagging costs). South Africa data for 2008 to 2012 was extended to earlier years using the producer price index for ordinary and extended cement. Calculated in US$ using average annual exchange rates.

major investor), a further 25 per cent reduction from the 2012 levels after the cement cartel.[20]

There are three main implications from the experience of the cement industry. First, as also illustrated by fertiliser, cartels are likely to operate at a regional level. In the SACU cement cartel some countries with relatively small cement markets were effectively allocated to a single producer. Viewed from the perspective of the country it appears to be a single dominant firm and supra-competitive pricing would appear to be unilateral conduct, in the form of excessive pricing. It is not possible to tell whether the single substantial Zambian producer was the result of market division arrangements. What is clear is that none of the other regional producers entered Zambia and only when Dangote entered did prices drop substantially to

---

[20] T. Vilakazi and S. Roberts, 'Cartels as "Fraud"? Collusion in Southern Africa in Fertilizer and Cement', *Review of African Political Economy* (2018).

levels in line with what appear to be competitive levels (of around $4–$6/bag on an ex-factory basis).

Second, as competitive rivalry or cartel arrangements operate across countries, trade restrictions can be used to effectively allocate markets. Firms can lobby to protect small local markets and to raise entry barriers using national champion type arguments while the government is unaware that this may be simply reinforcing a regional cartel arrangement. Trade flows can also be used to monitor market shares. The SACU cartel used monthly sales data to monitor adherence to the market division arrangement which was an agreement on market shares for the whole SACU market. Sales volumes by regions within South Africa and the other countries in SACU were used by firms to be able to identify where they were gaining or losing sales in order to continually adjust to meet the targeted shares. List prices were transparent and effectively set by the lead firm. The agreement on market shares meant there was no competition in terms of discounting from these list prices to win customers. The only aspect which may be observed by the competition authority of a country is the information exchange and, unless the scope of the geographic market over which arrangement operates is correctly identified, the stability in market shares will not even be observed.

Third, there can be very substantial benefits from entry by 'outsider' firms rather than entry or expansion by those across the border in a neighbouring market. However, the economies of scale combined with the need to secure critical inputs, in particular, limestone and energy, mean that expansions in output are more likely to come from insiders than outsiders. The limestone deposits for Sephaku's plant in South Africa were only secured as the 'use-it-or-lose-it' provision in the mining laws meant it came up for sale.[21] Exclusive supply arrangements for extenders such as fly ash from coal fired power stations can also weaken the ability of entrants to be efficient low-cost producers. Industrial policies may therefore be required to create competition, which becomes easier as economies grow, as long as the temptation to simply support the expansion of incumbent(s) is resisted.

8.2.3 *Summary*

The examples of fertiliser and cement illustrate that cartel enforcement is very difficult at a national and even a regional level where the arrangements are international in nature. In addition, the available margins and rents to be earned mean that there is a strong incentive for businesses to lobby for rules and regulations which bolster their position and keep out rivals.

While we can decry corruption and rent-seeking, it is naive to do so without recognising the globally concentrated nature of the industry and the ability for large

---

[21] Amunkete et al., 'Regional Cartels'.

suppliers to control markets. Lobbying governments is simply one tool in their arsenal for maintaining control.

More importantly, enforcement is likely to be limited in its impact where there are range of other restrictions on competitive markets. The competition agenda also effectively overlaps with a regional trade agenda where trade restrictions are the result of lobbying by firms to divide markets. The competition agenda must in addition be an industrial policy agenda if competitive markets and investment in increased local production are to go hand in hand.

8.3 COMPETITIVE DYNAMISM IN NETWORK INDUSTRIES: THE CASE OF MOBILE MONEY

Mobile money refers to mobile telecommunications network operators (MNOs) offering money transfer services, payments and banking services, including through partnerships with banks. The rapid growth of mobile money has led to dramatic improvements in financial inclusion.[22] For example, in Kenya and Tanzania, which have led the way in Africa, financial inclusion measured by the ability to access banking services, including through mobile money facilities, covered the great majority of adults in 2015.[23] Uganda has followed closely behind its East African neighbours.[24] Zimbabwe has also seen a rapid take-up of mobile money services.[25] I draw on these country experiences to consider the implications for a constructive competition and development agenda.

Allowing MNOs to offer money transfer services has substituted for the transfer of physical cash between people such as where urban wage earners are seeking to transfer funds to family members in rural areas. Where there is latent demand due to basic infrastructure deficits, light regulation (not requiring licensed banks to manage the transfers, but simply trust accounts in which funds are held against the mobile wallets) and the growth of an agent network hand in hand with subscribers, then mobile money has achieved critical mass, takeoff and explosive growth.[26]

---

[22] J. Aron, '"Leapfrogging": A Survey of the Nature and Economic Implications of Mobile Money', Centre for the Study of African Economies Working Paper (2015).

[23] R. Macmillan, K. Lloyd and S. Roberts, 'A Comparative Study of Competition Dynamics in Mobile Money Markets across Tanzania, Uganda and Zimbabwe: Synthesis Report', report for Bill and Melinda Gates Foundation (2016); J. Blechman, 'Mobile Credit in Kenya and Tanzania: Emerging Regulatory Challenges in Consumer Protection, Credit Reporting and Use of Customer Transactional Data', *African Journal of Information and Communication* (2016) 17, 61–88; R. Mazer and P. Rowan, 'Competition in Mobile Financial Services: Lessons from Kenya and Tanzania', *African Journal of Information and Communication* (2016) 17, 39–60.

[24] R. Macmillan, A. Paelo and T. Paremoer, 'The "Evolution" of Regulation in Uganda's Mobile Money Sector', *African Journal of Information and Communication* (2016) 17, 89–110.

[25] G. Robb and T. Vilakazi, 'Mobile Payments Markets in Kenya, Tanzania and Zimbabwe: A Comparative Study of Competitive Dynamics and Outcomes', *African Journal of Information and Communications* (2016) 17, 9–38.

[26] D. Evans and A. Pirchio, 'An Empirical Examination of Why Mobile Money Schemes Ignite in Some Developing Countries But Flounder in Most', Coase-Sandor Institute for Law and Economics Working Paper No 723 (2015).

The services have evolved from simply transfers to payments, and to mobile banking where subscribers have access to deposit and loan facilities with potentially very substantial benefits, for example, to small-scale farmers in accessing credit.

There are substantial network effects in mobile money services. The more users there are, the more valuable the service is. And it is necessary to secure a critical mass of agents to provide a sufficiently ubiquitous service to attract customers, but also a critical mass of customers to generate commissions necessary to attract agents to come on board.

The dynamic and innovative services raise a number of competition and regulatory issues. The services do not exist in the first place unless the regulatory regime is permissive.[27] As new services, it was not possible to predict in advance how rapidly they would evolve. The M-Pesa product of Safaricom in Kenya was piloted with development funding as a small test case and the rapid take-up was unanticipated. The services straddle different regulatory regimes, most obviously financial services and telecommunications. In some countries, the central bank has played a lead role while in others it has been the telecommunications authority. There is a range of competition issues which has seen competition enforcement actions in Kenya and Zimbabwe by the respective competition authorities. The issues are complex as they involve balancing network regulation concerns of investment and access, as well as prudential considerations relating to the payments and banking systems.

The initial investments by providers to build a network leverage off the MNOs' existing network and agents who sell airtime. There is also a need to raise awareness and encourage uptake to ensure a critical mass of subscribers for the network to be attractive. The first mover bears a greater share of these costs and reaps competitive advantages from being in pole position. At the same time, dominance and substantial market power in mobile money can reinforce a dominant position in mobile telecommunications. For example, in Kenya while Safaricom's mobile money market share measured in terms of subscribers was around 77 per cent in 2015, in terms of active users its share is above 95 per cent.[28] The lack of interoperability meant that to use mobile money required being on the Safaricom network raising concerns for competition in mobile telecommunications more broadly than just mobile money.

There are a range of restrictive arrangements which can protect the investments made by the incumbent but also enable it to entrench its position.[29]

---

[27] M. Bourreau and T. Valletti, 'Enabling Digital Financial Inclusion through Improvements in Competition and Interoperability: What Works and What Doesn't?', CGD Policy Paper 065 (Center for Global Development, Washington, DC, 2015).

[28] This is corroborated by 99 per cent of active mobile money account users reporting using Safaricom M-Pesa in 2014, where 'Active' means accounts used within the previous ninety days (Intermedia, 'Kenya. Digital Pathways to Financial Inclusion 2014 Survey Report' (2015); Mazer and Rowan, 'Competition in Mobile Financial Services').

[29] Robb and Vilakazi, 'Mobile Payments Markets in Kenya'; MacMillan, Paelo and Paremoer, 2016; Mazer and Rowan, 'Competition in Mobile Financial Services'.

The first set of issues is agent exclusivity. An agent network is crucial as it enables cash-in and cash-out by users. While exclusivity supports investment in building a network by the lead operator, it also undermines rivals' ability to compete as the ideal agents are existing retailers. The systems typically remain independent meaning that there is no free-riding on the investment in the physical equipment itself. Tanzania prohibited agent exclusivity in 2010, two years after the launch of mobile money. The removal of agent exclusivity came later in Kenya, Uganda and Zimbabwe, in each case after legal and regulatory proceedings relating to possible anticompetitive conduct by the incumbents.

The second set of issues relate to access. The initial growth of mobile money transfer has been for the is unbanked. However, the rapid growth in these countries has meant that mobile money services soon overlapped with those who are banked. In addition, banks can use the mobile money subscriber base to extend branchless banking services. This means banks can provide access to their services through a mobile platform, typically using unstructured supplementary service data (USSD). However, the MNOs control USSD. MNOs can simply refuse to provide this access or can charge such high prices that it is unattractive. This has been the case in a number of countries, including Kenya, Uganda and Zimbabwe.

The incentive of the incumbent MNO is to block those offering services which do, or may, compete with the MNOs' mobile financial services offering. This stifles creativity and responsiveness to the needs of different groups of consumers as the incumbent MNO seeks to keep everything under its umbrella. By comparison, where there is rivalry between MNOs they are incentivised to offer reasonable terms to attract customers, as in Tanzania. USSD pricing and access has been an issue in each of the countries except Tanzania. In Uganda, private litigation was brought against the incumbent.[30] In Kenya and Zimbabwe, the competition authorities have engaged with it.[31] A lack of transparency further hinders competition through increasing search costs and making comparability more difficult.[32]

Countries have also had different experiences with interoperability, which is the third set of competition issues. In Tanzania interoperability arrangements have been negotiated bilaterally under the firm encouragement of the central bank.[33] In the other countries there has been no interoperability between mobile money networks and transactions can only be made on-net. Non-members of the network are treated as if they had no mobile money account at all. The harm to competition from the absence of interoperability is greatest where the market is highly skewed in favour of

[30]   Macmillan, Paelo and Paremoer, '"Evolution" of Regulation'.
[31]   Robb and Vilakazi, 'Mobile Payments Markets in Kenya'.
[32]   Mazer and Rowan, 'Competition in Mobile Financial Services'.
[33]   J. Blechman, F. Odhiambo and S. Roberts, 'Competition Dynamics in Mobile Money Markets in Tanzania', CCRED Working Paper 2017/22.

a dominant firm. This is also where it is very unlikely that interoperability will be agreed without regulatory intervention.

The fourth set of issues relate to the importance of data on credit records. A critical consideration in the mobile credit offering is ability to evaluate risk. Information from money transfers is an important source of data on subscribers' behaviour which can be used in mobile credit extension, which is typically in the form of small short-term loans.[34] In turn, an individual's track-record built-up from mobile credit is a valuable source of information for credit worthiness for longer-term loans. But, the credit record is controlled by the mobile money service provider and, as of 2016, is not shared with credit bureaus in Tanzania and Kenya.[35] This is possible due to a regulatory patchwork in Kenya and Tanzania with many gaps with respect to provisions and their enforcement.

How should the challenges of this field be addressed when it straddles telecommunications, financial services, competition and consumer protection? A nuanced approach is required to making judgements which take into account challenges in prudential regulation of the financial system, economic regulation to address market failures and consumer protection.[36] It bears repeating that privileging the existing prudential regulations and placing banks ahead of MNOs in the provision of services stifles their development at birth.[37] All of the countries here have chosen not to go down that path.

The countries demonstrate quite different approaches to the balancing of the concerns. However, all are grappling with the challenges recognising the economic value of the services and the need to support their growth. In Tanzania Kenya, Tanzania, Uganda and Zimbabwe all have similarly high levels of mobile money adoption but different market structures. In Kenya and Zimbabwe, the emergence of overwhelmingly dominant firms has seen the competition authorities take action while in Uganda there has been private enforcement. In mobile money transfer (MMT) services, extended agent exclusivity and lack of interoperability appear to have further bolstered the lead of incumbents in Zimbabwe and Uganda, while there is no interoperability and little effective rivalry in Kenya even after the ending of agent exclusivity. *Ex poste* enforcement has meant that a single dominant mobile money provider is reinforcing its dominance in telecoms and enforcers find themselves grappling with very powerful interests. The leading MNOs in Uganda, Kenya and Zimbabwe also appear to seek to retain greater control over aggregators' ability to innovate on their mobile money platforms than in Tanzania.

Tanzania by comparison has had effective rivalry in mobile telecommunications and has adopted a 'test and learn' approach to mobile money which has

---

[34]   Blechman, 'Mobile Credit in Kenya and Tanzania'.
[35]   Ibid.
[36]   Blechman, 'Mobile Credit in Kenya and Tanzania'; Mazer and Rowan, 'Competition in Mobile Financial Services'.
[37]   Evans and Pirchio, 'Empirical Examination'.

been fostered by the central bank through engagement. Expectations were set in broad terms with early interventions regarding agent exclusivity and to promote interoperability which were not, in fact, binding. Participants recognised the objectives and believed that other steps would be taken if necessary. Competition was nurtured by the broad rules for the services. Active competition between the MNOs for improved MMT services also appears to have driven greater cooperation of the MNOs with the banks, such as to facilitate transfers between bank accounts and mobile wallets, and with independent third parties (aggregators) in developing innovative services. Maintaining competition *in* the market through ongoing engagement has in fact been more effective than allowing competition *for* the market and *ex post* enforcement.

8.4 BARRIERS TO ENTRY

The third set of issues and one which goes beyond the standard prescriptions for competition enforcement is that of barriers to entry by local firms. Barriers to entry are typically part of an initial market analysis by competition authorities, following on from market definition as part of the consideration of whether there is substantial market power. Reducing barriers may be part of the advocacy efforts of a competition authority, especially targeted at regulations and government policies which harm competition. However, understanding the barriers to the entry and growth of effective competitors is also important for understanding why markets are configured in the way that they are and how this might be changed to foster the kind of rivalry we seek, namely one which encourages investments in capabilities. If we care about the identity of market participants and care about whether indigenous firms can compete and not just multinationals then this is something to consider when evaluating entry barriers.

An assessment of barriers to entry is critical for the correct balance between the risks of over and under enforcement and is one reason why countries should adopt different standards.[38] Barriers are higher in the context of market failures, including imperfect information. Along with economies of scale and scope, they provide the context for strategic behaviour by dominant firms. For example, if there is little consumer switching because of imperfect information and brand loyalty then the contestable market will be smaller and a dominant firm can more effectively employ retroactive rebates to further undermine rivals. Financial markets which are relatively underdeveloped also raise the likelihood of exclusionary strategies. In smaller less developed markets, as characterise most developing countries, this is all the more important.[39]

---

[38] See D. Evans, 'Why Different Jurisdictions Do Not (and Should Not) Adopt the Same Antitrust Rules' (2009) 10(1) *Chicago Journal of International Law* 161–88.

[39] P. Brusick and S. Evenett, 'Should Developing Countries Worry about Abuse of Dominance?' (2008) 269 *Wisconsin Law Review* 274–77.

A very narrow view can be taken of what constitutes entry barriers as being the costs that an entrant has to incur which were not incurred by the incumbent.[40] This, however, allows for substantial incumbent advantages where the incumbent was able to recoup its investment costs while the prospective rival incurring the same costs is likely to be deterred, including because of possible strategic behaviour by the incumbent. In other words, incumbency advantages can be 'locked in'. Some sunk costs and network effects are exogenous, incurred due to the nature of the product and the set-up costs required to produce at minimum efficient scale. Other sunk costs are influenced by the incumbent such as the level of spending on advertising.[41]

A series of studies in South Africa assessed entry barriers in practice through examining the experience of entrants in a number of selected markets. These markets are telecommunications, agro-processing, supermarkets, banking, renewable energy supply, airlines, fuel distribution, beer and mobile money.[42] The markets were selected based on their importance in the economy as well as those where there had been entry.[43] The main types of barriers to entry identified are as follows.

8.4.1 *Routes to Market, Consumer Behaviour and Switching Costs*

The experiences of firms highlighted the importance of being able to reach consumers – physically as well as importantly through building the profile and positioning which induces consumers to switch. Behavioural economics has identified the many ways and reasons for consumer inertia.[44] This follows earlier literature on the justifications for advertising which can be a very large and sunk cost.[45] Related to consumer behaviour and advertising are the costs associated with packaging, promotions and display.

---

[40] See D. Carlton and J. Perloff (2004) *Modern Industrial Organisation* (Harper Collins, 2004), following G. Stigler, *The Organization of Industry* (University of Chicago Press, 1968).

[41] J. Church and J. Ware, *Industrial Organisation: A Strategic Approach* (McGraw Hill, 2000).

[42] The studies are: G. Makhaya and N. Nhundu, 'Competition, Barriers to Entry and Inclusive Growth: Retail Banking Capitec Case Study', CCRED Working Paper 2015/12; R. Hawthorne, P. Mondliwa, T. Paremoer and G. Robb, 'Competition Barriers to Entry and Inclusive Growth: Telecommunications Sector Study', CCRED Working Paper 2016/2; R. das Nair and C. Dube, 'Competition, Barriers to Entry and Inclusive Growth: Case Study on Fruit n Veg City', CCRED Working Paper 2016/7; C. Matumba and P. Mondliwa, 'Competition, Barriers to Entry and Inclusive Growth: Soweto Gold Case Study', CCRED Working Paper 2015/11; G. Montmasson-Clair and R das Nair, 'The Importance of Effective Economic Regulation for inclusive Growth: Lessons from South Africa's Renewable Energy Programmes', CCRED Working Paper 2015/10; P. M. Ncube, T. Nkhonjera, T. Paremoer and T. Zengeni, 'Competition, Barriers to Entry and Inclusive Growth: Agro-processing', CCRED Working Paper 2016/3; A. Paelo, G. Robb and T. Vilakazi, 'Study on Barriers to Entry in Liquid Fuel Distribution in South Africa', CCRED Working Paper 2014/13.

[43] See www.competition.org.za/barriers-to-entry

[44] See J. Mehta (ed.), *Behavioural Economics in Competition and Consumer Policy* (University of East Anglia, Centre for Competition Policy, 2013).

[45] Church and Ware, *Industrial Organisation*.

Retail and distribution arrangements are obviously important for consumer goods, where they quite literally shape the routes to market for products. For producers of consumer goods such as food products, the costs of packaging, advertising and display and the ability to access the major supermarkets is an important consideration.[46] There are a number of practices which make it difficult for smaller brands to establish a presence, including category management practices of supermarkets where the organisation of a set of products in the supermarket is handed over to a lead supplier.

The example of beer, as a consumer product, highlighted the advertising and promotional costs required to establish a brand and the scale economies associated with advertising expenditure which does not increase proportionate to sales but is necessary to establish the product in the market.[47] Beer also has to be in fridges/coolers in taverns and bars, and on draught (on the bar top), for consumers to buy it. The same applies to other products, such as soft drinks, as well as more broadly to display space in outlets. Exclusive arrangements typically in place mean that small rivals are shut-out from a large number of outlets. In some countries competition enforcement has addressed this, however, the South African Act requires demonstrating a *substantial* lessening or prevention of competition which has been interpreted as showing that there would have been lower prices and higher quantity supplied in the market in the absence of the conduct. Small rivals can often not prove their product would be cheaper and there would be more supply to the market as a whole, while large firms claim their conduct aids the efficiency and lowers costs in their own supply chain.

For supermarkets there are also questions of entry barriers. The study of supermarkets[48] highlighted the importance of location in appealing to consumers. Transport costs and time can be reinforced by habit and convenience which means consumers gravitate to shopping malls. In South Africa, exclusive leases have blocked rival supermarkets as well as grocers, bakeries and butcheries from shopping malls. Such leases are a straightforward block to entrants in accessing potential markets and mean they have to look at alternative and inferior locations. The justification for exclusive leases is that they support investment in shopping malls as they ensure an anchor tenant. This applies in some locations and for a period, but not to support the ubiquitous practice for durations that last decades. It is also not clear that it justifies outright exclusivity as opposed to long-term leases for prime space in a given mall.

In many important services network effects mean there are natural first-mover advantages as consumers value the number of members a network has. This is reinforced where investment is required in the extension of network infrastructure

---

[46] Ncube et al., 'Regulation and Rivalry'.
[47] Matumba and Mondliwa, 'Competition, Barriers to Entry and Inclusive Growth'.
[48] R. das Nair and S. Chisoro-Dube, 'Growth and Strategies of Large, Lead Firms – Supermarkets', CCRED Working Paper 8/2017, University of Johannesburg.

such as ATMs and branches in banking and mobile phone masts in telecommunications. Regulation to ensure interoperability and the terms on which this happens is critical for there to be effective competition in such industries.

Banking services require people being able to obtain cash and make payments and the study of Capitec's entry[49] found branches and an ATM network remain critical in South Africa. However, allowing cash back at point-of-sale (supermarket tills), as has been possible for a number of years, means an ATM network can be bypassed while mobile payments opens up opportunities to use more cost-effective solutions and points the way to substantially cheaper 'branchless banking' models. Switching costs are also significant and consumers do not readily switch to rivals even where they may be offering cheaper prices and better products and services. Consumers find it difficult to compare bank charges and services across banks, and banks spend large amounts on advertising their brand simply to establish and maintain their reputation.

The entrant, Capitec bank, first attracted customers to micro-loans, while customers retained their own bank account if they were already banked. Customers were only converted to also use banking services once becoming familiar with Capitec through the loans. It took over ten years for Capitec to be an effective rival and, in many respects, it appears to be the exception that proves the rule. It had a banking licence from its parent, it benefitted from the reputation of its main owner and it had a base of micro-loan clients. Even with all of these advantages it struggled for a long time to gain a foothold.

There are also substantial network effects and switching obstacles in telecommunications. This is reinforced by large promotions and advertising expenditures which arguably obscure rather than assist in understanding the range of options of offer. Customer inertia can be compounded in mobile telecommunications by network operators which can make the switching process difficult and inconvenient even while number portability has been enforced. This has been compounded by a range of strategies such as on-net discounts which firms can use to lock-in the network effects which operate in telecoms.[50]

In electricity supply, access to market has been an important obstacle for renewable energy independent power producers who require access to the grid to be able to sell the power generated.[51] There have been concerns around Eskom's incentives to undermine independent generators which led independent power producers to seek guarantees from National Treasury. These concerns appear to have been born out over time.

---

[49] Makhaya and Nhundu, 'Competition, Barriers to Entry and Inclusive Growth'.
[50] Hawthorne et al., 'Competition Barriers to Entry and Inclusive Growth'.
[51] Montmasson-Clair and das Nair, 'Importance of Effective Economic Regulation'; G. Montmasson-Clair, 'Commissioning Renewable Energy: A Review of South Africa's Regulatory and Procurement Experience', *Journal of Economics and Financial Sciences* (special issue, 2014) 7.

The case studies all emphasise the importance of routes to reach consumers for entrants to be effective competitors and the challenges that they face in this regard.

8.4.2 Scale Economies, Vertical Integration, Learning Effects and Access to Patient Finance

Economies of scale and scope may not be entry barriers as a firm can enter at a size which reaches minimum efficient scale if it can raise the finance to do so. However, financial market imperfections handicap entrants who are potentially efficient competitors with a strong proposed offering, not yet proven, and yet little finance of their own. Scale and scope effects further mean that strategies can be employed by incumbents to undermine the rival's access to segments of market demand such as to ensure the rival operates at below installed capacity, so raising its average costs. Larger rivals, such as multinationals, are better placed than smaller local firms.

Economies of scale were highlighted as important across the studies. The effects are obviously very large in mobile telecommunications and retail banking. In supermarkets, there are large-scale effects in distribution, in particular, the investment in distribution centres. In manufacturing activities such as dairy, poultry and beer, there are economies of scale in processing and packaging facilities. In poultry, these effects are greatest in breeding and abattoirs which means independent broiler producers may be subject to market power at different levels of the value chain. In dairy production, the processing of value-added products necessary to diversify away from being reliant only on commodity milk production requires larger-scale investments (in powdered milk, yoghurts and cheese).

It is important to appreciate that building competitive capabilities is more than simply attaining minimum efficient scale and also involves a learning-by-doing process. This refers to the range of internal practices and knowledge which need to be developed to operate efficiently. It is also necessary to take into account the building of external relationships for supply. These are not necessarily barriers in their own right but reinforce existing advantages of incumbents and provide opportunities for them to undermine entrants.

For example, in poultry, the systems and flow of production (from breeding stock at great-grandparent, grandparent and parent levels, through to broilers) means it takes three years or more to become competitive. The incremental building of capabilities by the brewing entrant Soweto Gold highlights a similar need for 'patient' finance to support the growth of brewing, packaging and distribution over a number of years. Industrial policies and long-term development finance are required to support the development of productive capabilities. Across the studies the duration required to build-up the business was a feature.

Supplier and customer relationships come up against the vertical integration of incumbents emphasised in a number of the case studies. An entrant at just one level of the supply chain is reliant on their integrated rivals for key inputs and/or key markets. Again, this provides incumbents with a potential lever over entrants and smaller rivals to undermine them. Alternatively, the rival has to enter simultaneously at the different levels as a vertically integrated operator, significantly increasing the entry costs.

In telecommunications, the failure to implement local loop unbundling mean rivals to Telkom in delivering fixed line services, such as 'value-added network services' (VANS), have been dependent on the incumbent and main rival.[52] The slow-moving former state-owned fixed line company has undermined entrepreneurial activity across a range of these services. Long-running competition cases have slowly unlocked parts of these activities. Similarly, the integration from generation through transmission and distribution of the state-owned supplier has proved a major obstacle to independent power producers. While there may be good arguments in theory for integration, in practice, it has undermined investment in alternative sources of generation. A separated state-owned transmission and distribution system could act in the public interest to support upstream investment in generation of renewable energy.

The existence of critical infrastructure and facilities, along with network effects, are rationales for regulation to ensure competition. Regulation can, however, itself can be a barrier, such as where onerous licencing conditions block entry. For example, banking regulations in South Africa have prevented the growth of mobile money transfer by mobile network operators. Ineffective regulation has also played an important part such as where network access should be opened up through regulation.

8.4.3 Summary

The way the economy works in terms of microeconomic outcomes is the product of many small decisions and some big ones. There are also 'non-decisions', where the established trajectory continues because no decisions are taken to change its direction. The studies of barriers to entry to the economy highlight the range of often mutually reinforcing microeconomic factors which stack-up to block greater participation in the economy by people as entrepreneurs/producers. For example, finance is often highlighted as the main block to new businesses and, indeed, the sunk investments required to get commercially viable enterprises off the ground means finance obviously matters. But, providing development finance without addressing the other barriers to effective entry is likely to be a waste of money.

The studies also point to the importance of entry by outsiders and indicate what is at stake if entrants are blocked or undermined. Several studies considered where incumbents have substantial unilateral market power while others have found that entry barriers have shielded a small group of 'insiders' from competition who can

---

[52]   Hawthorne et al., 'Competition Barriers to Entry and Inclusive Growth'.

tacitly coordinate. The studies suggest gains from entry in lower consumer prices of similar orders of magnitude to cartel mark-up calculations (of 15 per cent–25 per cent).[53] In services (banking, telecoms) which are at the core of economic activity the mark-ups imply very wide-ranging effects on economic participation. While changes to bring more competition have brought improvements, the point is that the magnitude involved could have been achieved earlier and point in the direction in which much wider impacts can be realised.

8.5 AN AGENDA TO FOSTER COMPETITIVE MARKETS

A productive and inclusive economy which rewards effort, innovation and creativity requires a constructive approach to competition. It can be understood in terms of fairness, as has been part of the mandate of the Korean Fair Trade Commission.[54] The approach adopted is explained by Kyu-Uck Lee[55] who observed the following regarding competition law and policy in Korea at the time:

> Competition is the basic rule of the game in the economy. Nevertheless, if the outcome of competition is to be accepted by the society at large, the process of competition itself must not only be free but also conform to a social norm, explicit or implicit. In other words, it must also be fair. Otherwise, the freedom to compete loses its intrinsic value. Fair competition must go in tandem with free competition. These two concepts embody one and the same value.

The intrinsic value of the freedom to compete implies evaluating the competitive market mechanism in terms of its accomplishments in promoting individual freedoms (to produce, develop productive capabilities, and make autonomous choices), as opposed to the conventional welfarist framework of assessment.[56] In the context of African development this means opportunities for the citizens of the countries. The identity of the market participants matters. As noted by Fox, this approach is, however, outside the antitrust mainstream and means that consumers may bear the costs of support for participation by local producers, at least when looked at in the partial terms of individual products and markets rather than holistically.[57]

The qualification is critical. While apparent market distortions may undermine static allocative efficiency in terms of consumers decisions, they may well be required to improve the direction of resources to investments for the development of productive capabilities (such as in the presence of technology spill-overs, or learning-by-doing

---

[53] Connor, 'Price-Fixing Overcharges'.
[54] E. Fox, 'We Protect Competition, You Protect Competitors' (2003)26(2) *World Competition* 149–65.
[55] A. Kyu-Uck Lee, '"Fairness" Interpretation of Competition Policy with Special Reference to Korea's Laws', in *The Symposium in Commemoration of the 50th Anniversary of the Founding of the Fair Trade Commission in Japan, Competition Policy for the 21st Century* (KFTC 1997).
[56] A. Sen, 'Markets and Freedoms: Achievements and Limitations of the Market Mechanism in Promoting Individual Freedoms' (1993) *Oxford Economic Papers*, 45
[57] Fox, 'Competition, Development and Regional Integration'.

effects). In other words, following Khan (2012),[58] we are concerned not simply with the governance framework for markets, but what the markets generate, namely whether they foster growth-promoting competition. It is not about 'getting prices right' but about building dynamic comparative advantages.[59] In the context of African countries, this is about the incentives and opportunities for investments in improved production capabilities to achieve technological catching-up.[60]

The three areas examined in this chapter question the standard competition prescriptions and indicate that there is a number of key considerations for an agenda to foster such competition in developing countries, such as the African economies in which the case studies examined here are located.

First, it is very difficult for developing countries to enforce against international cartels due the difficulties in obtaining information.[61] And, even when cartel conduct is identified, more competitive outcomes do not necessarily result. The coordinated arrangements can effectively be maintained through trade and industrial policies shaped by lobbying by individual firms to protect their rents and/or by tacit arrangements.

Second, there can be substantial gains from the entry of new producers who are 'outsiders'. The entry of Dangote and others into cement production in countries across Africa has dramatically reduced prices. A narrow enforcement agenda against cartelisation in cement could not achieve this outcome but instead appears to have stimulated increasingly sophisticated ways of coordinating through information exchange. The gains from entry indicate that industrial policies which support investments at scale by new suppliers of products such as cement and fertiliser need to be distinguished from those that protect incumbents.

Third, the mobile money experience demonstrates how the balance can be struck by regulators and competition authorities to ensure innovative new markets evolve. In particular, the Tanzanian experience illustrates a 'test and learn' approach where expectations and principles are communicated to the lead firms, including the importance of ensuring markets will be open to new participants in future. Complex issues such as network effects can be addressed and rules evolved to ensure dynamic rivalry. Rather than the common criticism that institutions are weak and so governments should not intervene, there is instead institutional 'learning-by-doing' underway from the interventions.

Fourth, the different and mutually reinforcing nature of barriers to entry needs to be understood. For example, addressing market failures in access to finance is unlikely to support effective competitors while other obstacles such as with routes

---

[58] M. Khan, 'Governance and Growth Challenges for Africa', in A. Noman et al. (eds.), *Good Growth and Governance in Africa: Rethinking Development Strategies* (Oxford University Press, 2012).
[59] A. Amsden, 'Asia's Next Giant' (Oxford University Press, 1989).
[60] Khan, 'Governance and Growth Challenges'.
[61] E. Fox, 'International Antitrust and the Doha Dome' (2003) 43 *Virginia Journal of International Law* 911.

to market and obstacles to consumer switching remain unaddressed. A critical insight is that interventions need to be on a number of fronts. Just as the barriers have a combined effect, so addressing one area in isolation will make little difference.

Fifth, while regulation perhaps naturally favours incumbents given the information asymmetries, vertically integrated incumbents can also 'self-regulate' their sector. And, potential rivals will struggle to plausibly show the costs of their exclusion. Competition policy therefore needs to imagine alternatives. One source of this is through international comparisons in order to learn from other countries' experiences. Government policies are important in opening up sectors to wider participation including through assistance enabling new firms to compete with incumbents who have often inherited advantageous positions.[62]

There are a number of rules which determine how markets work. These can tip the balance in favour of one side or the other. In this chapter, I have argued that a proactive policy to generate competition is needed. We should ask ourselves whether the competition law regime is 'fit for purpose', with reference in particular to nurturing performance-based competition through investment in productive capabilities. In some cases, regulations blocking entry can be removed, in others, proactive regulation *for* competition may be required given market failures and intrinsic obstacles. It is also critical to distinguish between industrial policies that result from lobbying for protection of incumbents from industrial policies which support new rivals, the adoption and adaptation of improved technologies, and spur productivity improvements. Simplistic arguments which pit industrial policy against competition policy miss the fact that the embedded economic structures of countries reflect earlier favouring of some interests over others.

The comparative analysis highlights the importance of learning, in incremental and iterative processes, and maintaining an openness to different ideas and contributions. Advice and technical support can be a valuable part of this process, but not a 'cookbook' or ideal-type models being transplanted.

---

[62]   O. Budzinski and M. Beigi, 'Generating Instead of Protecting Competition', in M. Gal et al. (eds.), *The Economic Characteristics of Developing Jurisdictions* (Edward Elgar, 2015).

B

Competition against Power

9

The Australian Controversy over
Abuse of Market Power Law

A *Study in Political Economy*

Alan Fels

9.1 INTRODUCTION

This chapter seeks to provide a legal and political account of a major controversy about a proposed legislative change of the Australian abuse of dominance law, and to illustrate how efficiency and equity considerations have influenced the shaping of the law.

After briefly describing the nature of the current and proposed law and the key interest groups and political players in the controversy, there is a history of the evolution of the law from its introduction in 1974 until now. That history also refers to some important legislative changes that have been triggered as a by-product of the inability of governments to resolve directly controversies regarding the abuse of dominance law.

The chapter then turns to an economic and legal analysis of the proposed law in order to provide an understanding of the technical issues involved in the proposed changes and of the reasons why a recent review of the law led to the proposed changes.

The chapter then returns to the political side to describe the political pressures that different parties applied to support or oppose the change and of the path that was followed on the way to a political outcome.

The chapter concludes with a discussion of some of the political lessons.

9.2 THE CURRENT AND THE PROPOSED MISUSE
OF MARKET POWER LAW

Australia's current abuse of dominance law (known as the 'misuse of market power' law) is largely captured in s. 46(1) of the Australian Competition and Consumer Law (2010).

> (1) A corporation that has a substantial degree of power in a market shall not take advantage of that power in that or any other market for the purpose of:

I am grateful to Dr Jill Walker (who originally suggested the test) advocated by me (and adopted by the Harper review) and Professor Caron Beaton-Wells for comments.

(a) eliminating or substantially damaging a competitor of the corporation or of a body corporate that is related to the corporation in that
or any other market;

(b) preventing the entry of a person into that or any other market; or

(c) deterring or preventing a person from engaging in competitive conduct
in that or any other market.

While the full provisions of s. 46 are lengthy, subsection 1 above includes some of
the key features that have been the subject of controversy. They include:

- The law only applies to behaviour that has an anticompetitive purpose.
  The effect of the behaviour is irrelevant.
- The law also stipulates that there is only an offence if a firm 'takes advantage' of
  its market power.

Two other features of the law stand out to the foreign observer:

- The statutory language above refers to behaviour that damages competitors
  rather than competition. At first sight this of deep concern. In practice, however, the courts have made it very clear that the concern is harm to competition,
  not to competitors.
- The law is based on the concept of 'substantial market power', not
  dominance or monopolisation. However, the case law on substantial
  market power differs very little in result from the case law in Europe
  and North America on the nature of market power and is not pursued in
  this chapter.

The proposed law recommended by the Competition Policy Review headed by
Professor Ian Harper is as follows:

1. A corporation that has a substantial degree of power in a market shall not
   engage in conduct if the conduct has the purpose, or would have or be
   likely to have the effect, of substantially lessening competition in that or
   any other market.
2. Without limiting the matters that may be taken into account for the purposes
   of subsection (1), in determining whether conduct has the purpose, or would
   have or be likely to have the effect, of substantially lessening competition in
   a market, the court must have regard to:
   (a) the extent to which the conduct has the purpose, or would have or be
       likely to have the effect, of increasing competition in the market
       including by enhancing efficiency, innovation, product quality or
       price competitiveness in the market; and
   (b) the extent to which the conduct has the purpose, or would have or be
       likely to have the effect, of lessening competition in the market including
       by preventing, restricting or deterring the potential for competitive con-
       duct in the market or new entry into the market.

Other proposed provisions are not set out here as they constitute minor clarifications.

The proposed new law constitutes a radical simplification of the previous law.

- It is aimed at giving the law a sharper economic focus. It provides that behaviour which has an anticompetitive purpose, effect or likely effect is prohibited.
- 'Taking advantage of market power' is no longer a requirement for breach of the law.
- The references to behaviour that 'harms competitors' have been removed and replaced with a simple test of behaviour that 'substantially lessens competition'.

The proposed change has triggered a fierce debate.

Before undertaking a legal and economic analysis of the two competing laws we give an account of the political background.

9.3 POLITICAL BACKGROUND

Before discussing the interest groups that have been involved in the controversies concerning the abuse of dominance law, it is worthwhile to set out the broad political consensus which governs the general character of abuse of dominance laws around the world.

As a political matter, abuse of dominance laws can be seen as a compromise between two sets of views. The first is the view that big business is too big, too powerful and harmful to the economy and society. This view may be supported by concerns that markets may operate in ways that are unfair to small business and farmers. The second is the laissez-faire view that business should be left free to act as it wants. Competition law steers a middle ground – it accepts the existence and value of big business and does not in general try to break it up. Nor does it generally regulate monopoly prices and output. In the case of pure monopoly, there is, however, price regulation but typically this is not done by competition regulators. In short the consensus view accepts dominance and does nothing fundamental to break it up or regulate it.

However, it prohibits 'monopolisation' or 'the abuse of dominance', i.e. it prohibits firms with dominance or substantial market power from acting in a way that harms competition. This is what is embedded in abuse of dominance laws.

Viewed from an economics lens, the same picture emerges. A monopoly is defined as a firm with no competition (and a dominant firm as one without substantial competition). A profit-maximising firm will price above the level it would achieve in a competitive market and thereby will harm efficiency. This suggests two basic policy options. One is to regulate prices. The other is to break up the dominant firm, at least in circumstances where the public benefit exceeds the cost. Neither of these policies, however, are generally part of the consensus economics approach to monopoly or dominance. The consensus is that the only form of regulation should be the prohibition of anticompetitive behaviour by dominant or monopoly firms. This may make good economic sense but it can also be viewed as a compromise.

At the level of daily business expressions of view, the following are the main concerns, typically voiced by small and medium-sized business people, especially in the retail context, as well as by consumers:

- Retailer concentration: the two big retailers in Australia, Coles and Woolworths, share a very large part of the retail grocery and fresh food and meat markets. This gives rise to concern that the prices they set may be uncompetitive. It would be healthier for competition if there was a third or fourth big player in the market. In recent years, competition from Aldi and Costco has had some tempering effect.
- Predatory behaviour: retailers and wholesalers operating at the same level as major retailers claim that there is predatory behaviour by the big retailers. Using their buying power, they are said to be able to extract more favourable supply deals for themselves than are smaller competitors such as the wholesaler (Metcash) that supplies small independent outlets around Australia, and thereby drive smaller competitors out of business. There are also complaints about big retailer entry into small markets with 'oversized' stores.
- Abuse of buyer power: suppliers of the two big retailers allege that there is exploitation of them as a result of the buyer market power that the two big retailers have. These retailers are able to extract supply prices that suit them and that are likely to have the effect of driving the suppliers out of business. Another complaint is about ex post rent extraction, e.g. once a supply relationship has been established, big retailers exploit sellers even more e.g. disregarding contracts, imposing unreasonable demands and so on: this is so-called unconscionable conduct.
- Conglomerate issues: big retailers are spreading into a range of new fields from big discount outlets, petrol, insurance and a range of other activities. Critics argue that this also is also harmful to competition and consumers.

The above discourses are usually conducted in the language of these practices being 'unfair'. The importance of 'fairness' often carries more weight with the public than the concept of 'harm to competition'.

Against this background it is worthwhile now to turn to the alignment of various interest groups and political actors.

9.3.1 Government

Government has a broad interest in competition law. Government relies upon markets to deliver goods and services. Markets do not work well if they are uncompetitive. As the ultimate custodian of the health of the economy, governments need competition law to break up anticompetitive behaviour, such as abuse of market power, as discussed in this chapter. Government also has an interest in not having laws that harm or limit competition. A successful competition law and policy is key to a good performance of the whole economy and to the success of a government.

In the real world, there are pressures on government not to act in the benevolent way suggested above. Most organisations and businesses like to be supplied competitively and to sell into competitive markets, but are less keen on being subject to competition, let alone competition law, themselves, and lobby government to that effect.

Nevertheless, in broad terms, governments adopt and support competition laws (some 133 governments currently around the world do so) because they contribute to better economic performance which is what citizens ultimately want and judge them by.

Accordingly, at the base of any political analysis of competition law lies a broad government wish to get competition law right, driving out anticompetitive practices while encouraging the maximisation of competition. In short, government is an important political driver of a proper competition law.

Nevertheless, a number of forces work for as well as against competition law in any government. At the institutional level, forces in favour of competition law and its proper application generally include ministers and officials in key economic agencies such as treasury, finance and prime minister (or cabinet) areas.

9.3.2 *Big Business*

'Big business', the top firms in terms of revenue or capital, is represented by the Business Council of Australia (BCA) whose membership is about 130 of such firms. Its views, especially when the majority are united, carry much weight with all sides of politics.

Big business has always strongly opposed any measures which strengthen the application of the competition law to them. It vehemently opposed the introduction of the Trade Practices Act (now the Australian Competition and Consumer Act 2010) in 1974 (as well as earlier weaker laws in 1965). It fiercely opposed the strengthening of the merger law in 1993 to a prohibition on mergers that substantially lessened competition laws; laws to regulate 'access to essential facilities' insofar as they affected big business; and laws about unconscionable conduct. Initially it opposed criminalisation of cartel law but eventually acquiesced.

The core approach, though buttressed by sophisticated arguments, has been simple: opposition to stronger competition law insofar as it affects key businesses (although it has supported the extension of competition laws to other areas of the economy, such as to the government-owned public utilities, the professions and to the health, education and public services sectors). It has consistently opposed strong enforcement of the Act by the regulator. In the case of the author it constantly pushed against his reappointment.

Big business opposition in Australia to abuse of dominance laws has always been especially strong. The Australian economy is relatively concentrated because of its size and distance from world markets, and because of weak merger law before the 1990s. Many key businesses are not, in practical terms, affected by nor concerned by cartel and merger laws (for a dominant firm there may be no one to merge or conspire with). This causes their focus on abuse of dominance laws to be even sharper. In addition, business does not like the slur with its moral overtones of being found guilty of abuse of market power.

Like most business groups, there is, however, some division of opinion amongst members of the BCA about the proposed changes to the abuse of dominance laws. The two dominant retailers are highly opposed and conducted a strong campaign of opposition. In some respects this is very understandable, since this is the industry always cited as the prime target of the changes (even though when the time comes it will be able to argue that currently there seems to be an (unusually) high degree of competition between the two and even though new entrants, especially Aldi, are making some difference to competition).[1]

As noted elsewhere in this chapter, the two big retailers attract critics from everywhere – suppliers, competitors and consumers. The two retailers, Coles and Woolworths, have not been well regarded in Parliament because of their treatment of suppliers.

The two big retailers were not alone in their concerns. However, there were also a number of BCA members with no concerns about the proposed law and preferring the BCA to focus its efforts on other issues. The net outcome, however, was strong BCA opposition.

Big businesses, whether acting through the Business Council of Australia or directly, deploys a normal full range of political influence such as political donations, research, advocacy, meetings with politicians, threats of not investing and so on.

The Competition and Consumer Law Committee of the Law Council of Australia mainly made up of lawyers representing big business also usually opposes laws that strengthen the application of competition law to clients. In recent times, a rival Law Council of Australia Committee concerned with small and medium enterprise law has significantly undermined such influence as it has. Also, a number of members of the Competition and Consumer Law Committee personally support the Harper review changes, but do not say so publicly, because of concerns at client reactions and its impact on their image as supporters of big business.

---

[1] The ACCC itself has wavered in its assessment of the state of competition between the big two. A 2008 ACCC market study, headed by previous chair, Graeme Samuel, had few concerns. His successor, Rod Sims had more concerns as did his predecessor, the author.

9.3.3 *Small Business*

The most vocal representative of small business is the Council of Small Business of Australia (COSBOA). In the early years of competition law in Australia, the sector was not well organised nor did it have much appreciation of the potential value of a competition law. Its knowledge, however, has grown over time, partly assisted by lobbying and education from Australian Competition and Consumer Commission (ACCC).

Although not well resourced, COSBOA has been successful in having its voice heard by politicians.

The National Farmers Federation shares many of the views of COSBOA.

Small business does not have a sophisticated understanding of competition law but it supports any change in the law that strengthens its protection from big business. It has an exaggerated set of expectations as to what a change in the law of abuse of dominance would do, just as big business does.

Now that small business has come to appreciate the power of competition law it often tends to seek amendments to the law that harm competition. In the case of s. 46, however, arguably it has been on the side of economic rectitude, as we will suggest below.

9.3.4 *Other Business*

There is a range of other business groups, which include the influential Australian Chamber of Commerce and Industry (ACCI), which is close to the Liberal Party. It has strongly supported a strengthening of the abuse of dominance laws and has probably carried more weight than COSBOA.

In earlier epochs it has been neutral on issues involving a conflict of big and small business, but its support of the Harper changes has been important in itself and in demonstrating that the voice of big and medium business is not united on the changes. Another major industry group, the Australian Industry Group (with a substantial manufacturing industry representation) has been relatively silent.

9.3.5 *Australian Competition and Consumer Commission*

The Australian Competition and Consumer Commission (ACCC) has played an important role in shaping legislation, both by public advocacy and by using its access to the bureaucracy, politicians and ministers. It also brings a good grasp of the technical issues to the table. While generally supporting a strengthening of the competition law, its approach to abuse of dominance has varied from one chair of the Commission to the next. It has never been neutral, nor, some would say, disinterested.

In the 1990s under the chairmanship of the author it sought a stronger misuse of market power law, particularly via the addition of an 'effects' test. However, this change was not at the top of its list of reform priorities and it pressed harder on other reforms. In the period from 2003 to 2011 when Graeme Samuel was chair, there was opposition to substantial reform of the abuse of dominance laws. Rod Sims, the current chair, has vigorously prosecuted the case for change and been influential. A former official, he has known which levers within the government to pull to get legislation changed.

9.3.6 *The Coalition Government*

The coalition government is made up of the Liberal Party and the smaller National Party. The Liberal Party is pro-business. It experiences the usual tensions of a party that supports competitive markets but is wary of government intervention to achieve this goal. It also experiences tensions when it is caught in the middle of conflicts between big business and small business. The National Party, the former Country Party, has considerable power in the coalition and has a number of members in the cabinet. It is pro small business and pro farmer.

Generally, the Liberal Party has been cautious in its support for changes that strengthen competition law, while the National Party has strongly and openly supported strengthening of abuse of dominance laws in the interests of small business and farmers.

A key player was Bruce Billson, the Small Business Minister. He tirelessly promoted the changes publicly and in his important capacity as a cabinet member.

9.3.7 *The Labor Party*

Traditionally the Labor Party has been a strong supporter of a competition law. However, it has somewhat uncharacteristically opposed the strengthening of s. 46. A decade ago the then Opposition Leader Mark Latham proposed a strengthening of s. 46 by the establishment of an 'effects' test. In essence, Latham was concerned that before an abuse of dominance breach could be established, the plaintiff (usually the ACCC) had to prove that the 'purpose' of the behaviour was to lessen competition. He advocated the adoption of a test based on the economic effect of the behaviour (including the effect on prices and/or other variables). This was, however, effectively blocked by a senior Labor politician, Lindsay Tanner, close to the Shop Distributive and Allied Trades Association. That union covers retail employment and has a close relationship with the two dominant retailers, Coles and Woolworths. The union opposition is a by-product of its dealing with those major retail enterprises. It is clear that some kind of deal had been done between the retailers and the union and under that deal the union quid pro quo is to stop the Labor Party from proposing any changes in the law. To this day, the union influence seems strong – Coles, for example, has hired former Western Australian Labor Premier, Alan Carpenter to represent it in many forums.

The Labor Party, in more recent times, has also opposed a strengthening of the law because it has listened to two other voices closely. The first is the BCA and the second is Graeme Samuel, the chair of the ACCC from 2003 until 2011. Graeme Samuel has always had major reservations about the need for a s. 46 in the law at all and has vehemently opposed any substantive strengthening of the section.

Armed with this background we can now turn to the history of the law.

9.4 HISTORY

9.4.1 *The Trade Practices Act 1974 (Cth)*

The 1974 Act provided as follows:

> 46.(1) A corporation that is in a position substantially to control a market for goods or services shall not take advantage of the power in relation to that market that it has by virtue of being in that position-
>   (a) to eliminate or substantially to damage a competitor in that market or in another market;
>   (b) to prevent the entry of a person into that market or into another market; or
>   (c) to deter or prevent a person from engaging in competitive behaviour in that market or in another market.

The core, internationally accepted, principles regarding the abuse of dominance law were well understood by the founders of the law.

In introducing the law in 1974, the Attorney General said:

> The provision is not directed at size as such. It is confined to the conduct by which a monopolist uses the market power he derives from his size against the competitive position of competitors or would-be competitors ... A monopolist is not prevented from competing as well as he is able, e.g. by taking advantage of economies of scale, developing new products or otherwise making full use of such skills as he has ...
> In doing these things he is not taking advantage of his market power.[2]

Drafting of the legislation was driven by the view that the provisions should be set out in detail for the benefit of a judiciary that was new to this kind of law. Accordingly, instead of simply stating that a firm with market power should not act in a way that lessens competition, the law provided examples of forms of behaviour that would be deemed unlawful if they harmed competition. Thus provisions (a), (b) and (c) refer to forms of behaviour that could do harm to competitors.

It is clear why, at that time, the words 'shall not take advantage' were inserted. If they not been inserted, then there would have been a prohibition on corporations with market power from engaging in behaviour that by virtue of provisos (a)–(c)

---

[2] Australia, Senate, Debates, 14 August 1974, p. 923.

simply damaged competitors, but not necessarily competition. It was clearly necessary to put in some words that limited the kind of behaviour that would be prohibited
by s. 46; with the benefit of hindsight it might have been wiser to have put in
a general proviso that stipulated that the specified form of behaviour was only
prohibited if it had the purpose or effect of substantially lessening competition.
The term 'take advantage' may have taken the law down a path not fully appreciated
in 1974.

In the current context that is if a substantial lessening of competition test is added
to s. 46 in the way that the Competition Policy Review has proposed, the original
rationale for 'take advantage' disappears. There is no need for there to be additional
words about taking advantage of market power. Once there is a substantial lessening
of competition test, as Harper recommends, it is clear that the words 'take advantage'
add an additional test over and above the test of 'substantial lessening of competition'. We refer to this point later.

9.4.2 *The Period 1976–91*

There was a fightback by big business against the 1974 Act, bringing about the
1976 Swanson Review. The author knew the business members of the review,
both Mr Swanson (who had a senior role at ICI) and Mr Jim Davidson (CEO
of Commonwealth Industrial Gases). They both came from dominant firms.
At that time, the author was involved in regulating prices of dominant firms
under the Prices Justification Act. Both mentioned to the author that the
Committee had proposed a considerable watering down of s. 46. Mr
Davidson compared big business with a big fish swimming in the pool, wag-
gling its tail and inadvertently killing some small fish without having had the
intention of doing so. On the basis of that analogy, he believed there should be
a purpose test.

As a result of the Swanson Report, the current law with its purpose test was
adopted.

In 1986 Labour introduced 'substantial market power' in place of dominance as
the market power threshold. This has not proved to be especially controversial.

9.4.3 *QWI v.* BHP

An important development in the 1980s was High Court clarification of the meaning
of s. 46.

The courts have understood the core principles well.

In the first major case in 1986, *Queensland Wire Industries Pty Ltd* v. *Broken Hill
Pty Co Ltd*, the High Court of Australia made the aims of the law clear.

Mason CJ and Wilson J. stated that the object of s. 46 was the protection of
consumer interests which is to be achieved through the promotion of competition

even though competition by its nature is deliberate and ruthless and competitors injure each other by seeking to take sales away from one another.

In the same case, Deane J. stated that:

> The essential notions with which s. 46 is concerned and the objective which the section is designed to achieve are economic not moral ones. The notions are those of markets, market power, competitors in a market and competition. The objective is the protection and advancement of a competitive environment and competitive conduct.[3]

In *Boral Besser Masonry Limited* (now Boral Masonry Ltd) v. *Australian Competition & Consumer Commission* Gleeson CJ and Callinan J. recognised 'the danger of confusing aggressive intent with "anticompetitive behaviour"'.[4]

In short, the courts have interpreted the law in such a way that the provisions about harm to competitors have been largely neutered. There are however other problems with the statute which I discuss below.

Since that decision, the broad character of the abuse of market power law in Australia has been clear – it is aimed at promoting competition not competitors.

9.4.3.1 Since 1991

From 1991, the Trade Practices Commission (TPC), the predecessor of the ACCC, advocated the adoption of an effects test in s. 46.

The author became chairman of the TPC in 1991. He was the first economist appointed to that role (albeit he did have a law degree). He gave early thought to the Act and to what needed to be reformed, as well to what the appropriate economic role of the TPC was.

As he saw it there were a number of priorities: to have a Trade Practices Commission that enforced the law more strongly 'without fear or favour'; to change the merger test from dominance to substantial lessening of competition; to increase the penalties and at a later point seek criminal sanctions for cartels; to get more economics into the Commission; to do something about the many restrictions imposed by governments on competition; to get the drafting of the act simplified; to introduce an effects test into s. 46; and, one day, to get a divestiture power.

The author sought to change the very badly worded s. 46 and, in particular, to overcome the obvious deficiencies of it. The author's major concern was that s. 46 was based on the wrong principle (purpose) and that it thus deviated from what applied and was generally agreed in North America and Europe. As an economist the author had long believed that the purpose of the Act was to stop harmful economic behaviour, irrespective of its intent, so it was clear to him that the emphasis on purpose was misplaced and the words 'or effect' should be added.

---

[3] *Queensland Wire Industries Pty Ltd* v. *Broken Hill Pty Co Ltd* (1989) 167 CLR 177 at 194.
[4] See S. G. Corones, *Competition Law in Australian* (6th edn, Lawbook Co, 2014), 428

The author considered the inclusion of the word 'effect' as a simple, basic piece of economics. This view has had considerable support over the years from the influential economics departments such as treasury.

Each of these reforms looked difficult. As discussed before, big business has had a long history of fiercely opposing changes that would strengthen the competition law.

The author was aware of how difficult it was to get reforms and the best that could be done was to get a big reform through every few years. So the sequence was higher penalties, mergers and criminalisation of cartels, with s. 46 dropping off the list of top priorities for some years.

9.4.4 *Dawson Report*

The Dawson Review (2002–3) was principally about criminalisation of cartels and also the vigorous law enforcement and associated publicity brought about by the ACCC.

However, there was a debate about s. 46 during the inquiry. As ACCC chair, the author personally held a substantial discussion with Mr Justice Dawson in which they discussed at some length the question of whether there should be a redesign of the whole of s. 46 and start all over again with the same proposition that the Harper Committee has now proposed. Both saw the logic. Dawson asked the author how he felt about it and, after acknowledging the logic of the proposal, the author 'blinked' and said that he was not pressing that reform now. The reason was that from the perspective of getting results as a law enforcer, s. 46 in its form then (and now) is drafted in a way that in some respects makes getting court results for the regulator easier than under a test, which requires proof of a substantial lessening of competition. This is because, as noted above, the provisions of s. 46 refer specifically to certain forms of behaviour that damage competitors (not competition). While it is true that the High Court has imposed an underlying competition test into s. 46, the fact is that in one case after another it was obvious that judges liked to look very carefully at whether the behaviour breached conditions (a), (b) and (c) in s. 46(1) (those are the provisions that refer to damage to competitors) and use it as a major hook in determining guilt under a s46 even if they also conducted a substantial lessening of competition test.

In the event Dawson offered no change and rejected the Commission proposal that the words 'or effect' be added to s. 46. His report was marred by some errors. The first involved a misstatement of US law. Contrary to his claim, it does have an effects test. The second was that although Dawson conceded that in the EU there was an effects test, he claimed that the EU was different because the law only related to dominant firms whereas in Australia it relates to firms with 'substantial market power'. He seemed to be unaware that in Europe the term 'dominance' covers 'collective dominance', which brings it very much into line with the Australian law.

In any case, that distinction is not relevant to the debate about whether purpose or effect is the right standard.

9.4.5 *Changes after Dawson*

In the period until the author's departure from the ACCC in 2003 there had been litigation under s. 46 with some wins and some losses. One important political side effect was that when pressures from small business and farmers built up for a more effective s. 46, the government would usually point to the fact that the ACCC was conducting several cases and it could suggest that everyone waited until their resolution. However, for several years after 2003, no cases were instituted under s. 46 because the ACCC chair, Graeme Samuel was sceptical about the value and practicality of cases under the section. This left a political vacuum which was soon filled.

Subsequently, the Parliament took two actions. First, the Howard government with apparent support from the then chair of the ACCC, introduced a number of amendments to s. 46 which did not amount to a change in the law at all. The amendments simply embodied conclusions of the High Court in some of the s. 46 cases and put their conclusions into statutory form. They were, in short, a form of window-dressing.

In the political vacuum, the then Senator Barnaby Joyce, a leading member of the National Party, orchestrated a very effective campaign to add some quite substantial changes to s. 46. He was aided in getting the changes through the system also by the proximity of elections and the need for mutual support and agreement between the Liberal Party and the National Party.

The 'Birdsville' Amendments were introduced; this meant that within s. 46 there were now two separate tests of abuse of market power, a 'world first'. It is claimed that the words of the test were first written by the current Deputy Prime Minister of Australia and Leader of the National Party, Mr Barnaby Joyce, in a hotel bar in the remote country town of Birdsville.

Section 46 (1AA) provides:

(1AA) A corporation that has a substantial share of a market must not supply, or offer to supply, goods or services for a sustained period at a price that is less than the relevant cost to the corporation of supplying such goods or services, for the purpose of:

  (a) eliminating or substantially damaging a competitor of the corporation or of a body corporate that is related to the corporation in that or any other market; or
  (b) preventing the entry of a person into that or any other market; or
  (c) deterring or preventing a person from engaging in competitive conduct in that or any other market.

(1AB) For the purposes of subsection (1AA), without limiting the matters to which the Court may have regard for the purpose of determining whether a corporation has a substantial share of a market, the Court may have regard to the number and size of the competitors of the corporation in the market.[5]

Another factor was the growing belief that a stronger s. 46 would be able to solve all the problems, or at least many of the problems encountered by small business in its relationship with big businesses.

There was also disappointment about the outcome of earlier changes to the law. In 1974, Australia had enacted the price discrimination provisions of the Robinson–Patman Act. They were symbolically important, but little used as they included a hard to prove requirement that for price discrimination to be unlawful, it had to substantially lessen competition. In the mid 1990s the provision was dropped from the Act with the promise that price discrimination concerns could be met by the existence of the abuse of market power law, i.e. s. 46. In fact, no cases of price discrimination were taken under s. 46. Disappointment at this was a factor in the campaign for the Birdsville amendments.

A late attempt in 2007 to review the law or some variation, seemed likely to succeed with a proposed proviso in the statute about below cost pricing, but this was headed off by the inclusion of a 'recoupment' requirement before below-cost pricing was unlawful.

It is difficult to see merit in the Birdsville amendments. A firm with market share does not necessarily have market power. Pricing below cost is not necessarily harmful to competition.

As yet there has been no litigation. One reason is that the ACCC is unenthusiastic about the provision although that does not prevent private action. Another reason is uncertainty about the meaning of 'below-cost pricing for a sustained period'.

There is a good case for removing the provision from the law before it does harm. At the political level it is worth noting that the small business advocates of changes to s. 46 are effectively accepting the removal of the strongly pro-small business provisions that are incorporated in the Birdsville Amendments. Big business opponents of changing s. 46 in the way the Competition Policy Review recommended are missing the opportunity to remove the undesirable Birdsville amendments, not to mention the damage to competitor provisions.

It was partly the worrying Birdsville Amendments that led the author to believe it was best to go down the path discussed with Mr Dawson.

9.5 UNCONSCIONABLE CONDUCT

There has been much political pressure from small business, farmers, large and small suppliers, and competitors for the law to be strengthened in relation to anticompetitive behaviour by firms with market power.

---

[5]   Ibid., 541.

Governments have felt the need to respond but they have encountered fierce resistance by big business, especially big retailers.

Rather than strengthen s. 46, they have often sought a way out of the conflict between big and small business by strengthening some other provisions of the Act. In particular, they have introduced a statutory prohibition on unconscionable conduct by business against other businesses (unconscionable conduct has previously been thought of as mainly a form of consumer protection) and by giving the ACCC the power to apply and enforce the law. There have also been laws about unfair contracts.

There has been considerable case law. The most significant concerns the retail giant Coles, which shares 60–80 per cent of the retail market with Woolworths. The ACCC successfully applied the law to Coles[6]. In essence Coles appeared to treat its suppliers harshly. For example, Coles's managers were assigned quarterly profit targets. If they fell short of the target, many had the habit of having 'a profit day' in which they required suppliers to make up the missing profit by means of a payment. The Federal Court of Australia saw this as a breach of the unconscionable conduct law. The resulting fine was $10 million and damages.

More recently, a case with many similarities concerning Woolworths went in favour of Woolworths.[7] Accordingly the case law is not very settled in this area.

Politicians have also made statutory provision for the application of codes of conduct e.g. a retail code of conduct. This has not been especially effective. Unfair contract terms legislation recently introduced will have an impact as well. This is not to say that those laws are unnecessary, nor that they are substitutes for a proper abuse of dominance law.

Small business and farmers have been appeased by other policy measures – tax cuts, access to finance, etc. for SMEs and for farmers, major investment (AU$5bn) in infrastructure (water, transport and telecoms), increasing access to premium markets through FTAs (particularly to the north in Asia), simplifying and making the tax system fairer for farmers, providing drought assistance and incentives to invest in R&D and a higher skilled workforce. Some of these measures could be regarded as a cost of government unwillingness to change s. 46.

9.6 ACCESS TO ESSENTIAL FACILITIES

Another product of the impasse over s. 46 has been the generation of a unique Australian addition to competition law – the establishment of a lengthy part (Part 3A) of the competition law which sets up a regime for providing access to 'essential facilities' of dominant firms by their upstream or downstream competitors, when access to the services provided by that facility is essential to them doing

---

6   *Australian Competition and Consumer Commission* v. *Coles Supermarkets Australia Pty Ltd* [2014] FCA 1405.
7   *Australian Competition and Consumer Commission* v. *Woolworths Ltd* [2016] FCA 1472.

business. A key reason was the belief of the Hilmer Review in 1993 that on economic grounds, there was a case for granting access to certain facilities if they were key inputs controlled by a monopolist that was vertically integrated. Hilmer believed that it was inappropriate to decide these matters by using s. 46 partly because of its purpose provision (which seemed irrelevant to an economic question), although a bigger factor was that s. 46 cases could require regulatory remedies such as determining prices better left to a regulatory process.

9.7 SECTION 46 IN DETAIL

Against this background we consider the law. As noted, although the provisions of s. 46 occupy several pages, the core of the prohibition is set out in s. 46(1).

A corporation that has a substantial degree of power in a market shall not take advantage of that power in that or any other market for the purpose of:

  (a) eliminating or substantially damaging a competitor of the corporation or of a body corporate that is related to the corporation in that or any other market;
  (b) preventing the entry of a person into that or any other market; or
  (c) deterring or preventing a person from engaging in competitive conduct in that or any other market.[8]

There are many problems with s. 46:

- The purpose test is inappropriate. There should be an effects test. This is discussed in more detail below.
- The term 'take advantage' has been problematic and seems unnecessary. This is also discussed in more detail below.
- It is out of line with international standards. Only New Zealand and Papua New Guinea have the same law.
- As discussed, a set of amendments of s. 46 introduced in 2008, 'the Birdsville amendments', sets up an inappropriate test of abuse, additional to the core one set out above, as discussed above.
- The section refers to behaviour that harms competitors, not competition, although this is partly mitigated by court interpretation as discussed above.
- It is unnecessarily long. This distracts from its key focus, and also encourages politicians to keep adding additional provisions.
- The provisions are the subject of much heat between small and large business. As noted, politicians have responded to this by tinkering with the section and adding other whole sections to the Act, including sections regarding 'unconscionable behaviour' between big and small business and industry codes of conduct and laws about access to 'essential facilities' as discussed below.

[8] See Corones, *Competition Law in Australian*, 427.

An approach proposed by this author and by the current ACCC, now largely adopted by the Competition Review, is to replace the entire s. 46 with a new law – which simply states that:

> a firm with substantial market power shall not engage in conduct that has the purpose or effect or likely effect of substantially lessening competition in a market.

9.7.1 *Purpose and/or Effect and Likely Effect*

The purpose test seems odd. It means that even if the behaviour by a firm with substantial market power has the effect of harming competition and therefore damaging the economy, it is not unlawful, unless the behaviour can be proven in a court of law to have had the purpose of harming competition.

There are several problems with this provision:

- It is based on the wrong principle. If a firm with market power engages in conduct that has the effect of harming competition it should be prohibited. The statute is an economic one designed to prevent harm to the economy, irrespective of purpose. This principle is accepted in virtually every jurisdiction in the world.
- It is sometimes difficult to prove that behaviour with an anticompetitive effect has been done with that purpose.
- The emphasis on 'purpose' tends to divert attention from the economic effect of the behaviour to a 'cops and robbers' style of investigation into the motivations of the behaviour with much attention given to the contents of emails and other internal or external communications by executives. (While there is economic evidence in such cases, its usefulness is somewhat restricted by the emphasis on purpose.)

Several defences of the purpose test have been proffered. None are convincing.

- A business should not be exposed to punitive sanctions for behaviour whose effect it did not intend. A counterargument is that 'purpose' or 'intent' could possibly be relevant to the level, if any, of the fine imposed for the behaviour but absence of proved purpose should not lead to the lack of a prohibition of behaviour that harms the economy, nor to an absence of award of damages.
- The great danger of an abuse of dominance law is that it inadvertently deters pro-competitive conduct. A 'purpose' test is a useful way of preventing abuse of dominance laws from deterring pro-competitive behaviour. A counterargument is that while it is important that the law should not deter pro-competitive behaviour, the job is best done, as in other countries, by the application of well-established relevant economic principle rather than by a purpose test, which may shield seriously anticompetitive behaviour.

- The provision is badly drafted and could be interpreted as prohibiting behaviour that harms competitors, not competition. Accordingly, it should not be strengthened or extended. However, the courts have not interpreted the law in this way. This is not to say, as discussed below, that the law should not be redrafted to exclude reference to 'harm to competitors'. There is a need to redraft the section as a whole, but a new version of this section of the Act should be based on the right principles and include an 'effects test'.
- A change in the law would lead to uncertainty. However, there is much uncertainty about the present law.

9.7.2 *Take Advantage*

Section 46 provides that a firm with substantial market power should not 'take advantage' of it to harm competition.

No other country except New Zealand and Papua New Guinea has a comparable provision. All other countries simply provide that firms with market power may not engage in behaviour that harms competition.

As discussed earlier, 'take advantage' adds an additional requirement before a breach of s. 46 can be found. It makes it necessary to demonstrate that the anticompetitive behaviour was 'taking advantage' of market power.

It greatly complicates the law to add the words 'take advantage', made worse with its particular overtones, compared with 'misuse'. There have indeed been cases where firms with substantial market power have been found by the Federal Court to have engaged in behaviour that substantially lessens competition but not to have breached the Act.[9]

The courts have ruled that 'take advantage' means that they have to ask whether the same behaviour could have occurred in a competitive market. If it could have, then the firm is not breaching the law because the behaviour could have occurred in any context and does not particularly result from using market power even if it is anticompetitive. The courts thus have to answer a hypothetical question. Could the same behaviour have occurred in a hypothetical competitive market? It is very hard to answer this question. There are many possible forms of behaviour that have to be considered in an abstract non-real world setting. It is difficult to predict what would happen in a market where everything else is the same except the firm's own market power. It also distracts attention from the key issue about whether the firm is harming competition. The actions of a hypothetical firm in a hypothetical market would seem largely irrelevant. It also ignores the fact that the effects on competition of conduct by firms with a substantial degree of market power can differ from the effects of the same conduct in a competitive market. Unilateral conduct by a firm

---

[9] Examples include *Rural Press* v. ACCC (2003) 216 Commonwealth Law Report, 53; ACCC v. *Cement Australia Pty Ltd* (2013), Federal Court of Australia 909.

with a substantial degree of market power is much more likely to distort the competitive process than the same conduct by a firm without market power.

'Take advantage' is an unnecessary addition to a law. The aim of the law is to prevent firms with substantial market power from engaging in conduct that has the purpose or effect of substantially harming competition. This is a simple principle and calls for a simple test. Moreover, there is great deal of law already available in ss. 45, 47 and 50 about behaviour that has the purpose or effect of substantially lessening competition. We know what it means. We do not need to add the words 'take advantage'.

9.7.3 Drafting

The drafting of the law is a further disadvantage.

Australia's law is the longest in the world. The competition prohibitions alone are nearly 20,000 words and occupy seventy-four pages. The Sherman Act in the United States is a couple of sentences. The European Treaty is less than a page. Even if we add a few 'bells and whistles' such as the Clayton Act in the USA, the law is still only a thousand words or so.

The UK has a slightly longer Act than in those jurisdictions but it is nowhere near as detailed as the Australian law.

As mentioned, the original rationale of the 1974 provisions was the need to spell out in detail for judges new to an economic law exactly what was, and was not, prohibited.

While that is the main reason for the lengthy nature of the law with its emphasis on form rather than result, there is another cause of its length: once there is a long law, there is a temptation to lengthen it further to capture more and new details. There is also political temptation to add further provisions. The Birdsville amendments described above are an example. So are the 2008 amendments, which lengthened the law without adding any substance.

Another example concerns the provisions of s. 47 which prohibits exclusive dealing that substantially lessens competition. These are set out over several pages and are extremely long and seem unnecessary as they are covered by s. 46 and by s. 45 (the cartel provisions).

Section 48 prohibits resale price maintenance per se. It provides a further example. In most countries there is a one-sentence prohibition. In Australia, however, ss. 96–100 contain lengthy provisos defining legal resale price maintenance, which seem entirely unnecessary.

The courts have done a reasonably good job in interpreting the economic provisions of the Act. There is sufficient jurisprudence both in Australia and overseas for them to be able to be trusted to apply a shortened law properly. The shorter form would enable a sharper focus on the economic effects of business behaviour rather than on its forms and motivations. In addition, it would be useful for the regulator to publish guidelines on the possible application of the law.

9.8 THE COMPETITION POLICY REVIEW

From at least 1990 there has been continuous small business pressure for
protection from the actions of big business. These demands have naturally
found their way onto the competition law agenda with demands for
a strengthening of the law about the abuse of market power. During the last
ten years, there have been some particular triggers for this pressure as noted
earlier. First there was a period of mixed outcomes for the ACCC when it
pursued actions under s. 46. Although it was successful against Safeway and had
some other successes, it also lost a major case, the *Boral* case, in the High Court
of Australia. In another case concerning compact discs, the Full Federal Court
of Australia found certain record companies to have been guilty of behaviour
involving exclusive dealing that substantially lessened competition but strangely
refused to find that there had been an abuse of dominance law under s. 46.
More significantly however as mentioned earlier, from the period 2003 until
about 2008, the Australian Competition and Consumer Commission instituted
no cases under s. 46. This probably reflected the policy inclination of that chair
together with his view that it would be difficult to win cases. This, especially
ACCC inaction, set the scene for political action as noted earlier.

9.8.1 *Factors Giving Rise to Review*

Small Business was encouraged to press for reform in s. 46 when it saw that a major
reform player, namely the Australian Competition and Consumer Commission,
supported significant changes to s. 46. Having suffered many rebuffs to their proposals to strengthen s. 46, when the small business saw the ACCC was pushing for
change, change which the ACCC considered fair, reasonable and rational, it was
encouraged to press harder.

Prior to the election in 2013 and in response to small business pressures the
Shadow Small Business Minister, Bruce Billson announced that if the coalition
was elected an inquiry would be held into s. 46. This proposal was quickly broadened into there being a 'root and branch' review of the whole of the act. Upon
election, the inquiry was further broadened into including a review of the whole of
competition policy including government restrictions on competition. One reason
for this was to defuse the sharp focus on s. 46.

In the event the competition review made over fifty far-reaching recommendations. However, the only recommendation, which generated heat, was the recommendation concerning s. 46 (to the dismay of Professor Harper and others who
regarded the other far-reaching recommendations as all-important).

The Competition Review Panel was chaired by Professor Ian Harper,
a distinguished economist with strong pro-market leanings and with a cautious
attitude to government intervention in markets. Other members of the Panel

included a leading barrister and two members with some sympathy for small business and farmer concerns. The Panel held numerous hearings, consulted widely, studied the law, and issued a draft report before publishing its report in 2015.

9.8.2 *The Competition Policy Review*

The Competition Policy Review 2015 led by Professor Ian Harper concluded that:

> Section 46, dealing with the misuse of market power, is deficient in its current form. It does not usefully distinguish pro-competitive from anti-competitive conduct. Its sole focus on 'purpose' is misdirected as a matter of policy and out of step with international approaches.[10]

It concluded that s. 46 should instead prohibit conduct by firms with substantial market power that has the purpose, effect or likely effect of substantially lessening competition, consistent with other prohibitions in the competition law. It should direct the court to weigh the pro-competitive and anticompetitive impact of the conduct.

The Review appeared to favour a very short version of s. 46 and this is reflected in its core recommendation, but having regard to the heat and emotion surrounding the debate, it concluded that the one sentence law should be surrounded by some provisos that were, in effect, explanatory.

It also concluded that the prohibition on exclusive dealing in s. 47 should be repealed as a properly drafted s. 46 together with amendments to s. 45, which concerns horizontal and vertical anticompetitive agreements, made it unnecessary. It could have but chose not to repeal the detailed provisions spelling out the meaning of resale price maintenance.

The Panel pointed out that the proposed test of 'substantial lessening of competition' is the same test as is found in s. 45 (anticompetitive agreements), s. 47 (exclusive dealing) and s. 50 (mergers) of the CCA, and the test is well accepted and understood, within those sections.

The review stressed that the issue for courts, and for firms assessing their own conduct, is to weigh the pro-competitive and anticompetitive impacts of the conduct to decide if there has been a substantial lessening of competition. To clarify the law and mitigate concerns about over-capture, the Panel propose that s. 46 include legislative guidance with respect to the intended operation of the section. Specifically, it recommended that the legislation should direct the court, when determining whether conduct has the purpose, effect or likely effect of substantially lessening competition in a market, to have regard to the extent to which the conduct:

---

[10] I. Harper, P. Anderson, S. McCluskey and M. O'Bryan, QC, *Competition Policy Review – Final Report* (March 2015), 9.

- increases competition in a market, including by enhancing efficiency, innovation, product quality or price competitiveness; and
- lessens competition in a market, including by preventing, restricting or deterring the potential for competitive conduct in a market or new entry into a market.

The review said that the proposed reform to s. 46 was intended to improve its clarity, force and effectiveness so that it can be used to prevent unilateral conduct that substantially harms competition and that has no economic justification.

The coalition government fairly quickly adopted most of the recommendations but said it needed more time to consider the recommendations regarding s. 46. During and after this time there was ferocious lobbying and advocacy by all sides of the debate. Big business claimed that the new law would have a powerful effect on deterring competition and that it would hold back innovation. The big business lobby circulated a list of business actions which it thought would not be possible under the new law, a list which most experts thought was highly improbable. It also argued that if a firm was highly innovative and efficient and thereby eliminated competitors and acquired dominance or otherwise enhanced dominance, it would be found to have 'substantially lessened competition'.

The ACCC and others argued against this proposition, claiming that there was significant case law, which showed that this was not the way that the courts viewed 'substantial lessening of competition'. From the other side, the small business lobby stepped up its campaigning and in doing so, it felt that the prospects of getting the reform were good given the support coming from the ACCC and this author.

During this period, the government held its own consultations and hearings. It also searched for a compromise between the old law and the new law. Something like this had been tried many years earlier when the Labour government was faced with a recommendation that it should change the merger law from 'dominance' to 'substantial lessening of competition'. It explored using words like 'collective dominance', 'joint dominance', 'shared dominance' rather than the term 'substantial lessening of competition' but eventually it accepted the recommendation in full without these somewhat ambiguous provisions. In 2015, the government too found that halfway houses were not workable.

Eventually the government decided to accept the Competition Review recommendation.

An important reason was the extremely strong support from the National Party. Of particular relevance is that during the time of the debate, the Liberal Party replaced its leader, Prime Minister Abbott with a new leader, Prime Minister Malcolm Turnbull. Turnbull won the position as a result of a vote in the Liberal Party. Following that, Turnbull, whose support for National Party policies was thought to be less strong than that of his predecessor, had to gain the support of the Nationals for his Prime Ministership. In the negotiations that occurred, the National Party made it a condition of their support that Prime Minister Turnbull would support a change in the s. 46 test. Turnbull appears to have given a commitment that he would very probably support the change in the law. In the event he did so, and the coalition adopted the new law with the qualification that there would be some discussion later about the exact wording of the change in the law.

This interesting event should not be seen out of context. It was not the key reason for the change in the law. The key reason for the proposed change in the law was the sound arguments for change, which carried much of business and much of the government with them. Very often in the face of such circumstances, key business interests such as that of the BCA would still prevail. In this instance, pressure from the National Party got the change in the law over the line. This is not unusual. The ACCC push for a removal of parallel import restrictions in the 1990s also got over the line by one vote in the Senate, when Senator Brian Harradine, previously cool to the changes, voted for them because of his anger at the Labour Party (opposed to changes) over what he saw as disrespect for religion earlier in that day in Parliament. But the bigger picture was successful ACCC advocacy that got the changes in the law over the first forty-nine hurdles to change. Senator Harradine was only the fiftieth! Likewise, the support of the prime minister and then the whole cabinet was only one of many hurdles on the path to reform.

Draft legislation reflecting exactly the Harper proposals has been introduced into the Parliament, and despite Labour Party opposition, it seems certain to be enacted.

9.9 CONCLUSION

This chapter argues that in accepting the Competition Policy Review proposal for reform of the abuse of market power law, the Australian government has adopted an economically and legally sensible change that brings Australian law into line with the rest of the world.[11]

It follows that a rational economic and legal approach to competition law policy making has prevailed notwithstanding very strong opposition from big business in Australia. The approach adopted accords with the requirements of both economic efficiency and equity. It earns high marks for a clear statement of a simple economic principle that underlies competition law; It also earns high marks for being fair and equitable in that it aims to strike down abuse of market power by businesses with market power.

The principal reasons for this outcome were:

- A strong economic and legal argument prevailed on merit despite opposition and noise from big business opponents.

[11] For a notable omission from the Australian abuse of dominance law, however, see Appendix 1.

- A further factor was a degree of negativity in community attitudes to big businesses, especially big retailers coupled with sympathy to views that there was unfairness to suppliers and small competitors of big business again especially in the retail sector.
- The change in the law was made much easier by the support of other powerful business groups, especially the powerful Australian Chamber of Commerce and Industry which represents medium and larger and some small businesses and the Council of the Small Business Organisations of Australia (COSBOA), which pushed extremely hard for the changes.
- At the political level, despite the tendency of a conservative coalition government led by the Liberal Party to be very cautious in adopting changes to the law that are opposed by big business, a degree of support in the Party buttressed by extremely strong support from the National Party members of the coalition government (who largely represent rural areas and farmers) made a big difference.
- The consumer voice was not heard very much during the debate.
- The media was relatively neutral on the topic with the Australian Financial Review basically opposing the change.
- Big business lost some support through voicing exaggerated concerns about the impact of the proposals. This lost them credibility.
- Timing was relevant and appropriate. Previously it was not possible to have full debate on the proposal because such debate was crowded out by debate about other competition law reforms in earlier years. The policy bandwidth in competition law is quite narrow.
- Adoption of the changes was facilitated by events described in the paper relating to the change in prime ministership. This removed one final hurdle in a field littered with hurdles on the way to reform.

APPENDIX 1

Divestiture

There is one notable omission from the Australian law – the absence of a divestiture power as a remedy for abuse of market power. The arguments for it are:

- It is a measure that addresses what is often the root of the problem that is an over-concentrated market. It contrasts with the current remedies, which may simply suppress certain ways in which market power is exercised without removing it.
- Section 46 is widely regarded as ineffective and the Harper changes will only make it slightly more effective. Providing a sanction with real teeth could force firms with market power to take this part of the law more seriously.

- It is sometimes suggested that there could be constitutional difficulties about a divestiture power insofar as the Constitution prohibits appropriation of property without due compensation. However, if divestiture is a sanction for breaches of the law (such as breaches of s. 46) rather than a direct appropriation of property, it is unlikely to be caught by this part of the Constitution.
- The track record of divestiture in the United States is strong. Successful divestitures included oil, tobacco, and chemicals a century or so ago and AT&T more recently. However, divestiture has a mixed academic press. The Harper Review opposed divestiture on the grounds that it could prevent the achievement of economies of scale and that it might be better for Parliament to exercise its power rather than a court of law. Whatever the merits or demerits of the Harper's view, divestiture is not an issue in the current climate. However, once the Harper recommendations are enacted, the scene would be set for a further inquiry into the Act in the next few years and at that time there could be a much fuller debate about divestiture.

Antitrust Enforcement and Market Power in the Digital Age

Is Your Digital Assistant Devious?

Ariel Ezrachi and Maurice E. Stucke

10.1 INTRODUCTION

The antitrust laws have been, and should be, about market power. Promoting efficiency, in and of itself, was never the goal. Nor can it be. The pursuit of efficiency is an unworkable antitrust objective. The efficiency paradox, as Professor Eleanor Fox identified, is where US conservative enforcers and courts in the name of efficiency protect inefficient conduct by dominant and leading firms, thus protecting inefficiency. We have paid the price from the efficiency paradox. The wreckage from the economic crisis includes financial institutions deemed too big to fail (or criminally prosecute) and complaints of crony capitalism.

But US antitrust enforcement still has not come to grips with power. This is especially troubling going forward with the rise of big data, big analytics, and super-platforms. Reflecting on Prof. Fox's warnings about the efficiency screen and assumptions, this chapter uses digital personal assistants to explore the pitfalls of "antitrust light" in the data-driven economy. With the agglomeration of data through the internet of things, individuals will have even less privacy, control and autonomy, and the private sphere will shrink. Individuals will continue to struggle with the imbalance of power that yields take-it-or-leave-it privacy notices that few people can afford to leave, if they wish to connect with friends and family. If the market power is left unchecked, the privacy harms will go straight to our democratic ideals of a loss of autonomy and freedom.

Who wouldn't want a personal butler? Technological developments have moved us closer to that dream. Intelligent, voice-activated digital helpers already provide a wide range of services and are likely to increase in appeal and sophistication. Virtual or digital personal assistants are (or can be) installed on our smartphones and smart watches, or are placed, like Amazon's Echo, in our homes. With ever-increased sophistication, these computer bots promise to transform the way we access information and communicate, shop, are entertained, control our smart household appliances, and raise our children.

Indeed, digital assistants already seek to interact with us in a human-like way, providing relevant information and suggesting restaurants, news stories, hotels, and shopping sites. Many of us already benefit from basic digital assistants. Apple iPhone users may have Siri call their mom on speaker. Siri can 'predict' what app they might want to use, which music they would like to listen to. Amazon's voice recognition personal assistant, Echo, can shop for you (knowing everything you previously bought through Amazon); plan your mornings, including upcoming meetings, traffic, weather, etc.; entertain you with music; suggest movies, shows, or audio-books; and control your house's smart appliances.[1] Our navigation apps already anticipate where we are heading throughout the day and provide traffic updates and time estimates. Other applications encourage use by ranking you in comparison to others and updating you during the day. Even your favorite coffee outlet may send you a notification and prepare your loyalty card on your device whenever you're near an outlet.

In 2016, Google showed a video of a suburban family undergoing its morning wakeup routine: "The dad made French press coffee while telling Google to turn on the lights and start playing music in his kids' rooms. The mom asked if 'my package' had shipped. It did, Google said. The daughter asked for help with her Spanish homework."[2] As the artificial intelligence and communication interface advance, digital assistants will offer an unparalleled personalized experience. These digital assistants – or 'digital butlers' – can provide us not just with information, but can anticipate and fulfill our needs and requests. They can do so, based on our connections, data profile, behavior, and so forth. As technological developments enhance the available features, our time will be too important to worry over life's little details. As the digital butler seamlessly provides more of what interests us and less of what doesn't, we will grow to like and trust it. Communicating in our preferred language, they can quickly execute our commands.

Yet, despite their promise, can personalized digital assistants actually reduce our welfare? Might their rise reduce the number of gateways to the digital world, increase the market power of a handful of firms, and limit competition? And, if so, what are the potential social, political, and economic concerns?

Our chapter explores these propositions. The Internet and e-commerce have brought us closer to the promised land of competition – where ample choice, better quality, and lower prices reside. New technologies and better networks, are see-mingly delivering waves of innovation and competitive pressure. Efficiency and welfare await us at every turn we take – we get more of what we need, with lower search costs and greater speed. Yet, behind the facade of welfare-enhancing compe-tition, a more complex reality exists, which may claw back some of the promised benefits and leave us worse off. We explore these developments more fully in *Virtual*

---

[1] www.wallstreetdaily.com/2015/08/04/amazon-echo-assistant

[2] D. Yadron, 'Google Assistant Takes on Amazon and Apple to Be the Ultimate Digital Butler'; www .theguardian.com/technology/2016/may/18/google-home-assistant-amazon-echo-apple-siri

Competition.[3] In this chapter we wish to focus on one example of innovation, which may undermine our welfare – the rise of digital butlers. The ease with which they may be used by leading platforms to cement their market power, depends, in many ways, on one's understanding of the scope and role of competition law.[4]

We illustrate how the digital butler will likely be a key gateway between the user and the World Wide Web. With this unique position of power, and with our trust and consent, it will act as a gatekeeper in a two-sided market. In such a market, its allegiance will likely lie with its creator or provider, not the user. We show how network effects, big data and big analytics will likely undermine attempts to curtail its power, and will likely allow it to operate below the regulatory and antitrust radar screens. As a result, rather than advance our overall welfare, these digital assistants – if left to their own devices – can undermine it.

10.2 HOW A DIGITAL BUTLER COULD FORTIFY THE LEADING PLATFORM'S GATEKEEPER POSITION

The notable developers of digital personal assistants all involve the leading online platforms: Google Assistant, Apple's Siri, and Amazon's Alexa. These super-platforms, all heavily investing to improve their offering, are jockeying as to "who gets to control the primary interface of mobile devices."[5] The stakes are great and will have effects that go beyond the mere use of the digital assistant. In the competitive race, the winning platforms will likely control a significant interface. In essence, each super-platform wants its personal assistant to become our key gateway. Let us see why.

We are all aware of the power at the hands of current search engines and interface owners, who can determine the order of search results, access to the market, and likely action by the user. While the competitor may be a 'click away,' the gate keeper may influence the likelihood of us being aware of it, or our incentive to click.[6] That power has increased as we shifted to mobile operating systems. Due to the characteristics of the mobile interface, we increasingly rely on the top recommended

---

[3] For further discussion, see A. Ezrachi and M. E Stucke, *Virtual Competition – The Promise and Perils of the Algorithm Driven Economy* (Harvard University Press 2016).

[4] On the range of values embedded in competition law analysis in the EU, A. Ezrachi 'Sponge' (2017) 5 (1) *Journal of Antitrust Enforcement* 49 – and the US – see M. Stucke, 'Reconsidering Antitrust's Goals' (2012) 53 *Boston College Law Review* 551.

[5] C. Mims, 'Ask M for Help: Facebook Tests New Digital Assistant: Single Interface Could Replace Web Searches and Apps on Mobile Devices', *Wall Street Journal*, November 9, 2015, www.wsj.com/articles/ask-m-for-help-facebook-tests-new-digital-assistant-1447045202

[6] On that point, illustrative is the recent European Commission Google decision: http://europa.eu/rapid/press-release_IP-17–1784_en.htm

search results and on a limited number of providers. As the European Commission noted, following its Google decision:

> The evidence shows that consumers click far more often on results that are more visible, i.e. the results appearing higher up in Google's search results. Even on a desktop, the ten highest-ranking generic search results on page 1 together generally receive approximately 95% of all clicks on generic search results (with the top result receiving about 35% of all the clicks). The first result on page 2 of Google's generic search results receives only about 1% of all clicks. This cannot just be explained by the fact that the first result is more relevant, because evidence also shows that moving the first result to the third rank leads to a reduction in the number of clicks by about 50%. The effects on mobile devices are even more pronounced given the much smaller screen size.[7]

Looking forward, these trends will intensify, as we shift to individualized, AI-dominated platforms, and to voice activation. As we converse primarily with our head butler, who increasingly predicts and fulfils our needs, we will less frequently search the web, look at price-comparison websites, or download apps. As the digital butler, powered by sophisticated algorithms, learns more about us, our routine, wants and communications, it can excel in its role. In a human-like manner, it can be funny – at just the appropriate level – and trustworthy. After all, being privy to so many of our activities, it will become our digital shadow. This is unsurprising. Many of us already rely on Google's search engine to find relevant results, Facebook to identify relevant news stories, Amazon for book recommendations, and Siri to place phone calls, send text messages, and find a good Chinese restaurant nearby. So, with an eager (and free) butler whose capacity to help us improves, we will increasingly rely on it.

Our digital butler can undertake mundane tasks and free our time. As Google's CEO noted, "Your phone should proactively bring up the right documents, schedule and map your meetings, let people know if you are late, suggest responses to messages, handle your payments and expenses, etc."[8] With time, we will happily relinquish other less personal and useful interfaces, and rely on our butler to surf the web.

That increased reliance on the digital assistant and subsequent reliance on the provider's online platform is the holy grail for the super-platforms. Their aim is to increase the time we spend on their platform – on the gate which it controls – the gate that delivers the income from advertisements, referrals, and purchasing activities. The key is to control as many aspects of our online interface and reap the associated benefits. Take, for example, the Google assistant, which forms part of the

---

[7] European Commission, press release, 'Antitrust: Commission Fines Google €2.42 Billion for Abusing Dominance as Search Engine by Giving Illegal Advantage to Own Comparison Shopping Service' (Brussels, June 27, 2017), http://europa.eu/rapid/press-release_IP-17-1784_en.htm

[8] http://economictimes.indiatimes.com/tech/internet/google-ceo-pichai-sees-the-end-of-computers-as-physical-devices/articleshow/52040890.cms

company's "effort to further entrench itself in users' daily lives by answering users' queries directly rather than pointing them to other sources."[9] Also illustrative were efforts by Facebook, which in 2015 announced a beta version of its digital assistant – M. It can replace most of one's web searches and apps with a function within Facebook Messenger.[10] The leading platforms' plans are clear: they "envision a future where humans do less thinking when it comes to the small decisions that make up daily life."[11] Each super-platform seeks to be the one primarily undertaking our tasks and many decisions for us. As Google's CEO wrote in a 2016 letter to shareholders, "The next big step will be for the very concept of the 'device' to fade away. Over time, the computer itself – whatever its form factor – will be an intelligent assistant helping you through your day."[12]

As our personal assistant becomes our default, so too will its operating platform's applications and functions. As we discuss below, some of these apps (like mapping and navigation apps) benefit from data-driven network effects. So, the more we use a personal assistant for our morning commute, the more data it has of traffic patterns, and the better it is relative to rivals. The removal of the human element from the search activity, and partly from the decision-making, transfers more power to the platform. The personal assistant will use its own tools and may exercise its own judgment as to prioritizing and communicating the results. Default and first-move advantage matter.[13] Finally, as more people use the personal assistant, more advertisers migrate to that platform. This creates another positive feedback loop: the leading platforms, with more advertising revenue and profit, can expand their platform further with smart appliances and driverless cars, all of which yields more data for the personal assistant.

Given the high stakes in the shift from a mobile first world to an AI first world, it is of little surprise that the powerful super-platforms are working hard to capture the lead position. Using the scale of data obtained through their existing network and their analytical capacity, they each want to become the key gatekeeper, who's the butler wins our trust, tasks, and online time. With these abilities, our personal assistant may recognize a busier than usual day. From our phone's geolocation data, it will know when we are heading to our car. Our personal assistant may suggest, "How about treating yourself to Chinese food tonight?" Our personal

9   J. Nicas, 'Google's New Products Reflect Push into Machine Learning', *Wall Street Journal*, May 18, 2016, www.wsj.com/articles/googles-new-products-reflect-push-into-machine-learning-1463598395? mod=ST1

10   Mims, 'Ask M for Help'.

11   Yadron, 'Google Assistant Takes on Amazon and Apple'.

12   Microsoft, 'Other Tech Giants Race to Develop Machine Intelligence', www.wsj.com/articles/tech-giants-race-to-develop-machine-intelligence-1465941959

13   As noted by Commissioner Vestager, "if Google's apps are already on our phones when we buy them, not many of us will go to the trouble of looking for alternatives. And that makes it hard for Google's competitors to persuade us to try their apps." Margrethe Vestager, "How Competition Supports Innovation," speech, Regulation4Innovation, Brussels, May 24, 2016, http://ec.europa.eu/commis sion/2014-2019/vestager/announcements/how-competition-supports-innovation_en

assistant might recommend a popular place. It might then direct the order to a restaurant it believes we would like, arrange for the food's delivery shortly after we arrive home, and pay for the food. All we need to do is grab the food at the door. So, like a good butler, our personal assistant will seamlessly anticipate and satisfy our needs, condensing all the steps to one or two commands.

10.3 HOW THIS GATEKEEPER POSITION MAY PROVIDE THE OPPORTUNITY TO EXERCISE MARKET POWER AND UNDERMINE COMPETITION

'So what?' You may ask. 'What if I decide to use one of these digital butlers and not others? After all it is my decision. I chose the gatekeeper, and can freely choose another.'

You may indeed choose your preferred butler, but may be unaware of some of the tactics it deploys to increase its own profitability while undermining your welfare. Further, your future ability to switch butlers may be more limited than you might anticipate. Let us explore this in more detail.

We already see today abuses by powerful intermediaries, such as price comparison websites and search engines. As more customers rely on the intermediary, the more attractive it becomes to sellers, who will find it important that their products be included on the platform. Sellers know that their products' and services' inclusion on a platform's search results may be crucial for their visibility. As these "information and referral junctions" become a crucial gatekeeper between suppliers and consumers, the platform's bargaining power and ability to distort competition increase.[14]

Some platforms, for instance, may allow for preferential placement based on the level of payment or commission they receive from sellers. For instance, pay-for-placement fees allow a platform to charge higher rates to sellers for the right to be positioned at the top of the list on the default page result. Such positioning may distort competition when the user is unaware of the preferential positioning and assumes that the top results are the best (or most relevant) ones objectively picked by the websites' algorithms. One example of such manipulation of results is in online air and hotel bookings.[15] Following Expedia's 2015 acquisition of Orbitz, for example, "the online travel agency implemented a new program that enables hotel

---

[14] See e.g. I. Lianos and E. Motchenkova, 'Market Dominance and Search Quality in the Search Engine Market' (2013) 9 *Journal of Competition Law & Economics* 419, 422, discussing how search engines "act as 'information gatekeepers': they not only provide information on what can be found on the web (equivalent to yellow pages), but they also are 'an essential first-point-of-call for anyone venturing onto the Internet'" and how they differ from other two-sided platforms, as "search engines detain an important amount of information about their customers and advertisers (the 'map of commerce')."

[15] The factors which could influence the default ordering of hotels on hotel booking intermediaries includes: "customer ratings and complaints"; "if hotels are willing to pay larger commissions"; "photo quality"; and "if a hotel is quicker to turn shoppers into buyers." S. McCartney, 'How Booking Sites Influence Which Hotels You Pick', *Wall Street Journal*, January 27, 2016, www.wsj.com/articles/how-booking-sites-influence-which-hotels-you-pick-1453921300. The methods that hotel booking

properties to move to the first page of Expedia's listings for an additional 10 percent commission."[16] Another example is gas and electricity aggregators.[17] Thus some intermediaries today have power to extract greater rents from suppliers of goods and services, in the form of higher commissions, fees for preferential placement, or advertising. The user may be unaware when the intermediary platform degrades quality. This is true even when competition is a click away.

Thus we can expect such exercises of market power, when: (1) the platform has the ability and economic incentive to intentionally degrade quality; (2) consumers cannot accurately assess the quality degradation; and (3) it is difficult or costly for others to convey to consumers the products' or services' inherent quality differences or to prompt them to switch.[18] These three factors suggest that the risk of anticompetitive strategies will significantly increase as we progressively rely on personal assistants.

10.3.1 Our Personal Assistants Have the Ability and Economic Incentive to Degrade Quality

Consider for instance the following question: who pays our butler? We pay for the hardware, such as the iPhone to access Siri. But none of the super-platforms charge a monthly fee for using its butler. Once you buy Amazon's Echo, you can access Alexa without additional charges. This appears extraordinary: each super-platform encourages us to use its free butler for as many tasks as we can. If a company offered you a human butler, upon whom you could heap as many tasks as possible, without incurring any charge, would you accept the offer? Would you trust the butler? Will the butler ultimately promote your interests or the company's?

---

intermediaries use to tailor search results have come under criticism by some hotels. The American Hotel & Lodging Association told the *Wall Street Journal*, "Biased or misleading search results from these sites or via web searches can be highly problematic, particularly on those booking websites that purport to be helping consumers comparison shop based off of less than objective information" (ibid.).

[16] 'Vista/Cvent: High Combined Market Share and Entry Barriers in Strategic Meeting Management Could Create Hurdle to Clearance; Increased DOJ Interest in Data Privacy May Drive Additional Scrutiny', Capitol Forum, July 20, 2015.

[17] "The executives at uSwitch, MoneySupermarket, Compare the Market, Confused.com and Go Compare were hauled in front of the MPs after it was claimed . . . that some were 'hiding' the best gas and electricity deals from their customers" (Rachel Rickard Straus, 'Price Comparison Website Bosses under Attack from MPs for Not Showing Customers the Best Deals', *This Is Money* (February 4, 2014), www.thisismoney.co.uk/money/bills/article-2939364; Price-comparison-website-bosses-attack-MPs.html. Among other things, platforms were accused of "not showing the cheapest tariffs by default if it meant they wouldn't earn a commission" (ibid.). Following this criticism, the price comparison websites have since ensured that the default search setting will include the full range of tariffs available, regardless of whether or not a commission is charged upstream.

[18] Using these three conditions, we explored elsewhere how a dominant search engine like Google could degrade quality (by providing less relevant responses to a search inquiry), even with competition from Bing, Yahoo!, and DuckDuckGo (M. E. Stucke and A. Ezrachi, 'When Competition Fails to Optimize Quality: A Look at Search Engines' (2016) 18 *Yale Journal of Law and Technology* 70, http://papers.ssrn.com/sol3/papers.cfm?abstract_id=2598128).

The issue concerns whether we are the true employers/principals of these virtual and digital assistants. On a superficial level, yes. The digital assistant will dim the lights on our command. But our new trusted alter ego, to whom we outsource our decision-making, while perhaps charming, is also partial. After all, being the 'free' part of a multisided market, we don't directly pay for the butler's services. Our butler must ultimately cater to the needs of its real employer – the platform. Of course, we can still benefit when the platform's interests are aligned with our own. But we may often be unaware of when such alignment is absent.

The gatekeeper may charge, like the powerful price comparison websites, an entrance fee (commission) from sellers for the right to be featured in the butler's options.[19] It may also delist sellers which are disruptive to the platform's operation (or advertising-driven business model). Such strategy may further intensify in markets in which the gatekeeper vertically integrates. Now the gatekeeper may likely use the butler to push its own services and products. For instance, the platform may insist its sellers and buyers to use its payment system or other related products.[20] Such integration might enable the gatekeeper to leverage its power to related markets, pushing out independent operators.

10.3.2 We Cannot Accurately Assess When, and the Extent to which, Our Butler Degrades Quality

As our butler learns to accommodate our particular tastes, it will be harder for us (and competitors) to identify when the butler degrades quality. It may be easier to assess quality degradation for objective queries (such as the distance between two cities or the current temperature outside). Here we can tell whether a butler answers incorrectly. But for these types of objective queries, the butler typically lacks the incentive to intentionally distort quality. After all, its platform won't profit by telling us it is 28 degrees Celsius, when it is actually 26 degrees. The danger lies in more subjective queries (or tasks that the butler undertakes automatically).

Voice activation and verbal communication are likely to distance us from the data, and lead us to rely on the butler's recommendations. Our environment will become less transparent, and our dependency on the butler that learns by doing will increase. The platform – through its butler – will benefit from unparalleled access to our data and communications. This may assist it in building a profile about us, including our likely reservation price, likely knowledge of outside options, shopping habits, general interests, and weaknesses, such as when our willpower is tired. This information can enable the platform to induce us to buy products that we otherwise

---

[19] This is common in many services, from take-away services to information ranking.
[20] See for example: 'Google Tweaks Policy, All Google Play Apps Must Use Google's Payment System', www.adweek.com/socialtimes/google-drops-the-hammer-on-third-party-android-billing-services-apps-must-use-googles-billing-system/528816

wouldn't, at prices higher than what others would be willing to pay. We call this behavioral discrimination.

As our butler accumulates more information about us, it will be aware of the extent to which we venture out and seek other options. Its aim is to deliver the right product or service at a price that we are willing to pay. So, the line between personalization and behavioral discrimination will blur. As we increasingly rely on the personal assistant for suggestions, it can increasingly suggest things or services to buy, and the price it has successfully negotiated. While helping our son with his Spanish, our digital assistant might suggest a particular app or private tutor that tremendously helped other students struggling with the same issue. Because the tutoring is customized for our son, it will be harder to assess whether the price the tutor charges is the fair market price or simply a price we would tolerate. Moreover, if the tutoring service is helping other children improve their grades, we would not want our child to be at a competitive disadvantage – especially if we are all eyeing the same highly selective universities. So, the digital assistant can prompt purchases that we otherwise wouldn't consider.

For behavioral discrimination to succeed, the platform and the butler will have to limit our exposure to outside options. To accomplish this, the butler may use its gatekeeper position. It may block offerings by other sellers or recommend applications and sites within its ecosystem. The butler may scan our communications and ensures that its credibility is intact. When price is of prime concern, it will beat the competition, as long as we are aware of it. If the personal assistant identifies signs of discontent, possibly in a discussion, tweet or chat, or due to us not completing a purchase, the platform will push a discount voucher or other benefits to keep us engaged. No longer will we be an anonymous shopper browsing the clothing racks. Instead our butler will be always by our side, learning how we react to different product offerings and pricing, learning which ads and promotions work better to induce us to buy and which ones to avoid, and when we can be induced to buy, even though we know we shouldn't.

Lastly, the control over our personal information has privacy implications. The data can be sold to others or used to optimize advertisement income. The platform may have an incentive to offer us certain goods and services sponsored by interested sellers. Think of it as sponsored ads in a non-transparent universe, in which limited benchmarks for comparison exist (as your interface is personalized).

10.3.3 *It Will Be Difficult or Costly for Others to Convey to Consumers the Inherent Quality Differences among the Butler's Suggestions or to Prompt Them to Switch Butlers*

With the increase control over our interface with the World Wide Web, our digital butler may be in a position to take actions which reduce our welfare. For instance, the more we communicate only with our personal assistant, the less likely we will independently search the web, read independent customer reviews on, use multiple price-comparison websites, and rely on other tools. We will entrust our butler to search the web, consider the customer reviews, find the bargain, and report to us its results. In relying on our butler, we become less aware of the outside options. This makes us vulnerable to the platform abusing its market power.

For these subjective queries or tasks, the personal assistant decides whom it admits, thereby increasing the power to exclude others. Exclusionary practices can enhance the platform's market power and lessen the threat (and viability) of rival downstream competitors. Perhaps, most worrying may be the gatekeeper's ability to exclude others from the market while providing us with a distorted view of available options and market reality. The more we rely primarily on the butler, the less we search for outside options. Even if we search the web, the ads, products, or search results we see may be orchestrated by our butler.

Accordingly, it may become harder for retailers unaffiliated with the platform's advertising business to reach that customer. Even if the retailer can reach the customer, it is less likely to succeed in selling the increasingly customized products or services (such as tailored shirts in the styles and colors that appeal to the customer). And even if the retailer can gain the customer's attention, the personal assistant may interject with its own recommendation, suggesting that he consider a special deal by another haberdashery, one that is part of the platform's ecosystem. In this multisided market, the assistant may subtly push certain products and services and degrade or conceal others, all in the name of personalization.

Moreover, even if we discover some quality degradation, we may not switch. The European Commission in 2015 announced its Statement of Objections over Google's intentionally degrading its general search results to systematically favor its own comparison-shopping services.[21] In 2017, it fined Google €2.42 billion for abusing its dominance as a search engine. The Commission noted that in an attempt to address the poor market performance of its comparison shopping service, Google demoted rival comparison shopping services in its search results. "Evidence shows that even the most highly ranked rival service appears on average only on page four of Google's search results, and others appear even further down."[22]

Despite Google's demotion of competitors' services, there has not been a mass exodus to rival search engines. Few people use multiple search engines (even though it is very easy to multi-home).[23] When the search engine yields results that are not directly responsive to our query, most of us will attempt a different search query, rather than a different search engine.[24] So if we don't multi-home search engines, it is less likely we will train new digital butlers.

---

[21] European Commission, press release memo/15/4781, 'Antitrust: Commission Sends Statement of Objections to Google on Comparison Shopping Service' (April 15, 2015), http://europa.eu/rapid/press-release_MEMO-15-4781_en.htm [https://perma.cc/T7UM-3Z5U].

[22] European Commission, 'Antitrust: Commission Fines Google €2.42'.

[23] Stucke and Ezrachi, 'When Competition Fails to Optimize Quality'.

[24] For example, one survey asked search users "what they would do if a Google search result did not contain the expected information"; 34 percent of respondents indicated they would "return to the

Over time, the scope of data and the personalization that follows will make it harder for users to switch digital assistants. Switching cost may also require users to change the underlying operating system and related applications (such as mapping technology); it may involve the need to retrain our digital butler. Indeed, once we choose and train a head butler, we may tolerate mistakes rather than train a new butler from another platform. We will likely repeat or rephrase our request. Accordingly, our initial choice of provider may later result in us unintentionally being locked in.

10.4 WHY THE LEADING PERSONAL ASSISTANT WILL LIKELY BE FROM GOOGLE, APPLE, FACEBOOK, AMAZON (OR PERHAPS MICROSOFT)

With the possibility that our digital assistant can act against our interest, one would expect and hope for the introduction of a 'virtuous assistant' – a class of independent assistants, developed by independent firms with *our* personal interest paramount. These virtuous assistants could warn us when behavioral discrimination is at play, when outside options are ignored, when price alignment seems out of order, or when our information is harvested. They may even deploy counter-measures to maximize our welfare in the face of such strategies. They will form a true extension of our interest – aware of our preferences and safeguarding our autonomy. Notably, as of 2018, no independent virtuous assistant has arisen.

Predicting the leading technology five years from now can be tricky. But several factors favor one of the super-platforms (Google, Apple, Amazon, and perhaps Facebook if it re-enters) capturing the personal assistant market, and disfavoring any independent virtuous assistant. To work well (and gain popularity), the digital butler will likely have to operate from an existing platform – such as a mobile platform – and be able to tap into the vast data it offers. This is for several reasons: first the scale and scope of data needed, second, the data-driven network effect of learning by doing, and third, the integration of the digital assistant with other apps and services, such as texts, mapping, photographs.

Personal data is the first key element. To provide you with relevant services and recommendations, the personal assistant must first learn your habits and preferences. To learn your preferences and predict your desires, personal assistants will require a significant volume and variety of personal data. Absent these features, an 'isolated' helper would be of little use and value – indeed, it would not be a *personal*

search results page and try a different result," and 25 percent said they would "return to Google to enter a new search." No respondents answered that they would try another search engine (A. Gesenhues, *Study: Top Reason a User Would Block a Site from a Search? Too Many Ads*, SEARCH ENGINE LAND (April 15, 2013), http://searchengineland.com/?p=155708 [https://perma.cc/6P59-GF56]). These results may suggest that users perceive the "switching costs" between search providers (or, alternatively, the "costs of spot-checks") as higher than the expected benefit of spot-checking.

assistant. Based on our personal data, including our chat history, geolocation, previous purchasers, and surf habits, the digital butler can provide us with recommendations, and effectively execute our instructions.

Learning by doing is the second key element. By learning through servicing us, digital butlers will not only be reactive but can also take a proactive role – anticipating our needs and wants, rather than following instructions. This requires the platform to have enough users, data and opportunities to experiment to train the algorithms.

The underlying code and algorithms of Facebook's M, for example, are largely open source. The key assets are not the algorithms. (Otherwise why share them?) Key are the scale of data and the algorithm's ability to learn by trial by error. As the *Wall Street Journal* reported, "Facebook Messenger already has more than 700 million users," which yields it the following advantage: "with access to so many users, Facebook has a plausible way to get the gigantic quantity of conversational data required to make a chat-based assistant sufficiently automated."[25] With more users making more requests, the digital assistant can quickly process more tasks easily. In effect, users help the super-platform's algorithm learn by noting and correcting mistakes. Only a few companies have the requisite volume and variety of personal data and opportunities to experiment for their personal assistants to be competitive: namely, the super-platforms Amazon, Facebook, Google, and Apple. Microsoft, in divesting its low-end smartphones, is aiming to become the fifth competitor in this space.[26]

Under this data-driven network effect, the strong can become even stronger as users and their data improve the assistant's algorithms, which attracts even more users. Ultimately these network effects will further weed out the five large platforms. We do not want multiple butlers, each asking us about movies tonight or food to order. Each super-platform will jockey for its butler to become our head butler. In discussing its digital personal assistant, Google's CEO said, "We want users to have an ongoing two-way dialogue with Google."[27] The more we converse with, and delegate to, the head butler, the better it can predict our tastes, and the more likely we are to rely on it for our daily activities. As our butler accumulates information over time, the switching costs between butlers will become higher. We could therefore be willingly locked into our comfort zone. New entrants will find it difficult to match the scale of data held by the super-platforms and to convince us to switch.

The third key element is the scope of services the personal assistant can offer, and the extent to which the personal assistant is integrated in these other services. For example, Google argues that given "its 17 years of work cataloguing the internet and physical world, its assistant is smarter and better able to work with its email, messaging, mapping and photo apps. And since Google makes software for

---

[25]   Mims, 'Ask M for Help'.
[26]   J. Greene and M. Verbergt, 'Microsoft Cuts Low-End Phones', *Wall Street Journal*, May 19, 2016, B1.
[27]   J. Nicas, 'Google Touts New AI-Powered Tools', *Wall Street Journal*, May 19, 2016, B1, B4.

smartphones, smartwatches and old-fashioned computers, Google says people will be able to have one conversation with multiple machines."[28] Google, as the head butler, can analyze our e-mails, texts, or photos, and suggest replies.[29] Looking at our calendar, it can determine the best time for the dog to be groomed.

These three elements can limit the success of the virtuous assistant. The super-platforms already possess far more personal data about us than any start-up could readily and affordably obtain. Any independent virtuous assistant will likely lack the scale and scope of products to attract new users.

Moreover, unless they develop their own operating system, the virtuous assistant will be dependent on the super-platform's services. The super-platform to nudge us to its personal assistant can seamlessly integrate it with its wide offering. They may exclude the virtual assistant from their online wallets, such as Apple Pay or Google Wallet. The super-platform can degrade the functionality of the virtuous assistant by reducing its performance and having them run slower. We would likely blame the virtuous assistant for its tardiness. Or the super-platforms may simply block the virtuous assistant by arguing that doing so protects us. For example, the super-platform may argue that privacy considerations restrict interoperability with the virtuous assistant.

Although these three factors favor the super-platform, a popular virtuous assistant may still be possible. With the possibility for such a virtuous assistant, you may rightly ask why we are pessimistic. Perhaps the easiest way to explain our prediction is to ask the following: which search engine did you use today (or this past week)? Did you opt for one which does not harvest information and retains your anonymity (such as DuckDuckGo) or for one which tracks your behavior to better target you with personalized ads? Did you limit the ability of your phone apps to access personal and geo-location information? Do you often change the default option? When downloading an app or update, do you read the terms and conditions? Even if you did, did you still accept the terms – not understanding who will access your data and what they will do with it? Did you invest money in privacy measures, or were you happy with the joy of free? And if you did invest money, do you know if the promise of privacy and control was truly delivered by your service provider?

The likely answers to these questions may help us appreciate why the current forces favor the super-platforms. Key here are data-driven network effects, big data, big analytics, vertical integration, bundling of services, and interoperability.

So, a virtuous assistant may still be possible. Their presence can possibly limit the ability of the powerful gatekeepers to exercise market power and reduce our welfare. But if virtuous search engines, such as DuckDuckGo, haven't prevented the abuses

---

[28]   Yadron, 'Google Assistant Takes on Amazon and Apple'.
[29]   Ibid.

of the dominant search engine, we remain doubtful that a virtuous personal assistant (by DuckDuckGo or others) will fare any better.[30]

10.5 *THE TRUMAN SHOW*

So far, we illustrated how the rise of the trusted digital butler may afford its provider with the power to affect our welfare and view of available goods and markets. Importantly, the power does not stop there. The control over the key interface provides the platform with the ultimate power – to affect not only what we buy, but to affect our views and the public debate. The reliance on a gatekeeper could enable its operator to intellectually capture users, and subsequently decision-makers, in an attempt to ultimately ensure that public opinion and government policies align with the corporate agenda.

While such proposition may sound apocalyptic, it should not be brushed aside. We have discussed the fascinating link between market power and intellectual and regulatory capture in *Virtual Competition*. In what follows, we briefly illustrate how the use of digital butlers may facilitate such capture.

Man, Aristotle observed, is by nature a social animal. As we increasingly rely on our personal assistant, it will increasingly learn about our social and political views, behavior, and susceptibility to biases. Facebook, for example, "collects data on roughly 1.6 billion people, including 'likes' and social connections, which it uses to look for behavioral patterns such as voting habits, relationship status and how interactions with certain types of content might make people feel."[31]

Facebook does not simply passively collect data about us. It also has the power to affect our behavior. One study, which later proved quite controversial, sought to examine 'emotional contagion,' whereby people transfer positive and negative moods and emotions to others.[32] This was the "first experimental evidence for massive-scale emotional contagion via social networks."[33] People, when posting on Facebook, frequently express positive or negative emotions. Their friends later see these posts via Facebook's "News Feed" product. "Which content is shown or omitted in the News Feed is determined via a ranking algorithm that Facebook continually develops and tests in the interest of showing viewers the content they will find most relevant and engaging."[34] Facebook's News Feed algorithms, as part of the

---

[30] For a review of the possible ways in which algorithms could promote customer welfare, see M. S. Gal and N. Elkin-Koren 'Algorithmic Consumers' (2017) 30(2) *Harvard Journal of Law and Technology* 309.

[31] By D. Hernandez and D. Seetharaman, 'Facebook Offers Details on How It Handles Research', *Wall Street Journal*, June 14, 2016, www.wsj.com/articles/facebook-offers-details-how-it-handles-research-1465930152

[32] A. D. I. Kramer, J. E. Guillory, and J. T. Hancock, 'Experimental Evidence of Massive-Scale Emotional Contagion through Social Networks', *PNAS Early Review*, March 25, 2014, https://cornell.app.box.com/v/fbcontagion

[33] Ibid.

[34] Ibid.

study, were intentionally manipulated. The experiment examined whether exposure to less positive or negative emotional content led the 689,003 test subjects to post content that was consistent with the exposure.[35] It did. When Facebook surreptitiously reduced friends' positive content in the News Feed for one week, the users were less positive: a larger percentage of words in the users' status updates were negative and a smaller percentage were positive.[36] When Facebook surreptitiously reduced their friends' negative content in its News Feed, the Facebook users were less negative themselves. People who were exposed to fewer emotional posts (either positive or negative) in their News Feed "were less expressive overall on the following days."[37] Thus by manipulating the News Feed, Facebook could influence users' moods.

What is also interesting is that Facebook could manipulate users' emotions even though the users' search costs were low: their friends' content "was always available by viewing a friend's content directly by going to that friend's 'wall' or 'timeline,' rather than via the News Feed. Further, the omitted content may have appeared on prior or subsequent views of the News Feed. Finally, the experiment did not affect any direct messages sent from one user to another'"[38]

If Facebook can affect users' mood and engagement by simply promoting some content over another in the users' News Feed, just imagine the power of digital butlers to affect our moods, behavior, and views. Digital assistants will likely become more proactive – making recommendations on entertainment, or commenting on the music we listen to or the books we are reading. By complimenting and cajoling, sharing thoughts with us on recent events, sending personalized notes on special occasions, encouraging one to communicate with others on certain matters, reminding us of presents, suggesting popular gifts trending among the recipient's friends, and informing us about information from our smart meters and smart sensors, it will ingrain itself in our lives – and engage with us through out the day.

Consider, for example, the control our personal assistant may have over what news stories we see. Currently, the super-platforms do not report the news. But many people rely on the super-platforms' algorithms to find news of interest. One 2015 study found that 61 percent of millennials in the United States (those born between 1981 and 1996) were "getting political news on Facebook in a given week."[39] This was a much larger percentage than any other news source. A 2016 study found that Facebook "sends by far the most mobile readers to news sites of any social media

[35]   Ibid.
[36]   Ibid., at 2.
[37]   Ibid., at 3.
[38]   Ibid., at 2.
[39]   A. Mitchell, J. Gottfried, and K. Eva Matsa, 'Millennials and Political News: Social Media – The Local TV for the Next Generation?' *Pew Research Center*, June 1, 2015, www.journalism.org/2015/06/01/millennials-political-news

sites" – 82 percent of the social traffic to longer news stories and 84 percent of the social traffic to shorter news articles.[40]

While we appreciate this free service, we do not know its exact cost. By presenting more stories with a more negative spin, can our digital assistant sour not only our outlook, but the outlook of our Facebook friends? When our butler joins our chats to make suggestions, or at times makes suggestions counter to those made by other helpers, we may not know whether it is being helpful or simply manipulating our behavior. It may work in the background to undermine attempts to expose us to competing products, or it may monitor our tweets and chat rooms for signs of discontent with the service or discount offered – signs of anger that should trigger a behavioral action. The list is truly endless – all under the guise of catering to our needs.

Users rely on the super-platforms, in part, because they believe the algorithms objectively identify the most relevant results. But, as we saw above, a powerful platform can intentionally degrade the quality of its results to promote its corporate interests. Thus, we can see why conservatives were concerned over allegations in 2016 that the social network Facebook manipulated for political purposes the rankings of news stories for its users, suppressing conservative viewpoints.[41] (Facebook denied doing this.)

As the personal assistant expands its role in our daily lives, it can alter our world view. By crafting notes for us, and suggesting 'likes' for other posts it wrote for other people, the personal assistant can effectively manipulate us through this stimulation. "With two billion 'likes' a day and one billion comments," one doctor noted, "Facebook stimulates the release of loads of dopamine as well as offering an effective cure to loneliness.[42] Imagine the dopamine spike when the personal assistant secures a new record of 'likes' for a political message it suggested that you post. Others do not know that your digital assistant was heavily involved in drafting your note. You do not know the extent to which the personal assistant generated the likes. And none of us know how this note is helping sway the public discourse in ways that benefit the super-platform.

10.6 POSSIBLE INTERVENTION

The problem we identify reaches beyond antitrust. But the problem is a manifestation of a platform's market power. The problem also strikes at a current weakness of antitrust policy, namely its price-centric focus. Competition officials

[40] K. Eva Matsa, 'Facebook, Twitter Play Different Roles in Connecting Mobile Readers to News', *Pew Research Center*, May 9, 2016, www.pewresearch.org/fact-tank/2016/05/09/facebook-twitter-mobile-news

[41] D. Seetharaman, 'Uproar over Bias Claims Ignites Fears over Facebook's Influence', *Wall Street Journal*, May 11, 2016, A1.

[42] 'Facebook and Your Brain: The Inside Dope on Facebook', *Psychology Today*, May 24, 2012, www.psychologytoday.com/blog/vitality/201205/facebook-and-your-brain

generally assess market power in the form of higher prices. Rarely do they assess market power primarily in the form of non-price effects such as quality.[43] So what can we do to prevent the anticompetitive (and manipulative) conduct?

Some might argue, nothing. The introduction of a digitalized butler, advanced technology and artificial intelligence, all promise to improve our welfare. The possible adverse effects described above are too speculative. Dynamic market forces and disruptive innovation should be sufficient to challenge the incumbents and ensure that they refrain from abusing their gatekeeper position.

Others will likely disagree. The risk of chilling innovation, investment, and competition is real, but so is the risk of exclusionary dynamics and anticompetitive effects. Arguably, the stakes are even greater. Digital butlers, and the personalized environment they will offer, may enable firms to extract more wealth than before, and reduce market transparency and the availability of comparison benchmarks. The exclusionary and exploitative strategies go beyond our wallets, and can affect our privacy, well-being, and democracy.

Yet, the optimal level of intervention is difficult to ascertain. With that in mind we briefly sketch here ex-post intervention, merited when an abuse of dominance is present, and ex-ante intervention, which may address more fundamental market failures.

An ex-post approach may lead to intervention when the platform operating the digital butler holds a dominant position and abuses it. To establish dominance, market power will have to be sustained over time. In the context of our discussion, it is possible that network effects and switching costs may contribute to the emergence of such market power. Abuse may be established when the dominant undertaking engages in exclusionary or exploitative conduct. Such strategies have attracted the European Commission's scrutiny in the past in the area of operating systems and search engines. In *Microsoft*,[44] the Commission was concerned with the leveraging of market power from the operation systems by the bundling of Windows Media Player;[45] and, to restrict interoperability with a view to encouraging use of Windows PCs only with Microsoft group servers, thus discouraging investment in non-Microsoft group servers.[46] In its Google investigation, as we saw, the Commission raised concerns about Google degrading its search results and illegally leveraging its market power.

The difficulty in enforcement in such cases may stem from the nature of the service. First one may question the true market power of personal helpers and their ability to behave independently of others. Even if customers are deemed to be locked

---

[43]   This is explored in greater detail in M. E. Stucke and A. P. Grunes, *Big Data and Competition Policy* (Oxford University Press 2016).

[44]   Case COMP/C-3/37.792 – Microsoft; unsuccessfully appealed in Case T-201/04 *Microsoft Corp v. Commission* [2007] ECR II-3601.

[45]   Case COMP/C-3/37.792, recital 826-834; Case T-201/04, para. 856

[46]   Case COMP/C-3/37.792, recital 642-646, in particular; Case T-201/04, para. 651

in, one may have difficulties establishing some forms of abuse. The personalization of the service may make it difficult to ascertain an objective benchmark for comparison. Credible counterfactuals to quality degradation may be difficult to establish. As the primary interaction takes place at the personal-assistant level, the effects may be seen more as personalization (and thus a legitimate part of technological progress) than exclusionary.

An alternative ex-ante approach will seek to ensure having the preconditions to promote privacy competition, ensure that the platform's incentives are aligned with users' interests, and prevent some of the market dynamics which could give rise to exclusionary or exploitative effects. Such approach may be implemented through sector investigations, agreed commitments, or other regulatory instruments. For instance, basic measures would ensure that users retain autonomy, are made aware of outside options and can switch with limited or no costs. One could require digital butlers to indicate clearly, either in a pop up window or voice warning when their suggestions are 'sponsored' or when they offer service through their own platform network while excluding others. Users may be able to opt out of personalized ads or sponsored products.[47] All these measures, to be effective, require short and clear communications. Knowing and voluntary consent is key as often the consent in today's click-wrap is little more than a facade. When users have few, if any, viable options, consent is not real but forced. In addition, 'consent fatigue' or digital helpers managing consent forms on your behalf, could lead to meaningless agreement and undermine customer empowerment.

To allow switching between butlers, data mobility should be encouraged. With adequate safeguards, one should be able to transfer the core parameters, which will enable a new butler to start from a position of personalization. At the providers' side, mobility would require access to platforms and the provision of interoperability information. Mobility may require the development of basic industry standards for key data points and will need to take into account issues of licensing and IP rights. Their development should nonetheless allow sufficient freedom for developers, to enable disruptive innovation.

10.7 CONCLUDING REMARKS

A recent trip to a home-improvement store highlighted the rise of smart appliances, which can communicate with digital assistants. For those of us watching *The Jetsons* the prospect of our own automated helper that will serve our needs might seem marvelous.

In industries dominated with data-driven network effects, we could likely receive free butlers. They will excel at mundane tasks, and as AI develops, they will

---

[47] Transparency is key – Google, in its last update, allowed users to opt out of personalized ads, etc. This is a positive move, which ensures user control over their data and search environment.

increasingly assist us with our daily tasks. Seeing the salient, day-to-day benefits, we may trust and rely on our butler. Our assistant will no longer be simply making our French press coffee, and turning on the lights in our kids' rooms. It will be tutoring our children, entertaining our family, telling us happy or sad stories from around the world, ordering our food (and the books that it recommends), and summoning the driverless car to whisk us to jobs, where we, as a result of being freed from the many household chores, can spend more time and effort to meet the rising expenses.

As we welcome the digital assistants to our homes, we may not recognize their toll on our well-being. The next technological frontier of digital butlers may not be rosy. As the digital butler increasingly controls our mundane household tasks, like regulating room temperature, adjusting our water heater and playing our favorite music, it will be harder to turn off. It will also be tempting to increasingly rely on the butler for other activities, such as the news we receive, the shows we watch, and the things we buy.

Market forces, given the data-driven network effects, have the potential to increase entry barriers, make the strong platforms (and their butlers) even stronger, and weaken many independent personal assistants. Economic and political power would consolidate into fewer hands. Market forces, left unchecked, may yield a handful of devious butlers, even though the technology exists for an independent virtuous assistant. The large platforms could extract even more personal data and command even higher rents to allow others to access us. Not only will our pocketbooks be affected. Our political and social discourse could also be manipulated.

One of the striking issues is how our digital environment, on one level may appear competitive and free, but on another level is carefully designed to suit the platform's needs (and pecuniary interests) rather than our needs and interests. We may feel that we roam the fields of the free market and free ideas, and yet we are increasingly ushered by the super-platform's digitalized hand.

So, we need to be aware of the possible conflicts of interest. Such awareness translates to power. Our public awareness, at present, is limited. Too often we accept terms and conditions without questioning them and assume that greater powers – market or state – will ensure our autonomy and welfare. In reality, the innovation from which we benefit comes at a price which is rarely challenged. Indeed, this evolution may go unchallenged under current user behavior and current antitrust policies. The greater algorithm autonomy in a nontransparent, highly personalized interface with customers can stifle competition enforcement. One would hope that the antitrust agencies and courts understand the risks and work to minimize them, among other things, by educating the user about the cost of freeing oneself from the platform's shackles.

As we explore in *Virtual Competition*, super-platforms and their personal assistants present unique challenges. We cannot assume that market forces, given these network effects, will deliver the virtuous assistant or curb these abuses. We must consider outside options. We must ask our antitrust, privacy and consumer protection officials and legislators what steps they are undertaking to minimize the risks and protect our interests and freedom. Until then, rather than ask your personal assistant if she loves or respects you, you might just want to keep her focused on the more mundane aspects of your life (such as turning off the lights).

Economic Efficiency versus Democracy

On the Potential Role of Competition Policy in Regulating Digital Markets in Times of Post-Truth Politics

Josef Drexl[*]

11.1 INTRODUCTION

The Chicago School of economics claims to offer an apolitical approach to antitrust by advocating economic efficiency as the ultimate goal of competition policy. In contrast, by showing that the Chicago School actually stifles efficiency by trusting dominant firms and protecting monopoly, critiques described Chicago's 'efficiency paradox' and conservative political agenda.[1]

Whether Chicago School should therefore be called an ideology[2] is not so important. Rather, the question is whether a competition policy that limits its objective to economic efficiency will always serve society and, if this question is to be answered in the negative, whether there is an alternative. Indeed, such an alternative can be found in a concept of protecting the competitive process.[3]

This alternative has the potential of bringing about diverse benefits for society. These broader benefits can even be highly political. The potential of competition law to contribute to democracy was well understood long before the rise of the Chicago School. In particular, the United States promoted competition laws and policy in post-war Germany and Japan as an instrument to extinguish the economic foundations of ideology. In the field of media markets, the goal of promoting democracy can even be integrated as a consideration in the assessment of practical cases.[4]

---

[*] This chapter takes into account legal and political developments until August 2017.

[1] Eleanor M. Fox, 'The Efficiency Paradox', in Robert Pitovsky (ed.), *How Chicago Overshot the Mark: The Effect of Conservative Economic Analysis on U.S. Antitrust* (Oxford University Press, 2008) 77.

[2] The term 'ideology' is used by Marina Lao, 'Ideology Matters in the Antitrust Debate' (2014) 79 *Antitrust Law Journal* 649, 651–2(assuming that current antitrust debate is not just about economics but that it is also influenced by 'ideological differences' between antitrust conservatives and antitrust liberals).

[3] See, in particular, Eleanor M. Fox, 'Modernization of Antitrust: A New Equilibrium' (1981) 66 *Cornell Law Review* 1140, 1179 (putting the competitive process at the heart of antitrust).

[4] See Josef Drexl, 'Competition Law in Media Markets and its Contribution to Democracy – A Global Perspective' (2015) 38 *World Competition* 367.

In line with these insights, this chapter discusses the question of whether there is also a role for competition policy to play in modern western societies in the service of fighting newly emerging ideologies, religious fundamentalism and populist politics in the context of regulating modern digital markets for ideas. In the light of the way radical Islamism has spread even among western societies through the Internet and, even more so, after the Brexit referendum in the United Kingdom and the more recent presidential campaign in the US, this question is more topical than ever.

In the following, section 11.2 takes up the discussion about the impact of dissemination of news over the Internet on democracy. It builds on recent interdisciplinary research on the topic and tries to assess the business model of the relevant online intermediaries, by taking Facebook as the most important example, in the light of the efficiency paradigm. Then, section 11.3 briefly looks at where media regulation comes from, namely, the protection of markets for ideas against concentration of private media undertakings that would negatively affect markets media plurality. Section 11.4 reports on how both national and European legislatures and regulators react to the migration of the distribution of news from the analogue to the digital world and how they conceive and react to the very new role of online intermediaries in disseminating news. Section 11.5 will then briefly sketch the very narrow constitutional framework for holding such intermediaries liable for false information, whether the information violates criminal laws or not. Finally, section 11.6 aims to apply competition law to the business models of online intermediaries to the extent that they disseminate news both as regards economic competition and competition in the political market for ideas. In the case of Facebook in particular, applying uniform principles is most convincing since the same algorithm applies irrespective of whether commercial or political information gets exchanged. In this most important section, the chapter argues in favour of competition-based media regulation that pursues to increase the availability of high-quality and reliable information and facilitates the identification of non-reliable information. The analysis concludes in section 11.7 by pointing out that media plurality should also be safeguarded by competition agencies through non-intervention where the business model by online intermediaries, such as news aggregators that facilitate access to the newspaper publishers, promote rather than restrict media plurality.

11.2 HOW INTERNET COMMUNICATION IMPACTS THE MARKET FOR IDEAS

As regards the Brexit referendum and the more recent presidential election in the US, there is common understanding that the Internet had a major impact on the voting. Criticism is now widespread that the dissemination of fake news over social platforms, such as Facebook's News Feed, could have considerably contributed to Donald Trump's election.[5]

11.2.1 *The Phenomenon of Post-Truth Politics*

Of course, it is debatable whether current populist movements can be categorised as ideologies in the traditional sense. As a common denominator, these movements all seem to rely on 'post-truth politics'. While truthfulness and adherence to facts have always constituted a cornerstone of modern democracies and high-quality journalism, modern populists – indeed similar to the ideologists of the twentieth century – do not seem to care whether factual statements are true or false. Quite to the contrary, they often create false statements on purpose. These politicians fully understand that they will not be punished by voters as long as their statements respond to the feelings of large parts of the electorate. The British referendum on Brexit on whether or not to remain in the EU and the US presidential campaign resulting in Donald Trump's election are among the most recent and apparent cases in which post-truth politics has been successful.[6]

For citizens, these wonderlands of populism may often appear as the 'cheaper' option to the burdensome, and therefore expensive, democratic debate on solving complex issues. Yet the problem is not only the advent of a different political style. What is more important is that post-truth politics seems to be contributing to the emergence of a 'post-factual society'. Citizens seem less interested in facts and complex expert analyses, which they may even consider as elitist.[7] Whether factual statements are well received nowadays seems to depend much more on how well they correspond to the individual, highly emotional and subjective preferences of voters than on their veracity.

These observations do not explain why populist movements and post-truth politics are currently thriving in western democratic societies and beyond. There are certainly manifold current political problems and challenges – war, terrorism, crime,

---

[5]   See Olivia Solon, 'Facebook's Failure: Did Fake News and Polarized Politics Get Trump Elected?' (20 November 2016) www.theguardian.com/technology/2016/nov/10/facebook-fake-news-election-conspiracy-theories (accessed 31 August 2017).

[6]   See, for instance, William Davies, 'The Age of Post-Truth Politics' (24 August 2016) www.nytimes.com/2016/08/24/opinion/campaign-stops/the-age-of-post-truth-politics.html?_r=0 (accessed 31 August 2017).

[7]   In the US, journalist and Trump supporter Jeffrey Lord defended Trump's disregard for truthfulness by calling fact-checking 'one more sort of out-of-touch, elitist, media-type thing'. He further argued that factual statements by candidates are best rejected by their actual political opponents. See Callum Borchers, 'Jeffrey Lord's Claim that Fact-Checking Is Elitist' (27 June 2016) www.washingtonpost.com/news/the-fix/wp/2016/06/27/jeffrey-lords-absurd-claim-that-media-fact-checking-is-elitist (accessed 31 August 2017). Similarly, in the UK, former Justice Minister and Brexit supporter Michael Gove claimed that 'Britain has had enough of experts'. Labour MP and leave supporter Gisela Stuart went a step further by saying: 'There is only one expert that matters, and that is you, the voter' (Michael Deacon, 'Michael Gove's guide to Britain's enemy . . . the expert' (10 June 2016) www.telegraph.co.uk/news/2016/06/10/michael-goves-guide-to-britains-greatest-enemy-the-experts (accessed 31 August 2017)).

immigration, economic recession, the challenges of globalisation, the impression of being left behind – that explain why people react emotionally. But there is enough evidence that modern digital communication significantly contributes to the success of populist movements.

11.2.2 *The Role of the Internet*

Within a relatively short period of time, research has been carried out by computer scientists, psychologists and experts in communication studies that is able to explain the mechanism of modern digital communication. This research, as explained in the following, largely concentrates on communication over social platforms such as Facebook. According to this research, the algorithms of social platforms that pre-select news for individual users create so-called 'filter bubbles' in which news items are selected according to the preferences of individual users. This news therefore tends to be void of any content that would challenge the user's established perceptions and beliefs. Following the logic of 'likes' and 'friends', individuals are only exposed to the views of like-minded individuals. In this way, self-contained communities emerge whose members share the same worldviews and believe in the same virtual reality. Such communities act as protected 'echo chambers' where narrow political views and false perceptions of reality, often based on false conspiracy theories, are constantly confirmed and strengthened.[8] Of course, members of such communities know that there is 'another world'. However, they often accuse the established media of being part of a conspiracy with the political class against 'the people'.[9] The 'Internet' becomes the only 'reliable' source on the reality members of these communities believe in.

This mechanism of social platforms and how it contributes to the spreading of conspiracy theories is well described in a study conducted by a group of computer scientists from the University of Lucca in Italy and some other universities.[10] The

---

[8] The World Economic Forum lists conspiracy theories distributed through social media as one of the main threats to society. See L. Howell, 'Digital Wildfires in a Hyperconnected World', WEF Report (2013) http://reports.weforum.org/global-risks-2013/risk-case-1/digital-wildfires-in-a-hyperconnected-world (accessed 31 August 2017).

[9] A typical example of this from the world outside the Internet is PEGIDA (Patrioten Europas gegen die Islamisierung des Abendlandes, Patriots of Europe against the Islamisation of the Occident), which emerged as a grass-roots populist movement against immigration in Saxony in late 2014. In organising demonstrations every Monday, this movement adopted the slogan '*Wir sind das Volk*' ('We are the people') of the 1989 democratic revolution and Monday demonstrations against the former Communist regime in East Germany. PEGIDA accuses the established media of lying, using the term '*Lügenpresse*' ('lying press'). More information available at: https://en.wikipedia.org/wiki/Pegida (accessed 20 November 2016).

[10] Michela Del Vicario et al., 'The Spreading of Misinformation Online' (2016) 116 *Proceedings of the National Academy of Sciences of the United States of America (PNAS)* 554, www.pnas.org/lookup/suppl/doi:10.1073/pnas.1517441113/-/CDSupplemental (accessed 31 August 2017).

study is of a quantitative nature. It assesses how information spreads on Facebook depending on whether it is of scientific or of a conspiracy nature.

According to the study, conspiracy theories 'simplify causation, reduce the complexity of reality, and are formulated in a way that is able to tolerate a certain level of uncertainty', while 'scientific information disseminates scientific advances and exhibits the progress of scientific thinking'.[11] But the study does not distinguish conspiracy theories and scientific information according to contents. Rather, the distinguishing criterion is verifiability.[12] While the generators of scientific information and the methods they apply can easily be identified, the origin of conspiracy theories typically remains obscure. Thus, the study classifies the belief that vaccines cause autism as a conspiracy theory.[13]

The study argues that the dissemination of conspiracy theories and scientific information can indeed be compared, since they take place in highly homogeneous clusters of segregated communities often referred to as 'echo chambers'.[14] The study demonstrates that 'consumers' of both scientific information and conspiracy theories show the same 'consumption pattern', but that the cascade dynamics of distribution for the two kinds of information turn out to be very different.[15]

To show this, the researchers measured the dissemination of scientific news from thirty-five Internet pages, conspiracy theories from thirty-two pages and intentionally false information from two 'troll pages' whose intention is to mock the public and expose its credulity online[16] through Facebook posts, where the scientific information or the conspiracy theory is commented upon. All three groups were monitored over a period of five years from 2010 to 2014. The consumption pattern relates to how dissemination takes place during the lifetime of posts – measured as the period between the first user and the last user sharing a post on Facebook. In this regard, the lifetime was basically the same for all categories. As regards the cascade dynamics,

---

[11]   Ibid., 554.
[12]   Ibid.
[13]   Ibid.
[14]   Ibid., 554–5.
[15]   Ibid., 555.
[16]   Troll messages can also be described as 'parodies of conspiracy theories' (ibid., 556). Yet there are also other websites that try to help users to find out whether information disseminated on the Internet is correct or not. See in particular the Italian website 'Bufale' (the Italian word for 'hoaxes'): www.bufale .net (accessed 31 August 2017). In Italy, at the time before the national elections in 2013, a story circulated widely on the Internet according to which the Italian Senate, on the motion of Senator Cirenga, had voted in favour of a law that would provide for payment of a total of €134bn to Italian MPs to enable them to find new jobs if they failed at being re-elected. This story rapidly spread on social platforms with major criticism of the political class, although it was very obvious that the information was false. There was no senator with the name Cirenga, the sum mentioned amounted to about 20 per cent of the Italian state budget and the number of votes mentioned went considerably beyond the number of seats in the Senate. On this story, see 'BUFALA Il senatore Cirenga e il fondo per i parlamentari in crisi' (30 June 2015), www.bufale.net/home/bufala-il-senatore-cirenga-ed-il-fondo-per-i-parlamentari-in-crisi-bufale-net (accessed 31 August 2017). The website reports that the news first appeared on Facebook in 2012; it was still being shared on Facebook three years later.

however, the study shows that scientific information is assimilated and reaches a higher level of diffusion much more quickly. Conspiracy theories take longer to be assimilated, but show a positive correlation between lifetime and size, meaning that conspiracy theories are much more intensively discussed. The study interprets this as an indication that conspiracy theories are highly resistant to corrections once they are adopted by an individual.[17] As the authors put it:

> Users tend to aggregate in communities of interest, which causes reinforcement and fosters confirmation bias, segregation and polarization. This comes at the expense of the quality of the information and leads to the proliferation of biased narratives fomented by unsubstantiated rumors, mistrust, and paranoia.[18]

In another study, researchers of Facebook itself looked at the pattern of how users react to the Facebook News Feed.[19] These researchers examined the reactions of 10.1 million US Facebook users who identified themselves, ranging from very conservative to very liberal, to equally ranked political news shared over Facebook.[20] Hence, the purpose of the study was to find out about the exposure of Facebook users to diverse political information by also taking into account the users' own behaviour. Indeed, the way Facebook's algorithm filters news is only one part of the news flow. First, users select information on the Internet to share with friends. Then, Facebook's algorithm filters the information that will finally appear in the news feed of the individual user based mostly on two criteria: the user's degree of affinity to the friend who posted the news and the interest in the kind of content the user has shown in the past. Finally, this user still has to click on the news. The study shows that Facebook users are exposed to cross-cutting news – defined as news that does not align with the political views of the individual user – on their news feeds. This is not surprising since Facebook users are connected with 'friends' who belong to diverse social communities of the real world (schools, universities, professional environments, etc.).[21] Yet the study also shows that the percentage of cross-cutting news being conveyed continuously goes down at every point along the sharing chain as compared to a random selection of news shared on Facebook. At its highest point

---

17 Del Vicario et al., 'Spreading of Misinformation', 558.
18 Ibid.
19 Eytan Bakshy, Solomon Messing and Lada Adamic, 'Exposure to Ideologically Diverse News and Opinion on Facebook, Science Express (7 May 2015) http://cn.cnstudiodev.com/uploads/document_attachment/attachment/681/science_facebook_filter_bubble_may2015.pdf (accessed 31 August 2017).
20 In responding to this study, the Wall Street Journal made available a selection of this news on the Internet relating to the two presidential candidates, Donald Trump and Hillary Clinton, to demonstrate in parallel how different very conservative and very liberal news can be. See Jon Keegan, 'Red Feed, Blue Feed – See Liberal Facebook and Conservative Facebook, Side by Side' (18 May 2016) http://graphics.wsj.com/blue-feed-red-feed/#methodology (accessed 31 August 2017).
21 Roughly 20 per cent of the friends of both liberals and conservatives belong to the other side of the political spectrum. It is to be noted that the study also stresses that the exposure to cross-cutting news will be considerably lower if individuals communicate within other fora, such as political blogs.

when friends first decide to select news for sharing, the percentage is lower when the news actually appears in the user's news feed and lower still when users actually click on a certain selection. The single most important factor involved is the decision of users to share news with friends.[22] In general, the study may prove that the effect of Facebook in segregating political debate within the society is less pronounced than other studies may have assumed so far. More importantly, the study highlights the role of the individual user's behaviour, especially that of sharing information, in creating this effect.

In addition, it is to be noted that, according to this study, liberal users are considerably less exposed than their conservative counterparts to cross-cutting news. Hence, although they may be less receptive for 'post-truth politics', liberals live in their own echo chambers. This could explain why liberals in the US were not aware of the large popular support that ultimately led to Trump's election. Similarly, in the UK, the supporters of EU membership did not expect the Brexit supporters to win the referendum. In sum, the kind of Internet communication studied here tends to divide modern societies into separate polities that do not sufficiently communicate with each other.

More recently, another story that gained high media coverage additionally underlined the psychological effects of communicating over social platforms. In March 2016, Microsoft launched Tay, a teen chatbot, as an experiment in artificial intelligence. Tay, a virtual 19-year-old girl, was expected to communicate on Twitter and to learn by communicating with human beings. However, within one day, Tay's character became completely racist and sexist and, ultimately, Microsoft quickly removed her from the Internet.[23] Indeed, artificial intelligence is meant to mimic human beings, including their capacity to learn. Tay obviously learned to adopt the prejudicial language she observed on the Internet. Chatbots have a commercial background as future tools of entertainment on the Internet. Yet the Tay experience shows that chatbots can also be used to distort public opinion. Hence, 'political chatbots' appear to be just another technological step after the appearance of 'political bots', computer programs that produce fake political statements by citizens on communication platforms as a new form of political propaganda. Such political bots were used during the latest presidential campaign very strategically in support of the Trump campaign and, to a lesser degree, to support Hillary Clinton.[24]

---

[22] The reduction of cross-cutting information is highest among liberals, namely, from about 45 per cent (random) to about 24 per cent shared by friends. In the case of conservatives, there is only a reduction from 40 per cent to 35 per cent.

[23] See, for instance, James Vincent, 'Twitter Taught Microsoft's AI Chatbot to Be a Racist Asshole in Less Than a Day' (24 March 2016) www.theverge.com/2016/3/24/11297050/tay-microsoft-chatbot-racist (accessed 31 August 2017) (with examples of her offensive tweets).

[24] See the analysis by Bence Kollanyi, Philip N. Howard and Samuel C. Woolley, 'Bots and Automation over Twitter during the U.S. Election', COMPPROP Data Memo 2016.4 (17 November 2016), http://comprop.oii.ox.ac.uk/2016/11/17/bots-and-automation-over-twitter-during-the-u-s-election (accessed 31 August 2017). This study conducted at Oxford University reports that one third of the tweets on

11.2.3 Is the Distribution of News over the Internet Efficient?

From the analysis, the question arises whether and how communication on the Internet should be regulated. As we can see, a negative impact on how public opinion develops can arise from various kinds of platforms on the Internet: social platforms such as Facebook, political blogs, Twitter and, to a lesser degree, search engines that list search results according to the user's preferences.

In the following the analysis will not focus on the content providers of ideologies such as post-truth politicians and parties or their supporters, but on the private operators of the digital platforms. These firms can be compared with private media companies of the old economy to the extent that they act as gatekeepers that select and filter information that the individual will ultimately receive on the Internet. In addition, their decisions on the criteria for selecting news for dissemination, including the design of their algorithms, follow an economic rationale. For instance, operators of social platforms have to attract as much traffic by users as possible to compete in the advertising market. They therefore provide news to users that the latter 'like' to consume and prefer to connect users with like-minded individuals ('friends') as a strategy to increase traffic. Search engines serve users better if they put the information that users can be expected to like most on top of the search list – and happy users are loyal users. This chapter focuses on the regulation of these Internet firms, since they act at the interface of economic markets and the political process. They are potential addressees of market regulation; but what this regulation should pursue is the objective of safeguarding democracy.

According to the Chicago School, the business decisions made by these Internet firms would probably have to be considered as efficient. The argument is that the market serves users with the news that they want. However, this conclusion could be questioned based on the consideration that efficiency depends on rational behaviour of the individual. Do users really act rationally when they prefer false statements and conspiracy theories to verifiable facts? Or are users boundedly rational when they consume and share news on the Internet? In the same vein, news consisting in false statements and conspiracy theories could be seen as news of low quality. Accordingly, the dissemination of false statements and conspiracy theories over the digital market for ideas could be considered a market failure in the sense of adverse selection.

The argument that we are dealing here with bounded rationality seems particularly convincing, since it has a sound basis in psychology. Human beings suffer from confirmation bias, which leads to so-called 'motivated reasoning'.[25] Evolution has

---

Twitter for Trump were generated by computer programs. Of those in favour of Clinton, it was still 25 per cent. In Germany, most political parties have made a pledge to refrain from using political bots in the campaign for the federal elections in September 2017. The only party that announced that it would rely on such bots to promote its political views is the populist party Alternative für Deutschland (AfD). See 'AfD will Social Bots im Wahlkampf einsetzen', *Die Zeit* (21 October 2016), www.zeit.de/digital/internet/2016-10/bundestagswahlkampf-2017-afd-social-bots (accessed 31 August 2017).

[25] See Robert T Carroll, 'The Skeptic's Dictionary', http://skepdic.com/motivatedreasoning.html (accessed 31 August 2017).

conditioned humans to select data in a way that confirms their convictions in order to help them to win arguments. 'Motivated reasoning' in this context describes emotion-driven reasoning that is designed to avoid emotional dissonance. Such reasoning often works as a defence to contrary evidence and often discredits the source of such evidence. Motivated reasoning makes the individual feel better. A typical example of motivated reasoning is Donald Trump's tweet of 2012 according to which climate change is a hoax created by the Chinese to make US manufacturers less competitive.[26] He thereby provided a seemingly plausible conspiracy theory to all US Americans who do not want to believe in climate change.

While this psychological analysis of the underlying mechanisms may be astute, it cannot counteract the fact that individual Internet users and citizens indeed feel better when they believe in false conspiracy theories. If one defines general welfare as the maximisation of the well-being of all users of a society, a market of ideas would have to be considered to work efficiently if this market provides users with the ideas that best correspond to the consumers' preferences. And even from a democratic perspective, there is nothing wrong about appealing to the emotions of citizens in political debates. Citizens often vote for the candidates they find more likable. In this sense, digital markets seem to be extremely efficient, since they give each and every Internet user the most preferred information. In contrast, the argument of bounded rationality and adverse selection seems rather paternalistic and even anti-democratic.

In addition, it is not possible to argue that digital markets for ideas are inefficient since they make societies that vote for post-truth politics 'economically' worse off. On the one hand, such an argument will often be based on pure speculation on the kind of economic policy post-truth politicians will implement once they get elected. On the other hand, even in a case where voters support a decision that has a direct negative impact on the national economy, such as in the case of the Brexit referendum of the UK, the fact that support for Brexit among British citizens has not necessarily gone down after the referendum, although the negative economic effects are now openly admitted by more and more pro-Brexit politicians, shows that voters sometimes prefer emotional well-being to economic well-being.

The relevant question, then, is not what economic efficiency means in the context of digital markets for ideas, but: can and should democratic societies accept the way in which modern digital markets provide news? The answer is a clear no. The way this type of market works is in conflict with fundamental principles that should apply in democratic societies. Citizens should not be lied to, and markets for ideas in democratic societies should help citizens make better-informed decisions. It is reliable information that democratic societies need to expect from functioning

---

[26]   This led to official protests of the Chinese government at the Marrakech UN climate conference shortly after Trump's election. See Neil Conner, 'Beijing to Donald Trump: Climate Change Is Not a Chinese Hoax' (17 November 2016), www.telegraph.co.uk/news/2016/11/17/beijing-to-trump-climate-change-is-not-a-chinese-hoax (accessed 31 August 2017).

markets for ideas, and not purely that they respond at best to the emotions of citizens. This conclusion derives from constitutional considerations beyond economic efficiency. Such constitutional considerations are key to the regulation of the economic activity of private actors in markets for ideas. This is indeed not a new insight. Safeguarding the democratic process in the context of markets is one of the objectives of the regulation at the interface of competition law and media law in democratic jurisdictions.

11.3 WHERE WE COME FROM IN THE FIELD OF MEDIA REGULATION

Before discussing how digital markets for ideas should be regulated in the future, it is worthwhile to remember how media markets are traditionally regulated.

The major concern has so far been on the negative impact of concentration on media plurality. This brings merger control into the picture. Media mergers can affect both 'economic competition' in the market and media plurality. Yet it is important to distinguish between the two.

In this regard, any jurisdiction has to answer two questions: the first question is whether a media merger should be assessed just like any other mergers by concentrating on the impact on economic competition, or whether the particular impact on media plurality should also be taken into account. The second question regards the institutional framework, namely, whether the assessment of a media merger should fall within the general jurisdiction of the competition authority or a sector-specific media regulator.

From a comparative perspective, jurisdictions may choose among three possible options: (1) media mergers are exclusively assessed by a sector-specific regulatory agency; (2) media mergers are only assessed by the competition agency; or (3) media mergers are assessed in parallel within the general institutional framework of competition law for assessing mergers and by a sector-specific regulatory body.[27] Indeed, it is extremely rare that a country that has a general merger control regime concentrates the assessment of a media mergers in the hands of a sector-specific regulator. An example for such a jurisdiction is Singapore.[28] Conversely, the fact that in a given jurisdiction media mergers are only assessed within the competition law framework, does not exclude that the merger control body is also required to look at the impact on media plurality as a second reason for prohibiting the merger. This is in fact the case in Austria.[29] A similar system exists under the Enterprise Act 2002 in

---

[27] For a comparative analysis of such different approaches, see Josef Drexl, 'Copyright, Competition and Development – Report by the Max Planck Institute for Intellectual Property and Competition Law on behalf of the World Intellectual Property Organization' (2013) 178–87, www.wipo.int/export/sites/www/ip-competition/en/studies/copyright_competition_development.pdf (accessed 31 August 2017).

[28] Ibid., 179. In Singapore, media mergers are assessed by the Media Development Authority.

[29] Ibid., 179–80. Section 13 Austrian Cartel Act (2005) expressly establishes a distortion of media plurality as an additional reason for prohibiting a merger. On the Austrian practice, see Drexl 'Copyright, Competition and Development', 179–80.

the UK where the Secretary of State for Trade and Industry can refer a merger among broadcasting entities to the competition authority if there are concerns regarding media plurality.[30]

An example of a country with a bifurcated system is Germany. There, media mergers are assessed by the Bundeskartellamt, the German competition agency, according to the rules of the general competition law – the Act against Restraints of Competition.[31] In cases of mergers between private TV stations, it will hence typically assess the competitive effect on advertising customers and, thereby, not take into account the public TV stations that are largely restricted in their possibilities to offer advertising space.[32] As regards the impact on media plurality, mergers of private TV stations in Germany are assessed by the Kommission zur Ermittlung der Konzentration im Medienbereich (KEK, Commission for the Assessment of Media Concentration), which is an authority established by the German *Länder*.[33] The role of the Commission is to safeguard plurality of opinion in the sector of private TV by preventing the emergence of 'prevailing opinion power' (vorherrschende Meinungsmacht) either through mergers or internal growth. Hence, in a case of media merger, KEK will assess the impact on the total TV audience while also taking into account the public TV stations, rather than limiting its assessment to the commercial effects in the advertising market.[34] In individual cases in Germany, a merger may have to be cleared in both systems in order to be implemented.[35]

11.4 HOW MEDIA REGULATORS REACT TO DIGITISATION?

In times of digital communication over the Internet and convergence of the media, the traditional focus of regulation on concentration along the boundaries of specific

---

[30] Following this procedure, in 2007, the former Competition Commission both held that the acquisition of ITV shares by Sky led to a substantial lessening of competition and confirmed the Secretary of State's concerns about a negative impact on media plurality. See Drexl, 'Copyright, Competition and Development', 180–1 (also with regard to judgment of the Court of Appeal finally upholding the Commission's decision).

[31] *Gesetz gegen Wettbewerbsbeschränkungen*; English translation available at www.bundeskartellamt.de/SharedDocs/Publikation/EN/Others/GWB.html (accessed 31 August 2017).

[32] See, for instance, Bundeskartellamt, Decision of 19 January 2006, Case B6-103–05, *Axel Springer AG/ProSiebenSat.1 Media AG*, 23–4, available at: www.bundeskartellamt.de/SharedDocs/Entscheidung/DE/Entscheidungen/Fusionskontrolle/2006/B6-103–05.pdf?__blob=publicationFile&v=3 (accessed 31 August 2017).

[33] For further information, see www.kek-online.de/?L=1 (accessed 31 August 2017).

[34] See *Rundfunkstaatsvertrag* (*Staatsvertrag für Rundfunk und Telemedien*, Treaty on Broadcasting and Electronic Media concluded among the German *Länder*), s. 26(2). According to this provision prevailing opinion power is presumed if a private TV operator reaches a 30 per cent share of the total TV audience in a given year.

[35] More broadly on the interface between competition law and media law, see Ralf Müller-Terpitz, 'Schnittstellen aus medienrechtlicher Perspektive' (2016) 8 *Zeitschrift für Geistiges Eigentum* 329.

types of media, such as TV, appears rather outdated and is in need of being revisited. There are two reasons for this need.

First, there seems to be less of a need to interfere in mergers of classical media, such as mergers of private TV stations, with a view to protecting media plurality. The role of TV stations as a major source of information and a principal gatekeeper for politically relevant information is rapidly decreasing. Younger people especially stay away from TV and use the Internet as their major source of information. In general, citizens can form their opinions by making use of multiple sources of information. For traditional broadcasting, digitisation and the Internet appear as disruptive technologies and as 'game changers'. Digitisation raises the question of whether existing regulations can and should be reconsidered.[36]

This, however, does not necessarily argue for giving up existing forms of regulation. Most recent experience in countries such as Hungary, Poland and Turkey, where governments challenge the independence of media companies, and particularly public TV stations, in order to control public opinion, still produces enough evidence that TV continues to play a key role in the formation of the political views of citizens. Another worrying example of this trend is that the Alternative für Deutschland (AfD), the young German party that has recently spoken out against immigration and consequently achieved major successes in regional and federal elections, includes the objective of diminishing the role of public TV in Germany in its political agenda.[37] In general, media that supports independent and often expensive investigative journalism remains key, perhaps now even more than ever, to making transparent the lies of post-truth politics and populism.

Second, in the light of the role digital communications platforms have today, dominance of media providers should no longer be considered the only case for intervention. Anybody can nowadays create fake news quite easily and distribute it on the Internet. In a changed world where every politician can address the public by opening a Facebook account and where citizens are no longer doomed to be passive consumers of news, but can actively participate in political debates over the Internet, media regulators should also look at the Internet intermediaries that offer platforms for direct communication between politicians and citizens as well as among citizens.[38]

---

[36]   In general on this role of the Internet, see Rupprecht Podszun, 'Digitalisierung, Medienvielfalt und die Rolle des allgemeinen Wirtschaftsrechts' (2016) 8 *Zeitschrift für Geistiges Eigentum* 350, 360–1 (also mentioning the service of Uber as a new digital business model that challenges existing regulation of taxi services).

[37]   Alternative für Deutschland, 'Grundsatzprogramm', Leitantrag der Bundesprogrammkommission und des Bundesvorstandes (30 April/1 May 2016), at section 7.5, https://correctiv.org/media/public/5d/22/5d222f06-a052-46a4-bef7-7586d0da01ec/20160324_afd_programmentwurf.pdf (accessed 31 August 2017).

[38]   According to KEK, in 2013, 90 per cent of national MPs in Germany had a Facebook account. There was evidence that having a Facebook account led to higher awareness of these politicians in the classical media as well. See Kommission zur Ermittlung der Konzentration im Medienbereich

Indeed, media regulators have become aware of the need to reconsider the traditional approach of regulation in the light of the digital revolution. For instance, the German media regulator KEK, in a report of December 2014, confirmed that the existing regulatory system no longer corresponds to the reality of how citizens use the media.[39] The report also looked at how social media influenced media plurality and public opinion.[40] In this context it noted that Facebook's algorithm led to a preselection of news based on the preferences of the individual user and his or her friends, which, in particular, excluded exposure to any views not shared by the user.[41] Therefore, KEK considered Facebook a 'gatekeeper', similar to classical media companies that preselect news for the public.[42]

However, there are also differences. Rather than directly selecting information, Facebook only 'indirectly' influences the selection of information through its algorithm.[43] KEK also noted that social platforms are predominantly platforms for exchanging views socially, which it did not consider substantially different from communication in any other social forum.[44] It therefore concluded that, for the time being, social media do not pose a particular threat for public opinion.[45]

It is however questionable whether this conclusion of 2014 can still be maintained given the rise of populist movements, not least in Germany, especially after large numbers of refugees started to enter the country in the second half of 2015. Yet, already in 2014, when KEK published its report, there were studies on the dissemination of information through digital platforms that indicated the negative impact of such platforms in Germany as well.[46]

More recently, a Commission with representatives of the Federation and the *Länder* was established with the task of considering the need for platform regulation. However, the focus of this Commission was still very much on the concept of dominance. Its major task was to take into account new platforms of distribution

---

(KEK), *Von der Fernsehzentrierung zur Medienfokussierung – Anforderungen an eine zeitgemäße Sicherung medialer Meinungsvielfalt, Bericht über die Entwicklung der Konzentration und über Maßnahmen der Sicherung der Meinungsvielfalt im privaten Rundfunk, Schriftenreihe der Landesmedienanstalten 14* (December 2014), 281–2.

[39] Ibid.
[40] Ibid., 281–4.
[41] Ibid., 282.
[42] Ibid.
[43] Ibid., 283.
[44] Ibid.
[45] Ibid., 284.
[46] For studies on the use of social platforms in Germany, see, in particular, Marcel Machill, Markus Beiler and Uwe Krüger, *Das neue Gesicht der Öffentlichkeit – Wie Facebook und andere soziale Netzwerke die Meinungsbildung verändern* (Landesanstalt für Medien Nordrhein-Westfalen 2013) http://lfmpublikationen.lfm-nrw.de/modules/pdf_download.php?products_id=343 (accessed 31 August 2017). This report contains an impressive list of available studies with informative summaries. One of these studies shows a very strong anti-Jewish attitude among young people using Facebook in Germany. However, the study could not prove whether Facebook contributed to the emergence of such an attitude. See Christian Hardinghaus, *Der ewige Jude und die Generation Facebook – Antisemitische NS-Propaganda und Vorurteile in sozialen Netzwerken* (Tectum 2012).

of content and TV programmes on the Internet for the purpose of developing the existing regulatory system to protect media plurality.

Yet a subgroup of this Commission also had the task of assessing specifically the role of intermediaries, such as Google, with its search engine, but also social platforms, such as Facebook. In June 2016 the Commission produced its report, which includes a contribution of the subgroup on intermediaries.[47] In particular, for legislation on the EU level, the subgroup recommends introducing an obligation on the part of the intermediaries to inform users about the criteria according to which the algorithm selects information.[48] This rule is supposed to enable users to make a more informed decision on whether they want to use a given service. In addition, the German media authorities have also mandated a study on the role of these intermediaries as regards the formation of their users' opinions.[49]

Another forum for addressing the impact of the Internet intermediaries on media pluralism would be European law. EU law addresses media regulation in two ways: first, it refrains from providing proper European rules for protecting media pluralism against mergers, but explicitly allows Member States to do so.[50] Second, the EU provides for sector-specific media regulation that goes beyond the control of concentration in the form of the Audiovisual Media Services Directive (AMSD).[51] In May 2015, the Commission published a proposal for a reform of this Directive,[52] which is meant to respond to the challenges of media convergence and to adapt the Directive to the ways individuals nowadays use media on the Internet. In its current version, the AMSD, despite its technology-neutral approach, which was implemented in 2010, does not apply to social platforms. Rather, it only regulates online services that are 'TV-like' in the sense that providers assert editorial responsibility. This would not change under the new rules proposed by the

---

[47] Bund-Länder-Kommission zur Medienkonvergenz, 'Bericht' (June 2016) 31–9, www.bundesregier ung.de/content/de/_anlagen/bkm/2016/2016–06-14-medienkonvergenz-bericht-blk.pdf?__blob=publi cationfile&v=3 (accessed 31 August 2017).

[48] Ibid., 35.

[49] This study was expected by the end of 2016. It is to be prepared by the Hans Bredow Institute for Media Research at the University of Hamburg; see www.hans-bredow-institut.de/en (accessed 31 August 2017).

[50] According to Council Regulation (EC) No. 139/2004 of 20 January 2004 on the control of concentrations between undertakings (the EC Merger Regulation) [2004] OJ L24/1, art. 21(4)(2). EU merger control law does not prevent Member States from controlling media mergers for the purpose of safeguarding media plurality.

[51] Directive 2010/13/EU of the European Parliament and of the Council of 10 March 2010 on the coordination of certain provisions laid down by law, regulation or administrative action in Member States concerning the provision of audiovisual media services (Audiovisual Media Services Directive) [2010] OJ L95/1.

[52] Proposal of the Commission of 25 May 2016 for a Directive of the European Parliament and of the Council amending Directive 2010/13/EU on the coordination of certain provisions laid down by law, regulation or administrative action in Member States concerning the provision of audiovisual media services in view of changing market realities, COM(2016) 287/4.

Commission. The Commission argues that the Directive 'should remain applicable only to those services the principal purpose of which is the provision of programmes in order to inform, entertain or educate'.[53] This requirement is not fulfilled by Internet intermediaries and platforms, such as Facebook, where information is selected based on general criteria and implemented in the form of an algorithm.

Hence, EU law, at least for the moment, provides no basis for regulating the distribution of information through Internet intermediaries such as social platforms, or for addressing the challenges they bring with them for the democratic process. Still, the European Commission has more recently conducted a consultation on the regulation of platforms and online intermediaries.[54] But this consultation largely focused on the commercial aspects of what online intermediaries are doing, their liability for illegal content and the lack of transparency regarding the treatment of personal data. Nothing in the consultation related to the particular business models of online intermediaries, such as social platforms in particular, when they distribute politically relevant information, or to the need to regulate this activity in order to safeguard the democratic process. The part of the consultation that comes closest to this issue relates to the 'duties of care' for online intermediaries. But in this context, the consultation only referred to 'illegal content'.[55] As regards the responses to the Commission's questions, again none of which focuses on the topic of this chapter, sharing of content was considered a 'cornerstone of freedom of speech' and its goal 'to promote a more informed and inclusive world'.[56] Moreover, participants in the consultation argued that intermediaries should not act as judges and should therefore not monitor the content they disseminate.[57]

This is where the discussion stood before the debate started to change in 2016. Indeed, under the impression of the Brexit vote and the Trump election, there is now much more awareness of politicians and regulators both on the national and European level that something needs to be done.

As regards the national level, Germany attracted major international attention in the summer of 2017 when the Parliament adopted a most severe new law challenging the operators of social platforms with fines of up to €50m if they do not delete illegal hate speech within very short deadlines.[58] A clear sign that the problem is now also

---

[53] Ibid., recital 3.

[54] See European Commission, Synopsis report on the public consultations on the regulatory environment for platforms, online intermediaries and the collaborative economy' (25 May 2016) http://ec .europa.eu/newsroom/dae/document.cfm?doc_id=15877 (accessed 31 August 2017).

[55] Ibid., 19.

[56] Ibid., 20.

[57] Ibid., 21.

[58] *Gesetz zur Verbesserung der Rechtsdurchsetzung in sozialen Netzwerken (Netzwerkdurchsetzungsgesetz)*; Act to Improve Enforcement of the Law in Social Networks (Network Enforcement Act), adopted 7 July 2017, expected to enter into force on 1 October 2017. English translation available at: www.bmjv.de/SharedDocs/Gesetzgebungsverfahren/Dokumente/NetzDG_engl.pdf;

taken much more serious on the European level was sent out at about the same time on the occasion of the appointment of the new Commissioner for the Digital Single Market, Mariya Gabriel. In his Mission Letter, the President of the Commission gave the new Commissioner the explicit mandate 'to look into the challenges the online platforms create for our democracies as regards the spreading of fake information'.[59]

11.5 THE GENERAL LEGAL FRAMEWORK FOR DISSEMINATING NEWS THROUGH INTERNET INTERMEDIARIES

Before the analysis can turn to new approaches to regulating Internet intermediaries such as search engines and social platforms from a competition-policy perspective, at a preliminary step, it is important to better understand the larger legal framework already in place that is relevant for such regulation.

The preceding analysis has already indicated that Internet firms act at best as facilitators of conspiracy theories and populist, ideological and fundamentalist ideas and beliefs. Through their services they only assist others to disseminate their 'news'. They themselves are not the source of information and content that undermines the democratic process.

Against this backdrop, the question is even whether it is possible to regulate the conduct of the Internet intermediaries. To answer this question a distinction has to be made between content that violates criminal laws or personality rights, on the one hand, and legal content on the other hand. In case of the former, the operator of the platform is indeed under a duty to delete that information from its server.[60] This is where the new German Act to Improve the Enforcement of Law in Social Networks kicks in.[61] It only applies in specific cases of hate speech that violates criminal law and provides for severe administrative fines if the content is not deleted within certain deadlines after a complaint has been brought, namely, within twenty-four hours in case of content that is manifestly unlawful and within seven days in other cases.

jsessionid=B37BF62B1158A3A8F4EA95BBD8715022.2_cid334?__blob=publicationFile&v=2 (accessed 31 August 2017). See also 'Germany Approves Plans to Fine Social Media Firms up to €50m', *The Guardian* (30 June 2017) www.theguardian.com/media/2017/jun/30/germany-approves-plans-to-fine-social-media-firms-up-to-50m (accessed 31 August 2017).

59 Jean-Claude Junker, 'Mission Letter' (16 May 2017) 5 https://ec.europa.eu/commission/commis sioners/sites/cwt/files/commissioner_mission_letters/mission-letter-mariya-gabriel.pdf (accessed 31 August 2017).

60 See Directive 2000/31/EC of the European Parliament and of the Council of 8 June 2000 on certain legal aspects of information society services, in particular electronic commerce, in the Internal Market (Directive on electronic commerce) [2000] OJ L178/1, art. 14. This provision guarantees privileged treatment of host providers under EU law. Accordingly, the host provider is not auto-matically liable for content that is stored by somebody else. However, the host provider has to remove illegal content or block access to this information once it has been made aware of the presence of illegal content on its server. See Directive on electronic commerce, art. 14(1)(b).

61 See n. 58.

Although this law is limited to crimes, it still raises major concerns as regards the respect of the constitutional guarantee of the freedom of expression in particular. While the online intermediary still enjoys some judicial protection since the administrative fine cannot be imposed without prior court decision on the illegality of the content, the Act does not establish any possibility of judicial recourse for the content provider against unjustified removal. In addition, since both the criminal law provisions in the field are difficult to apply and the provisions of the new law also lack precision, in particular as regard to the term of 'manifestly illegal', there is the concern that the online intermediaries will now overshoot the mark and engage in self-censorship to avoid any risk of being fined. In sum, this legislation tries to outsource the enforcement of criminal law to the online intermediaries as private entities without providing any legal redress for the content providers in case of unjustified removal.[62]

Even more, false information disseminated by online intermediaries will not automatically violate criminal laws or personality rights. Information spread by pro-Brexit politicians about the annual contributions of the UK to the EU was blatantly wrong.[63] But this does not make the statement as such or its communication to the public illegal.

Of course, this insight does not prevent the legislature from introducing further regulation per se. But any form of regulation will have to take account of the fundamental rights of the parties involved. This includes the freedom of expression of both the information provider[64] and the recipient of the information,[65] since any regulation of the intermediaries would indirectly affect these fundamental rights of the providers and recipients of information. In addition, if one takes the constitutional order of the EU as the point of reference, the intermediaries can rely on their freedom to conduct a business.[66] In its case law on the duty of Internet access providers to take measures against copyright infringement, the CJEU has particularly highlighted the need to create a 'fair balance' between the interest in protecting copyright and the freedom of Internet access providers to conduct a business.[67]

---

[62] For a critical view on the Government Bill, see Josef Drexl, 'Bedrohung der Meinungsvielfalt durch Algorithmen' (2017) 61 *Zeitschrift für Urheber- und Medienrecht* 529, 539–40.

[63] Boris Johnson, former mayor of London, who has become the UK's Foreign Minister after the Brexit referendum, claimed in his pro-Brexit campaign that the UK contributes a weekly amount of £350 million to the EU that could be used for healthcare instead. This information was most visibly shown on Johnson's campaign bus. Yet this number was declared to be misleading plain and simple by the UK Statistics Authority. See 'Why Vote Leave's £350m Weekly EU Cost Claim Is Wrong', www .theguardian.com/politics/reality-check/2016/may/23/does-the-eu-really-cost-the-uk-350m-a-week (accessed 20 November 2016).

[64] EU Charter of Fundamental Rights, art. 11(1), first sentence.

[65] Ibid., second sentence.

[66] Ibid., art. 16.

[67] See judgments in *Promusicae*, C-275/06, ECLI:EU:C:2008:54, [2008] ECR I-271; *Scarlet Extended*, C-70/10, ECLI:EU:C:2011:771, [2011] ECR I-11959; *UPC Telekabel Wien*, C-314/12, ECLI:EU: C:2014:192. On this case law, see also Josef Drexl, 'European and International Intellectual

Against the backdrop of the constitutional situation, it is to be noted that maintenance of media plurality is considered part of the constitutional guarantee of the freedom of expression and the freedom of information in the media sector.[68] From the perspective of media regulation, the primary question should not be whether information can be made available on the Internet or not. The question is only whether regulation should control the very economic rationale of the business models of Internet intermediaries such as search engines and social platforms.

11.6 COMPETITION LAW AND POLICY AS A BASIS FOR INTERVENTION

In the light of the constitutional limitations for regulating content on the Internet and its removal outside the criminal justice system, the question is whether a solution could be found by regulating the business model of the online intermediaries. This also brings competition law into the picture. Competition law seems relevant for two reasons: first, competition law applies to all sectors of the economy and, with severe administrative sanctions at its disposal, provides for powerful enforcement measures. In addition, such measures can be taken on the supranational level of the EU, while sector-specific regulation would typically be placed on the national level. However, the question is whether a restraint of competition can be identified when Internet intermediaries disseminate news created by others through the Internet. Second, competition policy provides a general framework of economic analysis on which 'pro-competitive' sector-specific regulation can rely for pursuing goals that lie outside of the realm of competition law. In this regard, competition policy can also provide guidance for other fields of regulation.

11.6.1 *Direct Application of Competition Law*

Accordingly, it is of paramount importance first to clarify the extent to which competition law can directly be applied to Internet intermediaries that disseminate news. Since such firms engage in economic activity, they are potential addressees of competition law. The design of their business models, including the design of the algorithms used for the functioning of a social platform or a search engine, is to be classified as unilateral conduct. This leads to a general and important limitation of the availability of competition law remedies. Unilateral conduct can only be

Property Law between Propertization and Regulation: How a Fundamental-Rights Approach Can Mitigate the Tension' (2016) 47 *University of the Pacific Law Review* 199, 214–16.

[68] EU Charter of Fundamental Rights, art. 11(2), expressly mentions media plurality as a constitutional value: 'The freedom and pluralism of the media shall be respected.'

considered a restraint of competition if the Internet intermediary holds monopoly power (US)[69] or market dominance (EU).[70]

This raises the question of how to define the relevant market. Would it be correct to only look at the economic market for advertising, or is it necessary to accept a separate market for ideas? Indeed, the former would be the natural starting point of the analysis under competition law, since an economic transaction only takes place between the Internet intermediary and the advertising customers. While the latter pay for the advertising service, the user on the other side of the platform gets the news service for free.[71] Yet such a limited analysis is only satisfactory in cases of two-sided markets, where the interests that need to be protected on the other side of the market where the users do not have to pay are still fully taken into account due to the economic interaction between the two sides of the market. This is indeed doubtful in this case. Advertising customers are interested in addressing a maximum of consumers. Hence, it is this economic rationale that convinced Facebook to apply a business model based on the key criterion of affinity expressed by a system of sharing among friends for disseminating news. According to this rationale underlying Facebook's algorithm, any information, even if it includes blatantly false statements and conspiracy theories, that increases traffic on Facebook makes the social platform more attractive to advertising customers. Hence the negative effects for the democratic process are produced by this very economic rationale.

If, thus, one accepted the proposal to analyse the effects on a separate market for ideas, it would still be difficult to distinguish separate markets for ideas as regards different kinds of news distributors, namely, social platforms, blogs and search engines. The same news and opinions can be disseminated through all these channels, and individuals often use these channels in parallel to gain access to political information. To argue that there is monopoly power or market dominance of firms such as Facebook, Twitter or Google would be extremely difficult.

Apart from the difficulties in showing monopoly power or dominance, it is also quite questionable whether the specific conduct of disseminating populist or ideological views, including conspiracy theories, can be considered as anticompetitive. This is indeed where the discussion on whether a pure economic-efficiency approach should be applied appears in the assessment of the individual case. A pure efficiency and consumer-welfare analysis would not take into account the broader implications of the information disseminated through such services for the democratic process.

---

[69]   In application of US Sherman Act, s. 2, on monopolisation.

[70]   In application of TFEU, art. 102.

[71]   In general, on the competition law implications of goods and services 'for free' provided on the Internet, see Michal S. Gal and Daniel L. Rubinfeld, 'The Hidden Costs of Free Goods: Implications for Antitrust Enforcement' (2016) 80 *Antitrust Law Journal* 521.

11.6.2 *Protecting the Competitive Process in a Market for Ideas*

In contrast, the alternative approach could rely on the model of protecting the competitive process. Yet, in this context, it would not suffice to restrict the analysis to competition among economic rivals. Rather, the key here is to apply the analysis to the market of political ideas. This transfer of competition policy analysis from the economic to the political market seems particularly feasible, since the same economic rationale and the same technological tools, namely, algorithms, apply irrespective of whether users on the Internet make economic decisions as purchasers of goods or services or whether they 'shop' for political ideas. What we learn from the preceding analysis is that the algorithms of intermediaries may lead to an adverse selection of the information that is delivered to users based on their emotional biases, which may even favour the dissemination of false information on the Internet.

If one makes this step from economic rivalry to political rivalry, the question still remains whether this is a case for competition law. What seems to be missing is identifiable harm to economic competition. Most notably, this case is not on exclusionary practices, with dominant Internet intermediaries harming competition by excluding competing intermediaries from the market by disseminating false information.

In the EU, Article 102 TFEU and similar provisions of the national competition law of the Member States also prohibit acts of exploitative abuse. In this regard, the Bundeskartellamt, the German competition authority, has made a courageous decision to explore uncharted territory by opening investigations under German competition law against Facebook for violating rules on personal data protection.[72] Indeed, this case raises the question whether competition law can be used as an enforcement tool for other fields of law. Yet the Bundeskartellamt may still integrate this case into the more classical competition law framework. The authority argues that the contract terms used by Facebook on data protection can be seen as the imposition of unfair conditions on users.[73] In line with this, personal data protection could be seen as a particular quality feature of the service on which firms could in principle be expected to compete (data protection as a competition parameter). Excessive use of personal data could hence be conceived as an exploitative abuse, not on price but quality. Moreover, users can be considered to provide data as a counter-performance for the service they receive.[74]

---

[72] See Bundeskartellamt, 'Bundeskartellamt Initiates Proceedings against Facebook on Suspicion of Having Abused Its Market Power by Infringing Data Protection Rules', press release (2 March 2016), www.bundeskartellamt.de/SharedDocs/Meldung/EN/Pressemitteilungen/2016/02_03_2016_Facebook.html (accessed 31 August 2017). See also Robert McLeod, 'Novel But a Long Time Coming: The Bundeskartellamt Takes on Facebook' (2016) *Journal of European Competition Law & Practice* 367 (2016); Podszun, 'Digitalisierung, Medienvielfalt', 354–5 (highlighting the use of competition law as an enforcement instrument for other fields of the law).

[73] Bundeskartellamt, 'Bundeskartellamt Initiates Proceedings'.

[74] This perspective has also been adopted by the Commission in its proposal for a Digital Content Directive, where the provision of personal data is perceived as a counter-performance of the consumer for digital content. See art. 3(1) Proposal of the Commission of 9 December 2015 for a Directive of the

Accordingly, online intermediaries would appear as market dominant customers in data markets that exploit data suppliers by taking more data than should be expected under competitive circumstances.[75]

In the case of disseminating news that includes false information such as conspiracy theories, however, such exploitative abuse cannot be argued. Quite on the contrary, it seems that economic competition works perfectly fine. Internet intermediaries follow the same business rationale of providing consumers with information according to the individual preferences of the latter.

To conclude, competition law as such does not seem to provide sufficient justification for intervention. Yet there is nonetheless a case for intervention under media law for the purpose of combatting false factual statements and the dissemination of unfounded conspiracy theories over the Internet.

11.6.3 *Competition-Oriented Media Regulation*

Media regulation should be competition-oriented in the sense that the concepts of economic competition are applied to political competition for the best ideas. Citizens should be correctly informed to make political decisions. In the light of these objectives, the economic rationale underlying the business models of Internet intermediaries results in adverse selection of false factual statements and unfounded conspiracy theories. Without regulation, such a market for ideas will create incentives for making strategic use of the Internet by misinforming the public. Intervention is hence needed to exclude incentives for politicians, third parties and even foreign governments to spread fake news and conspiracy theories on the Internet. For such regulation, there is no need to show that Internet intermediaries are dominant in the sense of economic competition. It suffices that individual Internet intermediaries have a major impact on the opinion of citizens. As regards the situation in the US, there can be no doubt that this is the case with Facebook. According to recent data, 62 per cent of US Americans receive news on social media and 44 per cent of US Americans do so on Facebook.[76]

The last question regards the remedies that should be available and should be imposed. In the larger framework of possible regulation, the two extremes are the following:

Least interventionist are measures that improve the availability of better-quality information on the Internet. Public TV in Europe in particular comes from a time

European Parliament and the Council on certain aspects concerning contracts for the supply of digital content, COM(2015) 634 final.

[75] Data markets have already been accepted in the competition law practice of the European Commission. See, in particular, the merger case Thomsen Corp./Reuters Group, Case COMP/ M.4726 – Thomsen Corp/Reuters Group, [2008] OJ C212/5.

[76] Jeffrey Gottfried and Elisa Shearer, 'News Use Across Social Media Platforms 2016' (26 May 2016) www.journalism.org/2016/05/26/news-use-across-social-media-platforms-2016 (accessed 31 August 2017).

when scarcity of frequencies argued for guaranteeing media pluralism within the organisational structure of public broadcasting corporations. When private TV was accepted in European countries, it quickly became clear that private TV largely addressed the preferences of mainstream viewers.[77] Private TV leads to more channels, but not necessarily to more diverse content or quality information. While it seems that the advent of the Internet argues against the universal-service justification for maintaining a system of public TV, the preceding analysis in fact shows that there is a need for public action to promote high-quality information and high-quality journalism on the Internet in order to promote plurality in opinion in the digital era as well.

The other extreme would consist in prohibiting and controlling the content that is made available on the Internet at its source. This, however, should only be done very restrictively, most importantly based on existing rules of criminal law and private-law rules concerning personality rights. Thereby, the legislature should not overshoot the market, as the German legislature nevertheless seems to have done most recently with the adoption of the new Network Enforcement Act. Media plurality does not provide a general justification for censorship on the Internet. New forms of regulation under the umbrella of electoral law could prohibit political parties from applying specific forms of computational propaganda such as political bots and chatbots. However, it is more difficult to lay hands on third parties using such tools of computational propaganda, especially in foreign territories.

Between the two extremes, there appears to be quite some scope for regulating the conduct of intermediaries. The target of regulation should be the business model including the algorithm that decides on the selection of news provided to users. The recent idea of German media regulators, to inform users about the criteria that are used for designing the algorithm in order to enable users to make informed decisions, however, does not appear to be very effective. It is very doubtful whether users would indeed refrain from joining social platforms such as Facebook if they knew about these criteria. This chapter shows that the user's conduct and psychology are key to the adverse selection as identified. The question therefore is whether public regulators should directly control the criteria applied by Internet intermediaries in filtering and disseminating news to users. Such regulation indeed faces major challenges. Most importantly, firms like Facebook consider their algorithm as their most important business secret. Facebook seems to have discontinued its former EdgeRank algorithm a few years ago, but it did so very

---

[77] Indeed, it has long been accepted in economics that competition among private media businesses does not necessarily lead to more diversity of content. See, for instance, Peter O. Steiner, 'Program Patterns and Preferences, and the Workability of Competition in Radio Broadcasting' (1952) 66 *Quarterly Journal of Economics* 194.

silently, without informing the public.[78] The new algorithm is said to use more than 100,000 different criteria for selecting information, but still relies strongly on the three criteria of EdgeRank: 'affinity' (as expressed by the closeness of the user and the source, in particular the 'friend' that shares the news); 'weight' (as expressed by the user's past action as to the type of content);[79] and time decay (how recent content is). In addition, the same algorithm and criteria apply to political and commercial communication. To monitor the operation of constantly changing algorithms applied by Internet intermediaries therefore appears as the most difficult enforcement issue. These problems may even increase with the implementation of 'machine-learning' features in the algorithm.

Before such regulation is introduced, a more intensive discussion of the underlying problem is nevertheless needed. It is only now that media authorities are beginning to understand the problem. The same is true as regards the Internet intermediaries themselves. Since the implications of their current algorithms for plurality of opinion and the dissemination of populist and even ideological views are gradually becoming better understood, the Internet intermediaries themselves could come up with alternative models for improving the quality of the information they convey. Implementation of techniques for identifying false information and conspiracy theories on the Internet could be one way of improving the reliability of news. This does not mean that intermediaries should necessarily withhold such information from users; they could also continue to apply the 'economic logic' of their algorithms, but they could 'red-flag' problematic information as potentially false information or as not scientifically reliable. Such additional service could further help Internet activists and initiatives that consider it their mission to identify and eradicate false information on the Internet.[80]

11.7 PROMOTING MEDIA PLURALITY BY NON-INTERVENTION

In the preceding part of this chapter the question was asked whether competition law can be relied upon to regulate how Internet intermediaries select news that they disseminate to users. But it is also possible for competition agencies to promote media plurality by non-intervention. Such a scenario can typically arise when businesses bring complaints against Internet intermediaries where their conduct promotes rather than harms dissemination of politically diverse news.

This mechanism can best be illustrated by the 2015 decision of the Bundeskartellamt, the German competition agency, in the Google case. In this

---

[78] See Matt McGee, 'EdgeRank Is Dead: Facebook's News Feed Algorithm Now Has Close to 100K Weight Factors' (16 August 2013) http://marketingland.com/edgerank-is-dead-facebooks-news-feed-algorithm-now-has-close-to-100k-weight-factors-55908 (accessed 31 August 2017).

[79] For instance, if a user likes to download videos, it is more likely that this user will get videos in his or her news feed.

[80] See the Italian website www.bufale.net (n. 16).

case, the authority rejected a complaint brought by both VG Media, a collective rights management organisation representing German press publishers, and several individual publishers relating to the representation of the search results by Google's search engine.[81] The dispute arose after the German legislature introduced an ancillary copyright for press publishers for the use of snippets taken from the original articles. The new ancillary right was expected to enable press publishers, which face huge economic challenges due to the Internet, to participate in the advertising income generated by Google. However, once the legislation was adopted, Google requested press publishers in Germany to make a decision to either grant a licence for free or accept that Google would no longer set a link to the websites of the press publishers. In their complaint to the Bundeskartellamt, the press publishers argued an abuse of market dominance by Google by discriminating against publishers who had not granted a licence for free. The Bundeskartellamt rejected the complaint, holding that there was at least an objective justification available to Google, namely, that there was a need to avoid the infringement of intellectual property rights by refraining from copying snippets from the original websites.

This case is of direct relevance for the topic of this chapter. In comments on the case, the argument was made that it is essential for maintaining media plurality on the Internet that dominant operators of search engine do not discriminate against individual content providers such as newspaper publishers.[82] This is in line with the idea currently under consideration by German media regulators[83] that intermediaries also operate as gatekeepers for media on the Internet. However, this does not necessarily mean that the Bundeskartellamt was wrong in its assessment. Both Google's search engine and the Google News service help users to find news reports on the Internet. Hence, Google's business models serve the very interests of the press publishers who want to generate traffic on their own websites. It seems that in Germany only large press publishers resisted the pressure to grant licences for free. Indeed, the large press publishers can expect more users to directly go to their websites to find relevant information. By rejecting the claim of the press publishers, the Bundeskartellamt prevented a result that would only have served the interest of the big publishers.

The situation is even worse in Spain. There, after the adoption of a similar ancillary right, Google completely withdrew its news service from the country.[84]

---

[81] Bundeskartellamt, Decision of 8 September 2015, Case B6-126/14, *Google*, www.bundeskartellamt.de/SharedDocs/Entscheidung/DE/Entscheidungen/Missbrauchsaufsicht/2015/B6-126-14.pdf?__blob=publicationFile&v=2 (accessed 31 August 2017). See also the English case report: Bundeskartellamt, 'Bundeskartellamt Takes Decision in Ancillary Copyright Dispute' (9 September 2015), www.bundeskartellamt.de/SharedDocs/Meldung/EN/Pressemitteilungen/2015/09_09_2015_VG_Media_Google.html (accessed 31 August 2017).

[82] See Boris Paal, 'Internet-Suchmaschinen im Kartellrecht' (2015) *Gewerblicher Rechtsschutz und Urheberrecht Internationaler Teil* 997, 1003–4 and 1005.

[83] See section 11.4.

[84] Jeremy Malcolm, 'Google News Shuttered in Spain Thanks to "Ancillary Copyright" Law' (10 December 2014), www.eff.org/deeplinks/2014/12/google-news-shuts-shop-spain-thanks-ancillary-copyright-law (accessed 31 August 2017).

This produced an obvious disadvantage for smaller publishers, whose websites are less easily found and less frequently visited than the sites of larger competitors. A recent study shows that Google News's withdrawal from the Spanish market caused considerable harm to media plurality in that country.[85]

Hence, rather than Google's conduct, it was the decision of the legislature to introduce an ancillary right for press publishers that created a situation in which media plurality was harmed. Small publishers benefit from news aggregators much more than large publishers.[86] Creating the ancillary right without evidence of a market failure only has the potential of undermining the business of news aggregators and ultimately reducing access to a large variety of newspaper content.[87]

In contrast, the decision of the Bundeskartellamt shows that competition agencies can also promote media plurality by non-intervention where intervention would be directed against intermediaries when they facilitate access to media that contributes to media plurality. Current plans of the European Commission to introduce a respective ancillary right on the EU level[88] therefore need to be evaluated critically.

11.8 CONCLUSION

At its very beginning, this chapter rejected the Chicago School's claim of being apolitical by focusing on economic efficiency. The truth is that the very act of choosing between different kinds of competition policy has a political dimension because of the possibility to make such a choice, the assumptions that underlie the different competition policies and the consequences they produce.

In particular, competition policy becomes highly political in media markets, which are both economic markets and political markets for ideas. This chapter highlights the fact that the business models of Internet intermediaries, including the operators of search engines and social platforms, which nowadays attract major attention from both competition law experts and enforcers, also have a great impact on the market for ideas. Indeed, the same economic rationale applies whether

---

[85] NERA Economic Consulting, 'Impacto del Nuevo Articulo 32.2 de la Ley de Propriedad Intelectual', Study for the Spanish Publishers Association (9 June 2015), www.nera.com/content/dam/nera/pub lications/2015/090715%20Informe%20de%20NERA%20para%20AEEPP%20(VERSION%20FINAL). pdf (accessed 31 August 2017).

[86] In the same vein, see also Jakob Kucharczyk, 'German and Spanish Competition Authorities Got It Right on the Ancillary Copyright for Press Publishers' (17 September 2015), available at: www.project-disco.org/intellectual-property/091715-german-and-spanish-competition-authorities-got-it-right-on-the-ancillary-copyright-for-press-publishers/#.Vo4i601JmUk (accessed 31 August 2017).

[87] Experts from the academic field mostly opposed the adoption of the ancillary right in Germany. See, for instance, Max-Planck-Institut für Immaterialgüter- und Wettbewerbsrecht, 'Stellungnahme zum Gesetzesentwurf für eine Ergänzung des Urheberrechtsgesetzes durch ein Leistungsschutzrecht für Verleger' (27 November 2012), www.ip.mpg.de/fileadmin/ipmpg/content/stellungnahmen/leis tungsschutzrecht_fuer_verleger_01.pdf (accessed 31 August 2017).

[88] See Proposal of the Commission of 14 September 2016 for a Directive of the European Parliament and of the Council on copyright in the Digital Single Market, art. 11, COM(2016) 593 final.

Internet intermediaries disseminate purely commercial information or political information.

Recent research explains that such intermediaries and the algorithms they employ play a major role in facilitating the dissemination of populist and even ideological ideas, as well as conspiracy theories. Social platforms allow users to gather in homogeneous communities where various biases are easily reaffirmed and almost never challenged. The economic logic of the algorithms of Internet intermediaries contributes to this development by targeting the users with information that appeals to them.

However, regulating this issue is not an easy task. Disseminating and receiving such information is part of the freedom of expression and the freedom of information that form the legal backbone of Internet communication. Outright censorship has no place on the Internet. Yet there is a case for regulation. While the Chicago School antitrust approach would most likely deny the existence of any problem, protecting the competitive structure argues in favour of enhancing access to high quality content and the development of policies that identify false or scientifically unproven information on the Internet. Potential regulation should target the criteria on the basis of which the algorithms for selecting information are designed. While it would be difficult to justify such regulation in the framework of competition law, such competition-oriented regulation could be implemented in the framework of a reform of media law. In addition, legislatures and competition agencies should refrain from unnecessarily intervening where Internet intermediaries facilitate access to media content that contributes to media plurality. The battle over the ancillary right for press publishers in Europe and the need to use additional competition law intervention show that legislatures have gone too far in adopting these rights and that competition agencies are well advised to refrain from intervention as a tool to enforce such rights.

C

Competition, Inequality, and Industrial Policy

Competition Policy versus Industrial Policy

Challenging the Mainstream Orthodoxy

David Lewis

12.1 INTRODUCTION

Equity considerations have a legitimate claim to be considered the fount of competition law. Certainly, in its origins competition law represented a statutory effort to limit the economic and political power of great concentrations of wealth. Competition law was thus broadly perceived as a charter for the 'little guy', the atomised consumer and the small producer. Arguably it is this understanding of competition law that, to this day, constitutes the basis for the popular appeal still accorded this complex, esoteric and frequently counter-intuitive branch of law and economics.

However, in current competition law and policy orthodoxy, equity considerations, certainly distributional considerations, do not, to put it mildly, loom large. Indeed, one of the first bits of advice that a new entrant into the world of competition enforcement will receive from her more experienced peers is to avoid polluting competition decisions with multiple policy objectives, particularly where the introduction of equity objectives may compromise the efficiency objectives widely held to be at the heart of competition law.[1]

That first lesson will be followed by those that teach that market power is not to be confused with size. The power of a very large firm may be constrained by the presence of other very large firms; or by low entry barriers; or by dynamic innovation. As Judge Scalia (in)famously noted in *Trinko*:

> The mere possession of monopoly power, and the concomitant charging of monopoly prices, is not only not unlawful; it is an important element of the free-market system. The opportunity to charge monopoly prices – at least for a short period – is what attracts 'business acumen' in the first place; it induces risk-taking that produces innovation and economic growth. To safeguard the incentive to innovate, the

---

[1] See Chapter 13 in this volume.

possession of monopoly power will not be found unlawful, unless it is accompanied by an element of anti-competitive conduct.[2]

This is, of course, not to suggest that all competition lawyers and economists are unmoved by equity considerations. But, citing the dangers of introducing multiple conflicting objectives into the competition decision, they would prefer to consign the goal of efficiency and productivity enhancement to competition law policy (CLP), while assigning the attainment of preferred equity and redistributive outcomes to fiscal, social and labour market policy.

The competition practitioner may even reluctantly concede that the disruption generated by enhanced competition may bring with it severe adjustment costs – jobs may be lost, small producers may be forced out of the market, particular regions may be disproportionately prejudiced by the loss of jobs and productive capacity. While some countries have inserted equity-inspired public interest factors into competition decisions, this is generally frowned upon by the competition orthodoxy.[3]

If obliged to make a case for the equity or anti-poverty credentials of competition law, it is generally rooted in its claimed ability to generate great firm-level efficiency, thus producing better-quality products at a lower price, effecting a transfer from powerful producers to consumers. But for anything beyond these competition-induced equities our competition practitioner's strong preference will be to call on active labour market policies and the creation of social safety nets in order to mitigate the adjustment costs.

This orthodoxy is challenged by the search for a CLP that addresses poverty and equality, particularly in developing countries. And, moreover, a CLP that will do all this and not be called upon to bend its fundamental principles in order to realise these 'non-competition' objectives. As Eleanor Fox put it in a recent paper:

> What is the role of competition law and policy? How does it fit or not fit with the (expected) SDGs? Is it in sympathy or in tension? Where it is in tension, must it take second seat i.e., should we presume that where poverty, equality and the environment are at stake, anti-trust law should bend.[4]

and

---

[2] *Verizon Communications Inc* v. *Law Offices of Curtis* v. *Trinko* LLP (02-682) 540 US 398 (2004).

[3] South Africa's competition statute, particularly the preamble outlining the principles governing the statute and provisions governing the regulation of mergers, requires consideration of public interest factors. It is the aspect of South Africa's competition law regime that has attracted most attention, and widespread criticism from competition scholars and practitioners: see Competition Act, 89 of 1998, especially the preamble and ss. 2 and 12.

[4] E. Fox (2015) '"Making Markets Work for The People" as a Post-Millennium Development Goal' (2015), http://unctad.org/meetings/en/Contribution/CCPB_7RC2015_HLRTCompSusDev_Fox_en .pdf, p. 3.

The second involves exemptions from antitrust and expansions of antitrust: authorizing anticompetitive agreements and conduct to advance non-competition goals such as the environment or promoting small businesses. Should antitrust bend? How readily and by what standard? Should antitrust expand to encompass 'fairness'?[5]

Fox's preferred case for CLP's progressive redistributive effects rests on its contribution to promoting ease of access to markets. This indeed appears to be the principal equity-related objective that underpinned the foundations of competition law – ensuring that the opportunity to participate in economic activity was not denied the 'little guy'.

CLP's claim to ease access for new entrants rests on several pillars:[6]

1. it lowers regulatory hurdles that restrict new entry;
2. it restrains dominant firms from abusing their dominant positions through exclusionary conduct that forecloses markets;
3. it restrains cartelisation of important intermediate goods markets; and
4. it drives innovation in products and services that facilitate market entry – e.g. mobile telephony, internet, Uber.

This chapter explores another not much considered dimension of the potential interfaces between two policy fields that are both focused on encouraging and enabling new entry and enhancing firm-level productivity, namely CLP and industrial policy.

12.2 FRAMING THE MAINSTREAM ORTHODOXY

Despite sharing near-identical objectives, these two policy fields are frequently cast as existentially opposed to one another. The root of this opposition is to be found in the popular presentation of the instrument of choice of the respective policy fields, namely market-centred CLP and state-centred industrial policy, thus revealing that in their mutual quest to secure new entry and firm-level efficiency, the debate between the protagonists of industrial policy and CLP is essentially concerned with where to draw the boundary between market and state.

The current state of this battle is that the respective protagonists of industrial policy and CLP have moved closer together. On the one hand, seminal contributions to economic theory have emphasised the ubiquity and impact of market

---

[5] Ibid.
[6] See, e.g., Fox, "'Making Markets Work'", p. 4: 'But if the farmers can obtain their inputs at a competitive price, they can produce a reasonable crop and even sell for export (if not blocked by developed country import restraints) ... Similarly, if budding entrepreneurs, poor and unconnected, can enter basic markets free of excessive, incumbent-protecting regulatory requirements that they cannot hope to hurtle, they can be a part of the economic enterprise rather than supplicants to it."

failures, and persuasive interpretations of successive Asian experiences of rapid and sustainable industrial development have emphasised the leading role of the state.[7]

On the other hand, evidence of state failure, particularly, but by no means exclusively, in poorly capacitated developing economies, combined with the constraints imposed on national policymaking by increasingly open international capital and product markets and the rise of global supply chains, have conspired to put the proponents of CLP in front by a short head.

The upshot is that the proponents of industrial policy are challenged – the onus is on them, so to speak – to develop and pursue *market-friendly* industrial policies, whose key features are:

- 'far-from-market' generic support – that is, an industrial policy focused on the provision of economic infrastructure and human capital rather than support directed at particular firms or even sectors;
- support provided through an 'open window' mechanism at which firms compete for state support;
- support programmes limited in time and constantly evaluated with the recipients, subject to disciplines that may see the withdrawal of support in the event of underperformance;
- an aversion to protection from international competition and any discouragement of direct foreign investment.

However, the force of the theoretical arguments against 'pure' market-driven outcomes and the empirical evidence that demonstrates the efficacy of market-friendly state intervention in promoting industrial development suggests that, in addition to being a bulwark against interventions that distort and undermine markets, the proponents of CLP should also be challenged to develop *inclusive growth-friendly CLP*.[8]

This challenge takes on particular significance as the market enquiry assumes an increasingly important role in the armoury of competition law. It strikes me that the focal point of market enquiries should be on overcoming entry barriers, particularly those that inhibit new entry, that is, entry into the market by new entrepreneurs and entry by incumbent operators into new lines of business. Likewise, CLP practitioners should not be content to confine their support for new entry to identifying and advocating against obstructive regulation and exclusionary private conduct. They should participate in designing incentive regimes that encourage new entry and that comport with CLP market principles.

---

[7] Alice Amsden, *Asia's Next Giant* (Oxford University Press, 1989); Ha-Joon Chang, *The Political Economy of Industrial Policy* (St Martin's Press, 2004).

[8] UNCTAD, 'The Role of Competition Policy in Promoting Sustainable and Inclusive Growth' (2015), http://unctad.org/meetings/en/SessionalDocuments/tdrbpconf8d6_en.pdf

12.3 CHALLENGING THE ORTHODOXY: THE INNOVATION CROSSING

It is widely understood that innovation is the principal driver of economic development and productivity growth and, in particular, of sustainable new entry.[9] It is also widely recognised that, if left unprotected, innovation may be easily emulated, depressing private returns with a consequent underinvestment in R&D. Accordingly, patent laws were formulated in order to protect the fruits of R&D from easy replication thus boosting private returns above those that would have operated in an unregulated market.

12.3.1 *The Developed Country Perspective: the Patent Exception*

The patent system thus constitutes the most widely accepted and productive interface between CLP and industrial policy. On the face of it, it may appear that it is CLP that has, to borrow Eleanor Fox's term, 'bent', insofar as it has permitted the existence of temporary, partial monopolies. However, it has made this apparent concession precisely in order to incentivise robust competition in important innovation markets on the premise that they will produce higher-quality products at lower prices, that is that competition will be stimulated in product markets.

So, in reality far from either policy field having bent before the other, the patent system constitutes a productive agreement between CLP and industrial policy, with practitioners in both fields alert to possible abuses that would extend the approved monopolies beyond the period or the scope necessary to ensure an equivalence of social and private returns.

However, patenting is generally confined to protecting new product development *by restricting imitative new entry* at too early a stage. Much of this new product development is R&D intensive, and, so, for the most part, it protects the sort of innovation, the major returns from which are overwhelmingly reflected in sustainable, dynamic growth in developed countries.

Intellectual property (IP) protection – or patenting – is thus construed as an overwhelmingly developed country issue (but, of course, for the fact that IP protection enables rent extraction in pharmaceutical markets of life and death significance for the people of developing countries). And, so, 'comparative advantage' between regions is reinforced by patenting practice. Developed countries with relatively efficient capital markets and skilled human resources generate patentable IP; developing countries with abundant unskilled labour and inefficient capital markets assemble the products innovated in developed countries.

---

[9]   OECD, 'Innovation and Growth: Rationale for an Innovation Strategy' (2007), www.oecd.org/sti/inno/39374789.pdf; OECD, 'Innovation for Development' (2012), www.oecd.org/innovation/inno/50586251.pdf.

While this bifurcation may help alleviate extreme poverty – in the form of labour-intensive jobs that move in increasing numbers to developing countries – it exacerbates inequality between and within nations because, aided and abetted by IP protection, significantly higher private returns accrue to skilled-labour-intensive and capital-intensive innovation than to unskilled-labour-intensive manufacture.

And so the inequality between developed and developing nations persists with the former, critically undergirded by IP protection, maintaining comparative advantage in high value-add innovation-intensive activities, with developing countries stuck in low value-add assembly. The best advice that economic orthodoxy can give to developing countries is to keep their jurisdictions open to direct foreign investment (DFI) because the technology transfers that accompany this form of investment will at least allow the developing country manufacturers to take advantage of the costly, skill-intensive innovation undertaken in the foreign investor's home country.[10] Hence although there may be much point in protecting innovation in developed countries, it cannot overcome, and indeed exacerbates, the divide between developed and developing countries because, the story goes, there is no innovation to speak of in developing countries – that is not where their comparative advantage lies.

However, the notion that developing country production requires no innovation is highly questionable. Instead the developing country problem may be identical to that of developed countries, namely that the essential innovation that does occur in developing countries is easily emulated with the same dis-incentivising consequences that would occur in developed countries were it not for IP protection. Is then the development problem not to temporarily restrict new entry, after the fashion of IP protection, rather than to leave the innovative developing country producer prey to easy emulation?

What then is this developing country innovation?

12.3.2 *The Developing Country Perspective: the Discovery Process*

It is reflected in what Hausman and Rodrik refer to as the 'discovery' process, the process of learning what one is good at producing.[11] Once one goes beneath the high-level comparative advantage categories of 'skilled or unskilled labour-intensive growth' or 'natural resource-based' growth, there is not much that economic theory can teach entrepreneurs or industrial policymakers about what to choose between the tens of thousands of subcategories to enter. So, it is important to know whether a country's 'labour-intensive comparative advantage' is in hats (Bangladesh) or bedsheets (Pakistan); footwear uppers (Dominican Republic) or ignition wiring sets (Honduras); bicycles (Taiwan) or air-conditioning units (Korea). The point is this: despite identical 'comparative advantages' these neighbours specialise in very

---

[10]   Ricardo Hausmann and Dani Rodrik, 'Economic Development as Self-discovery' (2003) 72 *Journal of Development Economics* 603.

[11]   Ibid. The empirical references used here are drawn from this paper (ibid., 613–23).

different products, each of which constitutes a very large share of their export earnings, and they produce hardly any of the products in which their neighbours specialise. Why is this? And how should it guide policy?

The costs of discovering which of these choices to settle on are considerable, involving, as it does, much experimentation and learning, that is, innovation. This innovation or discovery process includes the adaptation of imported technology to domestic conditions and requirements but it also covers a range of factors including the development of design skills, appreciation of fashion trends, familiarity with market networks, etc. However, and here's the problem, these innovations or 'discoveries' are not easily codified and so not easily patentable. But, like many skilled labour and capital-intensive developed country innovations, once these discoveries have been made they are very easily emulated. And so there is an undersupply of innovators willing to sink costs into discovery. The upshot, and the critical insight of Hausmann and Rodrik's thought-provoking paper, is that *ex ante* there is a shortage of discovery (innovation), and *ex post* there is an excess of diversification, a lack of specialisation. And so what should be done to encourage developing country innovation and how should developing country CLP practitioners engage with this problem?

12.3.2.1 Protect Process Innovation

Competition law enforcement agencies need to develop standards applicable to new entrants, particularly those producing competing products and services, but using new production methods.

These new production methods will inevitably involve non-patentable adaptations of existing methods. They may also require a degree of nimbleness and flexibility that large incumbents will have difficulty emulating. These new entrants will be a particular target of incumbents who will seek to keep them out of the market either through exclusionary conduct or through acquisition. If this is done at a sufficiently early stage the new entrant will not have the resources to defend itself and nor will antitrust law be able to defend it because taking out a new entrant in an established market is unlikely to pass a substantial lessening of competition test.

The South African competition authorities have in one instance adjudicated a case of a disruptive new entry into the important market for health insurance products in which an established competitor was prevented by the Competition Tribunal – South Africa's adjudicator of first instance – from acquiring a relatively new entrant that was beginning to make ground in this market utilising a new, but non-patentable approach that, if successful, may have successfully extended affordable health insurance to low- and middle-income consumers. The Competition Appeal Court reversed this prohibition thus enabling the incumbent operator to suppress the innovation.[12]

---

[12] *Medicross Healthcare Group (Pty) Ltd/Primecure Holdings (Pty) Ltd* (11/LM/Mar05).

12.3.2.2 Targeted Producer Subsidies

The doctrinaire opposition of CLP practitioners to producer subsidies should 'bend' before subsidies designed to reward new entrants, just as it 'bends' to accommodate patent protection for codifiable R&D-based innovations. In reality, innovator subsidies or protection do not entail any bending because they are pro-competitive. While it is difficult to imagine extending patent protection to adaptive innovation (although this should be explored), it's wholly possible to conceive of a subsidy programme that rewards adaptive innovators.

Of course, as with all targeted support the subsidy must not extend beyond the innovator, nor should it exceed the costs of discovery. While a subsidy to innovators – whether of the developed or developing country innovator variety – will, per definition, always be risky, the subsidy should be conditional upon submission of a credible business case. The subsidy should be contingent upon identification of quantifiable targets and it should be subject to termination in the event that the agreed targets are not met.

While the Pakistani adaptive innovators initial decision to go into bedsheet (rather than hat) production is likely to be serendipitous, evidence that there is a business case should justify the grant of the aforementioned subsidy to the entrepreneur in order to compensate for her costs of discovery.

However, for the Pakistan economy to graduate from one in which there is a random smattering of successful bedsheet producers to an economy that specialises in bedsheet production for the world market, it is necessary to attract new entry on a significant scale thus generating the prospective agglomeration economies that large-scale new entry will bring. In other words, rewarding the developing country innovator should not discourage the emulators whose presence will constitute the productivity enhancing 'industrial district'.[13]

This raises a number of important issues: first, it is important that the subsidy not exceed the costs of discovery. To the extent that it does the innovator will be able to use its subsidy to outcompete the new entrant emulators thus discouraging the latter from entering the market. The difficulty entailed in determining the discovery costs is acknowledged and so too is the possibility of error and abuse. But these risks are no greater than those entailed in determining the scope and duration of patent protection.

Second, there should be no competition policy obstacle placed in the way of state support for the sector. The subsidy could well be restricted to firms in targeted locales in order to prepare the ground for the powerful agglomeration economies that will follow the crowding in of the emulators. Agglomerations then offer the prospect of generic state support – for example, the building of infrastructure targeted at supporting the industrial district or the development of training programmes or marketing facilities designed to support the whole sector.

[13]   Hausmann and Rodrik, 'Economic Development as Self-discovery', 626–8.

There are, to be sure, some forms of support which frequently find favour with industry policymakers but which CLP should firmly resist. These are:

- export cartels, not because cartels, above all else, are deemed heretical in CLP but because the support which they provide cannot discriminate between efficient and inefficient firms; and
- the regulation of excessive pricing, which is commonly advocated by industrial policy protagonists and which finds expression in many antitrust statutes. These should be removed from antitrust statutes or, where they are present, antitrust authorities should refrain from enforcing these provisions. Antitrust authorities do not have the information or the decision-making procedures necessary for regulating prices, however tempting this may be in the name of securing favourable prices of intermediate goods in order to encourage downstream manufacturing. This does not mean that there are never grounds for price regulation. But it should not be within the remit of competition law practitioners.

None of the above – new substantial lessening of competition standards for conduct prejudicial to adaptive innovators, subsidies for adaptive innovators and sectorally and geographically targeted state support designed to extend agglomeration economies – requires much, if any, bending on the part of either CLP or industrial policy. All are pro-competitive and advance the mutual objective of both policy fields in their support for new entry and firm-level productivity enhancement.

Both do challenge the orthodoxies, indeed the prejudices, of their respective policy fields.

12.4 CONCLUSION

CLP and industrial policy are both focused on encouraging and enabling new entry and enhancing firm-level productivity. And yet they are widely considered, by their respective proponents no less, to be existentially opposed to one another. The reason for this appears to lie in the dominant instruments of each, with competition policy driven by the market and industrial policy by the state.

Although state-driven approaches are supported by evidence of ubiquitous market failure and the experiences of successful, predominantly Asian, developmental states, evidence of widespread state failure and the restraints imposed upon national industrial policies by liberalised global markets have conspired to give the CLP an edge in the policy debate. This is evidenced by the pressure imposed upon industrial policymakers to formulate market-friendly industrial policies.

However, this chapter argues that the force of the arguments against pure market-driven approaches are of sufficient weight to demand of competition law policymakers that they produce inclusive growth-friendly competition policy.

The imperative to protect innovation is the one important policy application in which competition policymakers are prepared to concede the importance of temporary market dominance and its accompanying rents. However, the form that IP protection takes nurtures the sort of innovation that predominantly occurs in the global north, the underlying assumption being that innovation is not a factor underpinning industrial development in developing economies.

Drawing on the theoretical insights and empirical evidence contained in a thoughtful paper by Ricardo Hausmann and Dani Rodrik, this chapter argues that innovation is indeed an important factor underpinning successful industrial development in developing countries. It argues that just as competition policy practitioners have embraced the importance of protecting innovation in the north because it is pro-competition, that is to say, because it produces better-quality products at lower prices, so too should it protect developing country innovation.

IP protection in the south is unlikely to take the form of codified patenting. It is more likely to take the form of subsidies to support innovation. Competition policy practitioners should actively participate in designing subsidy schemes that accept the importance of developing country innovation while simultaneously guarding against their abuse. This is, after all, the approach taken to IP protection in the north.

13

Antitrust, Industrial Policy, and Economic Populism

D. Daniel Sokol

13.1 INTRODUCTION

Whereas an antitrust policy that embraced multiple goals was of major debate into the 1970s, a sea change of case law that focused on economic analysis, agency evolution (including the introduction of merger notification in the 1970s), and shifts in economics and economic analysis of antitrust law meant that by the mid 1980s, US antitrust was solely based on economic goals.[1]

What in the US legal academy was the last dying gasp for a generation of legal scholars who defended populism (the exception is the notable and powerful work of Eleanor Fox) was the work of Robert ("Bob") Pitofsky in the famous symposium issue of the *Penn Law Review* that signaled the end not merely of populism but of the structure–conduct–performance paradigm. Pitofsky chastised antitrust scholars for "persuading the courts to adopt an exclusively economic approach to antitrust questions." He argued (at that time) that "[i]t is bad history, bad policy and bad law ... to exclude certain political values in interpreting the antitrust laws."[2] Pitofsky explained

---

Parts of this chapter are based in part uponD. D. Sokol, 'Tensions between Antitrust and Industrial Policy' (2015) 22 *Geo. Mason L. Rev.* 1247.

[1] The difference between the antitrust economic left and right in this sense is not as significant as between the populists and non-populists. Compare e.g. R. H. Bork, *The Antitrust Paradox* (Free Press, 1978), 56–66, with R. H. Lande, 'Chicago's False Foundation: Wealth Transfers (Not Just Efficiency) Should Guide Antitrust' (1989) 58 *Antitrust Law Journal* 631; R. H. Lande, 'Wealth Transfers as the Original and Primary Concern of Antitrust: The Efficiency Interpretation Challenged' (1982) 34 *Hastings Law Journal* 65. See also D. Besanko and D. F. Spulber, 'Contested Mergers and Antitrust Policy' (1993) 9 *Journal of Law, Economics, and Organization* 1; D. J. Neven and L.-H. Roller, 'Consumer Surplus vs. Welfare Standard in a Political Economy Model of Merger Control' (2005) 23 *International Law Journal of Industrial Organization* 829; J. B. Baker, 'Economics and Politics: Perspectives on the Goals and Future of Antitrust' (2013) 81 *Fordham Law Review* 2175; B. Orbach, 'How Antitrust Lost Its Goal' (2013) 81 *Fordham Law Review* 2253; S. C. Salop, 'Merger Settlement and Enforcement Policy for Optimal Deterrence and Maximum Welfare' (2013) 81 *Fordham Law Review* 2647; J. D. Wright and D. H. Ginsburg, 'The Goals of Antitrust: Welfare Trumps Choice' (2013) 81 *Fordham Law Review* 2405.

[2] R. Pitofsky, 'The Political Content of Antitrust' (1979) 127 *University of Pennsylvania Law Review* 1051.

political values in a populist manner by noting, "if the free market is allowed to develop under antitrust rules that are blind to all but economic concerns, the likely result will be an economy so dominated by a few corporate giants that it will be impossible for the state not to play a more intrusive role in economic affairs."[3] The irony, of course is that when Pitofsky headed the Federal Trade Commission (FTC) in the 1990s, he did not adopt any populism. Rather, he continued with economic analysis that was established by prior Republican and Democratic administration and is considered to be part of a time of a "golden age" of antitrust.[4] Similarly, in Richard Posner's antitrust law case book of 1976, the title he used reflected the tension within antitrust legal scholarship of that time. Posner's title was *Antitrust Law: An Economic Perspective*. At the time, Harry First criticized the book on more populist grounds, stating that "[Posner's *Antitrust Law*] comes at a time when the limits of traditional microeconomics as a tool of antitrust policy have become starkly apparent, limitations which suggest that antitrust law should be moving outside the economist's world rather than burrowing more deeply into it."[5] Two things are worth noting since that time. The first is that by the time of the second edition in 2001 of Posner's case book, Posner's title had been abridged to *Antitrust Law*. Anything further seemed superfluous. Second, Harry First went on to embrace economic analysis in his scholarship in his progressive vision of antitrust.[6]

This chapter suggests that once rigorous economic analysis was embraced, antitrust fundamentally shifted. Antitrust went through a change from a regulatory function to an enforcement function based on a singular economic goal. Once this goal was embraced, antitrust became limited in its reach. Certainly, this has been true in the United States. It has been less true in Europe but perhaps this is a function that in spite of unambiguous language by DG Competition as to the singular economic goal of consumer welfare, case law has not caught up with the stated policy goal and those within DG Competition who push back against economic analysis are emboldened by the lack of explicit case law with regard to efficiency in conduct cases. This chapter lays out these developments in the United States and Europe and suggests that as a normative matter, an antitrust that is limited to what it does best, market correction against illegal monopoly power, should remain the singular goal. In contrast, other non-economic factors are better served through other policy instruments.

13.2 THE REAL GOAL OF ANTITRUST IS AN ECONOMIC ONE

Sound antitrust law and policy is in tension with industrial policy. Antitrust promotes consumer welfare whereas industrial policy promotes government

[3] Ibid.
[4] W. E. Kovacic, 'Intellectual DNA of modern U.S. Competition Law for Dominant Firm Conduct: The Chicago/Harvard Double Helix' (2007) 1 *Columbia Business Law Review* 1–80.
[5] H. First, 'Book Review' (1977) 52 *NYU Law Review* 947.
[6] See e.g. H. First, 'Bork and Microsoft: Why Bork Was Right and What We Learn about Judging Exclusionary Behavior' (2014) 79 *Antitrust Law Journal* 1017.

intervention for privileged groups or industries.[7] Unfortunately, industrial policy seems to be alive and well both within antitrust law and policy and within a broader competition policy worldwide. This chapter identifies how industrial policy impacts both antitrust and competition policy. It provides examples from the United States, Europe, and China of how industrial policy has been used in antitrust. However, this chapter also makes a broader claim that the overt or subtle use of industrial policy in antitrust and competition policy is also a global phenomenon. The US experience teaches us that industrial policy can be pushed to the margins in antitrust (and the failure to push industrial policy to the margins produces economic inefficiencies). Further, successful competition advocacy can reduce the competitive distortions that industrial policy may have on competition policy more broadly.

Industrial policy threatens consumer welfare.[8] Yet, determining the scope of industrial policy may sometimes prove to be a challenge because industrial policy has multiple meanings.[9] For purposes of this chapter, industrial policy means political interference either within antitrust or from outside of antitrust (such as through the political process or sector regulation), in which economic analysis that is not based on antitrust economics (which is industrial organization economics as applied to antitrust) may shape antitrust enforcement. Optimal antitrust enforcement requires that political factors not play a part of antitrust and that a technocratic antitrust – characterized by economically justified outcomes, predictability, administrability, and respect for due process and transparency – be the driving forces of enforcement. Additionally, antitrust should try to limit the political impulse based on interest group capture in other parts of government as a function of a broader competition policy to improve national competitiveness.[10] Across the world, industrial policy asserts a more central position in antitrust enforcement than in the United States. Such situations allow for implicit intrusions of industrial policy, as agencies may be able to strategically pick and choose the economics that they adopt based on the outcome, reverse engineering a decision.[11] In other situations, industrial policy sneaks in more subtly, due to case law that supports agencies with

---

[7] Even capitalist countries inject industrial policy at various times. Sometimes the industrial policy has spillover effects that improve overall well-being but these policy interventions may be less efficient than less distortive policy interventionist that might have been done instead. Antitrust agencies have a role to play to limit anti-competitive policy distortions through their competition advocacy mission. For an overview, see J. C. Cooper et al., 'Theory and Practice of Competition Advocacy at the FTC' (2005) 72 *Antitrust Law Journal* 1091.

[8] L. J. White, 'Antitrust Policy and Industrial Policy: A View from the U.S.', in A. M. Mateus and T. Moreira (eds.), *Competition Law and Economics: Advances in Competition Policy Enforcement in the EU and North America* (Edward Elgar, 2010).

[9] See generally T. K. Cheng, I. Lianos, and D. D. Sokol, 'Introduction', in T. K. Cheng, I. Lianos, and D. D. Sokol (eds.), *Competition and the State* (Stanford University Press, 2014), 1–12.

[10] E. M. Fox and Deborah Healey, 'When the State Harms Competition – The Role for Competition Law' (2014) 79 *Antitrust Law Journal* 769.

[11] D. D. Sokol, 'Merger Control Under China's Anti-Monopoly Law', (2013) 10 *NYU Journal of Law and Business* 1.

aggressive enforcement because such case law was based in part on industrial policy goals.[12] In some systems, competitor effects still have some significance in antitrust analysis.[13] At some level, this focus on competitors rather than on competition is a form of industrial policy because it may favor outcomes inconsistent with consumer welfare.[14]

Government may intervene in the economy both within an antitrust system and outside of it.[15] An antitrust regime that makes economic analysis of competitive effects the sole method for analyzing consumer harm removes political factors from the analysis, shifting discretion from antitrust authorities to the market. That is, the market will determine winners and losers rather than antitrust policy. From a normative standpoint, this is more desirable because the incorporation of fairness-related concerns may lead to results that hurt consumers. This is true in part because "fairness" is a highly variable concept.[16] Professors Phillip Areeda and Donald Turner identified fairness as "a vagrant claim applied to any value that one happens to favor."[17] Fairness in antitrust can be misapplied by less efficient competitors to promote their own goals at the expense of consumers.[18] These special interests can capture the antitrust system and antitrust enforcers, whom such competitors can misuse for their personal aims to extort protection.[19] Antitrust is not an effective mechanism for these sorts of fairness trade-offs. Other areas of regulation are better suited to addressing such trade-offs than antitrust. Embracing antitrust economics promotes greater predictability and outcomes that are less likely to be hijacked by overtly political concerns not based on competition economics, which allows for better predictability in antitrust and a narrow focus on what antitrust does best – promote consumer welfare. Some of the introduction of industrial policy in antitrust is due to the particular language of the enacting legislation that provides for multiple and sometimes competing goals

---

[12] M. A. Bergman et al., 'Merger Control in the European Union and the United States: Just the Facts' (2011) 7 *European Competition Journal* 89.

[13] M. B. Coate and A. N. Kleit, 'Art of the Deal: The Merger Settlement Process at the Federal Trade Commission' (2004) 70 *S. Econ. J.* 977.

[14] H. First and E. M. Fox, 'Philadelphia National Bank, Globalization, and the Public Interest' (2015) 80 *Antitrust Law Journal* 307.

[15] T. W. Ross, 'Recent Canadian Policy Towards Industry: Competition Policy, Industrial Policy and National Champions', in A. M. Mateus and T. Moreira (eds.), *Competition Law and Economics: Advances in the EU and North America* (Edward Elgar, 2010).

[16] L. Kaplow, 'On the Choice of Welfare Standards in Competition Law', in D. Zimmer (ed.), *The Goals of Competition Law* (Edward Elgar, 2012).

[17] P. E. Areeda and H. Hovenkamp, 'Antitrust Law – An Analysis of Antitrust Principles and their Application' (4th edn, Wolters Kluwer, 2015), para. 111d; L. Kaplow and S. Shavell, 'Fairness Versus Welfare' (2001) 114 *Harvard Law Review* 961.

[18] R. D. Blair and D. D. Sokol, 'Welfare Standards in U.S. and E.U. Antitrust Enforcement' (2013) 81 *Fordham Law Review* 2497.

[19] W. J. Baumol and J. A. Ordover, 'Use of Antitrust to Subvert Competition' (1985) 28 *Journal of Law and Economics* 247; D. D. Sokol, 'Strategic Use of Public and Private Litigation in Antitrust as Business Strategy' (2012) 85 *S. Cal. L. Rev.* 689.

for antitrust. The original statutory schemes of many antitrust regimes contained multiple goals. These goals may create a path dependency in the case law, which then favors antitrust intervention even when such behavior may be economically justified on efficiency grounds. The good news is that most jurisdictions have adopted an antitrust-economics-driven goal (most often consumer welfare) as the sole criterion for antitrust analysis, with other goals falling by the wayside. Yet, even when industrial policy is not explicitly used (or no longer used) in antitrust law, in practice, its implicit use regularly occurs in many jurisdictions around the world due to this path dependency in the case law because bad old cases remain good case law until they are overturned.[20]

13.3 US EXPERIENCE OF INDUSTRIAL POLICY IN ANTITRUST

Much of US antitrust enforcement from the 1950s and 1960s is an embarrassment by today's standards.[21] Back then, big was bad,[22] merger efficiencies were ignored,[23] vertical restraints were per se illegal,[24] there was tightening of rules for refusals to deal,[25] intellectual property was subject to the nine no-nos,[26] horizontal restraints were unnecessarily applied,[27] and the Robinson–Patman Act was aggressively enforced.[28] In all of these cases, industrial policy that favored inefficient competitors was both a fundamental part of case law and government-enforcement priorities. Such economically misguided and aggressive enforcement hurt US competitiveness and contributed to the US's economic malaise.[29] This approach in US case law began to change in the late 1970s, although the change in merger case law lagged

---

[20] R. D. Blair and D. D. Sokol, 'The Rule of Reason and the Goals of Antitrust: An Economic Approach' (2012) 78 *Antitrust Law Journal* 471.

[21] D. H. Ginsburg, 'Originalism and Economic Analysis: Two Case Studies of Consistency and Coherence in Supreme Court Decision Making' (2010) 33 *Harvard Journal of Law and Public Policy* 217.

[22] *United States v. Von's Grocery Co.*, 384 US 270, 278–9 (1966); *United States v. Phila. Nat'l Bank*, 374 US 321, 371–2 (1963); *Brown Shoe Co. v. United States*, 370 US 294, 345–6 (1962); *United States v. Aluminum Co. of Am.*, 148 F.2d 416, 428 (2d Cir. 1945).

[23] *Fed. Trade Comm'n v. Procter and Gamble Co.*, 386 US 568, 580 (1967).

[24] *Albrecht v. Herald Co.*, 390 US 145, 151–4 (1968); *United States v. Arnold, Schwinn and Co.*, 388 US 365, 373 (1967).

[25] *Klor's, Inc. v. Broadway-Hale Stores, Inc.*, 359 US 207 (1959).

[26] B. B. Wilson, 'Special Assistant to the Assistant Attorney Gen., Antitrust Div., U.S. Dep't of Justice, Patent and Know-How License Agreements: Field of Use, Territorial, Price and Quantity Restrictions (Nov. 6, 1970)', in S.-A. Sanders (ed.), *Antitrust Primer: Patents, Franchising, Treble Damages Suits* (Boston Bar Association, 1970), 11, 12–14.

[27] *United States v. Topco Assocs., Inc.*, 405 US 596 (1972).

[28] *FTC v. Morton Salt Co.*, 334 US 37 (1948); *Utah Pie Co. v. Cont'l Baking Co.*, 386 US 685 (1967).

[29] D. A. Hyman and W. E. Kovacic, 'Can't Anyone Here Play This Game? Judging the FTC's Critics' (2015) 83 *Geo. Wash. L. Rev.* 1948 (identifying the limitations of excessive intervention by the FTC in the 1960s and 1970s). Note that economic competitiveness is a function of many factors, of which competition policy is only one such factor. See M. E. Porter, M. Delgado, C. Ketels, and Scott Stern, 'Moving to a New Global Competitiveness Index', in *Global Competitiveness Report 2008–09* (World Economic Forum, 2008).

behind the abolition of per se rules regarding conduct.[30] Overt political antitrust considerations (i.e. those not based on antitrust economics) are no longer part of the current antitrust policy discourse within the case law or agency practices. In the United States, antitrust liability has narrowed due to a better understanding of economics, and antitrust analysis is now driven by economic analysis.[31] One might suggest that there was a highly political decision by the US judiciary to remove overt politics going forward from antitrust through the creation of an efficiency goal. This policy choice to remove over politics based on a "public interest" framework found in regulatory fields is the mechanism that allows for more or less continuity across both Democratic and Republican administrations in antitrust.

Changes in priorities became embedded not merely in case law but also in agency practice with the rise in the importance of economics (and economists) in agency analysis.[32] In terms of how incentives impact the role of industrial policy in antitrust, discretion in the hands of lawyers will play out differently than in those of economists because discretion influences how centrally economic analysis will factor into case selection. Professor Luke Froeb and his colleagues explain that "[e]conomic methodology is particularly well suited for predicting the causal effects of business practices and for determining the effects of counterfactual scenarios that are used to determine liability and damages."[33] If economic analysis forms the basis of enforcement decision-making, effects become the focus. In this sense, overt political control can be removed from case analysis because economic inquiry is guided more by empirics. Lawyers, as part of an investigative team, may be less driven by the empirics of economics.[34] As a result, more overt political goals might factor into their analyses. This is not to say that economists are not subject to political motivation. However, economists exercise it less than lawyers because populism was never part of industrial organization's mantra. The greater institutionalization of economics as the central motivation for antitrust may have been a causal factor that changed the role of non-antitrust government intervention in antitrust. In particular, one can see this change in merger control and the shift in the United States from hostility to eventual embrace of efficiencies in both the Merger Guidelines and case law analysis. The US experience is worth noting as an example for other jurisdictions, even those with significantly different institutional designs, largely because of the

---

[30]   H. Greene and D. D. Sokol, 'Judicial Treatment of the Antitrust Treatise' (2015) 100 *Iowa Law Review* 2039.

[31]   V. Ghosal, 'Regime Shift in Antitrust Laws, Economics, and Enforcement' (2011) 7 *Journal of Competition Law and Economics* 773–4, 733; B. Orbach and D. D. Sokol, '100 Years of Standard Oil Antitrust Energy' (2012) 85 *S. Cal. L. Rev.* 429.

[32]   M. B. Coate, 'A Test of Political Control of the Bureaucracy: The Case of Mergers' (2002) 14 *Economics and Politics* 1 (2002).

[33]   L. M. Froeb et al., 'The Economics of Organizing Economists' (2009) 76 *Antitrust Law Journal* 569, 573.

[34]   F. S. McChesney et al., 'Competition Policy in Public Choice Perspective', in R. D. Blair and D. D. Sokol (eds.), *The Oxford Handbook of International Antitrust Economics* (Oxford University Press, 2015), vol. I.

important changes that the United States implemented. One notable change was the creation of a distinct group of economists within the antitrust agencies, including a chief economist and staff, who are not subordinate to agency lawyers. This institutional design allows for a distinct economic voice to influence case selection and analysis, helping to ensure that there is an economic basis for enforcement decisions.[35]

Empirical work suggests that overt politics not driven by antitrust economics has, for the most part, become a nonissue in US merger enforcement in recent decades. As one economist notes, "[p]opulism was forced to a fringe position."[36] Earlier studies of US merger control examining the 1980s suggested that there were noneconomic factors at play in merger control. The same work also found that the recommendations of economists carried less weight than those of agency lawyers.[37] A greater role for economists merely shifts "political" antitrust from noneconomic politics (such as industrial policy) to "politics" within economics (i.e. how to decide the difficult cases "on the margins" based on economic theory and empirics that may not always be clear).

13.4 INDUSTRIAL POLICY IN EUROPEAN ANTITRUST

In Europe, path dependency based on multiple goals of antitrust remains a fundamental characteristic of European case law, with more of an interventionist flavor than in the United States.[38] This is due to the multiple goals of European Commission (EC) competition law on the books, including industrial policy concerns.[39] Even if the Directorate-General of Competition (DG Comp) states that its sole goal is consumer welfare,[40] European case law remains more favorable for a finding of competition law infringement than in the United States, where the shift to a singular goal of antitrust and the primacy of economic analysis has led to more rule of-reason analysis and less intervention.[41] In Europe, the interventionist case law and enforcement also operates in the shadow of the law – serving as leverage

---

[35] L. J. White, 'Economics, Economists, and Antitrust: A Tale of Growing Influence', in J. J. Siegfried (ed.), *Better Living Through Economics* (Harvard University Press, 2010), 232.

[36] M. B. Coate, 'Bush, Clinton, Bush: Twenty Years of Merger Enforcement at the Federal Trade Commission' (Sept. 29, 2009), 19 (unpublished manuscript), http://papers.ssrn.com/sol3/ papers.cfm? abstract_id=1314924

[37] M. B. Coate, 'A Test of Political Control of the Bureaucracy: The Case of Mergers' (2002) 14 *Economics and Politics* 1.

[38] B. Van Rompuy, *Economic Efficiency: The Sole Concern of Modern Antitrust Policy? Non-Efficiency Considerations under Article 101 TFEU* (Wolters Kluwer, 2012), 16.

[39] D. J. Gifford and Robert T. Kudrle, *The Atlantic Divide in Antitrust: An Examination of US and EU Competition Policy* (University of Chicago Press, 2015), 8–9.

[40] P. Akman, *The Concept of Abuse in EU Competition Law: Law and Economic Approaches* (Hart, 2012).

[41] Ibid.

to be used against firms that are under investigation, in order to extract greater concessions in consent agreements.

Historical factors and path dependency explain the EC's greater orientation toward industrial policy in merger control. The core purpose of European competition law was to further market integration over other factors such as efficiency, although these at times converged with efficiency justifications.[42] This meant that efficiency played a lesser role in the original formulation of European competition law. One might suggest that a reading of Aerospatiale-Alenia/de Havilland[43] (a merger case arising soon after the 1989 merger rules on the failing-firm defense were established) expressed the tension between industrial policy and competition policy – at least within the failing-firm-defense context. Because lawyers originally played a significant role in merger enforcement, while economists historically played a minor role, the EC's decisions to challenge mergers may have lacked a rigorous economic justification. This too has changed due to the institutionalization of greater economic analysis, including the creation of a chief economist and an economics staff not subordinate to lawyers, as well as a series of cases that reversed EC challenges based on insufficient economic analysis.[44] The earlier case law and institutional approaches have impacted the current structure and nature of European merger and conduct enforcement in terms of state intervention.[45]

At present, Europe more strictly enforces merger regulation than the United States, although increasingly there is convergence.[46] Path dependency and earlier non-efficiency legacy may play some role in this orientation towards greater enforcement.[47] One could frame Europe's wariness regarding vertical restraints (including vertical mergers) as an expression of this same sort of legacy. Thus, more aggressive European challenges to vertical mergers may be as much political (based on a concern for the competitive process) as economic – and represent a key difference with the United States on competition law and economics.[48]

Another cause of the development of noneconomic factors in European merger control was what some claimed to be anti-US bias.[49] Empirical work analyzing the

---

[42] Gifford and Kudrle, 'Atlantic Divide'.
[43] Commission Decision 91/619, Case No. IV/M.053, 1991 OJ (L 334) 42 (EC).
[44] Gifford and Kudrle, 'Atlantic Divide'.
[45] Ibid.
[46] M. Bergman et al., 'Merger Control in the European Union and the United States: Just the Facts' (2012) 7 *European Competition Journal* 1744.
[47] Gifford and Kudrle, 'Atlantic Divide'.
[48] J. Cooper et al., 'A Critique of Professor Church's Report on the Impact of Vertical and Conglomerate Mergers on Competition' (2005) 1 *Journal of Competition Law and Economics* 791–2, 785, and n. 27.
[49] N. Aktas et al., 'Is European M&A Regulation Protectionist?' (2007) 117 *Economics Journal* 1109–11, 1096; N. Aktas et al., ' Market Response to European Regulation of Business Combinations' (2004) 39 *Journal of Finance and Quantitative Analysis* 755–6, 731; I. S. Dinc and I. Erel, 'Economic Nationalism in Mergers and Acquisitions' (2013) 68 *Journal of Finance* 2471, 2473; T. Duso et al., 'The Political Economy of European Merger Control: Evidence Using Stock Market Data' (2007) 50 *Journal of Law and Economics* 455, 470.

period of the 1990s found that there was protectionism involved in European merger control. DG Comp had a higher probability of intervening against non-European firms when there were European competitors in the same market.[50] Professor Nihat Aktas and his colleagues examined whether foreign acquiring firms were subject to greater antitrust intervention than domestic acquiring firms when local competitor firms were harmed, observing distinct cases from 1990 to 2000.[51] They found that the joint effect of a given bidder's nationality (foreign versus domestic European) and whether there were European competitors involved led to abnormal stock returns. They concluded that, "[f]aced with the empirical facts, a cynical observer might doubt the good intentions of European regulators."[52] There has been retreat from this approach, even in their subsequent work (and many other factors may have been at play). Professors Serdar Dinc and Isil Erel analyzed the largest twenty-five merger targets (measured by market capitalization of the respective target firms) from the first fifteen EU member states during the period from 1997 to 2006.[53] They found that, "instead of staying neutral, governments of countries where the target firms are located tend to oppose foreign merger attempts while supporting domestic ones that create so called national champions, or companies that are deemed to be too big to be acquired."[54] This legacy of European industrial policy has troubling implications for robust antitrust enforcement.

Going forward, EU level competition policy needs to be more mindful of "effects" in its antitrust policy. Further, it needs to shed the legacy of bad case law that does not appropriately put economic analysis at the forefront of case development. Anything short of this will harm European consumers and hurt European competitiveness and innovation exactly at a time where Europe is struggling globally.

13.5 CONCLUSION

Antitrust is better off today in the United States and Europe than in the past. The system is predictable, based on a (more or less) clear standard of economic harm and actual economic effects. Where changes are necessary to antitrust law, it is to tweak the application of changing industrial organization economics rather than to change the worldview of the overall application of antitrust. Though academic visionaries like Eleanor Fox have articulated a broader set of values in antitrust, these values are better actualized through broader legislation outside of antitrust for which democratic accountability can better mesh with larger policy goals. Antitrust has worked best where its function has been

---

[50] Aktas et al., 'European M&A Regulation'.
[51] Ibid.
[52] Ibid.
[53] Dinc and Ere, 'Economic Nationalism'.
[54] Ibid.

narrow – policy interventions to support markets rather than in a regulatory function. This chapter provides a brief overview of how and why such an interventionist policy works for antitrust. Broader public policy goals such as inequality and fairness have more precise and effective tools to reach such outcomes but antitrust is not within this set of tools.

PART III

Reconciling Equity and Efficiency

The Challenge of Effective Antitrust Enforcement

A

Designing Effective Enforcement Systems

14

Competition Culture and
the Cultural Dimensions of Competition

Albert Allen Foer

14.1 INTRODUCTION

The late political and linguistic pundit William Safire wrote that "ideology" was "originally a system of ideas for political or social action," but in what he mischievously declared was current political use, ideology means "a mental straitjacket, or rigid rules for the philosophically narrow-minded."[1] Professor Eleanor Fox's ideology is neither rigid nor narrow-minded. Indeed, the flexibility, tolerance, and cultural pluralism of her approach to "competition culture," both domestically and internationally, are some of its distinguishing characteristics. Her writings provide a background for consideration of both the concept of competition culture and the cultural dimensions of competition.

The Foxian ideology can be quickly summarized with respect to her academic home base of antitrust in the US: it is multidisciplinary and process-oriented, reflecting a passionate interest in broader political and normative values that were being squeezed out of the antitrust enterprise by a single-minded worship of efficiency.[2] Expanding to global horizons, the Foxian ideology emphasizes both the commonalities between jurisdictions and the diversity of national antitrust jurisdictions that must be respected as a fact on the ground and also as a natural outcome of the differences between political institutions, laws, and customs.[3] In this,

My thanks to American Antitrust Institute (AAI) former research fellow Arthur Durst for research and editorial assistance. This chapter does not purport to speak for the AAI.

[1] William Safire, *Safire's Political Dictionary* (3rd edn, Random House, 1978), 320.
[2] See e.g. the following by Eleanor M. Fox, 'Modernization of Antitrust: A New Equilibrium' (1981) 66 *Cornell Law Review* 1140, 1182; 'The Battle for the Soul of Antitrust' (1987) 75 *California Law Review* 917; 'The Efficiency Paradox', in Robert Pitofsky (ed.), *How the Chicago School Overshot the Mark: The Effect of Conservative Economic Analysis on US Antitrust* (Oxford University Press, 2008), 77, at 88; 'Against Goals' (2013) 81 *Fordham Law Review* 2157, 2160.
[3] See Eleanor Fox, 'Antitrust and Regulatory Federalism: Races Up, Down and Sideways' (2000) 75 *NYU Law Review* 1781; Eleanor Fox, 'Toward World Antitrust and Market Access' (1997) 91 *American Journal of International Law* 1, 2 ("I conclude that we need a vision of liberal antitrust to fit the

she agrees with Professor David Gerber by emphasizing that the laws of individual states govern global markets.[4]

Within the International Competition Network (ICN), Fox has supported efforts to create what is called "competition culture," while at the same time urging space for jurisdictions to reflect their own special backgrounds and needs. As she puts it, "[t]he idea that there is one right route is nonsense."[5] The Foxian ideology stresses that each jurisdiction must be understood as a system and that antitrust is only a part of the system.[6] Professor Fox is therefore suspicious of convergence efforts that fail to recognize deep-seated differences.[7]

Fox has called our attention to context,[8] institutional differences,[9] politics,[10] and culture.[11] Culture has probably been the least developed of these concerns, though always present, and it is to distinctions between the notion of a competition culture and the cultural dimensions of competition that I address this chapter.

worldview of liberal trade; not without derogations, but with a framework for permissible derogations").

[4] David J. Gerber, Global Competition (Oxford University Press, 2010), 3; Stephen Breyer, *The Court and the World* (Knopf, 2015), 99–107 (describing the considerations in the *Empagran* decision and the complexities in dealing with global commerce and national regulation); *F. Hoffmann-La Roche Ltd. v. Empagran SA*, 542 US 155 (2004).

[5] Email from Eleanor Fox to author (February 11, 2016) (quoted with permission; on file with author); Eleanor Fox, 'Monopolization and Abuse of Dominance: Why Europe Is Different' (2014) 59 *Antitrust Bulletin* 129, 130 ("[C]onvergence through derived international standards tends to obscure fundamental differences and may thereby detract from a deeper comparative understanding of the law. The efforts presume an ease of and incentive toward horizontal accommodation by each jurisdiction to the other free from loyalty to its own system, and thus they discount the reality that each system answers to its own drummer").

[6] Eleanor M. Fox, 'Linked-In: Antitrust and the Virtues of a Virtual Network' (2009) 43 *International Law* 151, 152.

[7] Eleanor M. Fox, 'GE/Honeywell: The US Merger That Europe Stopped – A Story of the Politics of Convergence', in Eleanor Fox and Daniel Crane (eds.), *Antitrust Stories* (Foundation Press, 2007), 331, 356–7 ("A single standard – whether achieved through soft harmonization or world rules – has its costs. Uniform rules, if too specific, would constrain the adaptation of law to a changing world. Moreover, they would frustrate localities' efforts to frame their own law according to their specific, contextual needs").

[8] Eleanor M. Fox, 'Why People Fail in the Struggle with Poverty', in Consumer Unity & Trust Society (ed.), *Better Governance for Inclusive Growth: CUTS 30th Anniversary Lecture Series 2013–14* (CUTS International, 2014) 91, 92.

[9] Eleanor M. Fox, 'Antitrust and Institutions: Design and Change' (2010) 41(3) *Loyola University Chicago Law Journal* 473, 487.

[10] Eleanor M. Fox, 'Chairman Miller, the FTC, Economics and Rashomon' (1987) 50(4) *Law & Contemporary Problems* 33–55, n. 107.

[11] Eleanor M. Fox, 'Monopolization and Dominance in the United States and the European Community' (1986) 61 *Notre Dame Law Review* 981, 983.

14.2 COMPETITION CULTURE AND THE CULTURE OF COMPETITION

14.2.1 *A Common But Narrow View of Competition Culture*

The concept of "competition culture" (perhaps coined as a global expansion of the business literature's "corporate culture") is frequently referenced in the global antitrust community.[12] The Advocacy Working Group of the ICN issued a "Competition Culture Project Report" ("the Report") in 2015.[13] The Report picks up on an earlier Working Group project that related "competition culture" to "competition advocacy." The latter refers to those activities conducted by the competition authority related to the promotion of a competitive environment for economic activities by means of non-enforcement mechanisms, mainly through its relationships with other governmental entities and by increasing public awareness of the benefits of competition.[14]

Development of a competition culture was then identified as "one of the key aims of competition advocacy," which the Report defined as "the awareness of economic agents and the public at large about competition rules. This included the business community, other governmental agencies, academia and society as a whole."[15]

The Report is largely based on a survey of ICN Members in 2013–14, in which forty-nine jurisdictions responded to a questionnaire. The working definition of competition culture used in the Report is:

> A set of institutions that determine individual and/or group behaviour and attitudes in the sphere of market competition. These are influenced by wider social

[12] E.g. the Turkish Competition Authority's website provides a paragraph on competition culture, which begins as follows: "The existence of a competition culture has an extremely important role in the succeeding of a competition policy. competition culture mainly involves being informed about the benefits introduced by competition, and the formation and development of the necessary awareness in the society as to the role possessed by the implementation of competition rules in securing such benefits" (www.rekabet.gov.tr/en-us/pages/competition-culture). Another example is a 2010 "Competition Culture" report of the Danish competition authority, whose foreword begins:

> This report is a first attempt to identify and describe aspects of the competition culture in Denmark. the term 'competition culture' refers to the behaviour of firms, consumers and the public sector in specific market situations and how their behaviour is affected by factors such as legislation and its enforcement, as well as norms and values. the competition culture is a determining factor for the actual intensity of competition in the Danish economy.

The focus of the report and of the supporting analyses is on describing and identifying key aspects of competition cultures in Denmark, Germany, and the UK. As the competition culture has not previously been analyzed, and inasmuch as it is characterized by a quite complex set of causal linkages, this report does not undertake to explain how the competition culture has developed or why it varies from one country to another (www.en.kfst.dk/media/3333/competition-culture-06012010.pdf).

[13] ICN Advocacy Working Group, *Competition Culture Project Report* (2015), at www.internationalcompetitionnetwork.org/uploads/library/doc1035.pdf

[14] Ibid., at 3.

[15] Ibid.

institutions and public policy choices and include customs impacting the degree of business competition and cooperation within a jurisdiction.[16]

It is further explained that:

> This definition recognises that each jurisdiction is situated differently with respect to public policies that promote market competition or cooperation. For example, transition economies and small island economies may be characterised by a more regulatory approach, in which there is greater state involvement in the running of markets and where markets are highly concentrated. It is also important to recognise that the objectives of promoting competition principles of efficiency and consumer welfare can be superseded by other public policy considerations, including social policy, public interest and national security. What may be considered a 'strong competition culture' in one jurisdiction may not be feasible or appropriate in another.[17]

And finally:

> Regardless of larger public policy contexts, the mission shared by competition agencies is to pursue enforcement based on sound legal and economic principles, to determine whether specific business conduct harms competition. This task is an anchor for effective competition advocacy and the foundation for building a strong competition culture.[18]

This framework recognizes the ICN membership's predominant antitrust ideology of efficiency and consumer welfare, while also recognizing these concepts have different meanings in different contexts and that they may be superseded by public interest values.

My concern is that neither the ICN nor more than a small handful of scholars has taken what might be thought of as the prior step of delving more deeply into the role of a nation's culture (or even multiple subcultures) in forming fundamental attitudes toward competition and cooperation.[19] In the remainder of this chapter I will explain what I mean and outline a research agenda.

---

[16]   Ibid., at 9. I would like to think that my remarks as a non-governmental adviser to the advocacy working group contributed to the references to institutions, choices, and customs (see American Antitrust Institute, 'Bert Foer Remarks from ICN Advocacy Working Group Workshop' (December 13, 2013), www.antitrustinstitute.org/content/bert-foer-remarks-icn-advocacy-working-group-workshop).

[17]   ICN Advocacy Working Group, *Competition Culture Project Report*, 9.

[18]   Ibid.

[19]   Te-Ping Chen, 'Wheat vs. Rice: How China's Culinary Divide Shapes Personality', *WSJ Chinarealtime* (May 9, 2014), http://blogs.wsj.com/chinarealtime/2014/05/09/wheat-vs-rice-how-chinas-north-south-culinary-divide-shapes-personality (contrasting the differences between north and south China – e.g. southerners are less individualistic than northerners – and attributing those differences partially to a reliance on cultivating rice in the south). A recent review of cross-cultural data comparing individualistic with collectivistic cultures may be found in Robert M. Sapolsky, *Behave: The Biology of Humans at Our Best and Worst* (Penguin, 2017), 266–82, 495–500.

As a starting point, let us look briefly at the ICN Competition Culture Report's survey results. "The survey reveals that just under a third of respondents feel confident their government officials understand the social benefits of competition and respect competition principles in its work."[20] "[O]nly a minority of respondents were confident their judges have both a high awareness of competition and are able to understand and interpret economic evidence."[21] "[Twenty-one percent] of respondents said there were no firms or lawyers specialising in competition law and general commercial lawyers dealt with competition law cases. These ten respondents are largely young competition agencies with limited enforcement experience."[22] Competition authorities were also asked to rate competition aware-ness among large businesses and SMEs within their jurisdictions. Basically (and not surprisingly), large businesses were thought to be more aware of the competition laws than smaller ones and "many firms are still not investing in the sorts of activities and initiatives that raise awareness of competition internally and make it less likely that an infringement will be committed within the firm."[23] Finally, the survey asked competition authorities to estimate competition awareness among members of the public. "The majority of the responses ... show some limited confidence that members of the public have basic competition awareness."[24]

This focus on awareness of competition laws indicates that we surely have a long way to go before key segments of governments, courts, the legal profession, busi-nesses, and the public will understand why we have competition laws, much less why they should voluntarily abide by such laws. *But the conception of culture as being contained in awareness of a law reflects an extremely narrow and potentially misleading view of culture.* Culture is a much broader and, frankly, more important topic, especially when we try to understand a rapidly changing economic institution.

14.2.2 *On Strong and Weak Cultural Dimensions*

Institutionalist economist Douglass C. North correctly observes: "It is not sufficient to describe societal change; rather we must attempt to find the underlying forces shaping the process of change."[25] The advent of global antitrust as an institution has occurred quickly. I believe that to a large extent, antitrust's expansion, running

---

[20] ICN Advocacy Working Group, *Competition Culture Project Report*, 10. The survey is subject to numerous methodological criticisms, but it seems to reflect what a self-selected group of responding national competition authorities thinks about how strong a competition culture exists in their nations; 77 percent of the respondents were authorities whose competition policy regime was at least 10 years old; 24 percent had no private enforcement (ibid., Appendix B).

[21] Ibid., at 14.

[22] Ibid., at 15.

[23] Ibid., at 20.

[24] Ibid., at 23. The report has many recommendations for how competition authorities can go about increasing the level of awareness in the various segments of society.

[25] Douglass C. North, *Understanding the Process of Economic Change* (Princeton University Press, 2005), 13.

alongside the dramatic changeover to and freeing up of market economies, has for a great many nations been imposed from the top down. What role was played – and will be played – by cultures? Does it matter whether the underlying cultures of these countries are historically in synch with market competition and its increasingly common antitrust protector? North stressed that "the intimate interrelationship of beliefs and institutions, while evident in the formal rules of a society, is most clearly articulated in the informal institutions – norms, conventions, and internally held codes of conduct."[26] While not focusing on antitrust as such, North comes close in this observation:

> Belief systems embody the internal representation of the human landscape. Institutions are the structure that humans impose on that landscape in order to produce the desired outcome. Belief systems therefore are the internal representation and institutions the external manifestation of that representation. Thus the structure of an economic market reflects the beliefs of those in a position to make the rules of the game, who enact rules that will produce the outcomes (i.e., the sort of market) they desire, whether those desires are to create monopoly or to create a competitive market (always with the caveat that their beliefs may be incorrect and produce unanticipated consequences).[27]

We can think of culture as a substructure upon which is built a society's economy, its political system, and ultimately its laws.[28] However, while it is entirely possible to have laws that are imposed from the top down, as opposed to bubbling up from the underlying culture, it is also possible for laws to shape culture. No doubt the co-evolutionary interactions between culture, politics, and law are complex, multi-directional, and variable.

If culture refers to norms of appropriate behavior that are widely shared in a society, the nature of the relationship with law will depend on how deeply imbedded within the culture a particular norm might be. Consider cigarette smoking. As I was growing up, smoking a cigarette was celebrated in the movies and on television, flaunted in high school halls, and even encouraged during brief breaks in Army basic training ("If you've got 'em, light 'em up!"). As information on the negative health impact of tobacco became more definitive and subject to both

---

[26] Ibid., at 50.

[27] Ibid., at 49–50. Economist Joel Mokyr recently observed, "[M]any mainstream economists are now committed to the significance of culture in the evolution of modern economics." In a book focused on the cultural underpinnings of the industrial revolution, he argues that "culture" affected technology "both directly, by changing attitudes toward the natural world, and indirectly, by creating and nurturing institutions that stimulated and supported the accumulation and diffusion of 'useful knowledge'" (*Culture of Growth: The Origins of the Modern Economy* (Princeton University Press, 2017), 7).

[28] Geert Hofstede, Gert Jan Hofstede, and Michael Minkov, *Cultures and Organizations: Software of the Mind* (3rd edn, McGraw-Hill, 2010). This is a key resource on cross-cultural research. The authors define culture as "the unwritten book with rules of the social game that is passed on to newcomers by its members, nesting itself in their minds" (ibid., at 26).

governmental regulation and non-governmental anti-smoking advocacy, the behavioral norm gradually but substantially changed. In this case, law and education combined to alter the behavioral norm, but it took roughly several generations to have a substantial impact, and even today there is a resurgence of tobacco use in certain segments of US society.

A more dramatic change apparently occurred with regard to the social acceptability of sexual lifestyles that were until recently widely condemned by law, religion, and social practices. In less than a generation, social practice and the law itself led the way toward change, so that today the federal law recognizes a constitutional right to same-sex marriage. Social practices have definitely changed in the direction of greater toleration but supporters of traditional marriage have indicated that the cultural and political battle to reverse the law or at least control the social acceptability of non-traditional lifestyles will go on. What does this have to do with competition?

These examples suggest that some types of cultural norms are susceptible to change from the top down, over varying durations and with varying intensities of change advocacy. The case of cigarette smoking involved political intervention by federal, state, and local governments as well as expanding scientific knowledge and its widespread dissemination, within a context that related to habits created by advertising and an addictive drug. The case of gay rights involved intervention by the courts more than by elected officials within a context of deeply held religious values. Using an analogy to the ICN Report's "strong or weak competition culture," one could say that change in smoking habits takes place within a relatively weak social culture while the evolution of gay rights takes place within a stronger and religiously based culture.

The question posed for the future of global antitrust convergence is whether cultural attitudes toward competition and cooperation are relatively weak or relatively strong. Are they malleable enough that universal standards can not only be formally imposed by governments, but also sustained through enforcement over a prolonged period of time? Or will we find out that fundamental attitudes and values are of such a strong nature that political systems will not adopt universal standards in their laws, or that even if they do, variations in enforcement will reflect diverse cultural attitudes that effectively undermine the formal law? Or, a third alternative: will there be a kind of compromise outcome where some areas of antitrust (such as civil anti-cartel enforcement) are susceptible to universal standards while others (such as unilateral conduct by dominant firms) are not? The future extent and success of antitrust convergence will depend to a significant degree on how we answer these questions.

14.2.3 *Cultural Clusters and Competition–Cooperation*

Multinational corporations are grappling with doing business around the world in varying cultural environments. David Livermore, president of the Cultural

Intelligence Center and a consultant to such multinationals, has written a book to prepare the businessperson to recognize and deal with diverse cultural contexts. He describes ten cultural clusters in terms of their key cultural value dimensions.[29] The cultural value dimensions of most relevance to antitrust would appear to be individualism/collectivism and cooperative/competitive.

Livermore says that "cooperative" cultures are characterized by "[e]mphasis upon cooperation and nurturing behavior; high value placed upon relationships and family." "Competitive" cultures are characterized by "[e]mphasis upon assertive behavior and competition; high value placed upon work, task accomplishment, and achievement."[30] His examples of clusters where cooperative values are highest include Nordic and sub-Saharan African clusters, while examples of clusters where competitive values are highest include Anglo and Germanic cultures. Clusters falling in the middle of the cooperation/competition scale include Arab, Confucian Asia, Eastern Europe, Latin America, and Latin Europe.[31]

Obviously, these dimensions, drawn from the study of cultural anthropology, are not intended to relate competition or cooperation directly to a particular form of government or economy, not to mention a particular approach to antitrust law. Nor can one necessarily jump from relationships in the home and family to attitudes toward marketplace competition, although one detailed critique of competition in the US pays roughly equal attention to sports, education, and the economy,[32] raising at least the possibility that a particular culture may hold a consistent view on competition that is reflected in all three of the principal categories of recreation,

---

[29] David Livermore, *Expand Your Borders: Discover 10 Cultural Clusters* (Cultural Intelligence Center, 2013). Appendix B defines seven pairs of cultural dimensions and examples of countries within ten different cultural clusters: (1) individualism ("individual goals and rights are more important than personal relationship"); collectivism ("personal relationships and benefiting the group are more important than individual goals"); (2) low power distance ("status differences are of little importance; empowered decision-making is expected across all levels"); high power distance ("status differences should shape social interactions; those with authority should make decisions"); (3) low uncertainty avoidance ("focus on flexibility and adaptability; tolerant of unstructured and unpredictable situations"); high uncertainty avoidance ("focus on planning and reliability; uncomfortable with unstructured or unpredictable situations"); (4) cooperative ("emphasis upon cooperation and nurturing behavior; high value placed upon relationships and family"); competitive ("emphasis upon assertive behavior and competition; high value placed upon work, task accomplishment, and achievement"); (5) short term ("values immediate outcomes more than long-term benefits (success now)"); long term ("values long term planning; willing to sacrifice short term outcomes for long-term benefits (success later)"); (6) low context ("values direct communication," emphasis on explicit words); high context ("values indirect communication. emphasis on implicit understanding"); (7) being ("social commitments and task completion are equally important; diffuse boundaries between personal and work activities"); doing ("task completion takes precedence over social commitments; clear separation of personal and work activities") (ibid., at 101).

[30] Ibid.

[31] Ibid.

[32] Alfie Kohn, *No Contest: The Case Against Competition* (Houghton Mifflin, 1992). Kohn observed, "[D]ifferent cultures depend on competition to different degrees in structuring their economic system or schooling or recreation. At one end of the spectrum are societies that function without any competition at all. At the other end is the United States" (ibid., at 1–2).

education, and the economy. Given the reciprocal impact of laws and institutions on culture, this seems to me unlikely.

The whole matter is complicated.[33] In Livermore's analysis, certain cultural dimensions such as individualism (rather than collectivism), low power distance, low uncertainty avoidance, low context, and doing orientation[34] would appear to be present for the US, UK, and Germany, which are categorized as the principal proponents of marketplace competition. On the other hand, the Nordic cluster is placed by Livermore within the extreme individualism end of the individualism/collectivism scale alongside the Anglo and Germanic cultures, but is also placed within the extreme cooperative dimension and the extreme "being orientation" whereas the Anglo and Germanic clusters are not only within the extreme competition end of the cooperative/competition scale, but also in the "doing orientation" extreme of the "being orientation/doing orientation" scale.

In other words, there is an interplay between the various cultural dimensions that relate to marketplace competition.[35] Stress on individualism may be typical of strongly pro-market countries, but can also characterize a highly cooperative culture. This fact might suggest caution about assuming that education, recreation, and economy within a given country will all reflect similar attitudes toward competition–cooperation.

It is intriguing to observe that the US is usually considered to be at the extreme competitive end of the individualism/collectivism scale, but a few years ago when I had a conversation with a group of competition lawyers in a former Soviet satellite country, I asked them if the competition lawyers there had their own organization. "No," they answered; in their country, everyone worries only about his own business. It is not, they pointedly said, like they perceive it to be in America, where people voluntarily join with their competitors for the betterment of the community. I was reminded of the American icon, Benjamin Franklin, advocate of the competitive norm ("time is money," "early to bed, etc.") and also founder of public libraries, post

---

[33] I go into this in more detail in Albert Allen Foer, 'Culture, Economics, and Antitrust: The Example of Trust' (2018) 63(1) *Antitrust Bulletin* 65. The literature on the relation of culture to human behavior is excellently related and evaluated in Sapolsky, *Behave*, fn. 19 supra.

[34] Livermore, *Expand Your Borders*.

[35] Andrew I. Gavil, 'Competition and Cooperation on Sherman Island: An Antitrust Ethnography' (1995) 44 *DePaul Law Review* 1225, 1226–7 (fn. omitted):

> More than just an economic policy reflected in the antitrust laws, competition is a pervasive component of the fabric of American life that emerges in discussions of all aspects of political, social and economic institutions. As a category of human relations, however, competition exists only in relation to other norms. 'cooperation' and 'individualism' are as much a part of the American culture as is 'competition', and at the source of each are 'relationships' – social, economic, and political. We define ourselves, our families, our governments, even our civilizations in terms of these relationships; be they 'competitive', 'cooperative' or 'individualistic.' Each of these concepts, however, masks a complex of assumptions about human behavior and character, the role of government and the character of business. those assumptions are deeply rooted in the American historical experience, indeed in the broader history of the development of western civilizations, and are in a continuing state of evolution.

offices, and social groups galore. We are a nation of joiners and cooperators and also a nation of competitors.

Exactly what characteristics should a researcher consider in evaluating how competitive a given culture actually is? And how far back in time should one look? For example, in the case of formerly communist countries, should one look for a tsarist culture, pre-communist culture, communist culture, or a post-communist culture? Where is the appropriate benchmark in any particular society?[36]

14.2.4 *Competition and Cooperation*

Another question worth pondering is whether it is appropriate to treat competition and cooperation as two ends of a cultural spectrum. Clearly the two concepts are closely related. A substantial amount of scholarship has investigated the relationship, including the disciplines of anthropology, evolutionary science, and game theory. We now think we know a good deal about how the earliest communities of hunter-gatherers were organized and how customs of cooperation developed over time. Game theorists have used computer simulations to test out various models over the equivalent of thousands of years of evolution, revealing the likely role of direct reciprocity, indirect reciprocity (the power of reputation), spatial selection and multilevel selection, kinship, and punishment in generating behaviors that are altruistic or otherwise cooperative.[37] We are even

---

[36] Ibid., at 1250 (fn. omitted):

> Americans throughout our history have simultaneously exhibited enthusiasm for economic growth and apprehension for the safety of our cherished political, social and economic freedoms in the face of large institutions, be they governmental or economic. And while early Americans formulated those feelings based upon their colonial experience, later generations have faced their own demons, only to arrive at the same state of cultural impasse. Ironically, despite the many differences among Americans that can flow from distinct historical encounters with authority, there persists common ground, a core American, and perhaps not so American, character, that desperately wants to balance the desire for personal autonomy, the profound need for community and the fear of the 'leviathan', however clothed. Culturally, we looked to antitrust in 1890, and continue to do so today, to resolve that imbalance. And that is a tall order for competition law to fill.

> See also Colin Woodard, *American Character: A History of the Epic Struggle between Individual Liberty and the Common Good* (Penguin, 2016).

[37] Albert A. Foer, 'Competition, Cooperation, and Martin Nowak's Supercooperators', American Antitrust Institute (July 28, 2015) (mimeo) (reviewing Martin Nowak, *The Supercooperators: Altruism, Evolution, and Why We Need Each Other to Succeed* (Free Press, 2011)). A great deal of thought has gone into the origins of cooperation, see: Ashley Montagu, *Darwin, Competition and Cooperation* (Schuman, 1952); Robert Axelrod, *The Evolution of Cooperation* (Basic Books, 1984); Robert Wright, *The Moral Animal: Why We Are the Way We Are* (Abacus, 1995); Matt Ridley, *The Origins of Virtue, Human Instincts and the Evolution of Cooperation* (Penguin, 1996); Robert Wright, *Nonzero* (Pantheon, 2001); Geerat J. Vermeij, *Nature: An Economic History* (Princeton University Press, 2004), 4–21; Samuel Bowles and Herbert Gintis, *A Cooperative Species:*

beginning to learn about neural mechanisms that may affect levels of competitiveness in individuals,[38] which suggests a truly exciting line of future inquiry: does the presence of the neuroactive hormone oxytocin, which may be linked to feelings of cooperativeness, vary from one culture to another, and if so, are these variations consistent with differences in observed attitudes toward competition and cooperation? And if there turns out to be a correlation, does causation run from oxytocin to cooperation or from cooperation to oxytocin? Or both?

Even if the starting point for natural selection is pure competition, we get to the possibility, indeed the necessity, of cooperation. But competition and cooperation are closely intertwined, as is increasingly being pointed out by some advocates of innovation and creativity.[39] From earliest history, anthropologists believe that small hunter-gatherer groups cooperated internally but competed against other groups.[40] Judge Frank Easterbrook, after acknowledging "the picture of 'pure competition' found in economic texts, is a hypothetical construct," draws on Ronald Coase's theory of the firm to succinctly describe the relationship of competition and cooperation within the antitrust context:

Human Reciprocity and Its Evolution (Princeton University Press, 2011); Yuval Noah Harari, *Sapiens: A Brief History of Humankind* (Harvill Secker, 2015); Sapolsky, *Behave*.

[38] Paul J. Zak, 'Values and Value', in Paul J. Zak (ed.), *Moral Markets* (Princeton University Press, 2008), 266–70 ("In sum, a large number of researchers have demonstrated that the neural representation of moral values is automatic and difficult to suppress, and often utilizes affective representations in the brain. I propose that values in economic transactions utilize similar neural mechanisms" (ibid., at 270)); Jonathan Haidt, *The Righteous Mind: Why Good People Are Divided by Politics and Religion* (Penguin, 2012), 270–4 ("The men who received oxytocin [via nasal spray] made less selfish decisions – they cared more about helping their group, but they showed no concern at all for improving the outcomes of men in the other groups"); Sapolsky, *Behave*, at 108–17, summarized at 135 ("Oxytocin and vasopressin facilitate mother–infant bond formation and monogamous pair-bonding, decrease anxiety and stress, enhance trust and social affiliation, and make people more cooperative and generous. But this comes with a huge caveat – these hormones increase prosociality only toward an us. When dealing with thems, they make us more ethnocentric and xenophobic. Oxytocin is not a universal luv hormone. It's a parochial one"). Sapolsky, a biologist and neurologist, provides the most recent summary of what is known (Sapolsky, fn. 19 supra).

[39] Charles Leadbeater, 'Why Co-Operation Will Be More Important Than Ever', *The Guardian* (January 3, 2012), at www.theguardian.com/sustainable-business/co-operation-more-important-competition-charles-leadbeater ("Milton Friedman argued that self-interest is fundamental to economic growth, actuating agents. He was wrong: most people, most of the time, are motivated by co-operation and fairness, as well as self-interest. An economy that neglects co-operation and fairness will not innovate and grow").

[40] Sapolsky, *Behave*, ch. 11. Consider this description of a relationship between competition and cooperation in keiretsu capitalism in Japan in the 1990s: "Despite the well-known Japanese desire for harmony, there is nothing sentimental about these unions; they can be ruthless. Each keiretsu resembles a fighting clan in which business families join together to vie for market share. Keiretsu and cartels or cartelized groups recognize one another as competitors, as 'us' versus 'them', just as competing companies elsewhere in the west do. And virtually all business activity is part of one or another keiretsu or cartel" (Robert L. Cutts, 'Capitalism in Japan: Cartels and Keiretsu' (July–August 1992) *Harvard Business Review*, at https://hbr.org/1992/07/capitalism-in-japan-cartels-and-keiretsu).

Every market entails substantial cooperation over some domain in order to facilitate competition elsewhere. Every firm has webs of internal cooperation. Exxon entails far more coordination than the average cartel. Every joint venture, every partnership, indeed every contract creates cooperation among people who might otherwise be rivals. Markets themselves are organized ... Antitrust law permits, even encourages, cooperation within a 'firm,' for such cooperation is the basis of economic productivity. But everything done within a firm could be done by market transactions as well.[41]

A specific example of the interrelationship of competition and cooperation is the way antitrust approaches the setting of standards by competitors and potential competitors. The cooperative setting of standards, even with its inherent risks of both horizontal and vertical collusion, is generally encouraged because of the value it can bring to the economy in the form of technological advancement, but certain activities within this context may be challenged as abusively anti-competitive. Antitrust draws the line between positive and negative, authoritatively approved and disapproved instances of cooperation. Similarly, antitrust as well as other laws such as those relating to arson, bribery, and murder, approves or disapproves of certain modes of competition. In this sense, *the fundamental purpose of antitrust should be seen as assigning both competitive and cooperative values to various classes of economic behavior, such as mergers, horizontal collusion, vertical restraints, monopolization, and natural monopoly.*

It seems to me, then, that we make a mistake in our rather modern conception of antitrust as being fundamentally about competition, as if what Easterbrook labeled 'pure competition' is the necessary default. Rather, antitrust is a nation's political tool for drawing lines defining when cooperation is the desired mode and when it is competition, or when some combination is most appropriate, and the line-drawing is likely to be influenced – to a degree that is not entirely clear – by the nation's cultural values.[42] Finally, when we attempt to place a national orientation on a competition–cooperation spectrum, à la David Livermore, we need to be clear

---

[41] Frank H. Easterbrook, 'The Limits of Antitrust' (1984) 63(1) *Texas Law Review* 1; see also his opinion in *Polk Bros.* v. *Forest City Enters., Inc.*, 776 F.2d 185, 188 (7th Cir. 1985) ("Cooperation is the basis of productivity. It is necessary for people to cooperate in some respects before they may compete in others, and cooperation facilitates efficient production ... Antitrust law is designed to ensure an appropriate blend of cooperation and competition, not to require all economic actors to compete full tilt at every moment").

[42] In the US, as many court opinions note, the Sherman Act is not read literally to bar every restraint of trade. The courts have been engaged in identifying the contours and particulars of appropriate and inappropriate cooperation and restraints for over a hundred years now. See generally FTC & Department of Justice, *Antitrust Guidelines For Collaborations Among Competitors* (2000), www .ftc.gov/sites/default/files/attachments/press-releases/ftc-doj-issue-antitrust-guidelines-collaborations-among-competitors/ftcdojguidelines.pdf; OECD, OECD *Reviews of Regulatory Reform: Indonesia Competition Law and Policy* 5 (2012), n. 5, www.oecd.org/indonesia/chap%203%20-%20competition% 20law%20and%20policy.pdf (explaining that Indonesian competition law has "concurrent purposes" with "Pancasila," a broad national philosophy that includes "(i) belief in one god; (ii) just and civilised humanity; (iii) the unity of the country; (iv) democracy guided by the inner wisdom in the unanimity

about whether we are really advancing a generalization about the culture's shaping of education, recreation, or economy, taken together; or whether we are focusing on one important aspect of a culture, say its attitude toward markets as compared to central planning, based on the coming together of a number of other cultural values in conjunction with the vagaries of history.

The close relationship of competition and cooperation finds its way into the title of a book by business school professors Adam Brandenburger and Barry Nalebuff: *Co-opetition*. As they put it, "[b]usiness is cooperation when it comes to creating a pie and competition when it comes to dividing it up."[43] Co-opetition may be a useful term for certain market phenomena, but it may mask the variety of proportions with which competition and cooperation are likely to be mixed under comparable circumstances within a diverse group of nations.

14.2.5 *Divergent Cultural Norms and Antitrust*

Several scholars based outside of the US/Western Europe tradition have reviewed social science literature and applied it to their local expertise in competition law. For instance, the invidious nature of cartels today seems to be one of the most widely shared perceptions in the international antitrust arena, while vertical relations tend to be viewed with more variations. Both cartels and vertical relations are used by Professor Thomas K. Cheng of the University of Hong Kong to make the point that "Divergent cultural norms mean that firms and consumers may behave differently across countries."[44] "Cartels in countries with a more trusting culture will tend to be more stable. Traditional mechanisms that have proved to be effective in breaking down the trust among cartel members may be less useful in these countries."[45]

Cheng cites the fact that stability and long-term relationships are more valued in some countries, such as Japan, than in others, illustrating that "the incentives to enter into vertical agreements may vary across cultures."[46] Cheng believes that the cultural value most directly implicated by abuse of dominance claims is

arising out of deliberations amongst representatives and (v) social justice for all the people of the country").

[43] Adam M. Brandenburger and Barry J. Nalebuff, *Co-Opetition* (Harvard Business School, 1996), 4.

[44] Thomas K. Cheng, 'How Culture May Change Assumptions in Antitrust Policy', in Ioannis Lianos and D. Daniel Sokol (eds.), *The Global Limits of Competition Law* (Stanford University Press, 2012), 205.

[45] Ibid., at 206; Foer, 'Culture, Economics, and Antitrust'.

[46] Cheng, 'How Culture May Change Assumptions in Antitrust Policy'. Apparently, East Asians process information differently from westerners. The former have a more holistic as opposed to focused manner. For example, typically westerners' eyes first look at a picture's center, while East Asians scan the overall scene. Sapolsky, *Behave*, at 276. A holistic approach toward vertical antitrust issues would be more likely to capture power relationships than the US approach which focuses more on in-market competition. Compare the US and Japanese/Korean handling of abuse of a supplier by a powerful buyer. The US involvement is limited to concern with abuse of monopoly power; both Japan and Korea have statutes outlawing abuse of superior bargaining power. See Albert A. Foer, 'Abuse of Superior Bargaining Position (ASBP): What Can We Learn from Our Trading Partners?', American

competitiveness, saying "there seem to be marginal differences in competitiveness across different cultures that may affect the likelihood of abusive conduct by dominant firms."[47] His overall conclusion is consistent with the Foxian ideology: "A drive for complete convergence is likely to be counterproductive and may even compromise the effectiveness of enforcement in jurisdictions with a significantly different cultural milieu from the mainstream antitrust jurisdictions in the West."[48]

Ki Jong Lee, a South Korean law professor, writes this:

> Countries with individualistic values are likely to have a more rigorous anti-cartel policy than those with collectivist ones; countries with high tendency to avoid uncertainty are inclined to have a relatively lax anticartel policy and countries with a similar combination of cultural values to that of the United States tend to have a more rigorous anticartel policy; Anglo cluster countries (United States, Canada, United Kingdom, Ireland, Australia, and New Zealand) tend to have a relatively rigorous anticartel policy.[49]

Based on similar value systems in Korea, China, and Japan, Professor Lee advocates the potential of promoting competition-friendly values on a regional level in northern Asia to promote the convergence of competition policies in the region. He concludes his discussion with these relevant insights:

> From a static point of view, the correlation between national culture and competition policy might simply represent the cultural limits on competition policy. But the correlation works both ways – culture affects competition policy and vice versa. Countries could maximize the receptiveness of their competition policies by aligning them with their national culture.[50]

The Latin American region is described by Julian Pena, an antitrust attorney in Argentina. Latin American countries, he says, "do not have a competition culture. Centuries of Spanish and Portuguese (in the case of Brazil) colonialism forged the roots of an anti-market institutional system where the government is omnipresent."[51] Moreover, based on Latin America's inherited Catholic values, he observes that individual success is relegated to social justice and to the prioritization of family and friendship. Also, "[i]ndividual success is not necessarily perceived by society as something positive and generally provokes distrust as to the means used to achieve such success."[52]

Antitrust Institute Working Paper No. 16–02 (2016), www.antitrustinstitute.org/sites/default/files/aai%20working%20paper%20no.%2016-02.pdf
[47] Ibid., 218–29.
[48] Ibid., 220.
[49] Ki Jong Lee, 'Promoting Convergence of Competition Policies in Northeast Asia', in Lianos and Sokol (eds.), *Global Limits of Competition Law*, at 222–3.
[50] Ibid., at 234.
[51] Julian Pena, 'The Limits of Competition Law In Latin America', in Lianos and Sokol (eds.), *Global Limits of Competition Law*, at 237.
[52] Ibid., at 240.

Pena's discussion highlights the problem of top-down imposition of antitrust rules:

> Since the late 1980s (at least until the late 1990s), Latin American countries started implementing the premarket policies included in the so-called Washington Consensus. In particular the different countries, at their own pace and manner (1) deregulated their economies, (2) privatized the state owned enterprises, (3) eliminated some government subsidies, (4) received strong foreign investments inflows, (5) liberalized their foreign trade, and (6) implemented competition policies. This overnight pendulum shift of the economic paradigm was not a result of a drastic self-examination and recognition of the failure of the previous paradigm. Instead, it was a set of "recommendations" from the Washington-based international financial institutions, which needed to be followed by the different countries in order to attain debt relief.
>
> The failure of the Washington Consensus policies to provide sustainable development with social welfare in the region resulted in a return to the greater state interventionism paradigm ... A common response to the crisis of the Washington Consensus in the region is characterized by a greater presence of the state in the market.[53]

All of which leads Pena to conclude that "competition laws in Latin America in theory look identical to those of developed countries but their enforcement differs substantially given different economic, political, institutional, and cultural environments."[54]

14.3 CONCLUDING REMARKS

I have provided in this chapter a sampling of culture-based commentary by a few antitrust scholars. I believe it is likely to be representative of what we would find if a more systematic effort were made to investigate the linkages between national cultures and national competition policies and their enforcement. On that basis, I want to offer several concluding observations and a proposal for further research.

First, I believe that the material presented here justifies a skeptical view of how far convergence of international competition policies is likely to go. A nation's culture, along with its particular history and institutions, contributes to the manner in which the state combines values relating to competition and cooperation. But causation is difficult to untangle and how cultural values manifest themselves in substantive policy, procedure, and enforcement is likely to vary not only by country, but by time period and by category of economic behavior (such as horizontal collaboration, merger controls, dominance, vertical arrangements, and sectoral regulation). Complexity also enters because different aspects of culture may be distinguished

---

[53] Ibid., at 237–8.
[54] Ibid., at 250.

by their susceptibility to change and because there is a co-evolution of culture with institutions, including law and economic knowledge.

Second, I believe that a multidisciplinary approach to the relationship of competition and cooperation undermines the teaching of some economic theorists that an efficiency-based, consumer welfare model should become a universal standard for all nations having market economies.[55] Deeply held values of fairness and sharing of power may be reflected differently by subcultures within a nation, and the generation of competition policy may reside more with an elite that shares a particular competition culture than with subgroups within the nation or, in the case of a democracy, the electoral majority. It is therefore possible that a national competition authority within which a particular competition culture predominates will be able to promote and extend its vision of competition policy to additional subgroups within the nation, as is encouraged within the ICN. But this should not be premised on the idea that there is a single universal conception of competition policy that captures all national competition authorities any more than it should be premised on an assumption that a single vision can be sold to cultural groups aligned with some different values.

And, third, I believe the conception of a continuum of competition and cooperation also undermines the neoclassical paradigm of antitrust based on the rational economic man. We've learned too much about the psychological aspects of economic behavior and the variability of cultural inputs to be satisfied with a model that oversimplifies by eliminating these complex factors. The determination of where to emphasize competition and where to emphasize cooperation, and how to combine

---

[55] In the overview and synthesis of an intriguing study of experimental games played by diverse groups in small-scale societies, the editors point out that:

> The institutions that define feasible actions may also alter beliefs about consequences of actions and the evaluation of these consequences. For example, a market-oriented society may develop distinct cognitive capacities and habits. The fact that almost everything has a price in market-oriented societies provides a cognitive simplification not available to people in societies where money plays a lesser role ... to take another example, extensive market interactions may accustom individuals to the idea that interactions with strangers may be mutually beneficial. by contrast, those who do not customarily deal with strangers in mutually advantageous ways may be more likely to treat anonymous interactions as hostile or threatening, or as occasions for the opportunistic pursuit of self-interest.
>
> Joseph Henrich et al. (eds.), *Foundations of Human Sociality: Economic Experiments and Ethnographic Evidence from Fifteen Small-Scale Societies* (Oxford University Press, 2004), 46

Importantly, the two principal lessons from these studies, at 5, are: first, "There is no society in which experimental behavior is even roughly consistent with the canonical model of purely self-interested actors; second there is much more variation between groups than has been previously reported, and this variation correlates with differences in patterns of interaction found in everyday life." In other words, the results of experimental games conducted with college students in western industrialized cultures and those conducted in non-industrialized small-scale societies reflect very different ways of thinking and valuing. The types of small-scale societies studied are not directly comparable to most nations with antitrust laws, but the variations found support the belief that cultural and institutional differences among antitrust nations deserve serious academic attention.

the two strategies, has to sip from the full cup of social science, including its recognition of cultural and social diversity. Finding the right mixture for a given culture is at essence a job for politicians.

These are my thoughts, but who can say for certain? Empirical and theoretical work needs to be done on a much-enlarged database. A large-scale and systematic study comparable to Michael Porter's four-year study of the national attributes that foster competitive advantage in particular nations and particular industries could be a useful model.[56] Researchers should be drawn from the ranks of legal and economic experts familiar with each target nation's competition policies and they should be tasked with absorbing both the international and local social science literature covering cultural anthropology, history, sociology, political science, religion, philosophy, law, and, yes, economics. Their work product should take the form of a series of ethnographies that describe the operative cultural forces and the extent to which these are reflected in the local history of competition policies and their actual enforcement, including their enactment and any transformation over time. A leadership team would draw generalizations from the ethnographies.

The objectives of such a study would include determination of the relationship between cultural values and national competition policies; assessment of cross-cultural generalizations that do or do not work; depiction of similarities and differences in competition policy regimes; identification of categories of economic behavior that are more or less likely to become subject to the same rules; and, ultimately, prediction of the extent and pace of convergence and harmonization of national competition policies.

At the same time, the study should explore the co-evolution of institutions and values, showing where the enactment of competition laws has or has not led to changes in culture more broadly or competition culture more narrowly.

Perhaps the following three more abstract questions are most basic: (1) what are the best standards for comparing the cultural dimensions of competition and cooperation among nations? (2) To what extent do these cultural differences influence thinking and action about competition laws, policies, and enforcement in specific countries? And (3), under what circumstances are cultural dimensions with respect to competition and cooperation more likely to be enduring or malleable?

---

[56] Michael E. Porter, *The Competitive Advantage of Nations* (Free Press, 1990). Porter focused on ten nations most closely and utilized over thirty researchers, most of whom were natives of, and based in, the nation they were studying (ibid., 24).

15

Formula for Success

A *Formula One* Approach to Understanding Competition Law System Performance

William E. Kovacic

15.1 INTRODUCTION

The modern field of international competition law has many architects. None surpasses Eleanor Fox. Individual competition law systems and global networks bear the enduring imprint of her work as a scholar, teacher, and mentor. Her extraordinary influence stems from her estimable professional accomplishments and admirable personal sensibilities. As a telling measure of who she is, on many occasions antitrust specialists across the continents have told me, with evident pride and affection, that they were Eleanor's students. In so many ways, she has taught all of us, and we too are proud of it.

Much of Eleanor's work has dealt with the design and implementation of competition law systems.[1] The remarkable growth in the number of jurisdictions with competition laws – from roughly thirty in the late 1980s to over 130 today – has focused ever closer attention on the institutional foundations of competition law and the links between specific institutional characteristics and system performance. The creation of new regimes, and the retooling of older systems, has led academics, policymakers, and practitioners to devote increasing attention to how design and process shape substantive outcomes.[2]

A fundamental, recurring question in the development of competition law systems, newer and older regimes alike, is what factors determine success in policy implementation.[3] Which factors – for example, the design of the institution, the

The author thanks participants in the 2017 CRESSE Competition Conference for many useful suggestions, and is especially grateful to Julian Pena who, in the course of many conversations, helped refine the analogy that informs the chapter. The views expressed here are the author's alone.

[1] See e.g. E. M. Fox and M. J. Trebilcock (eds.), *The Design of Competition Law Institutions: Global Norms, Local Choices* (Oxford University Press, 2013).

[2] See e.g. A. Ottow, *Market and Competition Authorities: Good Agency Principles* (Oxford University Press, 2015); D. A. Crane, *The Institutional Structure of Antitrust Enforcement* (Oxford University Press, 2011).

[3] See e.g. U. Aydin and T. Büthe, 'Competition Law: Policy in Developing Countries: Explaining Variations in Outcomes: Exploring Possibilities and Limits (2016) 79 *Law and Contemporary Problems* 1.

quality of leadership, the skill of the professional staff, the nature of the "enabling environment" that surrounds the competition agency – facilitate the formation of effective programs? Which factors are most significant – "must have" elements without which a system cannot achieve a high level of proficiency?

On a number of occasions since the early 1990s, I and various co-authors have tried to answer these questions in a more traditional academic format, sometimes looking in more detail at specific countries and sometimes trying to draw lessons from a broader range of experiences across jurisdictions.[4] To some extent, academic papers may provide useful guidance for competition authorities, but they do not satisfy the need, often expressed in my interactions with newer competition authorities, for a framework that concretely and vividly presents the ingredients of a well-functioning system.

In this chapter, the world of motor sport supplies an analogy that seeks to capture the institutional foundations for successful implementation of competition law commands. Formula One (or "F1") racing provides the inspiration for the framework set out here. The links between Formula One and competition law have emerged in the course of teaching competition law at King's College London and in serving on the board of the United Kingdom's Competition and Markets Authority. In these activities, I have come to know academics and practitioners who share my interest in Formula One. Our discussions about competition law and cars occasionally intersected and suggested parallels between the factors that predict success for a competition system and for a racing team, respectively.

From a quick glance, competition law and Formula One have various similarities. Both endeavors are global enterprises, with contests conducted around the world. Both fields have celebrities. For a general audience, Margarete Vestager, the European Union's Commissioner for Competition, may not be as recognizable as Lewis Hamilton, the reigning Formula One World Champion, but she seems to be gaining on him. In both domains, there is acute rivalry between teams (DG Comp and the US antitrust agencies strive for global preeminence no less strenuously than Ferrari and Mercedes pursue F1 championships) and within teams (the occasional tension between Hamilton and his driver teammates has a strong counterpart in the relationship between the Antitrust Division of the US Department of Justice and the US Federal Trade Commission). Both pursuits involve huge financial stakes – massive franchise fees, broadcast rights, and purses in Formula One, and immense

---

4   This chapter draws upon and extends themes explored in earlier works, including W. E. Kovacic, 'The Federal Trade Commission at 100: Into Our 2d Century' (January 2009), available at: www .ftc.gov/sites/default/files/documents/public_statements/federal-trade-commission-100-our-second-century/ftc100rpt.pdf (last accessed November 21, 2018); D. A. Hyman and W. E. Kovacic, 'Competition Agency Design: What's on the Menu?' (2012) 8 *European Competition Journal* 527; W. E. Kovacic and M. Lopez-Galdos, 'Lifecycles of Competition Systems: Explaining Variation in the Implementation of New Regimes' (2016) 79 *Law and Contemporary Problems* 85; W. E. Kovacic and D. A. Hyman, 'Consume or Invest? What Do/Should Agency Leaders Maximize?' (2016) 91 *Washington Law Review* 2395.

fines in competition law. And both activities produce smash-ups when things go wrong – spectacular crashes in Formula One, and interjurisdictional collusions in competition law enforcement.

Beyond these somewhat whimsical common traits, the Formula One analogy has serious aspects. In my conversations with antitrust specialists who are F1 enthusiasts, a recurring topic for discussion is the relative importance of the car and the driver. Both are important ingredients for success. A great driver can take an average car and finish respectably. Yet there is only so far that a great driver can take a team with a merely adequate vehicle. A great driver with an inferior car will not win championships.[5] At the same time, putting a great car in the hands of a deficient driver is not a winning approach. A weak driver will not exploit the possibilities that a superior vehicle provides and, at worst, may plough a great car into the wall. In competition law, great leadership (the drivers) can achieve decent results with merely adequate agencies (the car). At some point, even with superior leadership, a competition system will not excel without upgrades to the car (the agency and its supporting institutions). As with Formula One, the potential inherent in an exceptional car will not be realized with weak leadership. Thus, in Formula One and in competition law, good performance is a function of the quality of the car and the driver.

This chapter uses these and other similarities to illuminate system characteristics that affect successful implementation, and to highlight important interconnections across individual system features. In doing so, the framework seeks to help jurisdictions understand what they must do to improve the performance of their competition systems. The framework also serves to set realistic expectations for what a system is likely to achieve with a given set of institutional conditions while showing the way to improvements that tend to enhance overall performance. By identifying system traits that tend to foster success, the discussion can help individual jurisdictions take stock of their strengths and weaknesses today and see how to reinforce strengthens and correct weaknesses. The motivation to address this topic comes primarily from my experience with newer regimes, but the lessons are more universal. Older, more experienced systems would do well to study systematically what has accounted for failure and success, and to pursue a conscious strategy to correct weaknesses and exploit strengths.

The chapter proceeds in two parts. The first sketches the basic ingredients for success in Formula One racing. The second part draws connections to the counterparts of these characteristics for competition system design and policy implementation. Examples from actual experience with competition law systems illustrate major points.

---

[5]   See R. Brawn and A. Parr, *Total Competition – Lessons in Strategy from Formula One* (Simon & Schuster, 2016) 2 ("It is winning [the] engineering war that is the foundation of winning a World Championship. Sometimes, an exceptional driver will compensate for a car's weakness, but it is rare. No Championship has ever been won with a poor car").

Before getting underway, one notable limitation to the Formula One–competition law analogy deserves mention. Success in Formula One racing is considerably easier to measure than success in competition law. There are two championships in Formula One racing – one for the drivers and one for the "constructors."[6] The drivers' championship is awarded to the driver who accumulates the most points over the entire season. The constructors' award goes to the team whose drivers collectively have gained the most points. Triumph in an individual Formula One race is easily identified; the victor crosses the finish line first. Over the course of a full F1 season, the drivers on the preeminent team generally win more races than their rivals and finish high on the ladder when they do not.

In competition law, measures of success are murkier. The overall impact of a competition system on economic performance – on prices, quality, or innovation – can be hard to assess. Discussions about competition system effectiveness have tended to focus on activity-related proxies, such as the number of cases prosecuted, and the volume of fines imposed.[7] These activity-based measures of effectiveness are simultaneously important, informative, and misleading. A baseline level of activity is essential to establish awareness of the competition regime and gain credibility for the enforcement mechanism. Yet a single-minded focus on case levels, or fines recovered, does not tell us much about the system's ability to deter misconduct or its impact on economic performance. For example, big fines in cartel cases are a popular index of effectiveness; yet a system that achieves an ever-ascending level of fines recovered for cartel infringements has a serious deterrence problem.

The effort in competition law to devise better performance measures, and to assess the economic impact of specific programs, has strengthened in the modern era.[8] Expanded attention to performance measurement has spurred a contemporary debate about competition law enforcement in areas such as merger control. Competition law lacks the clarity of the checkered flag as the mark of success, but the tools for evaluating economic effects are better than they were thirty years ago. Improvements in assessing how institutional design influences system performance – a development that owes much to Eleanor Fox – have given us a better idea of which institutional configurations enable a competition law system to produce better economic results. The framework set out below seeks to sustain that direction of travel.

15.2 DETERMINANTS OF SUCCESS IN FORMULA ONE RACING

Success in Formula One racing depends on six principal factors: the owner, the car, the driver, the team, the circuit, and the weather. As noted below, these factors are

---

[6] Ibid., 7.
[7] See Kovacic and Lopez-Galdos, 'Lifecycles of Competition Systems', 94–5 (discussing value and limitations of activity measures of competition agency effectiveness)
[8] For a review of the modern literature regarding merger policy, see J. Kwoka, *Mergers, Merger Control, and Remedies* (MIT Press, 2015).

interdependent. Weaknesses with respect to one factor (e.g. a good but not great driver) can be offset by strengths in another area (e.g. a truly superior car). Each ingredient is described below.

15.2.1 *The Owner*

The owner of a Formula One team affects the success of the enterprise in several ways. As a starting point, individuals or consortia own F1 teams because they like the sport. There is no question about whether they are sympathetic to the aims of Formula One racing or see F1 as a worthy pursuit. Formula One owners generally agree on the purpose of owning an F1 team: to win races and championships.

Guided by the senior management team, the owner makes decisions fundamental to the team's success: its overall strategy, its investment in the development of racing vehicles, the hiring of drivers, and the assembly of a support team. Nothing about this comes cheaply, least of all the investment in vehicles. An owner who will not spend substantial sums to purchase and maintain state-of-the-art vehicles dooms the team. This includes maintaining and refining vehicles for the season at hand and preparing for later years. As two motor sport luminaries have observed, "In Formula One, the car is everything."[9] The best-funded teams tend to dominate the podium.[10]

Another major focus of expenditure is recruitment and retention of drivers and the technical team that supports them. Good owners have an eye for good talent, and are willing to seek it, own it, and keep it. Once the team is formed, however, good owners do not try to control routine operations. The owner closely follows the work of the racing team, monitors their progress, and points out areas for needed improvement. On racing day, the owner does not tell the drivers how to operate the car, least of all to give instructions via the communications network that connects the support team and the driver. The owner hires people who are proficient at making good operational choices and lets them do their job without interference.

15.2.2 *The Car*

F1 racing is a story of extraordinary technological dynamism – a constant pursuit of a better aerodynamic shape, more efficient engines, improved steering and handling mechanisms, and better tires. On their own and with partners, competitive F1 teams make regular, massive investments to extend the state of the art and achieve

---

[9]   Brawn and Parr, *Total Competition*, 8.
[10] See Fergus Ryan, Williams calls for a return of the competitive spirit, Financial Times, Special Report, December 17, 2017, at 2 (reporting that a handful of well-funded teams – notably, Ferrari, Mercedes, and Red Bull – have dominated the sport since 2000).

technological supremacy.[11] When evenly matched drivers face each other, the better car ordinarily prevails.

Superior cars have several characteristics that help produce championships. Perhaps most important is *power* in the form of an engine that functions to maximum effect within limits that F1 imposes on its members. An underpowered vehicle cannot race effectively. The wear and tear of racing also places a premium on *resilience*. Because testing and racing continuously reveal areas for improvement, *adaptability* is necessary if the F1 team is to make refinements that improve prospects for success. After each season, successful teams also install *upgrades* that strengthen the vehicle for the coming season. Because crashes and collisions go with the sport, teams sustain *redundancy* by having two or more cars in the racing inventory.

15.2.3 *The Driver(s)*

As noted earlier, the driver's capability is a major determinant of success. A truly superior driver can take an average car and run a respectable race. As noted above, great drivers cannot overcome the limitations of an inferior car. With evenly matched cars, however, the driver's skill can be decisive.

The rigors of F1 racing demand that drivers have courage and mental toughness that enable them to cope with intense pressure and move decisively when openings emerge. Success is attained through a mix of the technical skills of good handling and the intuition born of experience. Very young drivers have won championships, but even they accumulated significant experience – from go-karts to F1 cars – before they attained preeminence.

Formula One racing teams typically have two principal drivers and seek to qualify two cars for each race. The presence of multiple drivers puts a premium on establishing a common commitment to the attainment of team goals rather than individual achievement. One common team strategy is to maximize the chances for victory, or a high finish, for the lead driver on the team, and to engage other drivers in supporting that effort. Drivers assigned supporting roles do not always accept these willingly, and severe tensions within a single team are not uncommon.[12] Unless moderated, intramural conflicts can diminish the team's performance.

---

[11] Formula One teams spend huge amounts on the design and construction of racing cars. In 2016, for example, F1 teams spent well over $1 Billion on racing car design and manufacturing. Michael Pooler, Technical rivalry helps drive industry innovation, Financial Times, Special Report, December 16, 2017, at 2.

[12] See Brawn and Parr, *Total Competition*, 50–1 (describing conflicts that arise between drivers of the same F1 team).

15.2.4 *The Team*

A cadre of specialists backs up the driver and supports the car. One group designs, builds, tests, and maintains the racing vehicles. Another group monitors performance during the race (e.g. fuel consumption), communicates with the driver, and suggests adjustments in tactics. A third group, the pit crew, refuel the car and replace tires during the race. More than a few F1 races have been won or lost in the pits. Especially for members involved in the race-day operations, the ability to function effectively under extreme pressure is a distinguishing sign of a successful team.

Between evenly matched cars and drivers, the skill of a supporting team on race day easily can save seconds that are the difference between winning and losing. Building and sustaining a good team requires major investments in talent: recruiting adequate numbers of highly skilled personnel.

15.2.5 *The Circuit*

F1 racing venues vary considerably along many dimensions. These include the quality of the road surface, the number and severity of turns, and the length of straightaways. Some tracks lend themselves to faster times than others. The overall quality of the track determines how fast the car can travel and shapes the strategy that the team will follow in deciding how to run the race.

15.2.6 *The Weather*

Atmospheric conditions provide an important constraint on how the team and its drivers will approach the race. On a dry surface with little wind, the driver has more freedom to run at higher speeds and employ aggressive tactics in passing other vehicles. On a wet surface, or on a windy day, the driver must exercise more caution in operating the car.

15.3 COMPETITION SYSTEM LAW SYSTEM PARALLELS

Each of the determinants of success in Formula One racing has a parallel in competition law systems. The discussion below draws out the connections.

15.3.1 *The Owners: the Political Leadership*

In concept, the citizens of a jurisdiction "own" its legal regime, including its competition laws. Their agents are political leaders who adopt laws on the public's behalf and, in turn, delegate enforcement responsibility to expert bodies (and sometimes to private actors). In practice, this model features a significant separation between ownership and control. Citizens exercise severely attenuated control over the operation of the competition regime. In practical terms, the functional owner is the political leadership – notably, legislators and the head of state.

Political leaders influence the performance of the competition system in several major ways. In creating a system, they define its goals. But unlike Formula One, where the single-minded objective usually is to win races, political leaders frequently seek to achieve multiple aims in adopting a competition law. In many cases, the statement of aims embodies conflicting objectives (promote economic efficiency, but protect small and medium enterprises) without guidance about the hierarchy of aims to be pursued. Instead, the reconciliation of goals is left to courts and enforcement agencies.

Political leadership also influences the competition system's performance in decisions that affect policy implementation. Among other activities, the political branches of government set budgets, appoint enforcement agency heads, carry out oversight hearings, and sometimes earmark funds to be used for specific projects. If political leaders are sympathetic to the competition regime, they can make these decisions in ways to improve system performance. If they are hostile to the system's purposes, they can draw the system to a halt – by refusing to appropriate minimally necessary funds, or by appointing agency leaders with weak ability or indifference to the competition law.

Another issue for political leaders is how much to be involved in the operations of the competition agency. There is broad recognition of the need for political leadership to hold agencies accountable for their use of public funds and their policy choices. There also is wide agreement that political leaders ought not intrude in agency decisions about whom to investigate, prosecute, and punish. In order words, the owners properly can plan a role in devising an overall strategy and rightly can demand that drivers and the supporting team be accountable for their performance; owners degrade their teams when they seek to tell the driver how to operate the car during a race.

Experience with modern competition law clearly identifies how political support enables a system to improve over time. This experience also shows the severe limits to what a competition system can achieve if political leadership is hostile to competition law or, more generally, to the market processes that a competition system is designed to support. In other cases, a competition system suffers not from the outright hostility of political leadership, but from political turmoil that results from military conflict or other forces that paralyze public administration. In these adverse political conditions, the best a competition agency can hope to do is to survive and to sustain a basic level of knowledge that can support the restoration of the system when conditions improve.

15.3.2 *The Car: the Competition Agency*

The competition agency is the principal vehicle for attaining the competition system's objectives. In Formula One, weak or merely adequate cars do not win championships. In competition law, a truly superior agency design is essential to achieve superior results.

First-rate F1 racing cars share some common design features – powerful, reliable engines; efficient aerodynamic properties; and fine-touch handling systems. Racing teams spend massive funds on research, development, materials, and engineering to advance the state of the art in all of these areas.

Effective competition systems possess some common "must-haves": effective information-gathering powers, a substantive mandate that covers important categories of misconduct by private and public actors; credible sanctions; a strong internal quality control regime; a diversified portfolio of policymaking tools (including the power to prosecute cases, to issue rules, to perform studies, and to serve as an advocate for competition before other government bodies); and an evaluation mechanism to assess the quality of agency processes and the outcome of substantive programs.

Beyond these essentials, a variety of other competition system design choices present themselves: should the agency be governed by a single official or by a board? Should the agency's mandate be limited to competition law, or should the agency be entrusted with duties in multiple policy domains (e.g. consumer protection or public procurement)? Should the agency be a stand-alone institution, or be situated as a division of a larger government department? Should enforcement authority be distributed across two or more public institutions, or given to private parties – in effect, should the competition system have some redundancy, much in the way that a Formula One team builds several cars in case a single vehicle is disabled?

For competition systems, modern experience suggests that a jurisdiction need not begin its competition system by trying to copy the most sophisticated and powerful system that already exists. A jurisdiction may lack the resources to fund such a vehicle, or it may lack the critical mass of human capital to operate it effectively. It is a perfectly legitimate choice to begin with a weaker "car" and to progress toward a more powerful vehicle over time.

Virtually all systems have evolved from weaker designs to more powerful designs. Periodic upgrades, based on an assessment of the jurisdiction's own experience and its study of other systems, are vital to winning policy championships. One way to view the evolution of systems is to envision political leadership as testing, in the earliest stages of an agency's development, whether the agency's leaders and supporting team are capable of handling a weaker car effectively. The launch phase of a competition system is a period of testing in which the agency's leadership and staff gain experience with the initial framework and discover what it can and cannot do. If the agency performs well in this first phase, the case can be made that the system is ready for an upgrade – to step up in class to a more powerful vehicle.

As is true with Formula One, the cycle of experimentation, evaluation, and refinement is continuous. Successful F1 programs do not become complacent or satisfied with an immediate period of prosperity. Likewise, the effectiveness of a competition system requires a commitment to progressive improvement and the pursuit over time of better practices.

15.3.3 *Drivers: the Enforcement Agency Leadership*

Competition system performance depends heavily on the skills of the agency "drivers." The head of an agency plays a central role in persuading political leadership to provide needed powers and resources, describing the agency's aims, priorities, and projects to external audiences, assembling and motivating the administrative and professional staff, and, in many agencies, guiding the selection and development of individual programs. Even in systems in which the power to select investigations and prosecute cases is delegated to subordinate officials within the agency, the agency leader can influence project selection through the appointment of these subordinate officials or offering a vision for where the agency should go.

What background and skills make for a successful competition agency driver? From studying competition agency experience, my own list includes the following traits: experience in managing a significant institution, preferably a government unit with economic regulatory responsibilities; extensive knowledge of the jurisdiction's economy and the political environment; an understanding of the jurisdiction's history of economic regulation; a long-term orientation that recognizes how current investments shape the agency's ability to function well in the future (that the measure of great agencies, like the great F1 teams, is not simply success in the season at hand but repeated success over the years, and that repeated success requires major investments that build capacity for the future); courage to make difficult decisions; and mental toughness to cope with the demands of what can be a bruising series of races.

Notice that the list does not include deep expertise in competition law. As an academic in the 1980s and 1990s, I strongly believed that this was a "must-have" characteristic. From my subsequent experience as a government official and researcher in studying competition agency performance, I now regard competition policy expertise as a "nice-to-have" characteristic. I have seen many competition agencies in which an official with the desiderata listed above have proven to be highly effective leaders and have outperformed officials who came to their agencies with a deep background in competition law.

I also have seen agencies in which competition policy experts have been disappointing agency leaders. The latter category includes academics who had no feel for the political process, little skill in management, an aversion to performing necessary public relations tasks, and deficient instincts for the interpersonal relations that are necessary to motivate an agency's personnel. Agency leaders who lack extensive competition law expertise can excel if they surround themselves with advisers who are experts and apply themselves earnestly to learn the field as quickly as possible.

Of course, many of the best competition agency drivers score highly on all criteria – management experience, familiarity with the economy, political awareness, personal skills, facility for outreach, long-term orientation, courage, mental toughness, and, yes, competition policy expertise (and, even better, some previous experience in the agency which they have been appointed to lead). These drivers bring the mix of experience and intuition to guide their agencies with the greatest positive effect. To shift sports analogies, they have all of the attributes of an excellent point guard in basketball or a superb midfielder in football – a 360-degree view of the entire playing surface, a sharp awareness of how the game is played, no felt need to do all of the scoring, and an ability to take satisfaction from the success of the team and not simply individual achievement.

Just as one can identify the ideal driver, it is possible to spot a menace behind the wheel. Some individuals ascend to leadership positions in competition agencies mainly on the basis of political patronage alone, without any of the traits necessary to function effectively on their agencies' behalf. At heart, they are public service mercenaries. To these appointees, government service is a day pass to an amusement park; it offers exciting rides and other attractions. Enjoy the park and leave without any regard to its future success. If you are lucky, your day at the park will provide the opportunity to meet other visitors who can invite you to other, better amusement parks in the future. Great agency leaders take the job to do something with the job; the mercenary is happy simply to have the job – to receive invitations to glamorous events, to be driven about town in the agency's car, and to glow with happiness upon being addressed as "the honorable" or "the chair."

Many agency leadership appointees fall between the polar opposites of agency centeredness and self-centeredness. If one asks about what motivates agency leaders – to serve the public interest, or to serve ambitions for personal adulation and advancement – the answer for most human beings is probably some mix of both. In the right dose and properly channeled, the personal ambition is healthy and necessary; on a good day, it elicits the imagination and creativity to devise good programs, and it supplies the extraordinary drive required to carry them across the finish line. A core challenge of public administration is to harness the private ambition for the agency's gain, to develop a system norm that focuses the attention of leadership on doing things that build a better future, and to persuade incumbent leaders that their admission to the hall of fame will depend in major part on how well they set foundations that enabled the agency to prosper when their successors are in office.

There is an additional complication in the selection of leadership when the agency is governed by a board rather than by a hierarchy led by a single executive. The effective operation of a board demands that board members have an additional characteristic: a willingness to participate constructively in a collegial decision-making process and to see oneself as a member of a highly interdependent partnership. On the typical board, there is a chair and members who are not the chair. Being

a non-chair commissioner is somewhat like playing backup to the featured perfor-
mer in a band. There can come a time when backup players believe that they deserve
to play the lead role, or at least be standing at the front of the stage. In speaking with
the members of many boards, it is striking to see how often chairs lose sight of this
dynamic and forget that many non-chair colleagues believe they would be a better
chair than the existing chair.

The successful configuration for a board consists of a chair who broadly and
graciously shares credit and forthrightly accepts responsibility on behalf of the agency
when things go badly. At the same time, non-chair board members must suppress the
temptation to engage in look-at-me behavior – especially speeches, presentations, and
comments to the press – that promote personal interests at the expense of the
reputation and effectiveness of the partnership. In Formula One, rivalries among
the drivers on a team can destroy the team. The same is true for a board.

15.3.4 *The Agency's Team: the Administrative and Professional Staff*

In Formula One, the driver cannot do the job alone. As described above, success in
racing requires contributions from a large ensemble of specialists – from the
engineers who design and build the car to the pit crew that changes the tires.
A weak team will drag down even the best driver.

So it is with a competition agency. Show me the quality of the team, and I can
tell how the team will perform. The crucial task for an agency is not simply to
assemble large numbers of employees. For every agency, there are several informative fractions. One deals with the quality of agency personnel: here the denominator consists of the total headcount, and the numerator is the number of truly
superior employees. For no agency is the numerator equal to the denominator.
The aim of recruitment and retention over time is to make the numerator and the
denominator converge. For another fraction, the denominator, again, is the total
number of agency personnel, and the numerator is the number of agency personnel who perform operational tasks – who perform investigations, carry out studies,
and work on cases. A key aim of management and organization is to organize
overhead functions as efficiently as possible in order to focus a larger percentage of
an agency's resources on operations.

For a competition agency, the core of the team includes economists, lawyers, and
administrative managers. Depending on its programs, the agency will bring in other
specialists, such as accountants and investigators. If an agency aspires to run programs involving intellectual property issues, it should retain at least a few patent
lawyers. If the agency desires to be active in the digital economy, it is well advised to
hire technology specialists, such as an expert in computer science. An agency can
contract out to obtain certain capabilities; as it develops more extensive programs in
a particular area, it makes sense to have a greater internal capacity to perform
required analytical tasks.

There is only so far that an agency can go if it has a superior driver and a strong vehicle, but a weak team. A vital function for political leadership (the owner) and agency leadership (the driver) is to press for the continuing enhancement of the team. In key respects, upgrades to the team's capability are long-term in nature. They are investments that do not always generate immediate success; they set the foundation for future achievement. This condition demands that owners and drivers embrace a long-term perspective that encourages investments in capability for the longer term. The progression of successful agencies over time has depended upon the gradual accumulation of greater team skills. As the team improves, the agency undertakes more ambitious and difficult projects. It is natural that the agency will start with more modest projects and, in increments, take on harder matters. This requires some stretching – to undertake matters that force the team to improve. The combination of personnel upgrades and well-calculated stretching enables the agency to carry out ever more difficult projects successfully.

15.3.5 *The Circuit: Collateral Institutions*

Formula One teams race on a variety of circuits. The conditions of the circuit determine the selection of racing strategy and, to a great degree, govern how fast the cars can travel. Some circuits have longer, broader straightaways and fewer sharp turns. Others present fewer long stretches that facilitate overtaking and confront drivers with a series of tough turns.

For competition law systems, the "circuit" consists of collateral institutions whose quality deeply influences system performance. Prominent among these are the courts, civil and professional societies, news organizations that provide expert coverage of economic regulatory matters, university departments that teach courses in economics and law, and the overall quality of formal rules and norms that govern public administration. In many ways, the speed and overall performance of the competition law system depends on the quality of these institutions. They constitute the road over which competition policy travels.

The importance of these institutions to system performance is apparent. If courts are slow, corrupt, or incompetent, the litigation of competition cases becomes problematic. If there are no good university programs in economics or law within the jurisdiction or within the nearby region, a vital source of human capital that builds good agency teams will be missing. If the civic and professional societies (e.g. bar associations) are weak or nonexistent, the competition system lacks important networks for communicating its ideas, for receiving feedback on its programs, and for generating commentary on the development of competition policy. Without a competent business press, the jurisdiction lacks a valuable conduit for informing the larger society about the operation of the competition system and identifying possible areas for attention by the competition agency. Lax public administration ethical rules and norms can infect the competition agency or confront the agency with a widespread public perception that all public bodies are corrupt.

As these collateral institutions improve, the competition law system can travel faster. Their enhancement must be a central aim in the development of the competition law system. Otherwise, the fastest car driven by the best driver and supported by an expert term will be slowed down. Indeed, there is a danger that if the conditions of the circuit deteriorate to a certain point, it becomes exceedingly dangerous to race. There comes a point at which a circuit's hazards are so severe that fatal smash-ups are routine and inevitable.

15.3.6 *The Weather: the Economic, Political, and Social Atmosphere*

In Formula One, weather conditions determine how fast teams can drive and whether races take place at all. In competition law, the weather consists of the economic, social, and political environment that surrounds the competition agency. In setting its strategy, choosing priorities, and selecting projects, an agency must be attentive to the nature of this environment and how it changes. The agency's perceived legitimacy and, ultimately, its effectiveness depend significantly on its ability to address and respond to public needs.

This is why the ingredients of economic knowledge and political awareness are important characteristics of agency leadership. The agency must anticipate storms and take measures to protect valuable programs from destruction (e.g. in the form of political backlash aroused by effective lobbying by affected economic interests). At the same time, the agency can spot instances in which economic or social turmoil create political conditions in which it can make an effective case for upgrades to its powers or resources. There are still other moments of relative tranquility in which the agency can accelerate its research and development efforts to strengthen its own capabilities to prepare for future races.

15.4 CONCLUSION: THE VIRTUOUS CYCLE

Formula One teams advance through a three-step process of experimentation, assessment, and improvement. The best teams have a compulsion to do better by achieving better vehicle designs, adopting more efficient race procedures, recruiting a stronger team, and attracting more skillful drivers. Everything they do revolves around an intense regimen of self-evaluation and improvement. This is driven by a clear metric for success: winning championships.

The metrics for success of a competition system are less clear-cut. There is a way, however, to assess the prospects for a competition system and to identify how a system can put itself in the best position to succeed. The assumption here is that good system design, strong technique, and superior personnel will increase its prospects for success in selecting and executing programs that improve social well-being.

Routine evaluation and the pursuit of improvements are essential to achieving this end. The framework presented here, derived from the Formula One comparison set out above, identifies the determinants for success. It sets out what conditions facilitate and obstruct effective policy implementation. It also helps create reasonable expectations about what a system is likely to achieve at any one moment, and where ambition should be focused to gain needed enhancements. Realism about existing conditions and ambition to improve are the combination that can guide a competition system to greater effectiveness.

16

Evaluating the Performance of Competition Agencies

The Limits of Assessment Methodologies and Their Policy Implications

Edward M. Iacobucci and Michael J. Trebilcock

16.1 INTRODUCTION

In this chapter, we focus on one of our principal preoccupations in this field in recent years: the design of competition law institutions. Both of us were participants in a Global Administrative Law project jointly sponsored by NYU Law School and the University of Toronto Law School, and co-chaired by Professor Eleanor Fox and one of us, resulting in a published volume of papers, *The Design of Competition Law Institutions: Global Norms, Local Choices*,[1] where scholars from eight major competition law jurisdictions, developed and developing (along with an evaluation of the role of international institutions), provided descriptions and evaluations of key design features and decision-making processes in their respective competition law regimes.

As has now been widely acknowledged in much scholarly literature and commentary on competition law, economic globalization, where economic activities increasingly traverse national borders, including mergers, agreements, and other business practices, intensifies the potential for systemic conflicts between or among domestic competition law regimes that are seized with evaluating the same agreements or practices.[2] Some strands of the literature that have sought to evaluate the scope for such systemic conflicts have focused on substantive differences between and among domestic competition law regimes, while other more recent strands of scholarly literature have focused predominantly on issues of institutional design and *modus operandi*, on the assumption that even if substantive laws are largely the same or similar, differences in institutional design and decision-making processes (as the legal realists taught us long ago) are likely to generate sharply different outcomes in practice (the "familiar law in the books versus the law in action" distinction). Even if

---

[1] Eleanor M. Fox and Michael J. Trebilcock (eds.), *The Design of Competition Law Institutions: Global Norms, Local Choices* (Oxford University Press, 2012).

[2] See e.g. Richard A. Epstein and Michael S. Greve (eds.), *Competition Law in Conflict: Antitrust Jurisdiction and the Global Economy* (AEI Press, 2004).

international harmonization of substantive competition law were both normatively desirable and politically feasible, discounting differences in institutional design and decision-making *modus operandi* is still likely to yield major divergences in legal outcomes. The Global Administrative Law Project on the design of competition law institutions in which we both participated and which one of us and Professor Fox co-chaired, is very much in the spirit of this latter body of more recent scholarship.

It is from this institutional perspective that, in this chapter, we develop a critical perspective on a small but growing body of recent literature that advances various proposals for evaluating the performance of competition law agencies either in terms of their impact within their own jurisdictions, or comparatively relative to the performance of competition law agencies in other jurisdictions.[3]

The literature on evaluating the performance of competition law agencies can be seen as part of a much larger recent phenomenon: the development of legal indicators, typically on a comparative basis, for many dimensions of various countries' legal systems. The proliferation of these legal indicators – for example, the World Bank's Governance Indicators; the World Bank's Doing Business Indicators; the World Justice Project's Rule of Law Indicators; Transparency International's Corruption Indicators – has generated substantial controversy, typically around

---

[3]   C. D. Howe Institute Competition Policy Council, *Watching the Watchman: The Need for Greater Oversight of the Competition Bureau*, Tenth Report of the C.D. Howe Institute Competition Policy Council (2015). Available at www.cdhowe.org/sites/default/files/attachments/other-research/pdf/ Communique_Nov_5_2015_CPC.pdf; Fabienne Ilzkovitz and Adriaan Dierx, *Ex-Post Economic Evaluation of Competition Policy Enforcement: A Review of the Literature*, European Commission, Directorate-General for Competition (2015), http://ec.europa.eu/competition/publications/reports/ expost_evaluation_competition_policy_en.pdf; William E. Kovacic and David A. Hyman, 'Consume or Invest: What Do-Should Agency Leaders Maximize?' *Washington Law Review* (forthcoming). Available at SSRN: http://ssrn.com/abstract=2705919 (December 19, 2015); Jean Delgato, Héctor Otero, and Eduardo Pérez-Asenjo, *Assessment of Antitrust Agencies' Impact and Performance: A Proposal for an Analytical Framework* (2015). Available at SSRN: http://ssrn.com/abstract=2700751 (November 20, 2015); OECD, *Guide for Helping Competition Authorities Assess the Expected Impact of their Activities* (2014). Available at: www.oecd.org/competition/guide-impact-assessment-competition-activities.htm; OECD, Working Party No. 2 on Competition and Regulation, Directorate For Financial And Enterprise Affairs Competition Committee, *Evaluation of Competition Enforcement and Advocacy Activities: The Results of an OECD Survey*, DAF/COMP/WP2(2012)7/FINAL (2013). Available at: www.oecd.org/officialdocuments/publicdisplaydocumentpdf/?cote=DAF/COMP/WP2 (2012)7/FINAL&docLanguage=En;Enrico Alemani, Caroline Klein, Isabell Koske, Cristiana Vitale and Isabelle Wanner, *New Indicators of Competition Law and Policy in 2013 for OECD and non-OECD Countries*, OECD Economics Department Working Papers No. 1104 ECO/WKP(2013)96 (2013). Available at: www.oecd.org/officialdocuments/publicdisplaydocumentpdf/?cote=ECO/WKP (2013)96&docLanguage=En; William E. Kovacic, 'Rating the Competition Agencies: What Constitutes Good Performance?' (2009) 16(4) *George Mason Law Review* 903–26, 903; GWU Legal Studies Research Paper No. 2012–21 (2012); GWU Law School Public Law Research Paper No. 2012–21 (2012); Stephen W. Davies and Peter L. Ormosi, 'A Comparative Assessment of Methodologies Used to Evaluate Competition Policy' (2012) 8 (4) *J. Comp. L. and Econ.* 769–803, 769; James C. Cooper and William E. Kovacic, 'Behavioural Economics and its Meaning for Antitrust Agency Decision Making' (2012) 8(4) *J.L. Econ. and Pol'y* 779–800, 779; George Mason Law and Economics Research Paper No. 13–17 (2012); Keith Hylton and Fei Deng, 'Antitrust Around the World: An Empirical Analysis of the Scope of Competition Laws and Their Effects' (2007) 74 *Antitrust L.J.* 271.

whether the indicators in question are measuring variables that are valid indicators of the concept in question, or, even if they are, whether the indicators are reliable measures of the variable in question.[4]

By way of focusing our chapter on the challenges of measuring or evaluating the performance of competition law agencies either within their own jurisdiction or comparatively, we consider proposals advanced in a paper by William Kovacic, Hugh Hollman, and Patricia Grant, "How Does Your Competition Agency Measure Up?"; this article is provocative and thoughtful – scarcely a surprise given the vast comparative experience and well-justified eminence in the field of comparative competition law scholarship of its lead author (indeed, one of Professor Fox's few peers in these respects).[5] Our chapter outlines various obstacles to meaningful objective measurement of agency performance, first by identifying challenges to measurement that exist even where the objective for competition policy in a jurisdiction is clear and in principle measurable, and second by pointing out the compounding nature of the challenge in more realistic contexts where objectives are controversial and often competing with one another. Ultimately, the complex contexts in which most agencies operate suggests that, in practice, assessment of an agency will turn on the exercise of judgment.

The chapter next considers institutional design. Given that there is no easy metric against which to measure performance, competition agencies should be designed to facilitate good decision-making. This raises a different kind of challenge: there is no single, optimal structure for competition institutions. As we have outlined in previous work,[6] there are a variety of often inconsistent values and considerations that inform institutional design. One size does not fit all.

Finally, the chapter turns to the implications of the analysis for international comparisons. The evaluation of domestic competition agencies invites comparisons with peer institutions in other jurisdictions. Clearly learning from international experience holds promise for the improvement of local agencies, just as careful approaches to comparative law may yield useful insights for substantive legal reform. There are, however, reasons to be cautious, especially if the comparative evaluative exercise is understood to be officially or unofficially influential in encouraging local lawmakers to reform local agencies. Competition laws may have different goals, and with them different optimal institutional designs. Any comparative evaluative

---

[4] For an insightful review of the literature on legal indicators, see Kevin Davis, 'Legal Indicators: The Power of Quantitative Measures of Law' (2014) 10 *Annual Review of Law and Social Sciences* 37; Kerry Rittich, 'Governing by Measuring: The Millennium Development Goals in Global Governance', in Ruth Buchanan and Peer Zumbansen (eds.), *Law in Transition: Human Rights, Development and Transitional Justice* (Hart, 2014).

[5] William Kovacic, Hugh Hollman, and Patricia Grant, 'How Does Your Competition Agency Measure Up?' (2011) 7 *European Competition Journal* 25.

[6] See Michael J. Trebilcock and Edward M. Iacobucci, 'Designing Competition Law Institutions' (2002) 25 *World Competition* 361; Michael J. Trebilcock and Edward M. Iacobucci, 'Designing Competition Law Institutions: Values, Structure and Mandate' (2010) 41 *Loyola University of Chicago Law Journal* 455.

process risks inducing convergence across heterogeneous competition law land-scapes, something that in our view should be resisted. We recognize the frictions that variation in substance and process across competition agencies creates, and discuss possible, and admittedly partial, responses other than harmonization in the concluding section of the chapter.

16.2 MEASURING AGENCY PERFORMANCE

As Kovacic et al. point out, the easiest and most common methodology for evaluat-ing agency performance is to measure levels of activity in various categories, e.g., investigations undertaken, enforcement proceedings initiated, advocacy briefs sub-mitted, research studies completed, but none of these measures, of course, provide any assessment of outcomes or impacts within or across these categories of activity. As the authors note, "being busy" is not synonymous with "being effective," or as they put it more colorfully, measuring activity levels is somewhat analogous to an airport or airline announcing departures but providing no details on arrivals. However, while impacts or outcomes of competition agency activity are clearly of ultimate interest, impacts or outcomes are notoriously difficult to measure. In thinking about how best to measure institutional performance, and/or a comparative analysis of performance, it is important to keep these difficulties front and center.

Assume in the first instance that the objective function of competition law is straightforward and uncontroversial; maximizing consumer welfare, for example. (This is the assumption upon which Kovacic et al. generally rely, though objectives vary across and within jurisdictions as we review below.) A clearly defined objective facilitates measurement of performance, but even in this context, we are highly skeptical that objective measurement of performance would amount to much more than rough and highly contestable estimates.

For one thing, an accurate evaluation of an agency decision would require information about the counterfactual: what would economic performance have looked like had the agency made a different decision? Reaching a conclusion about economic outcomes in a counterfactual scenario is extremely difficult, as is well known. Indeed, competition agencies invest vast resources in merger cases attempting to determine *ex ante* economic impacts if a merger that has not yet occurred were permitted. An *ex post* assessment of a merger decision is not necessa-rily easier: whatever the decision, the assessor must determine what would have happened had the agency made a different decision.

There is a qualification to any conclusion that an *ex post* assessment is not much easier or more accurate to conduct than an *ex ante* assessment, but it is a qualification that raises its own problems: because of the importance of barriers to entry, it may be that mistaken intervention is easier to spot than mistaken permissiveness. If an agency prevents a merger, for example, on the belief that barriers to entry are high, yet subsequent experience reveals a steady stream of entry, then it would be apparent that the agency made a mistake. If, on the other hand, the agency prevents a merger and there is little entry, this could be the result of high barriers to entry, but could also reflect a robustly competitive market with little room for profitable entry. There is an intrinsic bias in favor of a finding of unwarranted intervention.

More generally, of course, there is the significant problem of measuring the deterrence impact of a given agency decision. It could be, for example, that prosecuting a price-fixing case costs the agency far more than the economic benefits of stopping collusion in a particular market. But that is not the right question to answer in determining whether it was a sensible decision. Rather, all the price-fixing in a country that is deterred by the knowledge of active price-fixing enforcement would need to be taken into account.[7] And of course, the time horizon for assessment raises another question. European authorities, for example, are thought to take a longer view of the impact of enforcement against dominant firms, understanding dominance to be problematic in its own right because of negative future effects on competition and innovation. This raises questions about the timeline that would be necessary to understand the impact of an agency's activities on deterrence. Thus, any claim that evaluation of the overall deterrence impact of an agency's activities is reliable would be optimistic.

Ex post assessment is especially difficult given selection bias problems that result from enforcement's deterrence effects. Effective agencies will deter conduct that clearly violates competition law. This implies that the conduct that an effective agency evaluates in detail, such as a proposed merger, will tend to be problematic cases: because of anticipated enforcement, clearly anticompetitive cases are less likely to be proposed. This means that the sample of cases being assessed will be especially difficult to decide correctly, rendering an *ex post* assessment biased in assessing the overall effectiveness of enforcement. There is another bias problem: hindsight bias. Even if the agency makes a clear mistake from an *ex post* perspective, it may well have been the right decision at the time it was made. Yet it is difficult in assessing a decision after the fact to eliminate the influence of factors that were not available to consider at the time of the decision.

If the benefits of competition agency activity are viewed dynamically as including the long-run impact of interventions on innovation and productivity, clearly quantitative assessments become increasingly speculative. If available forms of intervention are expanded beyond investigative and enforcement activity (as they should be) to include promulgation of guidelines, undertaking research studies, public consultation and education, and advocacy initiatives before other arms of government, impacts on long-run consumer welfare become almost impossible to evaluate. Moreover, exogenous factors that are likely to vary substantially, even dramatically,

---

7 Similarly, Kovacic et al., observe that small cases can generate significant and important precedent ('How Does Your Competition Agency Measure Up?').

from one jurisdiction to another may be a major determinant of a competition agency's effectiveness, for example openness to international trade and foreign investment; the scale and dominance of state-owned enterprises; the inherent thinness and fragmentation of many markets, especially in many developing countries.[8]

For all these reasons, even accepting a monolithic objective function for a competition agency, an accurate assessment of the quantitative impact of its activities will be, to understate it, challenging. But most agencies do not adopt a monolithic objective, rendering objective assessment even more problematic, as we discuss next.

16.3 SPECIFYING AN OBJECTIVE FUNCTION

In their paper, Kovacic et al. generally appear to assume that consumer welfare maximization is the objective of competition laws. While this may be true, broadly speaking, of antitrust laws in the US, it is clearly not the case in many other competition law jurisdictions. By way of examples, we take some of the eight jurisdictions surveyed in the volume edited by Professors Fox and Trebilcock (Australia, New Zealand, Canada, Chile, China, the European Union, Japan, South Africa, and the United States). The purpose clause of the Canadian Competition Act states that the purpose of the Act is inter alia to ensure that small and medium-sized enterprises have an equitable opportunity to participate in the Canadian economy, while the merger provisions in the Act provide an efficiencies defense, potentially even where a merger may result in higher prices for consumers.[9] This standard in subsequent jurisprudence has been qualified by a so-called "balancing weights" test where transfers of consumer surplus to a merged entity that is able to raise prices are not necessarily treated as wealth-neutral where these transfers would bear disproportionately on lower income consumers.[10] The Canadian Competition Tribunal must take fairness considerations into account, in other words, not just efficiency. The European Union in the formulation and administration of its competition laws has placed a heavy emphasis on the elimination of "distortions" within the internal market and thus has adopted as a major goal freedom of movement of goods, services, capital, and people within the European Union. Japan's anti-monopoly law has been interpreted as having as one of its major objectives the protection of small and medium-sized enterprises, and hence the

---

[8] See e.g. Michal Gal, *Competition Policy in Small Economies* (Harvard University Press, 2003); Michal Gal et al. (eds.), *The Economic Characteristics of Developing Jurisdictions: Their Implications for Competition Law* (Edward Elgar, 2015).

[9] See e.g. Edward Iacobucci, 'The *Superior Propane* Saga: The Efficiencies Defence in Canada', in Barry Rodger (ed.), *Landmark Cases in Competition Law around the World in Fourteen Stories* (Kluwer Law International, 2012), 63–87.

[10] See *Canada (Commissioner of Competition) v. Superior Propane Inc.* 2003 FCA 53, [2003] 3 FC 529; Iacobucci, '*Superior Propane* Saga'; Michael Trebilcock, 'The Great Efficiencies Debate in Canadian Merger Policy' (2004) 10 *New Zealand Business Law Quarterly* 298.

Japanese Fair Trade Commission devotes considerable resources to policing low prices in Japan's economy, presumably with a view to protecting small businesses from excessively vigorous competition. South Africa's competition laws have an extensive and ambitious list of goals, including addressing its exclusionary past by promoting participation of all citizens in the economy and promoting the fair distribution of ownership and control of markets among different racial groups and balancing the interests of workers, owners, and consumers. The objectives of China's anti-monopoly law include promoting efficiency, encouraging free competition, safeguarding healthy development of a socialist market economy and the public interest, protecting the state-owned economy and small business, encouraging the expansion of domestic enterprises and scrutinizing foreign takeovers, with no clear hierarchy established between these various objectives.

This sample reveals the plurality of objectives that different jurisdictions adopt, not always perfectly consistent with one another, and in some instances, mutually inconsistent. For example, the Canadian Act seeks to promote both competitive prices for consumers and productive efficiencies. How, then, to interpret the efficiencies defense to mergers? Are higher prices permissible if there are cost savings? Which objective prevails? The case law suggests that the Competition Tribunal must exercise its judgement on a case-by-case basis.[11] In general a plurality of sometimes inconsistent objectives makes an assessment of competition agencies' performance problematic.

Of course, the eight jurisdictions surveyed in detail in our comparative project are a small sub-set of the more than a hundred countries that now have competition law regimes (many of them adopted in recent years), so that it is almost certainly the case that the divergences in specifications of objectives in our sample of jurisdictions would be greatly amplified in a much broader sample. This divergence in objective functions may be viewed as supporting the inference that in evaluating the performance of competition law agencies, they should be treated as *sui generis* and evaluated in terms of their own objectives (internal validity) and comparative assessments treated with extreme caution (external validity). However, in terms of comparative performance assessments, it might be argued that subsets of jurisdictions can be identified that share common policy objectives and in such cases there are useful insights to be derived from comparative evaluations in identifying relative strengths and weaknesses of different agencies in advancing common policy objectives, e.g., jurisdictions subscribing either to a total welfare standard (maximizing the sum of consumer and producer surplus), or consumer welfare standard (maximizing consumer surplus). Even adopting this assumption, we believe that any comparative performance assessment exercise is likely to encounter formidable challenges, which we address below.

---

[11] See *Superior Propane* (n. 9).

16.4 FROM OUTPUT AND OUTCOME MEASURES TO INSTITUTIONAL DESIGN

Kovacic et al. are clearly aware of the challenges of generating quantitative, objective assessments of agency performance. They suggest that such assessments be supplemented by a more qualitative assessment of performance by an expert, detached panel. While we do not have strong views on the role of such an expert panel, it is important to acknowledge that many of the problems associated with quantitative measures of performance will ultimately affect the force of the conclusions of an expert panel. It is difficult in many jurisdictions, for example, to articulate precisely a clear, internally consistent and uncontroversial set of objectives for competition policy, which renders any qualitative assessment subject to the personal views of the experts about how best to weigh different considerations. Without shared foundational objectives, how is one to determine who the experts are, let alone whether their assessment reflects that expertise? But, again, even if objectives were clear and straightforward, how are the experts to determine whether the agency has met its objectives? The panel would not have objective measures of performance that are especially reliable before it, and it is hard to say in the abstract how effective a kind of expert audit of the agency would be. In addition, there is a danger associated with expert panels (especially international panels) that they would push for homogeneity in institutional design and priorities, which would be problematic given the legitimacy of heterogeneity across polities. We analyze the dangers of compelled homogeneity below, while in this section, we explore the challenges of institutional design, the inevitability of trade-offs, and the impossibility of a single, optimal approach across jurisdictions.

Because of the challenges of *ex post* review in both its quantitative and qualitative forms, we draw attention to the fundamental importance of the institutional design of competition regimes. Ultimately, effective agency performance will depend on the judgment that the people within the institutional framework exercise, judgment that as we have discussed will be very difficult to second-guess *ex post*. In our view, institutional design is crucial in creating the knowledge and appropriate incentives for decision-makers in competition agencies.

Institutional design raises another set of complexities, however, because it is impossible to specify what the "right" design is, in significant part because optimal institutional design depends on a variety of competing values. In our previous writing on the design of competition law institutions,[12] we identified at least three basic structural models for the design of competition law agencies: the bifurcated judicial model, where a specialized competition agency undertakes investigative and enforcement functions and remits disputed matters to the ordinary courts of the jurisdiction for adjudication; the bifurcated agency model, where a specialized competition agency performs investigative and enforcement functions, while

---

[12] See (n. 6).

adjudicative functions are remitted to a separate specialized competition tribunal; and the integrated agency model, where a single agency performs all three functions (investigation, enforcement, and adjudication). All three of these models, or variants thereof, are represented in the eight jurisdictions surveyed in detail in the project that Professors Fox and Trebilcock chaired. While various arguments can be made for and against each of these models, it is far from clear that any one of these models possesses decisive advantages over the other two. Moreover, with a variety of competing values at stake in designing legal institutions, the choice of institutional structure will, in large part, reflect the particularities of a given jurisdiction's history, institutional culture, political dynamics, etc., as recognized more generally in the path dependence literature that seeks to explain the mixed to weak recent record of externally sponsored institutional reforms in developing countries.[13]

In our earlier writing, we argued that while the normative criteria or values for evaluating competition law institutions may be relatively uncontroversial considered in isolation, each value implies an obverse value and indeed interactions with other values, thus rendering the weighting of, or trade-offs among, values a quintessential polycentric and highly contestable exercise. The key dyadic values are listed below.

16.4.1 *Independence: Accountability*

On the one hand, competition law institutions should be free from day-to-day political interference. Independence serves to depoliticize enforcement decisions, reduce the risk of perceived bias, and provide consistency from one political administration to the next.[14] On the other hand, at least in a representative democracy, it is difficult to defend institutional independence without some form of accountability; for example, with respect to appointments, budgetary allocations, financial expenditures, periodic mandate, and performance review.

16.4.2 *Expertise: Detachment*

Competition law matters typically require high levels of expertise in their resolution – expertise with respect to particular industries, expertise in marshalling and interpreting empirical data, and expertise in industrial organization theory. However, too close an involvement in the industry in question or excessively doctrinaire commitments to particular theoretical paradigms may compromise

---

[13] See e.g. Mariana Prado and Michael Trebilcock, 'Path Dependence, Development and the Dynamics of Institutional Reform' (2009) 59 *University of Toronto Law Journal* 341; Michael Trebilcock, 'Between Universalism and Relativism: Reflections on the Evolution of Law and Development Studies' (2016) 66 *University of Toronto Law Journal* 330.

[14] Canadian Competition Bureau, Options for the Internationalization of Competition Policy (August 2009), www.competitionbureau.gc.ca/eic/site/cb-bc.nsf/eng/01646.html

detachment in evaluating or adjudicating novel arrangements or evolving economic or theoretical environments.

16.4.3 *Transparency: Confidentiality*

In order to enhance the public credibility of competition laws, high levels of transparency in performing investigative, enforcement, and adjudicative functions are desirable. However, much of the information that a competition law agency is required to evaluate from the immediate parties involved and from competitors, suppliers, and customers is commercially highly sensitive, and public disclosure may be seriously damaging to legitimate business interests. The ideal degree of transparency therefore varies depending on the type of decision being made. For example, formal adjudications are normally on-the-record public proceedings whereas many interim or procedural matters may be determined in a much less open manner.

16.4.4 *Administrative Efficiency: Due Process*

Competing concerns also exist between administrative efficiency and due process protections. Many matters with which a competition law agency may be seized are time-sensitive (e.g., merger review). However, timelines in disposition are in tension with the value of due process in providing all affected or interested parties a right to be heard, to adduce evidence, and to contest the position of parties adverse in interest.

16.4.5 *Predictability: Flexibility*

In a legal system based on the rule of law, significant value is placed on the predictability and consistency with which laws are applied. In such a legal system, affected parties can order their affairs with a fairly high level of confidence in the nature of the rules that govern those affairs. But the value of predictability is in tension with the obverse value of flexibility where the evolution of economic theory and the idiosyncrasies of particular industries, transactions, or practices may require reevaluation and refinement of pre-existing rules, policy positions, or adjudicative decisions. This often leaves a large domain of uncertainty in the application of competition laws.

In balancing these values, a complex, subjective, and inevitably highly contentious optimizing calculus is involved. Moreover, the complexity of this calculus is, in fact, greater than the primary dyadic value tensions identified above in that many of the values interact with one another in polycentric, mutually reinforcing, or antithetical ways.

Even in the small subset of eight competition law regimes that were evaluated in the project led by Professors Fox and Trebilcock, these trade-offs have been resolved in very different ways, again in part reflecting different legal traditions, social values, and political dynamics in each of these countries.

As this brief discussion of the range of values at stake in institutional design reveals, a wide range of institutional arrangements are justifiable in principle. Ultimately, institutional design reduces to questions about the relative weighting of different values. We discussed above the enormous challenge of measuring performance of competition agencies on the basis of quantitative measures, in part because of a variety of values and objectives of substantive law. We have argued in this section that the range of values at stake in designing competition agencies render assessments of institutional design and performance problematic even if the substantive competition law goals of an agency were clear and uncontroversial. For example, an agency may not render timely decisions, but that may be the result of a conscious prioritization of due process; adjudicators in competition policy may not be particularly expert, but that could be the result of an emphasis on detachment; and, of course, the converse could be true in both cases.

16.5 REVISITING THE PROBLEM OF POTENTIAL CONFLICTS BETWEEN COMPETITION LAW REGIMES

We have reviewed the challenges with both quantitative and qualitative assessments of competition agency performance from both the perspective of competition law values, and values underlying institutional design. But that said, there clearly are some institutional practices that are better than others. In another recent paper,[15] Kovacic argues that good agency performance has two dimensions: one that focuses on outputs (or ideally outcomes) of initiatives, the second involves investments in long-term capacity, and that agencies should be graded on both dimensions. With respect to the latter, he proposes that one might appropriately ask the following questions of any competition agency:

- How clearly and coherently has the agency stated its objectives?
- Does the agency have a conscious process for setting a strategy and selecting programs that will fulfill its stated goals?
- Does the agency have a problem-solving orientation?
- Is the agency making adequate investments in acquiring and retaining the human capital it needs to perform its chosen projects?
- Is the agency making regular investments to improve its base of knowledge?
- Has the agency developed internal quality control procedures to ensure that theories and facts are tested vigorously?
- Is the agency making capital investments in the infrastructure of inter-agency networks?

[15] William Kovacic, 'Rating the Competition Agencies: What Constitutes Good Performance?' (2012) 16 *George Mason Law Review* 903.

- Does the agency have a mechanism for evaluating the effects of its programs and processes?

While it is difficult to disagree, as a matter of good public management, with the appropriateness of any of these questions, we close by discussing a different short-coming of evaluations of competition agencies: there is a risk that any comparative exercise will result in a push for convergence across jurisdictions, which is not, in our view, necessarily desirable. The variance across jurisdictions in both the ends and means of competition policy raises cautionary flags about the entire project of comparative competition institutional performance. In particular, while some comparative initiatives may self-consciously seek to promote institutional and substantive convergence across jurisdictions, we are concerned that even if this were not the objective, it is a natural product of the exercise. The proliferation of comparative legal indicators have been criticized in part because of their tendency to induce convergence across different polities with different priorities. Quantitative assessments would clearly push for homogeneity across jurisdictions – no jurisdiction would welcome a finding that it is "below" others on some quantitative metric. In addition, qualitative assessments of institutional performance, even if the assessments were to attempt to judge each agency on the basis of its local values, will tend to be the product of the assessors' own politically contestable judgments – both substantive competition law goals, and institutional design, are informed by politically contestable values. The politics and preferences of the assessors would tend to exert pressure to conform so as to avoid a low grade on a competition agency scorecard.

16.6 CONCLUSION

To summarize the foregoing, we are skeptical of the robustness of quantitative measures of agency performance even within a single jurisdiction, and even more skeptical of comparative ratings or rankings across jurisdictions, given substantial divergences in agency mandates, institutional structures, decision-making processes, and accountability regimes. Optimal competition regimes will vary across jurisdictions, and any effort to compare and evaluate agencies would tend to induce convergence on a uniform set of institutional norms, which would undesirably undermine efforts to match local competition law enforcement to local circumstances and priorities.

We do not discount the value of "soft law" efforts such as those undertaken by the International Competition Network, an international organization of more than a hundred domestic competition agencies, to forge at least a loose consensus around "best practices" on various issues. Convergence, for the ICN, is a matter of consensus, not coercion. Nor do we discount the value of mutual cooperation agreements between agencies where these are judged to be mutually beneficial. However, just as we have argued that coerced convergence on particular competition sub-stantive law norms is undesirable, we would also maintain that a concerted push to institutional conformity is also misguided, for example through aid conditionality or accession conditions for membership of preferential trade agreements, or simply "naming and shaming" through international legal indicators.

This begs the question of how global competition enforcement ought to unfold where there is variation in institutions and priorities across jurisdictions, along with market conduct that has multijurisdictional impacts. The possibility of conflict across jurisdictions has led to calls for the international harmonization of competi-tion laws, which in their most radical form envisage an international competition code, somewhat akin to the Trade-Related Intellectual Property Rights Agreement negotiated during the Uruguay Round of the GATT and now vested in the World Trade Organization.[16] As reflected in the controversies surrounding the TRIPs Agreement and the abortive efforts during the early years of the Doha Round to negotiate even a minimalist international agreement on competition policy, we are deeply skeptical of such proposals, both in terms of their normative desirability and their political feasibility.[17] Just as foreign traders and foreign direct investors do (and should) take a plethora of distinctive domestic laws as given in the markets in which they seek to trade or invest, in principle they should also accept differences in domestic competition law regimes. Rather, as we have proposed in earlier writing,[18] a more productive line of analysis would focus on rules of recognition designed to identify the governing jurisdiction in cases of potential conflicts between domestic competition law regimes.

In particular, with respect to in-bound commerce, we argue that foreign traders or investors should accept the competition law regimes of the countries of destination as they stand, provided that they are both framed and enforced in a non-discriminatory fashion with respect to domestic and foreign producers of like or competitive products, by way of application of the national treatment principle enshrined in the GATT and many other international economic agreements.[19] That is to say, they should not complain that they are subject to different treatment in countries of destination with respect to the application of competition laws than

---

[16] See Michael Trebilcock and Edward Iacobucci, 'National Treatment and Extraterritoriality: Defining the Domains of Trade and Antitrust Policy,' in Epstein and Greve (eds.), *Competition Laws in Conflict*, 169–72.

[17] Ibid.; David Leebron, 'Lying Down with Procrustes: An Analysis of Harmonization', in Jagdish Bhagwati and Robert Hudec (eds.), *Fair Trade and Harmonization: Prerequisites for Free Trade?* (MIT Press, 1996), vol. I; Michael Trebilcock and Robert Howse, 'Trade Liberalization and Regulatory Diversity: Reconciling Competitive Markets with Competitive Politics' (1998) 6 *European Journal of Law and Economics* 5; Dani Rodrik, *The Globalization Paradox: Democracy and the Future of the World Economy* (Oxford University Press, 2011).

[18] Trebilcock and Iacobucci, 'National Treatment'.

[19] The national treatment principle is crucial in our analysis of the optimality of heterogeneity. Beggar-thy-neighbor substantive law and/or enforcement, such as the ubiquitous permissibility of export cartels, violates this principle.

would obtain under the domestic competition laws of their countries of origin. A major part of the motivation for this proposal is that, despite the diversity in policy objectives of competition law regimes around the world, most share in common, as one element, the promotion of consumer welfare, so that jurisdictions where consumer welfare is potentially adversely affected by the agreements or practices of foreign parties who are selling goods to consumers in these jurisdictions have no basis for complaint that countries of destination seek to apply their competition laws to such agreements or practices, wherever the producers or suppliers in question happen to be located.

Conversely, with respect to outbound commerce, producers in countries of origin who complain about lack of access to markets in countries of destination, perhaps as a result of more stringent or more lax competition policies in the latter jurisdictions relative to their countries of origin, have no basis for asserting that their domestic competition policies should apply to agreements or practices in countries of destination. Rather, we argue, this should be viewed as a matter not of competition law but of trade law, and provided that countries of destination apply their competition laws in a non-discriminatory fashion as between domestic and foreign suppliers, producers denied access to foreign markets should resolve their grievances through conventional trade law mechanisms, including trade negotiations for improved access.

Of course, we recognize that there will be cases where agreements or practices impact consumer welfare in a number of different jurisdictions with distinctive competition laws, and all these jurisdictions may reasonably view their competition laws as legitimately engaged by the agreements or practices in question, creating the potential for conflicts or at least divergences in the application of these laws to the same agreements or practices. In some cases, tailoring and limiting remedies or sanctions to the consumer welfare injury sustained within a jurisdiction may resolve such conflicts. In other cases, especially in all-or-nothing scenarios such as many (but not all) multi-jurisdictional mergers, we see virtues in evolving rules that identify a lead jurisdiction with dispositive or recommendatory powers, principally based on where the potential consumer welfare impacts, in terms of value or volume of sales, are greatest, although we acknowledge that operationalizing such rules poses some complex and challenging issues.[20] Whatever the challenges with creating an appropriate set of recognition rules, in our view they are not only politically more feasible than the alternatives, but in addition, given variation in local market contexts and political priorities, are more desirable than a push for harmonization of substantive law or institutional arrangements.

---

[20]   For discussion, see Trebilcock and Iacobucci, 'National Treatment'.

17

Toward a Realistic Comparative Assessment of Private Antitrust Enforcement

Daniel A. Crane

Over the course of her extraordinary career, Eleanor Fox has contributed in many vital ways to our understanding of the importance of institutional analysis in antitrust and competition law.[1] Most importantly, Eleanor has become the leading repository of knowledge about what is happening around the globe in the field of competition law and its enforcement institutions. At a time when much of the field of antitrust was moving in the direction of theoretical generalization, formal modeling, game theory, and the like, Eleanor tirelessly worked the globe to discover the *actual practice* of competition law in the world. She left no doubt that she preferred an inductive, fact-based approach to studying competition law to armchair theorizing.[2]

Until recently, comparative institutional analysis in antitrust centered largely on comparing public enforcement institutions – for example, on comparing independent agency versus prosecutorial models, sectoral regulators versus generalist competition agencies, administrative versus criminal enforcement, and the like. However, the rise of private antitrust enforcement in many jurisdictions requires extending institutional analysis to comprehend comparisons between private enforcement systems, between public and private systems, and taking account of the complex interactions between public and private systems.

This chapter will propose a framework for conducting comparative analysis of antitrust systems given the rising growth of private enforcement. In particular, I shall argue that a realistic assessment of the country-specific practice of private antitrust litigation requires looking beyond the stated objectives and justifications for the practice – such as providing compensation to injured consumers or complementing public enforcement – and to the actual effects of private enforcement on the overall antitrust ecosystem. The evidence from the United States' long and not always felicitous experience with private enforcement suggests that private litigation has

---

[1] See e.g. E. Fox and M. J. Trebilcock, *The Design of Competition Law Institutions: Global Norms, Local Choices* (Oxford University Press, 2013).

[2] E. M. Fox and L. A. Sullivan, 'Antitrust-Retrospective and Prospective: Where Are We Coming From? Where Are We Going?' (1987) 62 *NYU Law Review* 936, 958–60 (criticizing Chicago School for being grounded in theory rather than fact and based on ideology rather than science).

important feedback effects on public enforcement and may, in some contexts, diminish the incidence and efficacy of public enforcement. As private antitrust enforcement grows around the globe, it will be important to study whether these effects are replicated or whether, instead, public enforcement remains predominant and relatively unmodified.

17.1 THE GROWTH OF PRIVATE ANTITRUST LITIGATION

Throughout much of the world, public enforcement of competition law principles remains the norm. Outside of the United States, private enforcement has been theoretically available but relatively rare. However, in recent decades there has been a surge of interest in private enforcement of competition law,[3] led particularly by the decade-long study of the issue in European Commission leading to the November 26, 2014 Council Directive on Antitrust Damages.[4] The Directive calls for expanded private antitrust enforcement throughout the European Union, and could, over time, lead to a dramatic increase in private antitrust litigation in Member States.

Private antitrust litigation seems to be breaking out in other parts of the world as well. Canada, which like the European Union has decided in favor of indirect purchaser standing,[5] has seen a steady growth in antitrust class actions, with twenty-five cases in 2013 and thirty-four cases in 2014.[6] South Korea has seen a similar growth in private antitrust damages cases filed in recent years, with an estimated thirty damages actions pending as of 2013.[7] Since the liberalization of Chile's rules on private antitrust enforcement in 2004, private litigants have filed over one hundred cases, 69% of all cases heard by the Competition Tribunal.[8] Many OECD countries report a steady increase in private antitrust cases in recent years.[9]

---

[3] See A. Andreangeli, *Private Enforcement of Antitrust: Regulating Corporate Behaviour through Collective Claims in the EU and US* (Edward Elgar, 2014); A. A. Foer and J. W. Cuneo (eds.), *The International Handbook on Private Enforcement of Competition Law* (Edward Elgar, 2010).

[4] Directive 2014/104/EU of the European Parliament and of the Council of 26 November 2014 on certain rules governing actions for damages under national law for infringements of the competition law provisions of the Member States and of the European Union Text with EEA relevance, http://eur-lex .europa.eu/legal-content/EN/TXT/?uri=uriserv:OJ.L_.2014.349.01.0001.01.ENG (hereafter EU Private Damages Directive).

[5] *Pro-Sys Consultants Ltd.* v. *Microsoft Corp.*, 2013 SCC 57 (Can.); *Sun-Rype Prods. Ltd.* v. *Archer Daniels Midland Co.*, 2013 SCC 58 (Can.); *Infineon Tech. AG* v. *Option consommateurs*, 2013 SCC 59 (Can.).

[6] Canadian Competition Bureau, 'The Relationship Between Public and Private Antitrust Enforcement' (June 10, 2015), www.competitionbureau.gc.ca/eic/site/cb-bc.nsf/eng/03926.html.

[7] CPI Overview of Current Antitrust Enforcement in Korea, www.competitionpolicyinternational.com/ overview-of-current-antitrust-enforcement-in-korea

[8] OECD Relationship Between Public and Private Antitrust Enforcement, Note by Chile (15 June 2015), www.oecd.org/officialdocuments/publicdisplaydocumentpdf/?cote=DAF/COMP/WP3/WD(2015) 14&docLanguage=En

[9] OECD, 'Public and Private Antitrust Enforcement in Competition', www.oecd.org/daf/competition/ antitrust-enforcement-in-competition.htm

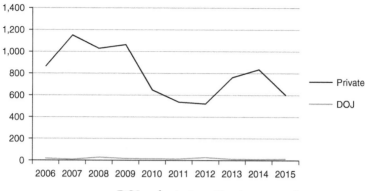

FIGURE 17.1 DOJ and private antitrust cases 2006–15

In the United States, private enforcement continues to far outstrip public enforcement, by a ratio of over 10:1. Figure 17.1 shows the trend lines for the last decade for antitrust filings by the Justice Department and by private parties suing under the antitrust laws in federal court. While there has been a good bit of volatility in the number of private antitrust cases initiated, the Justice Department's trend line has been flat and stuck in low single figures. The Federal Trade Commission (FTC) files a few additional cases, as do state attorneys general, but the overall numbers of public enforcement cases remain very small compared to the number of private cases filed.

Raw numbers of case filings do not always tell the story, since a single public case may have a much greater effect on the competitive landscape or the formulation of antitrust principles than a number of private cases. But by almost any metric, private antitrust litigation has wielded a greater influence on the shape of US antitrust law in recent decades. For example, since 1990 the US Supreme Court has decided thirty-six antitrust cases, thirty of which were private and only six of which were public. This means that antitrust norms have been overwhelmingly created in the context of private enforcement.

In short, private antitrust remains the bedrock of US antitrust enforcement and a growth industry around the world.

17.2 DISCREPANCIES BETWEEN PRIVATE ANTITRUST LITIGATION AS SCRIPTED AND AS PRACTICED

The worldwide growth of private antitrust enforcement raises new opportunities to study the actual effects of the private enforcement system. While there has been much written about the US private enforcement system, much of it may seem idiosyncratic to the framework of US civil litigation more generally – including such features as relatively permissive use of class actions, juries, and liberality on questions of proof and damages. As private antitrust enforcement becomes a more regular feature in other jurisdictions, it will be appropriate to ask how it actually operates – what are its actual patterns and effects.

While there are many different potential angles on understanding the practice of antitrust enforcement, two broad questions are of particular importance. First, does private antitrust enforcement achieve the purpose for which it ostensibly exists in most jurisdictions – providing compensated to injured consumers. Second, does private antitrust enforcement serve a complementary and supporting role to public enforcement – as it is advertised to do – or does it instead become competitive with, and to some extent displacing of, public enforcement?

17.2.1 *Compensation for Who?*

The US private enforcement system is oriented primarily around a deterrence goal. This is evident from the very way the courts speak of private enforcers – as "private attorneys general."[10] Treble damages are allowed as a bounty to encourage private suits in the public interest.[11] Standing principles – allowing direct purchaser suits without the pass-on defense despite the potential absence of any injury at all and disallowing indirect purchaser suits even though the indirect purchaser often incurs the real economic injury – are explicitly justified on deterrence grounds.[12] Similarly, the rule of joint and several liability without a right of contribution[13] is squarely grounded in deterrence.

Europe's recent movement in the direct of expanded private antitrust enforcement charts the opposite course, perhaps drawing from the continental tradition of more sharply distinguishing between private and public law than occurs in the Anglo-American tradition.[14] In contrast to common law systems, continental legal systems have long expressed skepticism about co-opting private plaintiffs into serving as surrogates for the public interest. For example, continental systems generally disfavor punitive damages,[15] and the qui tam action is an Anglo-American curiosity largely unknown on the continent.[16]

---

[10]   e.g. *Hawaii v. Standard Oil Co. of California*, 405 US 251, 262 (1972) ("By offering potential litigants the prospect of a recovery in three times the amount of their damages, Congress encouraged these persons to serve as 'private attorneys general'").

[11]   *Exxon Shipping Co. v. Baker*, 554 US 471, 511 (2008) ("We know, for example, that Congress devised the treble-damages remedy for private antitrust actions with an eye to supplementing official enforcement by inducing private litigation, which might otherwise have been too rare if nothing but compensatory damages were available at the end of the day").

[12]   *Illinois Brick Co. v. Illinois*, 431 US 720, 746 (1977) (justifying indirect purchaser standing prohibition by observing that, from a deterrence perspective, it is irrelevant whether the party receiving the damages was actually injured).

[13]   *Texas Industries, Inc. v. Radcliff Materials, Inc.*, 451 US 630 (1981).

[14]   R. B. Schlesinger, *Comparative Law* (5th edn, Foundation Press, 1988), 300 ("In a civilian mind, all law is automatically divided into private law and public law").

[15]   H. Koziol, 'Punitive Damages – A European Perspective' (2008) 68 *Louisiana Law Review* 741.

[16]   On the Anglo-American roots of the qui tam action, see J. Randy Beck, 'The False Claims Act and the English Eradication of Qui Tam Legislation' (2000) 78(3) *North Carolina Law Review* 539, 548–9.

The European Commission's initial intervention in the debate – the Commission's 2005 Green Paper – appeared to tilt in the deterrence direction.[17] It articulated both a compensatory and deterrence objective for private antitrust enforcement,[18] but espoused a damages multiplier in cartel cases,[19] expressed doubt on indirect purchaser standing and allowing the pass-on defense in light of its complexity.[20] By the 2008 White Paper, however, compensation had clearly won out. The White Paper stated emphatically that "Full compensation is ... the first and foremost guiding principle" of private antitrust litigation and that "More effective compensation mechanisms mean that the costs of antitrust infringements would be borne by the infringers, and not by the victims and law-abiding businesses."[21] The emphasis on compensation is also highly visible in the Commission's directive on private damages, which allows for the passing-on defense and indirect purchaser standing and prohibits damage multipliers.[22]

As jurisdictions outside the United States and Europe cautiously transition toward increased private enforcement, they will necessarily be confronted with similar choices. Early signs suggest that jurisdictions may tend to frame private enforcement around a compensation goal rather than thinking of private enforcement as a supplement to public enforcement designed to maximize deterrence. Jurisdictions such as Canada,[23] Germany,[24] and South Africa[25] have decided in favor of indirect purchaser standing with the pass-on defense (although other jurisdictions, such as South Korea, have rejected the pass-on defense).[26]

Although the impulse toward compensation is understandable given continental assumptions about the public–private divide and the role of private law, antitrust

---

[17] Green Paper – Damages actions for breach of the EC antitrust rules, https://eur-lex.europa.eu/legal-content/EN/ALL/?uri=CELEX%3A52005DC0672

[18] Ibid., at 1.1 ("Damages actions for infringement of antitrust law serve several purposes, namely to compensate those who have suffered a loss as a consequence of anti-competitive behaviour and to ensure the full effectiveness of the antitrust rules of the Treaty by discouraging anti-competitive behaviour, thus contributing significantly to the maintenance of effective competition in the Community").

[19] Ibid., at 2.3 ("[D]oubling of damages at the discretion of the court, automatic or conditional, could be considered for horizontal cartel infringements").

[20] Ibid., at 2.4 ("The 'passing-on defence' substantially increases the complexity of damages claims as the exact distribution of damages along the supply chain could be exceedingly difficult to prove. Evidentiary problems also burden actions of indirect purchasers, as they might be unable to prove the extent of their damages and the causative link with the infringing behaviour").

[21] 2008 White Paper, at 3.

[22] See EU Private Damages Actions Directive, recital 29, recital 36, arts. 2(3), 12–16.

[23] J. Bodrug, A. Fanaki, and C. Spagnola, 'Supreme Court of Canada Allows Indirect Purchaser Class Actions for Antitrust Claims 13-APR' (2014) *Antitrust Source* 1.

[24] Kartellteilnehmer haften auch mittelbar Geschädigten auf Schadensersatz, http://juris.bundesgerichtshof.de/cgi-bin/rechtsprechung/document.py?Gericht=bgh&Art=pm&Datum=2011&Sort=3&nr=56711&pos=1&anz=119

[25] Private anti-trust litigation 2014: South Africa, www.ensafrica.com/news/Private-anti-trust-litigation-2014-South-Africa?Id=1202&STitle=Anti-trust%20%7C%20Competition%20ENSight

[26] Korean Supreme Court rejects passing-on defense in private damages action arising out of price-fixing agreement, www.lexology.com/library/detail.aspx?g=32446d04-e8e0-41ed-8c5f-13b3b037b76f

litigation to date has done a poor job of achieving a compensatory goal, if by compensation we mean identifying an injured class for whose benefit the law exists – consumers – and providing financial redress in proportion to their injuries. As I have previously submitted,[27] antitrust enforcement is incapable of compensating consumers for two out of three major categories of injury – deadweight losses and dynamic injuries. That leaves wealth transfers or overcharges as possibly compensable. Yet, even as to this third category of injury, the prospects for adequate compensation to large percentages of injured consumers are remote.

The difficulties with providing compensation for overcharges are many. As the Council Directive recognizes in providing for indirect purchaser standing, large shares of overcharges are ordinarily passed on downstream to household consumers, who absorb the majority of the loss. They are the primary victims in need of compensation. But, by the time it reaches the household consumer level, the overcharge is often spread widely over thousands or millions of persons, each of whom incurs a relatively modest injury. Practically speaking, locating and providing compensation to the majority of the injured consumers is usually impossible.

To illustrate this point, I refer to important empirical work by Bob Lande and Josh Davis, who argue that the United States antitrust system has been successful in pursuing compensation for injured victims.[28] In a debate with Lande and Davis hosted by the American Antitrust Institute, I took their most recent study of sixty cases and provided an alternative perspective on the figures they reported. Lande and Davis report a total recovery of between $33.8 billion and $35.8 billion in these sixty cases,[29] an impressive-sounding number. But when one scrutinizes the numbers closely, the compensation claim appears much weaker. Even though over half of the states allow indirect purchaser suits under state antitrust law, only $2 billion out of the total pot was awarded to indirect purchasers. Of the total, $13 billion went to competitors – whose welfare is at best an incidental focus of antitrust laws – and $15 billion to direct purchasers, many of whom may have passed on nearly the full overcharge and hence suffered no substantial injury. Attorneys' fees ate up between 9 and 27 percent of the awards, and claims administration costs an additional 4 percent (notably, such costs went up by 50 percent in indirect purchaser cases).

Focusing now on the indirect purchaser claims, I calculated the average claims rate (meaning the percentage of all persons in the class who filled out the paperwork to be awarded a share of the judgment or settlement). In the seven cases for which this information was available, the average weighted (by magnitude of the award) claims rate was 12 percent, meaning that 88 percent of the injured class members did

---

[27] D. A. Crane, *The Institutional Structure of Antitrust Enforcement* (Oxford University Press, 2011).

[28] See R. H. Lande and J. P. Davis, 'Benefits from Private Antitrust Enforcement: An Analysis of Forty Cases' (2008) 42 *University of San Francisco Law Review* 879; J. P. Davis and R. H. Lande, 'Defying Conventional Wisdom: The Case for Private Antitrust Enforcement' (2008) 48 *Georgia Law Review* 1; J. P. Davis and R. H. Lande, 'Toward an Empirical and Theoretical Assessment of Private Antitrust Enforcement' (2013) 36 *Seattle University Law Review* 1269.

[29] Davis and Lande, 'Empirical and Theoretical Assessment of Private Antitrust Enforcement'.

not partake in the damages at all. In sum, 12 percent of indirect purchasers received 6 percent of between 70 and 87 percent of damages awarded in the sixty cases. Accordingly, only a small fraction of consumers received a share a small piece (about 5 percent) of the total damages generated by the United States' antitrust system, reflecting only one aspect of their injury.

One can, of course, argue that my interpretation of the data takes a "cup 88% empty" perspective and neglects the important compensatory benefit to the 12% of consumers who did receive some compensation for their injuries. And perhaps more could be done to improve the system and reach more consumers. Perhaps. For present purposes, my point is just that there is a large gap between compensatory justifications and compensatory practices. As new private enforcement systems develop, they should be judged by what they do rather than what they say.

17.2.2 *Spillover Effects on Government Enforcement*

Courts, antitrust enforcers, and legislators often assert that private antitrust enforcement complements and bolsters public enforcement. The US Supreme Court has explained that private enforcement should be secondary to, and never competitive with, public enforcement:

> The private-injunction action, like the treble-damage action under s 4 of the Act, supplements Government enforcement of the antitrust laws; but it is the Attorney General and the United States district attorneys who are primarily charged by Congress with the duty of protecting the public interest under these laws. The Government seeks its injunctive remedies on behalf of the general public; the private plaintiff, though his remedy is made available pursuant to public policy as determined by Congress, may be expected to exercise it only when his personal interest will be served. These private and public actions were designed to be cumulative, not mutually exclusive.[30]

The EU Directive also shows sensitivity to the relationship between public and private enforcement, asserting the need for "coordination of these two forms of enforcement in a coherent manner,"[31] and proposing mechanisms for preventing private enforcement from undermining public enforcement, such as limiting private access to self-incriminating materials received as part of leniency applications.[32]

The reality, however, is that private enforcement cannot help but have spillover effects on public enforcement – not all in the direction of making public enforcement more effective. To the contrary, the US experience shows that a swell of private enforcement can subtly undermine public enforcement, or even choke it off altogether.[33] Particularly if private enforcement in particular areas comes to

---

[30]   *US v. Borden Co.*, 347 US 514, 518 (1954).
[31]   EU Private Damages Directive, recital 6.
[32]   Ibid., recital 26.
[33]   See generally Crane, *Institutional Structure*.

significantly outstrip public enforcement in frequency, with the governing liability norms being predominantly created in private litigation, public litigation can become laden with the baggage of private litigation to the point if ineffectiveness or practical disappearance.

US monopolization law is a case in point. Historically, public antitrust enforcement of s. 2 of the Sherman Act has declined since a high in the 1970s, when the agencies were bringing over three cases a year,[34] to the last several administrations where very few monopolization cases have been brought. Over the eight years of the Bush administration, the Justice Department filed no monopolization cases. While running for office in 2007, Senator Barak Obama singled out this ostensibly weak enforcement record for condemnation, characterizing the failure to pursue monopolization cases as "lax enforcement" that harmed consumer interests.[35] His Antitrust Division immediately withdrew a report on monopolization offenses disseminated by the Bush administration and promised that the Justice department would be "aggressively pursuing" monopolization cases.[36] But, then, over seven and a half years, the Justice Department brought only one monopolization case. The case, against United Regional Health Care System of Wichita, Texas, was hardly a blockbuster antimonopoly action of the earlier Standard Oil, IBM, AT&T, or Microsoft variety. The Justice Department alleged that the relevant market was for the sale of inpatient hospital services to insurance companies in a geographic area "no larger than the Wichita Falls Metropolitan Statistical Area."[37] The government's theory – that United had a 90% market share in acute inpatient services and used exclusive dealing contracts with insurance companies to stifle competitors – broke no new theoretical or practical ground.

What happened to public enforcement against monopolization? Among the several contributing factors is the dramatic rise of private monopolization actions in the later part of the twentieth century. Figure 17.2 below provides a statistical summary of public and private monopolization cases in the federal appellate courts in the post-war period. From the 1950s to the 1970s, the federal agencies filed a modest number of monopolization cases during each five-year period – far fewer than private monopolization cases, but still enough to make a significant impact on the formation of legal norms and market circumstances. But, as private monopolization litigation skyrocketed from the mid 1970s to the early 1990s, public monopolization enforcement receded, both proportionally and absolutely. With a few notable exceptions such as the DC Circuit's *en banc Microsoft* decision, the monopolization

[34] W. E. Kovacic, 'The Modern Evolution of US Competition Policy Enforcement Norms' (2003) 71 *Antitrust Law Journal* 377, 448, table 4.

[35] Statement of Senator Barak Obama for the American Antitrust Institute, www.antitrustinstitute.org/files/aai-%20Presidential%20campaign%20-%20Obama%209-07_092720071759.pdf

[36] Justice Department Withdraws Report on Antitrust Monopoly Law, www.justice.gov/opa/pr/justice-department-withdraws-report-antitrust-monopoly-law

[37] Complaint at 7, *United States* v. *United Reg'l Health Care Sys.*, No. 7:11-cv-00030 (ND Tex. Feb. 25, 2011), available at www.justice.gov/atr/cases/f267600/267651.pdf

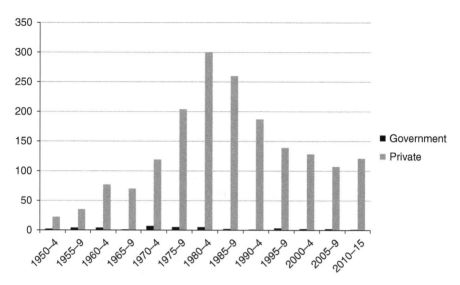

FIGURE 17.2 Monopolization cases in federal appellate courts by five-year period

law made from the 1970s forward was made in the context of private litigation. As the courts reacted to the dramatic rise of private monopolization cases by announcing new restrictions on a variety of exclusion theories – from predatory pricing, to tying, to duties to deal – private monopolization cases began to recede, reaching an apparently stable equilibrium at about half of their peak levels for the last two decades. This dramatic rise and then significant reduction of private monopolization litigation left in its wake public monopolization enforcement, which all but disappeared.

As with the previous comments on compensation, one can propose alternative explanations of the data and case trends. Again, my point in this chapter is not so much to argue for the correctness of my own interpretation, but to suggest the importance of asking questions of this nature in analyzing the actual relationship between public and private enforcement.

17.3 A FRAMEWORK FOR ANALYZING THE EFFECTS OF PRIVATE ANTITRUST LITIGATION

Having articulated some skepticism about two of the strong assumptions underlying many private antitrust enforcement systems – that they provide effective compensation to injured consumers and that private enforcement complements rather than substitutes for public enforcement – I will now propose seven questions that should be posed of emerging private enforcement systems in order to evaluate their actual incidence and effects. The answers to these questions will likely vary over jurisdictions and over time, and should provide a fruitful basis for comparative study and improvement in private enforcement.

17.3.1 *Who Receives Compensation Awards?*

As discussed above, the vast bulk of damages in the US system are going to competitors and direct purchasers. Even when damages payments are made to household consumers, only small fractions of the injured populations are receiving awards. To the extent that emerging private enforcement regimes are predicated on a compensatory rather than deterrence objective, the systems should be evaluated based on their effectiveness in achieving meaningful compensation to significant fractions of injured consumers.

In principle, this criterion can be assessed relatively simply: (i) what is the injured population; (ii) what is the amount of the alleged overcharge; (iii) what is the fraction of the injured population that actually obtains damages; and (iv) what is the percentage of the claimed overcharge recovered in damages. Obtaining data may be difficult, although studies such as Lande and Davis's in the United States show that it is not impossible.

17.3.2 *Are Private Cases Generally Congruent with Normative Theories of Antitrust Law?*

One of the abiding concerns with private antitrust litigation in the United States is that private litigants do not have optimal incentives when it comes to competition. Competitors, in particular, would often prefer a *less* competitive world, and hence may complain of behavior that harms them but benefits consumers. To address the problem of private antitrust cases that are incongruent with the purposes of the antitrust laws, the United States has developed an antitrust injury doctrine that requires symmetry between the plaintiff's theory of injury and the normative theories underlying the antitrust laws.[38]

The antitrust injury requirement is not only important as a doctrinal tool to weed out misguided cases, but it also may serve as evidence of the proclivities of a private enforcement system. Evidence that many private cases articulate theories of harm that are essentially complaints about *more* competition may show that the system has not been optimally calibrated to incentivize the right kind of cases to be brought.

Similarly, the mix of classes of private plaintiff and kinds of theories they advance can provide valuable insight on the practical effects of expanded private enforcement. One such study was particularly influential in shaping attitudes toward private antitrust litigation in the United States, and ultimately may have had a significant effect on the subsequent development of the law. The Georgetown Private Antitrust

---

[38] See Daniel A. Crane, *Antitrust* (Wolters Kluwer, 2014), 169.

Litigation Project studied 2,350 private antitrust cases filed in federal court in five judicial districts between 1973 and 1983.[39] The survey results provided some interesting insights into what kinds of cases were being filed and who was filing them. First, complaints of vertical misconduct outnumbered horizontal complaints.[40] Second, most private cases were brought by businesses vertically related to the defendant, such as dealers, licensees, and franchisees or by competitors.[41] Competitors brought 35.5 percent of all cases, dealers 27.3 percent, and suppliers 5.6 percent and franchisees and licensees cumulatively around 3 percent.[42] Customers – the ostensible beneficiaries of antitrust law – played a comparatively minor role. Final or end customers brought 8.7 percent of cases, perhaps not surprisingly in light of the Supreme Court's limitation of indirect purchaser standing.[43] But customer companies filed only 12.5 percent,[44] hence all customer complaints accounted for only about a fifth of antitrust filings.[45] One takeaway from the Georgetown Study was that the US private antitrust litigation system was incentivizing the wrong mix of cases to be filed and that corrections in both substantive and procedural rules were necessary to achieve a more desirable balance.

17.3.3 *Are There Indicia of Average Quality of Private Cases?*

Civil litigation case quality can be measured statistically. For example, the percentage of cases that survive pretrial screening motions such as motions to dismiss or for summary judgment may provide a rough measure of case quality,[46] giving an indication of whether the system creates incentives for meritorious cases to be brought or rather provides incentives for low-quality cases to be brought for reasons collateral to expected victory and recovery. There probably is not a uniform way of assessing case quality statistically across multiple jurisdictions, since different jurisdictions utilize differing procedural devices for case management and apple-to-apples comparisons may therefore be challenging. Nonetheless, jurisdiction-specific measures could be created to assess the percentage of cases that are allowed to advance to a determination on the merits or are instead screened out at some earlier stage.

---

[39] S. C. Salop and L. J. White, 'Economic Analysis of Private Antitrust Litigation' (1986) 74 *Georgia Law Review* 1001, 1001–2.
[40] Ibid., at 2005.
[41] Ibid.
[42] Ibid., at 1008, table 5.
[43] *Illinois Brick Co.* v. *Illinois*, 431 US 720 (1977).
[44] Salop and White, 'Economic Analysis', 1008, table 5.
[45] Ibid., at 1002–3.
[46] See e.g. J. B. Gelbach, 'Material Facts in the Debate Over Twombly and Iqbal' (2016) 68 *Stanford Law Review* 369, 381–2.

Similar analysis can be conducted around case settlement. Pretrial settlements provide some indication of the parties' respective view of the merits. Cases that settle for nuisance value reflect low-merit filings, whereas cases that settle for more significant sums signal higher-value filings.

These sorts of case quality indicia do not demonstrate that filed cases are meritorious in a strong sense – i.e. compared to some ideal of what competition rules should be and what kinds of cases should be allowed to proceed. But they do provide some insight into the merit of cases as judged from a system's internal norms.

17.3.4 *What Happens to Public Agency Budgets?*

If private litigation truly is a complement rather than a substitute for public enforcement, then the growth of private litigation should not lead to a decrease in government funding for public enforcement. (Indeed, in economic terms, if public and private enforcement truly are complements, an increase in the demand for private enforcement should lead to an increase in the demand for public enforcement as well.) Thus far, there is no historical evidence in the United States that the growth in private litigation has led to a diminution in public enforcement funding, since the FTC and Antitrust Division have been funded at near-historic highs in recent years, even adjusted for GDP growth.[47]

Still, with antitrust budgets quite limited and politically dependent in many newer antitrust enforcement jurisdictions, it would not be surprising to see a rise in private antitrust enforcement correspond with a decrease in public funding. Politicians eager to cut budgets may see little need for generosity to public agencies as to a public good supplied amply supplied by private markets. At any rate, as private enforcement grows throughout the world, it will be important to understand how, if at all, this affects legislatures' willingness to fund competition authorities.

17.3.5 *What Happens to Mix of Public Cases?*

The US experience suggests the following pattern: with a rise in private enforcement, the public agencies become more or less specialized in merger and anti-cartel enforcement, whereas private litigants take over monopolization enforcement and most other civil non-merger enforcement. Will this pattern be repeated elsewhere? Is this particular pattern a feature of US idiosyncrasies – criminal enforcement against cartels, two federal agencies, state attorney general enforcement, treble damages, fee-shifting, class actions, and the like – or does it have more general resonances?

Up until recently, these questions were largely unanswerable because there were few, if any, other natural experiments with the scale of private enforcement that has

---

[47]   Crane, *Institutional Structure.*

occurred in the United States. The emergence of other significant private enforcement regimes will begin to provide answers. Further, the effects on the mix of public cases need not resemble the US pattern to be significant. It would be surprising if a large increase in private enforcement did not affect the distribution of public cases, which in turn could have important effects on the emerging shape of competition law.

17.3.6 Does Public or Private Litigation Make the Law?

Even if public enforcement proceeds unabated by an increase in private enforcement, the efficacy of public enforcement may be hindered if an increasing amount of antitrust law is made in the context of private litigation and then applied wholesale to public enforcement. The US experience contains telling instances in which antitrust principles created in private litigation have been applied to defeat government claims in subsequent cases. Predatory pricing provides a case in point. After many years in which the government brought no predatory pricing cases but a very pro-defendant legal reform was occurring in scores of private predatory pricing cases, the Justice Department finally brought a predatory pricing case against American Airlines, which it then lost under the new predatory pricing case law.[48] Something similar occurred as to "pay-for-delay" patent settlements, where the FTC was stuck for a decade with a very pro-defendant legal rule created in private litigation.

17.3.7 Does Private Enforcement Weaken or Strengthen Enforcement Overall?

Finally, as a catch-all question, one should inquire whether private enforcement weakens or strengthens antitrust enforcement overall. Is there evidence that the growth of private enforcement inserts new vigor into the competitive landscape by effectively supplementing public enforcement, leveraging private resources (money, knowledge, creativity, and perspective), and creating new constituencies and public support for competition law? Or, does private litigation interfere with public enforcement by disrupting cooperative relationships between regulators and regulated entities, stealing public enforcers' power to set the enforcement agenda, and creating inconsistencies in the law or suboptimal norms by focusing litigation on the idiosyncratic positions and preferences of the individual litigants rather than the public interest more broadly.[49] While it may be impossible to answer these questions categorically, some effort should be made to understand and catalogue the subtle interplay between public and private enforcement as private enforcement systems grow.

---

[48] *US v. AMR Corp.*, 335 F.3d 1109 (10th Cir. 2003).
[49] M. C. Stephenson, 'Public Regulation of Private Enforcement: The Case for Explaining the Role of Administrative Agencies' (2005) 91 *Virginia Law Review* 93, 118–19.

17.4 CONCLUSION

Eleanor Fox's extraordinary career in antitrust should inspire everyone working in the field to pay careful attention to the facts on the ground, to learn how antitrust systems really work rather than just theorizing about them. In this chapter, I have attempted to suggest the kinds of questions that one might ask to understand the actual effects of expanded private antitrust enforcement around the globe. The list is certainly not exhaustive; it is to be hoped that comparative study will yield greater insights on private enforcement which, in turn, will prompt a richer set of questions.

18

Antitrust Enforcement in the US and the EU

A *Comparison of the Two Federal Systems*

Daniel L. Rubinfeld

18.1 INTRODUCTION

This chapter offers commentary on a normative question: to what extent should antitrust enforcement (and regulatory authority more generally) be centralized and to what extent should the authority be delegated to lower levels of government? While this question has implications worldwide, I will use the European Union and the US as the focal point of my analysis. The underpinnings of the antitrust enforcement structure are different in the two federal systems. In the US, the driving force is the state action exemption doctrine, based on the common law, which spells out instances in which the center can enforce its federal antitrust statutes against anticompetitive state and local regulation. In the EU, however, the driving force is the principle of subsidiarity, which delegates powers to Member States unless a strong case can be made that the externalities are so substantial as to require actions from the center.

Fortunately, the normative question at issue here has been analyzed previously by a number of authors, the primary of whom is my colleague Eleanor Fox. No one is better situated to analyze this issue than Professor Fox, since she has devoted a substantial part of her academic career to the study of comparative antitrust analysis. While seeing pros and cons, Eleanor claims that the EU has it (more or less) right. In the EU, federalism trumps the Member States – Member State authorities have a duty to take on Member State laws that run counter to the interests of the Union.[1] Whereas, in the US, we must rely on a less than clear set of guidelines that flow from state action case law and the dormant commerce clause of the US Constitution. Moreover, as Professor Fox has pointed out, the US gives too much weight to state sovereignty (e.g., the Eleventh Amendment prohibits

---

[1] See Eleanor M. Fox, 'State Action in Comparative Context: What if *Parker v. Brown* were Italian', in *International Antitrust Law and Policy: Fordham Corporate Law* (Juris, 2003), ch. 19; Eleanor M. Fox and Deborah Healey, 'When the State Harms Competition – The Role for Competition Law' (2014) 79 *Antitrust Law Journal*, 769.

suits in federal courts by citizens against states). In her view, the federal government should have greater authority to intercede when state actions affect national interests.

I offer a somewhat different perspective. While it may require a further statutory intervention, the US, as a fully formed political and economic system, has the ability to improve its federalism antitrust oversight. The same cannot be said of the EU, which is neither fully formed politically (witness the problems of Greece and Italy, Brexit, and a failure to deal coherently with the immigration problem) nor economically (witness the inability of the EMU to deal with the downturn of the European economy and a series of significant economic shocks). It has, however, had a relatively integrated/federal EU antitrust policy for decades and antitrust enforcement has one through various reforms, chiefly with decentralization and the adoption of Regulation 1/2003.

In the section that immediately follows, I briefly review the principle of subsidiarity and the state action exemption doctrine. Following that, I describe several of the important differences between the US and the EU; I explain why the two enforcement systems are unlikely to achieve convergence with respect to the antitrust enforcement of regulatory activities; I conclude with several suggestions for possible reform.

18.2 THE US REGULATORY FEDERALISM: THE STATE ACTION EXEMPTION DOCTRINE

Over the past several decades the US Supreme Court has offered a process-oriented test that balances to a reasonable degree the norms of economic efficiency and political participation. In essence, the validity of a particular state regulation now depends heavily on whether that regulation has been clearly authorized by the state legislature and, if so, whether that legislature actively supervises the regulatory activity. This section offers a brief overview of the development of the "state action doctrine."

The US courts have faced issues of regulatory federalism in their efforts to resolve the inevitable tension between federal antitrust law and state business regulation through an evolving doctrine.[2] The conflict between state and federal interests has been longstanding in US constitutional history. This conflict has typically been resolved by a constitutional interpretation in which federal laws trump their state counterparts – witness the Supremacy Clause of the US Constitution, which resolves conflicts in favor of federal law. In contrast, however, the "state action doctrine" has typically resolved the tension between federal antitrust regulations

---

[2] This section builds on Robert P. Inman and Daniel L. Rubinfeld (with Robert Inman), 'Making Sense of the Antitrust State Action Doctrine: Balancing Political Participation and Economics Efficiency in Regulatory Federalism' (1997) 75, May *Texas Law Review* 1203.

and the states' sometimes anticompetitive regulation of business activities in favor of the states.

As spelled out by the Supreme Court's opinion in *Parker* v. *Brown*, the doctrine largely exempts the actions of states (and to a lesser extent localities) from the federal antitrust laws. The relevant doctrine is a two-pronged test requiring state regulations to be "clearly articulated" and "actively supervised." Moreover, my federalism co-author Robert Inman and I see the current doctrine as providing institutional protection for the goal of political participation, a goal this is arguably consistent with the objectives of the Sherman Act, especially as espoused during the populist era. Unfortunately, the ideals of a federal system (as Professor Fox and I are likely to agree) are not currently well protected by the current Supreme Court's view of the state action doctrine. The current US doctrine allows many state regulations which adversely affect the economic well-being of non-residents to stand, at a cost in potentially significant lost economic welfare. Indeed, *Parker* v. *Brown*, the corner-stone of the current state action doctrine, is just such a case.

In *Parker* v. *Brown*, the Court was asked whether California's Agricultural Prorate Act violated the Sherman Act.[3] California had established such a program in order to maintain the prices of and competition for a number of agricultural products. Under the program, ten producers of any crop within a production zone could petition the Prorate Advisory Commission to implement a restrictive marketing program. If the Commission agreed, a proposed program would then be drawn up and submitted for ratification by at least 65 percent of the growers. The Agricultural Prorate Act was challenged by a producer of raisins on the grounds that the Act violated the Sherman Act and the negative Commerce Clause.[4]

The Court noted that the marketing program would violate the Sherman Act if it had been devised solely upon the initiative of the producers. However, the Court further asserted that while Congress had the power (under the Commerce Clause) to prohibit anti-competitive state programs, Congress did not intend to prohibit states from undertaking regulatory activities approved and directed by state legislatures.[5] Underlying the Court's decision in *Parker* was its primary concern to protect state legislative sovereignty in a federalist system; the Court was not unusually troubled by the fact that the Prorate Act was clearly "anti-competitive,"

---

[3] *Parker* v. *Brown*, 317 US 341 (1943). Without the Parker holding, the Supremacy Clause of the US Constitution would invalidate all regulations that violated federal antitrust laws.

[4] The negative Commerce Clause is largely a court-developed doctrine that restricts states from discriminating against out-of-state residents. As such it stands as a possible constraint on the ability of states to approve regulations which generate out-of-state spillovers. Because of its narrow focus on discrimination toward out-of-state residents, however, the negative Commerce Clause does not act to limit regulations affecting only within state residents. Where the negative Commerce Clause does have a potential role to play is when a state business regulation creates significant interstate monopoly spillovers.

[5] *Parker*, 317 US at 341, 350–1 (1943).

cartelizing California's raisin producers by restricting output and raising the price of raisins.

In its dormant Commerce Clause analysis, the *Parker* court did concern itself with the substantive economic facts of the California regulation on residents within and outside the state, but importantly, it chose to evaluate those facts in political, rather than economic, terms. The court seemed persuaded by the fact that the raisin production was confined largely to California. However, the fact that 95 percent of raisins consumed in the US were grown in California was interpreted by the court not as a source of potential monopoly powers capable of causing harmful economic spillovers, but rather as a fortunate configuration of interests for ensuring maximum political participation by all interested raisin producers. In the opinion, the court rested its judicial restraint on a view of federalism emphasizing state legislative sovereignty: "In a dual system of government in which, under the Constitution, the states are sovereign, save only as Congress may constitutionally subtract from their authority, an unexpressed purpose to nullify a state's control over its officers and agents is not lightly to be attributed to Congress."[6] To the court, only the legislature of the state of California, and no other governmental unit, had the proper incentive to worry about the plight of the raisin growers of California.[7]

It seems clear that the *Parker* court understood there were economic consequences outside of California, but that absent any explicit action by Congress to remedy such consequences, the court believed that the action by the state legislature was sufficient to warrant the state action exemption. Looking favorably upon decentralized political decision-making, the court set the path along which all subsequent state action doctrine would evolve: the economic consequences of state regulations would be largely ignored, provided those regulations were decided by an open, participatory political process, as evidenced by state legislative involvement.

The court's decision in *California Retail Liquor Dealers Association* v. *Midcal Aluminum, Inc.*[8] was the defining step in the development of the court's current political participation test for state action immunity. The court faced the question of whether the involvement of a state agency in a per se violation of the antitrust laws – supporting a resale price maintenance scheme for wine distributors – would render the scheme immune from the federal antitrust laws. The state legislature had clearly authorized price setting and provided an enforcement mechanism, but the state did

---

[6] 317 US at 351. But the *Parker* court was clear that this protection would not extend so readily to municipalities. Because municipalities are not sovereign entities, the immunity granted by the court to the acts of states would only translate to the acts of a municipality if the municipality were acting under the explicit authority of the state; *Parker*, at 350–1.

[7] Interestingly, the Supreme Court's interest in the California raisin business has been reinvigorated in this most recent session. In *Horne et al.* v. *Department of Agriculture* (October term, 2014), the court reviewed an arrangement in which a portion of the net proceeds of the sale of raisins went into a reserve that was given to the Department of Agriculture free of charge. The court held that compensation for a taking was required in this case, even though the transfer involved personal rather than real property.

[8] 445 US 97 (1980).

not establish prices, review the reasonableness of price schedules, regulate the terms of fair trade contracts, monitor market conditions, or engage in any "pointed reexamination" of the program.[9]

After reviewing the facts, the court put forth a two-part participation test to determine whether a state regulatory system should be immune from antitrust liability: (1) "the challenged restraint must be 'one clearly articulated and affirmatively expressed as state policy,'" and (2) "the policy must be 'actively supervised' by the State itself." The state interests identified by the state court were "to promote temperance" and to "[p]rotect small licensees from predatory market pricing policies of larger retailers." Although there was a clearly articulated state resale price maintenance policy approved by the state legislature, the liquor pricing program was deemed to violate the second prong of the court's proposed test. The court found there was no indication that the program was actively supervised, since there was no supervision or review of the prices set by the producers and wholesalers.

As an approach for protecting political participation of the citizens of the state in regulatory policymaking, *Midcal's* two-part test has proven to be an important step forward. Requiring the clear articulation of the regulatory policy by the state legislature, the first prong helps to ensure that all interested parties know of and have the opportunity to be involved in the original political agreement. Demanding that the legislature actively supervise the approved regulation, the second prong assures the original participants that their initial bargain will be enforced. The second prong gives meaning to the first, for without supervision, interested individuals cannot be assured that their initial participation in the political process will be meaningful. Subsequent cases have reinforced the importance, and clarified the reach, of each part of *Midcal's* two-part participation test.

Of particular interest to the antitrust community, it is notable that over time the court has tightened the constraint for regulations set by private parties. To illustrate, in *Ticor Title*[10] the Federal Trade Commission (FTC) sued six title insurance companies for unfair competition, alleging that they had fixed prices for title searches and examinations. The insurance companies belonged to rating bureaus which were licensed – but *not* appointed – by the state legislature, and which submitted rates to the state that went into effect if the state did not act within thirty days. Despite the fact that the insurers had participated in the rate-making process, the court denied state action immunity, holding that the state had not actively supervised the rate-making process. A rate-making policy that had been generated by the political process, absent active supervision by the state, may have been "captured" by the industry being regulated, a result contrary to the original regulatory goals.

---

9   Ibid., at 105–6.
10 *FTC v. Ticor Title Ins. Co.*, 504 US 621, 625 (1992).

More recently, in *North Carolina Dental* the Supreme Court supported a lower court's opinion that a state dental board's restriction on the provision of teeth-whitening services violated the Sherman Act because it was not adequately super-vised by an independent state authority.[11] Licensing boards present a thorny problem because they have characteristics of both public and private entities. On the one hand, states authorize them to regulate certain aspects of their respective professions. On the other hand, they are typically composed of market participants, thus raising the specter of regulatory capture. In *North Carolina Dental*, seven of the eight members of the board were market participants who had been elected by their peers. The dispute sprang from the growing provision of teeth-whitening services, which the state's Dental Practice Act defines as a dental service, by non-dentists. In response to complaints by dentists, the board opened an investigation and ultimately issued cease-and-desist letters that succeeded in pushing non-dentist practitioners out of the market. In 2011, the FTC had ruled that the board's conduct was anticompetitive and the board appealed to the Fourth Circuit in part on the ground that as a formal state agency it is not subject to the active supervision test. The court disagreed, holding that the board is essentially a private actor since it is operated by market participants and its members are elected by market participants.[12] The Supreme Court's affirmation was on a 6:3 vote.

As in its specification of its clear articulation test, the court has defined the domain of the active supervision requirement with the goal of maximizing political partici-pation clearly in mind. Local political participation is encouraged, as local residents are allowed to set local regulations subject to the limits of the enabling state statutes and to see those regulations enforced as they wish. Together the current state action doctrine's two-pronged *clear articulation* and *active supervision* test provides impor-tant safeguards for the goal of political participation. The most participatory of all political bodies – state and local government legislatures – are assigned a central responsibility for the design and enforcement of business regulations. Only when those branches of government have been pushed aside or ignored does federal government supervision through federal antitrust law come to bear. By showing a clear, but moderated deference to state and local legislatures – arguably the branches of government "closest to the people" – the Court significantly advances the goal of political participation in regulatory policymaking. It is in this sense that

---

[11] *N.C. State Board of Dental Examiners v. FTC*, 135 S. Ct. 1101, 2015.

[12] A number of circuits have taken a different approach. In *Earles v. State Bd. of Certified Pub. Accountants*, the court ruled that a licensing board consisting entirely of market participants was exempt from the active supervision test because it is "functionally similar to a municipality" and "the public nature of the Board's actions means that there is little danger of a cozy arrangement to restrict competition" (139 F.3d 1033, 1041 (5th Cir., 1998)). In *Hass v. Oregon State Bar*, the court applied a more nuanced analysis and exempted the Board of Governors of the state bar from the active supervision test after considering a number of factors that appeared to restrain the board's ability to pursue private interests, including: three of the board's fifteen members were non-lawyers; the records and accounts of the bar were open to public inspection; the members of the board were subject to a code of ethics applicable to all public officials (883 F.2d 1453, 1460 (9th Cir., 989)).

the US federal system of antitrust enforcement may have some advantage over the European system – a system that has some rigidity and substantial political uncertainty.

As currently constituted, however, the US system fails miserably with respect to the treatment of externalities. While the current state action doctrine offers citizens a clear political voice in determining regulatory policies *within* their state, the present doctrine offers no such protection for regulatory policies decided in neighboring states. Such protections are neither needed nor desired when state policies have no cross-border economic effects. But when one state's economic regulations create significant interjurisdictional economic spillovers, then affected residents in neighboring states may be harmed. More about this central, crucial issue momentarily.

18.3 EU ANTITRUST FEDERALISM: THE PRINCIPLE OF SUBSIDIARITY

In the context of the EU, subsidiarity is a principle of governance designed to give meaning to the divisions of responsibility between the center and the Member States. The principle seeks to allocate responsibilities for policy formation to the lowest level of government at which the objectives of that policy can be successfully achieved. Inman and I have explained that this principle is consistent with and supportive of a system of decentralized federalism.[13] In the context of the European Union, decentralized federalism would combine the Tiebout model of competitive Member State governments with Ronald Coase's model of efficient bargaining. The assignment of governmental functions in this world allocates all policy responsibilities, at least initially, to the Member States. Member states then have the option of jointly allocating some of their responsibilities to the center. Deciding what those centrally allocated policies should be, belongs (in principle) to the European Parliament and the Council of Ministers.

The success of a system of decentralized federalism that is consistent with the principle of subsidiarity is open to debate. As witnessed by recent events, there is a limit to the ability of Member States to protect individual rights to personal freedom, political rights, and property rights. A strong center is required to ensure the right of individual's to move freely and to support the rights of Member States to enforce policies that do not generate substantial externalities. From my perspective, the goal of a fully formed EU political entity should be modeled on a system of democratic federalism, one which builds on the advantages of a centralized EU "constitution" that protects rights and promotes political participation. However,

---

[13] Robert P. Inman and Daniel L. Rubinfeld, 'Subsidiarity and the European Union', in Peter Newman (ed.), *The New Palgrave Dictionary of Economics and Law* (Macmillan, 1998), 545; Robert P. Inman and Daniel L. Rubinfeld, 'Subsidiarity, Governance, and E.U. Economic Policy' (2002) 3(4) *CESifoForum* 3.

consistent with basic federalism principles, the assignment of governmental responsibilities should be made so that responsibilities are given to the governmental unit that can make the strongest contribution to ensuring personal, political, and economic liberties.

That is the theory; I now move on to consider how the two regimes have compared in practice.

18.4 A COMPARISON OF THE TWO REGIMES

On paper, application of the principle of subsidiarity to the allocation of responsibilities for the oversight of competition issues appears well suited to foster the principles underlying the ideals of a system of democratic federalism. Indeed, the application of the subsidiarity principle effectively codifies a reasonable and potentially efficient treatment of externalities. With respect to antitrust-related issues, there are a number of articles that provide a relatively rigid set of rules that define antitrust federalism. First, Articles 34 and 35 TFEU prohibit state measures that restrain imports or exports. This is strongly suggestive of a "no externality" rule.[14] Second, Article 4(3) TEU (ex Article 10 TEC) makes it clear that Member States "shall facilitate the achievement of the Union's tasks," and therefore do not undertake actions that would reduce the effectiveness of EU competition law.[15] Furthermore, there is no equivalent to the US's Eleventh Amendment which protects (under certain conditions) sovereign state entities from suit claiming certain violations of the federal antitrust laws.

Third, if there is conduct that is seen to violate Article 101 TFEU (restraints of trade), Member State competition authorities have a responsibility to "disapply" the national legislation and may impose penalties on conduct that was encouraged by the national legislation. Professor Fox provides a wonderful example that supports the clarity of EU law at least as seen in comparison to the US. In her 2003 "Italian paper," Fox takes a close looks at an important EU federalism case: *Italian Matches: Commission v. Italy*.[16] Italy had delegated the right to set tariffs to a competitor's association. The court concluded that the competitor's association had the ability to set minimum and maximum prices, and as such violated Article 101 TFEU. So, the

---

[14] As Fox, 'State Action', at 471 points out, "EC law has Articles 28 and 29 [now Articles 34 and 35 TFEU], which are stronger versions of the US Commerce Clause. While the US Constitution says merely that Congress can regulate commerce, and it impliedly prohibits state measures that constitute undue burdens on commerce (the dormant Commerce Clause), the EC Treaty states affirmatively that Member States may not impose 'quantitative restrictions' or 'measures having equivalent effect' on imports [Article 34 TFEU] or exports [Article 35 TFEU]."

[15] Note, in particular, the claim of Wainwright and Bouquet that Article 4(3) TEU (former Article 10 TEC) requires the EU "not to adopt or maintain in force any measure which could deprive [EC competition law] of its effectiveness" (Richard Wainwright and Andre Bouquet, 'State Intervention and Action in EC Competition Law' (2004) *Fordham Corp. L. Inst.* (B. Hawk ed.), 539, 540).

[16] (CNSD), Case 35-96, [1998], ECR I-3851.

US's *Parker* v. *Brown* decision, still relevant in US jurisprudence, would likely be overturned if subject to EU law.

Fox spells out a clear, articulate interpretation of the application of EU law to competition issues. Specifically, she comments that "[w]hen States violate EC law, injured private persons and the Member States' own antitrust authorities and courts may hold them to account. Indeed, Member State competition authorities may have a duty – among their many other tasks – to ferret out offending Member State law."[17] To further cement the point that the EU treats the externality question directly, Fox points out that "[t]he States cannot fulfill the task of harmonizing rights of state regulation with rights of free trade and competition as well as the center; too much deference to state sovereignty on this point and for this task will unacceptably undermine Community."[18]

For these and other reasons, as it currently stands the EU antitrust regime offers a clearer delineation of powers and functions than does the US system. Were the discussion to stop at this point, one would have to agree that with respect to antitrust federalism, the EU design trumps currently US law. But, to this outsider, the EU system is missing several elements that are not as easily remedied. First, there appears to be an incomplete accounting of the political economy of Member State regulatory politics – one that shows an appreciation of the benefits of local political participation – a reflection of the differing values of local cultures and local political and economic interests. Second, the EU relies heavily on a model of cooperative federalism – a model that is breaking down as Member State interests are beginning to trump federal interests – Brexit and Greece being two recent examples. Third, the agenda-setting powers of the Council of Ministers is limited and the politics of universalism (Member States acting in their self-interest rather than the federal interest) appears to characterize the behavior of the expanded European Parliament. A more ideal model – democratic (decentralized) federalism, which incorporates the principle of subsidiarity and a stronger system of EU governance, and which was largely the objective underpinning modernization and the adoption of Regulation 1/2003, seems less and less attainable.

Professor Fox's advocacy of the EU antitrust regime is compelling. Indeed, it is hard to disagree with her compelling argument that the European Union's law of state action is "significantly more competition-friendly than its counterpart in U.S. law."[19] But, as just described, its future is uncertain as the internal politics of the EU ebbs and flows. Furthermore, the structural design of the EU leaves the effectiveness of rights and activities relating to political participation uncertain. While preferences driven by local

---

[17] Fox, 'State Action', 473.
[18] For an updated perspective, see Fox and Healey, 'When the State Harms Competition', in which the authors point to areas in which nations' competition laws can usefully proscribe certain anticompetitive state acts while not interfering with the state's prerogative to govern; and discusses the normative implications of (more) antitrust coverage of state acts.
[19] Fox, 'State Action', 474.

culture and local political interests are readily expressed at the Member State level, the same cannot be said for participation at the EU level. In the US many citizens are active in elections for both the House of Representatives and the Senate, whereas the majority of residents of the EU appear to have little or no idea as to who represents them in the Europe Parliament or for that matter in the Council of Ministers.

While both the EU and the US federal systems can be improved with respect to antitrust enforcement, I am somewhat more sanguine about long-term prospects in the US. As I see it, the US system can be readily improved, through a combination of statutory and legal interventions. While great patience will be required, I see improvement as politically feasible. As has been noted, currently, the US courts require the answers to two questions: (1) is the regulation clearly articulated? (2) Is it actively supervised? If the answer to both is yes, the state action is exempt. I propose that the courts add a third question. Are there any interjurisdictional monopoly spillovers with the potential to significantly harm customers outside the state? If the answer to that question is yes, then there is no exemption. With the addition of this externality hurdle, a relatively weak (on efficiency grounds) state action doctrine can be transformed into one that can achieve both efficiency and participation goals.

As an alternative, the externality problem can be remedied through statutory action, action that would recognize the problems created by interjurisdictional spillovers in the current antitrust exemptions cases. Inman and I have offered one solution.[20] We suggest a detailed "spillover test" which the courts can use to identify those instances in which interjurisdictional economic harm may have been imposed on out-of-state residents without their prior political approval. If a state regulation fails the test, we argue it should be subject to Sherman Act review. Our proposed spillover test enhances overall economic efficiency in the regulatory economy and contributes to the goal of political participation. If this were to become law, either through the common law or through statutory intervention, I believe that the US federal system, one that is more mature than the European system both politically and economically, can provide a tool that allows us to determine the appropriate protections for active state policymaking, and can promote and protect a truly political process for setting regulatory policies.[21]

---

[20] Inman and Rubinfeld, 'Making Sense of the Antitrust State Action Doctrine'.

[21] A number of scholars, including Andrew Guzman and Eleanor Fox and Deborah Healey have discussed how the externality problem can best be handled by some form of international regulatory authority. Guzman believes that the regulation of international antitrust requires the adoption of substantive international standards and that the place to establish such standards is the World Trade Organization (WTO). See Andrew Guzman, 'Antitrust and International Regulatory Federalism' (2001), 76 *New York University Law Review* 1142; Fox and Healey, 'When the State Harms Competition'. At this point in time, it appears that the WTO is unlikely to take on such a task. The more operative question is whether the current International Competition Network can be transformed into Professor Fox's ideal of a world competition forum.

19

Galvanising National Competition Authorities in the European Union

Giorgio Monti

19.1 INTRODUCTION

Absent a global antitrust authority, Fox and Arena envisage a world where there is 'more and deeper coordination through regional and world systems'.[1] Their concern with this approach to global antitrust is whether the coordinating entities would apply 'global norms of procedure, process and performance' and who would monitor them.[2]

The European Union's competition authorities, brought together by the European Competition Network (ECN), might be seen as the prime example of deep regional cooperation: the Commission and national competition authorities (NCAs) apply the same antitrust provisions, coordinate enforcement through a reporting system, and the ECN serves as a site for discussion and deliberation. Indeed, when reflecting on the tenth anniversary of this system of enforcement, the then Director General for Competition Policy noted that in that first decade, the Commission had taken only 134 decisions while the NCAs had taken 736.[3] It followed, in the view of the Commission that 'EU competition rules are the law of the land'.[4] According to Commission officials, this successful system had two glitches: the first is that the NCAs could be even more effective if there was procedural harmonisation;[5] the second was that the new system did not seem to allow the Commission to increase its productivity.[6] This narrative falls nicely within the concerns

---

[1] E. M. Fox and A. Arena, 'The International Institutions of Competition Law', in E. M. Fox and M. J. Trebilcock, *The Design of Competition Law Institutions: Global Norms, Local Choices* (Oxford University Press, 2013)

[2] Ibid.

[3] A. Italianer, 'Completing Convergence' Speech at European Competition Day 10 October 2014 (http://ec.europa.eu/competition/speeches/text/sp2014_05_en.pdf).

[4] Commission, Ten Years of Antitrust Enforcement under Regulation 1/2003: Achievements and Future Perspectives COM(2014) 453, para. 23.

[5] Ibid., para. 46.

[6] W. Wils, 'Ten Years of Regulation 1/2003: A Retrospective' (2013) 4(1) *Journal of European Competition Law and Practice* 293.

expressed by Fox and Arena: it reveals how one regional group seeks to supplement coordination with regional procedural norms, and the kinds of monitoring mechanisms that may be designed to accompany them.

This chapter is organised as follows. Section 19.2 discusses this narrative and the steps currently being taken, in particular the 'ECN plus' project, which has culminated in a Directive to harmonise antitrust procedures across the Member States. However, as shown in section 19.3, this narrative suffers from a major defect: it is based on the premise that antitrust enforcement by NCAs is 'regional' in any meaningful sense. Instead, the evidence reveals that for the most part NCAs operate to address market failures at local level. Instances where NCAs apply EU competition law to anticompetitive conduct beyond their borders are exceptional and controversial. From this perspective, the ECN plus project appears premature. Thus, in section 19.4 we suggest that NCAs could usefully move in the following directions: further extraterritorial enforcement, deeper coordinated enforcement and more attention to competition advocacy. These measures would do more to achieve the ambition set out by DG Competition in the ECN plus project: that 'NCAs should, like the Commission, act in the general interest of the EU'.[7] The suggestions we make are accompanied by a governance structure which is atypical of antitrust.

19.2 MODALITIES FOR PROCEDURAL, PROCESS AND PERFORMANCE ALIGNMENT

There are three sites through which procedural convergence may take place: the European legislator, the ECN and the courts. Before considering each in turn, it is worth summarising how the system of enforcement of EU competition law has evolved to date.[8]

The NCAs of EU Member States work closely together and with the European Commission. The legal sources of this close working relationship are two. First, Member States adopted (in the period between 1990 and 2003) antitrust rules that mimic those of the EU. Furthermore, some Member States have introduced provisions by which the interpretation of national law is aligned to that of the EU.[9] The interpretation of national and EU Law is also rendered closer by the ECJ allowing references for a preliminary ruling on the interpretation of national law in a number of instances where national law provisions are very similar to the EU rules.[10] The second source is Regulation 1/2003, which came into force on 1

---

[7] DG Competition, Inception Impact Assessment 'Enhancing Competition in the EU for the benefit of businesses and consumers: reinforcement of the Application of EU Competition Law by National Competition Authorities' (2015).

[8] For a more detailed analysis, see D. Gerard, 'Public Enforcement: The ECN – Network Antitrust Enforcement in the European Union', in I. Lianos and D. Geradin (eds.), *Handbook of European Competition Law: Enforcement and Procedure* (Edward Elgar, 2013)

[9] The most notable example is found in the UK: Competition Act 1998, s. 60.

[10] e.g. Case C-32/11, *Allianz Hungaria* [2013] ECLI:EU:C:2013:160, paras. 17–23.

May 2004.[11] This Regulation contains certain provisions that bring the Commission and the NCAs (and national courts to a lesser degree) close together. In particular, Article 3 provides that if a suspected practice affects trade between Member States, then an NCA shall apply EU competition law (i.e. Articles 101 and 102 TFEU) in parallel with national law. Furthermore, save in certain circumstances, the application of national competition law cannot lead to a stricter approach than the application of EU Law.[12] The intended effect of this is that the same rules will apply irrespective of jurisdiction. In addition to this, the ECN was established as a forum for coordinating the activities of the network members.[13] The original aim of the ECN was to allocate cases among various NCAs should two or more authorities claim jurisdiction over a particular case. It was also designed as a forum to facilitate the transfer of information among authorities.

The economic rationale behind this framework is that convergent rules facilitate cross-border business, and coordinated enforcement can be more efficient. From the perspective of certain Member States, using EU law served as a means of upgrading national competition rules (e.g. for the UK and Italy). From the perspective of the European Union, it was also felt that the system would allow competition agencies to take cases where they have a comparative advantage, and this would leave the Commission better able to set its own priorities.[14]

19.2.1 The ECN Plus Project

The operation of Regulation 1/2003 was reviewed five and ten years after its coming into force.[15] Alongside much self-congratulation about the success of this initiative, the Commission took the opportunity of identifying ways to adjust this framework so as to improve its performance. This has resulted in a legislative initiative which is designed to harmonise some of the procedural aspects of competition law enforcement.[16]

---

[11] Regulation 1/2003, On the implementation of the rules on competition laid down in Articles 81 and 82 of the Treaty [2003] OJ L1/1.

[12] The exceptions are instances where unilateral conduct is regulated more strictly under some domestic laws, notably the German, French and Italian laws.

[13] The text establishing the ECN is the *Joint Statement of the Council and the Commission on the Functioning of the Network of Competition Authorities*, at http://ec.europa.eu/competition/ecn/join t_statement_en.pdf

[14] Commission, White Paper on Modernisation of the Rules Implementing Articles 85 and 86 of the EC Treaty (24 April 1999) [1999] OJ C132/1

[15] Communication from the Commission to the European Parliament and the Council, Report on the functioning of Regulation 1/2003 COM(2009) 206 final; Commission, Ten Years of Antitrust Enforcement under Regulation 1/2003.

[16] Directive 2019/1 empower the competition authorities of the Member States to be more effective enforcers and to ensure the proper functioning of the internal market [2019] OJ L11/3

The Directive is motivated by four considerations: improving enforcement tools, harmonising fining powers, making leniency regimes more coherent and enhancing the independence and resources of NCAs. It is beyond the scope of this chapter to examine this proposal in detail, but certain aspects are worth noting.[17]

The first is that harmonisation is grounded on procedures governing the Commission's own investigatory and decision-making powers. The assumption is that the Commission has the best-developed procedural system and this can be helpfully bequeathed to other NCAs. There may well be grounds for this stance in view of the Commission's experience but it is striking that the impression given is that no Member State has been able to identify a single procedural improvement to complement those at the hands of the Commission which might be usefully passed on to other NCAs. This approach is probably driven by the legal measure being used: rather than a 'Regulation 2', which might have served to reform the Commission's procedures as well as those of NCAs, the Commission opted for a Directive whose sole ambition is reforming NCAs. Thus, the rules on inspection and the provisions on remedies as well as those on fines largely replicate the powers the Commission has.[18]

The second is that many provisions of the Directive appear to be based on earlier attempts by the ECN to invite Member States to upgrade national procedures. The ECN released a number of documents detailing what agencies considered best practices; admittedly these instruments have not proved sufficiently persuasive for Member States. This shift from soft to hard law points to some limits in the role that networks can play in harmonisation. In this context it is striking that the Directive even covers leniency policies: one would have assumed that in this field, where NCAs can enact a policy independent of the legislature, the ECN would have served as a sufficient mechanism to encourage all Member States to adopt the same type of leniency policy, but it evidently was not the case.[19] Furthermore, the Directive's codification of leniency is limited in ambition: it shied away from creating a single registry so that a would-be leniency applicant could send a single bundle of documents to one address, irrespective of which agency takes the case: multiple filings will remain even after the Directive.[20]

---

[17]   For a critical overview, see G. Monti, 'The Proposed Directive to Empower National Competition Authorities: Too Much, Too Little or Just Right?' (2017) 3(3) *Competition Law and Policy Debate* 40–7.

[18]   Directive 2019/1, Arts. 6–16.

[19]   ECN Model Leniency Programme (2012), at http://ec.europa.eu/competition/ecn/mlp_revise d_2012_en.pdf. This is based on the earlier survey: ECN Model Leniency Programme: Report on the Assessment of the State of Convergence, at http://ec.europa.eu/competition/ecn/model_lenien cy_programme.pdf

[20]   Thus the difficulties that DHL found itself in have not gone away. See Case C-428/14, *DHL Express (Italy)* v. *Autorità Garante della Concorrenza e del Mercato* [2016] ECLI:EU:C:2016:27.

In sum, the most significant aspects of procedure which the Directive seeks to harmonise reveal a weakness of the ECN as an engine for convergence, and not just because of intransigent legislatures at national level.

19.2.2 *The ECN as a Site for Monitoring NCAs*

Article 11 of Regulation 1/2003 is a key provision to ensure coordination among the network of competition agencies: NCAs inform the Commission shortly after the first formal investigative measure; draft decisions are notified to the Commission before adoption and these may be discussed by the members of the Network via the Advisory Committee.[21] These discussions allow for an exchange of opinion among members of the network. Article 11(6) provides that the Commission can remove a case from the hands of an NCA, which reads like a threat should an NCA express a desire to take decisions that deviate from what the Commission would wish for.[22] This threat is also made explicit in the so-called 'Network Notice' that accompanies Regulation 1/2003 where the Commission explains the possible grounds upon which Article 11 (6) may be triggered, which include differences among NCAs taking parallel cases, unreasonable delay by an NCA in reaching a decision, or an NCA proposing a decision out of line with the appropriate interpretation of EU competition law.[23] At the time Regulation 1/2003 was being discussed, the fear among some was that NCAs might act politically and protect national firms: it was felt that Commission oversight might reduce this risk. This power has never been exercised. However, it likely serves as a 'nuclear' option if gentler nudging by the Commission and other NCAs fails to sway an NCA who is proposing to deviate from the rules. As with other matters of European law, it is likely that the Commission's power to influence NCAs varies depending on which NCA is under the radar: weaker agencies might feel more compelled to obey than those that are well established.

The ECN also performs a sort of peer-review function. It does so in two ways: informally when agencies discuss policy matters, this can provide the motivation to do one's best and not to be perceived by other NCAs as lagging behind. The club creates pressure to keep up with generally accepted standards. There is also a more formal mechanism for peer review, which are studies on the degree of convergence among the NCAs. For example, in the implementation of leniency policies the ECN studied how far the standards were convergent.[24] This serves as further peer pressure for NCAs to upgrade their enforcement tools to the required standards. However, as noted above, in this context peer pressure was not enough to align leniency policies.

---

[21] Commission Notice on cooperation within the Network of Competition Authorities OJ C 101/43, para. 61 [hereafter, the Network Notice].
[22] Regulation 1/2003, Art. 11
[23] Network Notice, para. 54.
[24] Above, n. 19.

The ECN has no legal personality and so it cannot be challenged. At the same time, it is an influential body insofar as it enjoys a degree of soft power to influence NCAs that deviate from the norm. In this setting, seeking to render the ECN judicially accountable would be disproportionate: in most instances where the ECN may suggest a course of action for one NCA the party who is adversely affected can seek judicial review of that NCA, and through this action the ECJ may be asked to provide advice on the proper interpretation of the competition rules. At the same time, a greater degree of transparency and participation might be provided when the ECN works on policy issues.

19.2.3 Courts

The ECJ has for many years served as a watchdog over the Commission's enforcement powers. While there is ongoing discussion about how far the ECJ's case law has served to control the Commission with sufficient alacrity, it is undeniable that appeals against Commission decisions have served to shape current procedural rules. While the Commission is largely kept in check by the ECJ, the powers of NCAs are checked against national constitutional provisions and by the benchmarks fixed by the European Convention of Human Rights.

For instance in *T-Mobile* the ECJ gave guidance on the meaning of the notion of concerted practice.[25] While the Dutch court followed the ECJ in holding that a concerted practice may be presumed by a finding that competitors exchanged information, it also added a further nuance, relying on the provisions of the European Convention on Human Rights. The national court held that this presumption should be rebuttable and it quashed the NCA's decision for failing to consider alternative explanations offered by the defendants about the conduct that occurred after the incriminating meeting.[26] Likewise, national procedures may be kept in check by the European Court of Human Rights, as occurred in *Menarini v. Italy* where the procedural soundness of the Italian appeals system was upheld by a majority if the judges.[27]

The merits of these judgments are beyond the scope of discussion here. The salient point for note is that national and supranational courts are capable of testing the degree to which procedures serve to safeguard the rights of the defendants. This scrutiny appears particularly important in light of the Directive, for it

---

[25] Case C-8/08, *T-Mobile Netherlands BV, KPN Mobile NV, Orange Nederland NV and Vodafone Libertel NV* v. *Raad van bestuur van de Nederlandse Mededingingsautoriteit*, ECLI:EU:C:2009:343.

[26] P. L. Parcu and Monti (eds.), *European Networking and Training for National Competition Enforcers ENTraNCE for Judges 2014: Selected Case Notes*, pp. 72–7. In subsequent judgments, the ECJ also refers to the importance of the presumption of innocence, see e.g. Case C-74/14, *Eturas and others v. Lietuvos Respublikos konkurencijos taryba*.

[27] A. Menarini Diagnostics S.r.l. v. *Italy* – 43509/08, judgment of 27 September 2011. For discussion, see R. Wesselig and M. van der Woude, 'The Lawfulness and Acceptability of European Cartel Law' (2012) 35(4) *World Competition* 573.

creates reassurances that the increased powers of NCAs will not go unchecked. Should the Directive be agreed, the review of some procedural matters will become bifurcated: while decisions of NCAs might be reviewed by the European Court of Human Rights, the decisions of the Commission will remain under the scrutiny of the ECJ. Time will tell how far these two courts will converge in the manner in which similar rights are recognised.

Taking stock of the discussion thus far, the European experience might be read to suggest that this regional group has succeeded in identifying superior regional procedural standards by which to apply EU competition law, and that it has created a soft law-based network of cooperation which includes some hard law monitoring of various types: the Commission retains ultimate responsibility for the integrity of the network through its oversight of national cases and its power to remove any NCA's competence; and national and supranational courts serve as independent arbiters to ensure procedural fairness standards balance effective enforcement with the respect of fundamental rights.

19.3 ENFORCEMENT PATTERNS OF NCAS

The above narrative is based on a misreading of what NCAs are actually doing. As we show here, the bulk of NCA enforcement of Articles 101 and 102 concerns issues of domestic concern; the sole reason that NCAs are applying EU law is because of the expansive interpretation of the notion of effect of trade between Member States.[28] Other than this, NCA enforcement is nearly always based on local problems. We review some of this evidence in section 19.3.1. Moreover, as suggested in section 19.3.2 this emphasis on domestic effects leads to an unnecessary duplication of procedures, which is inadvertently facilitated by the ECJ. True supranational enforcement by NCAs remains exceptional, and two examples are discussed in section 19.3.3.

19.3.1 *Provincialism*

It has been shown that in a number of the Member States which joined the EU in 2004 the NCAs reveal a tendency to apply national competition law more frequently than its EU counterpart.[29] The authors put this down to the narrow interpretation that is given to the notion of effect on trade between Member States. One might wonder why an NCA would be so motivated, after all in many cases the national and EU standards are aligned. As shown above, cases where Articles 101 and 102 are engaged are rendered transparent and may be discussed by other NCAs at ECN

---

[28] See on this the recent excessive pricing case.

[29] M. Botta, A. Svetlicinii and M. Bernatt, 'The Assessment of the Effect on Trade by the National Competition Authorities of the "New" Member States: Another Legal Partition of the Internal Market?' (2015) 52(5) *Common Market Law Review* 1247.

meetings. Could it be that in some instances NCAs are reluctant to undergo this form of peer assessment?

More generally, the significant number of instances where conduct is analysed under national competition law suggests that NCAs are even more important than the Commission seeks to acknowledge. After all, whether antitrust enforcement occurs through the application of national or EU competition law, the result should be the same: greater deterrence of conduct that reduces consumer welfare or raises entry barriers. The public good delivered by competition enforcement does not vary depending on whether the law applied is national or European.

Turning to the cases where the NCA applies EU competition law, nearly all cases are about domestic issues. Take any reference for a preliminary ruling that emanates from appeals against NCA decisions and you will see that the infringement is local, for example: in *Pierre Fabre*[30] the ban on internet sales is France-wide, in *Telia Sonera*[31] the margin squeeze only affected Sweden, in *Tele 2 Polska*[32] the non-infringements at stake involved the Polish market, in *DHL*[33] the cartel was situated in Italy, and *Eturas*[34] concerned collusion on the Lithuanian market. Even a more systematic review of all decisions of NCAs would reveal the same pattern: NCAs investigate local or national markets.

At the same time, it should be noted that whether EU or national law is applied, the fine tends not to change. Most NCAs have no power to impose a fine for the effects that conduct has outside the national borders. This leads to the paradoxical situation that NCAs apply EU law because the conduct in question has anticompetitive effects but are then unable or unwilling to vary the level of penalty based on the presence or absence of cross-border effects. For example, in the one cartel case taken by the UK NCA applying EU competition law there is an extensive analysis of the facts and the law when considering the application of the Chapter 1 prohibition of the Competition Act 1998, followed by a very short account of why that conduct also infringes Article 101.[35] However, one might expect that the level of the fine might change if conduct has cross-border impact, but no such alterations are made. But some NCAs have taken the view that they have no powers to impose fines for effects outside their borders.[36] Then, it is not clear what the practical, added value, of applying EU Law is: neither the competition analysis nor the fine is affected by the parallel application of national and EU competition law.

---

[30] Case C-439/09, *Pierre Fabre Dermo-Cosmétique SAS* v. *Président de l'Autorité de la concurrence*, ECLI:EU:C:2011:649.

[31] Case C-52/09, *Konkurrensverket* v. *TeliaSonera Sverige AB*, ECLI:EU:C:2011:83.

[32] Case C-375/09, *Prezes Urzędu Ochrony Konkurencji i Konsumentów* v. *Tele2 Polska sp*, ECLI:EU: C:2011:270.

[33] Case C-428/14, *DHL Express (Italy) Srl and DHL Global Forwarding (Italy) SpA* v. *Autorità Garante della Concorrenza*, ECLI:EU:C:2016:27.

[34] C-74/14, '*Eturas' UAB and Others* v. *Lietuvos Respublikos konkurencijos taryba*, ECLI:EU:C:2016:42.

[35] Office of Fair Trading, Decision No. CA98/01/2012, *Airline passenger fuel surcharges for long-haul flights* https://assets.publishing.service.gov.uk/media/555de2a24of0b666a200001c/fuel-surcharges.pdf

[36] Bundeskartellamt, Activity Report 2003/2004 p. XIII.

In addition to NCAs applying EU competition law solely within its borders, the advent of Regulation 1/2003 has not seen much change in the Commission's policy. It was thought that as a result of this reform the Commission would be better able to set priorities, and be more proactive. However, we see no major shift in the kinds of cases it takes, nor in the number of enforcement actions taken. Why not? We can only hypothesise: (1) the Commission had to handle a lot of state aid cases involving the banking sector as a result of the financial crisis; (2) the Commission takes more complex cases, which is clearly the case if one looks at the length of decisions like *Intel* (rebates, 518 pages) or *Lundbeck* (reverse patent settlements, 464 pages); (3) the Commission invests in market studies which allow it to better understand how markets work. However, even if all of these are true, is there not an enforcement gap? That is to say: if NCAs take local cases and the Commission is selective on the transnational cases it takes, are some transnational cases escaping scrutiny? If so, should not (some) NCAs step into the breach?

19.3.2 *Splitting up Cross-Border Cases*

An even more worrying phenomenon is that some cases with cross-border effects are divided up among NCAs. The most prominent example is the flour mills cartel. This was investigated and pursued by four NCAs contemporaneously.[37] The players were often the same undertakings in all jurisdictions and the nature of the infringement pursued by the NCAs was very similar: price fixing, coordinated shutdowns of mills and (in some) an agreement to divide markets. There was some coordination on the fines set because of the economic situation of some of the undertakings: the Dutch NCA lowered its fine 'provided that the combined fines for the undertaking concerned would be in line with the jointly assessed ability to pay of this undertaking'.[38] In obtaining this result, we are told that the two NCAs

> are happy with their cooperation on inability to pay in their parallel proceedings involving the same undertaking. This transnational cooperation, complex though as it was, proved efficient for the undertakings involved and for the competition authorities.[39]

Clearly this solution is pragmatic and based on common sense. On the other hand, it is not clear why it was the Dutch who had to lower their fine. The same result would have obtained if the second authority to impose a fine (the Bundeskartellamt, whose decision was given on 25 October 2011) were to take into consideration the fines imposed by the first (the Dutch NCA whose decision was taken on 16 December 2010). At any rate, it is an overstatement to say that this

---

[37] See press release from the BKA: www.bundeskartellamt.de/SharedDocs/Meldung/EN/Pressemitteilungen/2013/19_02_2013_M%C3%BCNBChlenkartell.html
[38] http://ec.europa.eu/competition/ecn/brief/01_2013/nl_de.pdf
[39] Ibid.

approach is efficient for the NCAs involved. Could not one NCA have handled the case and imposed fines accordingly, especially given the cross-border nature of some of the infringements, and the close link between all the forms of collusion identified?

Further complexities arose from the Belgian NCA's decision 2013, on the basis of Article 101 TFEU and Belgian law.[40] One of the parties challenged this decision for infringement of the principle of *ne bis in idem*, in view of the decision of the Dutch NCA. The appellant in question, Brabomills, had been acquitted by the Dutch NCA. Its concern was that it was not clear whether the fine imposed by the Belgian NCA (a lump sum of €100,000) was for the harm that it had caused in Belgium or could also have included harm caused in the Netherlands. In the latter case, it argued the fine would be in breach of his rights. The Belgian Court of Appeal upheld this claim – it found that it was impossible to work out whether the fine was calculated taking into account the effects in Belgium only or also in the Netherlands. To avoid any risk, the fine was annulled completely.[41] The court explained that, following the ECJ's ruling in *Toshiba*, it was possible for multiple NCAs to impose fines on the same cartel (and thus each NCA pursue cases to protect the same legal interest) provided that each then fines the undertaking for the actual consequences of the cartel that occur in its territory (and so there is no identity of facts). It follows that the NCA could not, as here, presume anticompetitive consequences, but it has to identify the actual consequences of the agreement in its territory to justify the penalty.

This somewhat clumsy approach to multi-jurisdictional cartels has the support of the ECJ, even if it is not clear that the judges had foreseen that their case law would lead to the kind of enforcement actions above. In *Toshiba* the ECJ was faced with a situation where the Commission had issued a decision against a cartel before the EU's eastward enlargement, so the fine was not imposed for the impact of the cartel on the Czech Republic. The question thus arose whether, after accession the Czech NCA could apply EU competition law to the same cartel for the effects on its jurisdiction. The ECJ confirmed that the second action was authorised, as it did not infringe the principle of *ne bis in idem*. There was, in other words, no second prosecution of the same matter because the Czech NCA was investigating a different aspect of the same cartel.[42] A similar approach was utilised in *DHL*, where the ECJ held that parallel antitrust investigations by the Commission and the Italian NCA concerning a cartel in the field of international freight forwarding were allowed because the Commission focused on the market for air freight, leaving the NCAs to carry out investigations in the markets for sea and road freight.[43] Seen on its own

[40] http://economie.fgov.be/en/binaries/20130312_beslissing_PUB_tcm327-216469.pdf

[41] http://economie.fgov.be/nl/binaries/20140312_eindarrest_HvB_Brabomills_tcm325-245407.pdf

[42] Case C-17/10, *Toshiba Corporation and Others* v. *Úřad pro ochranu hospodářské soutěže*, ECLI:EU:C:2012:72. For criticism, see G. Monti, 'Managing Decentralized Antitrust Enforcement: Toshiba' (2014) 51(1) *Common Market Law Review* 261.

[43] Case C-428/14, *DHL Express (Italy) Srl and DHL Global Forwarding (Italy) SpA* v. *Autortità Garante della Concorrenza e del Mercato*, ECLI:EU:C:2016:27.

terms, this judgment might be justified: the reason the matter was litigated was because the applicant had not submitted the proper leniency documents to all the NCAs that might have investigated the cartel so that in Italy it was unable to secure immunity from fines. The ECJ was not going to let an applicant circumvent its own error. At the same time, however, one has to wonder if the ECJ's view that each leniency application is autonomous from the others is really sustainable, given that the Commission and NCAs form a network of agencies that work together. Should not such joint work mean that undertakings might entertain a legitimate expectation that in allocating cases leniency policies would be shared as well? Leaving aside the merits of the two judgments, the upshot of this case law is that it is perfectly legitimate for cases like the flour cartel to happen again.

This approach appears an inefficient use of scarce resources, and it also seems to run counter to the Network Notice. It is inefficient because each agency gathers its bundle of information (and perhaps also makes inquiries of other NCAs to secure further information), and each applies Article 101 to different facets of what is in reality a set of conduct which is often only harmful if taken together. Moreover, each agency has to bear the costs of appeals. The Network Notice indicates that conduct affecting three or more Member States would be handled by the Commission, so it is not clear why neither the flour mills case nor the cases relating to online travel agencies (discussed below) were allowed to remain national. As discussed above, Article 11 and the Network Notice provide for ample guidance on the proper steps to take to reassign a case that one NCA has taken. Indeed, the Notice provides that '[i]n order to detect multiple procedures and to ensure that cases are dealt with by a well-placed competition authority, the members of the network have to be informed at an early stage of the cases pending before the various competition authorities'.[44] Granted, the Notice does not envisage that each case is dealt with by only one NCA, but it is the desired result for most cases.

One might wonder why it is that cases are divided up in this inefficient manner. A benevolent hypothesis would be that since NCAs are unable to impose a fine for conduct affecting other jurisdictions, then the only manner to impose an effective fine is for each agency to work on the case. A less benevolent explanation is that by dividing the case up, then each NCA can take credit for issuing a decision. Without discussing the reasons further, the fact that the Commission remains the sole actor able to take cross-border cases, is a worrying weakness of the system.

19.3.3 *Glimmers of a European Approach*

In contrast to the above, the NCAs of two small Member States have shown some leadership in canvassing a more European attitude to antitrust enforcement. The Dutch NCA, for example, imposed fines on a cartel of Dutch silver-skin

---

[44] Network Notice, para. 16.

onion producers in 2012 taking into consideration the adverse effects that their conduct had across the European Union. The choice to impose a fine to reflect the damage caused in other EU markets was upheld on appeal.[45] To a degree this case is relatively uncontroversial because all the undertakings are situated in the Netherlands and thus the enforcement action did not stretch to conduct of non-Dutch firms in other countries. Thus, there was no need to secure enforcement cooperation from other Member States.[46]

A more courageous step was taken recently by the Belgian NCA which imposed a global injunction against the actions of the International Federation for Equestrian Sports (FEI). The NCA was concerned about the rules of this association which forbade racers from participating in events organised by other federations. The NCA saw this as conduct which could foreclose competition in the market for racing events and imposed an interim injunction preventing the federation from enforcing its rules which affected races organised in other EU Member States and also outside the EU. An interim injunction was issued because a competing event was being organised (the so-called Global Champions League) and that absent an interim order this business would likely collapse. The FEI defended this restriction as a means to protect the well-being of horses and riders. However, the Brussels Court of Appeal upheld the injunction.[47] The court began by exploring the power that the European Commission has over conduct that takes place outside the EU. Drawing on the ECJ's jurisprudence it observes that the Commission has subject-matter jurisdiction when conduct outside the EU has immediate and substantial effects on markets in the EU.[48] The Belgian court then reasons that by analogy NCAs, whose task it is to apply EU competition law, must also have the power to apply those rules to conduct taking place outside of its jurisdiction since it is obliged to apply EU competition law, pursuant to Article 3(1) of Regulation 1/2003. The court further justifies this by exploring the role of NCAs in the network of competition authorities: by concluding that the Belgian NCA is well placed to act to apply EU competition law and that considerations of effectiveness militate in favour of this injunction having a reach beyond competitions set up in Belgium, otherwise the injunction would not prevent the anticompetitive effects noted by the NCA.[49]

---

[45] The District Court of Rotterdam upheld the entirety of the decision (ACM, District Court of Rotterdam rules in silver-skin onion cartel (16 April 2014); summary at: www.acm.nl/en/publications/publication/12894/District-Court-of-Rotterdam-rules-in-silverskin-onion-cartel).

[46] It will be recalled that in cases of extraterritorial enforcement, the Commission relies upon diplomatic channels to attempt to secure the payment of fines when firms are based outside of the EU.

[47] Brussels Court of Appeal, Case 2015/MR/1, *Fédération Equestre Internationale* v. *Autorité Belge de la Concurrence* (judgment of 28 April 2016), at www.abc-bma.be/fr/decisions/15-vm-23-gcl-ttb-vs-fei

[48] Ibid., para. 22. This broadly reflects the more recent approach found in *Intel*.

[49] Ibid., paras. 23–30.

19.4 MOVING FORWARD WITH REGIONAL ENFORCEMENT: ALTERNATIVES

Given the reality of what NCAs do, it is premature to move forward with the kinds of procedural measures that the ECN plus project has proposed. Granted, it cannot hurt if NCAs are afforded more resources and are made more independent, but it will be difficult to monitor Member State compliance with these requirements.[50] At the same time, harmonising procedures might stifle the discovery of even better approaches to cartel enforcement. In this final section, three suggestions are made that would enhance the work of pubic enforcement by NCAs in ways that are preferable if one wishes to galvanise them to act as regional agencies.

19.4.1 *More Extraterritorial Enforcement*

The first possible development one might wish to stimulate is further extraterritorial enforcement, like the Dutch silver-skin onion cartel and the Belgian case against the FEI. Cartels spanning more than one Member State could be taken by the Commission or by a single Member State. In these instances, the provisions of Regulation 1/2003 facilitate cooperation at the level of investigation and the sharing of information across NCAs.[51] It does not look as if these provisions have generated controversy, and their purpose seems to be to help the authority in one country to handle cross-border infringements effectively.

At the same time, some might wish for caution against this recommendation. This could be for two reasons: the first is that this recommendation requires a high degree of mutual trust among the Member States. In other fields of EU law, where mutual trust has been assumed, e.g. in the context of the European Arrest Warrant, it has given rise to some concerns: does mutual trust assume too much about the integrity of all Member States' procedural safeguards?[52] In other words, some might object that proposing extraterritorial enforcement before procedural harmonisation puts the cart before the horse.

A second reason for concern is that while extraterritorial enforcement in cartel cases may well be tolerated insofar as such conduct has undoubtedly damaging economic effects whether that conduct manifests itself in one state or several, matters may differ with conduct where the welfare effects are more ambiguous, like instances of abuse of dominance. Consider in this context the facts behind the controversial decision in *Intel*. The concern here arose because of rebates granted in China by Intel that had an adverse impact on

---

[50] These requirements are set out in Arts. 4 and 5 of the Directive.

[51] Regulation 1/2003, Arts. 12 and 22.

[52] For example, Case C-399/11, *Stefano Melloni v. Ministerio Fiscal* ECLI:EU:C:2013:107. And, more generally, see Evelien Brouwer and Damien Gerard (eds.), *Mapping Mutual Trust: Understanding and Framing the Role of Mutual Trust in EU Law*, MWP 2016/13, available at http://cadmus.eui.eu/bitstream/handle/1814/41486/MWP_2016_13.pdf?sequence=1

the EU market.[53] Assuming that the adverse impact is shown, a finding of abuse would appear to ignore any possible welfare-enhancing effect that the conduct might have in China.[54] If this is possible at global level, it may also be true at regional level. In this context, should we really allow one NCA to decide a case on behalf of all its members? One might suggest that the answer should be in the affirmative, because while we would not expect the Commission to weigh up the welfare losses in the EU with the welfare gains in China, we might feel more comfortable with one NCA balancing welfare effects across the EU. At the same time one wonders if the EU is, politically, ready to accept that national agencies act in the EU interest in this manner. In the framework of Banking Union, national regulators have been stripped of powers to supervise the most systemically significant banks so that a central authority can manage EU-wide risks. Banking Union reveals that perhaps decentralising enforcement is not such a wise move after all.[55]

19.4.2 *Joined-up Enforcement*

If trusting a single agency is asking too much, perhaps trusting a group of agencies becomes more palatable. Such a scenario emerged in the Booking.com saga. A brief account is followed by discussion of how this instance reveals a possible basis for NCAs taking a more significant role in the enforcement of EU competition law.

A spate of similar cases has arisen where an online platform like Booking.com requests that the hotels who wish to advertise on their website do not sell rooms online on their own website or on other competing websites at prices that are lower than the prices that are made available to Booking.com (in the jargon a wide MFN clause). The concern is that this softens price competition and raises entry barriers for new entrants, to the detriment of consumers.[56] Three NCAs took the lead (the French, Italian and Swedish). It appears that there were regular exchanges of ideas in the lead-up to the three agencies issuing a commitment decision phrased in similar terms on the same day.[57] What followed was that nearly all other NCAs accepted the approach of the leading three NCAs and issued similar decisions. Up to this point in the process, we observe an interesting approach to coordinate on an issue of significance for the EU as a whole: not a single decision, but multiple, simultaneous and identical decisions, which are then accepted by other NCAs.

---

[53] Case C-413/14 P, *Intel Corp. v Commission*, ECLI:EU:C:2017:632.

[54] See in this context the discussion in M. Gal and J. A. Padilla, 'The Follower Phenomenon: Implications for the Design of Monopolization Rules in a Global Economy' (2010) 76(3) *Antitrust Law Journal* 899.

[55] See e.g. P. G. Texeira, 'The Legal History of the Banking Union' (2017) 18(3) *European Business Organization Law Review* 535.

[56] The soundness of this theory of harm is beyond the scope of this contribution.

[57] https://webgate.ec.europa.eu/multisite/ecn-brief/en/content/french-italian-and-swedish-competition-authorities-accept-commitments-offered-bookingcom

If we pause at this moment, we might wonder if this approach could be refined further such that the three agencies issue a single decision affecting all of the territory of the EU. Having more than one NCA in charge might reduce mistrust since it is unlikely that multiple agencies may act in a beggar-thy-neighbour manner protecting national interests and imposing externalities. Moreover, conversations at ECN level could allow for deliberation informed by evidence from other Member States who are not leading the case.

However, before we take this as a case study on how to make decentralised enforcement more effective, we should add two further factors that render the example much less hopeful. The first is that the German NCA did not agree with the substantive line taken by the other jurisdictions, and took a tougher approach. In essence: the approach taken by the majority of the NCAs is that Booking.com cannot request that hotels offer other online travel agents the same price, but they can insist that the hotel's own website does not have better prices (a narrow MFN clause is tolerated). In contrast, the German NCA takes the view that any control on anyone's retail price is unlawful. The second is that the Italian, French and Austrian governments considered that the approach taken by their NCAs was not satisfactory from a public policy perspective, and decided that hotels should be free to set lower prices than the online travel agents. Each passed legislation of different kinds to ensure that hotels were free from price parity clauses. This shows how at times political considerations can still serve to undermine competition policy: we return to this in the following section.

However, even with these two caveats, this is an important precedent for cooperation among agencies. It mirrors what we see globally in merger cases, where there is cooperation among various agencies to coordinate theories of harm and possible divestitures. In merger cases, this is facilitated by confidentiality waivers by the firms to the merger; in EU law this is made easy by the power of NCAs to share information, provided by Regulation 1/2003. Furthermore, cooperation has continued as the NCAs carried out a monitoring exercise to test the impact of the commitments that have been agreed. While the impact assessment probably came too soon after the decision to provide any clear findings, it shows a willingness to continue to cooperate: notably even the German NCA participated, indicating that there is a willingness among the agencies to test which approach works best.[58]

19.4.3 *Joint Leadership and Experimentalist Governance*

Another phenomenon that we observe especially in the field of e-commerce is that a small number of NCAs have taken a leadership role, the Commission's resources possibly consumed by the *Google* case. For example, it is reported

---

[58] Report on the monitoring exercise carried out in the online hotel booking sector by EU competition authorities in 2016, http://ec.europa.eu/competition/ecn/hotel_monitoring_report_en.pdf

that in 2013 the German and the British NCA worked together to assess certain practices carried out by Amazon and they agreed not to pursue the matter having persuaded Amazon to drop the price parity clauses it set up in its marketplace. Amazon changed its practices across the EU.[59] Another example is that the French and the German NCAs are the most active in taking cases in e-commerce markets. The French NCA had also been quite influential in the review of the rules on vertical restraints in 2009–10. It remains to be seen what this leadership role achieves – does an NCA expect that its enforcement action will make the firms change their conduct across the EU, in the expectation that other NCAs will follow suit? Or does the lead NCA expect to exercise leadership such that other NCAs will follow it in other cases? There are too few instances of this approach to allow us to draw any firm conclusion.

What seems to transpire from the evidence, however, is that while leadership is tolerated, experimentation is not looked upon with much enthusiasm if it crosses a certain boundary. Any NCA that attempts to deviate from the line favoured by the Commission is challenged. A recent, and ongoing, matter is the incorporation of sustainable development/animal welfare in competition law decisions. In the Netherlands, the state is keen to facilitate farmers agreeing on production processes that are less harmful to animals, but the Commission has reprimanded some of the attempts to do so in harsh terms. This is a missed opportunity to approach divergences in a more optimistic line, by having different agencies taking different approaches, allowing a subsequent reflection on what might work best.[60]

In sum: when the Commission has not taken a clear policy line (as for example in many aspects of e-commerce) then NCAs may experiment or try and exercise some leadership role by, for instance, being very active, or by issuing joint reports as is the case for big data where the French and the German NCAs issued an exploratory document.[61] The commitment to experimentation and to identifying superior enforcement standards is also reflected by the ex post studies in the online travel agent cases. This creates a powerful governance method for a regional grouping which could be explored: NCAs sharing resources to confront novel policy issues, and engaging in reflections on how to best shape enforcement. Moreover, this approach can be implemented in such a way that the better-resourced agencies assist those with less experience and/or fewer resources. It could facilitate capacity building and a more efficient deployment of resources.

---

[59]   http://ec.europa.eu/competition/ecn/brief/05_2013/brief_05_2013.pdf

[60]   For discussion of the Dutch issue, see G. Monti and J. Mulder, 'Escaping the Clutches of EU Competition Law: Pathways to Assess Private Sustainability Initiatives' (2017) 42 *European Law Review* 635.

[61]   Competition Law and Data (2016), at www.autoritedelaconcurrence.fr/doc/reportcompetitionlawand datafinal.pdf

19.4.4 *Advocacy*

A final aspect for consideration is that agencies in a regional grouping are best placed to identify the source of the major restrictions to competition: national legislation.[62] As we see with the advent of disruptive forms of innovation like Uber and Airbnb, states are easily captured to protect the interests of established groups (taxis and hotels) against the competitive threat posed by new entrants. The Competition and Markets Authority's assessment of the taxi regulations stands out as an important evaluation of the anticompetitive risks posed by the legislator,[63] but it is Italy's advocacy rules that should serve as a model for all NCAs and the Directive on strengthening NCAs missed a vital opportunity by failing to incorporate a version of these provisions. In brief, the NCA can take legal action against general administrative provisions, regulations or measures of any public administration which infringe competition law. The NCA sends a reasoned opinion to the public administration with a request that the administration complies by reforming the restrictive regulation. If there is no response, then an appeal is brought to the administrative courts to force compliance.[64]

19.5 CONCLUSION

The lesson that emerges from this discussion is that we need to rethink the meaning of decentralisation: the sole ambition of the legislator when enacting Regulation 1/2003 is to ensure that firms investing across borders are faced with comparable legal regimes. Perhaps it is also hoped that the ECN can serve as a way of ensuring that NCAs do not take decisions that benefit national champions, but there is no vision of granting NCAs powers across borders. The aim is to empower businesses to trade across borders with more confidence. Thus, the proper word to describe the present process, when coupled with the Directive, is harmonisation. The driving force is to ensure that all NCAs act applying the same rules and very similar procedures, so that traders are treated the same in all Member States. This is not very different from the 'convergence' discourse we find at the International Competition Network level, but with greater legislative and executive control than is possible globally.

This chapter is a challenge to be more ambitious: to treat NCAs as agencies that serve the EU as a whole, and concomitantly to empower them with the capacity to act across borders. If the unilateral application of EU competition law by one NCA in such a way that conduct is challenged across the EU is seen as too daring, the

---

[62] R. A. Posner, 'The Social Cost of Monopoly and Regulation' (1975) 83(4) *Journal of Political Economy* 807.

[63] e.g. CMA Taxi and private hire regulation: CMA letter to City of Sheffield (28 September 2016).

[64] Italian Competition Act (1990, as amended in 2011) Art. 21 bis. The NCA carried out a study on the effectiveness of this instrument and reported a 52 per cent success rate (AGCM, *Relazione sull'attività svolta nel 2016*, p. 32).

chapter suggests that teams of NCAs might have greater legitimacy to impose a solution across the EU territory. This would save resources that presently go in parallel proceedings.

A second challenge in this chapter is to consider whether rather than merely top-down review of the performance of NCAs one might also engage in policy learning across the agencies. With joint decisions, the ECN could become a site for coordination and capacity building: teaming up agencies to pursue the same case in a manner that would allow newer agencies to benefit from the experience of those which are more experienced. This is analogous to what probably happens in many cross-border mergers where we see cooperation among NCAs. While in merger cases this is facilitated by confidentiality waivers by the parties who favour teamwork among agencies, this need not prevent NCAs from doing so in other instances.

Finally, if NCAs are to contribute to the creation of an internal market, then a legal framework to empower them to challenge anticompetitive regulations would seem necessary. The Commission has shown itself willing to exercise advocacy powers when major infrastructures were being liberalised,[65] but for local regulations that stifle new forms of business, NCAs have a comparative advantage. Here one could learn from the experiences of the Member States and derive either best practices or a legislative proposal to empower NCAs to challenge restrictive regulation resulting from state measures.

---

[65]   See W. Sauter, *Coherence in EU Competition Law* (Oxford University Press, 2016), ch. 9.

B

Effective Coordination of Enforcement Systems

A Global Governance Perspective

20

Extraterritoriality and the Question of Jurisdiction in Competition Law

Dennis M. Davis

20.1 INTRODUCTION

The challenges of globalisation hold significant challenges for the competition community, in particular the importance of extending its regulatory gaze beyond the strict confines of a national jurisdiction. To date Competition authorities and courts seized with regulating anticompetitive structures or behaviour appear to have lacked the legal imagination or determination to respond adequately to the challenges posed to the enterprise of competition policy and law by developments that have shaped the global economy over the past three decades.

For the purpose of examining the problem that the doctrine of jurisdiction has posed for the contemporary development of competition policy and law, it is useful to have recourse to the restrictions of national jurisdiction as contained in the US Restatement (3rd) of the Foreign Relations Law of the United States which provides a clear guide as to the limitation of a national court's jurisdiction. It states that nations may write rules to curb transactions that extend beyond the national boundary if the aim of these regulations is to protect municipal interests, such as domestic consumers and further that the regulation is proportional to its declared purpose. According to the Restatement, two further sets of consideration are critical to the enquiry:

1. where a command of the actor's nation directly conflicts with the requirements of the regulating nation; and
2. where assertion of jurisdiction is unreasonable in view of all the interests, contacts and regulations,

In which case jurisdiction must be limited.

In the context of competition law, these limits place very little constraint on a nation's permissible jurisdiction to prescribe. For example, as no country in a global world 'owns' a merger, the assertion of national jurisdiction is permissible where domestic consumers may be affected by the transactions that are a consequence thereof.

The potential elasticity of the concept of jurisdiction which flows from the Restatement raises questions about the disappointing nature of the contemporary application of jurisdiction and hence the 'effects' doctrine, as it was initially set out by Justice Learned Hand in the *United States* v. *Aluminium Company of America*.[1] As Eleanor Fox has noted,[2] in contrast to the *Alcoa* case, competition authorities now recognise, for example, that when it comes to a merger, where consumers are likely to be significantly adversely affected, no restrictive scope to jurisdiction should be applied and hence the effects of an offshore merger may be considered by a national authority. However, broader questions of competition law beyond merger law remain extremely narrowly based. As this chapter is concerned with the broad field of competition law and not only merger control, the decisions of the US Supreme Court in *Empagran SA* v. *F Hoffman-LaRoche Ltd*[3] and the critique offered of the opinion by Professor Fox assume critical importance.

20.2 EMPAGRAN

In *Empagran*, the Supreme Court held that Congress meant to exclude from the scope of the Sherman Act a private damages claim by victims who bought the relevant product abroad from a world cartel, unless it could be shown that the plaintiffs were harmed by the cartel's anticompetitive effects in the United States.

The case turned essentially on the interpretation of the Foreign Trade Improvements Act of 1982 (FTAIA). The critical sections of FTAIA provide thus:

Sections 1 to 7 of this title [the Sherman Act] shall not apply to conduct involving trade or commerce (other than import trade or import commerce) with foreign nations unless –

(1) such conduct has a direct, substantial, and reasonably foreseeable effect –
  (A) on trade or commerce which is not trade or commerce with foreign nations [i.e. domestic trade or commerce], or on import trade or import commerce with foreign nations; or
  (B) on export trade or export commerce with foreign nations, of a person engaged in such trade or commerce in the United States [i.e. on a US export competitor]; and
(2) such effect gives rise to a claim under the provisions of sections 1 to 7 of this title, other than this section.

[1]   *United States* v. *Aluminium Company of America*, 148 F.2 d 416 (2) d Cir. (1945).
[2]   E. Fox, *Antitrust Report* (2005) 4, 3; E. Fox, 'Extra Territoriality and Input Cartels' (September 2014) *CPI Antitrust Chronicle* 1.
[3]   *Empagran SA* v. *F Hoffman-LaRoche Ltd*, 542 US 115 (2004).

The complainants contended that the Sherman Act cannot both apply to conduct when one person sues but not apply to the same conduct when another person sues in the same case. The alleged conduct in this case had domestic effects, which effects were sufficiently harmful to US domestic consumers to give rise to a claim under the Sherman Act. The complainants with whom the Supreme Court were confronted, were non-US consumers of the relevant vitamins sold by defendants but in markets outside of the United States.

They argued that the language of FTAIA would not have employed the relevant words 'give rise to a claim' to suggest a geographical limitation. In the view of the complainants, this phrase was employed for a neutral reason, namely in order to make clear that the effect must be adverse as opposed to beneficial. In short, the complainants contended that the conduct which gave rise to litigation had both a direct substantial and reasonably foreseeable effect on trade or commerce which, given its impact on domestic US consumers, could hardly be called trade or commerce with foreign nations so as to fall outside the scope of the Act. Further they argued that the effect which gave rise to a claim under the Act, price-fixing, was adverse to consumers. In their view, it followed that this factual matrix was sufficient to bring the claim brought by those who suffered injury in foreign jurisdictions within the scope of the Act. Expressed differently, once a class of plaintiffs can show that price-fixing by a cartel has taken place which detrimentally affects them as a class of domestic consumers, another class of plaintiffs who have suffered the same or similar effect outside of the USA may join the action which, given the adverse effect in the USA, then also falls within the scope of the Sherman Act.

Justice Breyer, writing for the court, conceded that there was 'linguistic logic' in this argument. But, he then went on to say that a statute can apply and not apply to the same conduct depending upon other circumstances. This observation was followed by a critical passage:

> At most, respondents' linguistic arguments might show that respondents' reading is the more natural reading of the statutory language. But those arguments do not show that we must accept that reading.[4]

Justice Breyer says little more and thus offers no further legal justification as to why the natural and obvious words of the section should not be given their natural and obvious effect by the court. However, it is in the failure to justify adequately the linguistic choice made by the court that an answer can be found: this judgment is predicated on a policy choice, namely an unwillingness to extend jurisdiction to a class of plaintiffs whose claim was based on foreign injury as opposed to the other class of plaintiffs who suffered domestic injury. Indeed, Justice Breyer does state that policy considerations are important for, as he writes earlier in his opinion:

---

[4] Ibid., at 133.

Why should American law supplant, for example, Canada's or Great Britain's or Japan's own determination about how best to protect Canada's or Great Britain's or Japan's own determination about how best to protect Canadian or British or Japanese customers from anticompetitive conduct engaged in significant part by Canadian or British or other foreign companies?[5]

The answer to this question turns on locating the economic context in which goods and services are produced in the twenty-first century as opposed to a belief that Fordist modes of production continue to prevail. But that is to move too far ahead in the argument. Before substantiating this observation, it is necessary to examine additional US jurisprudence.

20.3 *MOTOROLA MOBILITY V. AU OPTRONICS CORP.*

The narrow view of jurisdiction as set out in *Empagran* was applied in a private damages claim against a foreign producer of an input that was sold abroad and was assembled into a final product sold in the United States in *Motorola Mobility LLC v. AU Optronics Corp.*[6]

Briefly, the facts were the following. In 2009 Motorola brought an anti-trust claim against major LCD manufacturers. It alleged that they had fixed the prices of LCD panels which are used as a component in Motorola's mobile phones. Specifically, the claim involved three categories of purchases, namely:

1. LCD panels imported into the United States (1 per cent of purchases);
2. LCD panels purchased outside the United States by Motorola's foreign subsidiaries that were employed as inputs in the finished products that Motorola later imported into the United States (42 per cent of purchases); and
3. LCD panels purchased outside of the United States that were employed as components in finished products that were sold outside of the United States (57 per cent of purchases).

Judge Richard Posner, on behalf of the Seventh Circuit, held that the FTAIA precluded the second and third categories of claim from being successful, leaving Motorola with only 1 per cent of its claim which was based upon purchases of LCD panels. The court summarily dispensed with the 'frivolous' category of claims (the third category) damages which was based on panels incorporated into cellphones sold in foreign countries because those panels never entered into the United States.

Turning to the second category of claim, the court acknowledged that there was 'doubtless some effect' that the defendants could have foreseen on US trade.

---

[5]   Ibid., at 123.
[6]   *Motorola Mobility LLC v. AU Optronics Corp.*, 746 F 3 d 842 (7th Cir., 2014).

Nonetheless, Judge Posner concluded that the connection to US commerce was too remote as 'the effect of component price fixing on the price of the product of which it is a component is indirect'. Judge Posner concluded that Motorola's claim was based 'on the effect of the alleged price fixing of Motorola's foreign subsidiaries'.[7] These subsidiaries could seek their own remedies in the countries in which they operated. If these countries did not offer adequate remedies, that was a risk Motorola as the parent company knowingly and voluntarily assumed.

In keeping with the policy approach expressed in *Empagran*, Judge Posner noted that there would be serious practical implications if Motorola's expansive interpretation of the domestic effects prevailed because it would 'enormously increase the global reach of the Sherman Act creating friction with many foreign countries and resentment at the apparent effort of the United States to act as the world's competition police officer'.[8]

Although the Supreme Court denied *certiorari* in Motorola, the decision did provoke a considerable measure of controversy. In an amicus brief seeking a rehearing *en banc* before the Seventh Circuit, the American Anti-Trust Institute argued in favour of looking through the separate corporate existence of the foreign subsidiaries in treating this as a case in which the US-owned manufacturer purchases price-fixed components abroad, incorporates them into finished products that the parent company imports into the United States and then sells them at a price that reflects the clear overcharging by a cartel.[9] The Institute argued that the panel's interpretation of FTAIA left US consumers vulnerable to harm caused by international cartels.[10] But a failure to hear the case leaves Judge Posner's opinion as persuasive precedent.

The upshot is that these decisions hold more significant implications for competition law than simply that FTAIA is a poorly drafted statute. Notwithstanding its linguistic difficulties, the Act did appear to reflect a balance that the United States struck between enforcement of arrangements that detrimentally affect US consumers and the principle of comity that has to be accorded to other countries.

The precedent created by these cases together with shifting patterns of production of goods and services which transcend national boundaries has meant that attention must be shifted from the attempt to employ a generous interpretation of the scope of the Sherman Act to different forms of international regulation or, at least, cooperation.

---

[7] Ibid., 853.

[8] Ibid., at 859.

[9] Brief of the American Antitrust Institute as amicus curiae in support of appellant's petition for rehearing, *en banc*, http//antitrustinstitute.org (accessed 7 August 2017).

[10] See however the opinion in *Minn-Chem Inc.* v. *Agrium, Inc.*, 10 1712 (7th Cir., 2012) where the court engaged with the test that the conduct in question must have a direct substantial and reasonable foreseeable effect on domestic commerce and thus adopted a definition of direct effect to mean 'a reasonably proximate cause or nexus' between anticompetitive activity and the domestic effect (opinion of Justice Diane Wood, at 22).

20.4 THE INTERNATIONAL CONTEXT

While international cooperation has improved, for example, through organisations like the International Competition Network (ICN) to harmonise aspects of national competition law, fairly modest proposals for a broader international regulatory regime which were placed on the agenda at the Doha Round of the WTO over a decade ago met with sustained opposition from developing countries which did not consider that international competition rules would be beneficial for them, many having already viewed with great scepticism the earlier Trade-Related Aspects of Intellectual Property Rights Agreements (TRIPS). Developing countries argued that not only did they not possess the necessary experience with the enforcement of competition law but they feared that international competition laws, based on either the EU or US model, would interfere with their chosen industrial policies and investment screening which they deemed critical to the vindication of their domestic economic objectives.[11]

Significantly the United States came to a similar negative conclusion, on the basis that it did not consider that international competition rules would hold benefit for the United States that could not be achieved by way of its own legislation. It was further of the view that such international regulation may reduce the efficacy of sound competition law.[12]

The failure of the Doha negotiations was a great disappointment for those who saw international competition regulation as necessary for the pursuit of the objectives of competition law in curbing cartels which transcend national boundaries, in prosecuting multinational corporations which abuse their market power and in constraining mergers which hold polycentric consequences in a multitude of jurisdictions.

This disappointment had been fuelled by some earlier optimism pursuant to the draft the ministerial declaration issued on 26 September 2001 which contained two options for a decision to be taken in Doha with regard to the nature of future work on competition policy in the WTO:

> We agree to negotiations aimed at enhancing the contribution of competition policy to international trade and development. To this end the negotiations would establish a framework to address the following elements: core principles, including transparency, non-discrimination, and procedural fairness and provisions on hard core cartels; modalities for voluntary cooperation; and support for progressive reinforcement of competition institutions in developing countries through capacity building. In the course of negotiations, full account shall be taken of the situation in developing and least developed country participants and appropriate

[11] E. Fox 'International Antitrust and the Doha Dome' (2003) 43 *Virginia Journal of International Law* 911.

[12] D. J Gerber, 'Competition Law and the WTO: Rethinking the Relationship' (2007) (10) *Journal of International Economic Law* 707.

flexibility provided to address them. We commit ourselves to ensure that appropriate arrangements are made for the provision of technical assistance and support
for capacity building both during negotiations and as an element of the agreement
to be negotiated.[13]

Neither of these initiatives were translated into a global reality. The formal attempt
to do more than the development of the softest of international cooperation through
institutions like the ICN ended with the Doha round and with it the development of
an international framework of regulation of either anticompetitive behaviour or
structures which enable the capture of excessive rents. The consequences of the
impasse and hence the failure at Doha was to exacerbate the vulnerability of
developing countries to the sharpest consequences of global trade. Professor Fox
explained this as follows:

> The vulnerability problem means that developing countries with poor legal systems
> are not only unlikely to deter incoming cartels but are unlikely to provide a system
> that will compensate their citizens even while victims abroad gets considerable
> recoveries. This is both unfair and inefficient ... This means that either the
> developing countries must accelerate their economic and institutional progress
> and capability in some substantial way to help themselves – perhaps through
> regional free- trade groupings which can give them critical mass (but this is a slow
> and uncertain process) or a world or transnational system of resource must be
> developed or the problem will remain unattended.[14]

In her reading of the consequences of the failure to develop international regulation, Professor Fox raised two further problems. Developing countries are often
unable to protect themselves from the anticompetitive actions of multinational
corporations that can detrimentally affect their economies. They have neither the
resources, information, nor the expertise to curb these practices. It follows that they
are vulnerable to international abuse. Furthermore, the rules of law, which work to
the advantage of developed economies with well-functioning markets, qualita-
tively less corruption, a long tradition of anti-trust law and expertise, are not
available to developing countries in any attempt to curb the abuse of transnational
practices.[15]

Professor Fox thus articulated concerns which are meaningful to both the developed and the developing world and assisted in the construction of a regulatory
scheme that curbs exploitative and exclusionary conduct, operate beyond the
national boundary and thus, all too often, are free of regulation by any competition
authority.

---

[13] World Trade Organization, 'Doha WTO Ministerial 2001 Briefing Notes'.
[14] E. Fox, 'Antitrust without Borders: From Routes to Codes to Networks: E 15 Expert Group on
   Competition Policy and the Trade System' (November 2015).
[15] Work by the OECD and UNCTAD and working groups of the ICN have greatly assisted developing
   countries to gain technical expertise required to build a bible competition authority albeit within the
   restrictive framework of a developing country.

These concerns have become of increasing importance to the future of a competition law that speaks to both developed and developing countries as can be shown by way of an examination of the current mechanisms of global production of goods and services. Conversely, an understanding of these mechanisms was so lamentably absent from the conceptual framework and hence the underlying premises upon which the *Empagran* and *Motorola* jurisprudence were based.

20.5 COMPETITION LAW IN AN AGE OF GLOBAL VALUE CHAINS

National antitrust law can no longer be confined to its country's boundaries. Global production of goods and services has paid put to legal chauvinism. As Eleanor Fox has observed:

> Anti-trust is not an island unto itself. It is deeply interrelated with trade; foreign investments; the free movement of goods; services and capital; law of intellectual property; sectorial regulations; and the wide variety of proposed and actual industrial policies.[16]

The world economy has changed radically from the economy that operated when competition law began to appear on the regulatory agenda following the introduction of the Sherman Act. Notwithstanding the rapid technological advances in the late nineteenth century by way of the steamship, telegraph and railroad, the multinational corporation of the twenty-first century is radically different in form and effect from its early twenty-century counterpart. For this reason, national antitrust regulation originally sought to curb cartels that were organised to reduce the welfare of national consumers, unilateral conduct took place within a national boundary and hence within the defined scope of the jurisdiction of a national regulator or court while mergers generally affected a clearly determined part of the national economy.

Over the past three decades, however, the organisation of industry, the production of goods and services and the nature of trade have all changed dramatically. Globalisation of production and trade which has been accompanied by the vertical disintegration of transnational corporations which have redefined their core competences to focus on innovation and product strategy, marketing and the highest valued segments of manufacturing services. At the same time, they have reduced their direct ownership over what they consider to be noncore functions while promoting the construction of networks or value chains.[17] As organisational structures stretch across the globe, local and national institutions matter but they have now to be viewed within terms of this global reach of a dominant organisational structure.

---

[16] Fox, 'Antitrust without borders', 6.
[17] See, for example, G. Gereffi, J. Humphrey and T. Sturgeon, 'The Governance of Global Value Chains' (2005) *Review of International Political Economy* 78.

The economic structure of the global economy can, in broad terms, be described as following: raw material extraction, agriculture and standardised manufacture take place in low–middle-income countries at the beginning of the value chain whereas consumer retail takes place at the end of the chain where substantial buying power is more likely to be located. Of critical importance for the regulatory enterprise in general and competition policy and law in particular, is the development that no single actor may be in formal control of another, although key segments of a value chain may represent the internal process of a multinational corporate group even as other links in the chain may be found between entities which, at least in theory, may be independent actors. Viewed in this way the control exercised by certain participants in the chain over other participants may take place without formal mechanisms of legal control which would traditionally form part of a corporate group.[18]

The firm that exercises ultimate control over the entire global chain is the lead firm which is located in the node in the value chain, which is generally characterised by concentration, centralisation and high barriers to entry. Nolan et al. summarise the shape of the twenty-first-century global chain as follows:

> If we define the firm not by the entity that is the legal owner, but, rather, by the sphere over which conscious coordination of resource allocation takes place, then, far from becoming 'hollowed out' and much smaller in scope, the large firm can be seen to have enormously increased in size during the global business revolution. As the large firm has 'disintegrated' so has the extent of conscious coordination over the surrounding value chain increased. In a wide range of business activities, the organisation of the value chain has developed into a comprehensively planned and coordinated activity. At its centre is the core systems integrator. This firm typically possesses some combination of a number of key attributes. These include the capability to raise finance for large new projects, and the resources necessary to fund a high level of R&D spending to sustain technological leadership, to develop a global brand, to invest in state-of-the-art information technology and to attract the best human resources. Across a wide range of business types, from fast-moving consumer goods to aircraft manufacture, the core systems integrator interacts in the deepest, most intimate fashion with the major segments of the value chain, both upstream and downstream. This constitutes a new form of 'separation of ownership and control', in which the boundaries of the firm have become blurred.[19]

Applying traditional competition law to a global value chain as described by Nolan et al. poses a fresh regulatory challenge. If a dominant buyer, such as a powerful corporation which operates across national boundaries like Wal-Mart, engages in conduct that harms producers of goods in country A but only consumers in country

---

[18] P. Gibbon, J. Bair and S. Ponte, 'Governing Global Value Chains: An Introduction' (2008) 37 *Economy and Society* 315; for a detailed analysis of chain governance, see R. Kaplinsky, 'Global Value Chains. Where They Came from Where They Are Going and Why This Is Important?' (Innovation, Knowledge Development Working Paper No. 68.OP, 2013).

[19] P. Nolan, J. Zhang and C. Liu, 'The Global Business Revolution, the Cascade Effect and the Challenge for Firms from Developing Countries' (2008) 32 *Cambridge Journal of Economics* 29, 44.

B because the product is exported, competition authorities in the countries where the producers are located would traditionally have little power to deal with the problems confronted by consumers. By contrast, if a competition authority enjoyed extraterritorial reach, it would be able, not only to protect the local producer, but also to have an impact on the welfare of consumers, albeit that the latter are located elsewhere.[20]

The effect thereof can be illustrated by reference to the Briefing Note of the UN Special Rapporteur on the Right to Food which emphasises 'the direct link between the ability of competition regimes to address the abuses of buyer power and supply chains and the enjoyment of the right to adequate food'. The Special Rapporteur argues in favour of the importance of global governance of competition law enforcement in the food sector in order that the right to food might be vindicated. In this document, the Special Rapporteur expresses concerns about the concentration of the retail sector, that is buyer power, which has admittedly attracted some attention from national competition authorities, which wish to deal with the bargaining power of large supermarket chains in both developed and developing countries, and which is seen to be linked to the growing concentration of agribusiness. This linkage impacts upon the effect of the realisation of the right to adequate food for the poorest and the most underprivileged segments of both developing and developed societies. Further, the downward pressure on producers' income flow forces the less efficient producer to merge without any significant benefit to consumers by way of the possible cost savings being passed on. There is also the practice of large retailers in the developed world, who pass the costs of compliance with retailers' standards in respect of hygiene and safety, onto small farm suppliers, which, again has a considerable effect on the latter's costs. In turn, this promotes a horizontal concentration as well as an increase in farms controlled by the exporters by way of vertical integration.

It is for this reason that the Special Rapporteur recommends that 'competition law regimes should be improved to comport with general human rights principles of

---

[20]   See the instructive paper by A. Darr and I. Lianos, 'The Hunger Games: Competition Law and the Right to Food' (unpublished draft paper 2016) particularly where the authors in dealing with the interface between the right to food as protected in both international and municipal instruments and competition law as means to deal with the impact of global value chains and food production write:

> The ability to exercise extra-territorial reach allows competition regimes to move further away from a pure consumer-centric approach towards market abuses that primarily impact agricultural producers within their jurisdiction. In the traditional approach to competition law, if a dominant buyer engages in conduct that harms producers in one country but consumers in another (because the products are exported), the competition regime in the country where the producers are located is rendered toothless. However, if competition regimes were allowed extra-territorial reach they would be able not only to offer protection to local producers but also thereby to protect the right to food in their jurisdictions. It is important to underscore that the common thread in examining buyer power or exercising extra-territorial reach is the need for balancing the competing values of fulfilling the right to food and to strive towards an outcome that finds the most optimum solution to a competition issue as well as the right to food without compromising the integrity of either.

equality and non-discrimination and to facilitate the realisation of human rights including among others the right to food, the right to work and the right to development'.[21]

At present, it appears to be fair to conclude that there is marked inability of competition authorities in developed countries to control excessive buyer power. As indicated in the discussion of the jurisprudence which was developed in both *Empagran* and *Motorola* and hence the content given to the effects doctrine and the manner in which this doctrine has been implemented, national competition law has not come to terms with the consequences of global value chains and hence the very basis by which the global economy operates in the twenty-first century – in turn a far cry from the economic model that was hegemonic when antitrust/competition law emerged as a regulatory mechanism to curb excesses of market power. At the same time, with reference to the concerns expressed by the Special Rapporteur, it is doubtful, given the lack of expertise, and limited resources as to whether developing countries, in which the majority of impoverished famers are located, could set up a credible competition deterrent.

20.6 CONCLUSION

The focus of competition law, in terms of this new economic context, requires a lifting of the regulatory gaze in order that greater global attention may be given to the reality of the global production process which, in turn, cannot be considered within the prism of a narrow 'effects' doctrine predicated on an antiquated Fordist notion of production and in which welfare is considered as a concept to be kept within national boundaries.

The inability of national courts to respond to the globalised economy is also reflected in another area of law which, in my view, only serves to highlight the difficulty regarding extraterritoriality and its challenges for a competition regime that can move from exclusive considerations of the nation state and its interests to a standard of global welfare that brings competition law and its objectives into congruence with the global economy as described in this chapter.

Take the jurisprudence which has vexed the Supreme Court of the United States on a number of occasions, that is, litigation fought in terms of the Alien Torts Claim Act. For example, in *Kiobel et al. v. Royal Dutch Petroleum Company*[22] Chief Justice Roberts wrote:

> On these facts, all the relevant conduct took place outside of the United States. And even where the claims touch and concern the territory of the United States they must do so with sufficient force to displace the presumption against extraterritorial

---

[21] Briefing Note No. 3 of 2010 United Nations Special Rapporteur on the Right to Food: www.ohchr.org/Documents/Issues/Food/BN3_SRRTF_Competition_ENGLISH.pdf (accessed 15 December 2016).

[22] *Kiobel et al. v. Royal Dutch Petroleum Company*, 133 SCt. 1659, at 1674 (2013).

application. Corporations are often present in many countries and it would reach far to say that mere corporate presence suffices. If Congress were to determine otherwise, a statute more specific than the ATS would be required.

Kiobel concerned plaintiffs who argued that the defendant company was involved in numerous acts of violence, torture, murder and harassment perpetrated by the Nigerian government; in particular Esther Kiobel and her co-applicants, who were all resident in the United States at the time that they launched the litigation requested the court to find the defendants which had a permanent presence in the United States responsible for what were described as violations of the law of nations as a consequence of their aiding and abetting the Nigerian government in committing extrajudicial killings, crimes against humanity, torture and cruel treatment, arbitrary arrest and detention, violations of the rights to life, liberty, security, association, forced exile and property destruction.

In its application of the Aliens Torts Claim Act, the court failed to grasp the manner in which a transnational enterprise such as the Royal Dutch Petroleum operates in globalised but unified markets.[23]

Tomaso Ferrando captures the underlying theory upon which the *Kiobel* judgment is based as follows:

> The court resurrects the nineteenth century's metaphysical approach to 'corporate separateness' [and] permits transnational corporations to subdivide their activities into wholly owned-and-controlled, watertight legal boxes in order to avoid taxes, minimize regulatory authority, and cabin liability for the unlawful acts of corporate agents.
>
> The reconstruction of the state system as divided into autonomous and impenetrable sovereign spaces is thus coupled with the idea that transnational corporations are constructed around a multitude of independent elements, rather than the expression of a unique economic entity.[24]

The approach adopted by the Supreme Court in *Kiobel* raises profound questions of what weight is to be given to a claim which can be shown to 'attach and be concerned' with the territory (in this case the United States). Does this approach meet the challenge of changing forms of global production? Can it continue to sustain the presumption against extraterritorial application and thus ignore the idea of multiple corporate spaces and hence the question as to whether the prevailing concept of jurisdiction remains relevant to the manner in which the corporations operate within the context of global value chains?

A decade ago, Eleanor Fox wrote:

---

[23] B. Neuborne, 'General Jurisdiction, Corporate Separateness, and the Rule of Law' (2013) 66 *Vanderbilt Law Review En Banc* 95, 108 (making this argument with reference to *Daimler* v. *Bauman*, but the fragmentation of the corporate structure is clearly present in *Kiobel II* too).

[24] T. Ferrando, 'Land Territory in Global Production: A Critical Legal Chain Analysis' (unpublished doctorate thesis, Sciences Po, 2015), 242.

Developing countries are hurt by international cartels and practices and are vulnerable to them. The violators know that developing countries have few resources to devote to antitrust (if any, after they serve other human priorities): Offshore firms direct exploitive practices at developing countries, often by acts taken and agreements made on their home shores.

In this article, she drew upon the precedent of an environmental convention, that is, the Basel Convention on the Control of Transboundary Movements of Hazardous Waste and their Disposal. Under this Convention, if a signatory country prohibits the imports of hazardous waste, all other signatories must render the shipment of hazardous waste to the country illegal. Professor Fox argued that the United States and other developed countries could and should adopt this model for hard-core export cartels which are 'the hazardous waste of antitrust'.[25] In turn, this suggests that the kind of international regulation to which she made reference in her 2007 article with regard to cartels is but one component of this comprehensive response. The other should be for courts to understand that the 'effects' doctrine has to be reinterpreted in the light of the dominance of global value chains and a new but prevailing economic reality. Hence courts must seek to develop the key jurisdictional basis of competition law to accord with the economic context in which the regulatory ambition of the field ought now to operate.

---

[25]   E. Fox, 'Economic Development, Poverty, and Antitrust: The Other Path' (2007) 13 *Southwestern Journal of Law and Trade in the Americas* 211, 223–4.

21

Competition Enforcement, Trade and Global Governance

A Few Comments

Petros C. Mavroidis and Damien J. Neven

21.1 INTRODUCTION

The debate on international antitrust has come from two perspectives. On the one hand, the trade community has emphasised the interface between trade policy and competition (policy and) enforcement. This interface, which was recognised from the outset of multilateral efforts to liberalise trade in what would become the GATT and eventually the WTO, focuses on the prospect that trade liberalisation through border instruments should not be undone by restrictive business practices (RBPs), placing a particular responsibility in this respect on competition enforcement. On the other hand, the antitrust community has emphasised the risk of inefficient enforcement when several jurisdictions can rule on the same case and thereby the need for coordination of enforcement across jurisdictions.

The chapter makes two simple observations. First, from the antitrust perspective, we find that both the deviation from the objective of the protection of consumer welfare and the scope for capture in enforcement are important root causes of conflicts across jurisdictions. This arises because, unlike what happens with other interests, the protection of consumer interests does not involve any direct external effects across jurisdictions. Some, admittedly casual, observations confirm that strategic enforcement in favour of (domestic) business interest remains a concern, so that the soft convergence across jurisdictions on objectives and institution design that has been achieved may not suffice. An international discipline on the enforcement of domestic rules may be desirable, possibly in the context of bilateral free trade agreements (FTAs).

Second, from the trade perspective, we observe that if the protection of market access commitments can in principle be achieved by non-violation complaints (NVCs), such complaints would trigger a competition enforcement that is not focused on the interest of the domestic constituencies that competition law is

We would like to thank participants at the symposium held in honour of E. Fox (Brussels, June 2016), for comments on an earlier version of this chapter. An earlier, shorter version of the material presented in sections 21.2–21.4 has appeared (in French) in *Reflets et Perspectives de la Vie Economique*, 2016(3).

meant to protect. This mechanism may thus prove ineffective unless supported by an international commitment. In addition, we find that when trade reflects the organisation of production along the vertical chain, NVCs involve the formulation of counterfactuals that is more challenging.

Whereas a commitment not to change the value of trade through domestic instruments will suffice when prices are determined by market clearing mechanism, a commitment to protect trade will no longer suffice to guarantee market access commitments when prices are determined through bilateral bargaining. Finally, we argue that new issues arise at the interface between trade regulation and competition, notably with respect to intellectual property, and that such issues may be best handled by a subset of like-minded countries in the WTO.

This chapter is organised as follows. We first present a taxonomy of the issues raised by enforcement actions having consequences beyond the scope of their jurisdiction (section 21.2) and of the governance mechanisms that can address them (section 21.3). We conclude (in section 21.4) that allowing for a challenge of decisions taken by foreign jurisdictions would be desirable, at least in terms of compliance with respect to domestic instruments. We also find that bilateral FTAs provide the most suitable framework for deploying such discipline. Section 21.5 considers international governance from the perspective of the interface between trade liberalisation and competition enforcement. Section 21.6 concludes.

21.2 A TAXONOMY OF CONFLICTS ACROSS JURISDICTIONS

This section develops a taxonomy of the circumstances which might lead to conflicts in enforcement decisions across jurisdictions. We first assume that the authorities involved pursue the same objective, namely consumer welfare and operate in the same way, so that different authorities confronted with the same facts will take the same decision and thus focus on difference in incentives resulting from different facts. We subsequently relax these assumptions and thus progressively uncover different sources of conflicts. This section also develops a positive analysis of divergences across jurisdictions without discussing whether the resulting outcome is inefficient. This normative aspect will be discussed in the next section.

21.2.1 *Conflicts When Agencies Protect Consumer Welfare*

An issue of international governance in competition enforcement can arise when two conditions are met, namely:

1. the existence of external effects across jurisdictions (so that the enforcement in one jurisdiction has effects in other jurisdictions);[1] and

---

[1] So that the authorities reviewing the case take different decisions (for instance authority A prohibits a merger that is allowed by authority B).

2. the pursuit of objectives that focus on effects taking place within the jurisdictions concerned.

This second condition is the default case.[2] The fact that authorities ignore the effects taking place outside their jurisdictions is only natural given that elected governments, as the ultimate principal of competition agencies, respond to incentives provided by domestic constituencies.

When the exercise of jurisdiction is determined by the effects doctrine (so that enforcement actions can be taken when effects are felt within the jurisdiction concerned), simultaneous enforcement actions arise, leading to external effects across jurisdictions.[3] To illustrate, a cartel in jurisdiction A, which involves export sales in jurisdiction B, could be investigated in both jurisdictions. An anticompetitive agreement between two firms or an abuse of a dominant position in jurisdiction A which had effects in jurisdiction B (for instance, because customers or competitors are located there) could be investigated by both authorities.

In the case of *ex ante* control (as in merger control), notification thresholds are also generally designed in such a way that transactions are notified in all jurisdictions in which they are expected to have significant effects. For instance, if the companies involved in a transaction have important sales in two jurisdictions, one expects that the notification criteria will be such that it is reviewed in both. The implementation of thresholds in different jurisdictions thus leads to simultaneous enforcement when the distribution of expected effects is sufficiently dispersed.

Hence, one can generally expect that international governance will be concerned with the simultaneous exercise of jurisdiction.[4] The simultaneous exercise of jurisdiction however, does not necessarily lead to a conflict, and thus does not necessarily require a mechanism of international governance.

One can identify two (sufficient) conditions[5] such that a mechanism of international governance is not required in the presence of simultaneous jurisdictions, namely the availability of remedies, which address the external effects, and the existence of incentives to cooperate. We examine these conditions in turn.

A conflict arises when the decision by one authority prevents the decision by another authority from fully deploying its effects. This arises, for instance, when two authorities review a concentration and one of them prohibits it (on the basis of the expected effects of the consolidation within its jurisdiction), whereas the other one clears it (on the basis of the expected effects of the consolidation in its own

---

2   Subject to the principle of comity as discussed below.
3   See D. J. Neven and H. Roeller. 'The Allocation of Jurisdiction in International Antitrust' (2000) 44 *European Economic Review* 845–85.
4   The simultaneous exercise of jurisdiction can be constrained by the application of general principles of international law. This constraint is discussed in the next section.
5   Besides the case, excluded by assumption, in which different authorities reviewing a case take the same decision.

TABLE 21.1 *Taxonomy of conflicts and governance mechanisms*

Circumstances	Governance mechanism
Simultaneous jurisdictions – remedies can be found in each jurisdiction	No conflict
Simultaneous jurisdictions – remedies cannot be found in each jurisdiction – repeated interactions	No conflict
Simultaneous jurisdictions – remedies cannot be found in each jurisdiction – repeated interactions	Comity principles
Very asymmetric distribution of outcomes across jurisdictions	Agreement on priority?
Simultaneous jurisdictions – remedies cannot be found in each jurisdiction – isolated transaction	Comity principles / Agreement on priority?
Objectives different from consumer protection	Convergence *ex ante* ICN/OECD Hard codes?
Differences in institutional framework/objectives	Convergence *ex ante*. ICN/OECD Hard codes?
Capture – deviation from the objectives	Mechanism to challenge decisions across jurisdictions

jurisdiction).[6] A conflict can also arise when the investigation of an agreement or an abuse of dominance leads to an infringement decision in one jurisdiction but not in the other one. These cases, however, involve *discrete* decisions in which the agencies effectively play a veto game. More generally, if transactions can be authorised with remedies in a jurisdiction without affecting them in the other jurisdictions concerned, there will be no conflict.[7]

The same reasoning applies to agreements and abuse of dominance cases, which affect several jurisdictions but can be subject to undertakings (for instance, in the context of a settlement procedure like that of Art. 9 of Regulation 1/2003).[8] This situation is presented in the first line of Table 21.1, which summarises our analysis.

Hence, the scope of potential conflicts can be limited to circumstances in which the operations of the companies concerned cannot be amended in each jurisdiction without affecting the operations in other jurisdictions. Even if it is difficult to formulate a prior on the likelihood of such circumstances, one can anticipate that business operations which are strongly integrated across jurisdictions can hardly be reorganised to meet constraints in individual jurisdictions without affecting their overall efficiency.

---

[6] Note that the existence of a conflict is not independent of the scope of the relevant geographic market. When the relevant market includes several jurisdictions, all of which are concerned about consumer welfare, there cannot be any conflict (D. J. Neven and L.-H. Roeller, 'On the Scope of Conflict in International Merger Control' (December 2004) *Journal of Industry, Trade and Competition* 235–49).

[7] See Neven and Roeller. 'Allocation of Jurisdiction', 845.

[8] Regulation (CE) No. 1/2003 of the European Council (16 December 2002) relating to the enforcement of Arts. 81 and 82 of the Treaty [2003] OJ L 1/1.

The second set of circumstances in which a mechanism of international govern-ance may not be required relates to the incentives to cooperate. In this respect, Cabral analyses the equilibria of a repeated game in which authorities review transactions, which have different, and potentially opposite, effects across their jurisdictions.[9] He shows that there is a unique equilibrium in this game, whereby authorities clear mergers even when they have negative effects within their jurisdic-tions up to a maximum level, which can be seen as a maximum concession. They do so because they anticipate that a negative decision would trigger the implementation of the static veto game forever after (see the second line of Table 21.1). Hence, cooperation can be sustained by repeated interactions and conflicts only arise for transaction which feature negative outcomes in excess of the maximum concession level in one jurisdiction, or in other words transactions which have significant and strongly asymmetric effects across jurisdictions (see third line in Table 21.1).

21.2.2 *Objectives Other than Consumer Protection Pursued, and Institutional Capture*

We are now in a position to relax our assumption that all agencies effectively pursue the objective of consumer protection. Let us first consider an objective, which is different from consumer protection but remains the same for all authorities. Let us assume for instance that the authorities maximise welfare in their jurisdiction, taking into account not only consumer surplus but also the profit of domestic companies. This objective introduces a new source of external effects across jurisdictions.

To see this, consider a situation in which a company from jurisdiction B operates in jurisdiction A. Consider a transaction, which can be remedied in jurisdiction A so as to protect its consumer surplus without affecting the consumer surplus in jur-isdiction B (and hence the objective function of the authority in jurisdiction B).[10] As mentioned above, there is no conflict across jurisdiction in this case.[11]

Assume now that jurisdiction B is concerned about the profit of its domestic firm. The modification of the transaction in jurisdiction A can directly affect the profit of companies from jurisdiction B but active in jurisdiction A. Hence, there is scope for conflict that would not arise if the jurisdiction B would pursue the objective of protecting consumer welfare. In principle, as soon as the modification of

---

[9]   L. Cabral, 'An Equilibrium Approach to International Merger Policy' (2005) 23 *International Journal of Industrial Organisation*, 39–751.

[10]   As discussed above, the protection of consumer welfare in jurisdiction A can still have indirect effects on the protection of consumer interest in jurisdiction B (when transactions cannot be amended).

[11]   Note that our example does not rely on the assumption that jurisdiction A effectively protects consumer surplus because it does not have domestic firms. Even if jurisdiction A had domestic firms and would pursue the interest of both domestic firms and domestic consumers and their interest could be protected by local remedies, the presence of foreign firms and of a foreign government defending their interest will add a source of conflict as long as intervention in A reduces the profits of foreign firms operating in A (as one would expect when consumer harm is given some weight in the decision).

a transaction that enhances domestic consumer welfare reduces the profit of a foreign firm operating there, there is a greater scope for conflict. The absence of such direct external effects in the case of the protection of consumer welfare follows from the fact that consumers are associated with a single jurisdiction and are affected only by the decisions taken in that jurisdiction. By contrast, companies can have activities across jurisdictions and will thus potentially be directly affected by decisions in more than one jurisdiction.

One can thus expect that conflicts across jurisdictions will be more frequent in the presence of such direct external effects. These external effects are also likely to be more significant when the distribution of the companies across jurisdictions is more asymmetric.[12]

Let us now consider the situation in which objective functions differ across jurisdictions or equivalently a situation in which different agencies de facto take different decisions with respect to the same case despite the fact that they pursue the same objective. Indeed, a situation in which an authority is captured by particular interests in the pursuit of the objective that it has been assigned (for instance, captured by the interest of companies when it is supposed to focus on consumer protection) can be seen equivalently as a situation in which the authority is meant to take into account these interests in its objective function. The pursuit of an objective different from consumer protection by one jurisdiction again introduces a direct external effect.

Consider for instance a transaction between companies in jurisdiction A, which has different effects in jurisdiction A and jurisdiction B. The transaction can, however, be amended in such a way that consumers' interests can be protected in both jurisdictions. If the authority in A takes into account the interest of its companies, a conflict can still arise. Indeed, by imposing remedies in its own jurisdiction to protect the interest of its customers, the authority of B will affect the profit of the companies from A and hence the objective function of the authority from A.

Some of the well-known conflicts between the US and the European Union in merger enforcement, like the Boeing–McDonnell Douglas, GE–Honeywell or Oracle–Sun transactions, could be seen in these terms.

To sum up (see Table 21.1), one can identify the following sources of conflicts in the presence of external effects across jurisdictions:

1. the absence of remedies in one jurisdiction which do not affect the outcome of the transaction in another jurisdiction and the absence of a mechanism of cooperation induced by repeated interactions (isolated cases); and

---

[12] See K. Head and J. Ries, 'International Mergers and Welfare under Decentralised Competition Policy' (1997) 30 *Canadian Journal of Economics*, 1104–23, who consider an objective function which includes the profit of domestic companies in a model of merger control. Their analysis illustrates this effect.

2. the absence of remedies in one jurisdiction which do not affect the outcome of the transaction in another jurisdiction and the presence of significant and highly asymmetric effects across jurisdictions.

In addition, the presence of objective functions which differ from the protection of consumer welfare and the heterogeneity of objective functions across jurisdictions, including the heterogeneity which results from a different capture of authorities by particular interests across jurisdictions will then exacerbate conflicts and the need for a mechanism of international governance.

21.3 GOVERNANCE MECHANISMS TO ADDRESS CONFLICTS

Once can distinguish between different governance mechanisms depending on their objective. Their objective could be:

1. to develop conditions likely to reduce the probability of conflicts, like fostering the convergence in objective functions, the adoption of a consumer surplus standard or the adoption of institutional arrangements and procedures likely to reduce the scope for capture in enforcement;
2. to impose a discipline through the challenge of decisions with respect to international norms or merely the respect of those prevailing in the jurisdiction concerned; and
3. to resolve conflicts when they arise (and before decisions are taken by authorities concerned).

A couple of preliminary remarks are warranted here. First, international law requires competition authorities to behave in a 'reasonable' way. The concept of 'reasonableness' is amorphous, and has been delineated somewhat as a result of some practice in this area, that has occasionally given rise to litigation.

If, for example, a transaction has effect over several jurisdictions, the authority of the jurisdiction in which the effects are the largest should have priority in enforcing its own laws. The other authorities should in principle only intervene if the enforcement is not satisfactory from their perspective. The manner in which the overarching 'reasonableness' standard is implemented in practice is exhausted in the customary international law principle of comity.

A for example, will desist from exercising jurisdiction in a case where a merger produces 99 per cent of its effects in B. Because comity is a matter of national discretion, states have through conventional means attempted to reduce the risk of haphazard exercise of discretion. For example, the European Union and the United States have signed an agreement endorsing 'positive comity'.[13] By virtue of this principle, affected states can pre-empt exercise of

---

[13]   http://ec.europa.eu/competition/international/bilateral/usa.html

jurisdiction by other states, and ask that the state about to exercise jurisdiction takes into account its own interests when doing so.

The second remark concerns our discussion of the objectives of international governance. One would in principle like to formulate these objectives with reference to a concept of efficiency and not only in terms of the deterrence or the resolution of conflicts. Any normative implication that could be derived from such an analysis would still remain contingent on some parameters that are difficult to observe like the distribution of effects across jurisdictions.

In this context, it seems preferable, even if it is a bit heuristic, to focus on the frequency of conflicts and to distinguish between mechanisms likely to reduce their incidence, through the development of favourable conditions and/or incentives, and those dealing with the resolution of the conflicts.

These objectives are however not necessarily independent and for each objective, different alternatives with different ambitions can be considered. For instance, regarding the objective of *ex ante* convergence of objective functions and institutions, one could consider the adoption of a common code or slower process of convergence through dialogue and the exchange of experience.

The first option was developed in the 1990s (in the context of the so-called 'Munich Group', but also within the OECD) with the ambition of adopting an agreement in the WTO on substantial norms and the ambition of enforcing it through the WTO mechanism of dispute resolution. This option turned out to be excessively ambitious. Remarkably, at the Cancun WTO Ministerial Conference (2003), it was supported only by the European Union and South Korea.

Given the reticence of the US and the frustration of the developing countries with the incomplete implementation of the Uruguay round, the matter was dropped even before the negotiation began. Ever since, the focus has been on dialogue, the exchange of experience and the development of best practices in the context of the OECD or the ICN. Discipline in the enforcement of such best practices also remains weak. Shame towards fellow enforcers is the only incentive that agencies have in avoiding blatant (observable) deviations from these practices.

If convergence through the adoption of a common code is no longer part of the multilateral agenda, it remains part of bilateral agreements. The European Union in particular has signed a number of bilateral trade agreements with 'close' countries in which the latter commit to adopt European competition norms (if not statutes). The agreement with Ukraine is a case in point.

The implementation of these agreements is however not subject to a formal discipline, in particular with respect to individual enforcement decisions. The US has adopted a different approach.[14] The FTAs, which it has concluded, merely insist

---

[14]   See H. Horn, P. C. Mavroidis and A. Sapir, 'Beyond the WTO? An Anatomy of the US and EU Preferential Trade Agreements' (2010) 33 *World Economy* 1565–88.

on the adequate implementation of national competition statutes.[15] Currently, there is however no discipline with respect to the enforcement of these national norms. There is no FTA which allows a government to challenge the competition decision of another government.

With respect to conflict resolution, existing mechanisms rely quasi exclusivity on bilateral cooperation agreements between jurisdictions which endorse a form of comity principle. Through the principle of so-called negative comity, the competition authorities commit to take into account the interest of other jurisdictions when they take a decision.[16] This principle is adopted, for instance, in all the recent agreements concluded by the European Union, with specific provisions involving different levels of commitment.[17] There is no need nevertheless to reflect negative comity in treaty language, as there is widespread acknowledgement that it has acquired the status of customary international law and binds all states anyway, irrespective of whether they have signed an agreement to this effect, unless they persistently object to it. To our knowledge, no state qualifies as persistent objector in this context.

Here again, the implementation of the comity principle is not subject to any discipline (except for the discipline induced by repeated interactions, discussed above). More powerful mechanisms which prevent unilateral actions have been proposed including the designation of a single authority in charge of enforcement as function on the concentration of interests.[18] In such a scheme, the jurisdiction with the strongest interest would be subject to the comity principle but would have a monopoly on the decision.

Overall, ambitions on the global governance of competition enforcement have receded over time. *Ex ante* convergence has shied away from hard codes to focus on soft mechanisms. International norms take the form of soft codes and there is no mechanism to ensure their implementation. The next section argues that this state of affair is unsatisfactory in light of recent cases in which several jurisdictions have seemingly deviated from the mission assigned to them. In these circumstances, a mechanism through which the respect of domestic norms could be challenged by other jurisdictions seems desirable.

---

[15] In the vast majority of cases, these FTAs merely endorse general objectives such as the development of competition. See e.g. F.-C. Laprévote, 'Competition Policy within the Context of Free Trade Agreements, E15 Initiative' (World Economic Forum, 2015); D. Sokol, 'Order without (Enforceable) Law: Why Do Countries Enter into Non-Enforceable Competition Policy Chapters in Free Trade Agreements' (2008) *Chicago-Kent Law Review* 231; O. Solano and A. Sennekamp, 'Competition Provisions in Regional Trade Agreements (OECD Trade Policy Paper Series, 2006), 31.

[16] See the various contributions in K. Meessen, *Extraterritorial Jurisdiction in Theory and Practice* (Martinus Nijhoff, 1996).

[17] See e.g. the agreements with Switzerland, Canada and Korea.

[18] E. Fox, 'Antitrust without Border: From Roots to Codes to Networks, E15 Initiative' (World Economic Forum, 2015).

21.4 IMPROVING GOVERNANCE THROUGH ADJUDICATION

Concern about the capture of competition enforcement is supported by a number of recent cases. To start with, the suspicion arises that some recent merger control decisions by Chinese authorities may have been motivated by the protection of domestic companies.[19] For instance, in the Inbev–Anheuser–Bush or the Wal-Mart–Niu Hai transactions, the Ministry of Commerce (MOFCOM), in charge of merger control, has imposed remedies which prevent the merging parties from developing certain products. In the Novartis–Alcon transactions, the parties had to commit not to reintroduce a Novartis product. In the Marubeni–Gavilon merger, the parties had to commit not to exploit synergies that might have given them a competitive advantage in the supply of soja in China. Hence, it would appear that the Chinese authorities have preferred to protect domestic competitors rather than allow for the development of competitive conditions to the benefit of consumers.

The protection and development of national champions can also be a concern for competition authorities in Europe. For instance, the Eon–Ruhrgaz merger, which had been prohibited by the Bunderskartellamt, was authorised by the German economy minister with the explicit motivation of encouraging the development of a national champion. More recently, the authorisation of the Telefonica–E-plus merger by the European Commission has proved controversial. The Commission had expressed concern in this case about the elimination of an aggressive competitor, in particular with respect to prepaid cards. The transaction was eventually allowed to go through with remedies such that the merged entity has to make capacity available to virtual operators only for half as much as what E-plus used before the merger. This remedy would not, at first sight, appear to be adequately calibrated to address the underlying concern and has been adopted in a political environment that may have been affected by the public intervention of the chancellor in favour of the transaction.[20] More generally, the Commission has never clarified the conditions in which the Member States can impose remedies on public interest ground in transactions reviewed by the Commission (under article 21(4) of the merger regulation).[21]

There is also a concern that interested parties might capture the authorities by affecting the public debate surrounding the cases, and thereby lead the authorities to

[19] The material in this section draws on M. Mariniello, D. J. Neven and J. Padilla, 'Antitrust, Regulatory Capture and Economic Integration' (Bruegel Policy contribution, issue 2015/11, 2015). Note that in the case of China, the protection of consumers is not the sole objective of competition enforcement. These cases thus reveal as much a concern about the objective itself as a concern about capture.

[20] See *Financial Times*, 8 May 2014.

[21] See D. J. Neven, 'European Champions and Merger Control Rules, Improving Enforcement in the Current Framework' (2014) *Concurrences* 4; M. Mariniello, 'Foreign Takeovers Need Clarity from Europe' (Bruegel Policy Brief, 2014) 7 also observed that for fourteen out of the twenty-two cases of significant intra-European consolidation in which national governments intervened (in the period 1999–2014), objectives other than the preservation of competition have been pursued (and have often led to the withdrawal of the consolidation).

take decisions that might not reflect the objective that have been assigned to them. It is interesting in this respect to observe how the public debate has progressively crystallised on the view that the Commission should (and will) impose significant remedies in the investigation of Google's practices, in particular regarding the search market (which has, so far, lasted for more than five years). Such remedies have then become a default case, making it difficult for the Commission to defend any other position.

These cases confirm that the capture of competition enforcement in favour of some interest groups and in particular in favour of domestic firms and at the expense of foreign firms remains a concern. These concerns were also present in some famous cases of conflicts between the EU and the US. In transactions like GE–Honeywell, Boeing–McDonnell Douglass or Oracle–Sun, the effects were clearly different across jurisdictions. Nevertheless, it is not unreasonable to presume[22] that in those cases, conflicts have been exacerbated by the protection of interests that the authorities are not meant to protect (in particular, the interest of US companies).

These observations suggest that international governance could be improved by implementing a greater discipline towards the respect of national norms. Bilateral (or regional) FTAs could also provide the appropriate framework to do so. As discussed above, the agreements signed by the US support the objective of an effective implementation of national norms with respect to competition enforcement. Bilateral FTAs also often include a dispute resolution mechanism but competition enforcement is systematically excluded from its scope of application. It would thus appear attractive to explicitly include competition enforcement in the scope of application of these mechanisms. It is a simple and pragmatic measure which does not require any institutional development and addresses what is arguably one of the most pressing issues. Such a measure is also less politically sensitive that the harmonisation of instruments that might involve issues of domestic preferences and sovereignty.

21.5 TRADE LIBERALISATION AND COMPETITION ENFORCEMENT

The interface between trade policy and competition policy focuses on the prospect that market access commitments might be undone by RBPs. For instance, a reduction of duties in country A on imports from country B (a market access granted by country A to country B) could be annulled in terms of its effect on country B by an import cartel; assuming that the country A is 'large' so that its imports affect the world price of the commodity concerned, a commitment not to exercise buyer

---

[22]   In light, for instance, of public statements by the executive branch of government (W. E. Kovacic, P. C. Mavroidis and D. J. Neven, 'Merger Control Procedures and Institutions: A Comparison of EU and US Practice' (2014) 59 *Antitrust Bulletin* 55–109).

power through import duties would thus be replaced by the exercise of buyer power through a cartel. An exclusive dealing arrangement between distributors and domestic producers might also foreclose firms. Alternatively, the market access commitments could be undone by providing subsidies to the import competing sector in market A. Competition enforcement in country A might play an important role in disciplining such practices, which deny the benefits of market access to firms from country B.

The interrelationship between the trade and the competition regimes has actually been discussed at the GATT level since its inception. The GATT framers were mindful that trade liberalisation would have been half-served only if private barriers would be 'tolerated' by the trading nations. Indeed, the GATT was but a chapter of the wider ITO project, the International Trade Organization (ITO). The GATT (Chapter III of the ITO) was addressing state barriers to trade, whereas Chapter V, aimed to address private barriers to trade, and could thus be seen as competition regime. As the ITO was never completed, Chapter V never saw the light of day.[23]

As things stand, the default discipline is non-discrimination. WTO members can design any antitrust policy they wish, and must apply it in a non-discriminatory manner. They incur an additional obligation under GATS to respond to requests regarding antitrust enforcement, and some additional obligations regarding telecoms, such as the obligation to adopt reasonable access pricing, and avoid a few RBPs.

Article XXIV of GATT still maintained the link between the GATT and Chapter V, requesting from GATT members to endeavour to implement Chapter V (and thus address RBPs within their jurisdiction). This provision also provides WTO members with a mechanism to address situations in which market access has been denied through inadequate competition rules or inadequate enforcement of these rules (and thus provides a discipline beyond non-discrimination). WTO members can raise NVCs and request compensation in case other WTO members had not addressed RBPs within their jurisdiction.[24]

Through an NVC, WTO members can request compensation in case a measure is taken subsequent to an agreement regarding a tariff concession that defies the legitimate expectations of the complainant. The US raised a claim to this effect against Japan. In Japan-Film,[25] the panel accepted that an NVC was possible, but the associated burden of proof was quite demanding (and the US lost).

At the Singapore Ministerial Conference (1996), the WTO members decided to establish a working group to examine the relationship between trade and competition.[26]

---

[23] D. A. Irwin, P. C. Mavroidis and A. O. Sykes, *The Genesis of the GATT* (Cambridge University Press, 2008).

[24] B. M. Hoekman and P. C. Mavroidis, 'Competition, Competition Policy and the GATT' (1994) 17 *World Economy* 121–50.

[25] Dispute DS44, Japan – Measures Affecting Consumer Photographic Film and Paper (1998).

[26] There was a lively debate at the time, going beyond merely addressing the interface between trade liberalisation and competition enforcement, and considering more generally the development of a competition discipline in the WTO. See e.g. E. Fox, 'Toward World Antitrust and Market Access'

Fred Jenny, a senior French bureaucrat, was asked to head it. The Jenny group[27] produced an impressive set of documents discussing the relationship between trade and antitrust policies. It started on a rather ambitious note, but considerably downsized the level of ambition as time passed. At the end of the process, the guiding idea was to raise awareness, to provide a mechanism for monitoring antitrust practice around the world, and to substantially contribute to increase technical capacity. Still, despite its limited ambitions, the work of the group was interrupted at the Cancun Ministerial Conference (2003) (as mentioned above).

Ever since, the matter has not received much attention. Some studies have highlighted the welfare implications of RBPs by foreign companies for developing countries. For instance, Francois and Wooton[28] discuss the potential gains for developing countries from dismantling transport cartels, and in similar vein, Mattoo makes a persuasive case when arguing that Zambia has more to gain from addressing effectively RBPs than from focusing on trade deals.[29]

In terms of enforcement, there is only one competition-related dispute reported since Japan-Film. In Mexico Telecoms, the panel was asked to pronounce on the consistency of termination rates imposed by the Mexican monopolist with Mexico's obligations regarding access pricing under the GATS Telecoms Reference Paper.[30]

Going forward, we only wish to make a few remarks on the prospect for further initiatives regarding the interface between trade liberalisation of competition enforcement.

First, the competition enforcement that is required in order to prevent the denial of market access through RBPs may not be consistent with the mandate that is given to competition agencies. Import cartels are a case in point. Assuming that competition agencies protect consumers' interest, and to the extent that import cartels benefit importers and those benefits are passed on to domestic customers, domestic agencies which follow their mandate should not intervene.[31] Of course, this does not come as surprise to the extent that a policy of giving market access (whose effects are denied by the import cartel) may not increase the welfare of domestic customers in

---

(1997) 91 *American Journal of International Law* 1–32; E.-U. Petersmann, 'International Competition Rules for Private Business: A Trade Law Approach for Linking Trade and Competition Rules in the WTO – The Institutional and Jurisdictional Architecture' (1996) 15 Chicago-Kent Law Review 545–82; M. Bacchetta, H. Horn and P. C. Mavroidis, 'Do Negative Spill-overs from Nationally Pursued Competition Policies Provide a Case for Multilateral Competition Rules?', in Claus-Dieter Ehlermann and L. Laudati (eds.), *European Competition Law Annual: Objectives of Competition Policy* (Hart, 1998), 271–309; S. Bilal and M. Olarreaga, 'Competition Policy and the WTO: Is There a Need for a Multilateral Agreement?' (EIPA WP98/W/02: Maastricht, 1998).

27   All documents issued by this group can be found at the WTO webpage, www.wto.org/english/tratop_e/comp_e/comp_e.htm

28   J. Francois and I. Wooton, 'Market Structure and Market Access' (2010) 33 *World Economy* 873–93.

29   A. Mattoo, *Services Trade and Development: The Case of Zambia* (World Bank, 2007).

30   D. J. Neven and P. C. Mavroidis, 'El Mess in Telmex: A Comment on Mexico – Measures Affecting Telecommunications Services' (2006) 5 *World Trade Review* 271–96.

31   This will also arise if the objective of the importing jurisdiction gives some weight to domestic firm.

the first place. It is only because trade liberalisation involves reciprocal market access that it is attractive for all partners (and enhances consumer welfare). Hence, any attempt to introduce a discipline on competition enforcement in those circumstances should follow the logic of trade agreements, à la Bagwell–Staiger.[32] In other words, the enforcement of competition law towards import cartels in country A (which hurts the exporters of country B) should be part of the agreement in which country B commits to enforce competition rules towards its own import cartels (which hurt exporters in country A). However, unlike what happens with commitments to reduce tariffs, that can be easily verified, a commitment to apply competition rules towards import cartels requires an enforcement mechanism (as it cannot be directly observed). That is, it is necessary for each country to be in a position to challenge the way in other countries effectively abide by their commitment, through a dispute resolution mechanism.

Overall, then, a discipline not to undo market access commitments through competition rules:

1. may not be a natural task for competition agencies, as it requires them to operate with an objective such that they will prevent practices which benefit consumers in their jurisdiction unlike what they do in their core activity;
2. requires a reciprocal framework; and
3. a dispute resolution mechanism.

Second, the interplay between the border instrument (tariffs) and the domestic policies that can undo the benefits of market access may become more complicated in a world in which trade is organised along global value chains. The consequence of this observation is that non-violation complaints, difficult as they were, are likely to become even more difficult to sustain.

The intuition for this argument comes from Antras and Staiger.[33] They consider a simple framework in which tariff commitments can be undone by domestic subsidies, first in a framework in which the prices paid by the importing country are determined by market clearing conditions, and second in a framework in which prices are determined by bilateral bargaining between producers and customers and in which producers need to invest in relationship specific capital. This second set of circumstances describes transactions along a value chain. They show that as long as prices are determined by market clearing conditions (even in the presence of market power), a commitment on behind the border policies, such that they will preserve the volume of trade implied by the tariff commitments and the behind the border policy at the time the agreement will suffice.

In this context, the counterfactual that is relevant for an NVC (against which observed trade needs to be compared) is simply the volume of trade at the time of

---

[32] K. Bagwell and R. W. Staiger, *The Economics of the World Trading System* (MIT Press, 2002).
[33] P. Antras and R. W. Staiger, 'Offshoring and the Role of Trade Agreements' (2012) 102 *American Economic Review* 3140–83.

agreement. The situation is however different when prices are determined by bargaining. In those circumstances, the simple rule does not apply because the behind the border policies can be used to affect the allocation of the surplus between producers and customers, while keeping the trade volume constant. Hence, the counterfactual that would have to be developed in non-violation constraint is more complex and would thereby further reduce the prospect of success for such a complaint.

Third, new issues arise with respect to the interface between liberalisation and competition enforcement beyond the preservation of market access. This is particularly striking with respect to intellectual property. For instance, the recent decision by the EU Commission and the FTC towards the monetisation of standard essential patents (such that standard essential patent holders are largely prevented from seeking injunctions) act as regulatory instruments which affect incentives to invest (much as the patent policy). These policies will thus interfere with the design of international agreements with respect to IP protection, including the TRIPS agreement.

Whether such issues can be tackled in the WTO is however unclear, given its malaise about the Doha round. As discussed by Hoekman and Mavroidis,[34] a contractual agreement between like-minded members of the WTO may be preferable and may act as a laboratory for future regulatory interventions at the multilateral level when the circumstances will permit.

21.6 CONCLUSION

The discussions that took place in the 'Jenny group' following the Singapore ministerial decision and the policy debates around it, to which Eleanor Fox contributed so much, were remarkable in a number of ways. There was genuine ambition to develop a harmonised competition code and to implement it through the WTO. Even though, eventually the original ambition dwindled down to something more manageable, members of the group still envisaged a role for the WTO in the trade and competition debate. Some argued for increasing transparency, what Coglianese called 'fishbowl transparency'.[35] In this vein, the WTO would be notified of laws, important decisions and practice in the realm of antitrust. Others wanted to add some critical evaluation of national practice, approaching thus, Coglianese's 'reasoned transparency', where beyond information there is also explanation of national experiences. In the end, nothing happened. Today, such ambitions seem almost like a pipe dream.

---

[34] Bernard Hoekman and Petros C. Mavroidis, 'Regulatory Spillovers and the Trading System: From Coherence to Cooperation', WEF E15 Initiative (2015), available at http://e15initiative.org/wp-content/uploads/2015/04/E15-Regulatory-OP-Hoekman-and-Mavroidis-FINAL.pdf

[35] G. Coglianese, 'The Transparency President? The Obama Administration and Open Government' (2009) 22 *Governance* 529–44.

The Jenny group was also a place where the antitrust tribe and the trade tribe met. The debates were rich but did not crystallise or were not allowed to do so. One can only speculate about the reasons behind this evolution.

In retrospect, however, one can see that concerns about external effects in enforcement may have been too far away from concerns about the protection of market access commitments. Indeed, it is also striking that while the antitrust community successfully developed soft mechanisms of convergence, little has been achieved in terms of the interface between trade regulation and competition enforcement ever since.

In some way, this chapter also supports the view that merging the antitrust and the trade perspectives was unlikely to develop as a happy marriage. One of the main challenges of the governance of external effects from antitrust enforcement might be today to develop a mechanism of adjudication. This was never a problem with the interface between trade regulation and competition. Its main challenge may be to develop domestic institutions that will have incentives to ensure that market access commitments are not undone.

22

International Enforcement Cooperation and the Dynamics of Convergence

Damien Gerard

22.1 INTRODUCTION

After years of stalled negotiations, the dropping of competition policy from the WTO Doha Agenda in 2004 was widely perceived as the ultimate failure of attempts at establishing a multilateral framework of competition rules.[1] That failure has been conceived in terms of (un)balance between equity and efficiency,[2] and ascribed in particular to a lack of sensitivity for the "internationally nuanced and culturally distinctive" nature of equity considerations as reflected, in one way or another, in domestic competition principles.[3] Since then, the dominant discourse in the field of international antitrust has been one of cooperation and convergence.[4]

Cooperation has taken many different forms over the years, notably the conclusion of bilateral enforcement cooperation agreements and the creation of international platforms for the sharing of experience and related knowledge. In turn, convergence has been generally presented as both the rationale for and outcome of enforcement cooperation arrangements. Remarkably, however, convergence has been consistently used without much referential substance or with significantly

---

[1] Decision of the WTO General Council, August 1, 2004, WT/L/579 (available at www.wto.org/english/tratop_e/dda_e/draft_text_gc_dg_31july04_e.htm).

[2] See, e.g., G. Hufbauer and J. Kim, 'International Competition Policy and the WTO', Peterson Institute for International Economics, 2008 (available at https://piie.com/commentary/speeches-papers/international-competition-policy-and-wto).

[3] See E. Graham and D. Richardson (eds.), *Global Competition Policy* (Institute for International Economics, 1997), 8.

[4] For a review of these developments, see E. Fox, 'Toward World Antitrust and Market Access' (1997) 91 (1) AJIL 1; E. Fox, 'International Antitrust and the Doha Dome' (2003) 43(11) *Virginia Journal of International Law* 911; E. Fox, 'Can We Solve the Antitrust Problems of Globalization by Extraterritoriality and Cooperation? – Sufficiency and Legitimacy' (2003) 48 *Antitrust Bulletin* 355; E. Fox, 'Antitrust without Borders: From Roots to Codes to Networks', in A. Guzman (ed.), *Cooperation, Comity, and Competition Policy* (Oxford University Press, 2010), 265.

different meanings ranging from the most general to the most specific,[5] thereby leading to what has been described as an "analytical chaos."[6]

In *Global Competition*, Gerber denounced indeed the use of convergence as "an easily-wielded rhetorical device" that often carries little meaning beyond the "increasing similarity among [legal] systems."[7] In that monograph, he then endeavored to sketch out the contours of convergence as "an increase in characteristics shared by competition law regimes and a reduction in non-shared characteristics,"[8] and to identify some of the key features thereof. First, for Gerber, convergence refers to "independent choices by states, i.e., choices that are not the subject of agreement,"[9] which distinguishes convergence from harmonization. Second, in his view, the concept of convergence "presupposes a point or points toward which individual decisions are moving."[10] Third, for Gerber convergence constitutes a sort of stand-alone process occurring outside any "framework of institutions and shared commitments," which would consequently deprive it from the possibility to "significantly improve the effectiveness of the jurisdictional system" because "it does not create obligations among states that can foster mutually supportive relationships or undergird continued convergence."[11] As a result of that limitation, Gerber prefers the idea of "commitment pathway" whereby "participants sketch a path towards agreed goals and establish obligations to support movement towards these goals."[12] While "[e]lements of the pathway are expected to take on sharper form as states interact in moving along it," commitments are "shared in the sense that the project's success would depend on the commitment of all participants to the project's goals."[13]

Following Gerber's pioneering work in the field, the present contribution aims to further substantiate the dynamics of convergence and hence to underline its potential as a means for balancing efficiency claims put forward by global trading interests and the diversity of equity considerations blended into the interpretation and enforcement of domestic competition principles applicable across the world. To do so, the contribution starts with a descriptive account of the stated achievements of the EU cooperative enforcement framework in terms of convergence. Subsequently, while acknowledging the uniqueness of the EU experience, it

---

[5] For illustration purposes, see J. Ph. Terhechte, 'International Competition Enforcement Law Between Cooperation and Convergence – Mapping a New Field for Global Administrative Law', *Working Paper CCLP (L) 26*, 2009, 8; A. Gerbrandy, 'Procedural Convergence in Competition Law' (2009) *Rev. Eur. Adm. L.* 110, 114, and 134; D. Geradin, 'Competition Law and Regional Economic Integration', *World Bank Working Paper no. 35*, 2004, 68–9.

[6] D. Gerber, *Global Competition: Law, Markets, and Globalization* (Oxford University Press, 2010), 281.

[7] Ibid., 282 and 292.

[8] Ibid., 282.

[9] Ibid., 281.

[10] Ibid., 282.

[11] Ibid., 291.

[12] Ibid., 295.

[13] Ibid.

attempts to derive a number of determinants of convergence but also to highlight some of the limits inherent to that concept and to formulate suggestions to overcome them. Eventually, at a time where the equity considerations embedded in antitrust enforcement receive renewed attention in various parts of the world and where multilateral international cooperation appears out of fashion, this contribution exposes the potential and limitations of convergence with a view to encouraging a reassessment of the cooperative strategies deployed since the decision to discontinue WTO negotiations on global competition norms.

22.2 CONVERGENCE IN EU COMPETITION LAW

In 2008, upon the fifth anniversary of the entry into force of Regulation 1/2003, the European Commission contended that the implementation thereof had prompted convergence both in substantive competition law principles and procedural enforcement rules. Thus, according to the Commission, the "constant dialogue" and "permanent exchange of experiences and views" between EU Member States' competition authorities within the European Competition Network (ECN) "has established confidence and trust between network members, increased the expertise and promoted convergence," thereby contributing to "a coherent approach and coherent application of the [EU] competition rules".[14] Similarly, the entry into force of Regulation 1/2003 was also deemed to have "generated an unprecedented degree of voluntary convergence of the procedural rules dedicated to the implementation of Articles [101] and [102 TFEU]."[15] In 2013, in a retrospective essay over ten years of EU competition law enforcement pursuant to Regulation 1/2003, a prominent DG COMP's official confirmed these earlier statements: "[t]he application of Regulation 1/2003 has also given rise to a significant degree of voluntary convergence of Member States' laws as to the procedures and sanctioning powers of national competition authorities, supported by the policy work in the European Competition Network."[16] While considering that "further alignment in terms of sanctions and procedure" is required in order to prevent "this system [to] lose ... its legitimacy in the long run," a director of the German Cartel Office otherwise equally acknowledged that "the path taken in the last ten years ... resulted undoubtedly in far more convergence than was expected ten years ago."[17] Interestingly, that view seems to be widely shared among EU Member State authorities, as apparent from a special issue of the ECN Brief published on the occasion of the tenth Anniversary of Regulation 1/2003.[18] A closer look at the various contributions to that publication indicates that convergence is associated in

---

[14] 1/2003 SWP, para. 249.
[15] 1/2003 Report, para. 31 and 1/2003 SWP, p. 201.
[16] W. Wils, 'Ten Years of Regulation 1/2003 – A Retrospective' (2003) JECL&P.
[17] K. Ost, 'From Regulation 1 to Regulation 2: National Enforcement of EU Cartel Prohibition and the Need for Further Convergence' (2014) JECL&P 131 and 136.
[18] ECN Brief 05/2012 – Extended Issue, 36–56 (available at http://ec.europa.eu/competition/ecn/brief/ 05_2012/brief_05_2012_short.pdf).

particular with three interrelated phenomena, namely: (a) the entry into force of Regulation 1/2003; (b) the operation of enforcement cooperation mechanisms; and (c) interactions within the ECN framework.

22.2.1 Convergence Prompted by the Entry into Force of Regulation 1/2003

The wording of many national antitrust provisions prohibiting collusive and abusive practices was already consistent with that of Articles 101 and 102 TFEU prior to the entry into force of Regulation 1/2003.[19] The prospect of enlargement,[20] on the one hand, and of the passing of Regulation 1/2003,[21] on the other hand, further stimulated that alignment in "new" and "old" Member States, respectively. The example of Hungary is illustrative of the impact of the enlargement process since "the 13 years spent in 'association status' between 1991–2004 had given Hungary the opportunity to gradually adjust the national competition rules to European Law" so that "on the eve of accession, Hungarian competition law was to a great extent harmonized with EU law."[22] The impact of the adoption of Regulation 1/2003 is then aptly exemplified by the situation of Austria where "the modernization process behind what was to become Regulation 1/2003 in late 2002 influenced the political and legislative process ... already from 2000 onward" and then culminated with the enactment of a new Cartel Act in 2005 that "marked the abolition of the notification system and aligned the text of Article 1 Cartel Act (as well as the conditions for exemptions foreseen in Article 2) with Article 81 EC Treaty (now Article 101 TFEU)."[23] The abolition of the notification system for agreements (not affecting cross-border trade) has been a recurrent feature of national competition law reforms in the early 2000s,[24] not only because the process leading to the adoption of Regulation 1/2003 had raised doubts about the alleged virtues of that system, but also because of the

---

[19] On the alignment of UK competition law on EU standards following the adoption of the UK Competition Act 1998, for example, see F. Barr, 'Has the U.K. Gone European: Is the European Approach of the Competition Bill More than an Illusion?' (1998) ECLR 139; J. Nazerali and D. Cowan, 'Importing the E.U. Model into U.K. Competition Law: A Blueprint for Reform or a Step into 'Euroblivion'?' (1999) ECLR 55; M. Cini, 'The Europeanisation of British Competition Policy', in I. Bache and A. Jordan (eds.), *Britain in Europe and Europe in Britain: The Europeanization of British Politics?* (Palgrave, 2006), 216.

[20] See, e.g., K. Cseres, 'Multi-jurisdictional Competition Law Enforcement: The Interface between European Competition Law and the Competition Laws of the New Member States' (2007) *Eur. Comp. J.* 465; L. Donnedieu de Vabres-Tranié, 'Nouveaux Etats membres: l'application du droit de la concurrence entre convergence et particularismes' (2007) *Rev. Lamy Conc.* 104.

[21] A large number of national competition statutes were amended shortly before, at the time of or shortly after the adoption and/or entry into force of Regulation 1/2003 (for an overview, see the Antitrust Encyclopedia available at www.concurrences.com).

[22] ECN Brief 05/2012, p. 44.

[23] Ibid., p. 36.

[24] See ECN Working Group on Cooperation Issues – Results of the questionnaire on the reform of Member States (MS) national competition laws after EC Regulation 1/2003, May 22, 2013, p. 2 (available at http://ec.europa.eu/competition/ecn/convergence_table_en.pdf).

uncertainty that the maintenance of such a system at national level would have caused for businesses. Likewise, new decisional competences granted to EU Member States' competition authorities (known as NCAs) by Regulation 1/2003, e.g. to accept commitments or order interim measures, were naturally extended to cases falling under national jurisdiction,[25] which led the ECN to conclude recently that "the decision-making powers in terms of prohibition decisions, commitment decisions, interim measures are very wide-spread."[26]

From a substantive point of view, the so-called "convergence clause" contained in Article 3 of Regulation 1/2003 prompted the alignment of national provisions dealing with coordinated practice with the wording of Article 101 TFEU, as it was the case in Austria or Finland,[27] but also ironed out national idiosyncrasies in relation to dominance. For example, in Latvia, "the previously existing 40% threshold as a mandatory indication for dominant position was removed, thus bringing the notion of dominance closer to the EU competition rules."[28] Similarly, once Romania accessed the EU, it "abolished the existing rebuttable presumption of 35% market share for establishing a dominant position in order to be fully convergent with Article 102 TFEU."[29] Generally, the reliance on a common language further promoted deep convergence in the interpretation of those similarly worded competition provisions,[30] notably by means of cross-references to EU cases and national cases applying EU law, even in purely national situations, and the development of and reliance on common analytical tools. Unsurprisingly, for instance, the Slovak NCA emphasized that it commonly "relies on EU case law in its decisional practice."[31] In Finland, the legislator sought to define key terms, such as that of "undertaking," along with the EU equivalent.[32] In Belgium, ensuring consistency in competition law enforcement went beyond a general commitment to rely on EU precedents even in purely domestic cases and was formalized by, e.g. the transplant of Articles 101 and 102 TFEU in domestic law, the

---

[25] Ibid., pp. 3–4. As a concrete example, the Bulgarian Law on Protection of Competition enacted in 2008 'empowered the [NCA] with new competences, namely to impose interim measures and approve commitments proposed by undertakings (in line with the provisions of Article 5 of Regulation 1/2003)' (ECN Brief 05/2012, p. 37). Likewise, Art. 12C of the 2004 Competition Act of Malta (Chapter 379 of the Laws of Malta), inasmuch as it allows undertakings to offer commitments to the Director General of the Office for Competition to meet his concerns, 'is essentially based on Article 9 of Regulation 1/2003' (ECB Brief 05/2012, p. 49).

[26] ECN Working Group Cooperation Issues and Due Process, *Decision-Making Powers Report*, October 31, 2012 (available at http://ec.europa.eu/competition/ecn/decision_making_powers_repor t_en.pdf).

[27] See, respectively, the 2005 Austrian Cartel Law and the 2004 Finnish Act 480/1992 on Competition Restrictions, as amended by Act 318/2004. Generally, the ECN considers that '[c]onvergence in substantive analysis in antitrust is achieved through the obligation for NCAs and national courts to apply Articles 101 and 102 TFEU pursuant to Article 3 of Regulation 1/2003' (ECN Working Group Cooperation Issues and Due Process, *Investigative Powers Report*).

[28] ECN Brief 05/2012, p. 47.

[29] Ibid., p. 37.

[30] 1/2003 Report, para. 21.

[31] ECN Brief 05/2012, p. 53.

[32] Ibid., p. 42.

incorporation of all EU block exemption regulations into Belgian law or the Supreme Court's refusal to apply "stricter" rules than foreseen by Article 102 TFEU and the equivalent Belgian provision to unilateral conducts engaged into by dominant companies.[33]

Over time, however, the original convergence toward rules and standards developed at EU level – which served as focal/starting points – has given place to a communalization of these standards as a result of the functioning of the ECN acting as a socialization and learning platform to the extent that, as Idot puts it, antitrust rules in the Union now amounts to "a law shaped in common" by the Commission and NCAs.[34] Yet, before examining evidence of that phenomenon, it is appropriate to explore convergence resulting from the operation of enforcement cooperation mechanisms inasmuch as it is primarily rooted in processes introduced by Regulation 1/2003, though largely supported by ECN initiatives.

22.2.2 *Convergence Resulting from the Operation of Enforcement Cooperation Mechanisms*

Regulation 1/2003 has established a number of enforcement cooperation mechanisms whereby NCAs and the Commission can exchange information and request each other's assistance in carrying out investigation duties. To that extent, the entry into force of Regulation 1/2003 has brought a "fundamental change" to the enforcement of antitrust law in Europe "by laying the foundation of effective cooperation between the competition authorities of the EU."[35] Over time, that cooperation has materialized in various cases involving primarily neighboring countries but also more distant Member States. Thus Denmark and Sweden are known to have mutually assisted each other on several occasions in recent years "in carrying out inspections and in sending out requests for information pursuant to Article 22" of Regulation 1/2003.[36] More surprisingly, the Romanian Competition Council has also reported having received assistance from the NCAs of Austria,

---

[33] Arts. 2 and 3 of the 2006 Act on the Protection of Economic Competition ('APEC' – *M.B./B.S.*, September 29, 2006, p. 50613) were deemed to be 'directly inspired by the European rules on competition' to the point of each being the 'carbon copy' of Arts. 101 and 102 TFUE (Projet de loi sur la protection de la concurrence économique, exposé des motifs, *Doc. Parl.*, Ch., sess. ord. 2005–6, no. 2180/001, pp. 11–12 – free translation from the original in French). The Belgian legislator also expressed the willingness that companies 'could mutatis mutandis rely on the case law developed by European institutions' (ibid., p. 8). Likewise, the notions of undertaking and dominant position defined in Art. 1 APEC 'are borrowed from the competition case law of the General Court of the European Union, in order of ensuring a greater legal certainty to companies which can refer to the interpretation given to these notions by the authorities of the European Union' (ibid.). Moreover, Art. IV.3 of the Code of Economic Law has also the effect of incorporating in domestic law the substance of all EU block exemption regulations.

[34] L. Idot, 'Réflexions sur la convergence des droits de la concurrence', *Concurrences*, 4/2012, p. 5 (free translation of 'un droit construit en commun').

[35] ECN Brief 05/2012, p. 42.

[36] Ibid., p. 39.

Bulgaria but also Italy, Netherland, and even Sweden in several investigative procedures.[37] In turn, the effective operation of enforcement cooperation mechanisms has prompted the convergence of substantive and procedural antitrust rules and principles across the Union.

First of all, the ECN has highlighted that "[c]onvergence in substantive analysis in antitrust" has been achieved not only by means of the conflict rules included in Article 3 of Regulation 1/2003 but also through "the mechanisms contained in this instrument to ensure co-operation and coherency (Articles 11 to 16 and 22)."[38] Intuitively, it is not difficult to understand how rules organizing the mutual information of openings of investigations or the peer review of proposed decisions may have indeed contributed to ensure consistency in the interpretation of Articles 101 and 102 TFEU and their national equivalents. Clearly, it was their intended purpose. The link between substantive convergence and investigative assistance mechanisms is more diffuse yet also understandable inasmuch as convergence constitutes an effective safeguard against possible objections to the execution of requests for cooperation rooted in the public policy nature of competition law principles. That said, enforcement cooperation mechanisms have primarily led to the convergence of procedural enforcement rules across systems.

The operation of these mechanisms has indeed prompted Member States to amend their enforcement framework so as to adequately respond to requests for assistance. As a result, based on an extensive survey of NCAs' investigative powers, the ECN concluded in 2012 that "[a] significant degree of voluntary convergence of Member States' laws has been achieved to date."[39] This is confirmed by various individual testimonies according to which national enforcement frameworks were amended to "enhance … the mechanisms for cooperation within the ECN" or "in light of practical experience gained in enforcing the competition rules" pursuant to Regulation 1/2003.[40] For example, Austria ensured that its NCA was "vested with the power to seal premises during inspections as well as to ask for explanations on facts and documents relating to the subject-matter and purpose of the inspection," but also to "issue requests for information by way of binding decisions (instead of obtaining a court order)."[41] Finland also strengthened its NCAs' investigatory powers, notably by allowing it to carry out inspections of private premises and to "summon a natural person for an interview if there is reasonable suspicion of their participation in a competition infringement."[42] Naturally, as for substantive convergence, the investigation powers of the Commission set forth under Regulation 1/

---

[37] Ibid., p. 52. See also the experience of the Portuguese NCA as reported on p. 51.

[38] ECN Working Group Cooperation Issues and Due Process, *Decision-Making Powers Report* and *Investigative Powers Report*, p. 5.

[39] ECN Working Group Cooperation Issues and Due Process, *Investigative Powers Report*, p. 48.

[40] ECN Brief 05/2012, pp. 36 and 52.

[41] Ibid., p. 36.

[42] Ibid., p. 41.

2003 initially served as a focal point for the approximation of procedural enforcement frameworks.[43] Yet, with time, one could witness a "trend to take account of developments elsewhere in the ECN" and,[44] eventually, the development of ECN model rules based on the input of a large number of ECN members and aimed to induce the hybridization of procedural enforcement powers and rules across systems.

The first such initiative consisted in the adoption of a ECN Model Leniency Programme (MLP) in 2006,[45] which was subsequently amended in 2012,[46] thereby testifying of the prominence of leniency in modern antitrust enforcement. The rationale for the development of the MLP lay primarily in the absence of a "one-stop-shop" system at Union level, so that applicants are forced to file for leniency with all authorities whose territory is affected by the potential infringement. Yet the incentive to do so depends to a significant extent on the characteristics of each domestic leniency program and on possible discrepancies between them, which may subject applicants to conflicting demands and thereby jeopardize the attractiveness of leniency in general. Conversely, greater convergence between national leniency programs is also such as to facilitate coordination between authorities in case of multiple applications, including for the allocation of the case and the coordination of subsequent inspections. Hence, ECN members "committed to make their best efforts to align their leniency programmes with the principles of the MLP,"[47] and so they did. In 2009, a ECN Report on Assessment of the State of Convergence concluded that "[t]he work within the ECN has been a major catalyst in encouraging Member States and/or authorities to introduce and develop their leniency policies and in promoting convergence between them."[48] For example, the MLP "served as a basis for the Cypriot Leniency Programme" and the implementation thereof was facilitated "[t]hanks to the exchange of experience with other ECN members."[49] Likewise, "[c]ooperation within the ECN was vital for the overhaul of the leniency programme [of the Portuguese NCA], including the development of the ECN Leniency Model Program and subsequent discussions and exchanges of experiences between competition authorities."[50] At the end of 2012, all but one

---

[43] See, e.g., the amendments brought to the Maltese Competition Act in 2011, which 'had the effect of aligning the procedures under the Competition Act with Regulation 1/2003' and of giving the NCA 'wide investigatory powers … akin to those found under Regulation 1/2003' (ibid., p. 48).

[44] ECN Working Group Cooperation Issues and Due Process, *Investigative Powers Report*, p. 49.

[45] ECN Model Leniency Programme, September 2006 (available at http://ec.europa.eu/competition/ ecn/model_leniency_en.pdf).

[46] ECN Model Leniency Programme (as revised), November 2012 (available at: http://ec.europa.eu/ competition/ecn/mlp_revised_2012_en.pdf).

[47] ECN Brief 05/2012, p. 40.

[48] ECN Model Leniency Programme – Report on Assessment of the State of Convergence (available at http://ec.europa.eu/competition/ecn/model_leniency_programme.pdf).

[49] ECN Brief 05/2012, p. 38.

[50] Ibid., p. 51.

ECN members operated a leniency program and "[t]hey broadly follow the shared principles agreed by the ECN."[51]

The MLP experiment was replicated on a much broader scale in 2013 with the endorsement and publication of a set of seven ECN Recommendations on key investigative and decision-making powers,[52] with the avowed objective "[t]o ensure further convergence within the ECN" and thereby "facilitate co-operation."[53] That initiative came as a follow-up to two surveys of procedural differences in Member States' antitrust enforcement frameworks which highlighted that, in spite of the observed convergence, "divergence subsists" though essentially "at a more detailed level."[54] The two reports aimed to "provide a basis for informed debate about the need for further procedural convergence within the ECN."[55] Yet, initially, they were prompted by the growing recognition of the risk created by procedural discrepancies for the proper functioning of the EU cooperative antitrust enforcement system. The German NCA, in particular, advocated the need for greater procedural convergence as "an important next step to ensure the good functioning of a system of parallel competences" that has otherwise "proven to be a great success."[56] Remarkably, though, the concerns of the German NCA extend beyond the scope of the 2013 ECN Recommendations to the issue of sanctions. Thus, "[i]n a system of flexible case allocation, the possible sanction imposed on a company for an antitrust infringement should not be too divergent" because,[57] essentially, "it is difficult to accept that a decision on case allocation which is not subject to appeal can decide on fundamental questions such as parental liability or succession in fines procedure."[58] These remarks touch upon a central and therefore highly sensitive enforcement aspect – that of sanctioning powers – in which diversity remains extremely wide. Today, the so-called ECN+ Directive(Directive 2019/1) has been adopted to precisely address key remaining procedural differences deemed to

---

[51] See European Commission, 'European Competition Network Refines Its Model Leniency Programme', November 22, 2012 (MEMO/12/887).

[52] See, respectively: (1) ECN Recommendation on Investigative Powers, Enforcement Measures and Sanctions in the Context of Inspections and Requests for Information; (2) ECN Recommendation on the Power to Collect Digital Evidence, including by Forensic Means; (3) ECN Recommendation on Assistance in Inspections conducted under Articles 22(1) of Regulation (EC) No. 1/2003; (4) ECN Recommendation on the Power to set Priorities; (5) ECN Recommendation on Interim Measures; (6) ECN Recommendation on Commitment Procedures; and (7) ECN Recommendation on the Power to Impose Structural Remedies (available at http://ec.europa.eu/competition/ecn/documents.html #powers).

[53] See, e.g., ECN Recommendation on Investigative Powers, Enforcement Measures and Sanctions in the Context of Inspections and Requests for Information, p. 5 and ECN Recommendation on the Power to Collect Digital Evidence, including by Forensic Means, pp. 2 and 4.

[54] ECN Working Group Cooperation Issues and Due Process, *Decision-Making Powers Report* and *Investigative Powers Report*, pp. 80 and 49, respectively.

[55] Ibid.

[56] ECN Brief 05/2012, p. 43.

[57] Ibid., p. 42.

[58] Ost, 'From Regulation 1 to Regulation 2', 131.

impede the effectiveness of antitrust enforcement, including in its cooperative dimension.[59]

22.2.3 *Convergence Resulting from Interactions within the European Competition Network (ECN)*

Various accounts reveal that interactions within the ECN and associated socialization and learning processes constitute a third source of convergence of substantive and procedural antitrust enforcement rules and principles. As noted, the peer review of enforcement outcomes and the exchange of local experiences can usefully contribute to the development of consensus and, with the translation thereof in the relevant forums, to convergence across systems. Hence, it was hypothesized that the ECN could grow into a platform for policy discussions and experience/expertise sharing, thereby prompting the emergence of common legal concepts. In effect, though the phenomenon is inherently complex and difficult to apprehend, the ECN seems to have induced a form of communalization of substantive antitrust principles and procedural enforcement tools. As Idot puts it, "the operation of the network, the constant benchmarking that it entails through exchanges of opinions and meetings among authorities at all levels, have enable an undeniable approximation of national legislations."[60] Moreover, instead of being imposed top-down by the Commission, that approximation "plays out and develops increasingly in an ascending way," i.e., as a bottom-up process.[61] This is indeed consistent with the Commission's own report of how the ECN was actively involved in the preparation of the 2009 dominance guidance paper and in the review of the EU block exemption regulations and guidelines on vertical and horizontal agreements.[62] Overall, "we are not just applying the same law," DG COMP's Director General Italianer once claimed, "[b]y working together, we are also fine-tuning the application of the law."[63] Testimonies of NCAs abound in the same direction.

Generally, the ECN is recognized by NCAs as having "achieved a much higher level of participation in the efficient and harmonious enforcement" of antitrust principles in Europe and thereby "facilitated greater convergence between the EU and national competition regimes."[64] The ECN's learning and socialization virtues appear to have particularly contributed to that phenomenon. For example, the

---

[59] Proposal for a Directive to empower the competition authorities of the Member States to be more effective enforcers and to ensure the proper functioning of the internal market, 22.3.2017, COM(2017) 142 final.

[60] L. Idot, 'Réflexions sur la convergence des droits de la concurrence', *Concurrences*, 4/2012, p. 7 (free translation from the original in French).

[61] Ibid.

[62] See, e.g., the 1/2003 SWP, pp. 72–4.

[63] A. Italianer, 'Completing Convergence', Rome, October 10, 2014 (available at http://ec.europa.eu/competition/speeches/text/sp2014_05_en.pdf).

[64] ECN Brief 05/2012, p. 48.

important role played by the ECN as a platform to "exchange useful information and expertise and participate in the formulation of policies as well as to coordinate on the application of competition policy," has been pointed out by the NCA of Cyprus, which further emphasized how the knowledge, information and guidance shared within the ECN "has enabled [it] to avoid pitfalls and bypass to a large extent the learning curve" in the enforcement of competition law.[65] "Informal exchanges of information" were also said to "have been extremely useful in broadening [the Portuguese NCA's] knowledge base in a very wide range of areas of competition enforcement and advocacy."[66] While also recognizing that its staff "has learnt and continues learning from the practice and expertise of other ECN members," the Hungarian NCA further praised the role of the ECN in "the widening of personal relations among the members of competition authorities on different levels (heads of authorities, general contact persons, chief economists, investigators)," which allows for "fruitful and lively exchange of views and close liaison with colleagues from other NCAs" and "makes cooperation smoother" as a result.[67] In turn, the exchange of experience and best practices among its members in the framework of various working groups "has kept the European Competition Network at the cutting edge of competition law and policy," it was reported,[68] which tends to confirm its experimentalist potential. For the Commission, indeed, "the ECN continuously stimulates the development and exploration of new paths,"[69] which can be logically explained by the fact that "on a daily basis, it is the NCAs that deal with issues, including new problems"; "given that experience," Idot explains, "they can then put forward their own viewpoint within the process leading to the adoption of generally applicable texts."[70]

While the entry into force of Regulation 1/2003 and the operation of enforcement cooperation mechanisms led to amendments to domestic laws and policy guidelines, interactions within the ECN seem to have rather enabled NCAs and the Commission to develop consensuses on interpretative standards and analytical frameworks for the application of Articles 101 and 102 TFEU and their national equivalents, i.e., to induce a form of deep convergence at the level of applicable principles. This is also apparent from the various reports published by ECN sectoral subgroups on competition enforcement in, e.g., the food or banking and payment sectors.[71] Still, the socialization and learning functions of the ECN have also

---

[65] Ibid., p. 38.
[66] Ibid., p. 52.
[67] Ibid., pp. 58–9.
[68] Ibid., p. 52.
[69] Ibid., p. 1.
[70] Idot, 'Réflexions', 5 (free translation from the original in French).
[71] See Report on competition law enforcement and market monitoring activities by European competition authorities in the food sector, May 24, 2012; Information paper on competition enforcement in the payments sector, March 20, 2012 (both available at http://ec.europa.eu/competition/ecn/documents .html).

influenced the formulation of domestic policies and the drafting of local laws. Amendments to the Polish Act on Competition and Consumer Protection, for example, "benefited from contributions from the ECN members, who provided a detailed overview of their relevant national legislation."[72] Likewise, the provisions of the 2008 Bulgarian Law on Protection of Competition drew "on the enforcement practices of the European Commission" but also of "other NCAs."[73]

Ten years after the entry into force of Regulation 1/2003, the Commission and NCAs concurred to claim that "the developments which have taken place at European level and within the ECN have led to a high degree of convergence."[74] As noted, the regulation itself – and even the prospect of its adoption – induced a fair amount of convergence, notably because of the obligations contained in Article 3 thereof. As a result of these obligations, combined with repeated interactions through peer-review mechanisms and policy discussions within the ECN, "[t]he substantive standards under which anti-competitive practices are assessed throughout the EU have been aligned to a large degree."[75] At the same time, the diversity of domestic procedural enforcement frameworks has been progressively accommodated by the operation of enforcement cooperation mechanisms and the development at ECN level of common model rules. In effect, multilateral work within the ECN is considered to have been "a catalyst in promoting greater convergence," in particular of procedures.[76] Even if "divergences subsist" and, indeed, lasting differences in terms of investigative powers, sanctions, and due process continue to raise important concerns for the legitimacy of the system set forth by Regulation 1/2003, which constituted the main rationale for the adoption of the ECN+ Directive, that regulation is said to have "played a significant role for improving the legal framework for the protection of competition in the EU and increasing the effective implementation of both EU and national competition rules, thereby creating favourable conditions for the development of a coherent competition policy in the EU."[77]

If convergence appears to be a widespread phenomenon in EU competition law enforcement, it is certainly not foreign to the context in which it developed. In particular, as observed, the pre-existence of established substantive antitrust standards and procedural enforcement rules at EU level, backed by a sophisticated body of precedents, appears to have played the role of focal point(s) and to have thereby ignited the convergence process. As such, increasing similarities in statutory language says little about actual convergence in practice, yet these similarities stirred the convergence process with the help of the largely positive perception of the EU enforcement system among NCAs. In truth, from a substantive point of view, Article

---

[72] ECN Brief 05/2012, p. 50.
[73] Ibid., p. 37.
[74] Ibid., p. 36.
[75] Ibid., p. 42.
[76] Commission Communication, 'Ten Years of Antitrust Enforcement under Regulation 1/2003: Achievements and Future Perspective', COM(2014) 453, p. 9.
[77] Ibid., p. 38.

3 of Regulation 1/2003 established an obligation going beyond convergence when it comes to coordinated practices. Yet that provision also fueled incentives to converge in other areas, such as dominance, and contributed to stimulating a culture of convergence extending to procedural enforcement rules. Both substantive and procedural convergence were subsequently enhanced by the dynamism of the ECN, a close-knit network with the defined task of facilitating enforcement cooperation mandated by binding rules but whose operations rapidly extended behind that original task to develop into a knowledge-sharing platform. The mutual learning resulting from the policy discussions conducted at ECN level then contributed to foster deep convergence in the interpretation of antitrust concepts, as sometimes translated in policy guidance, and to develop model rules in the form of recommended best practices aimed to drive convergence further beyond the scope of Regulation 1/2003.

In the end, it appears that the effective – but by no means perfect – convergence observable in the field of EU competition law results from a very sophisticated strategy that seems hardly replicable outside of the EU framework, if for the sole reason that competition is the only field in which the Union possesses enforcement powers of its own, and since more than fifty years. At least, expectations are that convergence would take different forms and occur with a (very) different degree of effectiveness in other international frameworks. Still, precisely because convergence appears to have occurred on a uniquely wide scale within the EU since the entry into force of Regulation 1/2003 and the beginning of the ECN operations, the EU experience carries significant value in identifying key determinants of convergence and informing the design of enforcement cooperation arrangements on a wider scale. Hence, the remainder of this contribution substantiates a number of said determinants and then discusses their limits and those of convergence as such.

22.3 THE DYNAMICS AND LIMITS OF CONVERGENCE

This section builds on the intuition that the achievement of convergence is related to features specific to enforcement cooperation arrangements. Naturally, because of the indirect, autonomous, and diffuse nature of convergence, it is inherently difficult to establish clear causation relationships between occurrences of convergence (or not) and specific cooperation fixtures. Still, the present section ventures into discussing mechanisms capable of generating and sustaining convergence in order to contribute to a better understanding of how it can be expected to function. The ambition is therefore to advance beyond "vague and perhaps little recognized assumptions" on which claims of convergence appear to often rest.[78] After reviewing different determinants of convergence, the limits thereof are equally considered. Indeed, because it typically results from a combination of multiple and dispersed

---

[78] Gerber, *Global Competition*, 283.

forces, convergence presents an inherent complexity and instability which raise questions in terms of effectiveness, due process, and accountability. These questions also need to be investigated in order to inform policy choices beyond the EU, and possibly also beyond competition law.

22.3.1 Conditions for Convergence

The following paragraphs attempt to single out some of the determinants of convergence, i.e., factors that are likely to actually cause domestic policymakers to take steps to reduce the divergences of their legal framework relative to that of other domestic legal orders, on the one hand, and to influence the reach, depth, and speed of convergence, on the other hand. Naturally, no single factor is determinative, as convergence is an incremental process that relies on the interplay between a set of factors. Moreover, the study of these factors and of their respective contribution to the promotion of convergence appears to remain to date an open field of research approached here from a narrow legal angle whereas it would benefit from a wider range of expertise cutting across the social sciences.

22.3.1.1 The Peculiarity of the EU Context

To start with, it is a fact that the EU context constitutes a peculiar environment characterized by an upfront commitment to "the process of European integration,"[79] the existence of a large body of common norms and meta-principles by which Member States are expected to abide and sophisticated institutions dedicated to the management of common problems. That environment is naturally conducive to the formation of shared beliefs (e.g. on the welfare benefits of competition and some high-level equity considerations), the fostering of interactions between legal orders (e.g. due to the free movement of goods and persons) and the search for mutually agreeable solutions, which entail the exposure of local differences, the reliance on comparative analyses and the development of a culture of accommodations.[80]

The magnitude of interactions between Member States creates interdependences, shared interests, and shared challenges, the reach of which requires overcoming lasting differences in legal traditions and *"mentalités"*. To that end, institutions have traditionally acted as catalysts for the devising of common solutions through a wide variety of hard and soft tools. In turn, the level of integration already achieved in the EU allows for – and sometimes mandates – experimenting with more relaxed forms of approximation.[81] That existing framework of shared

---

[79] See the first recital of the preamble to the Treaty on European Union.

[80] For a discussion on the role of comparative law in the EU context, see, e.g., K. Lenaerts, 'Interlocking Legal Orders in the European Union and Comparative Law' (2003) ICLQ 873.

[81] In that respect, Krisch generally observed that "[m]any articulations of pluralism … arise out of context of close integration," notably because they "reflect processes of resistance to the rise of regional

commitments and established institutions distinguishes the EU framework from other – global or regional – contexts in which convergence has been discussed, sometimes with skepticism.[82]

The link between convergence and cooperation constitutes a second important distinguishing factor between the EU and other contexts entertaining claims of convergence. Thus, convergence in the EU does not rest on ethereal assumptions about the alleged power of rationality, socialization, or hortatory efforts,[83] but is rooted in elaborated regulatory schemes structuring and promoting iterative inter-actions between domestic legal systems by means of coordination mechanisms taking the form of conflict (including recognition) rules and of the organization of enforcement agents in networks. This means that convergence results albeit indir-ectly from the setting up of binding instruments, even if procedural in nature, generating obligations capable of fostering mutually supportive relationships but also of creating common constraints calling for solutions to ease them while complying with the gist of the decision to tackle the relevant policy issue in common in the first place. In other words, the cooperative strategy being pursued, and in particular the willingness to secure the benefits of entering into that cooperative strategy, creates incentives to accommodate tensions arising from local idiosyncra-sies and thus generates an impetus to converge. Moreover, in such context, conver-gence can also encompass more traditional spillover phenomena resulting from the need to remedy irritations caused to the domestic legal system by the adoption of cooperation instruments and from the willingness to maintain coherence within the legal system in question.[84] Eventually, it can be said that convergence as understood in the EU context is inherently coupled with cooperation so that the relevant question is less how to prompt convergence in such a cooperative environment than what factors are likely to weight on the reach, depth, and speed of convergence as an approximation strategy.

22.3.1.2 Competition Law as a Locus of Convergence

First of all, the EU experience reveals that the nature and extensiveness of the social field in question and associated legal framework targeted by cooperative regulatory schemes appear to affect the magnitude of convergence outcomes. Thus, the

---

or global institutions and their increasing impact" (N. Krisch, *Beyond Constitutionalism – The Pluralist Structure of Postnational Law* (Oxford University Press, 2010), 227).

[82] Gerber, *Global Competition*, 291. Others, like Cheng, view convergence as "the most important development in international competition law in recent years" but then question the "wholesale harmonization of competition laws" notably given the need to "incorporate economic development considerations" in the assessment of market practices (Th. K. Cheng, 'Convergence and Its Discontents: A Reconsideration of the Merits of Convergence of Global Competition Law' (2011–12) *Chi. J. Int'l L.* 433).

[83] As suggested by Gerber, *Global Competition*, pp. 283–5.

[84] For a discussion on spillover and convergence, see, e.g., Van Gerven, 'Open Method', 35.

narrower or wider-ranging scope of the social field concerned directly impacts the complexity of the cooperative regulatory scheme to put in place in order to organize interactions between legal systems, notably as it bears upon the size of the relevant epistemic community within which mutual learning is to take place in order to induce a communalization of the applicable legal concepts, and therefore the complexity of stimulating convergence. In turn, the fact that that social field is regulated by public law, i.e., that public authorities are endowed with the enforcement of the rules regulating it, appears relevant because it facilitates the organization of enforcement agents in networks, simplifies the operation of reflexive mechanisms and allows for reactive convergence initiatives by means of legislative and non-legislative mechanisms (e.g. guidelines and recommendations). The texture of the applicable rules can also be relevant, for whether they take the form of more or less general/specific rules of conduct can have a bearing on the scope left to enforcement agents for adapting the interpretation of the scope thereof to external constraints. So does the technicality of the necessary interpretations and the required expertise to do so for the closer the community of experts, the greater the incentive they may have to share knowledge and settle on common core assumptions.[85] The (relative) novelty of the issues encountered and of the associated body of rules can further influence the willingness of actors to make the (nascent) solutions adopted domestically converge,[86] whereas departing from settled principles deeply entrenched in the domestic culture would typically require greater incentives and/or constraints. Likewise, the degree of dissimilarity between the contemplated domestic solutions would tend to increase the costs of them moving toward each other, whether in terms of creating mutual understanding or of accommodating the impact of disruptions to each legal system's equilibrium, thereby slowing down the emergence of convergence signs and/or confining them to secondary issues. Conversely, similar considerations suggest that convergence is a self-reinforcing process that gets facilitated as legal systems do actually move toward each other because a certain degree of similarity improves the "readability" of foreign systems, incentivizes enforcement agents to cooperate and facilitates the benchmarking of local solutions.[87]

---

[85] For an account of the relationship between communities of experts and legal approximation, see, e.g., David J. Galbreath and Joanne McEvoy, 'How Epistemic Communities Drive International Regimes: The Case of Minority Rights in Europe' (2013), *Journal of European Integration* 169. See also, generally, P. M. Haas, 'Introduction: Epistemic Communities and International Policy Coordination' (1992) IO, 1.

[86] The lack of expertise in particular legal issues in certain legal systems may also facilitate knowledge transfer from more experienced jurisdictions, as illustrated by the experience of certain EU Member States within the ECN.

[87] Along the same lines, comparative law scholarship teaches that "l'affinité des situations culturelles, sociales, économiques peut être décisive pour déterminer, ou pour rendre possible, une imitation" and that "[s]i deux systèmes se ressemblent, les influences et les imitations (unilatérales et réciproques) sont plus intenses que s'ils diffèrent nettement" so that "les difficultés à surmonter seront d'autant plus grandes que seront grandes les différences d'ordre général entre les deux systèmes" (Sacco, *Comparaison juridique*, 123–5).

22.3.1.3 The Importance of Focal Points

Second, as noted, the importance of focal points to initiate and structure convergence processes cannot be overstated. Beyond the open promotion of convergence
by specific actors in the cooperative regulatory scheme in question, through the
voicing of concerns at specific obstacles to the smooth functioning of coordination
mechanisms and the proposition of solutions thereto, the existence of authoritative
focal points surfaces indeed as a major incentive to support a process of hybridization across legal systems. Thus, the existence of a fully articulated body of substantive
and procedural rules at EU level appears to have been decisive in paving the way
toward convergence in the field of competition law. Yet, it cannot be excluded that
more limited sets of rules can have a similar, even if more gradual, effect. Generally,
though, from a methodological point of view, the reliance on convergence focal
points can be related to a more general phenomenon known as "modeling," defined
by Braithwaite and Drahos as "observational learning with a symbolic content,"[88]
which has long been an instrument of choice for the promotion of regulatory
emulation across legal systems.[89] The effectiveness of model rules at being emulated
is said to be largely a function of their authority, which in turn results from their level
of details, comprehensive character, and technical validity, but also from the
recognized expertise – or "prestige"[90] – of their originator.[91] In line with reflexive
regulation theories,[92] one may equally postulate that the origination of model rules
in deliberative processes involving directly (potential) addressees thereof, is capable
of further contributing to the effectiveness of their emulation. Hence, the ability of
transnational networks of enforcement agents to translate domestic knowledge
shared by means of peer-review and other learning mechanisms into common
guidance would seem to combine many features of a successful mechanism for
triggering "mutual emulation," i.e., convergence, as observed with the issuance of
recommendations and model rules by the ECN. As such, that ability is a function
of network design strategies, which constitute a third important determinant of
convergence.

---

[88] J. Braithwaite and P. Drahos, *Global Business Regulation* (Cambridge University Press, 2000), 539.
[89] The adoption of model rules at international level also falls within the "modeling" category, whether
      it originates in the framework of international institutions or at the initiative of non-governmental
      organizations. Well-known examples include the UNCITRAL Model Law on International
      Commercial Arbitration, Codes of Practice of the International Labour Organization or the FIATA
      Model Rules for Freight Forwarding Services.
[90] On the notion of 'prestige' as a key driver of legal transplants and receptions, see, e.g., Sacco,
      Comparaison juridique, 123; and M. Graziadei, 'Comparative Law as the Study of Transplants and
      Receptions', in M. Reimann and R. Zimmermann (eds.), *The Oxford Handbook of Comparative Law*
      (Oxford University Press, 2000), 457–8.
[91] Braithwaite and Drahos, *Global Business Regulation*, 541–2.
[92] See generally, e.g., J. Lenoble and M. Maesschalck, 'Renewing the Theory of Public Interest:
      The Quest for a Reflexive and Learning-based Approach to Governance', in O. De Schutter and
      J. Lenoble (eds.), *Reflexive Governance – Redefining the Public Interest in a Pluralistic World* (Hart,
      2010), 3.

While empirical observations tend to support a correlation between the degree of interaction and communication among legal systems in the social field in question with the magnitude of convergence outcomes, a possible correlation between convergence and the sophistication of conflict rules developed to coordinate these interactions appears inconclusive. To be sure, the obligation of national competition authorities to jointly apply EU and equivalent national provisions to anticompetitive practices affecting trade between Member States constitutes a powerful convergence mechanism, but one may question whether it is replicable in other forums, given the peculiarity of EU competition law and of its enforcement by the Commission.

22.3.1.4 Institutional Determinants

In contrast, there seems to be a high degree of correlation between convergence and the design of enforcement networks, notably as to their objectives, composition, ability to pool knowledge, and align incentives. From an institutional design perspective, and somewhat counter-intuitively, the extent to which networks are brokered appears of little significance – or at least secondary – when it comes to encouraging convergence. After all, the ECN is largely governed by the organizations that comprise it and not by a centralized network broker, i.e., it's a participants-governed network where "[p]ower ... at least regarding network-level decisions, is more or less symmetrical, even though there may be differences in organizational size, resource capabilities, and performance."[93] Still from an institutional point of view, however, two other elements seem more determinative of the production of convergent solutions.

The first such element pertains to network goals commitment on the part of members and does in fact relate to network governance inasmuch as shared governance, in particular, is considered to foster commitment by promoting "community capacity."[94] This is clearly observable at ECN level, which is characterized by a strong network goals consensus, including as to the recognition of convergence as an objective of network interactions.

A second important institutional element conditioning the aptitude of networks to produce convergence outcome relates to the composition thereof. Composition has a quantitative side, for the number of organizations (potentially) participating in the network has a direct impact on the complexity of network governance, on the level of network commitment and alignment of network objectives, as well as, importantly, on the closeness of network interactions.[95] In turn, it complicates the pooling and dissemination of knowledge, and thus the possibility and depth of mutual learning

---

[93] K. G. Provan and P. Kenis, 'Modes of Network Governance: Structure, Management, and Effectiveness' (2007) JPART 235.
[94] Ibid., 234.
[95] Provan and Kenis, 'Modes of Network Governance', 238.

experiences. In addition, composition has a qualitative side, which pertains to the nature of network members' powers and institutional positioning. When it comes to producing convergence, specifically, the fact that these members have decisional – instead of or in addition to prosecutorial – powers may be such as to facilitate peer-review discussions, the emulation of foreign solutions and their translation into domestic practice. In addition, the fact that network participants are (or originate from) the sole or ultimate domestic enforcement agent in the social field in question is such as to enhance peer recognition and the authority of the network as a whole, to increase the salience of network discussions, the communalization of normative beliefs and the openness to foreign considerations, as well as to create common incentives to grow from an enforcement coordination to a lawmaking role reflecting a shared sense of contribution to a meaningful policy enterprise.[96]

Eventually, given their overall objective of facilitating interactions between network participants, process-management strategies also appear naturally relevant as determinants of convergence. Certainly, the endowment of the network with operational tasks such as cross-border investigative procedures and joint fact-finding mechanisms is such as to provoke interactions and to require the disclosure of domestic constraints, thereby creating opportunities for mutual learning and the production of joint solutions prone to elicit convergence, including on technical issues. The degree of effectiveness of these procedures is equally likely to strengthen the interdependency between network actors and to multiply interactions, while equally exposing local idiosyncrasies and increasing the incentives to question the necessity thereof or to explore the possibility to amend them.

Organizational arrangements such as peer-review procedures constitute another powerful way to enhance mutual learning and turn experience into a source of shared knowledge that can possibly be translated in common policy guidance. The frequency of peer-review procedures and the transparency of the outcomes thereof, with the associated reputational costs, then surface as strategic variables influencing their ability to support the formation of shared knowledge and, as a corollary, to induce the convergence of local practices. Moreover, the structuring of network interactions by means of dedicated working groups within which the functioning of the network is evaluated and other questions of common policy interests are openly discussed, appears further capable of contributing to the emergence of joint solutions or common approaches that are all the more likely to be replicated domestically that they are partly informed by local experiences.

In turn, the recurrence of these working group meetings is such as to induce the development of goal-achieving strategies likely to translate into tangible work products reflecting a convergence in the perception of problems and solutions. Overall, the organization of forums dedicated to reflecting on issues encountered in joint enforcement efforts and to processing the outcome of peer reviews with the objective

---

[96]   For supportive theoretical considerations, see, e.g., Haas, 'Introduction', 1.

of pooling together policy-relevant knowledge, appears particularly amenable to shaping over time common regulatory cultures capable of supporting deep and lasting convergence across systems.[97]

22.3.2 *Limits of Convergence*

Resorting to convergence as a strategy to accommodate efficiency/unity and equity/ diversity entails trade-offs' for convergence also has limits. Some of these limits surface "in counterpoint" from the determinants of convergence discussed in the previous section. However, even when the necessary conditions are present, convergence raises questions. This is because, as noted, convergence presents an inherent complexity and instability, largely due to its voluntary and incremental character, insofar as it is premised on the coexistence over time of closer but not (necessarily) identical substantive norms and may occur through practices (sometimes informal) developed by enforcement agents. As further discussed below, convergence appears to challenge indeed traditional understandings of concepts such as unity, accountability, and the rule of law while offering at the same time an opportunity to reflect on the meaning thereof in a transnational context.

22.3.2.1 The Limit of Effectiveness

A first limitation of convergence relates to its effectiveness at achieving the approximation of domestic solutions, thereby questioning its pace but also, more fundamentally, its tolerance for lasting diversity. That objection, which fundamentally raises the question of unity, calls for a threefold response. First, convergence achieves approximation precisely through the autonomous adaptation of divergent domestic legal concepts. Thus, convergence does not claim to achieve uniform substantive solutions and cannot therefore fail to reach that objective. Second, the effectiveness of convergence should be appreciated against existing alternatives, or rather lack thereof. In the realm of competition law enforcement, for example, "global convergence in ... legal and economic analysis is [viewed as] essential to ensuring effectiveness of ... enforcement and creating a level playing field for businesses across ... jurisdictions" and to "increase legal predictability by reducing the risk of incoherent intervention."[98] Third, convergence's incrementalism – as the source of its apparent imperfection – is one of its major strengths: because it proceeds at a limited pace and by means of the gradual adjustment of local rules and practices, convergence is less prone to antagonize key actors and more likely to succeed in reframing issues in a new light and inducing approximation over time in

---

[97] See, e.g., the multiple references to the willingness to build a "common competition culture" in 1/ 2003 SWP.

[98] J. Almunia, 'Cooperation and Convergence: Competition Policy in the 21st Century', ICN Annual Conference, Istanbul, 27 April 2010 (SPEECH/10/183).

areas where less flexible approaches would be met with greater resistance. This is not
to say, though, that convergence efforts cannot also generate opposition and, in
truth, a case can be made that a convergence strategy would be vulnerable to
such opposition and ill-equipped to overcome it.[99] However, as presently
understood, convergence consists in second-order effects induced by cooperative regulatory schemes creating concrete – if procedural – obligations capable of supporting local attempts at overcoming that opposition, and the
development of informal tools and practices can also assist in that regard.
As to the instability of convergence outcomes, i.e., the risk of reversal/repeal
of converging domestic solutions, it can be countered by regulatory strategies
designed to solidify them into common hard rules, or threats of doing so. For
example, in the competition enforcement area, the Commission pointed out
as an "issue of concern" the fact that "the level of convergence achieved to
date remains fragile, as changes in national laws or practices could result in
the roll-back of improvements which have been made at any time."[100] Hence,
it suggested that "appropriate initiatives" could be sought at EU level to
secure the convergence outcomes achieved so far,[101] which led to the adoption of the ECN+ Directive at the end of 2018.

22.3.2.2 The Limit of the Rule of Law

A second limit of convergence, which is a corollary to the first, pertains to its relation
with the rule of law, as it does not afford the level of predictability expected from an
integrated legal system when it comes to determining the rules to take into account
when adjusting one's behavior or practices, of a cross-border nature. In other words,
convergence allows for uncertainty to endure and for diverging rights and obligations to apply. In effect, convergence aims to achieve approximation through the
medium of domestic solutions, which are by definition multiple. By doing so,
however, convergence openly tolerates the assertion of jurisdiction over the same
factual situation by different legal orders with their own respective substantive
solution. The question then arises as to whether such a strategy is necessarily
suboptimal in terms of legal certainty. Indeed, even if convergence does not entail
the upfront application of one and the same solution across legal systems, it

---

99   As suggested by Gerber, *Global Competition*, 289.
100 Commission Staff Working Document, 'Enhancing competition enforcement by the Member
     States' competition authorities: institutional and procedural issues', SWD(2014) 231/2, para. 54.
     More specifically, while considering the significant degree of convergence achieved across EU
     Member States in relation to leniency following the adoption of the ECN Model Leniency
     Program, the Commission observed that: "there is no requirement at EU level to have a leniency
     programme in place and the exemplary level of convergence can always be put into question"
     (Communication of the Commission, Ten Years of Antitrust Enforcement under Regulation 1/2003:
     Achievements and Future Perspectives, COM(2014) 453, p. 11).
101 Ibid., pp. 11–12.

guarantees the submission of the situation in question to a coherent set of rules and to an "approximated" solution anchored in a certain domestic legal architecture and consistent with its underlying legal tradition and *mentalité*, including due process standards. It thereby ensures a degree of predictability that is not per se inferior to that associated with the application of a facially uniform but "foreign" solution by a multiplicity of local law-enforcement bodies, which may result in significant frictions and insecurity even if concealed under the reliance on similar language. Moreover, the risk of arbitrariness in the determination of the applicable solution is attenuated by the application of distinctive features of the cooperative regulatory scheme supporting convergence in the social field in question, chiefly common conflict rules designed to achieve improved predictability.

Fundamentally, though, convergence is premised on the confrontation of differing local solutions, so that it inherently implies a tension with certainty and predictability ideals. Conceptually, convergence favors argumentative logics creating space for contestation and change as a means for achieving optimal and fair outcomes over formal rule-of-law standards that are not easily replicable in a transnational context.[102] As it materializes, however, and despite its constant state of flux, convergence should be capable of achieving levels of predictability comparable to those observable in unitary legal orders, discounting for the intrinsic indetermination of law, notably as converging outcomes benefit from a presumption of consistency with domestic legal cultures.

22.3.2.3 The Limit of Accountability

A third important limit of convergence relates to its democratic credentials, or lack thereof, and in particular its uneasy relationship with the notion of accountability, understood as "the obligation to explain and justify conduct" and be responsible for the consequences thereof.[103] This is because convergence is a diffuse – and therefore opaque – process producing consensus as a result of multiple influences from multiple sources and actors, which can materialize in multiple ways. As a result, it is particularly complex to disentangle the relevant factors of convergence and the role of individual actors, to hold them accountable and even to determine the appropriate accountability forum.[104] This is even more so when convergence and the associated modification of applicable domestic standards is prompted by soft law measures or administrative practices, implemented directly by enforcement agents. The accountability issue arising from the complexity of the convergence method

[102] On contestation as a surrogate for rule-of-law standards in a post-national order, see, e.g., Krisch, *Beyond Constitutionalism*, 282–4.

[103] M. Bovens, 'Analysing and Assessing Accountability: A Conceptual Framework' (2007), *European Law Journal* 450.

[104] The nature of convergence as an EU approximation strategy effected through domestic means also questions the determination of the appropriate forum of accountability, which as such undermines accountability in either forum.

and the involvement of multiple actors echoes concerns raised at the grounding of transnational governance in democratic values and at the accountability of network structures, including as to the resistance of network actors to general public interest considerations.[105] In turn, ways of addressing that issue are essentially twofold: focusing on compensatory values inherent to convergence, on the one hand, and highlighting its submission to domestic accountability mechanisms, on the other hand.

Thus, first, the interplay of different influences and actors with their respective interests and traditions, on which convergence relies, can be said to act as an accountability mechanism in and of itself, i.e., as a non-institutionalized check against regulatory excesses rooted in a system of "peer-to-peer" responsiveness. Put otherwise, convergence results naturally from the confrontation of a multiplicity of voices and contestation by different collectives, which are as such building blocks of democracy. Moreover, the instability of convergence and its reliance on soft guidance and enforcement practices also ensures the revisability of its outcomes, which is another key element of democratic orders. Admittedly, the channeling of multiple voices does not exclude a possible capture of convergence processes by specific actors benefiting from greater capacities, information, and expertise. However, the interests of powerful actors are not necessarily aligned and rivalry between them can also contain the risks of capture. Likewise, the sharing of knowledge and mutual learning processes induced by cooperative regulatory schemes tend to create a dynamic of empowerment, as observed in the context of the ECN, capable of balancing over time an uneven distribution of resources. In addition, the revisability of convergence outcomes does not exclude a form of stickiness due to the burden of reforming a consensus reached by multiple actors and to its dependence on domestic procedures to turn it into practice.

Second, convergence occurs through domestic means available at local level, which are subject to classic accountability mechanisms available in their respective forums, including representative democracy, responsiveness toward elected bodies and judicial control. Thus, the voluntary nature of convergence implies its subjection to established democratic values and processes, and leaves room for local resistance to outcomes perceived as undesirable. Convergence therefore occurs under a shadow of anarchy sometimes complemented, like at EU level, by a shadow of hierarchy embedded in the possibility of resorting to more hierarchical approximation initiatives, which act(s) as (an) accountability safeguard(s).

In the end, it is unclear to what degree convergence actually suffers from an accountability deficit. Because it takes shape through the medium of domestic lawmaking procedures, it is immune from many of the criticisms traditionally voiced

---

[105] For general discussions, see, e.g., G. de Búrca, 'Developing Democracy Beyond the State' (2008) *Columbia Journal of Transnational Law* 221 and Y. Papadopoulos, 'Cooperative Forms of Governance: Problems of Democratic Accountability in Complex Environments' (2003) 42(4) *European Journal of Political Research* 473.

toward substantive norms adopted at supranational level. Moreover, the complexity of convergence and the multiple actors involved therein may well have democracy-enhancing effects, first by broadening the range of information, experience, and argument available to and involved in domestic rulemaking processes and, second, by contributing to the ongoing formation of a public sphere to which international arrangements are to be held ultimately accountable.[106]

22.4 CONCLUSION

This contribution has sought to substantiate some of the determinants and discuss related limits of convergence as the dominant value in the international antitrust enforcement discourse since the failure of attempts at establishing a multilateral framework of competition rules at WTO level. The overall objective of that inquiry has been to encourage a reassessment of existing cooperative strategies at a time where the increasing global trade and its associated consequences have triggered renewed sensitivity for equity considerations and distrust in binding supranational solutions.

In doing so, the contribution started by describing the EU experience in achieving a significant level of convergence by means of the setting up of a sophisticated cooperative enforcement system in the early 2000s. Deriving lessons from that arguably unique experience, and mindful of the need to test the proposed considerations against a broader set of empirical findings and to seek additional input from other social sciences, it then undertook to relate convergence outcomes and the reach, speed and depth thereof to five main determinants, as follows:

- the magnitude and intensity of interactions between legal orders, which tend to distinguish the Union from other regional/global contexts entertaining claims of convergence;
- the organization of these systemic interactions by means of cooperative regulatory schemes taking the form of binding legal instruments creating procedural obligations affecting the implementation of local solutions;
- characteristic features of the social field in question, notably its scope and complexity, and of the legal framework regulating it, including the involvement of public authorities in the enforcement of applicable rules, the extensiveness, technicality and novelty of these rules and the degree of dissimilarity of local solutions;
- the existence of convergence focal points capable of leading convergence and of supporting the hybridization of solutions across legal systems (including their own communalization), whether they consist in a more or less comprehensive

---

[106] For a discussion of similar virtues associated with the increasing rulemaking taking place in global institutions, see J. Cohen and Ch. F. Sabel, 'Global Democracy?' (2005) *New York University Journal of International Law and Politics* 763.

set of binding EU-wide rules or in other forms of model content, including of a soft law nature; and

- network design strategies, both of an institutional and process-management nature, pertaining to network goals commitment and composition, on the one hand, and organizational network arrangements, on the other hand, including the execution of operational tasks, the more or less systematic recourse to peer-review procedures and the structuring of the network in working groups engaged in evaluating the network operations and in open policy discussions in the framework of recurring meetings.

As a result, convergence appears essentially contingent on the production of joint knowledge through operational mechanisms of a cooperative nature inherently designed to stimulate mutual learning, and the processing thereof by structured networks committed to contribute to the perfection of these mechanisms. As a result, convergence does seem to largely depend on the effectiveness of cooperative regulatory schemes, which is itself conditional on the defining features of the social fields they seek to organize on a cross-border basis, and on the incentives of network participants to reflect on their own experience and to enter into logics of appropriateness.[107]

The limits arising from the complexity and instability of convergence were subsequently discussed, in particular as to its effectiveness at achieving the approximation of domestic solutions, its relation with rule-of-law standards and its democratic credentials. In terms of effectiveness, and among other considerations, the tolerance for legal diversity inherent to convergence and the incremental character thereof were found to count among its main strengths in inducing approximation in areas where less flexible approaches would be met with great resistance. With respect to its compliance with the rule of law, it is a fact that convergence aims to achieve approximation through the medium of domestic solutions, which are by definition multiple. However, the predictability of convergence outcomes is also guaranteed by their incorporation in a coherent domestic legal system and consistency with the underlying legal culture. Finally, as to the tension between the complexity of convergence and the notion of accountability, it appears eventually compensated by, on the one hand, the confrontation of multiple voices inherent thereto and the intrinsic revisability of its outcomes and, on the other hand, the subjection of these same outcomes to established accountability mechanisms available at domestic level.

---

[107] Through logics of appropriateness, actors seek to fulfill the obligations associated with the membership in a particular social community and to internalize the rules produced by that community, which they tend to view as natural, rightful, expected, and legitimate. For a theoretical discussion, see, e.g., J. G. March and J. P. Olsen, 'The Logic of Appropriateness', in M. Rein, M. Moran, and R. E. Goodin (eds.), *Oxford Handbook of Public Policy* (Oxford University Press, 2006), 689.

Afterword

23

Competition Policy at the Intersection of Equity and Efficiency

The Developed and Developing Worlds

Eleanor M. Fox

In the last quarter of the last century in matters of economic law, it was common cause that we could pursue either efficiency or equity but not both; the twain would not meet. I never believed it.

The gospel of efficiency was ushered into US antitrust by the Chicago School, whose beautiful proofs,[1] dating at least from the 1960s,[2] were resisted by US law and policymakers until the early 1980s. They gained traction with the presidential election of Ronald Reagan (1980), validating national sentiment that government had wormed its way too deeply into the business of business; that business was essentially efficient, and that if we simply let business free to do the work of business we would all be better off. Pursuit of equity was regarded as wrong-headed. If we pursued equity, we would undermine efficiency. The pie would shrink and we would all be worse off.

Arthur Okun's book, *Equality and Efficiency: The Big Tradeoff*,[3] laid a foundation for this thesis. In the book, which itself was a gospel until the early twenty-first century, Okun concluded from theory that as we equalize the distribution of income we decrease the efficiency of the economy and that therefor society should forgo greater equality for a healthier economy. Empirical research indicated the contrary, e.g. Lane Kenworthy, *Equality and Efficiency: The Illusory Tradeoff*,[4] but seems to have attracted little attention in the United States. At least in the US antitrust

---

[1] See P. Krugman, 'How Did Economists Get It So Wrong?', *New York Times*, September 6, 2009, magazine section, at 36: The economists failed to see the financial crisis of 2008 coming because they so unquestionably trusted markets. "[T]he economics profession went astray because economists, as a group, mistook beauty, clad in impressive-looking mathematics, for truth" (at 37).

[2] In this chapter, I do not make a distinction between efficiency, consumer welfare, or total welfare. The welfare standards are aspects of efficiency. Efficiency is calculated as an outcome of a particular transaction or course of conduct. The analyst asks: does it or does it not lessen welfare? In large markets such as the United States, consumer welfare usually coincides with total welfare. Indeed, in Robert Bork's famous book, *The Antitrust Paradox* (Free Press, 1978), Bork defines total welfare as consumer welfare (see ch. 5).

[3] A. M. Okun, *Equality and Efficiency – The Big Tradeoff* (Brookings Institution, 1975, repub. 2015).

[4] L. Kenworthy, 'Equality and Efficiency: The Illusory Tradeoff' (1995) 27 *European Journal of Political Research* 225.

community, since the third quarter of the twentieth century, there has been a widely shared belief that efficiency is the holy grail, and moreover, that US antitrust precedents in the 1960s to the mid 1970s (which constructed an antitrust of the underdog and equated antitrust with economic democracy) was erroneous if not also contemptible.

There was in any event a missing link. The literature on equality and efficiency normally referred to income equality, which is equality of outcome, and the equality (or equity) embedded in 1960s US antitrust was equality of opportunity and inclusiveness. This seemed an unimportant distinction to the Chicagoans of the 1970s–1980s, who adopted a line taken out of context from the *Brown Shoe* opinion of the Supreme Court in 1962 enjoining what today we would call a trivial merger: "It is competition, not competitors, which the Act protects."[5] The epithet was and is commonly used as an iteration of the equity–efficiency trade-off: do not give weight to the position of (smaller) competitors or you will harm efficiency. Equity, equality, opportunity, fairness – don't go there. The science of antitrust economics is about efficiency. Equity undermines efficiency.

The break did not come until the turn of the twentieth century, both through experience and research. The experience was a harsh one; it was the brutal recession of 2007–8. Alan Greenspan, who was chairman of the Federal Reserve Board and thus the leader of monetary policy for the United States, had to admit that there was "a flaw [in my] model."[6] Some blame was laid at the feet of the economists, who were so sure that the market would work that they opposed regulation of new financial instruments derived from mortgages sold to low-income home buyers who could afford the mortgage only so long as house prices continued to rise. Theory had outrun reality. One might have thought that US antitrust jurisprudence (which by then was extremely laissez-faire with respect to the monopoly violation)[7] would take on board the lesson of too much trust in the market. But it did not.

Second, as to research: at least since 2014 with publication of the important research paper by Ostry, Berg, and Tsangarides[8] of the International Monetary Fund, and in the same year the publication of *Capital in the* Twenty-First *Century* by Thomas Piketty,[9] our understanding of the economics of inequality has fundamentally shifted.[10] Ostry, Berg, and Tsangarides show "that greater inequality in society strongly retards economic growth." An *Economist* article summarizing the literature concludes that:

5   *Brown Shoe Company* v. *United States*, 370 US 294, 344 (1962).
6   See 'Greenspan Admits "Flaw" to Congress, Predicts More Economic Problems', *PBS Newshour*, October 23, 2008), at www.pbs.org/newshour/bb/business-july-dec08-crisishearing_10-23
7   See *Verizon* v. *Trinko*, 540 US 398 (2004) (hereafter *Trinko*).
8   J. D. Ostry, A. Berg, and C. G. Tsangarides, 'Redistribution, Inequality, and Growth' (IMF Staff Discussion Note, February 2014), www.imf.org/external/pubs/ft/sdn/2014/sdn1402.pdf
9   T. Piketty, *Capital in the Twenty-First Century* (Harvard University Press, 2014).
10 Matthew Yglesias, 'Inequality and Efficiency: The Last Casualty of the Cold War' (*The Economist*, April 23, 2014).

with Soviet-style state socialism having departed the scene, the supposed tradeoff between growth and egalitarian distribution may no longer describe anything important about the world . . . Greater equality seems to be simply good for growth. Once the effects of that shift in economic thinking filter into political discourse, we'll know the cold war is finally dead.[11]

Piketty speaks especially to tax policy, and thus explicit redistribution of wealth. Antitrust is not tax policy. Equity in antitrust means tilting the scales away from powerful business and for powerless people; away from protecting the (freedom of) the incumbent and toward protecting the access and opportunity of young challengers.[12] Safeguarding opportunity for outsiders is a far cry from handing them money. It has obvious efficiency properties. US antitrust orthodoxy protects the freedom of the incumbent on grounds that protecting the incentives of (even) the monopolist will preserve its incentives to invest and invent; that imposing duties on (even) the monopolist will chill its inventiveness; and that providing a cause of action to elbowed-out rivals will only induce nuisance suits that drain the time of executives and the pocketbooks of their firms.[13] This is one way of thinking about efficiency (and of efficiency without equity). US antitrust orthodoxy says it is *the* efficient way. I do not agree.

Efficiency is an elastic term when we use it as the object of an antitrust system. It is common cause that antitrust systems are designed to create or preserve an economy of dynamic, competitive, and innovative firms. We do not know how to create this dynamic end result and we agree that we should not try to engineer it. The solution of US orthodoxy is to leave business alone unless the case for intervention (the case that there is unjustified accretion or misuse of market power) is very clear; and, under US precedents, business is assumed to be efficient and market power is assumed to be hard to get and harder to keep.[14]

The world view of the critics is quite the opposite. They would place their bets on a diverse and competitive market rather than on incumbent firms; they would rather preserve an environment that promotes incentives of outsiders to contest markets than incentives of a monopolist to invest. Both philosophies can be found in the jurisprudence of US district and appellate courts, but the balance of the US Supreme Court is with the orthodoxy.[15]

---

[11] Ibid.

[12] See *Trinko*, and *Brooke Group Ltd.* v. *Brown & Williamson Tobacco Corp.*, 509 US 208 (1993), which show how the US scales are tilted distinctly toward the incumbent.

[13] See *Trinko*; and *Pacific Bell Telephone* v. *LinkLine Communications, Inc.*, 555 US 438 (2009); *Credit Suisse Securities* v. *Billing*, 551 US 264 (2007).

[14] If plaintiff cannot prove that the conduct limits output in the market, or if defendant had a good business reason such as choosing to deal with whom it likes, the conduct is normally lawful.

[15] See *Trinko*; LinkLine; *Novell* v. *Microsoft*, 731 F.3d 1064 (10th Cir., 2013) (Judge, now Justice, Gorsuch). See also E. Fox, 'The Efficiency Paradox', in R. Pitofsky (ed.), *How the Chicago School Overshot the Mark: The Effect of Conservative Economic Analysis on U.S. Antitrust* (Oxford University Press, 2008), 77.

I am very much involved in considering good competition rules and policy in the developing world. Perhaps my unease with the efficiency gospel of US antitrust led me in this direction. Surely it was not the only spur, for I am fascinated by the people and problems in the countries I visit and I feel that I can make a better contribution in the developing than in the developed world.

One cannot help but observe that, in the developing world, efficiency and equity meet. Yes, there are also trade-offs. But efforts to enhance efficiency and efforts to enhance equity (such as by antitrust enforcement) coincide where barriers to markets are high, where most of the population have been excluded from the economic life of the country, where oligarchs and their families control the cream of the economic opportunities, and where powerful state-owned enterprises occupy the lion's share of trade. In those circumstances, efficient moves to bring competition to the market are equitable, and equitable moves to bring competition to the market are efficient.

Cartel enforcement is an easy case and not controversial in the context of this chapter. It is equitable and efficient in developed and developing worlds alike.

As for merger control, the most difficult problems for developing countries are not along the equity–efficiency axis. They relate to powerlessness of developing country authorities to impose the best remedy (normally, injunction) to protect their people against power created by multinational mergers. But equity and efficiency coincide in the analysis of monopsony-creating multinational mergers that squeeze poor farmers in Africa (including efficient ones who produce at lower cost than their western counterparts) in the name of welfare of western consumers and producers.

Monopoly/abuse of dominance cases see the greatest divergence from US efficiency/consumer welfare standards. Developing countries might wish to protect entry opportunities for people without power more than freedom of action of the incumbent – and if put to the test could probably prove that enforcement to do so is efficient for their society, both in the particular case and in terms of the effort to create an environment that best promotes incentives to compete, invest, and invent.

It is a fourth category that intrigues me the most in my work in developing countries. That is the area of competition policy beyond enforcement. It is called advocacy in the West, but it is a larger-than-life advocacy and is adjunct to nothing. In the United States, advocacy entails, for example, the Justice Department Antitrust Division's arguing with a regulatory agency to allow or disallow a merger.[16] In Kenya it is about identifying the stubbornest economic barriers that keep hundreds of thousands of people out of the market – restraints likely to be much more damaging competitively and personally than any private restraint; and assessing whether it is politically and practically possible to tear the barriers down. Working with the World

---

[16]   It may also involve much more such as fighting against excessive licensing regulations. See M. Ohlhausen, 'Advancing Economic Liberty', remarks at George Mason Law Review's 20th Annual Antitrust Symposium, February 23, 2017. In this respect, advocacy of developed and developing countries distinctly overlaps.

Bank team, developing country competition authorities have had notable successes in confronting serious government and hybrid (public–private) restraints.[17] Equity and efficiency meet.

In developing countries, competition policy can make the difference between life and death; between severe poverty and a dignified life.[18] It can promote opportunity, inclusiveness, and, indeed, efficiency. To echo *The Economist*, the supposed trade-off between equity and efficiency does not describe anything important about the developing world.

CONCLUSION

The old gospel of efficiency, not equity, is dead. The two pursuits can move together, in tandem, or apart. Equity can take many forms. I make two concluding observations in the context of opportunity to contest markets.

First, the more unequal and exclusionary a society, such as South Africa under apartheid, the more it may be necessary to do equity to get efficiency – let alone to do equity as moral imperative. Second, apart from historical exclusions, law tempered by a consciousness of equity to the outsider can produce not only more equity but more efficiency. Often it is the case: the outsider has the best ideas.[19]

---

[17]   See 'Boosting Competition in African Markets Can Enhance Growth and Lift at Least Half a Million People out of Poverty' (July 27, 2016), available at www.worldbank.org/en/news/press-release/2016/07/27/boosting-competition-in-african-markets-can-enhance-growth-and-lift-at-least-half-a-million-people-out-of-poverty

[18]   Ibid.

[19]   See *United States* v. *United Shoe Machinery Corp.*, 110 F. Supp. 295, 346 (D. Mass. 1953) (Wyzanski, Judge), aff'd, 347 US 521 (1954).

Index

during Progressive Era, 132, 133
under Sherman Act, 133
customs union, with EU, 124–5
CUTS International, 139–40, 150–1

data-driven network effects, 232–3, 240
Davidson, Jim, 206
Davis, Josh, 346
Dawson Report, 208–10
Birdsville Amendments and, 209–10
changes after, 209–10
deliberative democracy, 80
democracy
competition law and, 242
deliberative, 80
in Turkey, 112
developed countries: *see also specific countries*
CLP in, 275–9
IP protections, 275, 276, 280
patent system exceptions in, 275–6
industrial policy in, 275–9
IP protections, 275, 276, 280
patent system exceptions in, 275–6
developing countries
CLP in, 275–9
discovery process in, 276–9
IP protections, 275, 276, 280
patent system exceptions in, 275–6
process innovation in, 277
targeted producer subsidies, 278–9
competition law in, 1, 153
competition policy in, 138–9, 444–5
crony capitalism in, 111
distributive justice in, 1
economic efficiency in, 155
economic inequality in, 59, 97–103
equity in, 1
industrial policy in, 275–9
discovery process in, 276–9
IP protections, 275, 276, 280
patent system exceptions in, 275–6
process innovation in, 277
targeted producer subsidies, 278–9
micro-business enterprises in, 161
development-friendly competition law, 153–6
formulation of, 154–6
goals in, 155–6
inclusiveness in, 156
open markets in, 154–5
substantive rules in, 156
in sub-Saharan Africa, 153
difference principle, 53–4, 92–3
digital assistant technologies
Amazon, 232–5

under antitrust law, 223–32
enforcement of, 237–9
Apple, 232–5
data-driven network effects, 232–3, 240
Facebook, 232–6
Google, 225–6, 232–5
quality degradation issues with, 231
industry gatekeepers for, fortification of, 224–35
consumer choice issues for, 230–2
default advantages, 226
through exclusionary practices, 231
first-move advantages, 226
market power of, 227–32, 237–9
through quality degradation, 228–30, 231
intellectual and regulatory capture and, 235–7
Microsoft, 232–5
super platforms in, 236–7
Digital Content Directive, 261–2
Dinc, Serdar, 289
direct taxation, 60
distributive justice
through competition law, 49–54
fairness-driven, 82–3
competition law and, 49–55
in Canada, 54
in developing countries, 1
economic inequality and, 49–54
divestiture power, 220
due process, in competition law agencies, 336

East Africa, competition in: *see also* barriers to
market entry; mobile telecommunications
network operators; *specific countries*
cement industry, 179–81
cartel control of, 179–82
pricing for, 180
SACU and, 179–81
commodities in, competition over, 175–82
under competition laws, 173–4
fertilizer industry, 175–9
cartel enforcement of, 181
in Kenya, 175
in Malawi, 177–8
in Tanzania, 177–8
in Zambia, 177–8
Easterbrook, Frank, 305, 306
EC: *see* European Commission
ECA: *see* Egypt Competition Authority
ECJ: *see* European Court of Justice
ECN: *see* European Competition Network
ECN Plus Project, 367–9
economic efficiency: *see also* economic inequality
allocative, 29
Chicago School on, 65, 242–3

Index

CPSIA information can be obtained
at www.ICGtesting.com
Printed in the USA
BVHW091827110522
636808BV00007B/49